About Pearson

Pearson is the world's learning company, with presence across 70 countries world-wide. Our unique insights and world-class expertise comes from a long history of working closely with renowned teachers, authors and thought leaders, as a result of which, we have emerged as the preferred choice for millions of teachers and learners across the world.

We believe learning opens up opportunities, creates fulfilling careers and hence better lives. We hence collaborate with the best of minds to deliver you class-leading products, spread across the Higher Education and Test Preparation spectrum.

Superior learning experience and improved outcomes are at the heart of everything we do. This product is the result of one such effort.

Your feedback plays a critical role in the evolution of our products and you can contact us – reachus@pearson.com. We look forward to it.

SOCIOLOGY

Deepanshu Singh

Pearson

Chapter Opener Image Credit: Merkushev Vasiliy / Shutterstock

The aim of this publication is to supply information taken from sources believed to be valid and reliable. This is not an attempt to render any type of professional advice or analysis, nor is it to be treated as such. While much care has been taken to ensure the veracity and currency of the information presented within, neither the publisher nor its authors bear any responsibility for any damage arising from inadvertent omissions, negligence or inaccuracies (typographical or factual) that may have found their way into this book.

ISBN 978-93-615-9663-6

First Impression

Published by Pearson India Education Services Pvt. Ltd, CIN: U72200TN2005PTC057128.

Head Office: 1st Floor, Berger Tower, Plot No. C-001A/2, Sector 16B, Noida - 201 301, Uttar Pradesh, India.

Registered Office: 6th Floor, Tower A, Unit A and B International Tech Park, CapitaLand Chennai, 200 Feet Radial Road, Zamin Pallavaram, Old Pallavaram Chennai – 600117, Tamil Nadu India

Website: in.pearson.com, Email: companysecretary.india@pearson.com

Compositor: Saksham Printographics, Delhi
Printed in India at Rajkamal Electric Press, Kundli, Haryana-131 028.

Table of Contents

Preface

Sociology is not just a subject — it's a mirror that makes us laugh, reflect, and occasionally wince at our own contradictions. Over years of teaching this discipline, I've come to believe that sociology is best understood not as a collection of theories, but as a living conversation between thinkers and society — between Comte's positivism and India's daily pragmatism, between Durkheim's 'social facts' and our everyday WhatsApp forwards.

This book attempts to bring sociology alive for UPSC aspirants by combining conceptual clarity with real-world relevance. It goes beyond definitions to ask the 'why' behind social behaviour — why gender roles persist in modern offices, why class lines blur on digital platforms, or why the Indian joint family continues to outlive every sociological prediction of its demise. Through examples from India and the world — from Kerala's human development story to Silicon Valley's work culture, from caste to consumerism, and from social movements to memes — the book connects global theories with Indian realities.

To make complex ideas easier to grasp, every chapter is supported with **flowcharts, mind maps, tables, and diagrams** that summarise theories, thinkers, and linkages across Paper I and II. These visual aids have emerged from years of classroom interaction, simplifying abstract sociological thought into quick, exam-ready recall.

At its heart, this book is a synthesis of academic depth and lived experience. It is meant not just to help aspirants score marks, but to cultivate what C. Wright Mills called the *sociological imagination* — the ability to see the connection between private troubles and public issues. I often tell my students: once you begin to think sociologically, you can never truly unsee society. You will find it in your family dinner table, in your workplace hierarchies, and even in your Instagram feed.

If this book helps you see the invisible threads that hold societies together — and find humour and empathy in that understanding — it will have served its purpose.

— Deepanshu Singh

Acknowledgements

This book is the product of many minds, hearts, and patient shoulders.

To my **wife**, whose calm and clarity kept me grounded even when deadlines didn't. To my **family**, who taught me the first lessons of human behaviour long before I read Durkheim. To my **friends**, for keeping laughter alive through the sociology of stress.

I owe deep gratitude to my **mentors, friends and students in the Civil Services**, and **my teachers** who shared invaluable insights into how policies and social realities intersect. Their practical wisdom shaped the applied dimension of this book. My thanks also to the dedicated **Pearson editorial team** for their professionalism and belief in this project, and to my students — the most relentless and rewarding critics of all.

To everyone who made this journey meaningful — thank you.

Foreword

By Asim Arun

Minister of State (Independent Charge) –
Social Welfare, SC/ST Welfare,
Government of Uttar Pradesh

It gives me great pleasure to write this foreword for Sociology by Deepanshu Singh, published by Pearson. Although my academic background lies in a B.Sc. from St. Stephen's College and an M.A. in Public Policy from the University of British Columbia, Canada, my engagement with Sociology began when I chose it as my optional subject during the Civil Services Examination. The subject fascinated me then—and continues to do so—because of how vividly its ideas explain the world we see around us.

Over the years, both in the Indian Police Service and now in a political role, I have often found sociological theories coming alive in everyday governance—whether it is understanding community dynamics, addressing inequality, or designing inclusive policies. Sociology helps us look beyond events to see the systems and behaviours that shape them, and in that sense, it remains one of the most practical disciplines I have encountered.

I have known Deepanshu for the past three years and have witnessed the thoughtful work he has been doing in mentoring UPSC aspirants and contributing to the field of public policy—especially his mission to guide underprivileged aspirants in Uttar Pradesh and beyond. His approach reflects a rare balance of academic depth and practical insight, which also comes through in this book—clear, relevant, and grounded in real-world understanding.

I congratulate Deepanshu Singh and Pearson for bringing out a work that will be valuable not only for aspirants but also for anyone curious about how society functions and how ideas can translate into impact.

About the Author

Deepanshu Singh is a seasoned mentor with over **12 years of experience** spanning **startups, government, and the private sector**. He brings together a unique blend of academic insight and policy expertise, having mentored more than **2,00,000 civil services aspirants**, including several top rankers. Currently, he leads a national non-profit in global mobility and skilling as the **Head of Partnerships and Government Relations**.

A **B.Tech in Computer Science**, he holds an **MBA from IIM Kozhikode** and a certification in **Public Policy from the London School of Economics**, with professional interests in **Artificial Intelligence, education, and governance**. A founding team member at Unacademy and former **Senior Director at Study IQ (a Google-backed EdTech)**, his **sociology courses have been viewed a record number of times**, making him one of India's **most sought-after educators**. He is also the author of **two bestselling books on International Relations**.

UPSC CSE Sociology (Optional) Paper 1, 2025

SECTION A

1. Answer the following questions in about 150 words each: (10 × 5 = 50)

   (a) What is common sense? How are common knowledge and sociology related to each other? Explain.

   (b) What is the relationship (similarities and differences) between sociology and history in terms of their area of study and methodology? Discuss.

   (c) What is a variable in social research? What are their different types? Elaborate.

   (d) Can Merton's reference group theory be relevant in understanding 'identity making' in digital world? Explain.

   (e) Is the social stratification theory gender-blind? Elucidate.

2. (a) What is positivism? Critically analyze the major arguments against it. (20 marks)

   (b) Highlight the main features of historical materialism as propounded by Marx. How far is this theory relevant in understanding contemporary societies? Explain. (20 marks)

   (c) What do you mean by reliability? Discuss the importance of reliability in social science research. (10 marks)

3. (a) Compare capability deprivation approach with that of social capital deprivation in understanding chronic poverty. (20 marks)

   (b) Are pressure groups a threat to or a necessary element of democracy? Explain with suitable illustrations. (20 marks)

   (c) What is hypothesis? Critically evaluate the significance of hypothesis in social research. (10 marks)

4. (a) Give an account of the recent trends of marriage in the Indian context. How are these different from traditional practices? (20 marks)

   (b) What would you identify as the similarities and differences in the elite theories of Mosca, Michels and Pareto? Discuss their main/crucial issues. (20 marks)

   (c) Critically analyze the sociological significance of informal sector in the economy of developing societies. (10 marks)

SECTION B

5. Answer the following questions in about 150 words each: (10 × 5 = 50)

(a) In what way is the scope of sociology unique? Explain.

(b) Does the structural-functionalist perspective on social stratification promote a status quo? Give reasons for your answer.

(c) Do you think that the formal workspaces are free of gender bias? Argue your case.

(d) How does Weber's Verstehen address the objectivity-subjectivity debate in sociology?

(e) To what extent can education and skill development be an agent of social change? Critically analyze.

6. (a) What is science? Do you think that the methods used in natural sciences can be applied to sociology? Give reasons for your answer. (20 marks)

(b) What do you understand by gender-based domestic division of labour? Is it undergoing a change in the wake of increasing participation of women in formal employment? Clarify your answer with illustrations. (20 marks)

(c) How can you assess the significance of social movements in the digital era? Explain. (10 marks)

7. (a) What is sampling in the context of social research? Discuss different forms of sampling with their relative advantages and disadvantages. (20 marks)

(b) How do theories of Marx, Weber and Durkheim differ in understanding religion? Explain. (20 marks)

(c) What is the nature of relationship between science and religion in modern society? Analyze with suitable examples. (10 marks)

8. (a) What do you understand by sustainable development? Discuss the elements of sustainable development as proposed in the UNDP's Sustainable Development Goals Report-2015. (20 marks)

(b) How do 'Civil Society Organizations' such as 'NGOs' and 'Self-Help Groups' contribute to grassroot level social changes? Discuss. (20 marks)

(c) In what way does queer kinship challenge the traditional kinship system? Substantiate by giving illustrations. (10 marks)

UPSC CSE Sociology (Optional) Paper 2, 2025

SECTION A

1. Answer the following questions in about 150 words each: (10 × 5 = 50)

   (a) 'Textual perspective is important in understanding of Indian Social System.' Discuss. (10 marks)

   (b) Justify that the Indian traditions are modernizing. Also discuss its contributing factors. (10 marks)

   (c) According to you, which social reform movement has played the most effective role in uplifting the status of women? Explain. (10 marks)

   (d) How did Colonial Policies for the tribes affect their socio-economic conditions in India? Discuss. (10 marks)

   (e) How would you appropriate to characterize G.S. Ghurye as a practitioner of 'theoretical pluralism'? (10 marks)

2. (a) Do you think that in a society like India, orthogenetic changes take place through differentiation? Do you observe continuities in the orthogenetic process? Elaborate your answer with suitable examples. (20 marks)

   (b) 'Agrarian class structure has been undergoing changes due to modern forces.' Critically examine. (20 marks)

   (c) How same sex marriages responsible for population dynamics in India? Discuss. (10 marks)

3. (a) What do you mean by nation building? What is the role of religion in nation building? Elaborate your answer. (20 marks)

   (b) Do you think that new economic reforms of British rule have disrupted the old economic system of India? Substantiate your answer with suitable examples. (20 marks)

   (c) Describe the main features of the Indian new middle class. How is it different from the old middle class? (10 marks)

4. (a) Who is said to be the pioneer of village studies in India? Illustratively describe contributions of some Indian sociologists on village studies. How their approaches are distinct from each other? (20 marks)

(b) 'Industrial class structure is a functions of social structure of Indian society.' Do you agree with this statement? Analyze. (20 marks)

(c) What is kinship? Briefly explain G. P. Murdock's contribution to the study of the kinship system. (10 marks)

SECTION B

5. Answer the following questions in about 150 words each: $(10 \times 5 = 50)$

(a) 'The transfer of land from cultivating to the non-cultivating owners is bringing about transformation in the Indian society.' Justify your answer by giving suitable illustrations. (10 marks)

(b) Bring out various factors responsible for declining of village industries in India. (10 marks)

(c) Discuss the social bases of political mobilization in independent India. Has some change occurred in these during the last 60-70 years? (10 marks)

(d) What are the major problems faced by the labour migrants while working in informal sectors of Indian States? Discuss. (10 marks)

(e) Do you think that the law has been able to abolish child labour in India? Comment. (10 marks)

6. (a) In what respects have the conditions of the Scheduled Castes and the Scheduled Tribes in India? Critically examine. (20 marks)

(b) Discuss the trend of urbanization in India. Do you think that industrialization is the only precondition of urbanization? Give you arguments. (20 marks)

(c) Which measures would you suggest for preventing caste conflicts in India? Justify your argument. (10 marks)

7. (a) What are the Private and Public network and support systems operative in Indian society for the aged? (20 marks)

(b) 'Educational development is the only Panacea for country's all ills and evils.' Critically examine the above statement with reference to NEP-2020. (20 marks)

(c) How Dalit movements in India have facilitated their identity formation ? Analyze. (10 marks)

8. (a) Is it possible to have sustainable development in India? Cite major environmental issues and suggest a few measures to achieve the sustainability. (20 marks)

(b) Do you think that forced displacement of labourers has caused their deprivation and resultant inequalities during the recent past years? Elaborate. (20 marks)

(c) What are the Indian government's schemes launched for poverty alleviation after the United Nations Declaration of 'Sustainable Development Goals-2015'? Briefly describe. (10 marks)

CHAPTER
1

Sociology: The Discipline

In this Chapter

- Modernity and Social Changes in Europe and Emergence of Sociology
- Scope of the Subject
- Comparison with other Social Sciences
- Sociology and Common Sense
- Previous Years' Questions

What is Sociology?

While growing up, we frequently hear the term 'society' or '*samaaj*' (in Hindi) in innumerable contexts. It is time and again reinforced that we live in a society, and there are things that are either good or bad in a society. The phrase that we hear too often is:- 'What will the society say?' It is natural to wonder what we exactly mean when we say 'society'. After all, an individual can only come in contact with a selective number of people in his/her lifetime. Do we refer to our family members as society? Or our friends and colleagues at work? Or the vast amount of unknown people who we will never meet and yet we know exist? These may sound like existential questions but in our day-to-day affairs, right from the international issues to our own individual circumstances, the amorphous entity of 'society' plays a significant role.

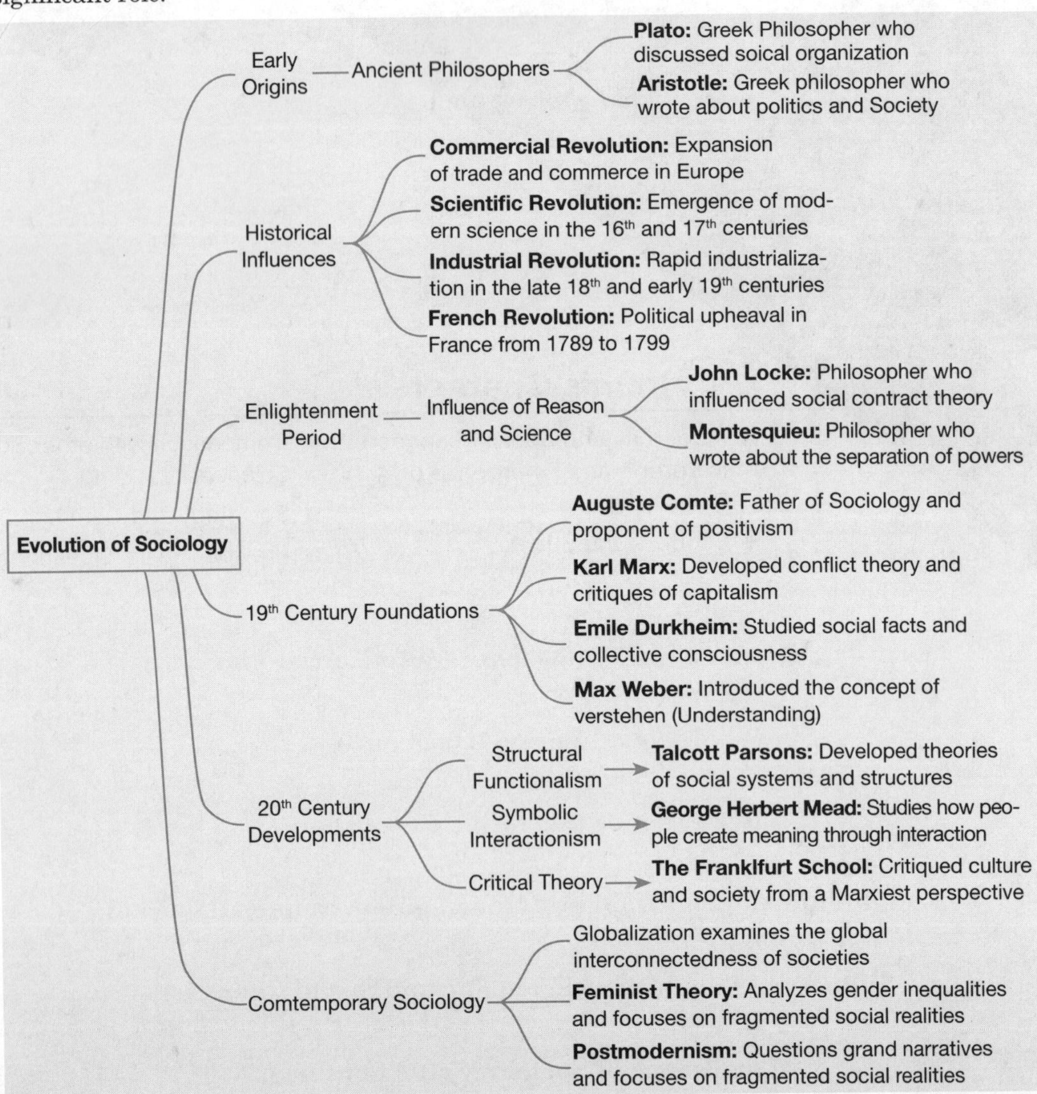

The discipline of sociology, in essence, refers to the study of society. Now, unlike objects in natural sciences, such as, a particular planet or a plant, society in social sciences is both abstract and real. It means that while the 'society' has no specific shape or appearance, it can be studied through study of things that constitute society—for instance, social groups, social relationships, social processes, social events, social spaces, social policies, social interactions, social practices, social structures, social rules, etc. The word 'social' implies the existence of two or more actors interacting with each other in a certain cultural setting in observable ways.

As per Anthony Giddens (2006), 'Sociology is the scientific study of human life, social groups, whole societies and the human world as such.' This definition highlights two traits of sociology—its subject matter and the scientific methods of study. It is a social 'science'. The term sociology was first coined in 1780 by the French essayist Emmanuel-Joseph Sieyès (1748–1836) in an unpublished manuscript. In 1838, the term was reinvented by Auguste Comte (1798–1857).

Modernity and Social Changes in Europe and Emergence of Sociology

Sociology emerged as a distinct academic discipline in the late 19th century, but its roots can be traced back to earlier philosophical and scientific traditions. Robert E Park commented that Sociology has a long past but only a short history. It is one of the youngest sciences at the same time one of the oldest areas of study as well. The origins of sociology can be traced back to ancient Greek philosophers, such as Plato and Aristotle, who wrote about the nature of society and the relationships between individuals and groups. However, it was not until the Enlightenment period in the 18th century that sociology began to take shape as a distinct field of study.

Sociology can be considered above all a science of the new industrial society. It emerged as a distinct science in nineteenth century Europe. Europe then was passing through a period of great changes which had set in with the French and the Industrial Revolutions. This period of change in the European Society is known as the Enlightenment Period as it embodied the spirit of a new awakening.

Ancient Greek Philosophers (Plato, Aristotle)

↓

Medieval Period (Dark Ages)

↓

Renaissance (Scientific Revolution)

↓

Enlightenment (Philosophers: Montesquieu, Rousseau, Locke)

↓

Industrial Revolution (Economic and Social Changes)

↓

Emergence of Sociology (19th Century)

Before the Onset of Modernity

- **Dark Ages:** The medieval period lasting roughly from fifth through the 13th centuries any have been called the Dark ages, because the common man was helpless, there was an arbitrary rule of the king, there was absence of national unity, there was a lack of education and people led miserable lives. Church during the medieval times emerged as the power centre and used to control the entire monarchy. It used to serve as the interfering power between the people and the Lords or Kings.

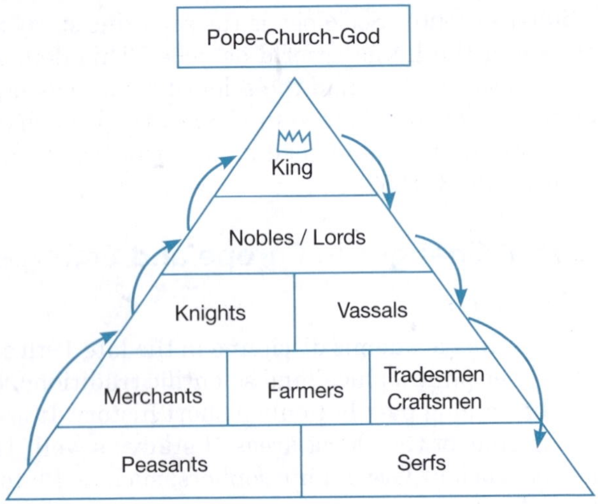

- **Feudalism**: It is a social hierarchy based on local administrative control and the distribution of land into units (fiefs). With feudalism, all the land in a kingdom belonged to the king. However, the king would give some of the land to the lords or nobles who fought for him. These presents of lands were called manors. The land was further given to knights (vassals) by their overlords. Fiefs were subdivided into manors and estates. This division of society based on land was also prominent in India. The Zamindar owned the land that was gifted to him by the provisional governors, Yavana, and ultimately it belonged to the king of the empire. Thus, the earliest division of society was based on status stratification and land-based power distribution.

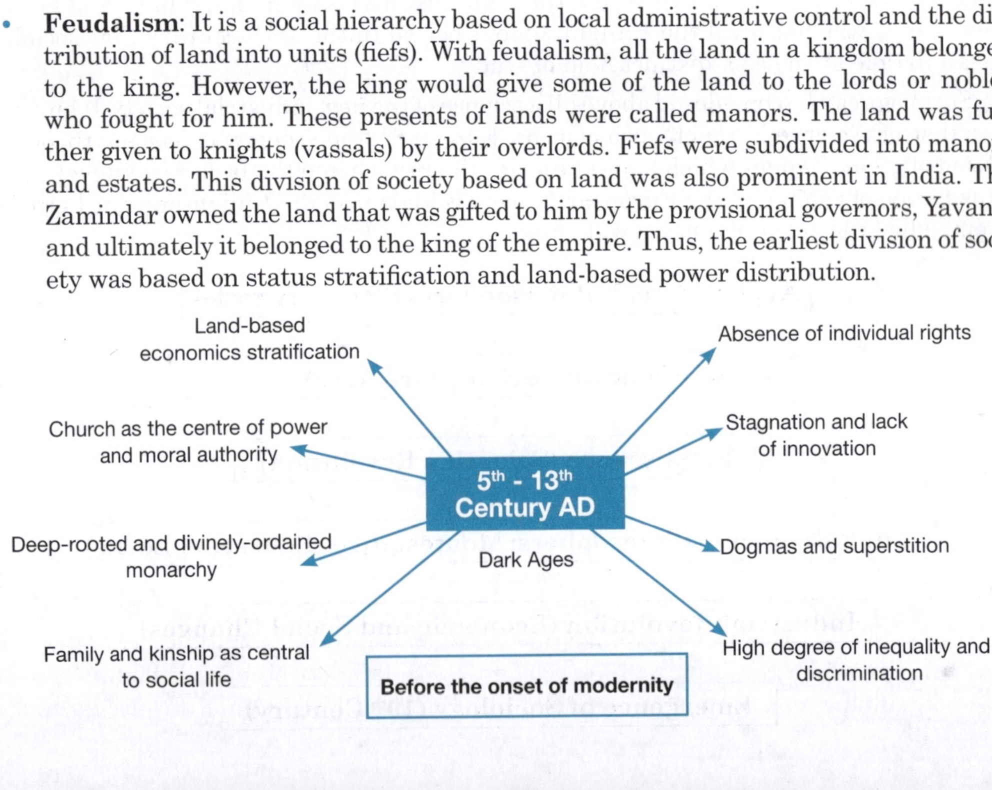

Pre-modern European society was characterized by several key features:

1 **Agrarian economy:** Land ownership and agricultural production formed the foundation of the economic system.
2 **Rigid social stratification:** Social classes were well-defined and relatively impermeable.
3 **Religious dominance:** The Church played a central role in shaping moral and social norms.
4 **Kinship-based social structure:** Family and extended familial relationships were integral to social organization.
5 **Monarchical political system:** Hereditary rule was prevalent, often justified through the concept of divine right.

The transition from this traditional societal structure began with the onset of the Renaissance in the 14th century. This period marked the beginning of significant shifts in European social, cultural, and political paradigms.

Modernity

The term modernity refers to a civilizational epoch. It is the 'period from the mid-eighteenth-century European Enlightenment to at least the mid-1980s, characterized by secularization, rationalization, democratization, individualization and the rise of science.' (Giddens & Sutton, 2014) While modernization refers to the process of making something contemporary, modernity has a much broader meaning referring to a historical period. Sociology itself is considered a product of modernity.

The clear demarcation of modernity as a distinct time period was a result of a series of social changes that the West, particularly Europe, underwent. However, it should be noted that the West was not the only region to do so. Besides being deemed as an epoch, during the twentieth century, many sociologists also theorized that modernity represented a 'societal model' that all nations would aspire to or be forced into eventually.

Walt Rostow argued that modernization was a process of moving through several stages 'as societies 'caught up' with the early modernisers and their economies began to grow. From a traditional, agrarian or agricultural base, societies could modernise by shedding their longstanding traditional values and institutions and investing for future prosperity in infrastructural projects and new industries. (Giddens & Sutton, 2014) According to Zygmunt Bauman, modernity represented a mentality in which order is privileged over randomness. Certain forces led to ushering in of modernity which further aided in the emergence of Sociology as a distinct discipline.

Social Forces

(a) **Commercial Revolution:** It refers to a series of events between 1450 to approximately 1800. The revolution signified the expansion of trade and commerce that took place from the fifteenth century onwards. The events shifted from a largely subsistence and stagnant economy of medieval Europe to a more dynamic and worldwide system. Major aspects included—a shift from land routes to sea-routes (Vasco da Gama landing in India, Christopher Columbus discovering America), destruction of monopoly in trade of Italian cities, flooding of European markets with new commodities such as spices, textiles, tobacco, cocoa, quinine, human slaves, etc., growth of banking, domination of countries like England, Holland and France, growth of companies, rise of the middle class which included bankers, investors, ship-owners, merchants, etc., strengthening of monarchy, decline of the Church, etc.

(b) **Scientific Revolution in the Renaissance Period:** Europe produced a 'scientific revolution' in the Renaissance period of 14th to 16th century AD. During the medieval period, church was the epicentre of power authority and learning. Learning was mostly of the religious variety. A scientific approach to nature and the human body became prevalent. Dissection of the human body became acceptable. Chemical processes like oxidation, reduction, distillation, amalgamation, etc., were studied. Copernicus's heliocentric theory (that earth revolved around the sun) drastically altered patterns of thought about the universe and human beings.

(c) **Political Revolutions:** Starting from the French Revolution in 1789, a long series of revolutions washed over well into the 19th century. While the impact of these revolutions was positive in many societies, the early thinkers were disturbed more by the chaos and disorder. They sought to seek ways to restore order to the society, some even attempting to return to the peaceful days of the Middle Ages. Some other sophisticated thinkers recognized that such a change would be impossible. The issue of social order was of central concern to thinkers like Comte, Durkheim and Parsons. The French Revolution, which erupted in 1789 marked a turning point in the history of human struggle for freedom and equality. It put an end to the age of feudalism and ushered in a new order of society. Even countries in other continents such as, India, were influenced by the ideas generated during this revolution. Ideas like liberty, fraternity and equality, which now form a part of the preamble to the Constitution of India, owe their origin to the French Revolution.

- The French society was divided into feudal 'estates'. The structure of the feudal French Society comprised the 'Three Estates'. Estates were defined as a system of stratification found in feudal European societies whereby one section or estate is distinguished from the other in terms of status, privileges and restriction accorded to that estate.
- The First Estate consisted of the clergy, which was stratified into higher clergy such as the cardinal, the archbishops, the bishops and the abbots. They lived a life of luxury and gave a very little attention to religion. They used to guide the monarch and were close to the administration of the kingdom.
- The Second Estate consisted of the nobility. The Nobels of the robe were nobles not by birth, but title. They were the magistrates and judges.
- The Third Estate comprised the rest of the society or the common people and included the peasants, the merchants, the artisans and other. As compared to the peasants, the condition of the middle classes, also known as the bourgeoisie comprising the merchants, bankers, lawyers, manufactures, etc., was much better. These classes too belonged to the third estate.
- After the French Revolution, the bourgeoisie, i.e., the bankers, merchants, etc., became rich and powerful, hence they started exploiting the weaker sections of the Third Estate.

(d) **Industrial Revolution and the Rise of Capitalism:** The industrial revolution though traced back to around 1760 AD, was not a single event but a culmination of a large number of a series of events – large number of people leaving farms for work in factories, factories transforming due to a large number of technological improvements, emergence of large economic bureaucracies, free exchange of products with money in the marketplace, etc. The emergent capitalism was resisted through labour movements. All these changes affected sociologists greatly, particularly Marx, Weber, Durkheim and Simmel.

(e) **The Rise of Socialism:** Marx opposed the excesses of capitalism and industrial system by favouring socialism. However, many other sociologists favoured reforms within the framework of capitalism itself. As a result, a great deal of sociological theory emerged in reaction to Marx's approach.

(f) **Feminism:** Events, such as mobilization of women for securing voting rights, mobilization against slavery, etc., influenced the works of women thinkers such as Harriet Martineau, Charlotte Perkins Gilman, Jane Addams, Florence Kelley, Anna Julia Cooper, Ida Wells-Barnett, Marianne Weber, and Beatrice Potter Webb. However, their work was pushed to the periphery of the discipline by male theorists like Spencer, Durkheim, etc., who were organizing the discipline.

(g) **Urbanization:** Industrial revolution led to a large number of people migrating from the rural settings to urban areas. But the expansion of the cities produced a seemingly endless list of urban problems—overcrowding, pollution, noise, traffic, and so forth. The first major American School of Sociology, the Chicago School, was in large part defined by its concern for the city.

(h) **Religious Change:** Many early sociologists like Durkheim and Comte came from religious backgrounds and imposed religious objectives onto their sociological leanings. Thinkers like Marx and Weber also wrote on the role religion played in people's oppression and economic growth respectively.

(i) **The Growth of Science:** During this period, science was gradually permeating every area of life. Resultantly, even sociologists (especially Comte, Durkheim, Spencer, Mead, and Schutz) were preoccupied with science, and many wanted to model sociology after the successful physical and biological sciences.

Intellectual Forces

The Enlightenment and Renaissance: Catalysts for Sociological Thought

The Enlightenment period, spanning the 17th and 18th centuries, marked a transformative era of intellectual advancement and philosophical evolution in European history. This period, along with the preceding Renaissance, laid crucial groundwork for the eventual development of sociology as a discipline.

Key Enlightenment thinkers, such as Charles Montesquieu (1689–1755), Jean-Jacques Rousseau (1712–1778), and John Locke made significant contributions that would later influence sociological theory. Montesquieu, in his seminal work 'The Spirit of the Laws,' proposed the separation of powers and advocated for individual liberty. Locke posited the existence of inalienable individual rights, including the right to life, property, and personal freedom. Rousseau's 'The Social Contract' introduced the concept of popular sovereignty. Voltaire championed religious tolerance and freedom of expression.

While these ideas were instrumental in precipitating events like the French Revolution, their initial impact on sociology was complex. As Irving Zeitlin noted, 'Early sociology developed as a reaction to the Enlightenment. This dialectical relationship would prove formative for the nascent field.

Contemporaneous thinkers such as René Descartes and Thomas Hobbes emphasized the construction of comprehensive, abstract systems of thought grounded in rationality. This period also witnessed the application of scientific methodologies to social phenomena. The prevailing belief was that reason and empirical research could unlock universal understanding and control.

The Enlightenment's emphasis on reason and its challenge to traditional authority significantly influenced early sociological theorists. It contributed to the conceptualization of sociology as a scientific discipline, even as the field would go on to critique and build upon Enlightenment principles.

This era's intellectual ferment, with its focus on rationality, empiricism, and social progress, established a philosophical and methodological foundation upon which sociology would later construct its unique perspective on human society and social interactions.

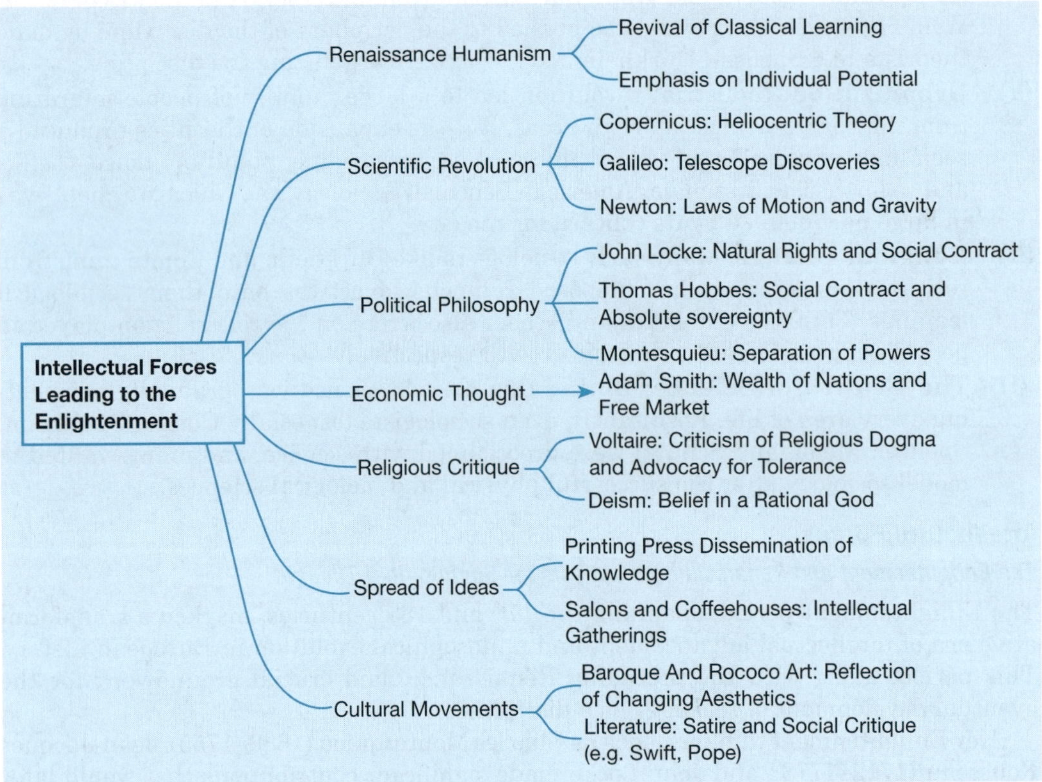

Important post-renaissance developments that had an impact on social theorists:

(a) The work of physicists and mathematicians like Galileo Galilei (1564–1642), Johannes Kepler (1571–1630) and subsequently, Sir Isaac Newton (1642–1727) brought to the forefront the experimental method.

(b) Circulation of blood was discovered by William Harvey (1578–1657). This led to the view of human organism in terms of interrelated parts and interconnected systems. This had its impact on social thought of Comte, Spencer, Durkheim, to name a few.

(c) In 'Origin of the Species'(1859), Charles Darwin put forward the theory that various living organisms compete for the limited resources the earth has to offer (the survival of the fittest as the natural law). Darwin also studied 'human evolution', tracing it in his work, 'Descent of Man' (1863) and traced the origins of the human species to some ape-like ancestors. This book created a huge uproar as the conservatives' idea of God having created all human beings was contested by his theory. As a result, even social theorists saw societies as constantly 'evolving' or developing from a lower to a higher stage.

The intellectual forces of the 18th century influenced the emergence of sociology in the following ways:

(a) Firstly, the 18th century thinkers began to study the human conditions in a scientific way using the methods of the natural sciences. They consciously applied scientific principles of analysis to the study of human beings in a way that had not been adopted before.

FYI

How Conservative Reaction to Enlightenment Led to the Emergence of Sociology?

Irving Zeitlin provided a series of propositions emerging from conservative reaction to Enlightenment that formed the basis of French Sociology, these include:

1. As opposed to Enlightenment thinkers who emphasized on the individual, the conservative reaction led to a larger sociological interest in society and other large-scale phenomena.
2. Society, by producing the individual, was deemed as the most important unit of analysis.
3. Instead of the individual, the basic components of society were considered to be roles, structures, relationships, positions, institutions, etc.
4. The parts of society were seen to be interrelated, leading to the argument that any change in one part will cause a change in the others.
5. Change was seen as a threat to both the society and the individuals.
6. The various large scale components were seen as useful for the society and the individuals.
7. Small units such as family, neighbourhood, religious groups, etc., were also seen as essential for the survival of individuals in modern society.
8. Modernising changes such as urbanization, bureaucratization, industrialization, etc., were seen to have negative effects.
9. The emphasis was on non-rational factors such as ritual, ceremony, worship, etc.
10. The conservatives also supported the hierarchical system of status and reward for the well-being of society.

(b) Secondly, the 18th century thinkers upheld reason as a measure to judge social institutions.

(c) Thirdly, the 18th century thinkers believed that human beings are capable of attaining perfection. They believed that social institutions can be changed to actualize the potential creative powers.

Three other intellectual influences current in the post-Enlightenment period influenced the emergence of sociology in Europe:

(a) **The Philosophy of History:** The basic assumption of this philosophy was that society must have progressed through a series of steps from a simple to complex stage. Associated thinkers included Abbe Saint Pierre and Giambattista.

(b) **The Biological Theories of Evolution:** Sociology moved towards an evolutionary approach and was modeled on biology. It led to strengthening of conception of society as an organism. Associated thinkers included Herbert Spencer and Durkheim.

(c) **The Surveys of Social Conditions:** Social survey as a method of inquiry emerged due to two reasons, one was the growing conviction that the methods of the natural sciences should and could be extended to the study of human affairs; that human phenomenon could be classified and measured. The other was the concern with poverty as a social, not natural problem.

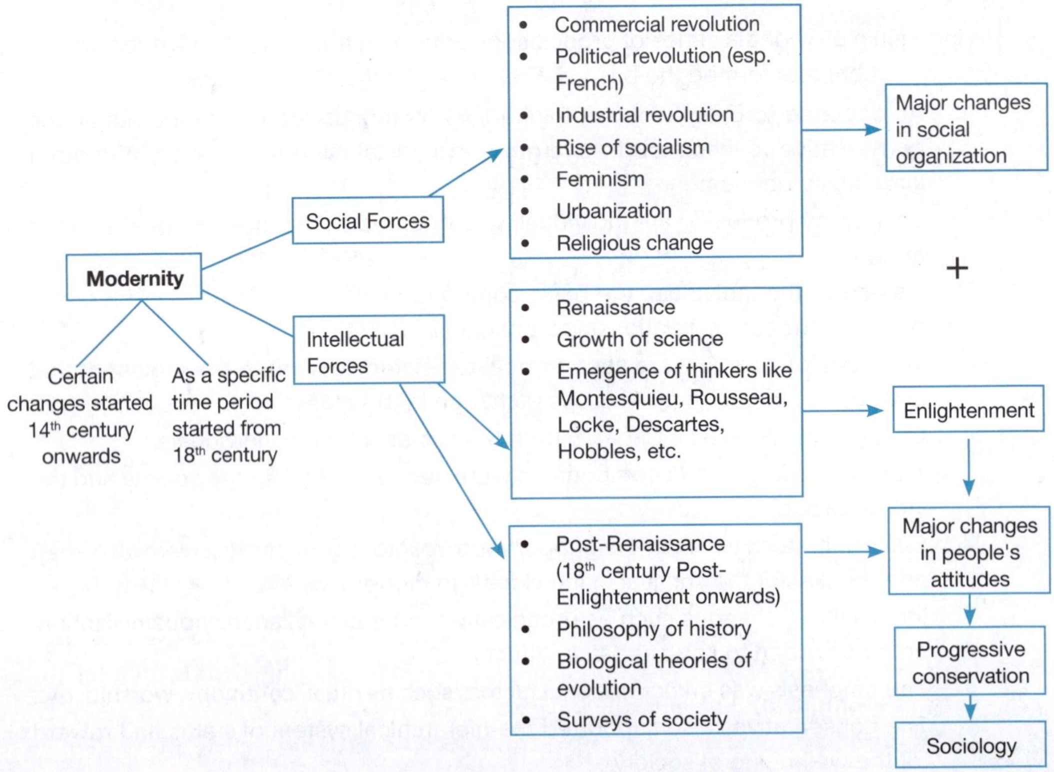

Scope of Sociology

For a sociologist,

(a) a society is more than the sum of its parts, meaning society is more than the actions, thoughts, values, beliefs and wishes of its individual members.

(b) a society is a complex and abstract reality.

The word 'scope' refers to the available space for activity or the variety of subjects that can be studied. In order to understand the scope of sociology, one should know what sociology concerns itself with.

Sociology deals with:

(a) **Society:** As a relatively self-sufficient, large group of people who maintain direct or indirect contact with each other through a culture.

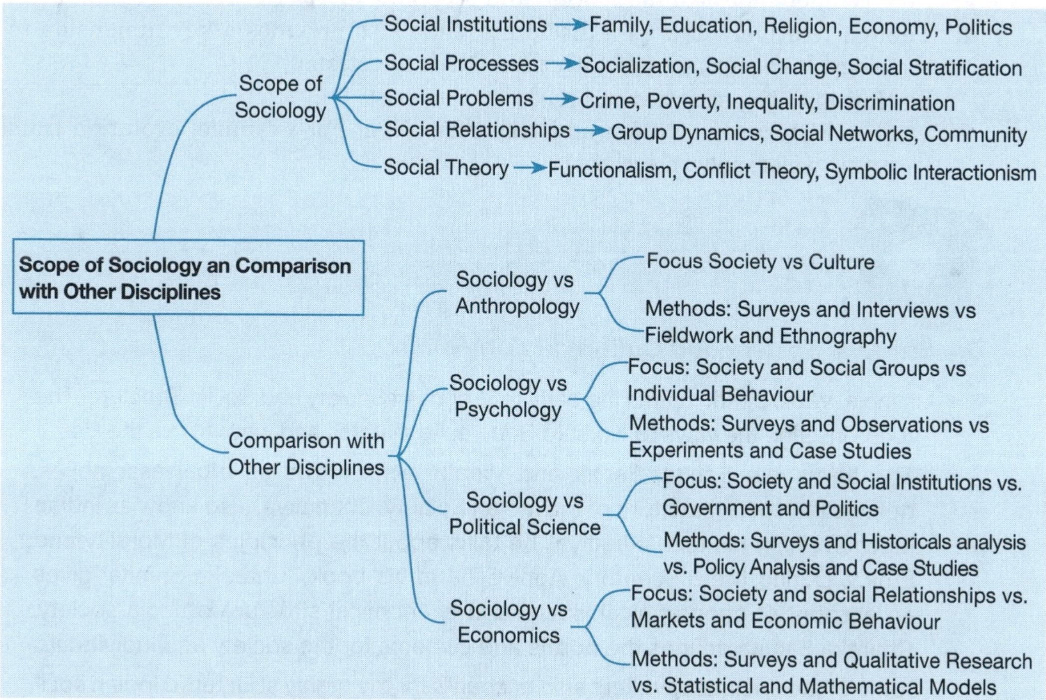

(b) **Sociological Imagination:** Studying anything sociologically entails breaking free from personal circumstances and putting them in a wider context. C. Wright Mills coined the term 'sociological imagination' to cultivate our imagination in order to look at even the routine processes anew. For example, unemployment is not just reflective of personal abilities but also symptomatic of the larger economic scenario.

(c) **Culture:** Shared beliefs, goals, artifacts, experiences, language, etc., that combine to form a unique and observable pattern.

1. **Social Groups:** Groups of two or more people with patterned interaction sustained over a period of time.

i. Charles Horton Cooley identified two types of social groups: 1. Primary groups—relatively small, homogenous groups with members having face-to-face contact and intimate cooperative relationships (e.g. Family), 2. Secondary groups—generally large size groups with members having limited, formal and impersonal relationships (e.g. a trade union).
ii. German sociologist Ferdinand Tonnies distinguished between Gemeinschaft (small traditional homogenous societies where primary groups and informal intimate relationships dominate) and Gesellschaft (large modern heterogeneous societies where secondary groups and contractual relationships dominate).

2. **Social Processes:** The dynamic aspects of social relations which contribute to both maintenance and change, such as socialization, social control, cooperation, conflict, social stratification, etc.
3. **Social Institutions:** Structures that provide stability, such as family, education, religion, political institution and economic institution.
4. Though relatively new as a discipline, time also provides a key dimension to sociology. It concerns itself with three basic questions:
   i. How and why societies emerge?
   (The historical evolution and transformation. For example, evolution from primitive to modern society.)

FYI

The Study of Society and Culture in Early India

- In India, Vedic period marks the early reference of Society and Social Structure. The Vedas inscribe the ways to worship God, recite mantras and ways to live the life.
- The terms like Sabha, Samiti and Vidath, also knows as tribal assemblies, defines the social structure of the Indian Society. Chanakya, also know as Indian Machiavelli, in his text, 'Kautilya', he talks about the principles of Morality and Ethics. During the 8th century, Agnivesha in his book, 'Charaka Samita' gives an account of geographical, social and economical structure of India society. Charaka Samita defines the norms and customs for the society and individual.
- Some of the ancient travellers also accounts for the highly structured Indian society. Megasthenes, a greek traveller who travelled during the Mauryan Empire writes about the system of classes. In his book, 'Indica', he talks about the distribution of society into seven classes: the wise man (Brahmins), farmers, herdsmen, artisans, soldiers, over lookers and government officials including army and navy officials. A Chinese traveller, Faxian who traveller India from China on foot around 337 BC–442 BC i.e., during the empire of Chandragupta-II was deeply impressed by the ideal and mild administration affected by Buddhism, economic prosperity and the simplicity of the people. This division of society based on the caste is called stratification, in sociology.

ii. How and why societies persist?
(The status quo and changes in the present. For example, role of structures like the State, bureaucracy, traditions, customs, etc.)

iii. How and why societies change?
(The predictions for the future based on recurring patterns or unprecedented changes. For example, the role of technology, inventions, social movements, etc.)

Based on the aforementioned concepts, units of study and concerns, it can be readily implied that the scope of sociology is extremely wide. In practical terms, it can range 'from analysis of passing encounters between individuals on the street to the investigation of international relations and global forms of terrorism.' (Giddens, 2006).

Though the discipline is concerned with the 'general' study of society as opposed to others that deal with the more specific areas like psychology, economics, political science, etc., the boundaries between sociology and other areas have become increasingly blurred over time. Streams like social psychology, social anthropology, sociology of economics, political sociology, etc., all combine sociological aspects with other areas of study.

Schools of Thought

There are two main schools of thought regarding the scope of Sociology i.e., the specialist or formalistic school and the synthetic school.

(a) **The Specialist or Formalistic School:** The major approach of thinkers under this school was to keep the subject matter of Sociology limited. Their objectives were to keep the discipline very compact. They treated sociology as a specific and independent science. The supporters of this school of thoughts were George Simmel, Vierkandt, Max Weber, Vonwise and F. Tonnies. George Simmel says that the study of sociology should be limited to formal behaviour of the individual.

Key points of this school of thought includes the following:

- Vierkandt wanted that sociology should also include the study of love and emotions. He emphasized the study of emotions of love, hate, and togetherness.
- Vonwise categorized social relationships. His work divided the social relationships into 650 human interactions and their study was to be termed as Sociology. Max Weber advocated interpretative understanding. Ferdinand Tonnies divided sociology into Gesellschaft (society) and Gemeinschaft (community). Simmel believed that sociology should deal with social relationships from different angles.
- This school emphasized the importance of specialized knowledge and the use of scientific methods to study social phenomena. The specialist school focuses on the study of specific social institutions, such as the family, education, and religion, and examines their functions and structures in isolation from other social institutions.
- Its main features include:
  (i) Sociology is a specific, pure and independent social science.
  (ii) Scope of sociology is very narrow and limited.
  (iii) Sociology deals with specific form of human relationships.
  (iv) Sociology need not to study all the events connected with social science.

- The main achievements of the Specialist School include:
    - (i) Development of specialized knowledge—The school emphasized the development of specialized knowledge with a focus on specific social institutions and processes.
    - (ii) Scientific methods—The school emphasized the use of scientific methods, such as surveys, observations, and experiments, to study social phenomena.
    - (iii) Objectivity—The Specialist School aimed to achieve objectivity in sociological research, focusing on empirical data and quantitative analysis.
- However, the Specialist School has also faced criticism for its narrow focus and lack of consideration of the broader social context.

(b) **The Synthetic School:** The Synthetic School emerged as a response to the criticisms of the Specialist School. This approach emphasises the importance of understanding society as a whole and the interconnectedness of social institutions and processes. The Synthetic School focuses on the study of social structures, such as class, race, and gender, and examines how these structures shape social institutions and individual behaviour. The thinkers of this school wanted to make sociology as the general science like social science. This school emerged as a reaction to the Formalistic School. The thinkers of this school said that Sociology should be a synthesis of social science and general sciences. Sociology is not a thing to be studied in silos or within compartments; this should be wide open with diverse reach. The main proponents of the synthetic school are the sociologists like Ginsberg, Durkheim, Comte, Sorokin, Spencer, F. Ward, and L.T. Hobhouse. According to this school:

- Sociology is a general and systematic social science.
- Scope of Sociology is very vast.
- Sociology needs help from other social science.
- It is synthesis of social science.
- Sociology is closely related with each other social science.
- The significant achievements of the Synthetic School include:
    - (i) **Holistic Understanding:** The Synthetic School contributed to a more comprehensive understanding of society, highlighting the interconnectedness of social institutions and processes.
    - (ii) **Critical Perspective:** The school emphasized a critical perspective on society, examining how social structures and institutions perpetuate inequality and social problems.
    - (iii) **Integration of Multiple Disciplines:** The Synthetic School drew on multiple disciplines, such as sociology, psychology, anthropology, and history, to provide a more comprehensive understanding of society.
- Durkheim divided Synthetic school in three major divisions:
    - (i) **Social Morphology:** The main focus here is the structure of society. According to Durkheim, Social Morphology includes all those components which relate to human population, geography of area, size, distribution, density, etc., and all these factors will decide human behaviour.
    - (ii) **Social Physiology:** In this, Durkheim emphasized on functions and mechanism of society i.e., culture, religion, laws, practices, etc.

(iii) **General Sociology:** Durkheim underlined that the general laws of society should be studied in general sociology. This will include the general theory of social science.

- However, the Synthetic School has also faced criticism for its broad focus, which some argue lacks the depth and specialized knowledge of the Specialist School.

Formalistic school believes in the study of the parts, which makes up the society and synthetic school advocates the study of the whole society. Both the schools complement each other. They are not opposed to each other. Therefore, we can say that Sociology is both a general science of society and at the same time also a specialized discipline. Therefore, it is neither possible nor desirable to restrict its scope.

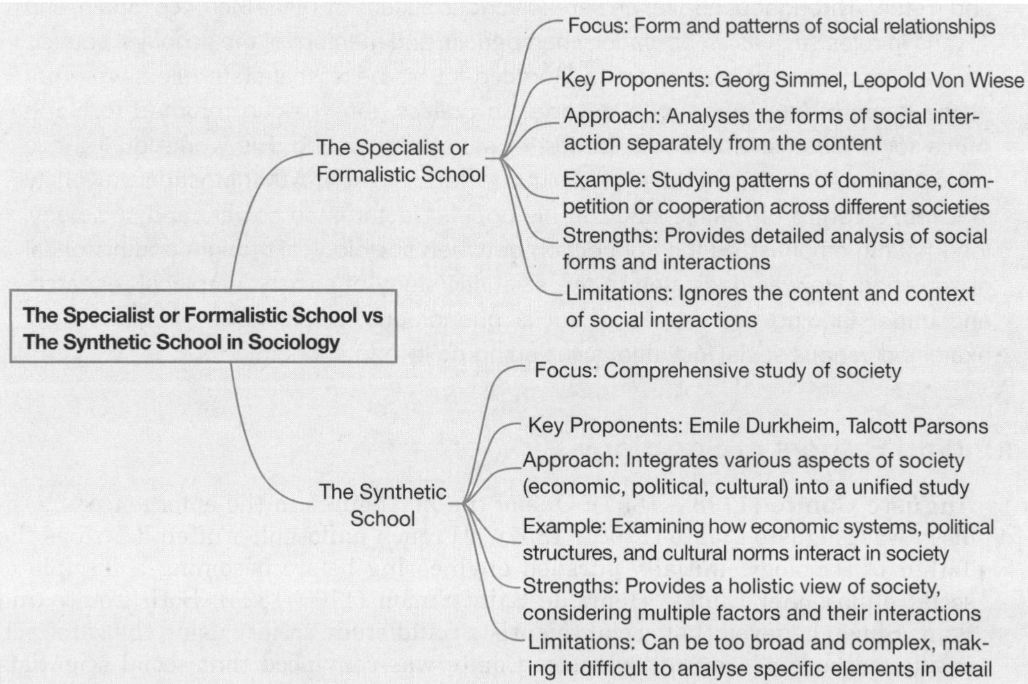

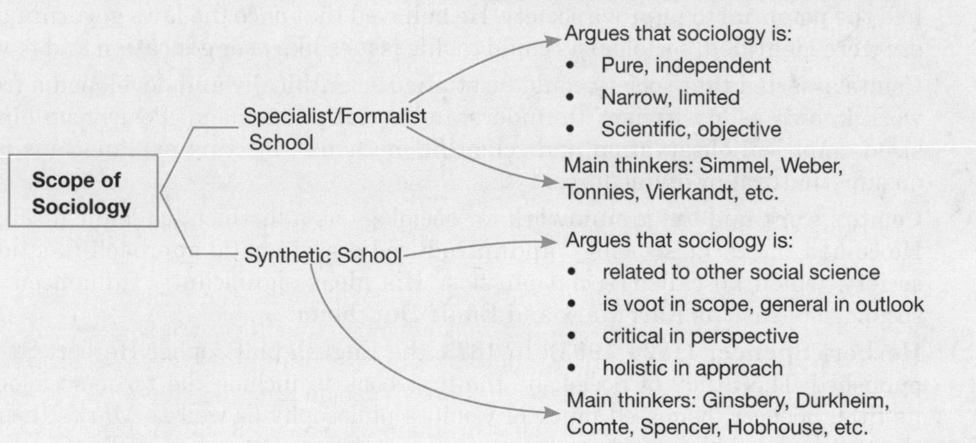

FYI

Is Sociology Exclusively Modern and European?

Sociology is often regarded as a modern, Western phenomenon. However, sociological ideas and theories were being developed long ago and in other parts of the world. One notable example is Abdel Rahman Ibn-Khaldun, born in Tunis, North Africa, on May 27, 1332. Coming from an educated family, Ibn-Khaldun studied the Koran, mathematics, and history. Throughout his life, he served various sultans in Tunis, Morocco, Spain, and Algeria in roles such as ambassador, chamberlain, and member of the scholars' council. He was imprisoned for two years in Morocco for his belief that state rulers were not divine leaders. After about two decades in politics, Ibn-Khaldun returned to North Africa for an intensive five-year period of study and writing. His works during this period elevated his fame and earned him a lectureship at Al-Azhar Mosque University in Cairo, a centre of Islamic study. In his popular lectures on society and sociology, Ibn-Khaldun emphasized the connection between sociological thought and historical observation. He was dedicated to the scientific study of society, empirical research, and understanding the causes of social phenomena. Additionally, he extensively examined various social institutions, including polity and economy.

Founding Fathers of Sociology

(a) **Auguste Comte (1798 – 1857):** One of the key figures in the emergence of sociology was Auguste Comte (1798 – 1857), a French philosopher often hailed as the 'father of sociology,' initially pursued engineering before becoming a disciple of social philosopher Claude Henri de Saint-Simon (1760–1825). Both Comte and Saint-Simon believed that social scientists could study society using the same scientific methods as natural sciences. Comte was convinced that social scientists had the potential to improve society. He believed that once the laws governing society were identified, sociologists could tackle issues like poor education and poverty.

Comte asserted that society could be studied scientifically and developed a framework known as 'positivism' to understand social phenomena. Positivism emphasized empirical observation and scientific methods, rejecting explanations based on supernatural or divine forces.

Comte's work laid the groundwork for sociology as a distinct academic discipline. He coined the term 'sociology' and introduced a systematic approach to studying society, which he called 'social physics.' His ideas significantly influenced later sociologists such as Karl Marx and Emile Durkheim.

(b) **Herbert Spencer (1820–1903):** In 1873, the English philosopher Herbert Spencer published 'The Study of Sociology,' the first book to include the term 'sociology' in its title. Spencer dismissed much of Comte's philosophy as well as Marx's theory of class struggle and his advocacy for communism. Instead, he supported a government structure that allowed market forces to control capitalism. Herbert Spencer's sociological works, such as 'Social Statics' (1850), 'The Study of Sociology' (1873), and 'Principles of Sociology' (1876 – 96), are heavily influenced by the concept of evolution. Spencer believed that social evolution has consistently progressed from a simple, uniform, or homogeneous structure to a complex, diverse, or heterogeneous one. Deeply influenced by Charles Darwin's 'The Origin of Species' (1859), Spencer's work significantly impacted many early sociologists, including Émile Durkheim (1858–1917).

(c) **Harriet Martineau (1802–1876):** Regarded by many as the first female sociologist, she was a prolific writer who tackled a broad spectrum of social science topics. She was an early observer of various social practices, such as economics, social class, religion, suicide, government, and women's rights. Her writing career commenced in 1931 with a series of stories titled *Illustrations of Political Economy*, aimed at educating the general public about economic principles (Johnson 2003).

Martineau was the pioneer in translating Comte's works from French to English, thereby introducing sociology to English-speaking scholars (Hill 1991). She is also renowned for conducting the first systematic methodological international comparisons of social institutions in her notable works *Society in America* (1837) and *Retrospect of Western Travel* (1838). Martineau highlighted the inconsistencies between the principles of capitalism and the professed moral values of people in the United States, criticising the free enterprise system for exploiting and impoverishing workers while enriching business owners.

(d) **Karl Marx (1818–1883):** Marx, a German philosopher and economist, was a pivotal figure in the evolution of sociology. His work primarily explored the interplay between economic and social structures, asserting that social inequality and conflict stemmed from the economic system. Marx's insights into class struggle and its impact on society significantly influenced sociological theories regarding conflict and social change.

In 1848, he and Friedrich Engels (1820–1895) co-authored the *Communist Manifesto*, one of history's most influential political documents. This work outlined Marx's societal theory, which contrasted sharply with Comte's positivism. Marx believed that societal growth and change were driven by the conflicts between different social classes over production means. During his theoretical development, the Industrial Revolution and the rise of capitalism created stark wealth disparities between factory owners and workers. Capitalism, characterized by private or corporate ownership of goods and production means, expanded in many countries.

(e) **Emile Durkheim (1858–1917):** He was a French sociologist who made significant contributions to the field of sociology. Durkheim's work focused on the role of social solidarity and the ways in which social institutions, such as religion, helped to maintain social order. He argued that social facts, or the shared values, beliefs, and practices of a society, had a profound impact on individual behaviour and social outcomes.

Durkheim was of the opinion that sociologists could study objective 'social facts' (Poggi 2000). He also believed by conducting such studies it would be possible to determine if a society was 'healthy' or 'pathological.' He saw healthy societies as stable while pathological societies experienced a breakdown in social norms between individuals and society.

(f) **Max Weber (1864 – 1920):** Key figures in the development of sociology include Max Weber (1864 – 1920), who introduced the concept of 'verstehen,' or understanding social action through empathetic interpretation, and Ferdinand Tönnies (1855 – 1936), who developed the concepts of 'Gemeinschaft' and 'Gesellschaft.' These terms describe the difference between traditional, communal societies and modern, individualistic societies.

Weber posited that the individual is the fundamental unit of society. He believed that human motivations, actions, and relationships should be analysed scientifically. 'Verstehen,' or interpretative understanding, is an effective method for comprehending the dynamics of society and culture, which cannot be reduced to merely observable objects.

The social scientist's task is to discern the inner meaning of social phenomena. Society and culture are not elements to be quantified like natural objects; rather, they require interpretation. Social actions and human relationships are qualitative in nature. Thus, it is essential to use empathy along with objectivity for a thorough understanding of social phenomena.

Weber suggested that the 'ideal type' can serve as an appropriate methodological tool for this purpose. For him, sociology is the interpretative understanding of social action. His principal works include 'The Protestant Ethic and the Spirit of Capitalism,' 'Economy and Society,' and 'Methodology of Social Sciences.'

(g) **Georg Simmel (1858–1918):** Simmel is known for his work on urban sociology, social conflict, and the philosophy of history. He argued that urbanization and industrialization led to the breakdown of traditional social structures and the emergence of new forms of social organization. Simmel also developed the concept of the 'stranger,' which refers to the anonymous, impersonal relationships that characterise urban life. Additionally, he argued that social conflict arises from the struggle between individuals and groups for scarce resources and power. Simmel's work laid the foundation for the development of sociological theories of urbanization, social conflict, and social change.

(h) **Vilfred Pareto (1848–1923):** Pareto was an Italian sociologist who made significant contributions to the field of sociology, particularly in the areas of social stratification and the study of elites. He developed the concept of the '80/20 rule,' which suggests that 80% of social wealth and power is held by 20% of the population. Pareto also argued that social inequality is a natural and inevitable result of human nature, and that societies are divided into two main groups: the 'foxes' (those who are clever and cunning) and the 'hedgehogs' (those who are simple and honest). Pareto's work influenced the development of sociological theories of social stratification and elite theory.

(i) **Thorstein Veblen (1857–1929):** An eminent American sociologist, Veblen is renowned for his insightful analysis of conspicuous consumption and the social psychology underpinning consumer behaviour. He posited that within capitalist societies, individuals engage in consumption to exhibit their social status and differentiate themselves from others. Veblen introduced the concept of 'conspicuous consumption,' which describes the use of luxury goods and services to signal wealth and status. His critique of the excesses inherent in capitalist society highlighted how consumer culture influences social interactions. Veblen's work significantly impacted the development of sociological theories concerning consumer behaviour and the social psychology of consumption.

(j) **George Herbert Mead (1863–1931):** Mead was an American sociologist who made significant contributions to the field of sociology, particularly in the areas of social psychology and symbolic interactionism. He argued that social behaviour is shaped by the interactions between individuals and their social environment, and that people develop their self-concept through interactions with others. Mead also developed the concept of 'Generalized other,' which refers to the social norms and expectations that shape individual behaviour. His work emphasized the importance of understanding the ways in which social interactions shape individual behaviour and social relations. Mead's work influenced the development of sociological theories of social psychology and symbolic interactionism.

(k) **Talcott Parsons (1902–1982):** Talcott Parsons, a prominent American sociologist, perceives sociology as the examination of social relationships and cultural products. He endeavored to align social science closely with natural science, emphasizing the preeminence of reason in sociological theory. Parsons refers to social science as 'action science,' which encompasses the study of interactions and values. His notable works include 'The Structure of Social Action' and 'The Social System.' Key themes in his work are the action frame of reference, the social system, and pattern variables. According to Parsons, a social system comprises multiple individual actors interacting within a context. The essence of a social system is the structured normative order that collectively organizes the life of a population.

Comparison with Other Social Sciences

A sociologist focuses on the broad examination of social behaviour as it manifests within both large and small groups. The primary aim is to analyse social relations and dynamics comprehensively, rather than within a specific context. The term 'general' is employed because other social science disciplines concentrate on more specialized fields. For instance, a political scientist investigates governmental functions and activities, while an economist examines the production and distribution of goods. In this regard, a comparison of sociology with other sciences is given below:

Criteria	Sociology	Anthropology	Psychology	Political Science	Economics
Definition	The study of the development, structure, and functioning of human society.	The study of human societies and cultures and their development.	The study of the mind and behaviour.	The study of systems of governance and political activity.	The study of production, distribution, and consumption of goods and services.
Main Focus	Social groups, institutions, and patterns of behaviour	Cultural practices, artifacts, and human evolution	Individual and group behaviour and mental processes	Power, governance, and political behaviours	Scarcity, resource allocation, and market behaviours

Methods	Surveys, case studies, participant observation, and historical analysis	Fieldwork, participant observation, and ethnographies	Experiments, case studies, and surveys	Surveys, case studies, and comparative analysis	Mathematical models, statistical analysis, and case studies
Key Concepts	Socialization, social institutions, social change, and social stratification	Culture, ethnocentrism, kinship, and evolution	Cognition, emotion, motivation, and personality	Democracy, authoritarianism, and international relations	Supply, demand, elasticity, and utility
Subfields	Urban sociology, criminology, social theory, and medical sociology	Physical anthropology, archaeology, and linguistic anthropology	Clinical psychology, cognitive psychology, and social psychology	Comparative politics, international relations, and political theory	Microeconomics, macroeconomics, and econometrics
Interdisciplinary Nature	Often overlaps with other social sciences, particularly anthropology and political science	Overlaps with sociology, linguistics, and archaeology	Interfaces with biology (neuroscience) and sociology	Engages with history, law, and sociology	Interfaces with mathematics, political science, and history
Application	Policy-making, social work, and community development	Cultural preservation, human rights advocacy, and development work	Therapy, human resources, and education	Policy analysis, diplomacy, and public administration	Finance, public policy, and business consulting

Sociology Versus Psychology

Consider a large-scale family reunion as an analogy for understanding the distinction between psychology and sociology. While psychology can be linked to an in-depth analysis of an individual family member's personal narratives, cognitive processes, and emotional experiences, sociology takes a broader perspective. It examines the dynamics of the entire familial gathering, identifying recurring patterns of interaction and investigating the underlying factors that influence group behaviours.

For instance, a sociological approach might explore why certain family members consistently maintain physical distance from others, or how familial roles and power structures manifest in seating arrangements and social clustering. In essence, where psychology delves into the intricacies of individual minds and emotions, sociology focuses on collective behaviours, institutional influences, and broader societal trends that shape human interactions within groups.

Psychology versus Sociology		
S.No.	**Psychology**	**Sociology**
1.	Study of Behaviour and Mental Systems	Science of Society – Social System
2.	Sigmund Freud & John Stuart Mill emphasized the primacy of psychology, arguing that all social phenomena derive from individual minds and psyches.	Émile Durkheim established sociology as a distinct discipline.
3.	Man's Mental actvities and Behaviour	Weber – Social Behaviour + underlying Meanings
4.	More Scientific and Specific	Family, religion, Power, Individual Social Changes.
5.	To Study Individual Behaviour	To Study Collective Behaviour
Social Psychology : Bridges the gap between both		

Girth and Mills explored intersections between psychology and sociology.

Sociology Versus Economics

Picture a bustling marketplace. If economics is focused on how money changes hands, the price of apples, or why some stalls are busier than others, sociology might look at why certain groups of people tend to shop together, or how the market's design affects social interactions. In other words, while economics studies the production, distribution, and consumption of goods and services, sociology delves into the social relationships and structures around those activities.

Aspect	Economics	Sociology
Primary Focus	Study of production, distribution, and consumption of goods and services	Study of society, social relationships, and social behaviour
Scope	Relatively narrow, focusing on economic activities and markets	Wide, encompassing various social phenomena including economic activities

Methodology	More quantitative, often using mathematical models and statistical analysis	Mix of quantitative and qualitative methods, including ethnography, surveys, and interviews
Theoretical Approach	Tends to seek universal laws and generalizable principles	Recognizes context-dependent nature of social phenomena; less universal laws
Key Theorists	Adam Smith, John Maynard Keynes, Milton Friedman	Karl Marx, Émile Durkheim, Max Weber, Talcott Parsons
View of Economic Activity	Central focus, often analyzed in isolation	One aspect of broader social activity and structures
Treatment of Individual	Often assumes rational, self-interested actor (homo economicus)	Considers individuals as shaped by and shaping social structures and norms
Policy Implications	Often provides specific, technical solutions based on economic models	Offers broader, more nuanced interpretations of social issues and potential interventions
Interdisciplinary Overlap	Economic sociology: application of sociological perspectives to economic phenomena	Social economics: study of the relationship between economic activity and social life
Example of Unique Contribution	Theories of market equilibrium, supply and demand	Theories of social stratification, cultural capital
Emerging Areas	Behavioural economics, environmental economics	Digital sociology, sociology of climate change

Sociology Versus Anthropology

Think of sociology and anthropology as two friends watching a community festival. While sociology might comment on the current patterns and group behaviours – like how and why people are dancing in a certain way or the roles people play in the celebration while, anthropology might dig deeper into the origins of the dance, connect it to ancient traditions, and look at similar practices in other cultures. Anthropology often emphasises a broader cultural and historical context, while sociology focuses on contemporary societal patterns.

While both study human societies, their methods and focuses differ:

Aspect	Anthropology	Sociology
Research Methods	Anthropology emphasizes field work and qualitative analysis through observation	Sociology often employs survey methods and quantitative analysis using statistics and questionnaires

Aspect	Anthropology	Sociology
Scope of Study	Anthropology often examines primitive societies and the evolution of human civilization	Sociology typically focuses on developing and industrial societies
Theoretical Approaches	Anthropology often employs a functionalist approach	Sociology uses a variety of theoretical frameworks
Aspects of Study	Anthropology considers physical aspects, including biological evolution	Sociology concentrates on cultural and social aspects

FYI

Social Anthropology

Traditionally focuses on smaller-scale, non-Western societies, though this has expanded to include all human societies. Emphasizes on ethnographic fieldwork, participant observation, and qualitative methods.

For inference, a sociologist might study inequality in urban education systems, while a social anthropologist might examine how different cultures approach teaching and knowledge transmission.

Examples include:

- Bronisław Malinowski's immersive study of Trobriand Islanders
- **Claude Lévi-Strauss:** Structural analysis of kinship and myth
- **Clifford Geertz:** Interpretive approach and 'thick description'
- **Evans-Pritchard:** Study of belief systems and social organization
- Ethnographic studies of global corporations
- Analysis of refugee communities in urban settings
- Research on technology adoption in different cultural contexts

Sociology Versus History

Let's say our world is a vast ocean. If historians are the deep-sea divers who go into the depths to bring up artifacts from sunken ships (past events) to tell us stories of bygone eras, sociologists are the sailors on the boat, observing the currents, waves, and weather patterns (societal structures and changes) and analysing how they impact our voyage. While history focuses on past events and their significance, sociology concentrates on understanding the present-day societal structures and predicting future trends.

The relationship between sociology and history is symbiotic:

Aspect	History	Sociology
Interdependence	History without sociology is fruitless	Sociology without history is rootless
Approach to Events	Historians (e.g., R. Brown) tend to focus on unique events	Sociologists seek broader generalizations from historical data

Sociology Versus Political Science

Imagine a school. If sociology is like observing how students form groups, share lunch, or even bully others, political science is like studying the school's student council, understanding how decisions are made, and noting who holds power in the school setting. While sociology looks at the broader patterns in society, political science zeroes in on governance, power structures, and political behaviours.

Aspect	Political Science	Sociology
Scope	Political science concentrates on political theory and administration	Sociology studies a broader range of social relationships, including political structures
Theoretical Contributions	Marx's theories are applied differently: Political science focuses on revolution, while sociology examines economic systems and social classes.	Weber's work spans both fields, addressing political sociology and voting patterns

Sociology Versus Philosophy

Imagine a group of people around a campfire. If philosophy is the deep and thoughtful conversation about the meaning of life, our place in the universe, or the nature of truth, sociology is more about observing how people have arranged themselves around the fire, which stories they share, and how they react to each other's tales. Philosophy tackles big existential questions, while sociology focuses on societal patterns and the interplay between individuals and society.

Sociology versus Philosophy		
Aspect	**Philosophy**	**Sociology**
Scope and focus	Broad inquiry into fundamental questions about existence, knowledge, values, reason, and the nature of reality	Focused study of human social behaviour, institutions, and societies
	Often deals with abstract concepts and theoretical constructs	Emphasizes empirical observation and analysis of social phenomena

Sociology versus Philosophy		
Aspect	**Philosophy**	**Sociology**
Methodological Approaches	Employs logical reasoning, conceptual analysis, and thought experiments	Utilizes empirical research methods, including surveys, interviews, and statistical analysis
	Often uses dialectical methods to explore ideas and arguments	Emphasizes data collection and interpretation to understand social patterns
Historical Development	Has a longer history, dating back to ancient civilizations	Emerged as a distinct discipline in the 19th century
	Traditionally seen as the foundation for all academic disciplines	Developed in response to societal changes brought about by industrialization and modernization
Key Figures and Their Contributions	Plato: Theory of Forms, political philosophy	Émile Durkheim: Social facts, division of labour
	Immanuel Kant: Critique of pure reason, ethical theory	Max Weber: Social action theory, bureaucracy
Theoretical Orientations	Epistemology: nature and limits of knowledge	Functionalism: society as an interconnected system
	Ethics: moral principles and values	Conflict theory: focus on power dynamics and inequality
	Metaphysics: nature of reality and existence	Symbolic interactionism: meaning-making in social interactions
Practical Applications	Informs ethical decision-making in various fields (e.g., bioethics, business ethics)	Informs social policy and program development
	Contributes to the development of logical and critical thinking skills	Provides insights for addressing social issues and inequalities
Interdisciplinary Connections	Philosophy intersects with: • Logic and mathematics • Cognitive science and psychology • Political theory and ethics	Sociology intersects with: • Anthropology and psychology • Economics and political science • History and cultural studies
Contemporary Developments	Increased focus on applied ethics and social philosophy	Growing emphasis on global and transnational social processes
	Engagement with issues of technology, AI, and environmental ethics	Increased use of big data and computational methods in social research

Sociology and Common Sense: A Comparative Analysis

Introduction

The relationship between sociology and common sense is a complex and nuanced one, often misunderstood by those outside the field. This chapter aims to elucidate the distinctions and interconnections between these two modes of understanding social phenomena, drawing on the insights of various sociological thinkers.

Defining Common Sense

Common sense refers to the basic, practical knowledge and understanding shared by most members of a society. It is derived from everyday experiences and observations, allowing individuals to perceive and judge situations in a rational and logical manner. However, it is important to note that common sense knowledge is often cursory and superficial, lacking the depth and rigor of scientific inquiry.

The Nature of Sociology

Sociology, as a social science, studies human society and social behaviour systematically. It examines the patterns of social relationships, institutions, and interactions within a society, analyzing how they shape individuals and groups. Sociology delves deeper than common sense, often challenging preconceived notions and revealing hidden complexities in social phenomena.

The Interplay Between Sociology and Common Sense

The relationship between sociology and common sense is dynamic and multifaceted:

1. **Source Material:** Common sense often provides the initial observations and questions that spark sociological inquiry. As Bouman and May (2007) note, sociology interprets and investigates the meanings of social actions and facts that have been branded by common sense.
2. **Critical Examination:** Sociology subjects common sense assumptions to rigorous scrutiny, often revealing their limitations or inaccuracies.
3. **Depth of Analysis:** While common sense offers surface-level explanations, sociology probes deeper, uncovering root causes and interconnections.
4. **Scope:** Common sense is typically limited to personal experiences, while sociology examines society as a whole. As Brown points out, society is an abstract concept - a conceptual web of relations between people and social institutions - that cannot be seen physically.
5. **Methodology:** Sociology employs scientific methods to test hypotheses and generate empirical evidence, whereas common sense relies on anecdotal evidence and personal interpretation.

Illustrative Examples

1. **Religion:** Émile Durkheim's work on religion demonstrates how sociology challenges common sense notions. While common sense might accept that 'God created

man,' Durkheim's sociological analysis reveals how social forces shape religious beliefs and institutions, suggesting that 'man created God and religion.'

2. **Suicide:** Durkheim's groundbreaking work on suicide challenged common sense notions, revealing complex social factors influencing suicide rates that are not immediately apparent to everyday observation.

The Value of Sociological Thinking

Peter L. Berger (1963) aptly noted that sociological questioning requires looking beyond the immediately apparent: 'To ask sociological questions, then, presupposes that one is interested in looking some distance beyond the commonly accepted or officially defined goals of human actions. It presupposes a certain awareness that human events have different levels of meaning, some of which are hidden from the consciousness of everyday life.'

This approach allows for a more comprehensive understanding of social phenomena, encouraging thoughts and ideas that transcend individuals' personal experiences and consider society as a whole.

Misconceptions and Criticisms

It is often argued that sociological thinking is merely an extension of common sense, analyzing the obvious and providing circular reasoning without empirical validation. However, this view misunderstands the nature and purpose of sociological inquiry. While sociology may draw initial insights from common sense observations, its methodologies and analyses go far beyond everyday understanding.

Conclusion

While common sense and sociology both offer insights into social life, they operate on different levels of analysis. Sociology builds upon and critically examines common sense knowledge, providing a more rigorous, systematic, and comprehensive understanding of social reality. As Bouman and May (2007) suggest, sociology interprets and investigates the meanings that common sense has already labeled and attached to social facts.
By recognizing the strengths and limitations of both approaches, we can develop a more nuanced and accurate comprehension of the social world around us. Sociology, with its scientific approach and broader perspective, offers valuable insights that complement and often transcend the limitations of common sense understanding.

Differences Between Common Sense and Sociology

- **Foundational Basis:** While common sense derives from personal experiences and casual observations, sociology relies on systematic research methodologies and rigorous analysis of data.
- **Approach to Generalization:** Common sense often employs broad generalizations and may perpetuate stereotypes. In contrast, sociology strives to provide a nuanced and comprehensive understanding of social phenomena, acknowledging the complexity of human behaviour and social structures.

- **Contextual Considerations:** Common sense is inherently subjective, varying across individuals and cultures. Sociology, however, aims to develop an objective and scientific understanding of society, taking into account diverse cultural and historical contexts.
- **Scope of Analysis:** The purview of common sense is typically limited to individual perspectives and immediate situations. Sociology, on the other hand, explores broader social structures, processes, and their interconnections across various levels of society.
- **Analytical Perspective:** Sociological thinking employs methodological approaches to view and analyze the social world from an objective standpoint. Common sense, being a product of subjective experiences, lacks this scientific rigor.
- **Knowledge Base:** Common sense knowledge often stems from beliefs, personal experiences, and assumptions. Sociological knowledge is grounded in rigorous qualitative or quantitative research. While common sense tends to reflect and reinforce generally accepted notions, sociology—particularly conflict theory—often challenges the status quo and argues for systemic change.
- **Reliability and Validity:** The common sense view, lacking systematic verification, may not always be reliable or valid. The sociological perspective, built on empirical research and theoretical frameworks, strives for high levels of reliability and validity in its findings and interpretations.

Similarities Between Common Sense and Sociology

1. Both common sense and sociology aim to understand human behaviour and society.
2. Both draw upon observations and experiences to make sense of social phenomena.
3. Both contribute to our understanding of social norms, values, and interactions.

   Examples

   (a) Common sense in India might suggest that arranged marriages are the norm, as they have been a traditional practice for generations. However, sociology would analyse the underlying social, cultural, and economic factors that influence the prevalence of arranged marriages in Indian society.

   (b) Common sense might lead to the belief that caste discrimination is declining in India. However, sociology would examine the persistent social inequalities and the structural factors that perpetuate caste-based discrimination.

   (c) Common sense might assume that people in Western countries value individualism and personal freedom. Sociology would delve deeper to analyse the historical, cultural, and economic factors that have shaped Western societies and contributed to these values.

   (d) Common sense might suggest that democratic countries have better living standards compared to autocratic countries. Sociology would investigate the complex relationships between political systems, social structures, and quality of life indicators to provide a more nuanced understanding.

According to Thomas Reid, every research starts from common sense. 'Common sense might be sociological nonsense, but sensible Sociology cannot develop without common sense'.

Aspect	Common Sense	Sociology
Definition	Everyday knowledge derived from personal experience and cultural norms.	Systematic study of society and social behaviour using scientific methods.
Basis	Intuition, traditions, and anecdotal evidence.	Empirical research, theories, and structured methodologies.
Approach	Subjective and uncritical acceptance of widely held beliefs.	Objective and critical analysis of social phenomena.
Scope	Limited to individual or group experiences and observations.	Broad, encompassing various aspects of society, including institutions, relationships, and processes.
Methodology	Non-systematic, relies on observation and personal interpretation.	Systematic, employs qualitative and quantitative research methods.
Verification	Rarely subjected to rigorous testing or validation.	Regularly subjected to peer review, replication, and validation.
Flexibility	Often inflexible, resistant to change.	Open to revision and change based on new evidence and perspectives.
Examples from India	Belief that joint families are always more supportive.	Studies on changing family structures in urban India (e.g., nuclear families becoming more common).
Global Examples	Stereotypes about immigrants being a burden on the economy.	Research on the positive economic impacts of immigration in countries like the USA and Germany.
Implications	Can perpetuate stereotypes and biases.	Aims to challenge and deconstruct stereotypes and biases.
Application	Used in everyday decision-making and judgements.	Applied in policy-making, education, social services, and other fields.
Adaptability	Slow to adapt to new information or societal changes.	Continuously evolving with new research findings and social developments.

Some examples of comparison

1. **Common Sense: Belief in Joint Families in India**

   In India, a common sense belief is that joint families are inherently more supportive and provide better social security. This belief is based on traditional views and personal anecdotes. While joint families can offer strong support networks, this perspective does not account for conflicts and the autonomy limitations that may arise within such family structures.

   Sociology: Changing Family Structures in Urban India

   Sociological studies have highlighted a shift towards nuclear families in urban India. Researchers like Patricia Uberoi and Rukmini Bhaya Nair have documented the rise of nuclear families due to factors such as economic independence, urban migration, and changing gender roles. These studies use empirical data to illustrate the complexity and diversity of family structures in contemporary India.

2. **Common Sense: Immigrants as Economic Burden**

   In many parts of the world, there is a common sense notion that immigrants drain economic resources and take away jobs from locals. This belief is often fueled by media narratives and political rhetoric.

   Sociology: Positive Economic Impacts of Immigration

   Contrary to the common sense perspective, sociological research has demonstrated that immigrants contribute positively to the economy. Studies in the USA by economists like Giovanni Peri show that immigrants complement the native workforce, contribute to innovation, and help in addressing labour shortages. Similarly, research in Germany has highlighted the role of immigrants in sustaining the welfare state and addressing demographic challenges.

Ace Your Answers!

1. How did the Dark Ages come to an end and what social processes characterized the period starting 14th century?
2. Define modernity from a sociological perspective. How is it different from modernization and modernism?
3. Did modernity lead to the emergence of sociology or did sociological insights create the modernity? Substantiate your viewpoint.
4. Highlight the similarities and differences between feudal and contemporary society.
5. What role did the intellectual forces play at different time periods in the emergence of sociology?
6. How did the conservative reaction to enlightenment lead to the organization of sociology as a discipline?
7. While the scope of sociology is wide, its application needs to be specific. Elaborate.
8. How is sociology related to the following:
   a. Anthropology
   b. Psychology
   c. Political Science
   d. Philosophy
   e. Biology
   f. Economics
9. Sociology feeds on the common sense for ideas while common sense gets formed from sociological inquiry. Do you agree? Substantiate your viewpoint.
10. Common sense is not so common. Sociology is general yet nuanced. Examine the relationship between the two.

Previous Years' Questions

2024

1. Discuss the nature of sociology. Highlight its relationship with social anthropology. (10 marks)
2. Sociology is the product of European enlightenment and renaissance. Critically examine this statement. (20 marks)

   (See 'Model Answer Approach' on Pg 1.29)

2023

1. Discuss the relationship between sociology and political science. (10 marks)
2. Do you think that common sense is a starting point of social research? What are its advantages and limitations? Explain. (20 marks)

2022

1. Delimit the scope of Sociology in relation to other social sciences. (10 marks)
2. What aspects of enlightenment do you think paved way for the emergence of sociology? Elaborate. (20 marks)

2021

1. Europe was the first and only place where modernity emerged. (10 marks)
2. From the viewpoint of growing importance of multi-disciplinarity, how do you relate sociology to other social sciences? (20 marks)

2020

1. How did intellectual forces lead to the emergence of sociology? Discuss. (10 marks)
2. In the context of globalization, has the scope of sociology been changing in India? Comment. (10 marks)

2019

1. Discuss the historical antecedents of the emergence of sociology as a discipline. (10 marks)

2018

1. The focal point of sociology rests on interaction. How do you distinguish it from common sense? (10 marks)

2017

1. Explain how sociology has emerged as a distinct discipline based on rationality and scientific temper. (10 marks)
2. Discuss the changing equations of discipline of sociology with other social sciences. 20 marks)

2016

1. 'Sociology is pre-eminently study of modern societies.' Discuss. (10 marks)
2. Is sociology common sense? Give reasons in support of your argument. (10 marks)

2015

1. How has Enlightenment contributed to the emergence of Sociology? (10 marks)

2014

1. How did the emergence of industrial society change the family life in Western Europe? (10 marks)
2. How is sociological approach to human actions different from that of psychological approach? (10 marks)

Right Approach

2024 - Q. 2

Sociology is the product of European enlightenment and renaissance. Critically examine this statement.

Introduction: Sociology's origins are traditionally attributed to European intellectual movements, particularly the enlightenment and renaissance. However, examining this claim requires a nuanced understanding of both the discipline's European foundations and its diverse global roots.

BODY: Supporting Evidence for European Origins:

1. Enlightenment's Rational Foundation:
   - Auguste Comte's 'law of three stages' emerged from enlightenment rationality
   - Scientific method and empiricism became central to sociological inquiry
   - Max Weber's emphasis on rationalization reflects enlightenment principles
2. Renaissance Humanism:
   - Shifted focus from theological to human-centered explanations
   - Early sociologists like Montesquieu drew from renaissance's secular outlook
   - Renaissance spirit of questioning authority influenced sociological skepticism
3. Industrial Revolution Context:
   - European social transformations provided the laboratory for early theories
   - Marx, Durkheim, and Weber's works responded to European industrialization

Critical Counter-Arguments:

1. Non-European Contributions:
   - Ibn Khaldun's 14th-century 'Muqaddimah' predated European sociology
   - Ancient Indian texts like Arthashastra contained social analyses
   - Chinese philosopher Confucius developed complex social theories
2. Colonial Knowledge Production:
   - Andre Gunder Frank's concept of 'intellectual colonialism' shaped early sociology
   - Indigenous knowledge systems were marginalized
   - Power relations influenced knowledge production
3. Modern Synthesis:
   - Contemporary sociology incorporates diverse cultural perspectives
   - Raewyn Connell's 'Southern Theory' challenges Eurocentrism
   - Indian sociologists like G.S. Ghurye combined Western methods with Indian insights

Conclusion: The future of sociology lies in its ability to transcend its European origins while acknowledging their significance. The discipline is evolving towards a more inclusive, global perspective that synthesizes diverse intellectual traditions. This transformation promises richer insights into social phenomena through multiple cultural lenses. As sociology moves forward, it increasingly embraces methodological pluralism and indigenous knowledge systems, making it truly global in scope and application.

CHAPTER
2

Sociology as a Science and Major Theoretical Strands

In this Chapter

- Science, Scientific Method and Critique
- Major Theoretical Strands of Research Methodology
- Positivism and its Critique
- Fact Value and Objectivity
- Non-positivist Methodologies
- UPSC Mains PYQs

Science, Scientific Method and Critique

What is Science?

- The word Science has its origin in Latin. It comes from the Latin word *Scientia*, which means knowledge or 'acquaintance with facts'. *Scientia* is derived from the verb 'Scire,' which means 'to know.'
- Science, as a subject matter as well as method, encompasses the systematic study of the world, including its physical, biological, and social aspects, with the aim to understand, explain and predict the underlying principles and mechanisms governing it.
- The subject matter of Science spans through a wide range of disciplines, such as Physics, Chemistry, Biology, Astronomy, Geology, Sociology, and many others, each focusing on different aspects.

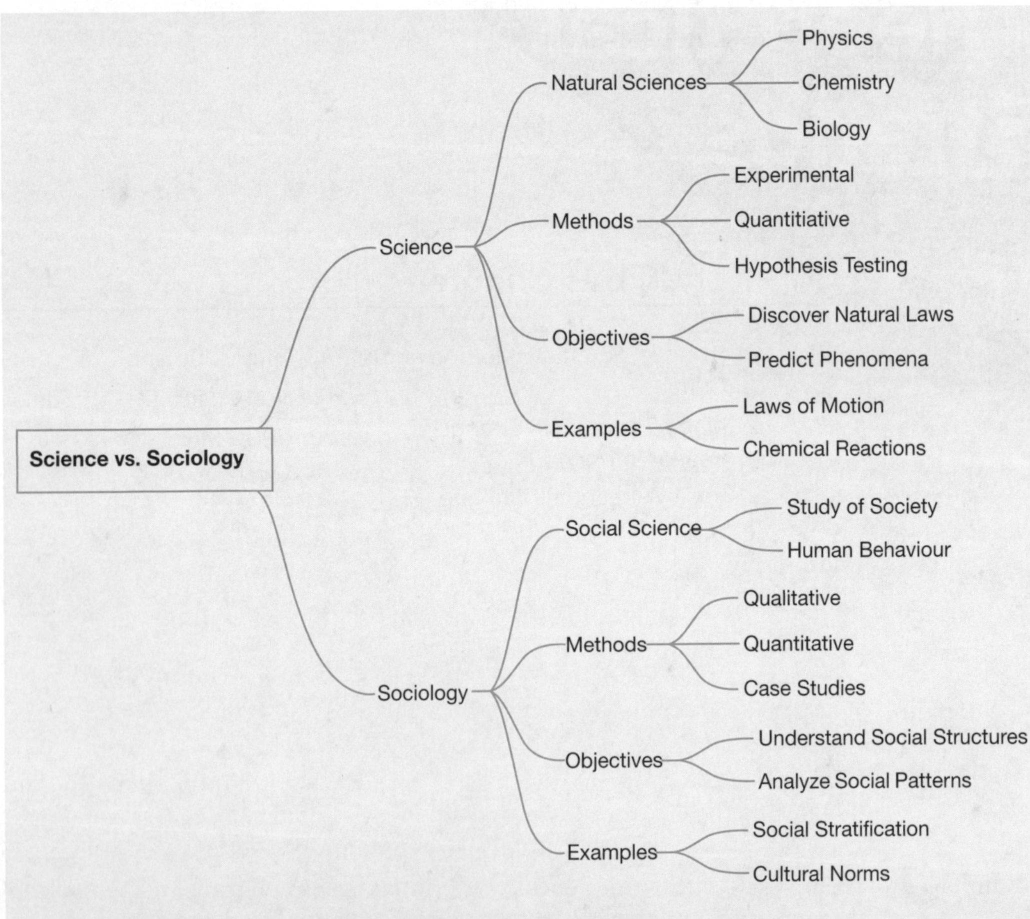

What are the Main Characteristics of Science?

The main characteristics of science include:

1. Empiricism—Role of sensory experience, observation, and evidence
2. Self-reflection and self-correction
3. Rational explanations based in facts, not assumptions
4. Objectivity in methods
5. Universality in application across time and space

What is a Scientific Method?

Scientific method is a systematic, organized approach to acquiring knowledge and understanding of the world.

What Makes Any Method Scientific?

Adherence to the following series of steps or criteria makes any method scientific:

- **Empirical Observation:** Gathering data through direct sensory experience or instruments
- **Hypothesis Formulation:** Developing testable explanations or predictions
- **Experimentation and Collection of Data:** Conducting systematic tests or observations to collect data
- **Data Analysis:** Quantitatively or qualitatively analysing the collected data
- **Objectivity:** Striving for impartiality and minimizing personal bias
- **Falsifiability:** Ensuring hypotheses can be proven false
- **Reproducibility:** Allowing other researchers to replicate experiments
- **Peer Review:** Expert evaluation of research for quality and validity
- **Cumulative Knowledge:** Building on existing scientific understanding

What are the Main Approaches to Scientific Method?

In terms of the nature of subject matter, there are two approaches—idiographic and nomothetic.

Aspect	Idiographic Approach	Nomothetic Approach
Focus	Focuses on understanding and explaining unique, individual cases or phenomena	Emphasises the identification of general laws, principles and patterns that apply to multiple cases or phenomena
Goal	Aims to provide in-depth, context-specific insights and explanations	Seeks to establish generalizable principles and regularities
Methodology	Often employs qualitative research methods, such as case studies, interviews, and ethnography	Typically uses quantitative research methods, such as surveys, experiments, and statistical analysis
Emphasis	Emphasises the uniqueness, complexity, and diversity of individual cases	Emphasises generalizability, seeking commonalities and patterns across cases

Aspect	Idiographic Approach	Nomothetic Approach
Use	Commonly used in disciplines like psychology, anthropology, and history, where the focus is on understanding individual experiences and cultural contexts	Commonly used in natural and social sciences to establish laws and principles that can be applied broadly
Example	Exploring the life experiences of a specific individual to understand their unique psychological development	Conducting a large-scale survey to determine factors that influence voting behaviour across a population

On the basis of methodology, the other two approaches are—inductive and deductive approaches.

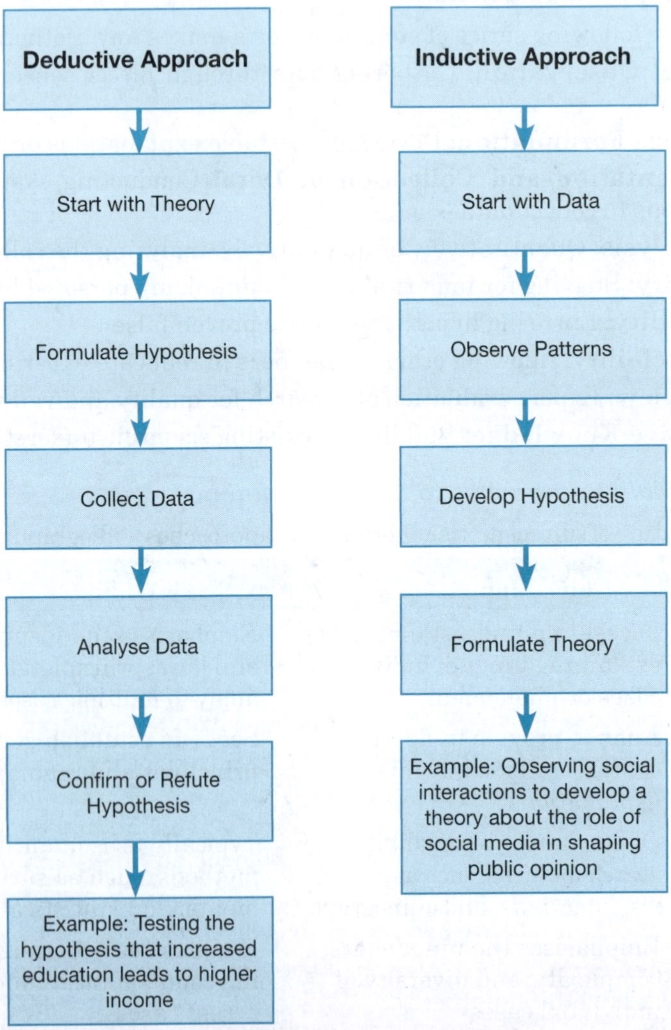

Aspect	Inductive Approach	Deductive Approach
Starting Point	Begins with specific observations or data	Starts with a general hypothesis or theory
Reasoning	Moves from specific observations to generalizations or theories	Moves from general hypotheses or theories to specific predictions or testable hypotheses
Research Objective	Often used for exploratory research, generating new ideas, and understanding complex or novel phenomena	Commonly used for hypothesis testing, confirming or refuting existing theories, and making predictions
Data Collection	Focuses on gathering empirical evidence and looking for patterns, trends, or regularities	Involves designing experiments or studies to test specific hypotheses, collecting data, and evaluating whether the data support or refute the initial theory
Hypothesis Generation	The formation of general principles or theories is the outcome of the process.	Specific predictions or testable hypotheses are generated based on the existing theory or hypothesis.
Commonly Used Methods	Qualitative research methods, case studies, and grounded theory	Quantitative research methods, controlled experiments, and surveys
Example	Studying the behaviours and interactions of a group of individuals to generate new theories about their social dynamics.	Testing a hypothesis that states 'Increased exposure to sunlight leads to higher vitamin D levels in the human body' by conducting experiments and collecting data.

Critique of Science and the Scientific Method

- **Falsifiability Challenge:** Karl Popper argued that no number of positive outcomes can definitively prove a theory true, but a single contradictory result can disprove it. Scientific knowledge is always tentative.
- **Value Neutrality Issues:** Thomas Kuhn emphasized the role of paradigms in shaping scientific research and the potential for bias within scientific communities.
- **Reductionism:** Some critics assert that the scientific method's reductionist approach oversimplifies complex phenomena by reducing them to measurable variables, potentially neglecting important aspects of reality. Philosopher Imre Lakatos recognized that science often simplifies phenomena for the sake of testing.
- **Lack of Inclusivity:** Feminist scholars have critiqued science for its historically male-dominated perspective and exclusion of diverse voices.
- **Ethical Concerns:** Robert Merton discussed the potential misuse of scientific knowledge for unethical purposes.

- **Cultural and Contextual Critiques:** Critics argue that scientific research sometimes disregards the cultural and contextual variations that shape social phenomena. Sandra Harding emphasized the importance of recognizing diverse standpoints and experiences.

Relationship between Sociology and Science

- Early sociological thinkers, such as Auguste Comte, Emile Durkheim, and Herbert Spencer, viewed sociology as a science.
- Auguste Comte, often regarded as the Father of Sociology, initially called the discipline 'social physics' and gave the concept of 'positivism' which emphasized the application of the scientific method to the study of social phenomena. His approach aimed to identify and discover social laws and principles, similar to how natural sciences uncover physical laws.
- Emile Durkheim, known for his work on 'social facts', sought to establish sociology as an empirical and scientific discipline by objectively examining external, measurable social facts rather than individual psychological factors to understand social order and change. His famous study on suicide rates used extensive statistical data to show that social factors, such as social integration and moral regulation, could influence individual behaviour.

FYI

In his book *Montesquieu and Rousseau*, published in 1892, Durkheim laid down the general conditions for the establishment of a Social Science (which also applies to Sociology)

a) Science has a specific subject matter and is not coextensive with all human knowledge or thought.

b) Social science must focus on objective realities and have a definite field of exploration.

c) Science deals with types or classes of subject matter, not individuals, to discover regularities of behaviour.

d) Social Science describes the normal form of social life within each type of society it classifies. This sense of 'normal' belongs to the classification of 'type' itself. For example, Indian society is classified as a traditional society. Whatever pertains to this type, is considered normal and therefore healthy.

e) The subject matter of Science yields general principles or 'laws'. Since all phenomena in the natural world are interrelated, human society which is part of this natural world also has regularities which should be discovered.

f) Social Science acknowledges continuity between the natural and social worlds but treats the social as a distinctive and autonomous sphere. Categories of human will and volition belong to psychology, not social science, which must assume societies have a certain nature.

g) To discern uniformities, types, and laws in society, a valid scientific method from the natural sciences is applicable to the social field.

- Herbert Spencer, often associated with social Darwinism, believed in the application of biological and evolutionary ideas to the study of society. His organismic analogy likened society to a biological organism, emphasizing interdependence and adaptation to maintain social stability and progress.
- Other scholars claimed that sociology has 'inter-subjective reliability', meaning that it has concepts (such as family, religion, status, etc.) with universal meanings irrespective of who is the investigator. Weber proposed the use of 'ideal types' (Idealtypen) as a method to approach objectivity in social science.

Criticism of the Approach of Modeling Sociology After Natural Sciences

Following are the scholar-specific arguments:

- Max Weber emphasized the importance of 'Verstehen' or understanding subjective meanings and motivations, suggesting that human behaviour is not always reducible to objective, scientific analysis.
- Alfred Schutz criticized the natural science model for not capturing the richness of subjective experiences and individual interpretations.
- Karl Popper argued that sociology often fails to meet the criteria of falsifiability due to the complexities of social phenomena.
- Peter Winch highlighted the limitations of applying natural science methods to socio-cultural phenomena and emphasized the need for interpretive understanding.
- Clifford Geertz advocated for interpretive, qualitative approaches in the social sciences, emphasizing the immersion in social contexts and the interpretation of meaning.

Major Theoretical Strands in Research Methodology

Research in Sociology is primarily conducted at two levels: macro level and micro level. The third way is an in-between which can be found in Robert Merton's Middle Range Theories Framework. A comparison between the three is presented below:

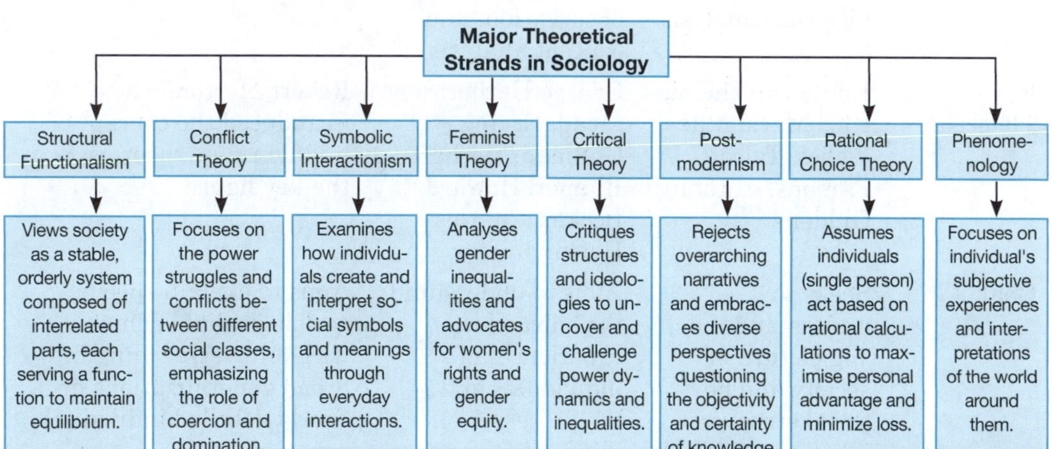

Aspect	Macro Approach	Micro Approach	Merton's Middle-Range Theories Framework
Scope	Examines society as a whole and focuses on large-scale social structures, institutions, and patterns	Focuses on individuals and small-scale interactions within society	Offers a bridge between macro and micro by focussing on specific, manageable, and intermediate-level phenomena
Level of Analysis	Analyses society at a broad level, looking at social institutions, organizations, and cultures	Analyses individuals and small groups, examining their behaviours, beliefs, and interactions	Examines phenomena that are more narrowly defined and offers a level of specificity between macro and micro levels
Research Questions	Addresses questions related to social order, stability, and large-scale social change	Focuses on questions related to individual experiences, identity, and interpersonal relationships	Addresses questions that lie between broad societal questions and specific individual experiences
Examples of Topics	Social inequality, globalization, political systems, economic trends, education systems	Family dynamics, friendship networks, identity formation, deviant behaviour	An example might be a study of 'role strain' or 'unintended consequences' that explores specific social mechanisms
Research Methods	Typically uses quantitative methods, such as surveys, statistical analysis, and historical analysis	Often employs qualitative methods, including in-depth interviews, participant observation, and content analysis	Utilises a combination of qualitative and quantitative methods to investigate intermediate-level phenomena.
Key Theorists	Emile Durkheim, Karl Marx, Max Weber, Talcott Parsons, Anthony Giddens	George Herbert Mead, Erving Goffman, Herbert Blumer, Howard Becker, Charles Horton Cooley	Robert Merton, who introduced the concept of middle-range theories, is the key figure.
Goal	Seeks to understand the 'big picture' of society and how social structures impact individuals	Aims to understand the subjective experiences of individuals and the processes of interaction in society.	Aims to explain specific sociological phenomena without overreaching into broad generalizations or overly detailed individual experiences.

Sociological theory has evolved over time, with various strands emerging at different points in history. Here's a list of key theoretical strands in sociology. These strands are presented in a chronological order from the earliest to more recent developments:

Classical Sociological Theory (Macro): Functionalism, Marxism, Social Action

- **Key Thinkers:** Auguste Comte, Karl Marx, Emile Durkheim, Max Weber
- **Major Works:** 'The Positive Philosophy,' 'The Communist Manifesto,' 'The Division of Labour in Society,' 'The Protestant Ethic and the Spirit of Capitalism.'
- **Examples:** Comte laid the groundwork for sociology as a discipline. Marx focussed on class struggle and capitalism. Durkheim studied social solidarity, while Weber explored the impact of religion on economic development.
    - Functionalism in Sociology is a theoretical perspective that views society as a complex system with interrelated parts, each serving a specific function to maintain social stability and order. It suggests that each element of society, including institutions and norms, contributes to the overall functioning of the social system. Functionalism emphasises the need for harmony, equilibrium, and balance in society to prevent dysfunction and social breakdown.
    - Marxism posits that societal inequalities and conflicts are primarily driven by the unequal distribution of resources and power, with the working class (proletariat) pitted against the capitalist class (bourgeoisie), and it calls for a restructured, classless society where resources are shared more equitably.
    - Max Weber's social action approach in sociology Focuses on understanding human behaviour through the lens of subjective meaning and individual interpretation. It emphasises the importance of examining the reasons and motives that individuals have for their actions.

Structural Functionalism (Macro-Level)

- **Key Thinkers:**
    - Emile Durkheim, 'The Division of Labour in Society'
    - Talcott Parsons, 'The Social System'
    - Robert K. Merton, 'Social Theory and Social Structure'
- **Core Idea:** Structural functionalism is based on the idea that society is like a biological organism, where each part has a function that contributes to the stability and well-being of the whole. Society is seen as having various institutions and elements, such as family, education, economy, religion, and government, each with its own function. These institutions are interconnected and interdependent, and they work together to maintain social order and equilibrium.
- **Contributions of Main Structural Functionalists:**
    1. **Emile Durkheim**
        - **Functional Integration:** Durkheim emphasized the idea of functional integration, meaning that different parts of society are interconnected and function together to maintain social order.

- **Anomie:** He introduced the concept of anomie, which refers to a breakdown in social norms and values. Durkheim argued that too much or too little integration in society could lead to anomie and social problems.
- **Solidarity:** Durkheim identified two types of social solidarity:
  (i) **Mechanical Solidarity:** In traditional societies, people are bound together by similarities and shared values.
  (ii) **Organic Solidarity:** In more complex, modern societies, people are interdependent, like the organs in a body, due to their specialized roles.

2. **Talcott Parsons**
   - **Functional Differentiation:** Parsons expanded on the idea of functional integration by introducing the concept of functional differentiation. He argued that as society evolves, institutions become more specialized in their functions.
   - **AGIL System:** He developed the AGIL system, which stands for Adaptation (to the environment), Goal Attainment, Integration (of different parts of society), and Latency (patterns of values and norms). This framework helps analyse how institutions serve these functions in society.
   - **Pattern Variables:** Parsons introduced the concept of pattern variables, which describe different social action orientations, such as affectivity versus affective neutrality and specific versus diffuse relationships.
3. **Robert K. Merton**
   - **Manifest and Latent Functions:** Merton expanded on the concept of manifest and latent functions within social institutions. He argued that institutions have both intended (manifest) and unintended (latent) consequences on society.
   - **Strain Theory:** Merton developed the Strain Theory, which explores how individuals adapt to the gap between cultural goals and the means available to achieve them. This theory is especially relevant in understanding deviant behaviour.
   - **Functionalism Revived:** Merton's work helped revitalize functionalism by addressing some of the criticisms it faced. He acknowledged that not all aspects of a society contribute positively to its stability and suggested that some aspects may be dysfunctional.

- **Examples:**
  1. **Family and Gender Roles:** Researchers have used structural functionalism to investigate family dynamics and gender roles within households. They have found that the manifest function of the family was to provide for the care and socialization of children. However, studies also revealed latent functions related to gender roles and divisions of labour within the family, which may have implications for the broader society in terms of gender equality and social expectations.
  2. **Religion:** Researchers used structural functionalism to study the role of religion in maintaining social cohesion in a diverse society. They explored how religion serves as a source of shared values, norms, and social integration.
- **Critique:** Critics argue that structural functionalism often ignores social conflict, inequalities, and change.

Conflict Theory (Macro-Level)

- **Key Thinkers:**
  - Karl Marx, 'The Communist Manifesto'
  - Ralf Dahrendorf, 'Class Conflict and the Industrial Revolution'
- **Core idea:** Conflict theory is a sociological perspective that views society as a place of competition and conflict over limited resources, such as wealth, power, and prestige. It emphasises the role of inequality and social struggle in shaping a society. It highlights how inequality in society is not just a random outcome but a result of deliberate actions and structures that benefit some groups while disadvantaging others.
- **Contributions of Main Conflict Theorists:**

1. **Karl Marx**
   - **Class Conflict and Historical Materialism:**
     (i) Karl Marx's primary contribution is his theory of class conflict. He argued that society is divided into two main classes, the bourgeoisie (capitalist class) and the proletariat (working class), and that the struggle between these classes is the driving force behind historical and social change.
     (ii) His theory of historical materialism posits that economic and material conditions shape society and history. Marx famously stated: 'The history of all hitherto existing society is the history of class struggles.'
   - **Concept of Alienation:** Marx introduced the concept of alienation, where he described how workers in a capitalist system become disconnected from the products of their labour, from their own creative potential, and from one another. This concept has been influential in understanding the dehumanizing effects of modern industrial society.
   - **Critique of Capitalism:** Marx provided a critical analysis of capitalism, emphasizing its inherent contradictions and exploitative nature. He argued that capitalism leads to the concentration of wealth and power in the hands of a few, while the majority of workers experience alienation and economic inequality.
   - **Ideological Influence:** Marx's ideas have had a profound influence on sociology, economics, political science, and philosophy. His writings laid the foundation for the development of Marxist theories and movements worldwide.
2. **Ralf Dahrendorf**
   - **Conflict in Modern Society:** He focused on the idea that social conflict is not solely based on class divisions, but also on authority and power relationships within various social institutions. Dahrendorf argued that in complex societies, individuals may occupy different positions of power and authority, leading to multiple sources of conflict.
   - **Authority and Social Change:** He explored the concept of authority and the tensions that arise when individuals or groups seek to exercise power over others. Dahrendorf's work highlighted how authority and power dynamics affect social change.

- **Pluralistic Approach:** Dahrendorf proposed a pluralistic perspective that acknowledged the existence of multiple conflicts in society. He argued that conflict is not necessarily negative and can contribute to social change and progress.

- **Examples:**
  1. **Labour unions and worker management relations:** Researchers examine how labour unions represent the interests of workers and engage in collective bargaining to address issues such as wages, working conditions, and job security.
  2. **Media ownership and bias:** Conflict theory is applied to analyze media ownership and bias. It highlights how media outlets can serve the interests of their owners and advertisers, potentially perpetuating certain ideologies or narratives that benefit those in power.
  3. **Gender Inequality:** It highlights how societal norms and power structures lead to disparities in opportunities, pay, and representation between genders. It has been instrumental in the study of the feminist movement.
- **Critique:** Critics argue that conflict theory can sometimes overly emphasize conflict and inequality at the expense of other important aspects of social life, such as cooperation, consensus, and shared values.

Symbolic Interactionism (Micro-Level)

- **Key Thinkers:**
  - George Herbert Mead, 'Mind, Self, and Society'
  - Erving Goffman, 'The Presentation of Self in Everyday Life'
- **Core Idea:** Examines how symbols and interactions shape individual behaviour and social reality. Individuals construct their self-concept through social interactions and the interpretation of symbols. Social reality is formed through the exchange of symbols and meanings in everyday life.

This theory has been discussed in further detail in the later sections of the chapter.

Feminist Theory (Various Levels)

- **Key Thinkers:**
  - Simone de Beauvoir, 'The Second Sex'
  - Bell hooks, 'Ain't I a Woman: Black Women and Feminism'
- **Core Idea:** Explores gender roles, inequalities, and the impact of patriarchy on society. Critiques the social construction of gender and advocates for gender equality. Addresses women's experiences and challenges patriarchal norms and practices.

This theory has been discussed in further detail in the later sections of the chapter.

Rational Choice Theory (Micro-Level)

- **Key Thinkers:**
  - James S. Coleman, 'Foundations of Social Theory'
  - George Homans, 'Social Behaviour: Its Elementary Forms'

- **Core Idea:** It views individuals as rational actors who make decisions based on a cost-benefit analysis. It assumes that people aim to maximize their personal utility, whether in economic terms (e.g., financial gain) or in terms of personal satisfaction. This doesn't necessarily mean selfishness but rather a rational pursuit of one's own goals and interests. People's decisions are influenced by constraints (limitations on their choices) and personal preferences (what they value). Rational choice theory considers how these factors affect decision-making.
- **Contributions of Main Rational Choice Theorists:**
  1. **James S. Coleman**
     - **Educational Attainment:** Coleman conducted influential research on educational attainment, highlighting how students and parents make rational choices about education based on the expected benefits. His 'Equality of Educational Opportunity' report (commonly known as the Coleman Report) studied factors affecting educational achievement and the role of schools in shaping student outcomes.
     - **Social Capital:** Coleman introduced the concept of social capital, emphasizing that social networks and relationships can be viewed as a form of capital that individuals use to make rational decisions.
  2. **George Homans**
     - **Exchange Theory:** Homans was instrumental in developing the foundation of exchange theory within the framework of rational choice theory. He emphasized that social interactions and relationships are based on exchanges of valued resources, such as time, money, and emotional support.
     - **Principle of Reciprocity:** Homans proposed that individuals are more likely to engage in social exchanges when they expect a fair and equitable return.
     - **Social Exchange Theory:** Homans' work laid the groundwork for the development of social exchange theory, which explores how individuals make decisions about forming and maintaining social relationships, including friendships, romantic partnerships, and cooperation in groups.
     - **Balance Theory:** He contributed to the development of balance theory, which examines how individuals seek to maintain psychological balance in their social relationships. This theory is particularly relevant in understanding attitudes and feelings in social exchanges.
- **Examples:**
  1. **Criminal Behaviour:** Rational choice theory has been used to understand criminal behaviour. It posits that individuals make decisions to engage in criminal activities based on a rational assessment of potential gains (e.g., theft) versus potential costs (e.g., arrest and punishment). For example, an individual may decide to commit a burglary if they believe the potential loot outweighs the risks of getting caught.
  2. **Voting and Political Participation:** In political science, rational choice theory is applied to analyse voting behaviour and political participation. Voters are seen as rational actors who weigh the expected benefits of their preferred policies against the effort and time required to vote. This theory helps explain why individuals choose to vote or abstain from voting.

- **Critique:** Critics argue that rational choice theory can oversimplify human behaviour by assuming that individuals always make perfectly rational and self-interested decisions. It may not fully capture the complexity of human decision-making, which often involves emotions, social norms, and cognitive biases.

Postmodernism (Various Levels)

- **Key Thinkers:**
  - Jean-François Lyotard, 'The Postmodern Condition'
  - Michel Foucault, 'The Birth of Biopolitics'
- **Core Idea:** This perspective emerged in the late 20th century. It challenges the traditional, modernist view of society, which is characterized by grand narratives such as Marxism or religious narratives, fixed meanings, and a belief in progress. Postmodernism emphasises the diversity, complexity, and uncertainty of contemporary society. It emphasises the role of language and discourse in shaping reality. It suggests that language is not a neutral tool but is embedded with power dynamics and subjectivity. It recognises that there is no single, objective truth and that different groups have their own interpretations of reality. It questions the legitimacy of experts and centralized power.

- **Contributions of Main Post Modernists:**
  1. **Jean-François Lyotard**
     - **Rejection of Metanarratives:** He argued that such narratives, like those found in science, religion, and politics, no longer hold the same authority they once did.
     - **The Inhuman:** In his book 'The Inhuman,' Lyotard explored the relationship between technology and society. He raised questions about the effects of technology on knowledge, communication, and social interactions, which are themes that continue to be relevant in the digital age.
     - **The Differend:** Lyotard introduced the concept of 'differend,' referring to conflicts or disputes that arise when one party's claims cannot be fully expressed or understood within the language or discourse of another party. This concept is influential in discussions about the limits of language and communication.
  2. **Michel Foucault**
     - **Discourse Analysis:** Michel Foucault argued that discourse shapes and regulates social norms and institutions. His work has been influential in understanding how power operates through language and how knowledge is constructed.
     - **Genealogy:** Foucault's approach to genealogy involves tracing the historical development of ideas, practices, and institutions. This method is critical in uncovering the hidden power structures and assumptions that underpin social systems.
     - **Archaeology of Knowledge:** In his work 'The Archaeology of Knowledge,' Foucault examined the production of knowledge and how it is organized into various discourses. He encouraged critical examination of the rules and systems that govern knowledge production and classification.

- **Panopticism:** Foucault's concept of 'panopticism' explores the idea of constant surveillance and self-regulation. He used the example of the Panopticon, a hypothetical prison design, to illustrate how individuals can internalize norms and control themselves due to the fear of being observed.

- **Examples:**
  1. **Identity and Gender:** Post-modernism emphasises that identity is not fixed but is a fluid, socially constructed concept. Scholars explore how individuals navigate multiple identities, and they challenge traditional binary understandings of gender.
  2. **Social Movements:** The Occupy Wall Street movement challenged the power of financial institutions and advocated for a more equitable distribution of resources, reflecting a postmodern skepticism of economic authority.
  3. **Media and Communication:** Researchers examine the blurring of boundaries between producer and consumer in the age of user-generated content. In the era of virtual reality and social media, individuals may curate online identities that may not reflect their offline lives, highlighting the idea of hyperreality.
- **Critique:** Postmodernism is often critiqued for lacking a coherent theoretical framework. It is seen as a collection of diverse and sometimes contradictory ideas, making it challenging to define and apply consistently.

Critical Theory (Various Levels)

- **Key Thinkers:**
  - Theodor Adorno and Max Horkheimer, 'Dialectic of Enlightenment'
  - Jürgen Habermas, 'The Structural Transformation of the Public Sphere'
- **Core Idea:** It originated in the Frankfurt School in the 1920s and is interdisciplinary in nature, drawing from fields such as sociology, philosophy, political science, and cultural studies. It emphasises the critical examination of society and aims to uncover and challenge structures of power, inequality, and injustice. It examines the ways in which dominant groups maintain their power and control, often at the expense of marginalized groups. It encourages praxis, which is the integration of theory and practice. It emphasizes that understanding society should lead to transformative action aimed at addressing social injustices.
- **Contributions of Main Theorists:**
  1. **Max Horkheimer**
     - **Dialectic of Enlightenment:** Max Horkheimer, along with Theodor Adorno, co-authored 'Dialectic of Enlightenment,' a foundational text for critical theory. This work critiques the effects of rationality and enlightenment on society, highlighting how they can lead to oppressive systems and a loss of individual autonomy.
  2. **Theodor Adorno**
     - **Negative Dialectics:** Adorno's work on 'Negative Dialectics' explored how contradiction and negativity can be important for critical thinking, and he emphasized the need to challenge fixed, dogmatic concepts.

- **Culture Industry:** Adorno, along with Max Horkheimer, introduced the concept of the 'culture industry.' They examined how mass culture and entertainment can homogenise and manipulate the masses, reinforcing conformity and passivity.

3. **Herbert Marcuse**
   - **One-Dimensional Man:** Herbert Marcuse's book 'One-Dimensional Man' analyses the conformist and repressive nature of advanced industrial societies. He argued that technological advancements can be used to maintain social control, and he called for a form of liberatory praxis to overcome this one-dimensionality.
   - **Critical Pedagogy:** Marcuse's ideas on critical pedagogy influenced education. He argued for teaching that empowers students to question and challenge societal norms and structures. This approach has had a significant impact on critical educational theory and practices.
4. **Jürgen Habermas**
   - **Theory of Communicative Action:** Jürgen Habermas developed the 'Theory of Communicative Action,' which focuses on the role of communication in society. He emphasized the importance of open, rational dialogue in achieving social change and justice.
   - **Public Sphere:** Habermas introduced the concept of the 'public sphere,' which refers to spaces where citizens can engage in rational discourse and critique public policies and institutions.

- **Examples:**
  1. The Black Lives Matter movement can be understood through critical race theory. It highlights systemic racism, police brutality, and racial inequalities in the criminal justice system. It calls for critical examination of power structures and the need for social change.
  2. Immigration policies and border controls can be analysed through critical theory to understand how they are used to maintain social divisions, limit access to resources, and perpetuate inequalities among migrant populations.
- **Critique:** Some critics argue that critical theory's intense focus on power dynamics and conflict can lead to an overly pessimistic view of society. It may not fully account for positive aspects of social change, cooperation, and functional institutions.

While they may deem similar in emphasis and approach, conflict and critical theory have certain key differences:

Aspect	Critical Theory	Conflict Theory
Origins	Originated in the Frankfurt School in the 20th century, with key thinkers like Horkheimer and Adorno.	Associated with Karl Marx and Friedrich Engels in the 19th century, focusing on class struggle.
Interdisciplinary Scope	Takes an interdisciplinary approach, drawing from various fields.	Primarily emphasises economic factors and class dynamics.

Aspect	Critical Theory	Conflict Theory
Focus in Society	Emphasises cultural, ideological, and institutional analysis.	Primarily focuses on power dynamics, social inequality, and class conflict.

While theories provide a larger framework to study social phenomena, there are different methods that are used to conduct research, the two major ones being positivist and non-positivist.

Positivism and Its Critique

- Positivism is a research paradigm and philosophical approach that emphasises the use of empirical, observable data and scientific methods to study and explain social phenomena. It is rooted in the belief that the social world can be studied using methods similar to those employed in the natural sciences.
- Positivism seeks to establish causal relationships, identify patterns, and develop generalizable theories about social phenomena. It assumes an objective reality that can be measured and studied.

Key Elements in the Origin of Positivism in Sociology

- **Comte's Scientific Vision:** Auguste Comte envisioned a science of society, sociology which 'has three principal sources of knowledge: observation of facts, reason, and historical documents.'
- **Hierarchical Science Framework:** Comte introduced a hierarchy of sciences, positioning sociology at the pinnacle, advocating that it could provide a scientific and empirical grasp of society, transcending prior speculative and theological approaches. He said, 'Sociology is the Queen of the Sciences.'
- **Three Stages of Intellectual Development:** Comte's theory of intellectual development for humanity consisted of three stages namely theological, metaphysical, and positive with the positive stage representing a shift towards scientific thinking and empirical methods

Key Characteristics of Positivism in Sociology

- **Empirical Data:** Positivist researchers rely on empirical data, which is data based on observations and measurable facts rather than subjective interpretations.
- **Quantitative Methods:** Positivism favours quantitative research methods, such as surveys, experiments, and statistical analysis, to collect and analyse data.
- **Objectivity:** Positivist researchers aim for objectivity and seek to minimise bias in their studies. They often adopt a neutral and detached role in their research.
- **Generalizability:** The goal is to establish general principles and theories that can be applied to larger populations or settings.
- **Causality:** Positivism seeks to identify cause-and-effect relationships between variables.

Critiques of Positivism in Sociology

(a) **Complexity of Social Reality:** 'The positivist approach oversimplifies the intricate nature of social reality, reducing it to quantifiable variables.' – Max Weber

(b) **Inadequate Understanding of Subjectivity:** 'Positivism neglects the subjective meanings and interpretations that individuals attach to their actions and experiences.' – Alfred Schutz

(c) **Limited Role of Values:** 'Positivism fails to address the role of values in research, leading to potential ethical and moral concerns.' – Karl Popper

(d) **Cultural and Contextual Variability:** 'Positivism struggles to accommodate the cultural and contextual variability of social phenomena.' – Clifford Geertz

(e) **Overemphasis on Generalization:** 'The quest for generalization may lead to a neglect of context-specific understanding.' – Peter Winch

(f) **Neglect of Unobservable Factors:** 'Positivism dismisses the significance of unobservable factors and emotions in social life.' – Emile Durkheim

(g) **Inadequate Treatment of Power Dynamics:** 'Positivism often fails to account for power dynamics and inequalities in society.' – Michel Foucault

(h) **Overemphasis on Causality:** 'Positivism's obsession with causality may lead to ignoring the interplay of multiple factors and complex causation.' – Anthony Giddens

Fact Value and Objectivity

A distinction should be made between fact and fact value to understand their role in Sociology. 'Fact' and 'fact-value' are terms often used in the context of epistemology to distinguish between descriptive statements (facts) and evaluative or normative statements (fact-values). They can be explained through the following:

Aspect	Fact	Fact-Value
Nature	Descriptive and verifiable	Combines description with value judgement
Objectivity	Objective; not influenced by personal values or opinions	Subjective; influenced by personal values, beliefs, and judgements
Determinability	Truth or falsity can be objectively determined through observation or evidence.	Evaluation involves subjective perspectives, and truth is context-dependent
Typical Examples	Water boils at 100 degrees Celsius at standard atmospheric pressure.	Pollution levels in the city have exceeded acceptable limits, and this is harmful to the environment and public health.
Areas of Relevance	Empirical observations, scientific research, objective reality	Morality, ethics, aesthetics, personal preferences, values, and beliefs

From the above, it can be understood that sociology involves the use of both facts and fact values.

Point to Note

Value Neutrality vs Objectivity

Value neutrality is a subset of objectivity. Objectivity encompasses a broader commitment to impartiality and neutrality throughout the entire research process, while value neutrality specifically addresses the researcher's need to minimise the influence of their personal values and biases. Both concepts are essential in maintaining the rigour and credibility of sociological research.

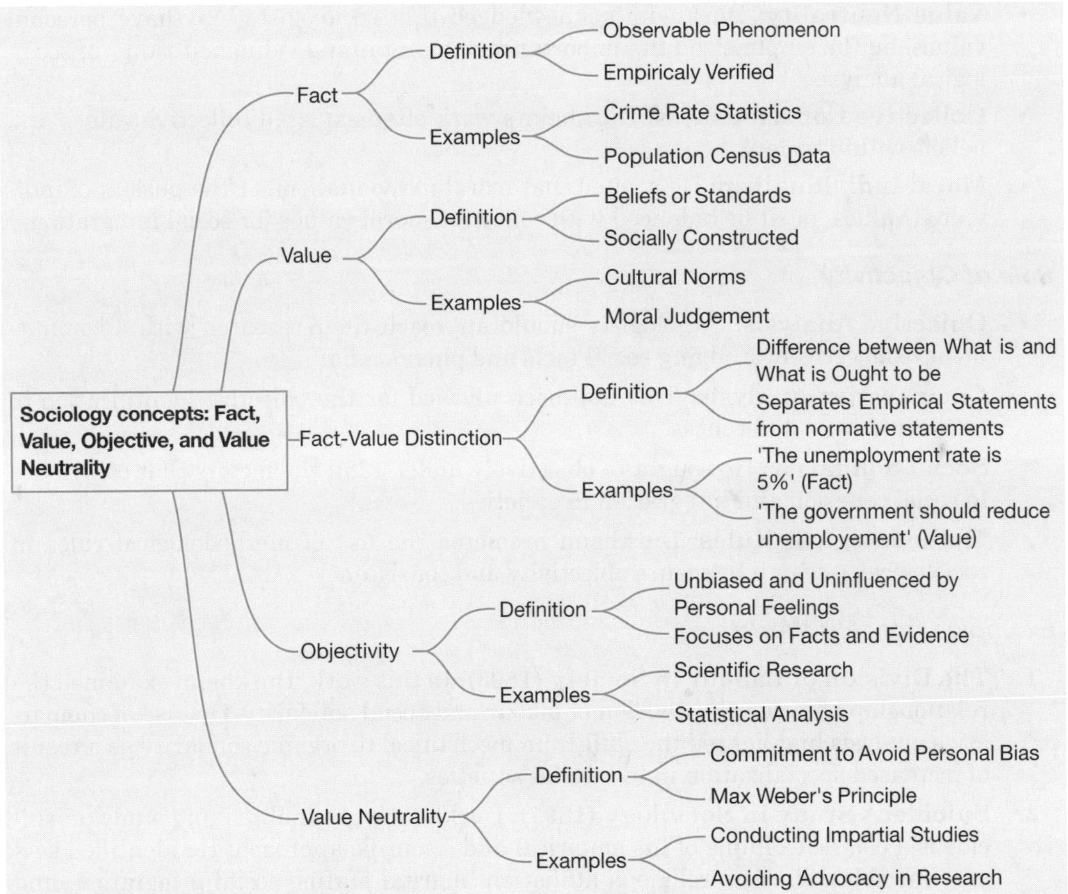

Durkheim's Ideas on Fact, Value and Objectivity

Role of Facts

- **Empirical Foundation:** He believed that sociologists should base their theories and analyses on concrete and observable data.
- **Social Facts:** Durkheim introduced the concept of 'social facts,' which are external, objective, and coercive elements of society.
- **Causal Relationships:** By examining the influence of social facts on individual behaviour, he aimed to uncover the causes of social phenomena.
- **Quantitative Data:** Durkheim advocated for the use of quantitative data and statistical methods to analyse social facts.

Role of Values

- **Value Neutrality:** Durkheim acknowledged that sociologists may have personal values, but he emphasized the importance of maintaining value neutrality in sociological analysis.
- **Collective Consciousness:** Durkheim's work often explored collective values and beliefs within society.
- **Moral Individualism:** He argued that moral individualism, or the pursuit of individual values, must be balanced with collective moral values for social integration.

Role of Objectivity

- **Objective Analysis:** Sociologists should approach their research with a commitment to objectively studying social facts and phenomena.
- **Comparative Analysis:** This approach allowed for the objective identification of similarities and differences.
- **Social Solidarity:** He sought to objectively understand the factors that contribute to social cohesion and integration in societies.
- **Methodological Rules:** Durkheim promoted the use of methodological rules in sociological research to ensure objectivity and consistency

Examples from His Works

1. **The Division of Labour in Society (1893):** In this work, Durkheim examined the relationship between the division of labour and social solidarity. His use of comparative analysis highlighted the shift from mechanical to organic solidarity as a result of increased specialization in industrial societies.
2. **Suicide: A Study in Sociology (1897):** Durkheim's groundbreaking study on suicide is a classic example of his empirical and scientific approach. He identified several variables, such as religious affiliation, marital status, social integration, and economic conditions, which could potentially influence suicide rates.
3. **The Rules of Sociological Method (1895):** He emphasized the study of 'social facts' that are external to individuals, such as marriage, law, and institutions and argued that sociologists should study these social facts as things.

4. **The Elementary Forms of Religious Life (1912):** In this work, Durkheim analysed the religious beliefs and practices of Australian Aboriginal tribes. He exemplified his focus on identifying the role of social institutions, such as religion, in shaping collective consciousness and maintaining social order.

Weber's Ideas on Fact, Value and Objectivity

Role of Facts

- **Empirical Foundation:** Weber also emphasized the importance of empirical facts in sociological analysis.
- **Factual Accuracy:** Weber advocated for the accurate and rigorous collection of facts in sociological studies.
- **Causal Understanding:** Weber was interested in identifying causal relationships between social phenomena.
- **Value Neutrality:** Weber acknowledged that sociologists bring their own values to their research, but he argued that they should strive for value neutrality by distinguishing between descriptive facts and their own evaluative judgements.

Role of Values

- **Verstehen (Understanding):** Weber introduced the concept of 'Verstehen,' which means empathetic understanding. Sociologists should strive to understand the social actors' values, beliefs, and motivations from their perspective.
- **Interpretive Sociology:** Weber's approach often involved interpretive or hermeneutic methods, where values play a crucial role in interpreting the meanings individuals attach to their actions.

Role of Objectivity

- **Ideal-Type Construction:** Weber developed the concept of the 'ideal type,' which is an objective and abstract representation of a social phenomenon as analytical tools to maintain objectivity.
- **Comparative Analysis:** Weber advocated for comparative analysis.
- **Causal Analysis:** Weber believed that sociologists should objectively assess the causes of social phenomena to understand their dynamics.

Examples from His Works

1. In his work 'The Protestant Ethic and the Spirit of Capitalism,' Weber used the concept of Verstehen to understand how the Protestant Reformation influenced the development of capitalism. He examined the religious beliefs and values of individuals to explain economic behaviour.

   We will understand the concept in detail here:

   Fact and Value in Weber's Analysis – Protestant Ethic and the Spirit of Capitalism

   Fact: In Weber's study, facts refer to objective, empirical observations about social phenomena. These include historical data, economic statistics, and observable behaviours. For example, Weber examines historical records to establish the rise of capitalism in Western Europe. He identifies key economic behaviours, such as the rational organization of work and systematic pursuit of profit, which he argues are characteristics of modern capitalism.

Examples of Facts in Weber's Work

- The historical development of capitalist enterprises.
- The systematic and disciplined approach to labour in Protestant communities.
- Statistical evidence showing a higher prevalence of capitalist economic activities among Protestants compared to Catholics during certain periods in history.

Value: Values, in contrast, pertain to the subjective, often ethical or moral beliefs held by individuals or groups. These values influence behaviour and can drive social change. In 'The Protestant Ethic and the Spirit of Capitalism,' Weber investigates how certain Protestant values, particularly those associated with Calvinism, contributed to the development of capitalist spirit. He argues that the Protestant ethic emphasized hard work, frugality, and a sense of calling, which collectively fostered a conducive environment for capitalism.

Examples of Values in Weber's Work

- The Calvinist belief in predestination, which led individuals to seek signs of salvation through success in worldly activities.
- The Protestant ethic that regarded hard work and economic success as virtuous and indicative of divine favour.
- The value placed on rationality, discipline, and frugality as moral imperatives.

Illustrating the Distinction with Examples

(i) **Historical Economic Behaviour (Fact):** Weber notes the empirical increase in capitalist enterprises among Protestant populations during the Reformation period. This observation is a fact based on historical economic data.

Example: In regions such as England and parts of Germany, where Protestantism was dominant, there was a notable rise in entrepreneurial activities and systematic economic planning.

(ii) **Religious Values and Beliefs (Value):** The Calvinist doctrine of predestination instilled a value system where economic success was seen as a sign of God's favour. This belief drove individuals to work diligently and accumulate wealth, viewing their economic success as a spiritual indicator.

Example: The idea that 'time is money' became a moral tenet among Protestants, driving them to avoid idleness and engage in continuous, disciplined work.

2. In 'The Theory of Social and Economic Organization,' Weber introduced the ideal type of the 'bureaucratic organization' to analyse the features and characteristics of bureaucratic structures in various institutions.
3. In 'Objectivity in Social Science and Social Policy,' Weber stressed the importance of value neutrality in sociological research. He argued that researchers should present facts without imposing their own judgements.
4. In 'The Protestant Ethic and the Spirit of Capitalism,' Weber explored the relationship between religious beliefs, economic systems, and cultural values as multiple causes contributing to the development of capitalism.

5. In 'Economy and Society,' Weber conducted historical and comparative studies of various religious, legal, and economic systems to trace their development and impact on societies.
6. In his essay 'The Objectivity of Social Science and Social Policy,' Weber discussed the difference between value relevance and value irrelevance in sociological research, arguing that both have their place but should be kept distinct.

Is Sociology a Science?

Below discussed are the arguments in favour and against.

Argument	In Favour of Sociology as a Science	Against Sociology as a Science
Empirical Evidence	Systematic data collection (e.g., crime rates) supports its scientific nature.	Systematic data collection (e.g., crime rates) supports its scientific nature.
Scientific Method	Follows scientific method with hypothesis testing and data analysis	Subjectivity and interpretation challenges objectivity
Theoretical Frameworks	Offers well-developed theories (e.g., functionalism) to explain social phenomena	Theories can be value-laden and biased
Replicability	Some sociological studies are replicable, enhancing scientific credibility.	Challenges in replicating social experiments due to unique settings.
Practical Applications	Inform policy-making and real-world interventions, akin to natural sciences	Subjectivity and disputes can limit the reliability of sociological findings

Conclusion

While sociology shares some characteristics with the sciences, such as systematic observation, empirical research, and theory-building, its subject matter introduces complexities that challenge its scientific status. Human behaviour, influenced by emotions, values, and social contexts, often eludes the consistency and predictability expected in natural sciences. Thus, sociology is considered a social science—a discipline with scientific aspirations but one that acknowledges the interpretative nature of human societies.

Non-Positivist Methodologies

Before we delve into the non-positivist methodologies, it is important to understand the difference between positivism, post-positivism and non-positivism to avoid any confusion.

Aspect	Positivism	Post-Positivism	Non-Positivism
Nature of Reality	Objective reality is independent of observers	Recognises objective reality but acknowledges the role of subjectivity and interpretation	Emphasises subjectivity, interpretation, and values
Approach to Knowledge	Empirical observation, measurement, and the scientific method as the path to truth	Empirical observation and the scientific method but with critical reflection and recognition of values	Diverse approaches that reject positivist principles and focus on subjectivity and interpretation
Example	Testing the effects of a drug on a specific ailment	Analyzing drug effectiveness while considering potential biases in research	Exploring the subjective experience of patients' pain and how it relates to their cultural context

Major Non-Positivist Methodologies

Interpretive Sociology

(a) Origin

Interpretive sociology, first used by Max Weber in his book - Methodology of Social Sciences (1949), is an umbrella term for various other streams like Phenomenology, Ethnomethodology, Symbolic Interactionism, etc. It seeks to understand social actions from the actor's perspective. It focuses on uncovering the meanings and interpretations that individuals attribute to their actions.

(b) Key Characteristics

- The basis of this approach is that an individual has a voluntary will, an unpredictable consciousness and his thoughts cannot be understood simply in terms of external influence, hence also known as voluntarist approach.
- It involves analysis of symbolic meanings, cultural interpretations, and the role of values and beliefs in shaping behaviour.
- Under this approach, Weber also proposed scientific methods such as Verstehen (understanding) of social actions, Ideal Type and Comparative methods
- Often involves qualitative methods like in-depth interviews.

(c) Example: Research on how religious individuals interpret and practice their faith within a specific cultural context. Like Max Weber stated, 'Adequate causal interpretation involves an understanding of the subjective meanings.'

Phenomenology

It is a philosophical and methodological approach that seeks to understand and describe human experiences from the perspective of the individuals living those experiences.

(a) Origin

Phenomenology, as applied in sociology, originated from the broader philosophical movement founded by Edmund Husserl. Its use in sociology gained prominence in the mid-20th century as sociologists adopted and adapted phenomenological principles to study human experiences and social phenomena.

(b) Essential Characteristics

- **Subjective Exploration:** Phenomenology in sociology prioritises the exploration of the subjective experiences, meanings, and interpretations of individuals and groups within a social context.
- **Bracketing of Preconceptions:** Researchers must suspend their preconceptions and biases to grasp the unmediated experiences and perspectives of participants.
- **Lifeworld Analysis:** A focus on the lifeworld (everyday world) of individuals, recognizing that social reality is constructed by how individuals perceive and experience it.
- **Empathy and Intersubjectivity:** Phenomenological sociology encourages researchers to empathise with the participants and achieve intersubjective understanding of their experiences.
- **Qualitative Methods:** It often employs qualitative research methods, such as in-depth interviews, participant observation, and content analysis, to access and interpret subjective experiences.

(c) Major Thinkers and Their Works

- **Alfred Schutz:** His work 'The Phenomenology of the Social World' laid the groundwork for applying phenomenology in sociology, emphasizing the significance of understanding everyday life.
- **Peter Berger and Thomas Luckmann** further systematized it in their book - The Social Construction of Reality (1967)
- **Anselm Strauss and Barney G. Glaser:** They developed grounded theory, a qualitative research method rooted in phenomenology, to generate theories from empirical data in sociology.

(d) Relevant Quotes

- **Alfred Schutz:** 'In phenomenological analysis, therefore, we should not try to achieve an 'objectivity' that denies the subjective world but should seek to reconstitute an intersubjectivity in which each participant can find again the significance of his own existence.'

(e) Critique

- Pierre Bourdieu critiqued phenomenology for its potential detachment from the structural and objective elements of society, suggesting it may neglect social context.
- Michel Foucault raised concerns about the potential reification of subjective experience, asserting that it could lead to the neglect of power dynamics and social institutions.
- Herbert Marcuse criticized phenomenology, asserting that it led to a withdrawal from the social and political sphere, focusing too heavily on individual experiences.

Ethnomethodology

It is a sociological approach that focuses on the study of how individuals create and maintain social order in their everyday interactions. This approach emphasizes the micro-level analysis of social interactions and is often concerned with the practical and taken-for-granted methods that individuals use to construct their social reality.

(a) Origin

Ethnomethodology emerged as a sociological approach in the 1960s and 1970s, primarily associated with the work of Harold Garfinkel. It developed as a reaction against structuralist and functionalist perspectives in sociology, aiming to understand how individuals create social order through their everyday interactions.

(b) Essential Characteristics

- **Microsociological Focus:** Ethnomethodology emphasises the micro-level analysis of everyday social interactions, emphasizing how people produce social order through their actions and conversations.
- **Emphasis on 'Members' Methods':** Ethnomethodologists seek to understand how individuals employ 'members' methods' (practical, everyday strategies and techniques that individuals use) to make sense of and navigate their social world. For example, during a handshake for greeting purpose, its firmness, duration and eye contacts are all part of the unspoken rules.
- **Indexicality:** It explores the indexical nature of language and meaning, recognizing that words and symbols gain their significance within specific contexts.
- **Breaching Experiments:** Researchers may use 'breaching experiments' to intentionally disrupt social norms and observe how individuals react and restore order. For example - The Elevator Standoff: In a crowded elevator, instead of facing the front as is customary, a researcher stands facing the rear.
- **Reflexivity:** Our sense of order is a result of conversations which are reflective in nature.
- **No Theoretical Framework:** Ethnomethodology generally avoids relying on pre-established sociological theories, favouring a more neutral stance.

(c) Major Thinkers and Their Works

- **Harold Garfinkel:** His work 'Studies in Ethnomethodology' is foundational for the approach, presenting breaching experiments and the concept of ethnomethods.
- **Harvey Sacks:** A prominent ethnomethodologist who contributed to conversation analysis, a method within ethnomethodology.

(d) Relevant Quotes

- **Harold Garfinkel:** 'The sociological feature of the sense of knowing that we may attribute to an actor (at any particular moment) consists of the actor's own working presumption that the formal orders of practical action exist, and will continue to exist.'

(e) Critique by Other Thinkers

- Pierre Bourdieu critiqued ethnomethodology for its potential neglect of larger structural and objective aspects of society, suggesting that it may overly focus on micro-level interactions.

- Erving Goffman raised concerns about the overly focused and sometimes contrived nature of breaching experiments, suggesting they may not fully represent real-world interactions.

Symbolic Interactionism

(a) Origin

It is a sociological perspective that emerged primarily in the United States in the early 20th century. It is closely associated with the work of American sociologists George Herbert Mead and Charles Horton Cooley. Herbert Blumer coined the term.

(b) Essential Characteristics

- **Symbolic Meaning:** It emphasises that people interpret and give meaning to symbols (e.g., words, gestures, and objects) in their social interactions.
- **The Self:** It explores how individuals develop a sense of self through social interactions, taking on the perspectives of others (the 'I' and the 'Me,' as described by Mead).
- **Role-Taking:** People engage in role-taking, which involves imagining themselves in the position of others and anticipating how they will react.
- **Social Reality Construction:** It asserts that reality is socially constructed through human interactions. The meaning of concepts, norms, and values is not fixed but evolves through social processes.
- **Socialization:** It is a dynamic process that allows people to develop the ability to think.
- **Micro-Level Analysis:** This perspective predominantly focuses on micro-level interactions and face-to-face encounters, emphasizing the significance of everyday interactions in shaping society.

Point to Note

Charles Horton Cooley's **'looking glass self'** concept can be summarized in three key points:

- **Imagined Perceptions:** Individuals imagine how they appear to others in social interactions, considering aspects like their behaviour and appearance.
- **Imagined Reactions:** They also consider how they believe others react to their perceived appearance and behaviour, whether positively or negatively.
- **Self-Concept Development:** Based on these imagined perceptions and reactions, individuals develop their self-concept and self-identity.

(c) Major Thinkers and Their Works

- **George Herbert Mead:** Mead's ideas on the self, role-taking, and symbolic interactionism are central to this perspective. His work, including 'Mind, Self, and Society,' significantly influenced the theory.
- **Charles Horton Cooley:** Cooley introduced the concept of the 'looking glass self'. His work 'Human Nature and the Social Order' is influential.

(d) **Relevant Quotes**

- **Charles Horton Cooley:** 'I am not what I think I am, and I am not what you think I am. I am what I think you think I am.'
- **Herbert Blumer:** 'Non-symbolic interactions don't require thinking, but symbolic interactions require thinking.'

(e) **Critique by Other Thinkers**

- Structural functionalists (e.g., Emile Durkheim) argued that Symbolic Interactionism focuses too narrowly on micro-level interactions and neglects the broader structural aspects of society.
- Proponents of Conflict Theory critiqued that Symbolic Interactionism does not adequately address power dynamics, class struggles, and social inequalities.
- Skidmore accuses symbolic interactionists of failing to explain why people consistently choose to act in given ways in certain ways instead of all other possible ways.

Dramaturgical Approach

It is a perspective in sociology that views social interactions as akin to a theatrical performance.

(a) **Origin**

The Dramaturgical Approach in sociology was developed by Erving Goffman, a Canadian sociologist, in his 1959 book titled 'The Presentation of Self in Everyday Life.' Goffman drew inspiration from theater and dramaturgy to understand how individuals present themselves in social interactions.

(b) **Essential Characteristics**

- **Front Stage and Back Stage:** Goffman introduced the concept of the front stage, where individuals perform for others, and the backstage, where they can relax and be themselves without an audience.
- **Impression Management:** Individuals engage in impression management, strategically controlling the information they present to create a favorable impression on others.
- **Role Distance:** People often maintain a distinction between their 'true self' and the roles they play, known as role distance, to cope with the demands of different situations.
- **Sign Vehicles:** Sign vehicles, including clothing, props, and non-verbal cues, are used to convey information about one's identity and social position.
- **Face-Saving Behaviour:** Goffman explored the ways individuals engage in face-saving behaviour to avoid embarrassment or maintain social dignity in interactions.

(c) **Major Thinkers and Their Works**

- Goffman is the key thinker associated with the Dramaturgical Approach. His works, including 'The Presentation of Self in Everyday Life,' 'Asylums,' and 'Frame Analysis,' have been influential in this field.

(d) Relevant Quotes

- **Erving Goffman:** 'All the world is not, of course, a stage, but the crucial ways in which it isn't are not easy to specify.'

(e) Critique by Other Thinkers

- **Critique of Oversimplification:** Some critics argue that Goffman's approach oversimplifies human interactions by reducing them to theatrical performances.
- **Neglect of Structural Factors:** Critics contend that the Dramaturgical Approach places too much emphasis on individual agency and neglects broader structural factors that influence.

Feminist Approach

It is a theoretical and analytical framework that focuses on understanding and addressing gender-based inequalities and the social construction of gender roles.

(a) Origin

The feminist approach in sociology emerged in the mid-20th century as a response to the limited inclusion of women's experiences and perspectives in sociological research. It has roots in various social movements advocating for gender equality and women's rights.

(b) Essential Characteristics

- **Gender as a Social Construct:** Feminism challenges the notion of gender as a biological given and emphasises its social construction. It explores how gender roles, norms, and expectations are shaped by societal forces.
- **Intersectionality:** Feminism incorporates an intersectional perspective, recognizing that individuals' experiences are shaped by the interplay of gender with other social factors like race, class, sexuality, and more.
- **Critique of Patriarchy:** Feminist sociology critiques patriarchal systems and power structures that perpetuate gender inequalities. It explores how these systems affect various aspects of life, from family dynamics to the workplace.
- **Voices of Marginalized Groups:** Feminism seeks to amplify the voices of marginalized and oppressed groups, including women of color, LGBTQ+ individuals, and those at the intersections of multiple marginalized identities.
- **Activism and Social Change:** Feminist sociology often aligns with activism and social change efforts. It aims to challenge and dismantle oppressive systems to achieve gender equality and social justice.

(c) Major Thinkers and Their Works

- **Simone de Beauvoir:** Her work 'The Second Sex' (1949) laid the foundation for feminist existentialism and explored women's oppression in a male-dominated world.
- **bell hooks:** Known for 'Ain't I a Woman: Black Women and Feminism' (1981), hooks addresses the intersection of race, gender, and class in the lives of Black women.
- **Audre Lorde:** Her work 'Sister Outsider' (1984) discusses the intersection of race, sexuality, and feminism, emphasizing the importance of self-care and self-empowerment.

(d) **Relevant Quotes**

- **Simone de Beauvoir:** 'One is not born, but rather becomes, a woman.'
- **bell hooks:** 'Feminism is a movement to end sexism, sexist exploitation, and oppression.'

(e) **Critique by Other Thinkers**

- **Critique of Essentialism:** Some critics argue that certain strands of feminism have been essentialist, assuming universal experiences for all women, which can overlook the diversity of women's experiences.
- **Backlash and Opposition:** Feminism has faced backlash and opposition from various quarters, with some questioning the need for feminism and gender equality.

Below are the key elements that highlight the distinctiveness of the feminist method of social research:

1. **Emphasis on Gender and Power Relations:** Feminist research places a central focus on understanding and analysing gender as a primary category of analysis. It examines power relations and seeks to uncover how these dynamics influence social structures and individual experiences. Feminist researchers aim to challenge patriarchal norms and highlight women's voices and experiences, which have historically been marginalized.
2. **Subjectivity and Reflexivity:** Unlike traditional positivist approaches that emphasise objectivity and detachment, feminist research embraces subjectivity and reflexivity. Researchers acknowledge their own positions, biases, and the influence these have on their research. Reflexivity involves a continuous process of reflection on the researcher's role, potential power imbalances, and the research process itself.
3. **Participatory and Empowerment Approach:** Feminist research often employs participatory methods that involve the subjects of the study as active participants rather than passive objects. This approach aims to empower participants by valuing their knowledge, experiences, and perspectives. It promotes collaboration and seeks to democratize the research process, ensuring that the outcomes benefit the communities being studied.
4. **Qualitative Methods and Rich Descriptions:** Feminist research frequently utilises qualitative methods such as interviews, ethnography, and participant observation. These methods allow for in-depth exploration of personal experiences and social contexts. Rich, descriptive data is valued over numerical data, as it provides a deeper understanding of the complexities of gendered experiences.
5. **Focus on Social Change:** A distinctive feature of feminist research is its commitment to social justice and advocacy. The goal is not only to generate knowledge but also to use that knowledge to challenge and transform gender inequalities. Feminist researchers are often engaged in activism and seek to influence policy and practice to promote equality.
6. **Interdisciplinary Approach:** Feminist research is inherently interdisciplinary, drawing from sociology, anthropology, psychology, literature, and other fields. This approach allows for a comprehensive understanding of gender issues, recognizing the interconnectedness of various social factors.

7. **Critique of Traditional Methodologies:** Feminist researchers critically examine traditional methodologies and the ways in which they perpetuate gender biases. They advocate for methodological innovations that are more inclusive and representative of diverse gender experiences.

Case Study: The Experience of Women in Academia

A notable example of feminist research is the study of women in academia. Research by scholars such as Joan Acker and Rosabeth Moss Kanter has illuminated the structural barriers and cultural biases that women face in academic institutions. These studies have used qualitative interviews and participatory methods to gather data, highlighting the experiences of women faculty members and advocating for institutional reforms to promote gender equality.

Contemporary Trends and Examples

1. **Workplace Inequality and Gender Pay Gap**

   Contemporary research on workplace inequality and the gender pay gap is a prominent area where feminist methodologies have been applied. Joan Acker's concept of the 'gendered organization' demonstrates how organizational structures and practices perpetuate gender inequalities. Acker's work emphasises the importance of examining power relations and the role of institutions in maintaining gender disparities.

   Thinkers:

   - **Joan Acker:** Her work on the theory of gendered organizations illustrates how workplaces are structured in ways that disadvantage women.
   - **Cynthia Cockburn:** Known for her studies on gender and technology, Cockburn explores how technological environments can reinforce gender inequalities.

2. **Sexual Harassment and #MeToo Movement**

   The #MeToo movement has brought significant attention to the issue of sexual harassment and assault. Feminist researchers have used participatory and qualitative methods to document personal testimonies and analyse the power dynamics involved. This movement has also sparked a wave of feminist activism and policy changes aimed at addressing and preventing sexual harassment.

   Thinkers:

   - **Tarana Burke:** Founder of the #MeToo movement, Burke's work highlights the importance of giving voice to survivors of sexual violence and advocating for systemic change.
   - **Catherine MacKinnon:** Her legal scholarship and activism have been pivotal in framing sexual harassment as a form of sex discrimination.

3. **Reproductive Rights and Health**

   Feminist research on reproductive rights and health examines how women's access to reproductive healthcare is influenced by social, political, and economic factors. Researchers use qualitative interviews and case studies to understand women's experiences with reproductive health services and advocate for policies that ensure equitable access.

Thinkers:

- **Loretta Ross:** An activist and scholar, Ross has contributed extensively to the reproductive justice movement, which links reproductive rights to broader social justice issues.
- **Barbara Katz Rothman:** Her work on the sociology of childbirth and reproductive technologies explores the medicalisation of women's bodies and the implications for women's autonomy.

4. **Intersectionality and Social Justice**

Intersectionality, a concept developed by Kimberlé Crenshaw, is central to contemporary feminist research. It examines how various social identities (e.g., race, gender, class, sexuality) intersect and create unique experiences of oppression and privilege. Intersectional analysis is used to highlight the complexities of identity and advocate for more inclusive social policies.

Thinkers:

- **Kimberlé Crenshaw:** Her foundational work on intersectionality has reshaped feminist research by emphasizing the interconnectedness of different forms of discrimination.
- **Patricia Hill Collins:** Known for her work on Black feminist thought, Collins explores the intersection of race, gender, and class, advocating for a more nuanced understanding of social inequalities.

5. **Digital Feminism and Online Activism**

The rise of digital feminism and online activism is another contemporary area of feminist research. Scholars examine how social media platforms are used to mobilize feminist movements, raise awareness about gender issues, and challenge misogyny. Research methods include digital ethnography and content analysis of online interactions.

Thinkers:

- **Jessalynn Keller:** Keller's research on digital feminism explores how young women use social media to engage in feminist activism and create online communities.
- **Zizi Papacharissi:** Her work on the networked self-examines how digital technologies influence identity formation and social movements, including feminist activism.

Non-Positivist Methods in Sociology: A Comprehensive Analysis

The emergence of non-positivist methods can be traced to Max Weber's concept of 'Verstehen,' which emphasized understanding social action through the meanings actors attach to their behaviour. Weber's seminal work, 'The Protestant Ethic and the Spirit of Capitalism,' demonstrated how interpretive methods could reveal complex relationships between religious beliefs and economic behaviour. This foundation was further developed by scholars like Alfred Schutz, who introduced phenomenological perspectives to sociology.

Strengths of Non-Positivist Approaches

- **Deep Contextual Understanding:** Non-positivist methods excel at uncovering rich, contextual meanings within social phenomena. Howard Becker's participant observation studies of jazz musicians revealed intricate social hierarchies and norms that would have been invisible to survey research. Similarly, Dorothy Smith's institutional ethnography demonstrated how everyday experiences connect to broader social structures, providing insights that quantitative methods might miss.
- **Flexibility and Emergent Discovery:** The flexible nature of non-positivist methods allows researchers to adapt their approach as new insights emerge. This advantage is particularly evident in Glaser and Strauss's development of Grounded Theory through their study of dying hospital patients. Paul Willis's 'Learning to Labour' similarly discovered unexpected ways working-class boys actively participated in their own social reproduction, findings that might have been overlooked with more rigid methodological approaches.
- **Voice and Agency:** Non-positivist methods excel at giving voice to research subjects rather than treating them as passive objects of study. Patricia Hill Collins's Black Feminist Thought emphasized the importance of marginalized voices, while Oscar Lewis's 'Five Families' provided detailed life histories of Mexican families. These approaches recognize human agency and complexity in ways that quantitative methods often cannot capture.
- **Cultural Sensitivity and Cross-Cultural:** Research Scholars like Clifford Geertz demonstrated the value of 'thick description' in understanding cultural phenomena, as evidenced by his analysis of Balinese cockfighting. Margaret Mead's work in Samoa, despite later controversies, showed how non-positivist methods could challenge Western assumptions about universal social phenomena.

Challenges and Limitations

- **Generalizability:** Issues one significant limitation of non-positivist methods is their limited generalizability. Critics of Michael Burawoy's extended case method point to difficulties in applying findings beyond specific contexts. William Julius Wilson argued that ethnographic studies of urban poverty, while valuable, couldn't fully explain broader structural changes affecting urban communities.
- **Subjectivity and Verification:** The subjective nature of non-positivist research raises concerns about bias and verification. The controversy surrounding Carlos Castaneda's work and debates about Alice Goffman's 'On the Run" highlight challenges in verifying ethnographic findings. Napoleon Chagnon's contested interpretations of Yanomami culture demonstrate how researcher bias can affect findings.
- **Resource Intensity and Practical Constraints:** Non-positivist methods often require significant time and resources. Loïc Wacquant's ethnography of boxing and Philippe Bourgois's five-year study of crack dealers exemplify the intensive nature of these approaches. This resource requirement can limit their practical application in many research contexts.

Contemporary Developments and Future Directions

Digital ethnography and new frontiers contemporary scholars like Christine Hine and Sarah Pink are adapting non-positivist methods to digital spaces, developing new approaches for studying online communities and digital culture. Daniel Miller's studies of social media use demonstrate how traditional ethnographic methods can be modified for digital contexts.

Participatory and decolonial approaches' recent developments include increased emphasis on participatory methods and decolonial approaches. Orlando Fals Borda's participatory action research and Linda Tuhiwai Smith's indigenous methodologies represent important advances in making research more inclusive and culturally sensitive. Methodological Integration Modern researchers increasingly recognize the value of combining methods. Pierre Bourdieu's integration of ethnography with statistical analysis in 'Distinction" demonstrates how mixed methods can provide more comprehensive understanding. Robert K. Merton's advocacy for middle-range theory suggests ways to bridge methodological divides.

Conclusion

In the debate over sociology as a science, it is essential to recognise that sociology employs scientific methods and principles to understand and analyze complex social phenomena. The discipline combines empirical research, theoretical frameworks, and systematic observation to unravel the intricacies of human behaviour and societal structures. While it may not conform precisely to the natural sciences, sociology's commitment to rigorous inquiry and the quest for objectivity solidifies its status as a valuable and distinct form of social science, allowing us to explore, explain, and ultimately contribute to a deeper comprehension of the social world.

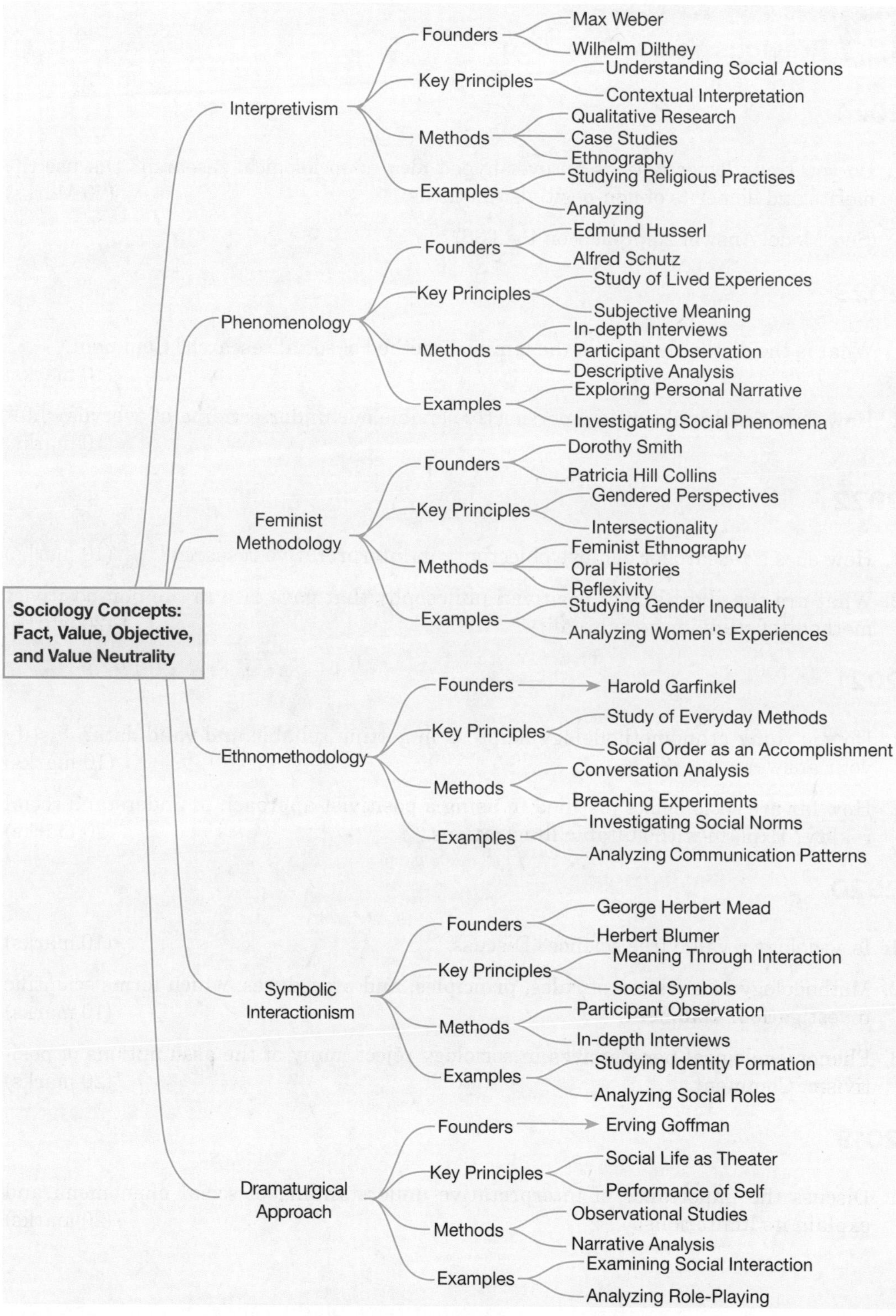
Sociology Concepts: Fact, Value, Objective, and Value Neutrality
Interpretivism
Founders
Max Weber
Wilhelm Dilthey
Key Principles
Understanding Social Actions
Contextual Interpretation
Methods
Qualitative Research
Case Studies
Ethnography
Examples
Studying Religious Practises
Analyzing
Phenomenology
Founders
Edmund Husserl
Alfred Schutz
Key Principles
Study of Lived Experiences
Subjective Meaning
Methods
In-depth Interviews
Participant Observation
Descriptive Analysis
Examples
Exploring Personal Narrative
Investigating Social Phenomena
Feminist Methodology
Founders
Dorothy Smith
Patricia Hill Collins
Key Principles
Gendered Perspectives
Intersectionality
Methods
Feminist Ethnography
Oral Histories
Reflexivity
Examples
Studying Gender Inequality
Analyzing Women's Experiences
Ethnomethodology
Founders
Harold Garfinkel
Key Principles
Study of Everyday Methods
Social Order as an Accomplishment
Methods
Conversation Analysis
Breaching Experiments
Examples
Investigating Social Norms
Analyzing Communication Patterns
Symbolic Interactionism
Founders
George Herbert Mead
Herbert Blumer
Key Principles
Meaning Through Interaction
Social Symbols
Methods
Participant Observation
In-depth Interviews
Examples
Studying Identity Formation
Analyzing Social Roles
Dramaturgical Approach
Founders
Erving Goffman
Key Principles
Social Life as Theater
Performance of Self
Methods
Observational Studies
Narrative Analysis
Examples
Examining Social Interaction
Analyzing Role-Playing

Previous Years' Question

2024

1. Do you think 'objectivity' is an over-hyped idea in sociological research? Discuss the merits and demerits of non-positivist methods. (20 Marks)

   (See 'Model Answer Approach' on Pg 3.38)

2023

1. What is the distinctiveness of the feminist method of social research? Comment. (10 marks)
2. How does the dramaturgical perspective enable our understanding of everyday life? (10 marks)

2022

1. How does a researcher achieve objectivity in interpretative research? (10 marks)
2. What are the shortfalls of positivist philosophy that gave rise to the non-positivist methods of studying social reality? (20 marks)

2021

1. Do you think ethnomethodology helps us in getting reliable and valid data? Justify your answer. (10 marks)
2. How far are sociologists justified in using a positivist approach to understand social reality? Explain with suitable illustrations. (20 marks)

2020

1. Is sociology a value free science? Discuss. (10 marks)
2. Methodology is a system of rules, principles, and procedures, which forms scientific investigation. Comment. (10 marks)
3. Phenomenological perspectives in sociology reject many of the assumptions of positivism. Comment. (20 marks)

2019

1. Discuss the importance of interpretative understanding of social phenomena and explain its limitations. (20 marks)

2018

1. Distinguish between fact and value in Weber's Protestant Ethic and the Spirit of Capitalism. (10 marks)
2. Is non-positivistic methodology scientific? Illustrate. (20 marks)
3. Does scientific method make sociology a science? Illustrate your answer with Durkheim's method. (10 marks)

2017

1. Examine ethnomethodology and phenomenological perspectives as critique of positivism. (10 marks)
2. Examine the basic postulates of positivism and post-positivism. (20 marks)
3. Elaborate the main tenets of interpretative sociology. (10 marks)

2016

1. What is 'value-free sociology'? Clarify. (10 marks)
2. Describe the basic postulates of 'scientific method'? How far are these followed in sociological research? (20 marks)
3. Examine Max Weber's method of maintaining objectivity in sociological research. (20 marks)

2015

1. Is Sociology a Science? Give reasons for your answer. (10 marks)
2. Examine the problems of maintaining objectivity and value neutrality in social science research. (20 marks)
2. 'Non-positivist methodology is essential for understanding human behaviour.' Discuss. (20 marks)

2014

1. How is objectivity different from value neutrality? Discuss with reference to Weber's views on methodology. (10 marks)
2. In what way is the interpretative method different from the positivist approach in the study of social phenomena? (20 marks)

2013

1. Critically examine positivistic approach in sociological studies. (10 marks)

Model Answer Approach

2024 - Q. 2

Do you think 'objectivity' is an over-hyped idea in sociological research? Discuss the merits and demerits of non-positivist methods.

Introduction: Objectivity, a central ideal in sociological research, refers to the unbiased and value-neutral approach to studying social phenomena. Positivist sociologists like Auguste Comte and Émile Durkheim championed objectivity, emphasizing empirical methods similar to natural sciences. However, non-positivist thinkers argue that complete objectivity may overlook subjective experiences, emotions, and meanings that shape human actions. Thus, objectivity's importance in sociology is often debated.

Body:

Merits of Non-Positivist Methods

1. **Understanding Subjective Experiences:** Non-positivist methods, such as interpretivism, emphasize verstehen (understanding) over mere observation. Max Weber advocated for empathetic understanding to grasp the subjective meanings that individuals attach to their actions.
2. **Focus on Depth Over Breadth:** Non-positivist approaches, such as ethnography and in-depth interviews, allow for a detailed understanding of social phenomena. Clifford Geertz's "thick description" exemplifies how in-depth analysis can reveal layers of meaning in cultural practices.
3. **Flexibility and Reflexivity:** Non-positivist methods allow researchers to adapt based on their findings and acknowledge their biases, enhancing the authenticity of results. This reflexivity, endorsed by sociologists like Pierre Bourdieu, helps the researcher engage more deeply with the social context.
4. **Revealing Hidden Meanings:** Non-positivist approaches reveal latent aspects of society, such as power dynamics and ideology. For instance, Michel Foucault's work on knowledge and power illustrates how societal structures influence thought processes, an aspect often missed by objective, quantitative methods.

Demerits of Non-Positivist Methods

1. **Challenges in Generalization:** Non-positivist methods, due to their focus on specific contexts, often face limitations in generalizing findings to broader populations. This affects the applicability of results across diverse societies.
2. **Risk of Subjectivity and Bias:** Non-positivist methods rely on subjective interpretation, making the research prone to researcher biases. This can lead to questions about the reliability and validity of the findings.

3. **Difficulty in Verification:** Non-positivist studies lack the replicability of quantitative methods, as they are deeply context-specific. This hinders the ability to independently verify findings, which is a critical scientific criterion.

Conclusion: While objectivity is crucial in ensuring unbiased sociological research, non-positivist methods bring valuable insights into subjective and complex social realities. Though these methods lack the precision of positivist approaches, they enhance the depth and authenticity of understanding. Hence, a balanced approach, combining objectivity with interpretative depth, may be ideal for capturing the full spectrum of human behaviour and societal dynamics.

Chapter 3

Research Methods and Analysis

In this Chapter

- Qualitative and Quantitative Methods
- Techniques of Data Collection
- Variables, Sampling, Hypothesis, Reliability, and Validity
- Previous Years' Questions

Introduction

A science of society became possible when it was clearly understood that society was a creation of man, not of God. Until the Medieval Period, the dominant idea was that society is of divine origin and was governed by God's will. Only through the Renaissance (a period of vigorous artistic and intellectual activity lasting from 14th till the 17th century) was this notion overturned.

Thinkers like Voltaire (1694–1778), Montesquieu (1689–1758) and Hume (1711–1776) gave ideas on the progressive evolution of societies. In 19th century, August Comte (1798–1857), proposed using the scientific methods of natural sciences to discover the laws governing human behaviour as part of what he called social physics, and later, sociology.

For Comte, the purpose of this approach was not to explain the origin of things or their reason of being, but to explain how things related to each other in terms of invariable and universal laws. Research essentially refers to the systematic study of one's chosen subject for arriving at new and valid conclusions.

What Constitutes 'Data' for Sociologists?

Social scientists use observation to identify the study material. However, unlike natural sciences where objects of study do not need interpretation, in social sciences, the observed phenomenon has a meaning attached to it. Thus, the data here consist of 'social constructs'. For example, cricket is a game. On plain observation, one can see different types of actions on the field—throwing the ball in a particular way, hitting it, players running between two points, other players running across the ground to catch the ball, etc. But all these actions can only be understood when one understands the meaning attached to those actions. Similarly, human actions in the social sphere encapsulate meanings and motives. Both the observable and unobservable part of human actions constitutes data for social scientists.

Moreover, sociologists study people 'in relation' to each other. Thus, the data consists of relationships and group behaviour as objects of investigation.

What are the Rules of Data Collection?

In the early years, scholars such as Auguste Comte, Herbert Spencer and Edward Burnett Tylor relied on accounts of missionaries, historians, and travellers to analyse societies. However, this approach was criticized for being too subjective wherein the 'armchair scholars' rely on biased selection and intuition.

Later on, scholars like Durkheim adopted the 'empirical approach' which advocated observing and studying only the observable phenomena (social facts). Over a period of time, certain rules have been identified to make data collection as scientific as possible:

1. The scientist must remain ethically and emotionally neutral.
2. Exercise cultural relativism and dispel the myth of 'what is natural'. The rule of cultural relativism requires that the researcher must not consider what does not belong to their own culture as 'strange' or 'wrong'. For example, Margaret Mead in

her work—Sex and Temperament in Three Primitive Societies (1935)—studied the Tchambuli culture in which men dressed up, put on make-up and flirted with the plain-looking women of the village.

3. Classification of social phenomena should be conducted with caution. For example, in certain primitive societies, on external observation, a political institution was not found. However, a deeper inquiry revealed that political functions were carried out through kinship structures such as clan, family, etc.

What are the Problems Encountered in Data Collection?

1. **Ethical Concerns**
   - **Informed Consent and Privacy:** Ensuring participants understand the study and give genuine consent can be difficult, especially with sensitive topics (e.g., studies on mental health, criminal behaviour). Becker's study on marijuana users faced criticism due to the ethical dilemma of studying illegal activities without full disclosure to authorities.
   - **Anonymity and Confidentiality:** Ensuring data protection is crucial, especially in studies involving stigmatized groups. For instance, Laud Humphreys' *Tearoom Trade* (1970), which studied gay men's sexual behaviours, was criticized for privacy violations, as he tracked participants without their consent.
2. **Access to Target Populations**
   - **Hidden and Vulnerable Populations:** Certain groups (e.g., marginalized communities, illegal immigrants) are hard to access due to their distrust of authorities and researchers. William Foote Whyte's *Street Corner Society* (1943) faced this when studying Italian-American slum communities, necessitating a prolonged engagement to gain trust.
   - **Gatekeeping Issues:** In institutional settings (e.g., schools, prisons), access to participants often requires the approval of gatekeepers, limiting researcher control. This challenge is highlighted by Michel Foucault's studies on institutional power structures, where gatekeepers can influence research outcomes.
3. **Respondent Bias and Social Desirability**
   - **Influence of Social Expectations:** Participants may respond based on what they think is acceptable rather than their true beliefs. Max Weber recognized this challenge, highlighting that understanding people's "verstehen" (subjective meaning) is essential but can be distorted by societal pressures.
   - **Hawthorne Effect:** Participants' behaviour may change simply because they know they're being studied. This effect was observed in the Hawthorne Works study, where workers improved performance due to the presence of researchers rather than changes in working conditions.
4. **Cultural Sensitivity and Language Barriers**
   - **Interpretive Differences:** Sociologists studying diverse cultures may misinterpret behaviours or concepts that do not translate well across cultural boundaries. Clifford Geertz's concept of "thick description" stresses the need for detailed cultural context to avoid such misinterpretations.

- **Language Barriers:** Translation can lead to misinterpretation. For instance, Pierre Bourdieu's study of Algerian society required nuanced understanding of local dialects, which added complexity to collecting accurate data.

5. **Researcher Bias**
   - **Personal Bias:** Sociologists may unconsciously impose their own cultural or social perspectives on the research. Alvin Gouldner argued for reflexivity in sociology, suggesting that researchers critically examine their biases to minimize their influence on data collection.
   - **Selective Observation:** Researchers might prioritize certain observations that align with their hypotheses. Howard Becker advocated for adopting a "sociological imagination" to recognize and mitigate this bias.
6. **Technical and Financial Constraints**
   - **Expensive Data Collection Methods:** Longitudinal studies and large-scale surveys require significant funding, limiting the scope of research for sociologists without institutional backing.
   - **Reliance on Technology:** While digital surveys and online interviews make data collection easier, they also exclude populations without internet access, leading to sampling bias. Mark Granovetter's work on social networks highlighted the limitations of digital tools in capturing complex interpersonal relationships.
7. **Changing Social Dynamics**
   - **Dynamic Nature of Social Groups:** Sociologists studying contemporary phenomena (e.g., social media behavior) face rapid changes in how people interact and communicate, making data quickly outdated. Zygmunt Bauman's concept of "liquid modernity" reflects this challenge, as social structures are continually evolving.

Purpose of Research in Social Sciences

The purpose of research in social sciences is a) exploratory or formulative—to understand a phenomenon that has so far not been researched and b) descriptive—to work further on some already known and explained phenomenon. The two objectives are interrelated as identification of new knowledge or recurring patterns lead to theory-building. Similarly, theories help generate hypotheses which when tested either validate the existing theories or lead to new insights.

What is Hypothesis?

A hypothesis is the statement about a relationship between at least two phenomena or variables. A variable is a social phenomenon that the researcher is either trying to explain in terms of causes or whose effects the researcher is trying to measure. The variable that the researcher is trying to account for is a dependent variable and the other whose effects the researcher is measuring is an independent variable. For example - suppose the hypothesis to be tested is that illiteracy in women leads to early marriages. Here, early marriage, the variable that the researcher is trying to account for, is a dependent variable. And illiteracy in women, the variable that has the potential to affect timing of marriage, is an independent variable.

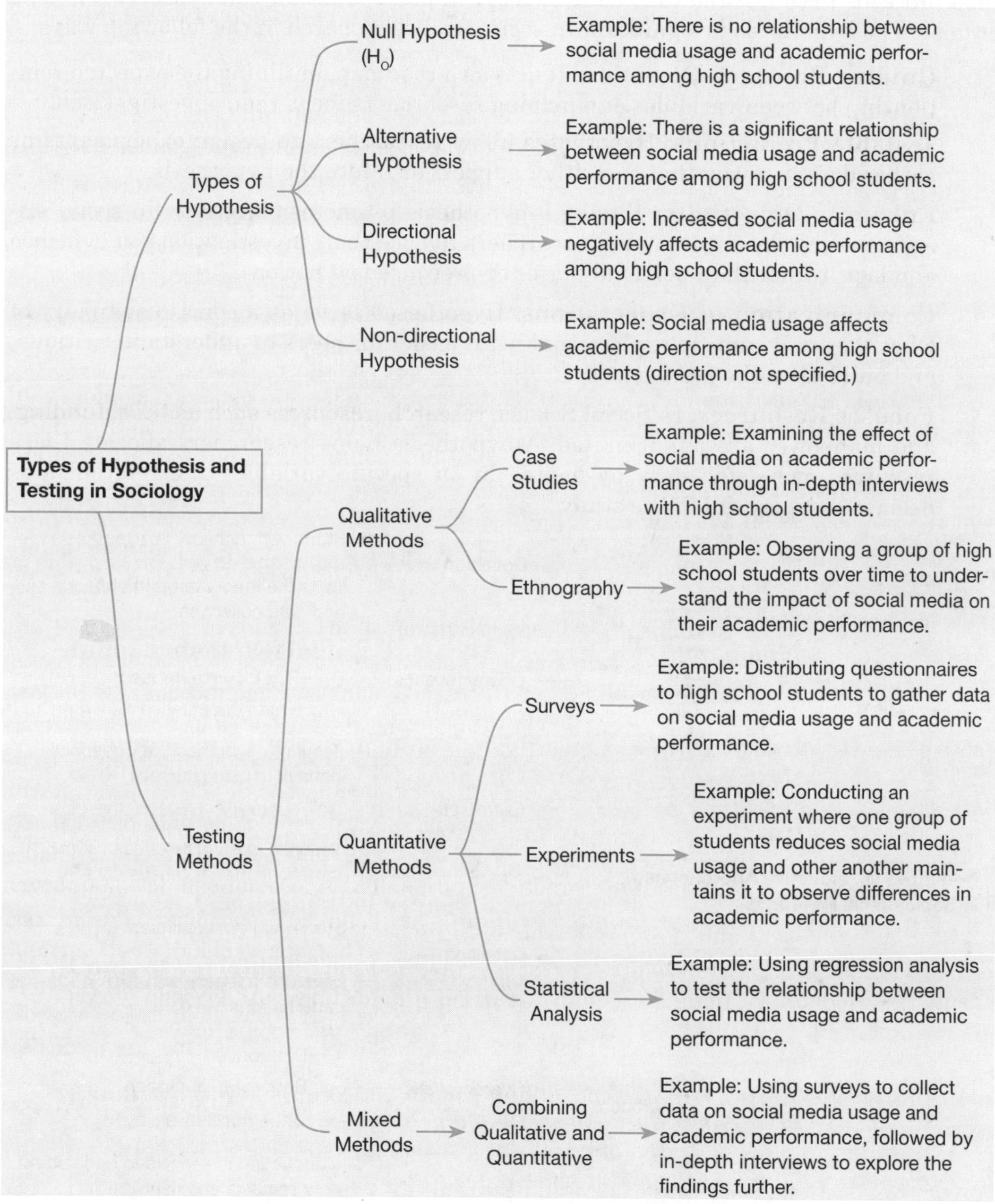

Significance of Hypothesis

Generating a hypothesis is part of the deductive approach to research. The researcher posits a statement reflecting a relationship between two or more social phenomena and then proceeds to collect relevant data in order to prove whether the hypothesis is true or false. The hypothesis is significant in social science research in the following ways:

1. **Guiding Research Direction:** It acts as a roadmap, outlining the expected relationship between variables and helping researchers focus their investigations.
2. **Testable Predictions:** Hypotheses allow researchers to design experiments or gather data in a way that can either support or refute the hypothesis.
3. **Enhances Objectivity:** Having a hypothesis promotes objectivity in social science research by encouraging researchers to base their investigations on evidence and logic rather than personal biases or preconceived notions.
4. **Communication of Expectations:** Hypotheses serve as a concise summary of what the study aims to explore, making it easier for peers to understand, critique, and build upon the research.
5. **Focuses Resources:** In Social Science research, resources such as time, funding, and manpower are often limited. A hypothesis helps researchers allocate these resources more efficiently by honing in on specific variables and relationships deemed most crucial to the study.

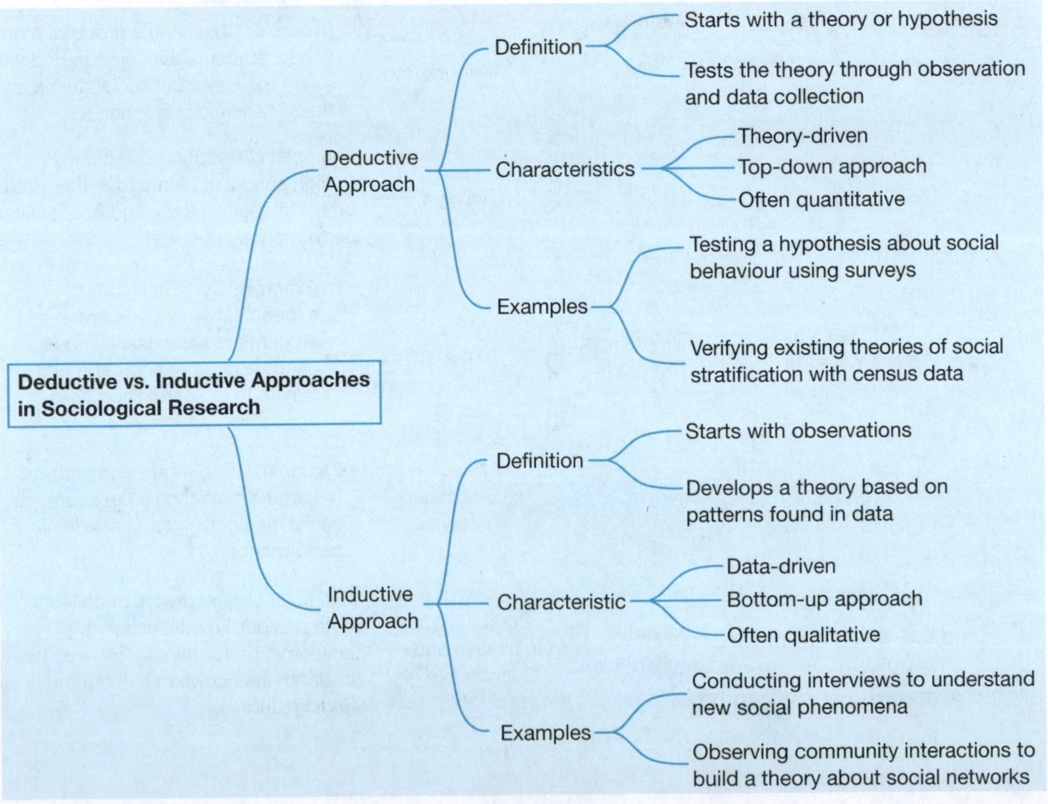

6. **Generates New Knowledge:** Hypotheses, even when disproven, contribute to the generation of new knowledge and sparking new avenues of inquiry.
7. **Contributes to Theory Building:** When a hypothesis is supported by empirical evidence, it strengthens existing theories or may even lead to the formulation of new theoretical frameworks.
8. **Supports Replication:** A well-crafted hypothesis facilitates the replication of research. Other researchers can replicate the study to test the same hypothesis, adding to the cumulative body of knowledge in the social sciences and validating the reliability of findings.
9. **Informs Policy and Practice:** Social science research often has real-world implications. Hypotheses that are substantiated by evidence can inform policy decisions and guide practical interventions, contributing to the application of research findings in addressing societal challenges.

Variables

In sociological research, variables are fundamental components that represent characteristics or properties of individuals, groups, or social phenomena that can vary or change. Understanding variables and their types is crucial for designing, conducting, and interpreting sociological studies. Variables are essential for testing hypotheses, establishing correlations, and drawing meaningful conclusions about social behaviour and structures.

Types of Variables

1. **Independent Variables:** These are variables that are manipulated or categorized to observe their effect on dependent variables. They are presumed to be the cause in a cause-and-effect relationship.

   Example: In a study examining the impact of education on income levels, education (measured in years of schooling) is the independent variable.
2. **Dependent Variables:** These are variables that are observed and measured to see how they are affected by independent variables. They represent the outcome or effect in a cause-and-effect relationship.

   Example: Continuing the previous example, income levels (measured in annual earnings) would be the dependent variable affected by the level of education.
3. **Control Variables:** These are variables that researchers keep constant to accurately observe the relationship between the independent and dependent variables. Controlling for these variables helps isolate the effect of the independent variable.

   Example: In the study of education and income, control variables might include age, work experience, and geographic location, ensuring these factors do not confound the results.
4. **Intervening (Mediating) Variables:** These variables mediate the relationship between the independent and dependent variables, explaining the process through which the independent variable influences the dependent variable.

Example: Job satisfaction might act as an intervening variable in the relationship between education and income, where higher education leads to better jobs, increasing job satisfaction, which in turn leads to higher income.

5. **Moderating Variables:** These variables affect the strength or direction of the relationship between independent and dependent variables. They indicate conditions under which certain effects hold.

   Example: Gender might moderate the relationship between education and income, with the impact of education on income potentially differing for men and women.

Examples in Sociological Research

1. **Study on Social Media Use and Academic Performance**
   - **Independent Variable:** Hours spent on social media daily
   - **Dependent Variable:** Academic performance measured by GPA
   - **Control Variables:** Age, socioeconomic status, type of school attended
   - **Intervening Variable:** Time spent on homework
   - **Moderating Variable:** Type of social media platform used (e.g., educational vs. entertainment-focused)
2. **Research on Urbanization and Crime Rates**
   - **Independent Variable:** Level of urbanization measured by population density
   - **Dependent Variable:** Crime rates measured by reported incidents per 1,000 residents
   - **Control Variables:** Economic conditions, policing policies
   - **Intervening Variable:** Social cohesion or community engagement
   - **Moderating Variable:** Availability of public amenities (e.g., parks, community centres)

Types of Research

The following are the major types of research in Social Science:

1. **Basic and Applied**
   - **Basic/Pure/Fundamental Research:** It pertains to the quest for knowledge about a phenomenon without concern for its practical use. For example, a sociological study to investigate the origin and function of rituals and practices in a particular community.
   - **Applied Research:** It focusses on analysing and solving social problems. For example, a mental health intervention study for gauging levels of mental illness and how to heal them.
2. **Descriptive and Analytical**
   - **Descriptive Research:** Its main purpose is to describe the state of affairs as it exists. It is also known as ex post facto research, implying the research is conducted on what has already happened or what is happening. In this, the researcher has no control over the variables. For example, a study on violence against women within a certain period of time to identify trends, frequency, causes, etc.

- **Analytical Research:** In this type of research, the researcher uses the facts and information already available and analyses them to make a critical evaluation. It aims at the establishment of a cause-and-effect relationship. For example, a study into the data available for social media usage can bring forth people's likes or dislikes, effects of viral trends, marketing campaigns, et

3. **Empirical and Exploratory**
   - **Empirical Research:** It relies on experiences and observations alone, often without due regard to systems or theory. It is data-based research and collection of certain first hand facts precedes a working hypothesis which is then subjected to experimentation. Evidence is gathered to prove the relationship between the concerned variables and the conclusions can be subject to further verification through observation and experiments. For example, a study on the relationship between social media usage and mental well-being of teenage adolescents.
   - **Exploratory Research:** It is usually qualitative in nature and leads to formulation of hypotheses and theories. Here, the assumption is that the researcher has little or no knowledge of the problem or situation under study. For example, a study on understanding attitudes of Gen Z towards work. Exploratory studies are also valuable for understanding some persistent phenomena like prevalence of corruption in politics, violence against women, new forms of slavery, etc.

4. **Quantitative and Qualitative**
   - **Quantitative Research:** It is based on the measurement of quantity or amount and is applicable to phenomena that can be expressed in terms of quantity. This type of research is designed around the principles of positivism, with definite criteria of measurement, strict sampling and statistical analysis.
   - **Qualitative Research:** It is based on phenomena relating to quality or kind. It is relevant where the aim is to discover the underlying motives of human behaviour. Projective techniques such as word association tests, sentence completion tests, story completion tests, etc., are used for this purpose. This kind of research does not involve specific numerical data, rather relies on in-depth exploration of specific social phenomena.
   - **Quantitative vs Qualitative:** At the technical level, both approaches provide a choice of alternative methods and one can select either or both according to the relevance of one's research. For example, in studying the relationship between literacy and early marriages among women, quantitatively, data can be collected to know the exact levels of literacy among a large sample of women and their marrying age. If there is a visible correlation between high levels of literacy and higher age for marriage, qualitatively, an investigation can be undertaken to study the difference in attitudes of women who choose to marry late and those who marry early.

     But at the level of epistemology, the two research approaches provide different perspectives on looking at the knowledge about the same social reality.

5. **Explanatory (Causal) and Longitudinal**
   - **Explanatory Research:** It explains the causes of social phenomena, establishing a relationship between the variables. For example, the study on the

relationship between broken families and juvenile delinquency will aim to answer - why do juvenile delinquents majorly come from broken families. This type of research mainly concerns itself with the 'why' and does not involve comparison.

- **Longitudinal Research:** It involves the study of a problem or social phenomenon over a period of time. For example, study of COVID cases in 2020, 2021 and 2022. The research can also be cross-sectional covering a broad range of phenomena at a single point in time.

6. **Experimental and Evaluative**
   - **Experimental Research:** In this type of research, the researcher shows that one type of variable causes another type of variable. It can consist of controlled experiments where manipulation of circumstances is involved. The identification of causal factors, introduction or exclusion of factors allow the researcher to observe their effects. Experiments rely on precise and detailed observation of outcomes and changes that occur following the introduction or exclusion of potentially relevant factors. The experiments can be conducted in either laboratory settings (less frequent in sociology since it is difficult to replicate the actual social reality) or natural settings. In natural settings, sociologists could go for a quasi-experimental approach wherein they study a 'naturally occurring experiment'. For instance, switch to online education during the COVID pandemic was a new setting for research on how education was getting affected in the new scenario.
   - **Evaluative Research:** It is generally conducted to assess the efficacy and efficiency of an activity and based on the former two, to answer whether the concerned activity should continue or not. So, for example, evaluative research can be conducted to assess the efficacy of the MGNREGA (Mahatma Gandhi National Rural Employment Guarantee Scheme) and to decide on the budgetary expansion for the scheme.

7. **Participatory Action Research**

   Action research is defined by the following four characteristics:

   (i) **Practical:** It is aimed at dealing with the real world problems and issues, typically at work and in organizational settings.

   (ii) **Change:** It is seen as something to be studied as part of social phenomena and also as ways to discover solutions for existing problems.

   (iii) **Cyclical Process:** The concluding findings generate a feedback loop, which when implemented is again evaluated for their impact in further research.

   (iv) **Participation:** Research practitioners are active participants in the research process.

All over, participatory action research consists of two stages: 1) in the first stage, research is carried out and 2) in the second stage, practitioners apply knowledge generated from the research. However, this type of research does not allow for full control on or manipulation of relevant factors which may be introduced as part of research. For example, a community health organization partners with local residents to explore and address health disparities in their neighbourhood.

Research Methodology

Quantitative Methodology

This type of methodology gained popularity with the emergence of Science as a predominant approach to understand the world. Sociology as a discipline emerged in the 19th century amidst the unprecedented changes brought through the industrial revolution. These changes took place along with the intellectual revolution that had begun in the 17th century with various thinkers advocating an evidence-based approach to study various phenomena. Resultantly, early sociological thinkers like Auguste Comte and Durkheim Spencer adopted the same approach as was used in the natural sciences to accord social sciences the same scientific character.

The word 'quantitative' is derived from the Latin word 'quantitas,' which means 'quantity' or 'size.' As part of quantitative methodology then, Comte argued for studying the observable and measurable aspects of society. This approach was called 'Positivism'.

Positivism, Durkheim and Sociology

Though both Durkheim and Comte emphasized on studying the external, observable aspects of the society, Durkheim's positivism was slightly different.

1. **Social Facts:** Durkheim proposed that the subject matter of sociology should be 'social facts' which are essentially social phenomena classified and treated as 'things'. However, he also focused on belief systems, customs and institutions that are not directly measurable or observable. In his opinion, social facts – collective beliefs, values, laws, etc., determine individual behaviour.
2. **Statistical Data:** Positivists believed that it was possible to count sets of observable social facts and so produce statistics. For example, Durkheim collected data on social facts such as the suicide rate and membership of different religions.
3. **Correlation:** A correlation refers to the tendency of two or more things to be found together, and it may refer to the strength of the relationship between them, For example, in his study of suicide, Durkheim found a correlation between the religion of Protestantism and high suicide rate.
4. **Causation:** In case of strong correlations, a positivist sociologist might suspect that one of these phenomena was causing the other to take place. For example, in case of correlation between class and crime, some like Robert Merton have speculated that working-class could be a factor causing people to commit crimes. However, such causation could be problematic as the same relationship could be explained through other scenarios.
5. **Multivariate Analysis:** Durkheim devised this technique to isolate the effect of a particular independent variable upon the dependent variables. For example, the role of gender can be isolated from the dependent variables of class and criminality. The crime rates can be compared between working-class men and working-class women to see if there is any difference. Since the class is same, any difference would indicate the role of gender.

Laws of Human Behaviour

The ultimate goal of positivism is to devise the laws of human behaviour, meaning, coming up with causal relationships that could explain and predict human behaviour in a universal and generalizable manner. For example, Durkheim suggested the law that suicide rate is high whenever there is economic boom or slump. Comte gave the law of three stages through which every society passed.

Positivism uses inductive methodology. It starts by collecting data, analysing it and out of this, theories are developed. This theory is tested against other sets of data for confirmation and if it is repeatedly confirmed, positivists assume they have discovered a law of human behaviour.

Criticism by Karl Popper, Hypothesis and Falsification Theory

- Instead of the inductive approach of the positivists, Karl Popper in his work—The Logic of Scientific Inquiry (1959)—suggests for a deductive approach. It starts with a theory and tests it against the evidence.
- Popper argued that scientists should start with a hypothesis or a statement that is to be tested. This statement should state what will happen in particular circumstances. These predictions are then tested against future events. Thus, Popper argues that it is not always necessary to observe and then theorise.
- Secondly, according to Popper, it is not possible to produce laws that will necessarily be found to be true for all time. There is always the possibility that at some future date, the theory will be proved wrong or 'falsified'. For sciences to be truly objective, scientists should endeavour to find evidence that contradicts their theory.

Practical Ways of Carrying Out Social Research

1. **Field Experiments:** Since it is difficult to conduct laboratory experiments to study social phenomena, social scientists test their hypotheses through field experiments. They isolate particular variables and test their impact in actual social settings. Some of the examples of field experiments are given below:
   - In 1968, Rosenthal and Jacobson tested the hypothesis that self-fulfilling prophecies can affect educational attainment. They manipulated the pupils' IQ (Intelligence Quotient) scores known to teachers. They found that the altered teachers' expectations towards certain students actually influenced the latter's academic performance.
   - An experiment on 'gender role socialization' was conducted at Sussex University. In that, girl babies were dressed up in blue and boy babies in pink, and the adults' reaction to them was recorded. The researchers found that due to inherent biases, restless 'boys' (in reality, girls) were perceived as wanting to play and be active. Similarly, restless 'girls' (in reality, boys) were perceived as emotionally upset and in need of comfort.
   - **Drawbacks of Field Experiments:**

     (i) The variables cannot be controlled to an extent as in the case of laboratory experiments.

(ii) Hawthorne effect: The fact that an experiment is taking place can affect the results. This was observed in an experiment conducted by Elton Mayo in 1933 at the Hawthorne works of the Western Electricity Company in Chicago. The study on workers' productivity showed that there was increase in productivity not due to the manipulation of variables but due to the knowledge of the experience being conducted.

2. **Comparative Method:** It is based on the analysis of what has happened or is happening in the society, rather than on artificially created situations. It involves comparing two or more societies, or groups within societies on different parameters. It can be used to study historical development of societies, which is not possible in case of field experiments. Early founders like Durkheim, Marx and Weber have all used the comparative method in their studies.

Qualitative Methodology

This approach developed as an alternative to the quantitative methodology. Proponents of this approach argue that the so-called scientific methods are inadequate to accurately study and analyse human behaviour, a subject-matter considerably different from that of the natural sciences. Hence, they proposed an interpretive approach which aims to study the meanings, motives, experiences, beliefs and unobservable aspects of human behaviour in social settings at a micro-level. Humans have consciousness which distinguishes them from natural things which respond to external stimuli without any thought process involved.

Within the interpretivist paradigm, there are three theoretical approaches through which qualitative methodology is applied:

1. **Weber's Verstehen Method:** Where the focus is on studying the meanings and motives behind social action.
2. **Symbolic Interactionism:** Where the focus is on studying how the concept of self is made through interaction with others.
3. **Phenomenology:** Where the focus is on individual consciousness and subjectivities.

The choice of research method to be used is influenced by many theoretical and practical considerations. However, the most important factor in this regard is the topic to be studied. If, for instance, one needs to know the number of users of a particular product, quantitative methods would be suitable. On the other hand, if one needs to study the role that conventional beauty standards play in influencing purchasing behaviour, then qualitative methods will be preferred.

In actuality, however, a mix of both—quantitative and qualitative methods is preferred. This approach is known as methodological pluralism. For example, even in Durkheim's study of Suicide, though he compared and analyses statistics on suicide in different societies, he also studied the traits of different religions and social institutions that played a role in encouraging or deterring suicidal behaviour.

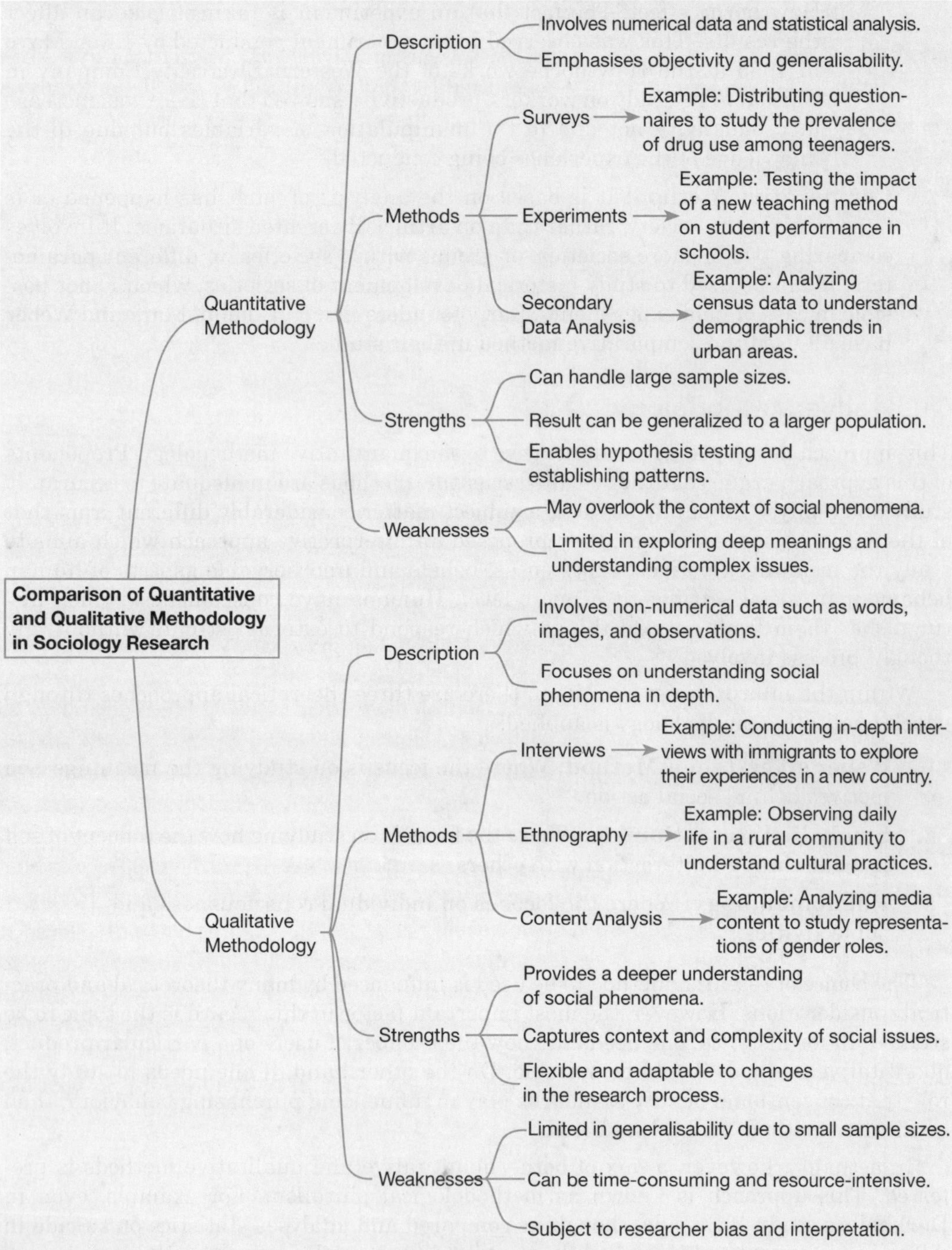
Comparison of Quantitative and Qualitative Methodology in Sociology Research
Quantitative Methodology
Description
Involves numerical data and statistical analysis.
Emphasises objectivity and generalisability.
Methods
Surveys
Example: Distributing questionnaires to study the prevalence of drug use among teenagers.
Experiments
Example: Testing the impact of a new teaching method on student performance in schools.
Secondary Data Analysis
Example: Analyzing census data to understand demographic trends in urban areas.
Strengths
Can handle large sample sizes.
Result can be generalized to a larger population.
Enables hypothesis testing and establishing patterns.
Weaknesses
May overlook the context of social phenomena.
Limited in exploring deep meanings and understanding complex issues.
Qualitative Methodology
Description
Involves non-numerical data such as words, images, and observations.
Focuses on understanding social phenomena in depth.
Methods
Interviews
Example: Conducting in-depth interviews with immigrants to explore their experiences in a new country.
Ethnography
Example: Observing daily life in a rural community to understand cultural practices.
Content Analysis
Example: Analyzing media content to study representations of gender roles.
Strengths
Provides a deeper understanding of social phenomena.
Captures context and complexity of social issues.
Flexible and adaptable to changes in the research process.
Weaknesses
Limited in generalisability due to small sample sizes.
Can be time-consuming and resource-intensive.
Subject to researcher bias and interpretation.

The Research Process

1. **Step 1 – Choosing a Topic for Research:** The choice of topic is influenced by a) one's own interests b) developments within the discipline c) developments in the society d) practical considerations such as availability of funding, availability of data, feasibility in collection of data, etc.
2. **Step 2 – Identification of Sources of Information**

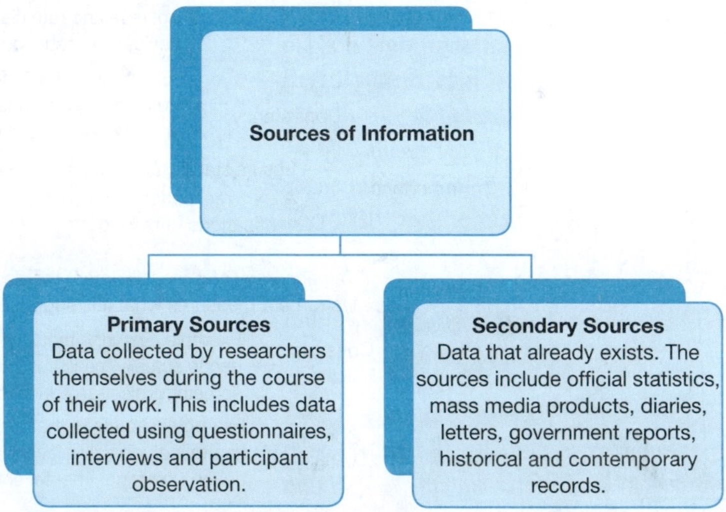

3. **Step 3: Choice of Research Method:** In case of primary sources, a primary research method has to be chosen. The researcher is expected to choose those methods which are practical and which maximise reliability and validity.
   - **Practicality:** Quantitative methods hold a greater appeal as they are less time-consuming and require less personal commitment. At the same time, they can be used for large samples. The qualitative methods, due to their time-consuming nature, are often limited to smaller numbers for practical purposes.
   - **Reliability**: Data is said to be reliable when other researchers using the same methods of investigation on the same material produce the same results. When replication of research leads to the same observation and measurement of results, the research is said to be reliable and further generalizations can be made. Quantitative methods are seen to provide more reliability as they present standardized data in a statistical form and the methods can be repeated in exactly the same manner to test the hypothesis. Qualitative methods, on the other hand, could be unsystematic and situation-driven, leading to lesser reliability as chances of replication results also go low.
   - **Validity:** Data is considered valid if it provides 'true' and 'accurate' picture of what is being studied. It should provide an accurate description of social reality. Data can be reliable without being valid. It means that studies could be replicated to produce the same results but it will not necessarily mean that the studies have accurately measured what they set out to study. For instance,

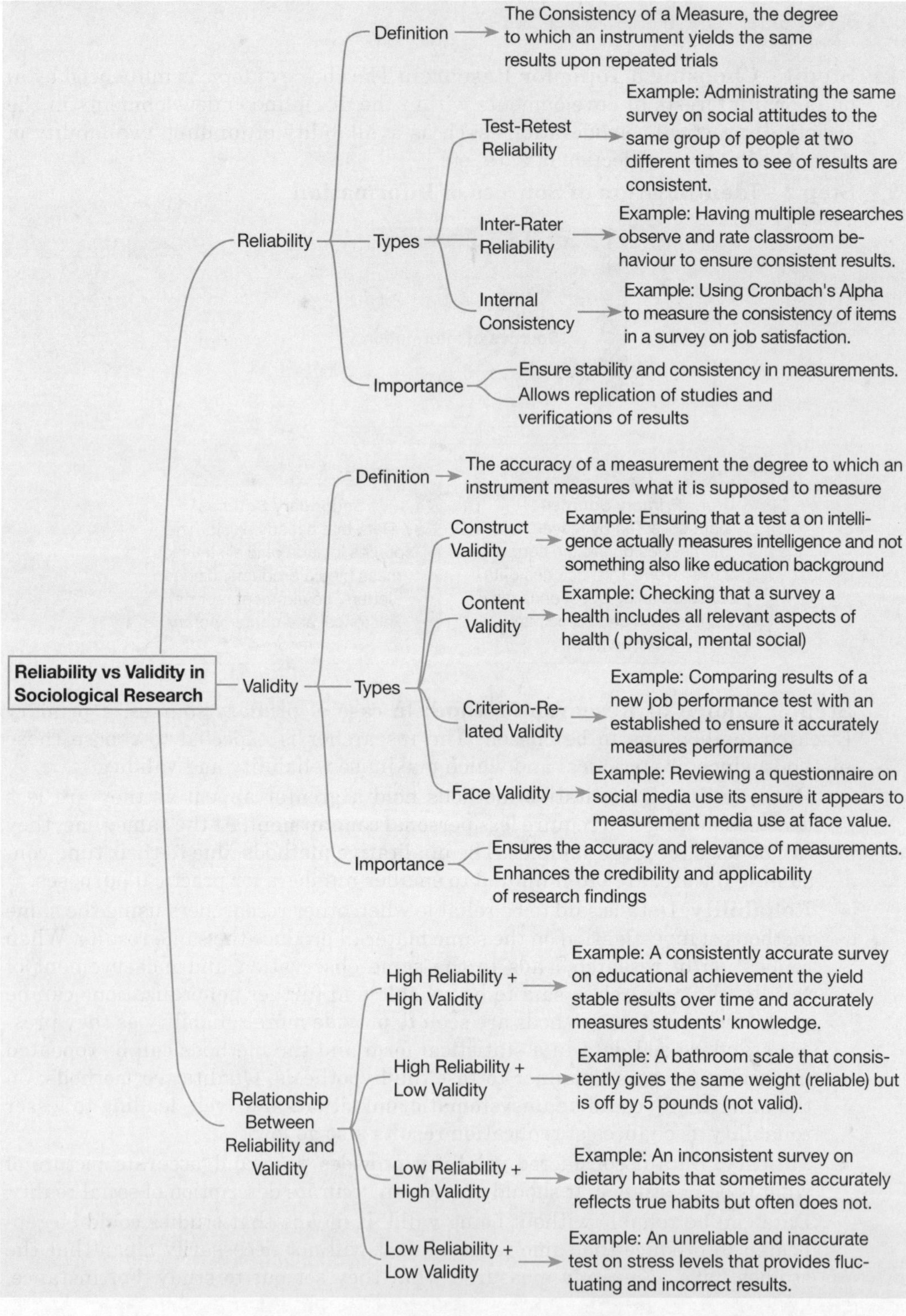

Reliability vs Validity in Sociological Research
Reliability
Definition
The Consistency of a Measure, the degree to which an instrument yields the same results upon repeated trials
Types
Test-Retest Reliability
Example: Administrating the same survey on social attitudes to the same group of people at two different times to see of results are consistent.
Inter-Rater Reliability
Example: Having multiple researches observe and rate classroom behaviour to ensure consistent results.
Internal Consistency
Example: Using Cronbach's Alpha to measure the consistency of items in a survey on job satisfaction.
Importance
Ensure stability and consistency in measurements.
Allows replication of studies and verifications of results
Validity
Definition
The accuracy of a measurement the degree to which an instrument measures what it is supposed to measure
Types
Construct Validity
Example: Ensuring that a test a on intelligence actually measures intelligence and not something also like education background
Content Validity
Example: Checking that a survey a health includes all relevant aspects of health (physical, mental social)
Criterion-Related Validity
Example: Comparing results of a new job performance test with an established to ensure it accurately measures performance
Face Validity
Example: Reviewing a questionnaire on social media use its ensure it appears to measurement media use at face value.
Importance
Ensures the accuracy and relevance of measurements.
Enhances the credibility and applicability of research findings
Relationship Between Reliability and Validity
High Reliability + High Validity
Example: A consistently accurate survey on educational achievement the yield stable results over time and accurately measures students' knowledge.
High Reliability + Low Validity
Example: A bathroom scale that consistently gives the same weight (reliable) but is off by 5 pounds (not valid).
Low Reliability + High Validity
Example: An inconsistent survey on dietary habits that sometimes accurately reflects true habits but often does not.
Low Reliability + Low Validity
Example: An unreliable and inaccurate test on stress levels that provides fluctuating and incorrect results.

studies on poverty could show the number of people living below poverty line but they cannot accurately describe the 'extent of poverty' the people below BPL suffer. The surveys in this regard would be reliable but not necessarily valid when designing schemes to address different levels and forms of poverty.

While quantitative methods are claimed to be more reliable, qualitative methods are used to increase validity as the latter focus on accurately grasping the social reality.

4. **Step 4: Choosing a Sample:** A sample refers to the set of individuals a researcher needs to study. It is part of a larger population and should be representative of the population that needs to be studied. Sampling refers to the process of selection of such units. Correctly choosing the sample can lead to generalizations for the larger population. The steps in this process are given below:

Step 1
- Identify the relevant population
- For example, in a study of voting, population would be all people who have the right to vote

Step 2
- Produce a 'sampling frame' (a list of all relevant sampling units in the population)
- For example, an electoral register or voting list carrying names of all eligible voters in a state or district, wherever the study needs to be conducted

Step 3
- Select a sample that contains the same proportions of people with relevant characteristics as are present in the population under consideration
- For example, if the population has 58 percent men and 42 percent women, the sample should reflect the same

Types of Sampling

(i) **Random and Systematic Sampling:** In random sampling, each unit has an equal chance of being selected in the sample. This is done by assigning numbers to each unit and then selecting the numbers through a random number table. For example – in lottery system, when chits are drawn at random or picking out numbers from a hat. If one introduces a system in this process, for instance, selecting every 5th, 10th, 15th ...unit, it becomes less random and then is known as systematic sampling. Random sampling is not ideal as it will not ensure adequate representativeness unless the sample is quite large. It does minimize biases in selection of units though.

(ii) **Stratified Random Sampling:** This involves division of sampling frame into groups in order to ensure a representative sample. The researcher identifies the variables that need to be controlled and then assign units to the groups based on these variables. The sample is then selected at random from each of these groups.

For example, if gender and age are variables in a study on voting behaviour in a district, the researcher may create separate groups of males and females in the age groups of 18–30, 31–50 and 51 and above, and then randomly select from each of these groups. Even though this sampling method is more representative and requires a smaller sample size, it is often not as practical as the sampling frame may not always contain the necessary information to divide it into groups.

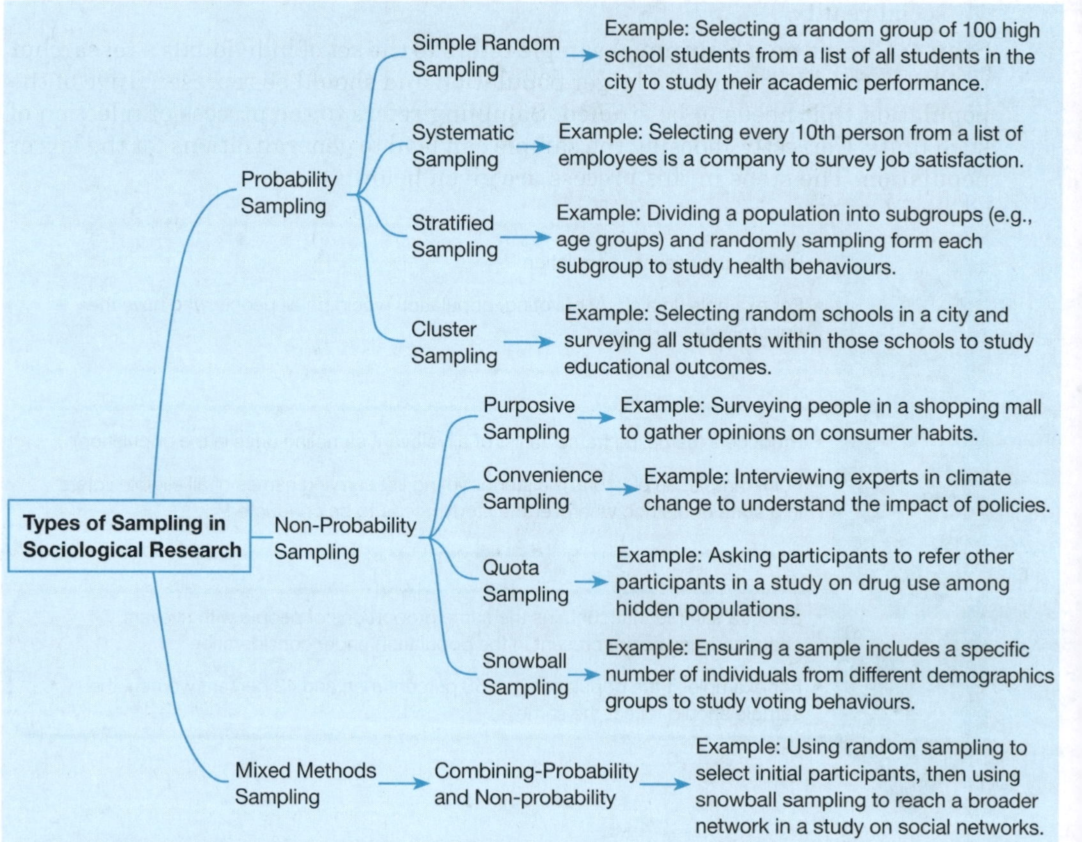

(iii) Quota Sampling: It is useful in the absence of a sampling frame when researcher has to control variables. For example, if a researcher knows that 20 percent of the population of a village is engaged in agriculture, a researcher will purposely choose and interview agriculturists to fill a quota which is representative of the village population. So, if the entire sample is of 100 people, the researcher will seek out 20 farmers only. If someone is not available or refuses to cooperate, the researcher will simply seek out another with the same traits. This method is useful when proportions of groups in the larger population are known. This method is also quicker and cheaper than using probability sampling. The drawbacks include that the method is not exactly random as every unit does not have an equal chance of being selected, the method of interviewing to identify whether the concerned unit is eligible or not may put the respondents on guard

(iv) **Multi-stage Sampling:** It involves selecting a sample from another sample. For example, in national opinion polls, it is not possible to go to every constituency to interview respondents. So, first, at the first stage, all states may be include, within the states, select number of districts may be identified, within the selected districts, one or two constituencies may be identified and within the constituency, either random stratified sampling (through electoral register) or quota sampling (interviewing at the election rallies) may be done. This type of sampling saves time and money for the researcher but because it is not random, it may not be fairly representative of all segments of the population.

(v) **Snowballing**: It involves using personal contacts to build up a sample to be studied. For example, to study parents who choose to adopt, one may begin with someone they know of personally and then ask if they know of others since adoptive parents could be part of special groups and communities. In modern times, even social media is used for this type of sampling. The drawback remains that the sample size cannot be too large. However, this type of sampling is helpful in studying those areas which are yet to be researched in-depth or those that signify new developments.

(vi) **Non-representative Sampling:** This type of sampling is done to purposively seek out samples which do not conform to the known theories or perceptions. For example, the theory on biological determinism explained behavioural differences between men and women on the basis of their different biology. To falsify this, as Karl Popper recommended, sociologists like Ann Oakley found women who exhibited traits traditionally known as masculine and *vice-versa*. Similarly, when election results defy opinion polls, it is common practice to interview political experts who may not represent the larger population but will be most-informed to present an analysis of the results.

5. **Step 5: Collection of data through various techniques**
    1. Case studies
    2. Life histories
    3. Social surveys
    4. Questionnaires
    5. Interviews
    6. Observation and Participant Observation
    7. Critical ethnography
    8. Postmodern ethnography
    9. Census

Techniques of Data Collection

Case Studies

A case study involves a detailed examination of a single example of something, like a community, institution, individual, event, etc.

- According to Howard Becker, case studies help arrive at a comprehensive understanding of the group under study. For example, Shane Blackman in 1997 conducted an extensive ethnographic study on the homeless in the Brighton area of UK to understand how that group experienced and saw the social world.

- Case studies help identify regularities in social structure and processes in order to further develop theoretical statements. They can falsify existing notions too. For example, Kathleen Gough's work on the Nayar society of Kerala showed that contrary to popular belief, family structures based on marital bond are not universal. Gough focused on the unique marital practices among the Nayars, particularly the system of 'sambandham.' In the Nayar society, formal marriages were less emphasized, and instead, there were more informal relationships termed *sambandham*.
- Case studies can be used to produce different typologies or a set of categories defining types of social phenomenon. For example, different types of suicide.
- Case studies can be useful for generating new hypothesis. For example, Paul Willis's study of a single school led to a number of hypotheses showing relationship between education and capitalism.

Drawback

A single case study cannot be used to generalize unless there are multiple case studies conducted on the same phenomenon at the same time.

Life Histories

Life history is a particular type of case study—the whole study concerns one individual's life. Most frequently used methods for this purpose include extended unstructured interviews and analysis of personal documents like letters, diaries, etc. Example—Robert Bogdan's study of Jane Fry, a trans-sexual.

- Life histories can be used as a sensitising tool. It enables the researcher to look at the world from the view point of the social actor. For example, Bogdan's study fought the notion among psychiatrists of trans-sexualism being a sickness.
- Multiple life histories can be used to develop theories. This process is known as 'analytic induction'.
- According to feminist researchers, life histories can be helpful for women in understanding their own situation and in changing it. For critical researchers too, life histories can help in raising people's consciousness and awareness of their own exploitation.

Social Surveys

These are research projects that collect standardized data about large numbers of people. They are based on carefully selected samples and are majorly used for generalization. The data are usually in statistical form and the most common method of collecting such data is through the use of questionnaires. Stephen Ackroyd and John A. Hughes have identified three types of survey:

(a) **Factual Survey:** It is used to obtain descriptive information. For example, Government census.

(b) **Attitude Survey:** It is conducted by opinion poll organizations. It attempts to discover the subjective states of individuals.

(c) **Explanatory Survey:** It tries to test theories and hypotheses or to produce new theories. In practice, however, a survey could include elements of one or more of the above types.

Questionnaire

It consists of a list of pre-set questions. In questionnaire research, the same questions are given to respondents in the same order. The questionnaire can be administered in the following ways:

(a) **Structured Interviews:** In this case, a trained interviewer gives the interview to the respondents and ensures that the interview is filled according to the instructions, clarifying any ambiguity involved. The drawback in this case is the potential for interviewer bias.

(b) **Postal Questionnaire:** This is mailed to the respondent with a stamped envelope for return to the researcher. In more recent times, this has been substituted with mailed questionnaires. Though inexpensive, the return rate is low in this type and based on the responses received, there could be biases in the results.

(c) **Administering in a Group in the Presence of the Interviewer:** This combines the advantages of the above two types. However, care must be taken to ensure the group respondents do not interact with each other during filling up of the questionnaire.

(d) **Administering via Telephone:** This is popular among market research firms and marketing departments of companies but less preferred by sociologists.

The formation of a questionnaire requires 'operationalization of concepts'. This means that the sociological concepts such as social class, caste, power, religion, etc., have their own definitions and meanings. Depending on the concepts that the researcher has chosen to study, the concept is broken into components. These components have indicators which are finally given the form of a question. For example, the concept of 'class' is further divided into the components of 'high class, middle class and the marginalized'. The indicators chosen for studying these components could be income and profession. Examples of resultant questions could be:

(a) What is your profession?

(b) What is your monthly/annual income?

In a questionnaire, questions are of two types:

(a) **Open-ended Questions:** These allow the respondents to reflect and develop their own responses. While these allow for deeper insights, the responses cannot be quantified or classified into fixed categories. The interpretation of these responses must be done carefully. They are included in unstructured interviews.

(b) **Closed or Fixed-choice Questions:** These questions come with a range of options for the respondent to choose from. The responses then can be easily classified. However, they do not generate in-depth explanation. They form structured interviews which are easy to administer, consume less time but yield relatively less rich data.

Among the two types, the social researchers often prefer unstructured, in-depth questionnaires. In this case, the responses are 'codified'. An analysis of all responses generates certain themes or categories in which the responses can be fitted into.

The final step is the analysis of data collected through questionnaires. Depending on the hypothesis, the data is analysed through different approaches such as multivariate analysis, statistical analysis, etc.

Advantages

(a) They are a practical way to collect large amount of data from large number of people in a small amount of time.
(b) They are relatively easy as a method in comparison to other techniques like participant observation.
(c) It is especially useful in collection of quantitative data and giving reliable results.
(d) They are useful when straightforward, descriptive data is required.

Disadvantages

(a) Critics argue that though the questionnaire might be reliable as a tool, the data they yield lacks validity.
(b) Phenomenologists argue that respondents may interpret the same questions and responses differently. This difference is not captured by the questionnaire.
(c) The questionnaire cannot capture whether the respondent is lying.
(d) The operationalization of concept can lead to the researcher imposing a form of social order on the respondents. Critics argue that this might lead to reinforcing the social structures that the research is aimed towards discovering. For example, the indicator of income as a sole determinant of class might reinforce the stereotypical notion of high class-low class.

    Despite the criticism, however, questionnaires remain a useful tool in the collection of data.

Interviews

Interviews are majorly of two types:

(a) **Structured:** These are based on structured questionnaires wherein the interviewer does not deviate from any of the provided questions and even probe the respondents' answers so that any clarification can be made, if necessary.
(b) **Unstructured:** These are more in the nature of a conversation. Some interviewers could refer to a schedule of topics they wish to cover

In terms of number of participants, interviews can be either single interviews where there is only one respondent at a time or group interviews where there are more. For example, Paul Willis in his study on education used to interview a group of boys at the same time. Group interviews allow for diverse sentiments to emerge and even put the respondents at ease.

Interviews should be conducted in a non-directive way wherein the interviewer refrains from offering opinions, approval or disapproval. Howard Becker, on the other hand, has advocated for a more active and aggressive approach in situations where the respondents are keen on hiding information. Others like Ann Oakley have used a more empathetic approach in which even the respondents were actively involved in the research process.

Advantages

(a) It is easier than methods like participant observation as it can be applied on a large sample and the responses can be codified to arrive at generalizable responses. It can be useful for both quantitative and qualitative research.

(b) Interviews can be useful in generating new hypotheses and theories.

(c) As a method, interviews are quite practicable and flexible. They combine the advantages of both questionnaire and participant observation.

(d) Interviews can be used to ask in-depth information and also withdraw when necessary.

(e) They allow for critical reflection on the part of both—the interviewers and the interviewees.

Disadvantages

(a) The responses given may not be accurate and may not reflect real behaviour.

(b) **Interviewer Bias:** Presence of the interviewer or directive nature of the interaction may lead the interviewees to give answers they perceive the interviewer wants to hear.

In summary, interviews are a useful tool in conducting the social research and are helpful in eliciting different types of responses.

Focus Group Discussions

Focus Group Discussions (FGDs) are a qualitative research method in which a small group of individuals, typically 6 to 12 participants, engage in an open and guided conversation about a specific topic, facilitated by a moderator.

Participants are selected based on criteria relevant to the research question, ensuring diversity of perspectives. A skilled moderator guides the discussion, encouraging participants to express their opinions, experiences, and insights. The discussion follows a semi-structured format, with predetermined topics or questions to explore. Participants interact with each other, providing a rich source of data through group dynamics. For example - Sociologists could employ FGDs to gather insights from teachers, students, and parents about the impact of educational policies on learning outcomes.

Advantages

(a) FGDs generate rich, in-depth data by tapping into group dynamics, allowing participants to build on each other's responses.

(b) The group setting encourages the expression of diverse perspectives and experiences on the topic.

(c) FGDs allow researchers to collect a significant amount of data in a relatively short time compared to one-on-one interviews.

(d) Observing non-verbal cues, such as body language and facial expressions, enhances the understanding of participant responses.

Disadvantages

(a) Group dynamics can lead to dominant voices overshadowing quieter participants, potentially limiting the diversity of opinions.
(b) Participants might conform to social norms or offer socially desirable responses, limiting the depth of insights.
(c) The moderator's influence, intentional or unintentional, can shape the direction of discussions.
(d) Findings from FGDs may not be easily generalizable due to the small sample size and potential biases in participant selection.
(e) Organizing and conducting FGDs may pose logistical challenges, such as scheduling difficulties and the need for a suitable venue.

Focus group discussions are a versatile tool in exploring a wide range of sociological topics and gathering diverse perspectives.

Observation and Participant Observation

The act of observation is part of conscious human behaviour. Though subjected to criticism for having the potential to alter the behaviour of respondents, observation as a research method, has been widely used, especially in qualitative research.

Ethnography and participant observation—Ethnography is the study of a way of life. It was first introduced by anthropologists who studied pre-industrial, small-scale societies. For example – Bronislaw Malinowski's study of the Trobriand Islanders is an example of the ethnographic study. It is used for qualitative study and mainly uses the following methods ofin-depth interviews, participant observation and use of qualitative documents.

The method of participant observation has been majorly associated with symbolic interactionists such as Herbert Blumer, Howard Becker and Erving Goffman. It entails joining a social group to collect and record data.

The participant observation can either be overt, where the researcher reveals their identity and true purpose or it can be covert, where the identity of the researcher is not revealed. In both cases, however, it is suggested that the researcher maintains some level of detachment in order to objectively record the data and accurately interpret it.

Advantages

The method allows for building of long-lasting and close relationships which provide greater opportunities for establishing trust and generate more valid data.

(a) Researcher is free to ask questions without any suspicion.
(b) Covert participation is beneficial in a way that members of the group do not change their behaviour
(c) Through acceptance by the group, the researcher gains the 'insider's view'.
(d) Observation helps the researcher refine his/her own approach and in development of questions that they would not have conceived at the beginning of the research.
(e) The ethnographic research can be used to generate and refine grounded theory. New theories can be grounded in the extensive qualitative data collected through this process.

Disadvantages

(a) The process can be extremely time-consuming.
(b) The researcher can only study a small group of people and has to be physically present for the research to proceed.
(c) There are limits on who can be studied as certain groups remain inaccessible.
(d) The knowledge that they are being observed can influence the subject group behaviour making them more self-conscious of their own actions.
(e) If the covert observer is uncovered, there is breach of trust and possibility of unwanted repercussions as in the case of study of marginalized crime, thefts, etc.
(f) Becoming too much of a participant can create the problem of 'becoming native'. The researcher might become unable to stand back and observe the situation objectively.
(g) To quantitative researchers, this method does not yield generalizable results.
(h) Such studies cannot be replicated and rely on the interpretation of a single individual. Thus. They lack reliability.
(i) The data recorded is dependent upon the method of selection and interpretation of the researcher. It may just be a fraction of all the data that could have been factored in.

Though the method of participant observation has been criticized for lacking objectivity and systematization, it is a rigorous approach to understand group behaviour in a deep and rich manner.

(a) **Critical Ethnography:** This type of ethnography is practiced by critical social science researchers who favour a close collaboration between the researcher and the participants to develop and test theories with the ultimate aim to reveal the oppressive structures of the society. For example, Paul Willis's study on transition of 'lads' belonging to working class, from education to work sphere, is a case of critical ethnography. Willis reveals how there are various factors in the education system which prevent upward mobility of the lads from working class, even though the aim of education is to enhance such mobility. This kind of ethnography is directed towards bringing about social change. The researcher partakes in the experiences of the oppressed and brings forth the oppression that is integral in social processes and structures.
(b) **Postmodern Ethnography:** This approach resists generation of any single account. Rather, it promotes putting forth different viewpoints present in the group. It does not put the researcher in a position of power who gets to decide how to analyse the generated data. The ethnography is 'fragmentary' in nature and does not produce a single, coherent account of things under study. However, this approach has been criticized for suffering with 'extreme relativism' and is generally not preferred.
(c) **Digital ethnography:** It is an approach within ethnographic research that focuses on studying people and communities in digital spaces. As society increasingly interacts and forms communities online, sociologists have adapted traditional ethnographic techniques to study these digital environments. Digital ethnography

involves observing interactions on social media platforms, forums, online communities, virtual worlds, and more to understand social behaviors, identities, and cultural trends in these settings

In digital ethnography, visual content like memes, GIFs, vlogs, and Instagram stories are particularly valuable, as these media reflect cultural symbols, social norms, and group identities. For example, sociologists can study the visual language of memes to understand humor, political sentiments, or generational values within specific online communities. Eg. Young people use Instagram to curate their self-image, often adhering to societal beauty standards. This offers insight into how visual culture reinforces body image norms. Digital ethnography, coupled with analysis of visual culture, shows the reciprocal influence between online trends and real-world practices. Sarah Pink, Daniel Miller are some prominent ethnographers.

Key Components of Digital Ethnography includes the following:

- **Online Participant Observation:** Researchers immerse themselves in digital communities to observe conversations, behaviors, and cultural expressions. This often includes studying text posts, images, emojis, and memes that convey social meanings.
- **Interviews and Surveys in Digital Spaces:** Digital ethnographers may conduct virtual interviews and distribute online surveys to collect data directly from users.
- **Data Analysis of Digital Artifacts:** This includes analyzing user-generated content like social media posts, videos, memes, and blogs to understand cultural expressions and community values.

Census Method

The census method is a comprehensive data collection approach used in sociological research to gather information about every member of a given population. Unlike sample surveys, which collect data from a subset of the population, the census method aims to include all individuals, providing a complete and detailed picture of the population under study.

Key Features of the Census Method

1. **Comprehensive Coverage:** The census method involves collecting data from every individual in the population, ensuring that no one is left out. This exhaustive approach is crucial for obtaining accurate and detailed demographic, social, and economic information.

   Example: National population censuses, such as the decennial census conducted by the United States Census Bureau or the Census of India, aim to gather data on every resident within the country.
2. **Detailed Data Collection:** Censuses collect a wide range of information, including demographic characteristics (age, sex, race), socioeconomic status (income, education, employment), and housing conditions (type of dwelling, ownership status).

   Example: The Census of India collects detailed information on housing, amenities, literacy, work status, and migration patterns, providing a holistic view of the population's living conditions and socioeconomic status.

3. **Periodic Administration:** Censuses are typically conducted at regular intervals, often every ten years, to track changes and trends over time. This periodic administration allows for the monitoring of population growth, migration, and social transformations.

   Example: The United States conducts its population census every ten years, providing a decadal snapshot of the nation's demographic and socioeconomic characteristics.

Importance and Application of Census method in sociological research

1. **Policy Formulation and Planning:** Census data is critical for government agencies and policymakers to design and implement effective social and economic policies. It helps identify areas of need, allocate resources, and plan for infrastructure development.

   Example: Data on population density and urbanization from the Census of India informs urban planning and the development of public services such as schools, hospitals, and transportation systems.
2. **Sociological Analysis and Research:** Sociologists use census data to analyse social structures, trends, and inequalities. The comprehensive nature of the data allows researchers to study various aspects of society, including demographic shifts, economic disparities, and social mobility.

   Example: Researchers might use census data to study the changing family structures in India, examining trends in household size, marital status, and living arrangements over time.
3. **Business and Economic Development:** Businesses utilise census data to understand market demographics, consumer behaviour, and regional economic conditions. This information is crucial for strategic planning, market research, and location decisions.

   Example: A company looking to expand its retail operations might analyse census data on income levels, population growth, and consumer spending patterns to identify potential new markets.
4. **Academic Research and Education:** Census data serves as a valuable resource for academic researchers and educators, providing empirical evidence for sociological theories and studies. It is widely used in research projects, dissertations, and teaching materials.

   Example: A sociology professor might use census data to teach students about demographic transitions, urbanization patterns, and socioeconomic inequalities, illustrating theoretical concepts with real-world data.

Strengths and Limitations

Strengths

- **Comprehensiveness:** The census method provides a complete dataset covering the entire population, allowing for detailed and accurate analyses.
- **Rich Data Source:** It offers extensive information on various demographic, social, and economic aspects, enabling multifaceted research.

- **Longitudinal Analysis:** Periodic censuses allow for the study of trends and changes over time, providing insights into social dynamics and transformations.

Limitations

- **Cost and Time-Intensive:** Conducting a census is expensive and logistically challenging, requiring significant resources and time.
- **Data Accuracy and Reporting Issues:** Despite efforts to ensure accuracy, censuses may suffer from undercounting, misreporting, and data collection errors.
- **Privacy and Confidentiality Concerns:** Collecting detailed personal information raises concerns about privacy and data protection, necessitating robust measures to ensure confidentiality.

Point to Note

Pilot Study

A pilot study is a small-scale preliminary study conducted before the main research in order to check the feasibility or to improve the design of the research. It is conducted on members of the relevant population but not on those who will be part of the final sample.

Feminist Method of Social Research

The feminist method of social research is distinct due to its focus on gender as a central category of analysis, its commitment to challenging traditional power structures, and its emphasises on reflexivity and inclusivity. It seeks not only to understand social phenomena but also to address and reduce gender-based inequalities.

Key Characteristics

1. **Gender as a Central Analytical Category**: Feminist research prioritises gender as a crucial variable in understanding social dynamics. This involves examining how gender intersects with other social categories such as race, class, and sexuality to produce different experiences and outcomes.

   Example: Studies on workplace dynamics often explore how gender roles and expectations influence career progression and job satisfaction differently for men and women.
2. **Commitment to Social Change:** Unlike traditional methods, feminist research is explicitly political and aims to contribute to social justice. It seeks to expose and challenge patriarchal structures and advocate for women's rights and empowerment.

   Example: Research on domestic violence not only documents the prevalence and impact of abuse but also aims to inform policies and support services to protect and empower survivors.
3. **Reflexivity:** This involves the researcher being aware of their own positionality and how their background, beliefs, and biases might influence the research

process. Feminist researchers often reflect on their relationship with the research subjects and the potential power dynamics involved.

Example: A feminist researcher studying single mothers might reflect on how their socioeconomic status or marital status affects their interaction with the participants and the interpretation of the data.

4. **Emphasis on Qualitative Methods:** Feminist research often employs qualitative methods such as in-depth interviews, ethnography, and participatory action research. These methods are valued for their ability to capture the complexity of women's experiences and give voice to marginalized groups.

   Example: Using life histories to understand the experiences of women in different cultural contexts allows for a rich, nuanced understanding that quantitative data might not capture.

5. **Inclusivity and Collaborative Approaches:** Feminist research prioritizes the inclusion of diverse voices, especially those of marginalized women. It often involves participants in the research process, ensuring their perspectives shape the research questions, methodology, and outcomes.

   Example: Participatory action research with indigenous women on land rights might involve them in designing the study, collecting data, and analysing results to ensure the research reflects their realities and needs.

Key Feminist Sociologists and Their Perspectives

1. **Dorothy E. Smith**
   - **Perspective:** Smith developed the concept of 'standpoint theory,' emphasizing that knowledge is socially situated. She argued that women's experiences and perspectives provide a valuable standpoint for understanding social realities, challenging the male-dominated viewpoints traditionally found in sociology.
   - **Contribution:** Smith's work underscores the importance of including women's voices and experiences in sociological research to uncover biases and promote more comprehensive understandings of social phenomena.
2. **Patricia Hill Collins**
   - **Perspective:** Collins introduced the concept of 'intersectionality' in her work on Black feminist thought. She highlighted how race, class, gender, and other social categories intersect to shape individual experiences and social structures.
   - **Contribution:** Her intersectional approach has been instrumental in feminist research, promoting the understanding of complex identities and the multiple layers of oppression individuals may face.
3. **Judith Butler**
   - **Perspective:** Butler's work on gender performativity challenged traditional notions of gender as a fixed and binary category. She argued that gender is a social construct that is performed through repeated actions and behaviours.
   - **Contribution:** Butler's ideas have influenced feminist research by encouraging the exploration of how gender identities are constructed and maintained in various social contexts.

4. **Nancy Chodorow**
   - **Perspective:** Chodorow's psychoanalytic feminist theory focuses on the reproduction of mothering and the socialization of gender roles. She examined how family structures and dynamics contribute to the development of gendered identities.
   - **Contribution:** Her research provides insights into the psychological and social processes that perpetuate gender roles and inequalities, highlighting the importance of family and early childhood experiences.

Contemporary Examples

1. **Intersectionality in Feminist Research:** This approach examines how various forms of oppression (e.g., racism, sexism, classism) intersect and affect individuals differently. It highlights the complexity of social identities and challenges simplistic analyses.

   Example: Research on healthcare disparities might explore how women of colour face unique barriers compared to white women, influenced by both racial and gender discrimination.

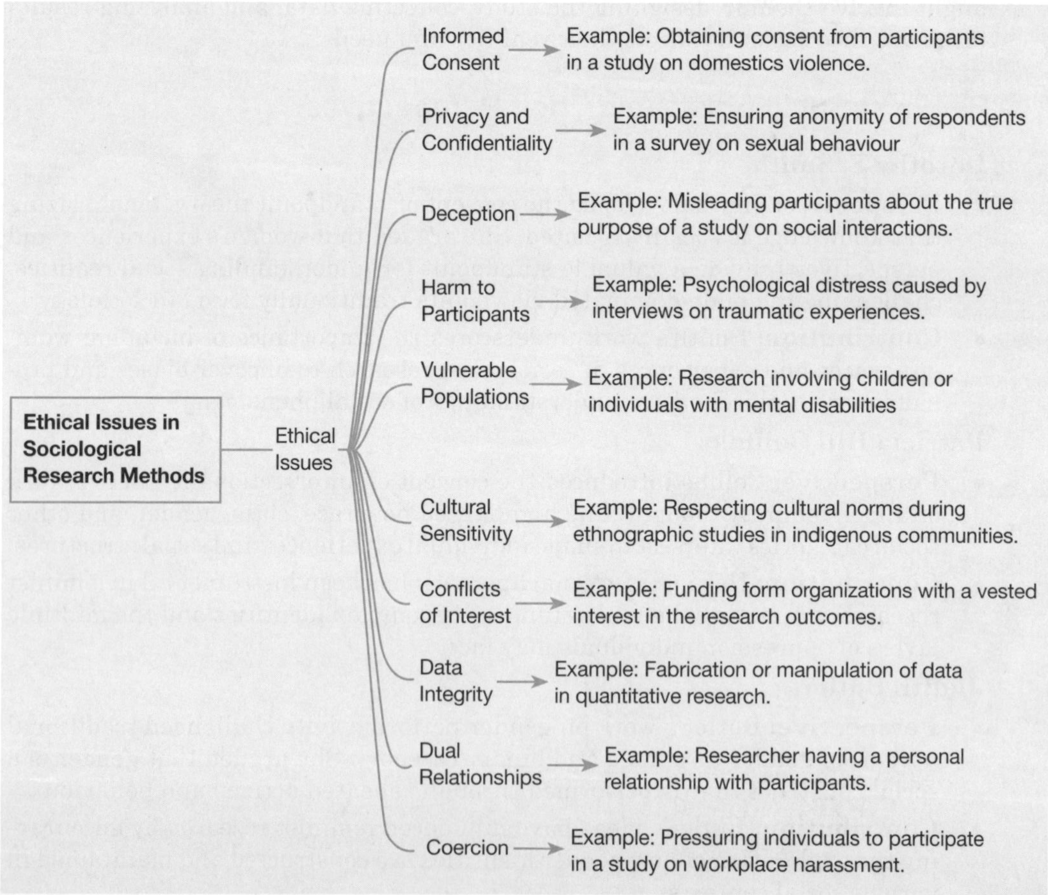

2. **Transnational Feminist Research:** This examines how global processes (e.g., migration, globalization) impact women differently across various cultural and national contexts. It challenges Western-centric views and incorporates perspectives from the Global South.

   Example: Studies on migrant domestic workers highlight the exploitation and rights violations they face, advocating for international labour rights and protections.

FYI

How to Maintain Objectivity in Qualitative Methods?

Qualitative research methods are often criticized for lacking objectivity and for possibility of the researcher influencing the process of data collection such as in interviews or participant observation. Here are several ways to promote and maintain objectivity in qualitative research:

1. **Engaging in Reflexivity:** Researchers should engage in reflexivity, reflecting on their own biases, assumptions, and preconceptions that may influence the research process.
2. **Prolonged Engagement:** Spending an extended period in the field allows researchers to develop a deeper understanding of the social context and helps minimize the risk of superficial interpretations.
3. **Triangulation:** Employ multiple data sources, methods, or researchers to cross-verify findings. Triangulation helps ensure that conclusions are not solely reliant on a single perspective, reducing the impact of researcher bias.
4. **Peer Review and Debriefing:** Regular discussions with peers or colleagues can provide an external perspective on the research process. Peer debriefing involves sharing experiences, challenges, and interpretations to minimize personal biases. Peer review involves evaluation of one's work by other members of the research community. External reviews provide an independent perspective on the study's rigor and objectivity.
5. **Member Checking:** This entails including participants in the research process by seeking their feedback on findings. Member checking allows participants to verify the accuracy of interpretations and adds another layer of validation to the research. It is to ensure that what is being recorded is what was actually intended.
6. **Transparent Documentation:** Clearly document all aspects of the research process, including data collection, analysis, and interpretation. Transparent documentation facilitates transparency and enables other researchers to assess the validity of the study.
7. **Codebook Development:** Based on extensive literature review and after repeatedly going over all the collected data, develop a clear and comprehensive codebook for data analysis. Coding should be systematic and based on pre-defined criteria.

8. **Researcher Training:** Ensure that researchers are adequately trained in qualitative research methods like interviewing, observation, moderating group discussions, etc., and in ethical considerations. Training helps standardise data collection and analysis procedures and minimizes individual biases.
9. **Balanced Sampling:** Aim for a diverse and representative sample to ensure that findings can be generalized within the specified context.
10. **Maintaining Neutrality:** Researchers should avoid imposing personal opinions or judgments that may influence participants' responses or the interpretation of data.
11. **Audit Trails:** This includes keeping detailed records of decisions made throughout the research process. An audit trail allows other researchers to follow the logic of decisions, ensuring transparency and accountability.
12. **Cultural Sensitivity:** Cultural sensitivity ensures that the research respects and accurately represents the perspectives of the studied community.

Mixed Methods of Sociological Research

Mixed-method research combines both quantitative (numerical data) and qualitative (descriptive data) approaches to gain a comprehensive understanding of social phenomena. This approach allows researchers to capitalize on the strengths of each method, integrating objective measurements with subjective insights. In sociological research, mixed methods can help in exploring complex social issues, validating findings, and providing a nuanced picture of social dynamics.

Key Features of Mixed Methods

- **Sequential Explanatory:** Quantitative data is collected first, followed by qualitative data to explain or elaborate on the quantitative results.
- **Sequential Exploratory:** Qualitative data is collected first to explore ideas, followed by quantitative data to test and generalize findings.
- **Concurrent:** Both methods are used simultaneously to compare and contrast results, often leading to a more comprehensive analysis.

Example of Mixed Methods in Sociological Research

A classic example of mixed-method research is a study on educational inequality. Researchers might:

1. Use quantitative surveys to measure factors like income level, access to resources, and academic performance across various socioeconomic groups.
2. Conduct qualitative interviews with students, teachers, and parents to understand perceptions, attitudes, and barriers to educational success.

This approach enables researchers to correlate quantitative patterns (e.g., lower academic performance in lower-income groups) with qualitative insights (e.g., personal experiences of discrimination, lack of motivation due to resource constraints) for a deeper understanding of educational disparities.

Strengths of Mixed Methods in Social Research

1. **Comprehensive Analysis:** Mixed methods provide a fuller, multi-dimensional perspective, as quantitative data offers breadth while qualitative data offers depth.
    - *Example:* In a study on workplace discrimination, quantitative surveys could reveal prevalence, while qualitative interviews provide context on the types and nuances of discrimination faced.
2. **Triangulation and Validation:** Using multiple methods helps validate findings by cross-verifying data, making conclusions more reliable.
    - *Example:* In community health research, triangulating survey data with interview insights ensures that both reported behaviors and perceived barriers are considered, reducing potential biases.
3. **Flexibility in Addressing Complex Issues:** Mixed methods are ideal for investigating social phenomena with both measurable aspects (like demographic data) and subjective dimensions (like personal experiences).
    - *Example:* In studies on climate change attitudes, quantitative polls might reveal support levels, while qualitative methods explore underlying beliefs and motivations.
4. **Enhanced Interpretive Power:** Mixed methods allow for interpretation of contradictions or inconsistencies in data, offering a more nuanced view of social reality.
    - *Example*: A study on technology use might reveal high smartphone usage quantitatively, while qualitative data might explain the negative impact of such usage on social interactions.

Limitations of Mixed Methods in Social Research

1. **Time and Resource Intensive:** Collecting and analyzing both types of data requires more time, resources, and effort, making this approach challenging for limited-budget research.
    - *Example:* Analyzing educational inequality quantitatively and qualitatively in a large population would require extensive resources for both data collection and analysis.
2. **Complexity in Data Integration:** Integrating quantitative and qualitative data can be difficult, especially when results do not align or are contradictory.
    - *Example:* A study on social media's impact might find positive effects quantitatively but negative personal impacts qualitatively, requiring careful interpretation to make sense of discrepancies.
3. **Researcher Bias:** Mixed methods are susceptible to researcher bias, particularly in interpreting qualitative data to fit quantitative findings, or vice versa.
    - *Example:* If a researcher has a hypothesis that gender affects job satisfaction, they might emphasize qualitative narratives that align with this, even if quantitative results are mixed.
4. **Difficulty in Balancing Methods:** There can be a tendency to prioritize one method over the other, which may lead to incomplete findings.

- *Example:* In a study of social movements, over-reliance on surveys might overlook the depth of activists' motivations that interviews could reveal, or vice versa.

Let us look at some other prominent examples.

1. In *The Protestant Ethic and the Spirit of Capitalism* (1905), Max Weber employed a mixed-method approach, although it was more interpretive in nature compared to modern methods.
2. In *Street Corner Society* (1943), William Foote Whyte used mixed methods to study Italian-American slum communities in Boston.
3. In *Unequal Childhoods: Class, Race, and Family Life* (2003), Annette Lareau combined qualitative and quantitative methods to explore how social class affects parenting styles and children's life outcomes.
4. In *Body and Soul: Notebooks of an Apprentice Boxer* (2003), Loïc Wacquant used mixed methods to explore urban poverty and the role of boxing gyms in marginalized communities in Chicago.

Point to Note

Triangulation

Triangulation is a research strategy that involves using multiple methods, data sources, theories, or researchers to study the same phenomenon. The idea is to enhance the validity and reliability of research findings by cross-verifying and corroborating evidence from different angles.

Operationalising Triangulation in Sociological Research

1. **Methods Triangulation:** This involves using a variety of methods. For example, a sociologist studying workplace dynamics might use both quantitative surveys and qualitative interviews to gather data. The combination of numerical data and in-depth narratives can provide a more comprehensive understanding.
2. **Data Triangulation:** This includes using data from multiple sources. For example, in a study on educational outcomes, a researcher may collect data from student test scores, teacher observations, and parent interviews. This diverse set of data sources helps validate findings.
3. **Theory Triangulation:** This includes analysing data from multiple perspectives. For example, in researching the impact of media on public opinion, a sociologist might employ different theoretical frameworks, such as functionalism and conflict theory, to analyse the same set of media content.
4. **Researcher Triangulation:** This involves collaborating with other researchers to remove biases through replication of study, administering of different research methods or in analysis. For example,multiple researchers might independently analyse the same set of interview transcripts to check for consistency in interpretation and reduce individual biases.

5. **Time Triangulation:** This involves conducting the research at different time periods. For example, a longitudinal study on changes in family structures could involve collecting data at multiple points over several years, allowing researchers to observe trends and variations.

Advantages

(a) Triangulation increases the credibility and validity of research findings by corroborating information from different sources or methods.
(b) It provides a more complete and nuanced understanding of complex social phenomena by capturing various dimensions.
(c) Triangulation can help mitigate the impact of individual biases, as findings are cross-verified through different perspectives or data sources.
(d) Researchers can gain a more holistic view of the research topic by considering diverse perspectives and approaches.

Disadvantages

(a) Triangulation can be time-consuming and may require additional resources, especially when using multiple methods or involving multiple researchers.
(b) Integrating findings from different sources can be challenging, and the analysis process may become intricate.
(c) Coordinating multiple data collection efforts or managing a team of researchers can present logistical challenges.
(d) In some cases, different methods or sources may yield conflicting results, posing challenges in interpretation.
(e) Triangulation may not be suitable for all research questions or contexts. Some studies may benefit more from a single, focused approach, like those on a small community or those that intend to analyse only one aspect in a detailed manner. It may also not be feasible in all circumstances. For example – During the COVID pandemic, fieldwork was not possible and so many researchers had to resort to connecting with participants through online modes.

Previous Year Question

2024

1. How do you view and assess the increasing trend of digital ethnography and use of visual culture in sociological research? (20 Marks)
   (See 'Model Answer Approach' on Pg 3.38)
2. What do you understand be 'Mixed method'? Discuss its strengths and limitations in Social research. (20 Marks)

2023

1. What is the distinctiveness of feminist method of social research? (10 marks)
2. What are variables? How do they facilitate research? (10 marks)
3. What are the different dimensions of the qualitative method? Do you think that the qualitative method helps to gain a deeper sociological insight? Give reasons for your answer. (20 marks)
4. What are the ethical issues that a researcher faces in making use of participant observation as a method of collecting data? Explain. (10 marks)

2022

1. The difference between information and data in social science is subtle. Comment. (10 marks)
2. Explain the different types of non-probability sampling techniques. Bring out the conditions for their usage with appropriate examples. (20 marks)
3. Suggest measures to minimise the influence of the researcher in the process of collecting data through focus group discussion. (10 marks)
4. What is reliability? Explain the different tests available to social science researcher to establish reliability. (10 marks)

2021

1. Discuss the challenges involved in collecting data through the census method. (10 marks)
2. How do qualitative and quantitative methods supplement each other in sociological inquiry? (20 marks)

2020

1. Discuss the importance and source of hypothesis in social research. (10 marks)
2. Analyse the strengths and weaknesses of social survey method in social research. (10 marks)

2019

1. Explain the probability sampling strategies with examples. (10 marks)
2. Bring out the significance of Ethnography in social research. (20 marks)

2018

1. Distinguish between quantitative and qualitative techniques of data collection with suitable examples from Indian society. (10 marks)
2. Explain with examples, the explanatory and exploratory designs of social research. (10 marks)

2017

1. Illustrate with examples the significance of variables in sociological research. (10 marks)
2. Examine the epistemological foundations of qualitative methods of social research. (10 marks)
3. How can one resolve the issue of reliability and validity in the context of sociological research on inequality? (10 marks)

2016

1. Analyse the importance of qualitative method in social research. (10 marks)
2. Hypothesis is a statement of the relationship between two or more variables. Elucidate by giving example of poverty and illiteracy. (10 marks)
3. 'Participant observation is the most effective method of collecting facts.' Comment. (20 marks)

2015

1. What are variables? Discuss their role in experimental research. (10 marks)
2. Why is random sampling said to have more reliability and validity in research? (20 marks)

2014

1. In what way biographies could be used to study social life. (10 marks)
2. Which research technique would be most suitable to study consumer behaviour and its social correlates? Explain. (20 marks)
   (See 'Model Answer Approach' on Pg 3.39)

2013

1. Analyse the limitations of quantitative methods in social research. (20 marks)

Model Answer Approach

2024 - Q. 2

Introduction: Digital ethnography and the use of visual culture are rapidly emerging as innovative methods in sociological research, particularly with the rise of digital media and online communities. Unlike traditional ethnography, which relies on in-person observations, digital ethnography explores social interactions in virtual spaces, making it well-suited for studying contemporary societies where online interactions are integral. Visual culture, including photos, videos, and social media imagery, offers researchers new tools to capture and analyze social realities.

Body:

Merits of Digital Ethnography and Visual Culture

1. **Access to Diverse and Global Communities:** Digital ethnography allows researchers to study communities and cultures that may be geographically dispersed. This broadens the scope of research, providing insights into global trends and cross-cultural phenomena without physical travel.
2. **Capturing Real-Time Social Dynamics:** Visual culture and digital platforms enable researchers to capture real-time social interactions and cultural expressions, making it easier to study changing trends, identities, and beliefs.
3. **Richness of Visual Data:** Visual culture provides context-rich data that allows researchers to analyze nuances in behavior, emotions, and social symbols. As Pierre Bourdieu suggested, visual media can reflect cultural capital, class distinctions, and social identity.
4. **Empowering Participants:** The participatory nature of digital ethnography often involves users sharing their perspectives directly, which fosters inclusivity. This aligns with the reflexive approach advocated by Clifford Geertz, where "thick descriptions" emerge from participants' interpretations of their own culture.

Challenges of Digital Ethnography and Visual Culture

1. **Ethical Concerns:** Digital research can raise privacy and consent issues, especially when studying online communities without direct interaction. Ensuring informed consent remains a challenge in public digital spaces.
2. **Authenticity of Online Interactions:** Online personas may not always reflect genuine behavior, as individuals often curate their digital identities. This can affect the authenticity of data collected.
3. Risk of Over-Interpretation: Visual data can be subject to researcher bias, leading to misinterpretation. The subjective nature of visual analysis requires careful reflexivity and contextual understanding.

Conclusion: Digital ethnography and visual culture are transforming sociological research by offering innovative ways to understand digital communities and visual expressions. While these methods provide valuable insights into modern societies, ethical concerns and interpretive challenges must be managed to maintain research integrity. Combining traditional and digital ethnography may offer a balanced approach to studying both offline and online social worlds.

2014; Q2.

Introduction: The study of consumer behaviour and its social correlates requires a research technique that can capture both quantitative data (purchasing patterns, preferences) and qualitative insights (motivations, cultural influences). Mixed methods, combining quantitative surveys with qualitative methods like focus groups and ethnography, offer a comprehensive approach. This approach is essential to understand not only what consumers purchase but also why they make these choices and how social factors influence them.

Body:

Merits of Using Mixed Methods for Consumer Behaviour

1. **Quantitative Surveys for Broad Patterns:** Surveys can gather data on consumer preferences, spending patterns, and demographic details on a large scale. Statistical analysis allows researchers to identify correlations between social factors (like income, education) and purchasing behavior. For instance, a survey could reveal that high-income consumers prefer eco-friendly products, correlating wealth with environmental awareness.
2. **Qualitative Methods for Deeper Insights:** Techniques, like focus groups and in-depth interviews allow researchers to explore the motivations, attitudes, and cultural influences behind consumer choices. For example, Pierre Bourdieu's concept of "cultural capital" highlights how consumption can signal social status, something quantitative data alone may overlook.
3. **Ethnography for Contextual Understanding:** Ethnographic methods, such as participant observation in retail settings or digital ethnography on social media, offer a close view of consumers in their natural environment. This approach is crucial for understanding the influence of peer groups, media, and cultural trends on purchasing behavior, aligning with Anthony Giddens' theory of reflexive modernity, where consumers make choices based on lifestyle identities.

Challenges of Mixed Methods:

1. **Time and Resource Intensive:** Combining quantitative and qualitative methods can be costly and time-consuming, often requiring specialized skills.
2. **Complex Data Integration:** Merging quantitative data with qualitative insights can be challenging, demanding careful analysis to ensure coherence.

Conclusion: A mixed-methods approach is ideal for studying consumer behavior and its social correlates, as it captures both large-scale trends and the nuanced motivations behind consumption. This comprehensive approach allows for a holistic understanding of consumer behavior, revealing the influence of social, economic, and cultural factors on purchasing decisions.

Chapter

4

Sociological Thinkers

In this Chapter

- Emile Durkheim
- Karl Marx
- Max Weber
- Talcott Parsons
- George H. Mead
- Robert Merton
- Previous Years' Questions

EMILE DURKHEIM (1858-1917)

Introduction

Emile Durkheim is credited with laying the early foundations of sociology and giving it an identifiable niche among the vying disciplines of philosophy and psychology. There are two main themes in his work: 1) primacy of the society over the individual and 2) the belief that society can and should be studied scientifically through the examination of external, observable things called 'social facts,' contributing significantly to the development of sociology as a discipline.

FYI

A Brief Biographical Sketch

Emile Durkheim was born in France in 1858 into a family of rabbis, but later in his teenage years, he disavowed his religious heritage. Over a period of time, he developed a keen interest in scientific methods and moral principles to study and guide social life.

Initially, Durkheim taught philosophy in various provincial schools in the Paris area and sought scientific training, which led him to Germany. He published significant works such as "The Division of Labour in Society," "The Rules of Sociological Method," and "Suicide," pioneering the field of sociology. In 1896, he became a professor at the University of Bordeaux and played a significant role in establishing sociology as a discipline.

Durkheim actively defended Alfred Dreyfus, a Jewish army captain, during a controversial court-martial trial. His interest in the Dreyfus affair stemmed from his lifelong concern with morality and the moral crisis facing modern society. He had an interest in socialism but had a different perspective from Marx, focusing on applying scientific moral principles rather than short-term political gains or economic aspects. Durkheim's influence extended beyond sociology, influencing fields like anthropology, history, linguistics, and psychology, with his journal "L'année sociologique" at its center.

Emile Durkheim passed away in 1917, and his work gained significance in American sociology through Talcott Parsons's "The Structure of Social Action" in the late 1930s.

Social Facts

- **Core Idea:** According to Durkheim, social facts are social structures, values and cultural norms that are external to and coercive of actors. For example, for a citizen, the institutions of bureaucracy, police, Government, etc., pose external constraints. For a woman, patriarchal cultural norms can seem coercive. In order to distinguish sociology from other disciplines, Durkheim proposed the study of 'social facts' as the subject matter of sociology. He treated them as a separate reality and referred to them with the Latin term sui generis which means unique, and not reducible to individual consciousness. For example, language is not simply a collection of words with private meanings, it is social in nature, exerts constraints on its users and any change in it, like slang or accent, has to be used by a sizeable majority of people to be identified so.

- **Methodology to Study Social Facts:** In Durkheim's view, social facts are to be treated as 'things' that exist outside the minds of both actors and the researcher. As a result, they need to be studied through empirical ways of observation and experimentation. Further, they are explained with the help of other social facts. For example - Durkheim analyse the social fact of suicide with the aid of other social facts like the levels of integration, anomie, etc.

Point to Note

'A social fact is every way of acting, fixed or not, capable of exercising on the individual an external constraint; or again, every way of acting which is general throughout a given society, while at the same time existing in its own right independent of its individual manifestations.'

—Durkheim

Point to Note

Major characteristics of Social Facts

1. External
2. Coercive
3. General
4. Can be empirically studied
5. Can be explained by other social facts

Types of Social Facts

Material Social Facts: These are the physical, tangible elements of society that exert social influence on individuals. They include:

1. **Architecture and Urban Planning:** Consider how the layout of a university campus influences student behavior—designated study spaces encourage academic focus, common areas promote socialization, and lecture halls establish hierarchical teaching relationships. These physical structures shape how people interact and behave within the institution.
2. **Legal Documents and Systems:** Birth certificates, marriage licenses, and property deeds are material social facts that organize society and define individuals' rights and responsibilities. For example, a marriage certificate isn't just paper—it creates legal obligations and social expectations that influence how married couples behave.

Non-Material Social Facts: These are intangible but powerful forces that shape individual behaviour through collective consciousness. They include –

- **Social Norms and Values:** The unwritten rule of standing in line at a grocery store illustrates this perfectly. Disapproval demonstrating its coercive power over individual behaviour.
- **Religious Beliefs:** Consider how religious dietary restrictions influence eating habits.
- **Cultural Practices:** Language usage patterns show how non-material social facts operate. The use of formal versus informal pronouns in languages like French (tu/vous) or German (du/Sie) reflects and reinforces social hierarchies and relationships.

The Interplay: Material and non-material social facts often work together. For example, a courthouse (material) represents and reinforces the authority of law and justice (non-material). The physical structure gives concrete form to abstract concepts of justice and social order.

Types of Non-Material Social Facts

1. **Morality**
   - As a social fact, Durkheim argued that morality is a social fact, meaning it is a tangible phenomenon that needs empirical investigation. It is closely tied to the social structure. The morality of any institution can be understood by asking questions like how is the institution constituted, how did it come to assume its present form, what is its place in the overall structure of society, etc.
   - **Drives the Society:** Durkheim believed that society must have a strong common moral framework and in many ways it was synonymous with morality. Durkheim believed that society is the source of morality, personality, and life itself. He believed that society has the resources, respect, and power to cultivate morality in individuals.
   - **Freedom and Moral Bonds:** Durkheim held a unique view of freedom, suggesting that individuals needed external moral constraints to be truly free. These moral restraints were necessary to prevent individuals from becoming slaves to their own uncontrolled passions and desires.
2. **Collective Conscience**
   - **Core Idea:** Durkheim defined the collective conscience as the totality of beliefs and sentiments shared by the average members of a society. It forms a distinct and self-sustaining system, separate yet derived from individual consciences.
   - **Independence and Influence:** Durkheim emphasized that the collective conscience is not merely a reflection of material conditions, as suggested by Marxist views. Instead, he saw it as an independent force that can shape and determine other social facts. For example, while economic changes can promote mass consumption, religious beliefs serve as a reminder that true happiness lies beyond materialistic achievements, thereby toning down greed-based consumerism.
   - **Primitive vs. Modern Societies:** Durkheim used the concept of the collective conscience to argue that 'primitive' societies had a stronger collective conscience characterized by more shared understandings, norms, and beliefs compared to modern, more individualistic societies.

3. **Collective Representations:** Durkheim uses this term to refer to a collective concept and a social 'force'. Examples include religious myths, symbols and popular legends. These represent ways in which society reflects on itself. They emerge from social interactions and can be studied easily as they are connected to material symbols such as flags, icons and pictures. Example - A New York Times cartoon had mocked India in 2014 when it had accomplished the Mangalyaan mission. Years later in 2023, when India successfully achieved the *Chandrayaan* 3 feat, netizens called out the cartoon for its racist undertone. Such pictures reflect how the West conceives of developing countries like India. A counter to such a cartoon, which appeared in 2017, reflected Indian patriotism.
4. **Social Currents:** Not associated with social organizations, unlike other social facts, social currents include phenomena like waves of enthusiasm, indignation, and pity in public gatherings. For instance, in Eastern European communist governments, rock concerts and their potential to create social currents were seen as a threat, as they could create cultural standards, fashions, behaviours independent of the control of political parties. These are sets of shared meanings within a collectivity. They can only be understood at the level of interactions and are intersubjective in nature.
   - **Critique and Response:** Durkheim's idea of non-material social facts, particularly of social currents has been criticized for assuming that such facts have an autonomous existence, separate from the actors. In response, however, Durkheim has recognized that these facts are a product of interactions between individuals. This collective consciousness is formed through the exchange of symbols and the interpenetration of individual minds. It is a shared 'consciousness of consciousnesses.'

Some Common Examples of Social Facts

1. **Laws and Regulations:** Legal systems encompass a wide range of rules and norms that govern behaviour within a society. These laws exist independently of individuals and exert coercive power, compelling adherence through sanctions. For instance, criminal laws deter theft and violence by imposing penalties, thereby shaping societal conduct and maintaining order.
2. **Moral Norms and Values:** Morality comprises shared beliefs about what is right and wrong, which guide individual behaviour. These norms are internalized through socialization but originate from the collective conscience of society. Examples include the taboo against murder and the expectation of honesty, which are upheld by societal approval and disapproval.
3. **Religious Beliefs and Practices:** Religious systems consist of beliefs, rituals, and moral codes that are external to the individual yet deeply influence behaviour. Religious institutions, such as churches and temples, enforce these norms. For example, practices like attending weekly services or observing religious holidays are social facts that individuals follow as part of their religious community.
4. **Educational Institutions and Curricula:** The structure and content of educational systems are social facts that shape the knowledge and skills imparted to individuals. These institutions standardise education, setting expectations

for attendance, performance, and behaviour. For instance, the curriculum dictates what is taught in schools, influencing the collective knowledge and societal values.

5. **Economic Systems and Practices:** Economic structures, such as market regulations, labour laws, and financial institutions, are social facts that govern economic behaviour. These systems determine how goods and services are produced, distributed, and consumed. For instance, wage standards and employment contracts regulate labour relations and economic activities.
6. **Language and Communication:** Language is a social fact that exists independently of individuals but is essential for communication within a society. It includes the rules of grammar, syntax, and vocabulary that individuals must learn and use to interact effectively. Language shapes thought processes and cultural transmission.
7. **Marriage and Kinship Systems:** Family structures and related norms, such as marriage practices and kinship roles, are social facts that dictate family dynamics and responsibilities. These norms vary across societies but universally influence personal relationships and social organization. For example, the expectation of monogamy in many societies is a social fact that guides marital behaviour.
8. **Professional Codes and Standards:** Professional norms include ethical codes, standards of practice, and organizational regulations that guide behaviour within specific professions. For instance, medical ethics dictate the conduct of healthcare professionals, ensuring standards of care and patient rights.

Division of Labour in Society

- The division of labour is a fundamental economic concept that involves breaking down complex production processes into specialized tasks, with different workers focusing on specific aspects of production to enhance efficiency and productivity. This idea gained prominence during the Industrial Revolution and was notably discussed by Adam Smith in '*The Wealth of Nations*,' where he used the famous example of a pin factory to demonstrate how task specialization could dramatically increase output. While Smith emphasized the economic benefits of specialization, Karl Marx later criticized its alienating effects on workers, arguing that it reduced them to mere cogs in the industrial machine. Émile Durkheim, however, approached the division of labour from a sociological perspective, seeing it as more than just an economic phenomenon. He argued that specialized labour creates "organic solidarity" in modern societies, as people become interdependent through their complementary differences rather than being bound by common beliefs and traditions (mechanical solidarity). For Durkheim, this interdependence serves as the foundation of social cohesion in modern societies, though he acknowledged that excessive or poorly regulated specialization could lead to social anomie. Max Weber further contributed to this discourse by examining how the division of labour led to bureaucratization and rationalization of modern society, viewing it as part of the broader process of modernization that brought both efficiency and potential dehumanization.

- **Core Idea:** The division of labour in modern society makes people dependent on each other and thereby generates a new kind of solidarity. It is not simply an economic necessity but also produces a significant moral effect. It was a material social fact for Durkheim.

Types of Solidarity

1. **Mechanical Solidarity:** Mechanical solidarity is present in pre-modern societies where people are generalists and share similar activities and responsibilities. People are self-sufficient in this type of society. The collective conscience is stronger here.
2. **Organic Solidarity:** This is found in modern society where people are held together by their differences. Everyone specialises in certain tasks and hence are dependent on other people, groups, structures and institutions for fulfilment of other needs. Increasing division of labour diminishes the collective conscience.

FYI

'Dynamic Density' as the Cause of Transition from Mechanical to Organic Solidarity

Dynamic density refers to the number of people in a society and the amount of interaction that occurs among them. As people increase, so does the competition for scarce resources. The division of labour then becomes a way to resolve such problems caused by increased dynamic density.

Mechanical Solidarity	Organic Solidarity
1. Present in pre-modern, simpler societies with less dynamic density	1. Present in modern societies with more dynamic density
2. People are generalists and share similar activities and experiences.	2. People are specialists in different activities and share diverse experiences.
3. People are self-sufficient and held together by common values, norms, etc.	3. People are dependent on each other and held together by differences and interdependence.
4. Stronger collective conscience	4. Weaker collective conscience
5. Both less competition and less differentiation. There is no significant need for people to cooperate with each other.	5. Less competition and more differentiation allow people to cooperate more and to be supported by the same resource base
6. Lesser solidarity and individuality	6. More solidarity and more individuality

Mechanical Solidarity	Organic Solidarity
7. Repressive law - All people believe in one common morality and any offence against it is met with a severe punishment, such as cutting off of one's hand, removal of one's tongue, etc.	7. Restitutive law – Offence is deemed to be committed against a particular individual or section. The common morality is weak and hence, people do not react emotionally. Offenders are required to make restitution for their offences to those that they have harmed and they are not severely punished.
8. Normal forms of division of labour	8. Pathological forms of division of labour can take place

According to Anthony Giddens, the collective conscience in the two types of society can be differentiated across the following four dimensions.

Solidarity	Volume (no. of people it covers)	Intensity (the depth of feeling)	Rigidity (how clearly it is defined)	Content (nature of beliefs)
Mechanical	Entire society	High	High	Religion
Organic	Particular groups	Low	Low	Low

Source: The Sociological Theory - George Ritzer

Abnormal Forms of Division of Labour

- Durkheim distinguished between the concepts of normal and pathological of labour. Normal refers to that which is found in all societies at similar stages and pathological to that which departs from what is normally found. By this definition, he argued that crime is normal as it is found in every society and provides the useful function of helping societies strengthen their collective conscience.
- He used the idea of 'pathological' to identify three abnormal forms that division of labour takes in modern societies:
  (a) **Anomic Division of Labour:** Lack of regulation in society, celebration of isolated individuality and people do not know what they should do.
  (b) **Forced Division of Labour:** Outdated norms and expectations can force people, groups into roles they are ill-suited for. Traditions and status could determine allocation of opportunities overshadowing talent and qualification, creating a pathological state.
  (c) **Poorly Coordinated Division of Labour:** When people's specializations lead to increased isolation rather than interdependence.
- **How to solve pathological forms of divisions of labour?**—Durkheim suggested 'social justice' to make social relations more equitable. This will ensure that division of labour works as a moral and solidifying force in the modern society.

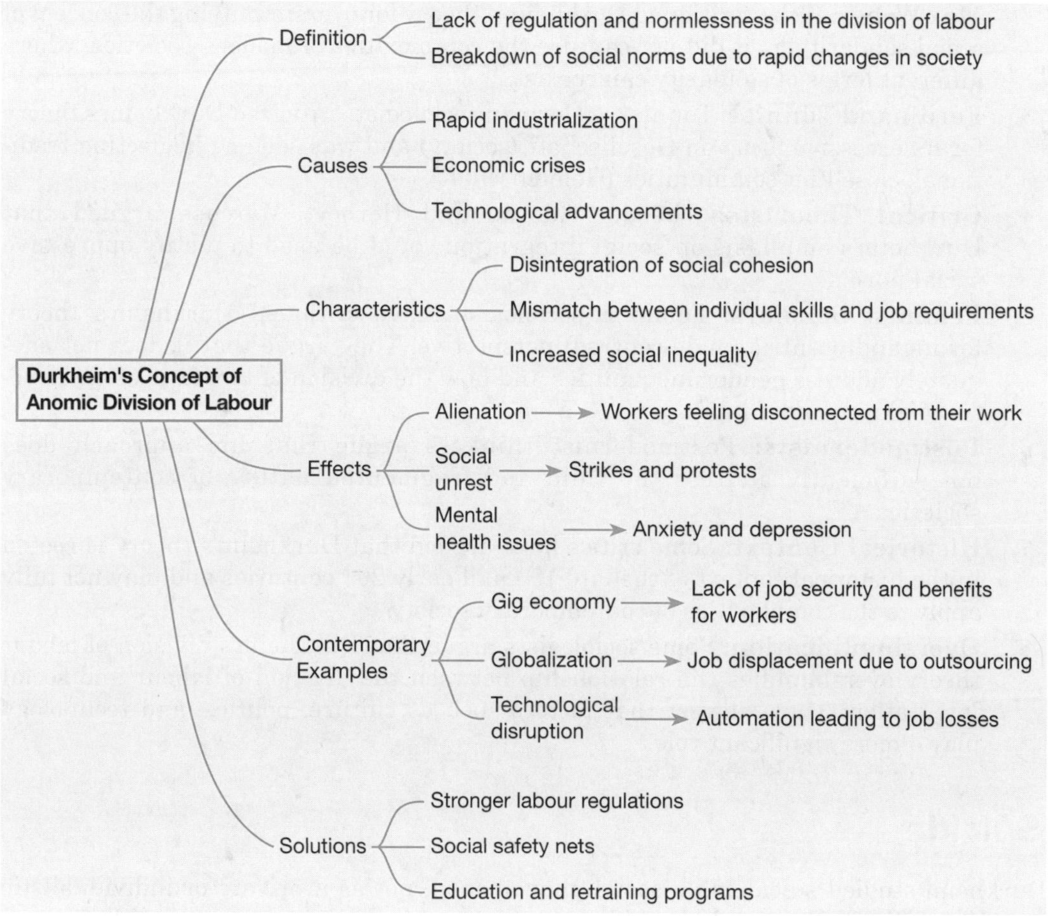

Contemporary Relevance

- **Global Relevance:** In the modern globalized world, Durkheim's theory of the division of labour is relevant in understanding economic interdependence. For instance, international supply chains and the global workforce exemplify complex divisions of labour.
- **Indian Example:** In India, the IT and software services sector showcases the division of labour, with specialized roles contributing to global tech solutions, reflecting Durkheim's concept of organic solidarity in a diverse society.

Critique

Emile Durkheim's theory of the division of labour in society has been subject to various critiques by other sociologists and thinkers. Here are some of the notable critiques:

1. **Karl Marx:** Marx argued that the division of labour primarily serves the interests of the capitalist class and perpetuates class inequalities, which Durkheim did not emphasise.

2. **Max Weber:** Weber critiqued Durkheim's theory for oversimplifying the concept of social solidarity as it did not capture the complexities of modern societies, where different forms of solidarity can coexist.
3. **Ferdinand Tönnies:** Tönnies, a German sociologist, criticized Durkheim's theory for its excessive focus on Gesellschaft (society) and was seen as neglecting traditional, close-knit communities (Gemeinschaft).
4. **Critical Theorists:** Theodor Adorno and Herbert Marcuse argued that Durkheim's emphasis on social integration could be used to justify oppressive social norms.
5. **Feminist Scholars:** Feminist sociologists have critiqued Durkheim's theory for its androcentric (male-centred) perspective. They argue that it does not adequately address gender inequalities and how the division of labour is often structured along gender lines.
6. **Postmodernists:** Postmodernist thinkers argue that his approach does not sufficiently address the fluid and fragmented nature of contemporary societies.
7. **Historical Context:** Some critics have argued that Durkheim's theory is rooted in the historical context of the late 19th and early 20th centuries and may not fully apply to the complexities of contemporary society.
8. **Oversimplification:** Some sociologists argue that Durkheim's division of labour theory oversimplifies the relationship between the division of labour and social integration. They suggest that factors such as culture, politics, and technology play a more significant role.

Suicide

Durkheim studied suicide as a social phenomenon, not as a private or individualistic one. He studies how and why suicide rates vary among different groups. He proposed to study suicide in two ways–by comparing between different societies or collectivities (that is, cross-culturally) and another by comparing within the same group from one time period to another (historically).

Types of Suicide

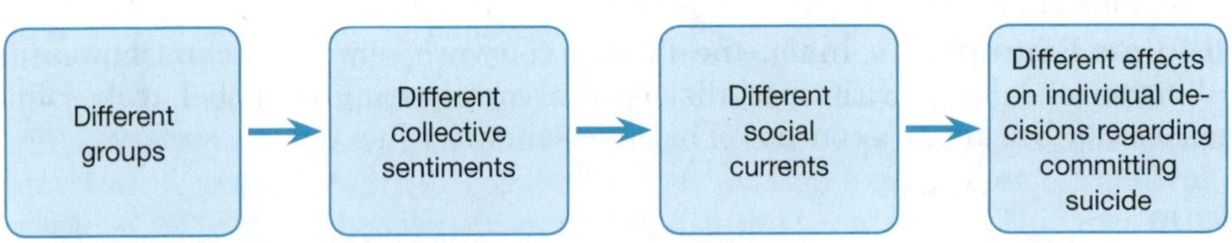

- The social facts that determine the type of suicide include
  (i) **Integration:** the strength of attachment that people have to society
  (ii) **Regulation:** the degree of external constraint on people
- Based on the different levels of integration and regulation, he identified the following four types of suicide

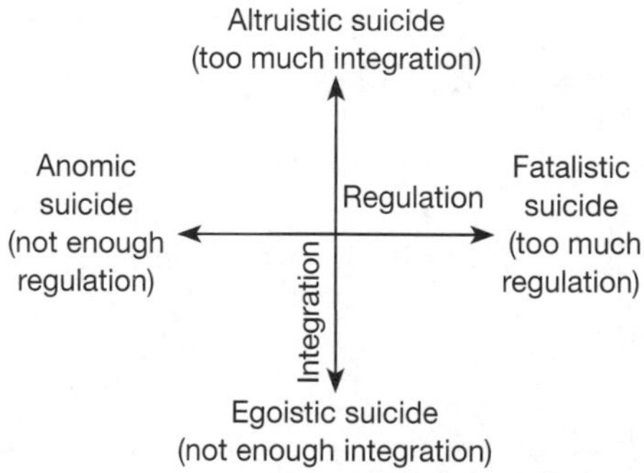

Durkheim's four types of suicide (after Pope 1976)

- Émile Durkheim, in his seminal work '*Le Suicide*' (1897), categorized suicide into four distinct types based on the relationship between the individual and society. These categories are grounded in the concepts of social integration and moral regulation.

Type of Suicide	Definition	Cause	Examples
Egoistic Suicide	Occurs when an individual feels detached or insufficiently integrated into society.	Low social integration.	1. Elderly people who feel isolated from their families and communities. 2. Urban professionals experiencing loneliness despite living in bustling cities. 3. A young adult unable to find a sense of belonging in peer groups or family circles.
Altruistic Suicide	Happens when an individual is excessively integrated into a group, leading to a willingness to sacrifice oneself for the collective.	Excessive social integration.	1. Soldiers who sacrifice their lives for their country or comrades in war. 2. Sati practice in historical India, where widows would immolate themselves on their husband's funeral pyre. 3. Suicide bombers driven by ideological or religious commitments to their cause.
Anomic Suicide	Results from a breakdown of social norms or a sudden disruption of social equilibrium, leaving individuals feeling purposeless or adrift.	Low moral regulation.	1. Stock market crash victims losing financial stability and life direction. 2. Farmers in rural India facing distress due to debt and crop failure. 3. Individuals affected by personal crises like divorce or unemployment in rapidly changing societies.

Type of Suicide	Definition	Cause	Examples
Fatalistic Suicide	Occurs when individuals feel excessively regulated by oppressive discipline or restrictions, leading to a loss of hope and sense of autonomy.	Excessive moral regulation.	1. Prison inmates enduring long-term sentences under rigid rules and inhumane conditions. 2. Women in patriarchal societies with no escape from oppressive norms (e.g., honour-based suicides). 3. Slaves or serfs under repressive systems feeling a complete lack of agency over their lives.

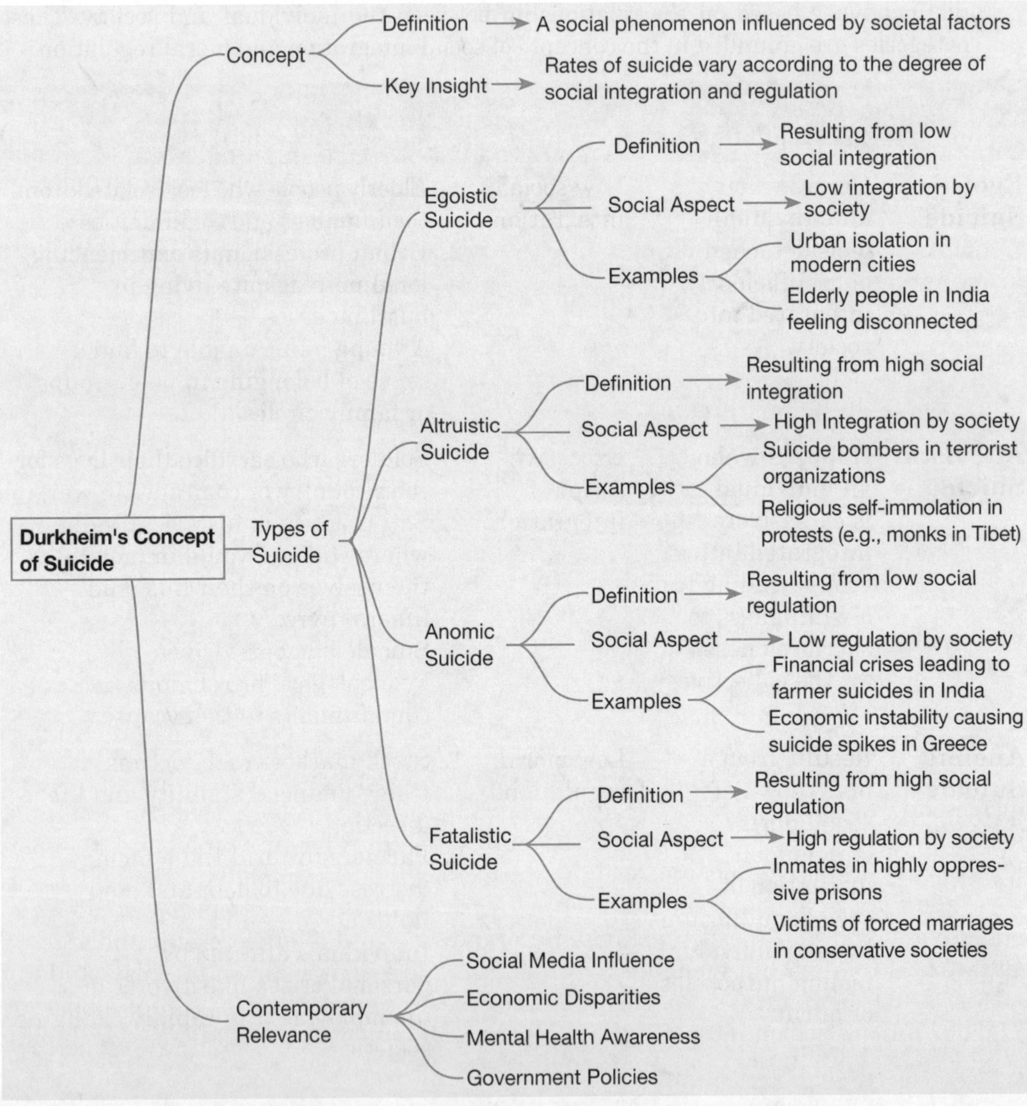

Anomic Suicide (Low regulation, normal integration perhaps moderate-high integration)	Fatalistic Suicide (High regulation, possibly low integration or overwhelmed regulation)
Occurs when society's regulatory norms (over goals, desires, behaviour) break down — people lack guidance about what is permissible, what to aspire to, or what counts as reasonable.	Occurs when regulation is extreme and oppressive — individuals' futures are blocked, desires curtailed, rules are inflexible and suffocating.
Typical during rapid social or economic change (boom or bust), when old norms no longer fit, and new ones have not crystallized.	In contexts like slavery, prison, totalitarian regimes, or other situations where individuals are trapped in an unchangeable role.
Leads to feelings of expectation-disappointment mismatch, disorientation, normlessness, purposelessness.	Leads to hopelessness, bitterness, sense of being overruled or crushed by external forces, lack of agency.
Examples: massive economic crises, sudden prosperity raising expectations, loss of social position, breakdown of moral norms.	Examples: slaves seeing no exit, prisoners with no possibility of parole or change; extreme caste or gender restrictions; oppressive institutional settings.
Less empirical data than for some other types, but many modern studies find correlations of social deregulation with suicide risk.	More theoretical; rare cases, often difficult to observe in data; less frequent in Durkheim's own empirical base.

References

Durkheim, Émile. Suicide: *A Study in Sociology*. (1897). Translated editions e.g. 1951 (Free Press / Routledge). Fundamental source. durkheim.uchicago.edu

'Suicide' summary, including the definitions of anomic and fatalistic suicide. durkheim.uchicago.edu+2SpringerLink+2

Secondary sources summarising anomic suicide risks in recent contexts: '*Anomic suicides on rise during recently emerging crises (revisiting Durkheim's model)*' (2023), Cambridge.

'Occupational Associations' as a Solution

In case of modern society, Durkheim has observed an increase in anomic and egoistic suicides due to low levels of regulation and integration and high levels of isolation. Durkheim suggests formation of occupational associations for this problem. Durkheim believed that all individuals involved in a particular industry, including workers, managers, and owners, should come together in an association. This association would serve both professional and social functions. By organising into a single group, individuals from various roles within the industry would recognize their common interests and the need for a shared moral system. He considered these occupational associations superior to labour unions, which intensified differences, and employer associations, which only protected owners' interests. The proposed associations would serve as a platform for developing and implementing an integrative moral system.

Contemporary Relevance

- **Global Relevance:** Durkheim's theory of suicide remains relevant due to mental health and societal factors. High suicide rates in developed countries, often linked to social isolation, reflect the concept of egoistic suicide.
- **Indian Example:** India has seen an increase in farmer suicides in the past due to high debt burden and student suicides lately driven by excessive pressure and social isolation. This is a real-life manifestation of Durkheim's theory on the impact of societal factors on suicide rates.

FYI

Distinct Sociological Methods used by Durkheim to Study Suicide

1. **Use of Quantitative Data:** Used actual numbers rather than focusing on individual instances
2. **Multivariate Analysis:** Involves evaluating multiple variables (more than two) to identify any possible association among them, for instance, association between religion, marriage and integration, economy, work and regulation, etc.
3. **Comparative Analysis:** Comparison between different groups across different periods of time
4. **Statistical Explanations:** Used official data on suicide rates to draw conclusions

The Elementary Forms of Religious Life

In the book, 'The Elementary Forms of Religious Life' (1912), Durkheim put forward both a sociology of religion and a theory of knowledge, 'religion cannot be defined except by the characters which are found wherever religion itself is found'.

Theory of Religion —The Sacred and The Profane

- Durkheim distinguishes between the sacred and the profane in religion. The sacred represents those aspects of social reality that are considered extraordinary and set apart from the everyday, while the profane encompasses ordinary, utilitarian, and mundane aspects of life. On one hand, the sacred brings out the attitude of awe, reference and obligation, on the other, these feelings are what transform ordinary things into sacred phenomena, making both the attitude and the sacredness of objects interdependent. The sacred and profane are kept apart because they are heterogeneous (different), antagonistic (in conflict) and isolated (separated).
- Durkheim acknowledged that religion is a powerful and pervasive social phenomenon with some truth, but this truth, he argued, is not supernatural.

Instead, it is rooted in society itself which is the source of superior moral power.

- Durkheim's central idea is that religion symbolically embodies society. Religious beliefs and rituals serve as a system of symbols through which society becomes conscious of itself. These symbols are a means through which society influences and inspires individuals.
- Durkheim contended that society, as a collective entity, possesses a superior moral power that transcends individual interests. This power influences individuals, demands sacrifices, suppresses selfish tendencies, and energises them. This power is expressed symbolically through religion.
- Durkheim noted that while all societies have religious beliefs, the specific content of these beliefs varies from one society to another. This variation underscores the idea that religion reflects the unique character and values of each society.
- According to Durkheim, in addition to the differentiation of the sacred and the profane, three other conditions are needed for the development of religion:
  (i) **Religious Beliefs:** A set of religious beliefs is essential. These beliefs represent the nature of sacred things and the relationships they have with each other and with profane elements.
  (ii) **Religious Rituals:** Rituals are rules of conduct that prescribe how individuals should behave in the presence of sacred objects. Rites are the rules of conduct that follow from beliefs, which prescribe how human beings must behave with regard to sacred things. They can be positive, where the sacred is sought to be brought closer to the world of men, for example, through '*havan*' or sacrifice. Rites can be negative, which means the sacred and profane are sought to be kept apart, e.g., purification rites, fasts, penance or suffering.
  (iii) **Religious Community (Church):** A religion requires a church, which serves as a unified moral community. The church brings together all those who adhere to the religious beliefs and practices, creating a single moral community.
- These ideas led Durkheim to comprehensively define religion as follows: 'A religion is a unified system of beliefs and practices which unite into one single moral community called a Church all those who adhere to them'.

Empirical Foundations of Theory of Religion

- Durkheim considered totemism, a religious system where animals and plants are revered as sacred emblems of clans, as the simplest and most primitive form of religion. He argued that totems are material representations of the non-material force, which is society. In the realm of totemism, three classes of things are connected: the totemic symbol, the animal or plant, and the members of the clan. For this purpose, Durkheim chose to study the 'primitive' culture of the Arunta tribe of Australia to understand the essential nature of religion.
- Durkheim contended that in modern society, religion's role becomes more specialized and narrow, occupying a smaller domain as other institutions like law and science express different aspects of collective morality. However, he also believed that most, if not all, collective representations in modern society have their roots in the all-encompassing religion of primitive society.

FYI

Religious Revivalism and Durkheim's Theory

Durkheim's theory of religion emphasizes its role as a unifying and moral force in society. It is relevant to understanding religious revivalism, where there is a resurgence of religious fervor and traditional values. Religious revivalism has been observed worldwide and in India, manifesting in various forms.

Worldwide Examples of Religious Revivalism

1. **Evangelical Christianity in the United States:** In the late 20th and early 21st centuries, the U.S. witnessed a resurgence of evangelical Christianity, characterized by mega-churches, faith-based political activism, and moral conservatism.
2. **Islamic Revivalism in the Middle East:** Countries in the Middle East, like Saudi Arabia and Iran, have experienced Islamic revivalism. The 1979 Islamic Revolution in Iran, led by Ayatollah Khomeini, marked a significant resurgence of Islamic influence in the political and social spheres.

Examples of Religious Revivalism in India

1. **Ayodhya Ram Mandir Movement:** The Ram Janmabhoomi movement aimed to build a Hindu temple at the site believed to be the birthplace of Lord Ram in Ayodhya. The movement led to a resurgence of Hindu religious sentiments and culminated in the construction of the Ram Mandir in 2020.
2. **Sikh Revivalism:** The Sikh community in India and Canada has experienced revivalism movements emphasizing religious identity and the preservation of Sikh traditions. The Khalistan movement in the 1980s was a significant manifestation of this revivalism.
3. **Yoga and Spiritual Tourism:** India's heritage of yoga and spirituality has experienced a global revival. Yoga centers and retreats attract people from around the world seeking spiritual growth and holistic well-being.

These instances of religious revivalism reflect Durkheim's idea that religion plays a central role in reaffirming collective values and social cohesion.

Theory of Knowledge

- According to Durkheim, as in totemism, objects from nature were classified into groups comprising sacred totems, so in other areas humans classify objects. This ability to classify and categorise stems from people's religious and social experiences. Because men exist in groups, they impose these divisions at a cognitive level too to group other things.
- Durkheim's theory of knowledge countered empiricism (that concepts are formed through sense impressions) and apriorism (that humans are born with certain

mental categories). He argued that our categories are social creations, collective representations.

- His sociology of knowledge posits that concepts and fundamental categories are collective representations created by society, primarily through religious rituals. Religion serves as the bridge between society and the individual, as these sacred rituals provide the basis for individual concepts. For example, the concept of time in various religions is associated with important events, like the Samvat era in Hinduism, Anno Domini in Christianity, etc., the concept of space is highly influenced by sacred and profane at both micro and macro levels; the Islamic concept of 'Tawhid' represents the oneness and totality of God, and this concept influences various aspects of Muslim life and thought.

Point to Note

Collective Effervescence

Durkheim's notion of collective effervescence refers to moments in history when a collective group experiences a heightened level of collective exaltation. These moments can lead to significant changes in the structure of society. Historical periods like the Reformation and the Renaissance are examples of such times.

Totemism, as examined by Durkheim, is a system of belief where clans or tribes are associated with particular totems, which could be animals, plants, or other natural entities. These totems are considered sacred and serve as symbols for the clan's identity, spirituality, and societal cohesion.

Key Elements of Durkheim's Analysis

1. **Collective Effervescence:** Durkheim observed that religious ceremonies involving totems generate a sense of collective effervescence, a heightened state of communal emotional unity and shared consciousness. This phenomenon occurs during rituals where individuals feel a connection to a greater social entity, reinforcing social solidarity.
2. **Social Function of Religion:** For Durkheim, the primary function of religion is not theological but social. Religion, including totemism, serves to bind members of a society together, fostering a collective conscience. This shared belief system and moral community are essential for the maintenance of social order and cohesion.
3. **Symbolism and Representation:** Totems act as tangible symbols of the clan's identity and unity. They represent both the sacred (divine) and the profane (ordinary) aspects of life, highlighting the dual nature of reality as perceived by the society. Through totemic symbols, the abstract concepts of society and divinity are made concrete and comprehensible.
4. **Sacred and Profane Dichotomy:** Durkheim's study delineates the division between the sacred and the profane, with the sacred being set apart and forbidden,

endowed with a sense of reverence. This dichotomy is fundamental to religious belief systems, including totemism, and serves to structure social life and moral boundaries.

Demonstrating the Reality of Religion

Durkheim's analysis of totemism illustrates that the reality of religion is grounded in its social function and collective nature rather than its doctrinal content. He demonstrated this through several key insights:

1. **Religion as a Social Construct:** Religion is a product of collective human activity. The reality of religion lies in its ability to bring people together, create shared beliefs, and foster communal identity. Totemism exemplifies this by showing how religious symbols and rituals originate from societal needs and collective experiences.
2. **Empirical Foundation:** By studying Aboriginal Australian societies, Durkheim provided empirical evidence that religion originates from the social structures and practices of human communities. This grounded his theoretical framework in observable reality, showcasing the tangible impact of religion on social life.
3. **Intrinsic Connection to Society:** Religion, including totemism, reflects and reinforces the social realities of the community. The sacred symbols and rituals of totemism embody the collective ideals and moral order of the society, demonstrating how religious life is deeply interwoven with social existence.

Moral Education and Social Reform

- Durkheim believed in the potential of social science for positive social intervention. His approach dictated that any reform should spring from society's morality itself, not from some abstract concepts. He saw aberrations as temporary not as inherent in society.
- **Morality:** For Durkheim, morality involves three components:
  (i) **Discipline:** Which resists individual arbitrariness
  (ii) **Attachment to Society:** Since society is the root of all morality
  (iii) **Autonomy:** Which involves an individual sense of responsibility towards one's actions
- **Moral Education:** Durkheim defined education as the process by which the individual 'acquires the physical, intellectual and moral tools to function in the society'. Durkheim saw the classroom as a miniature version of society, where students from diverse backgrounds come together, interact, and learn together. He believed that the collective energy and spirit within the classroom could be harnessed to teach moral values, for example, teachers and educators often aim to teach students values like honesty, respect, and responsibility. Education can pass on collective beliefs and values that are important for society. This includes discipline, devotion to society, and the development of autonomy. Most importantly, education, Durkheim argues, has the role to explain to students why they should

abide by society's rules and how it will benefit them. Without such understanding, they will be subject to an inferior morality.

Critique

1. **Functionalism and Positivism**
   - **Critique:** Durkheim's work is often associated with functionalism and positivism. Some critics argue that he was overly focused on macro-level social facts and searching for social functions in a way that resembled functionalism.
   - **Example:** Robert K. Merton, a prominent sociologist, criticized functionalism, arguing that it oversimplified complex social phenomena and didn't sufficiently address social change and conflict.
2. **Objective Nature of Social Facts**
   - **Critique:** Durkheim's concept of social facts as objective phenomena has been challenged. Critics argue that even seemingly objective social facts, such as suicide rates, are subject to interpretation and may not be as objective as Durkheim claimed.
   - **Example:** Erving Goffman emphasized the role of individual perception and interpretation in shaping social reality, which challenges the objectivity of social facts.
3. **Assumptions About Human Nature**
   - **Critique:** Durkheim's assumption about human nature, particularly the idea that people are driven by insatiable passions, has been criticized for lacking empirical evidence and for potentially being a product of social structures.
   - **Example:** Max Weber, a fellow classical sociologist, argued that social actions are driven by subjective meanings and interpretations, emphasizing the role of individual agency in shaping behaviour.
4. **Consciousness and Autonomy**
   - **Critique:** Durkheim's theories downplay the role of consciousness and individual mental processes treating them as dependent on social facts. Critics argue that consciousness and mental processes can develop autonomy, just like other social facts.
   - **Example:** George Herbert Mead, a symbolic interactionist, emphasized the active role of the self and consciousness in shaping social behaviour.
5. **Conservatism and Morality**
   - **Critique:** Durkheim's strong connection between sociology and morality has been criticized for potentially leading to conservatism as he advocated returning to society's morality. Critics argue that pluralist societies have different notions of morality and it is tough to make a singular choice.
   - **Example:** Herbert Marcuse, a critical theorist, argued that the scientific study of society should not be divorced from the pursuit of social justice and the critique of oppressive social norms.

Additional Concepts and Comparative Analysis

Character of Modern Society

Theorist	Prediction	Relevance	Critique
Ferdinand Tönnies	Transition from Gemeinschaft (community) to Gesellschaft (society), indicating a shift from close personal ties to impersonal relationships.	Accurately predicted increased individualism and decline of traditional community bonds in urban settings. Reflects fragmentation and impersonality in contemporary social interactions.	Oversimplifies modern societies, which exhibit both Gemeinschaft and Gesellschaft characteristics. Does not fully account for modern multicultural and globalized interactions.
Émile Durkheim	Shift from mechanical solidarity (homogenous, collective conscience) to organic solidarity (specialized, interdependent individuals).	Described increased specialization and interdependence in modern economies. Concerns about anomie resonate with issues of social isolation and alienation.	Emphasis on social cohesion and stability may downplay conflict and change. Concept of anomie may not fully encompass disconnection in the digital age.
Max Weber	Increasing rationalization and dominance of bureaucratic institutions, leading to disenchantment and the iron cage of bureaucracy.	Insights into rationalization and bureaucracy are relevant in understanding modern organizations, corporate culture, and government institutions. The 'iron cage' metaphor reflects dehumanising aspects of bureaucracy.	Pessimistic view of modernity may neglect emancipatory and innovative potentials of modern institutions. Underappreciates emotional, irrational, and non-bureaucratic influences.
Karl Marx	Historical materialism and class struggle, predicting capitalism's exploitative nature leading to its downfall and the rise of socialism.	Critique of capitalism remains influential in discussions about economic inequality, labour exploitation, and global capitalism. Class struggle framework aids in understanding social conflicts and movements.	Predictions of capitalism's collapse and socialism's rise have not materialized as expected. Economic determinism underestimates the role of culture, politics, and non-economic factors.

KARL MARX (1818–1883)

Introduction

Marx's work has been received differently in different parts of the world. Until well into the second half of the 20th century, his work was largely ignored in America. On the other hand, he was quite popular in Eastern Europe and variably influential in Western Europe. In some parts, his work was synonymous to sociological theory in the backdrop of the Cold War while in others, due to the abuses of Soviet-style communism, many turned away from his work. However, during the 1960s, the experiences in anti-Vietnam War, civil rights movements and student-rights movements led many to again start paying serious attention to Marx's work. Since then, there have been varied attempts to use Marx's work in understanding contemporary social changes.

FYI

A Brief Biographical Sketch

Image Credit: Everett Historical/Shutterstock

Karl Marx was born in Trier, Prussia on 5 May, 1818.

He received a doctorate in philosophy in 1841 from the University of Berlin, a school heavily influenced by Hegel. Upon moving to Paris in 1843, Marx encountered two new sets of ideas–French socialism and English political economy. The combination of Hegelianism with these ideas shaped up his intellectual orientation. At this point, he also met his future benefactor and lifelong friend - Friedrich Engels.

In 1844, Marx produced The Economic and Philosophic Manuscripts of 1844 which highlighted his increasing preoccupation with the economic domain.

Due to his increasing radicalism, he was again moved to Brussels in 1845. He became an active member of an international revolutionary movement and associated with the Communist League. In writing a document expounding the organization's aims and beliefs, Marx produced the Communist Manifesto of 1848. It contained stirring political slogans such as: 'Working men of all countries, unite!'

In 1849, he moved to London. In light of the failed political revolutions, he withdrew to more serious research on the workings of the capitalist system. These studies resulted in the three volumes of Capital. He lived in poverty during this time. In 1864, he became involved in political activity again and acquired fame as a leader and author. Eventually, however, the disintegration of revolutionary movements and personal illness took a toll. He passed away on 14 March, 1883.

Intellectual Influences

Marx was profoundly influenced by the German philosophy and idealism prevalent during his time, particularly the works of Georg Wilhelm Friedrich Hegel and Ludwig Feuerbach. Hegel's ideas are rooted in the broader framework of idealist philosophy, which emphasises the importance of ideas, specifically reason, for understanding social change. Hegel's dialectics are characterized by three elements: thesis, antithesis, and synthesis.

According to Hegel, historical progress occurs through a series of clashes between an idea (thesis) and its opposite (antithesis), resulting in the emergence of a new idea (synthesis). While Marx accepted Hegel's concept of dialectics, he rejected the focus on ideas. Instead, Marx introduced material forces into the framework and developed the theory of dialectical materialism.

Ludwig Feuerbach, another significant influence on Marx, was a German philosopher who challenged Hegel's notion that the 'real man' emanates from the divine. Feuerbach argued that the 'real man' exists in the 'real, material world.' He posited that human beings create an image of God, attributing to it ideal qualities they themselves cannot attain. In striving to be like God, humans fail to appreciate their own qualities, leading to what Feuerbach termed religious alienation. Marx was particularly drawn to Feuerbach's emphasis on the material foundations of religion. However, Marx believed Feuerbach should have connected religious alienation more directly with economic activity.

Historical Materialism

- **Idealism:** It is a theory positing that ultimate reality can be comprehended and interpreted through ideas. In contrast, materialism asserts that everything that exists is dependent on matter, focussing on the actual conditions of human existence. These two perspectives are fundamentally opposed: Idealism emphasises the significance of ideas, while materialism prioritizes material conditions. Marx's overarching views on society are encapsulated in his theory of historical materialism.
- **Core Idea:** The term 'historical' here refers to the dimension of time and history, how societies and human relations have developed and transformed over a period of time. The 'materialism' aspect refers to the material conditions–the economic and physical aspects of life play a fundamental role in shaping human and societal developments. Marx's historical materialism states that the way people meet their material needs determines their social relations, institutions, and dominant ideologies. The mode of production and economic relations constitute the 'base,' while non-economic relations, social institutions, culture and prevailing ideas form the 'superstructure.'

Main Features

(i) **Two-way Influence:** Marx's theory recognizes that the base and superstructure influence each other. The economic base develops in an attempt to satisfy human needs, which, in turn, gives rise to new needs and desires. This dynamic interaction leads to more changes in the base and then further in the superstructure, simultaneously shaping the society.

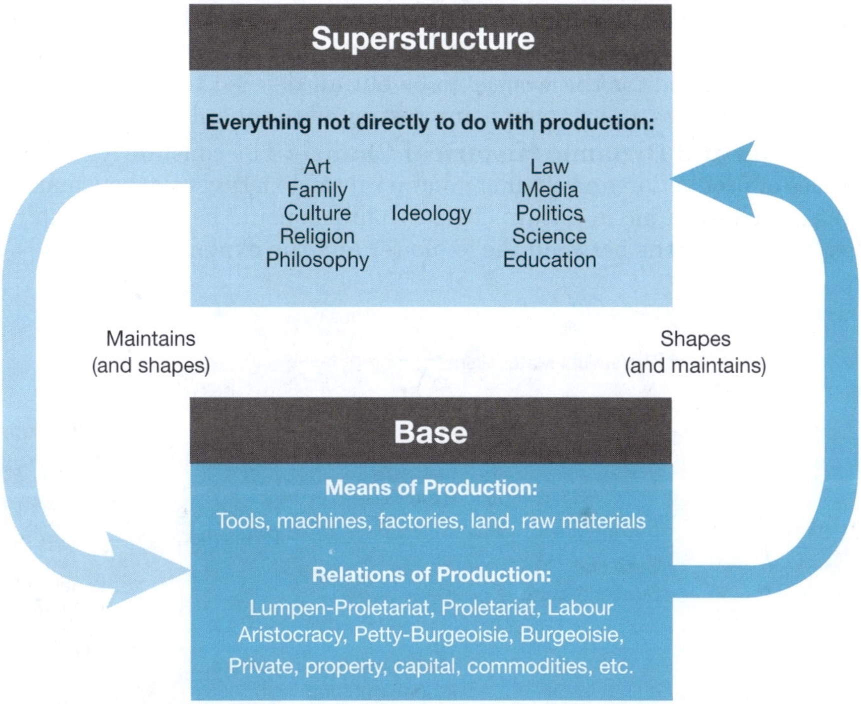

Point to Note

Base and superstructure always move in a spiral pattern, where the base is generally dominant.

(ii) **Material Forces of Production:** At any stage of social development, people use certain tools, machineries, technology, factories, etc., for their productive activities. These are referred to as the forces of production.

(iii) **Relations of Production:** In dealing with the forces of production, people enter into certain social associations which are referred to as the relations of production. The totality of the relations of production constitutes the economic structure of society, on top of which rises a political and legal superstructure to which correspond definite forms of social consciousness.

(iv) **Property Relations and Class Conflict:** At a certain stage, the material forces come into conflict with the relations of production or property relations (related to ownership of assets). The feudal relations, for instance, were incompatible with new forces of production which included technology, factories, etc., Capitalism, for example, is marked by the capitalist class owning the capital and wage labourers working for them. The hoarding of wealth by the capitalists and low wages for prolonged periods lead to class conflicts between capitalists and the working class.

(v) **Impact on Family and Personal Relations:** The socialization required to produce a good male worker also led to conditioning of a certain type of husband. Similarly, the need for the worker to be out all day led to mothers becoming the primary caretakers and women being restricted to the role of being a housewife.

(vi) **Revolution and Dynamic Historical Change:** The constantly evolving nature of forces of production and their conflict with the existing relations make for social change to be dynamic in nature. This dynamism could be marked by a revolution when the rift widens between the exploiter and the exploited.

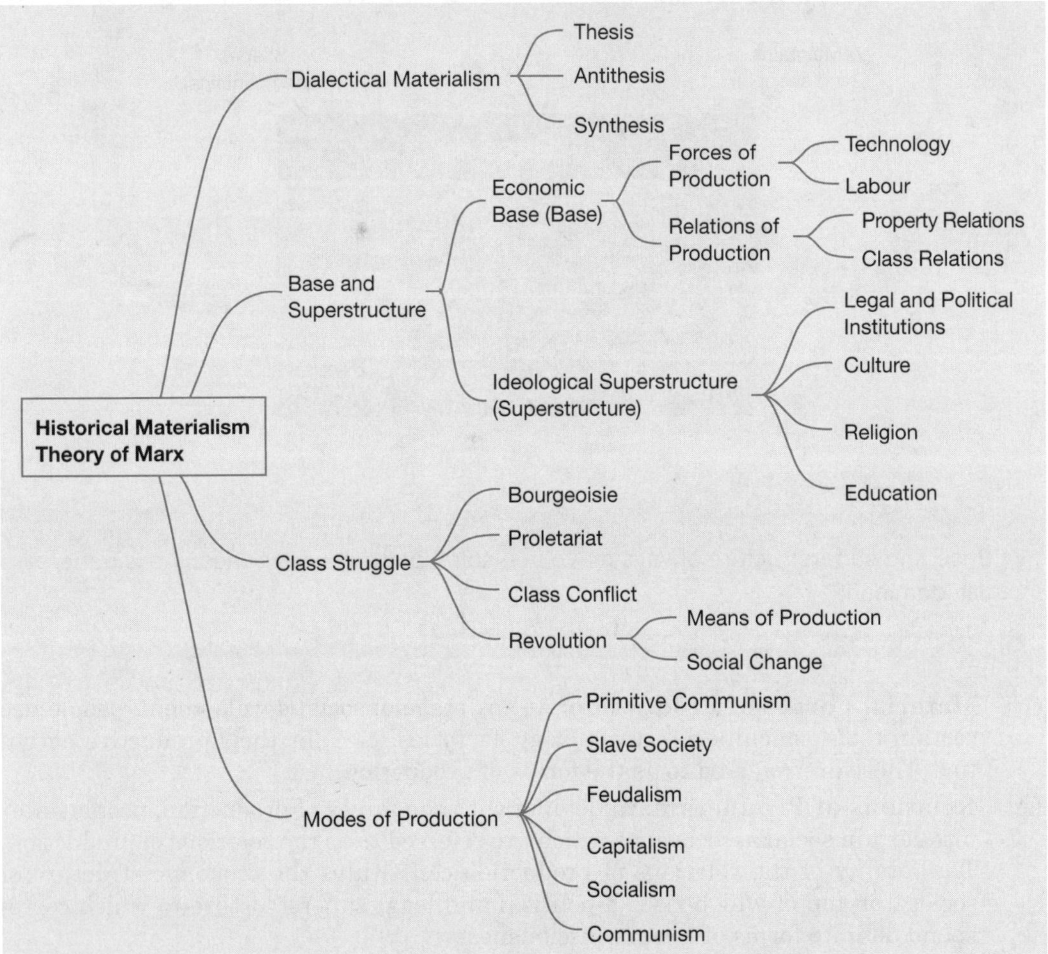

Historical Materialism as a Critique of Hegel's Idea of the Dialectic

Marx adopted the concept of 'the dialectic' from German philosopher G.W.F. Hegel. Dialectical philosophy posits that contradictions are inherent to reality and that understanding reality requires examining the evolution of these contradictions. While Marx concurred with the significance of contradictions in historical change, he diverged from

Hegel by asserting that these contradictions are not merely mental but are resolved through tangible, material struggles in the social sphere.

Under capitalism, Marx identified the primary contradiction as the conflict between capitalists, who strive to maximise their profits by exploiting workers, and the workers, who seek to secure a larger portion of the profits generated by their labour. Marx argued that every commodity possesses two types of value: 'use-value' and 'exchange-value.' The use-value of a commodity lies in its consumption, whereas exchange-value represents its worth when traded for other products.

The Labour Theory of Value, as proposed by Adam Smith and David Ricardo, contends that human labour power imbues any commodity with value in terms of both use and exchange. This theory significantly influenced Marx, who modified it to explain the concepts of surplus value and surplus labour.

Relevance of Historical Materialism in Contemporary Society

The theory of historical materialism can be used to understand the following:

(i) **Economic Inequality:** The increasing wealth gap between billionaires and the working class in contemporary capitalist societies. According to the Oxford Inequality Report, 2023, the top 10% of the Indian population holds ~77% of the total national wealth.

(ii) **Class Relations:** Class struggle in the form of labour unions bargaining for better wages and working conditions.

(iii) **Capitalism and Globalization**: Multinational corporations outsourcing manufacturing, for instance of smartphones, apparels, etc., to countries with lower labour costs such as Bangladesh, Vietnam, China, etc.

(iv) **Economic Crises**: The 2008 financial crisis, triggered by unregulated lending practices and speculative investments.

(v) **Labour and Exploitation**: Rise of the gig economy, where workers often lack job security and employment benefits.

(vi) **Social Movements**: Environmental activism demanding action against climate change and global warming driven by capitalist practices.

(vii) **Property Relations**: Disputes over land ownership and indigenous land rights, often tied to resource extraction. For instance, debate over the Forest Rights Act in India.

(viii) **Political Change**: The influence of corporate lobbying on government policies and regulations.

(ix) **Social Change and Revolution**: Protests and movements advocating for systemic changes, such as the Occupy Wall Street movement.

(x) **Environmental Issues**: Capitalism's contribution to deforestation, pollution, and resource depletion as seen in the Amazon rainforest.

Critique of Historical Materialism

(i) **Reductionism:** Critics argue that historical materialism reduces complex societal phenomena to economic factors, neglecting the role of culture, ideology, and individual agency. Antonio Gramsci's concept of cultural hegemony challenged historical materialism's neglect of cultural factors.

(ii) **Teleology:** Some see historical materialism as teleological, implying an inevitable march towards communism, which they find overly deterministic. Karl Popper criticized Marxism, including historical materialism, for its unfalsifiability and saw it as a form of historical prophecy rather than scientific theory.

(iii) **Inapplicability to Non-Capitalist Societies:** Some argue that historical materialism primarily applies to capitalist societies and is less relevant to understanding non-capitalist systems.

(iv) **Predictive Limitations:** Other criticize the theory's predictive limitations, as some historical events haven't conformed to Marxist expectations.

(v) **Human Agency:** Some argue that the theory sidelines human agency, implying people are passive products of economic forces.

(vi) **Role of Ideas and Culture:** Weber emphasized the role of ideas, values, and culture in shaping societies. He critiqued the economic determinism of historical materialism.

(vii) **Market as a Source of Order:** Friedrich Hayek criticized central planning and advocated for the market as a source of social order, in contrast to Marxist economic determinism.

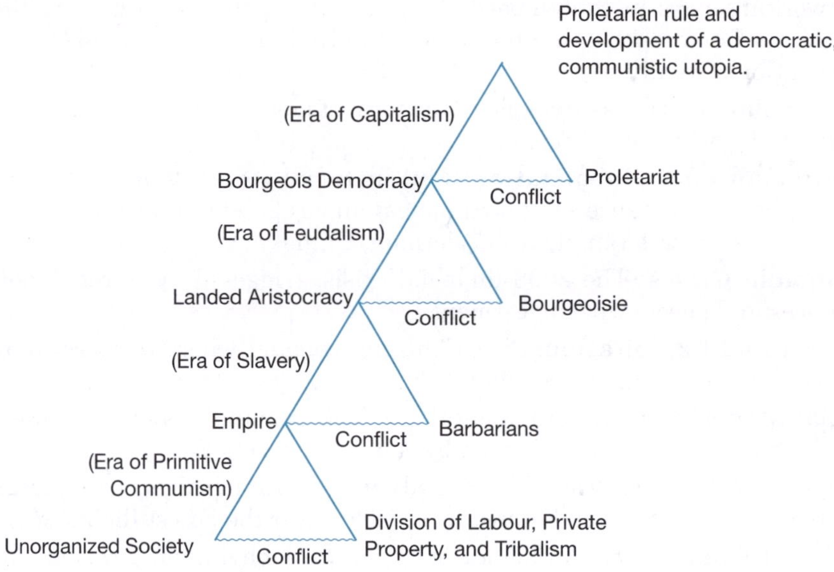

Fig 4.3: Dialectical Materialism: Marx's Theory of History

Marx's Dialectical Method

Marx's dialectical method to study the social phenomena consisted of the following features.

- **Fact and Value:** His method suggests that social values and social facts are intertwined, and hence should not be separated. A dispassionate, value-free sociology is both impossible and undesirable. Marx's emotional involvement in his analysis of capitalist society may have provided him with unique insights. His work shows how passion and commitment to one's ideas are often essential for in-depth research and analysis, as dispassion in science is considered a myth.

- **Reciprocal Relations:** This method does not view social phenomena in a simplistic, one-way, cause-and-effect manner. Instead, it recognizes the simultaneous occurrence and mutual influence of social factors, creating reciprocal relationships and further a complex totality of social life. Here, the focus is on understanding how various social factors interact and affect one another within the broader context of social life.
- **Past, Present and Future:** Dialectical sociologists aim at examining the relationships between contemporary social phenomena, their historical roots, and potential future directions. The importance of historical research is highlighted by this approach as it rightly emphasizes the effects that past circumstances continue to have on the present. Dialectical thinkers believe that the seeds of the future are found within the present social context and hence, find sociology deeply political.
- **No Inevitabilities:** Marx, in his dialectical view, did not imply determinism but rather recognized that the future is shaped by human choices and actions. Described as a 'political possibilist,' he believed in the potential for communism, but he emphasized that it required conscious active choices and struggles by the working class. The old model of the dialectic, involving thesis, antithesis, and synthesis, is considered inadequate for sociology as it oversimplifies complex social phenomena. Dialecticians study real relationships and reject formulating grand abstractions in favour of a more nuanced understanding of social dynamics.
- **Actors and Structures:** Dialectical thinkers have been concerned with understanding the dynamic relationship between individuals and the large-scale social structures they create. According to Marx, these structures can simultaneously enable human fulfilment and also pose a significant threat to humanity. This method also involves considering the continuous interplay between actors, structures and the historical context (past, present, and future circumstances), creating a multifaceted and nuanced perspective on social dynamics.
- **Human Potential:** Marx's analysis of the large-scale contradictions in capitalist society is built upon his micro-level analysis of human potential, labour, and alienation in the system. Marx recognized a general human potential which he called 'species being', denoting the unique human capacities that set humans apart from other species. However, he emphasized that this potential is subject to modification in different historical epochs according to differing circumstances. He believed that human potential is tangled with specific social relations and institutional contexts, and is neither unchanging nor does it function in isolation. It is shaped by the very same dialectical contradictions that also shape society's history.
- **Labour:** Marx defines labour as a 'process' through which humans engage with both nature and society, leading to the transformation of both the external world and their own human nature. Creative and purposeful labour is what sets apart humans from other species, turning their internal thoughts into external reality through their ability to objectify their purpose. Labour encompasses all activities that transform both - nature into objects and human nature itself. Labour propels human history as it satisfies human needs which beget more needs requiring additional forms of productive activity. It is inherently social, and in changing the individual it also changes the society. It defines the social nature of the collective consciousness, highlighting the link between individual and societal transformation.

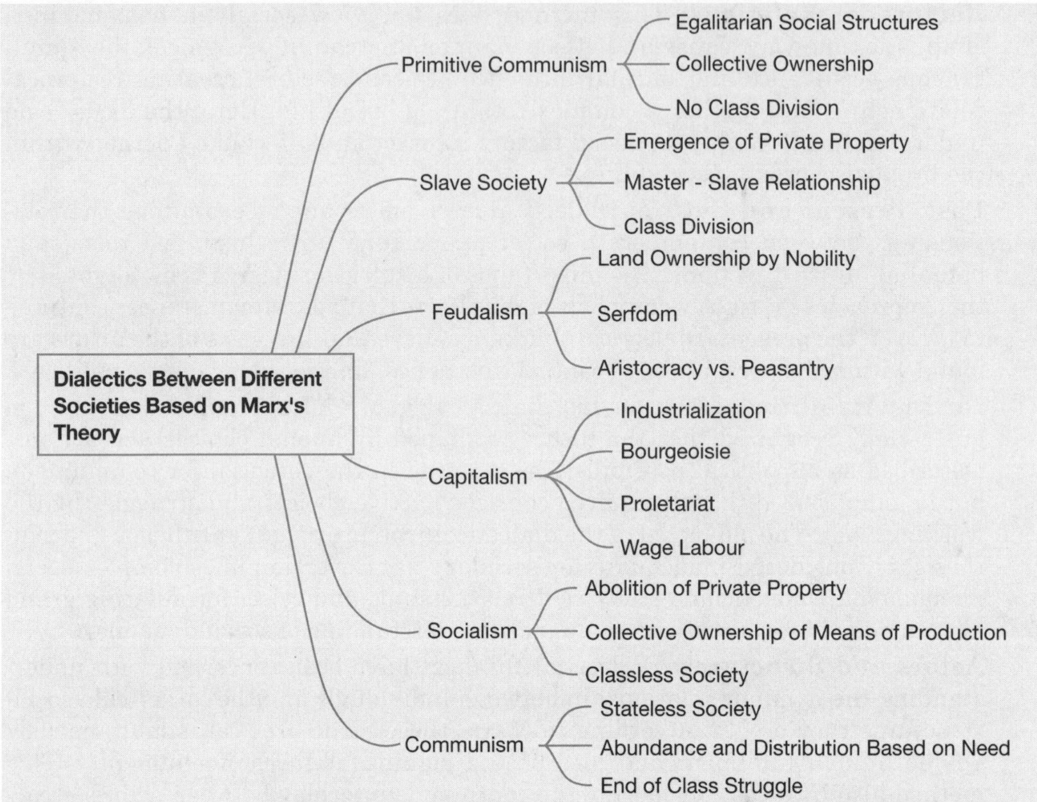

Marx's Theory of Mode of Production and Dialectics

Mode of Production	Key Features	Dialectics
Primitive Communism	Common ownership and communal distribution of resources.	Contradiction arises as societies grow, new forces of production emerge leading to inequality between people and rise of classes.
Slave Society	Class division between slave-owning elites and slaves. Slavery is the dominant mode of labour.	Conflict between masters and slaves, leading to slave uprisings and ultimately the decline of slavery.
Feudalism	The dominant mode of labour is serfdom, with peasants tied to the land. Feudal lords have control over land and resources.	Tension between lords and peasants over land rights, leading to revolts and the eventual rise of capitalism.

Mode of Production	Key Features	Dialectics
Capitalism	Wage labour becomes the primary mode of labour. New forces of production emerge with the rise in wealth, invention of new technologies, banking, investment, etc. Private ownership of the means of production.	Dialectical struggle between the working class and the capitalist class. Contradictions include economic crises, inequality, and exploitation.
Socialism (Transitional Phase)	Public or collective ownership of the means of production. Efforts to reduce class distinctions and inequality.	Transition marked by class struggle as the working class seeks to establish a more equitable society.
Communism	Classless society with common ownership of resources and means of production. Elimination of wage labour and exploitation.	The state 'withers away,' and true classlessness is achieved. Dialectics involve the ongoing construction of a society without class divisions.

Alienation

- **Origin:** In the 19th century, Europe was going through significant industrialization, as a part of which people were leaving traditional trades for factory work. This shift, characterized by harsh working conditions, triggered a huge sense of crisis and revolts in 1848. Germany, in particular, faced challenges which included cheap goods from England and France disrupting its less efficient manufacturing sectors. To address this, Germany introduced capitalism, resulting in unprecedented change, poverty, and alienation. Karl Marx's theory of alienation was a response to understand these economic, social, and political transformations. He sought to create a society where human potential could be fully realized. He identified capitalism as the primary cause of alienation.
- **Core Idea:** According to Marx, alienation refers to the distorted and estranged relationship between individuals and their labour as a result of capitalist processes. In capitalism, labour ceases to be an expression of the worker's purpose or a realization of one's capabilities. Instead of being an end in itself, it becomes a means to earn money for survival, with the capitalist at the helm, dictating the nature and purpose of work. By losing control over one's work, one also loses the capacity to positively transform oneself. With estrangement from work, comes estrangement from the self.

Sociological Basis of Alienation: Class-Based Division of Labour

In Marx's two class system, capitalists employ workers (and thereby own workers' labour time) and capitalists own the means of production (tools and raw materials) as well as the ultimate products. Without any money-generating means of their own, to survive, workers are forced to sell their labour time to capitalists. As a result, people feel free only in the animal functions of eating, drinking and procreating while the distinct 'species being' is subjected to a form of slavery.

The Four Components of Alienation

(i) **Alienation from the Productive Activity:** Workers do not produce objects to satisfy their own needs directly or according to their own ideas and creativity. They work for the capitalists for a subsistence wage in return. Those who work in highly specialized tasks have little sense of their role in the entire production process. For example, workers who tighten the bolts in engines may not know how their labour contributes to the production of the entire car.

(ii) **Alienation from the Product:** The object created by the worker is the capitalist's private property. Even for the satisfaction of their own needs, the workers will have to buy the product like anyone else. For example, a bakery worker will also need to buy the same bread that he makes even if he is suffering from starvation. As a result, people's sense of identity is derived from the things they buy, for example, clothes, cars, homes, etc., rather than from the things they make as part of their profession.

(iii) **Alienation from their Fellow Workers:** Capitalism forces workers to work as strangers even though labour as a productive activity, Marx argues, requires cooperation. The nature of technology induces a great degree of isolation. In modern times, the cubicle has led to increased competition and hostility between the workers. Provoking conflict, pitting one worker against another are all means to extract maximum productivity and please the superiors.

(iv) **Alienation from their own Human Potential:** Workplace, rather than being a source of transformation and fulfilment, is where people feel least human, least themselves as they are reduced to machines. Smiles and greetings become scripted formalities and consciousness is numbed as relations with other humans are increasingly controlled. As a result, people become incapable of expressing their human qualities.

Alienation is an example of contradiction in Marx's dialectical approach of understanding social changes under capitalism. According to Marx, this contradiction can only be resolved through real social change in the form of a revolution.

Contemporary Relevance

- **Global Relevance:** Marx's theory of alienation is seen in contemporary global labour practices. For example, workers in sweatshops in developing countries may experience alienation due to monotonous, repetitive tasks and exploitation by multinational corporations.
- **Indian Example:** In India, many workers in the informal sector, like those in textile factories, experience alienation as they lack job security, benefits, and face harsh working conditions, making them feel disconnected from their labour.

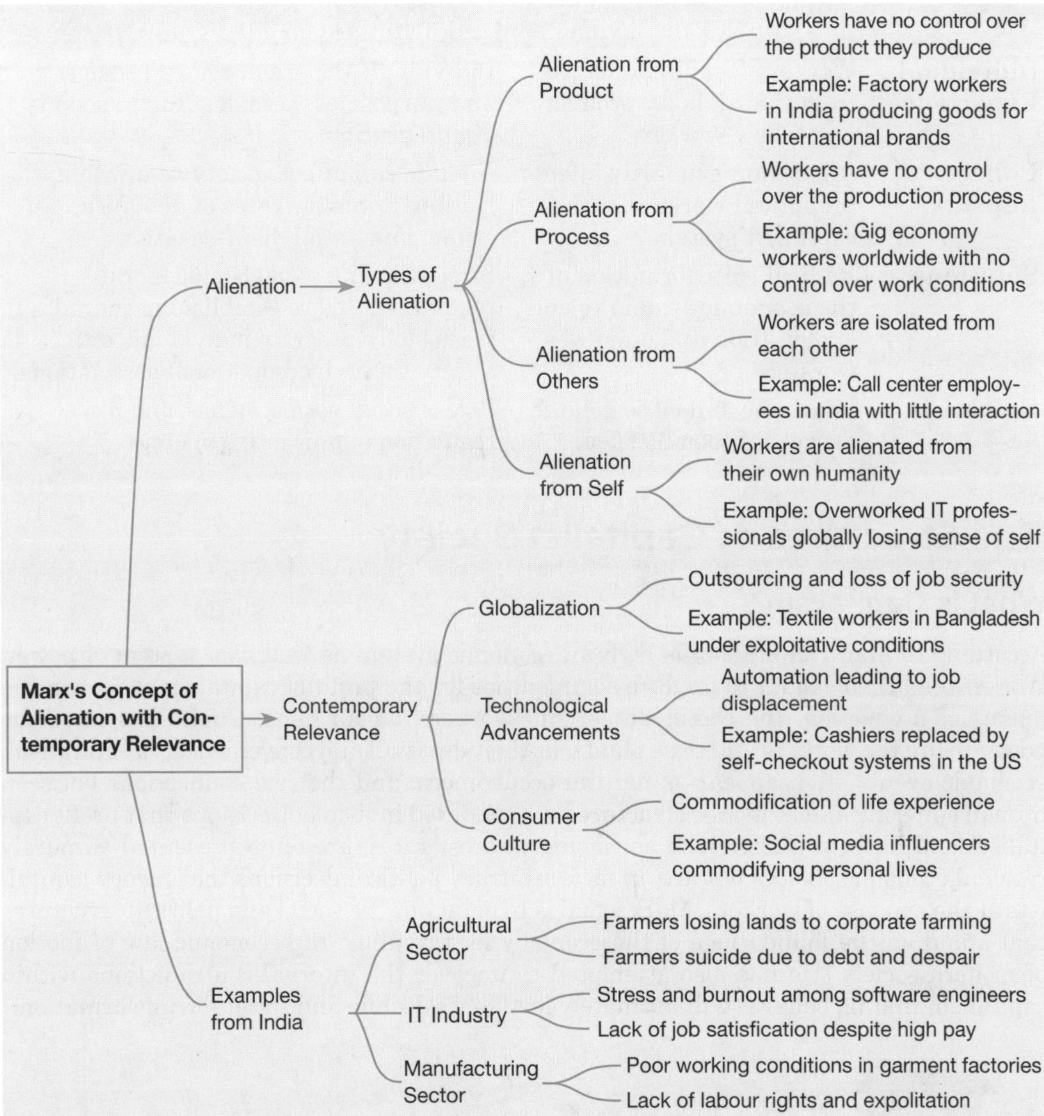

A tabular representation of the differences between Marx's theory of alienation and Durkheim's theory of anomie:

Aspect	Marx's Theory of Alienation	Durkheim's Theory of Anomie
Focus	Economic and labour relations within a capitalist system.	Social norms, values, and moral regulation in modern society.
Primary Concern	Critique of capitalist exploitation and the impact on workers.	Analysis of the breakdown of social integration and its consequences.
Causes of Social Issues	Capitalist economic structure and class struggle	Rapid social change, division of labour, and the weakening of collective conscience.

Aspect	Marx's Theory of Alienation	Durkheim's Theory of Anomie
Individual Experience	Workers feel disconnected from their labour, products, and fellow workers.	Individuals experience normlessness and purposelessness, leading to social disintegration.
Collective Impact	Alienation primarily affects individual workers in the capitalist system.	Anomie can affect society as a whole, leading to higher rates of deviance, crime, and social disintegration.
Solutions	Radical transformation of the economic system to end exploitation and empower workers.	Strengthening social bonds, moral regulation, and re-establishing shared norms to reintegrate individuals into society through occupational associations.
Emphasis	Economic and class-related aspects of social issues.	Role of social norms, values, and moral regulation in preventing anomie.

The Structures of Capitalist Society

What is Capitalism?

According to Marx, capitalism is both an economic system as well as a system of power. Workers sell their labour to produce commodities for the profit of capitalists who own the means of production, the commodities, and workers' labour time. Capitalists have the power to fire the workers and close plants, at their own will and convenience. In capitalism, economic events often appear as natural occurrences, and the real connections between human suffering and economic structures are rendered invisible. Decisions that profit capitalists and harm workers, such as raising interest rates, are often presented as purely rational economic choices but are, in fact, arbitrary political decisions that favour capitalists at the expense of workers. Marx's goal is to point out the social and political structures that stand on the foundations of the economy by revealing 'the economic law of motion of modern society.' He has also attempted to uncover the internal contradictions within capitalism that he believes will ultimately lead to its decline and societal transformation.

FYI

The Economic Law of Motion of Modern Society

- 'The economic law of motion of modern society' is a concept associated with Karl Marx. It refers to the innate principles that oversee how capitalist societies function and change.
- It includes the law of value, where the price of commodities is determined by the labour time needed for their production. Value of products thus is directly proportional to the efforts of workers and yet, workers are not proportionally compensated.

- The law of accumulation showcases the tendency of capital to concentrate in the hands of a few, usually through corporate mergers and acquisitions.
- This concept also incorporates crisis theory, stating that capitalism, due to its contradictions and inequalities, naturally leads to economic crises that have a worse effect on those who were not involved in the decision-making.
- Historical materialism is a related concept, indicating that economic structures have a deterministic influence in shaping other aspects of society, including politics and culture.

Commodities

Marx defines commodities as products of human labour that possess both use-value (utility for satisfying human needs) and exchange-value (the capacity to be traded for other commodities in the market). Under capitalism, commodities are produced not primarily for direct consumption by their producers, but for sale in the market, where their exchange-value often becomes more significant than their use-value in determining production decisions. A commodity has two key characteristics:

(i) **Use Value:** This represents the inherent utility of a commodity for satisfaction of human needs. It is connected to the physical characteristics of the commodity and its ability to fulfil certain specific needs. For example, food has the use value of satiating hunger, and clothing has the use value of providing cover and warmth. It is difficult to compare use value of different commodities, as it is based on their specific qualities and their ability to fulfil certain needs.

(ii) **Exchange Value:** In capitalism, commodities gain exchange value through the process of being exchanged in the market, typically for money. Exchange value makes way for the quantitative comparison of different commodities. For example, a pair of shoes might be exchanged for six loaves of bread or more money, showing that a pair of shoes is not just more expensive but also more valuable, while in reality the two are very different in terms of their usage. Capitalism operates through this transition.

Fetishism of Commodities

Marx's concept of fetishism of commodities refers to the process by which these commodities acquire an independent, almost mystical external reality.

- The market and its commodities are perceived as real and independent phenomena, separate from human needs and decisions.
- Marx sees this as synonymous to the worship of self-made objects as if they were gods. Thus, though they are made by humans, they are treated as naturally-occurring objects, endowed with different exchange value and appeal.

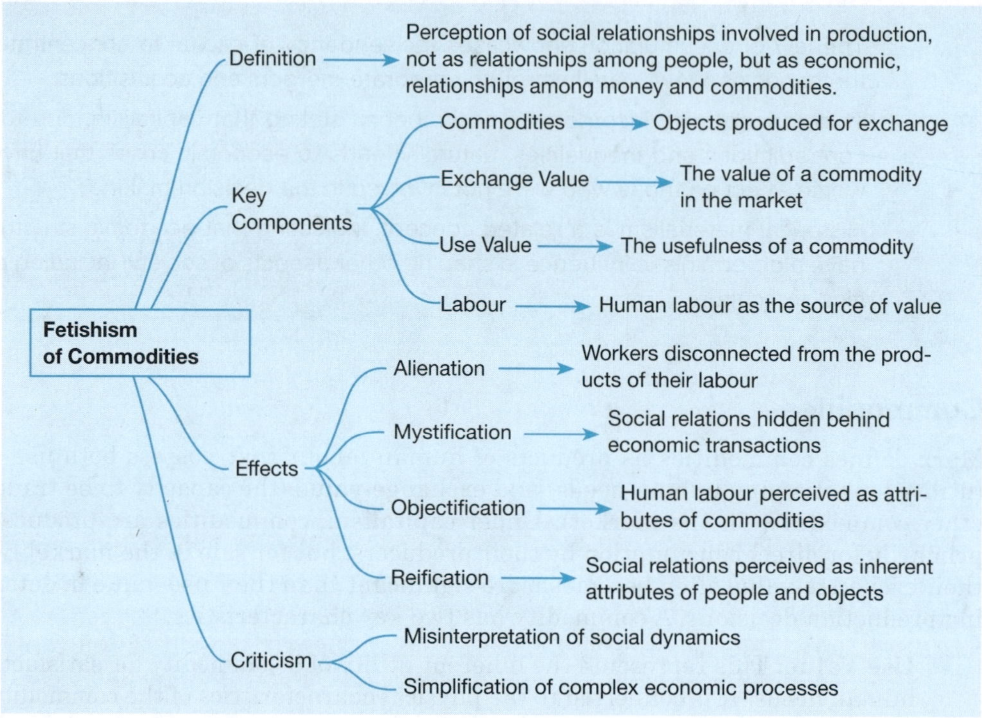

Fetishism and Reification

- Reification is the process of coming to believe that humanly created social forms and structures, including the economy, are natural, universal, and absolute things. Though produced by humans, these structures are perceived to be objective, authoritarian and unchangeable.
- Marx contends that the economy is a form of planned domination, and decisions made within it, such as interest rates and layoffs, are fundamentally political and even biased in nature.
- Reification goes beyond the economy to encompass other social relationships, religious practices, political structures, and systems.
- This is the defining feature of capitalism wherein social relations tend to become independent of the people involved, manifesting as impersonal structural imperatives that dominate individuals.

Capital, Capitalists and the Proletariat

The Proletariat

The proletariat consists of workers who sell their labour. They lack ownership of the means of production. They do not possess tools or factories and may increasingly lose their skills and even jobs as they work alongside machines. They can be both producers and consumers; they rely on wages to buy necessities, making them entirely dependent on their employers.

The Capitalists

- Capitalists are people who own the means of production. Capital symbolises money that is invested to create more money rather than being used to fulfill immediate human needs or desires.
- Marx introduces two types of commodity circulation, i.e., one reflecting capital's circulation (Money → Commodities → Money) and the other one (Commodities → Money → Commodities).
- In such circulation, the primary aim is to generate more money and profits, rather than utilising commodities for their inherent value.

The Capital

- Capital, as per Marx, encompasses more than just a monetary system; it represents a specific social relationship.
- The ability of capital to yield profit arises from a power dynamic embedded in an unequal social relation between the capitalists and the proletariat. Capitalists benefit from this exploitation, living off the profits generated through the labour of the proletariat.

Exploitation

- Marx explained exploitation as a situation, where workers produce more value than they receive in wages or compensation. This exploitation is intrinsic to the economic system itself.
- **'Free' Wage Labour:** Workers in capitalism may see to be 'free labourers' who enter into employment contracts by their own free will. However, Marx argued that workers have little to no choice because wages are necessary for their survival making them dependent on the capitalists. Moreover, there is always a reserve army of unemployed workers further limiting their bargaining power.
- **Surplus Value:** It refers to the profit obtained by capitalists when the workers receive less wages than the value they create. Capitalists reinvest this profit to expand their enterprises, propelling the continuous growth of capitalism.
- **Social Relations and Domination:** Surplus value and capital are not solely economic concepts but also represent social relations and a form of domination. Labour acts as the source of surplus value, and capitalism benefits from this exploitation of labour.
- **Competition and Accumulation:** Capitalism is characterized by constant competition between capitalists racing for more profit. The process of self-enrichment becomes an entrenched social mechanism in which capitalists constantly aim to accumulate and invest more capital. This drive for profit further intensifies the exploitation of the working class, eventually leading to class conflict.

Polarization of Classes by Karl Marx

- Polarization of Classes
  - Bourgeoisie
    - Owners of the means of production
    - Accumulate wealth and power
  - Proletariat
    - Workers who sell their labour
    - Exploited and oppressed by the bourgeoisie
- Capital Accumulation
  - Wealth concentrated in the hands of the bourgeoisie
  - Leads to increased inequality
- Class Struggle
  - Conflict between bourgeoisie and proletariat
  - Driving force of historical change
- Alienation
  - Workers are alienated from the products of their labour
  - Leads to loss of individual freedom
- Exploitation
  - Workers produce more value than they receive in wages
  - Surplus value extracted by the bourgeoisie
- Class Consciousness
  - Proletariat becomes aware of their exploitation
  - Leads to revolutionary potential
- Revolution
  - Overthrow of the bourgeoisie by the proletariat
  - Establishment of a classless society

FYI

Reserve Army of Labour and Feminist Perspective

Marx's Reserve Army of Labour:

- It is a concept in Marx's theory of capitalism and refers to the pool of unemployed or underemployed workers. It serves as a mechanism for capitalists to control labour and wages. Capitalists can hire from this reserve army in times of high demand, suppressing wage growth.
- It reflects job insecurity, poverty, and exploitation of vulnerable workers.

Feminist Perspective on the Reserve Army of Labour:

- Highlights the gendered nature of the reserve army;

- Argues that women are disproportionately part of this reserve due to gender inequalities;
- Women often work in precarious, low-paying jobs, making up a significant portion of the reserve;
- Reflects the intersection of economic and gender inequalities; and
- Feminists advocate for addressing both labour market disparities and gender-based discrimination to reduce the reserve army's size.

Class Conflict/Struggle as a Source and Consequence of Social Change

- **Class as a Concept:** Though not systematically defined, class in Marxism refers to a group of people who share similar situations with respect to their control over the means of production.

  Marx's conception of class is further rooted in its potential for conflict. Individuals are deemed to belong to a class when they participate in a common struggle over surplus value. In capitalism, this struggle arises due to the contradictory interests of capitalists (bourgeoisie) and workers (proletariat).
- **Awareness and Class Formation:** A class truly comes to exist when its members gain awareness of their conflicting relationship with other classes. Without this, it remains a 'class in itself', and when aware, it becomes a 'class for itself.'
- **Primary Classes in Capitalism:** Marx highlighted two primary classes in capitalism: The bourgeoisie (capitalists who own the means of production) and the proletariat (workers who sell their labour for wages). The conflict between these classes stems from the inherent contradiction between labour and capitalism.
- **Proletarianization:** Marx predicted proletarianization, where more individuals would be pushed into the ranks of the proletariat due to increasing mechanization and competition for profits.
- **Competition and Accumulation:** Capitalism is characterized by ruthless competition among capitalists, who are solely driven by the pursuit of profit and capital accumulation. This competition further intensifies the exploitation of the proletariat.
- **Capitalist System's Logic:** Marx did not blame the actors or individual greed, rather attributed the actions of individual capitalists to the systemic logic of capitalism. The system itself pushes capitalists to exploit labour.
- **Capitalists Turn Workers into their own Gravediggers:** The growing hostile proletariat, created by the capitalist system, would ultimately lead the revolution against capitalism.

- **Crisis Predictions:** Marx predicted various personal, economic, social and political crises in modern society due to capitalism. These include alienation, economic fluctuations (booms and depressions), and pointed to the state's role in protecting private property and intervening when economic coercion fails.

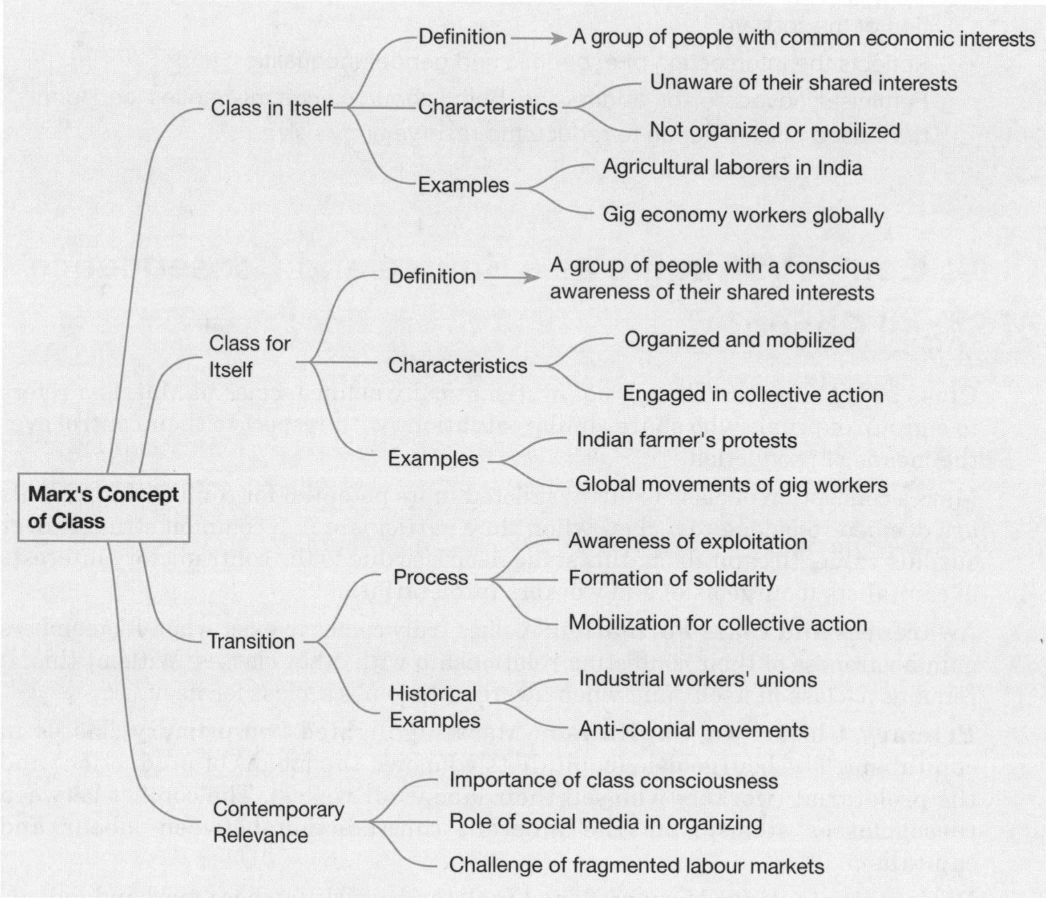

Polarization of Classes

The polarization of classes refers to the increasing division and inequality between different social classes, particularly the wealthy and the poor. This concept is rooted in Marxist theory, which predicts that capitalism will inherently lead to such divisions. Over time, wealth and resources become concentrated in the hands of a few, leading to a widening gap between the rich (bourgeoisie) and the poor (proletariat). This process of polarization exacerbates social tensions and economic inequalities, fostering conditions ripe for social unrest and potential revolutionary change.

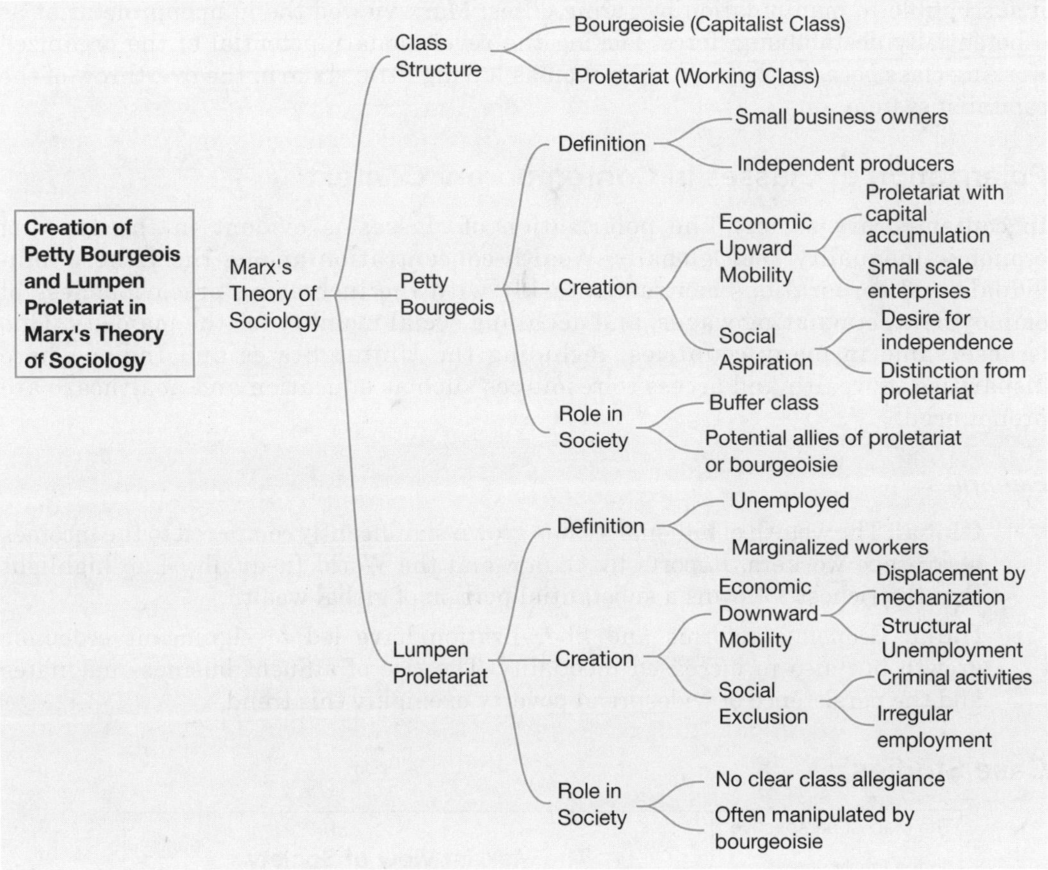

Concept of Petty Bourgeoisie

The term 'petty bourgeoisie' refers to a class situated between the bourgeoisie and the proletariat. This class includes small business owners, shopkeepers, and self-employed individuals who possess some means of production but not enough to be considered part of the bourgeoisie. Karl Marx and Friedrich Engels identified the petty bourgeoisie as having a dual character: they aspire to join the bourgeoisie but face the constant threat of proletarianization, or downward mobility into the working class. This dual character often results in a political ambivalence, as the petty bourgeoisie may support conservative measures to protect their interests or radical measures when they face economic decline.

Concept of Lumpenproletariat

The 'lumpenproletariat' is a term coined by Karl Marx to describe the segment of the proletariat that is chronically unemployed and marginalized. This group includes beggars, criminals, and those disconnected from the formal labour market. The lumpenproletariat is characterized by its lack of class consciousness and organization, making it susceptible to manipulation by ruling elites. Marx viewed the lumpenproletariat as a potentially destabilizing force, lacking the revolutionary potential of the organized working class because they are often seen as having little stake in the overthrow of the capitalist system.

Polarization of Classes in Contemporary Context

In contemporary society, the polarization of classes is evident in the growing economic inequality seen globally. Wealth concentration among the richest individuals and corporations contrasts starkly with the increasing precariousness of employment, stagnating wages, and declining social mobility for the majority. This is observable in many countries, including the United States and India, where disparities in wealth and access to resources such as education and healthcare are pronounced.

Examples

- **Global:** The wealth of billionaires has grown significantly compared to the incomes of average workers. Reports by Oxfam and the World Inequality Lab highlight that the richest 1% owns a substantial portion of global wealth.
- **India:** Economic reforms and liberalization have led to significant economic growth but also to increased inequality. The rise of affluent business magnates and the persistence of widespread poverty exemplify this trend.

Case Studies

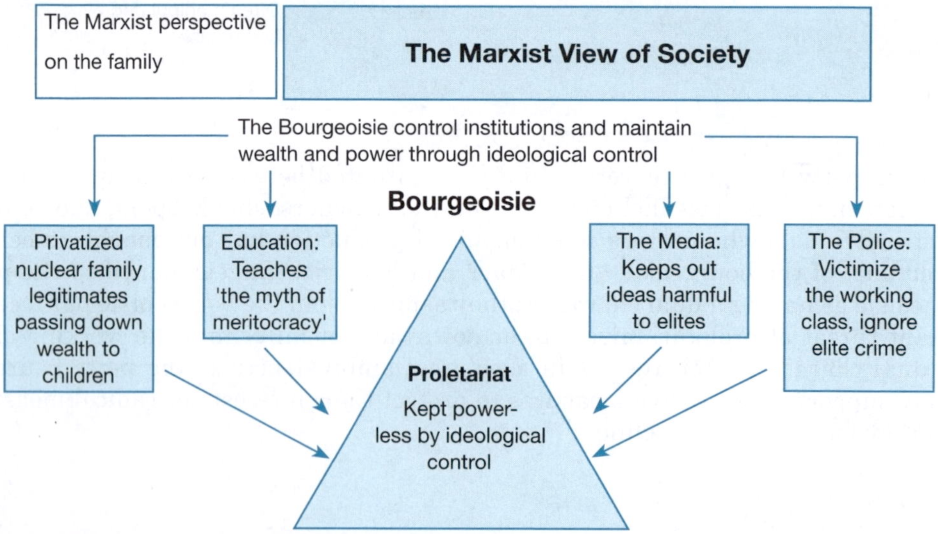

- **The United States:** The decline of manufacturing jobs and the rise of the gig economy have contributed to a shrinking middle class and expanding lower class.

- **India:** The informal sector employs a large proportion of the workforce, contributing to economic instability and social stratification.

Contemporary Relevance

- **Global Relevance:** Class struggle is evident in contemporary global economic disparities. For instance, the Yellow Vest movement in France, a socio-political movement that began in November 2018, was triggered due to economic hardships like rising living costs, low wages, and high unemployment.
- **Indian Example:** India has witnessed numerous labour strikes and protests, often rooted in class struggle. Movements like the farmers' protests against agrarian policies reflect class-based disparities in the country.

Capitalism as a Good Thing

Despite criticising it, Marx did see capitalism as primarily a good thing.

- **Freedom and Liberation:** Marx saw capitalism as a system that held the potential of freedom for the working class. It signified a break from the traditional values and constraints of pre-capitalist societies.
- **Economic Progress:** Marx also saw capitalism as having the potential to remove material deprivation and hunger. It offered the promise of bettering the living standards of the population.
- **Root of Modernity:** Marx believed that capitalism brought forth the defining characteristics of the modern age by challenging the traditional beliefs. Its inherent competition led to constant technological innovation and social change.

While acknowledging capitalism's revolutionary impact, Marx believed that its role in history had come to an end. He called for the overthrow of capitalism and the transition to a new stage, communism.

Conclusion

Karl Marx's contributions to understanding capitalism, historical materialism, alienation, and class struggle have profoundly shaped how we analyse society across various time periods. Marx's critique of exploitation, his call for a classless society, and his focus on the material conditions of human existence continue to inspire social movements, making his work influential and relevant.

MAX WEBER (1864-1920)

A Brief Biographical Sketch

Image Credit: ZUMA Press, Inc./Alamy

- Max Weber was born in Germany, in 1864, in a middle-class family. His father was a bureaucrat who rose to a prominent political position, was devoid of any idealism and used to enjoy earthly pleasures. His mother, completely opposite in nature, was a devout Calvinist concerned with asceticism and other-worldly affairs.
- The contrasting personalities of his parents not only led to marital tensions but also reflected in Weber's choice of subjects to work on afterwards. During his early college days, Weber chose his father's lifestyle to socialise and mingle. However, after military service and upon returning to his parents' home for further education, Weber gradually grew to like his mother's ways.
- Initially, he studied law but later on his interests shifted to economics, history and sociology.
- The increasing differences with his father and the latter's death following a violent argument negatively impacted Weber's psyche and he remained far from academic life for good 6–7 years. His work, The Protestant Ethic (1904–05), marked his return.
- Even though he studied religion extensively, he personally was not as religious but he did adopt the Calvinist rigorous ethics to produce works.
- In 19th–20th century, the social milieu in which Weber lived was characterized by the following:
  (i) Advent of modern industrial capitalist society in the wake of events such the industrial revolution, setting up of factories, mass production, urbanization, etc.
  (ii) The rise of the modern state brought forth bureaucratic structures; and
  (iii) A trend towards rationalization.
- Thus, both the social atmosphere he lived in and his personal experiences guided his work.

Weber's Overall Approach to Methodology in Sociology

Historical-Sociology

Weber was opposed to pure abstract theorising. His own ideas were rooted in empirical, usually historical research. Weber explained the difference between sociology and history as given below:

Sociology	History
It formulates type concepts and generalized uniformities of empirical processes. Example: Instead of, kinship, religion, stratification, etc.	It is oriented towards the causal analysis and explanation of individual events, actions, structures and personalities possessing cultural significance. Example: Instead of, explaining the chain of events leading up to the World Wars.

How did Weber Combine History and Sociology?

He developed concepts so that he could explain the causes of historical phenomena. During his time, an active debate was going on in Germany between the positivists who saw history on the lines of natural science and the subjectivists who denied such a possibility, between the nomothetic thinkers who believed history consisted of general laws and the idiographic thinkers who saw history as reducible to individual events. Weber, through his historical sociology, combined the two approaches. According to him, history is composed of empirical events and there can be no generalization at that level. What sociologists need to do is to separate the empirical world from the conceptual universe. The concepts so developed can be used as 'heuristic' devices to understand the peculiar events. As a result, he conceptualized 'ideal-types'.

Value-Relevance

Weber argued for teachers to control their personal values in the classroom. The students are obliged to listen to the teacher while the audience in any other place can make a choice. According to him, the academician should express facts, not personal values.

Values and Research: Weber believed in differentiating between existential knowledge – what is, and normative knowledge – what ought to be.

1. According to him, fact and value are not to be confused and values are to be restricted to the time before social research begins.
2. They should influence what we choose to study. In this regard, he devised the concept of 'value relevance'.
3. Researchers should always make themselves and the audience aware of their value position.
4. There is no way of scientifically choosing among alternative value positions. Thus, social scientists cannot presume to make choices for the people. Social science research can give factual conclusions but it cannot tell people what they 'ought to do'.

Point to Note

Value-relevance

Weber's concept of 'value relevance' was derived from the work of German historicist, Heinrich Rickert. In historical research, it means that the choice of objects to study would be made on the basis of what is considered important in the particular society in which the researchers live. 'They choose what to study about the past on the basis of the contemporary value system.' Weber, for instance, chose to study bureaucracy as it was a very important part of the society that he lived in.

Critique

- In application, Weber himself did not keep values out of his work and teaching. His views about the Roman state, Judaism, etc., showed that he was very much influenced by popular values of the day and it reflected both in his choice of research subjects and acquisition of knowledge for this purpose.
- Even though he advocated studying subjective motives in an interpretative framework, as discussed ahead, the majority of his works like Bureaucracy (1922), The Protestant Ethic and the Spirit of Capitalism (1904–05) were concerned with large-scale structures.

Thus, there were contradictions in his stated methodology and application in real works.

Social Action

Weber defined sociology as '*a science concerning itself with the interpretive understanding of social action and thereby with a causal explanation of its course and consequences*' (*Economy and Society*, 1921; English translation 1978). In this definition, Weber highlights three core elements: **(a) methodology**, which is *Verstehen*—the interpretive understanding of the subjective meanings individuals attach to their actions; **(b) subject matter**, which is *social action*, that is, action oriented to the behaviour of others; and **(c) outcome**, which is the *causal explanation* of the course and consequences of such action. In this way, sociology seeks not only to grasp meanings but also to explain how actions unfold and what effects they produce.

References:

- Weber, M. (1978). *Economy and Society: An Outline of Interpretive Sociology*. University of California Press.
- Ritzer, G. (2011). *Sociological Theory* (8th ed.). McGraw-Hill.

Weber defined Sociology as 'a science concerning itself with the interpretative understanding of social action and thereby with a causal explanation of its course and consequences.' (Weber, M. (1978). *Economy and Society: An Outline of Interpretive Sociology*. University of California Press.) In this definition, Weber outlines three things: a) methodology, which is interpretative understanding or the concept of Verstehen, b) subject matter or focus of study, which is social action and c) outcome, which is identification of adequate causes and consequences of social phenomena.

Definition

Social action, according to Weber, refers to the action which occurs when individuals attach subjective meaning to their social action and 'takes account of the behaviour of others and is thereby oriented in its course.' For example, an economic action is not simply driven by the necessity of meeting one's needs, but also by conscious orientation to produce and consume for different purposes like social mobility, status maintenance, etc. People often buy what is 'trending', thereby orienting their action to the behaviour of others. Similarly, an action which an individual does not think about is not social action. Screaming out of sudden shock, abruptly falling asleep or praying in private are not social actions.

Point to Note

Essential Features of Social Action

1. Actor attaches meaning to the act, that is, a conscious thought process is involved.
2. It takes into account behaviour or possible reaction of others, that is, it is oriented in its course.

Why did He Want to Study Social Action?

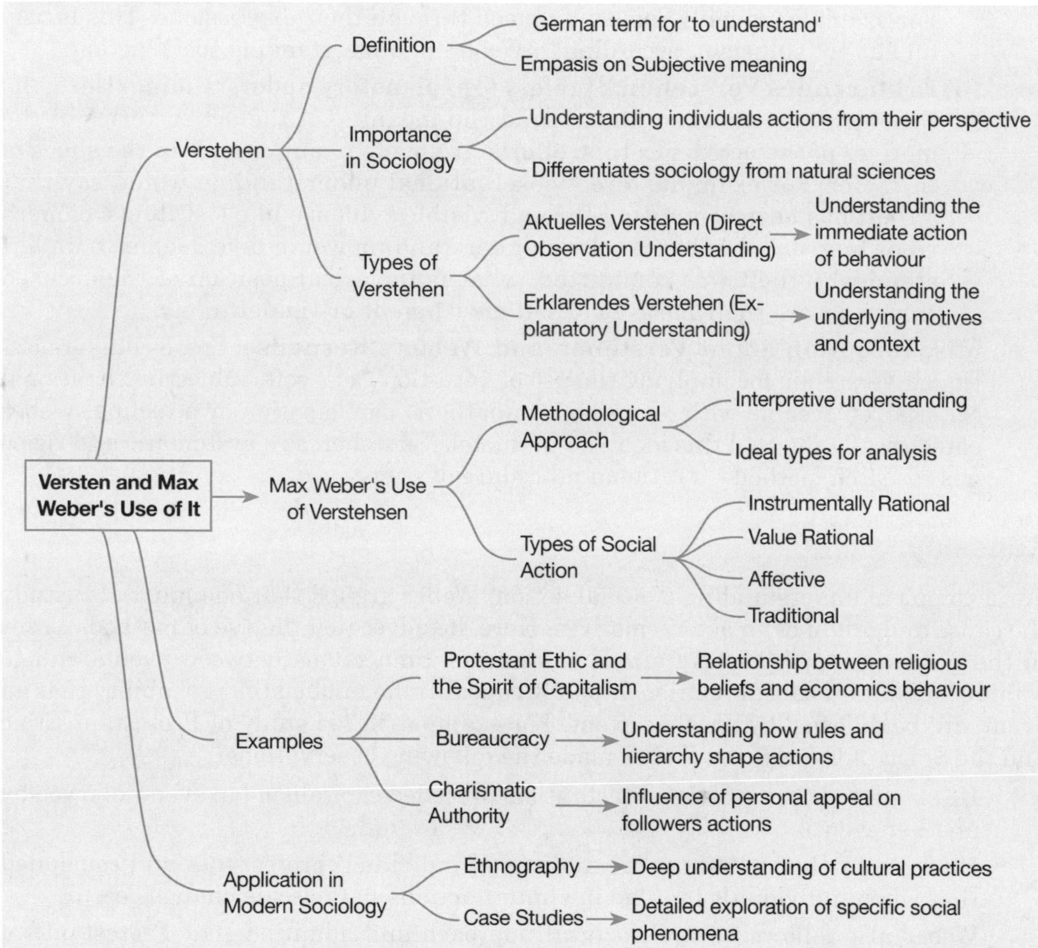

According to Weber, even large scale groupings such as bureaucracies, class, status groups, parties, etc., consisted of individuals who carry out social action. By studying individualist social actions, we can identify the patterns that influence the functioning of collectivities and the structural changes in collectivities that influence individual social action.

How did He Study Social Action?

Weber studied social action in two interrelated ways, first is Verstehen and second is causality or causal explanations.

1. **Verstehen:** It is the German word for 'understanding'. Weber's thoughts on verstehen were derived from a field known as hermeneutics. Hermeneutics was a special approach to understand and interpret the published writings. It sought to understand both the basic structure of the text and the thinking of the author. Weber extended this idea from the understanding of texts to the understanding of social action.

   Weber distinguished two types of understanding:

   (i) **Aktuelles Verstehen:** It is translated as direct observational understanding. For example, gauging someone's mood through their expressions. This is useful but not sufficient, according to Weber, in understanding social action.

   (ii) **Erklarendes Verstehen***:* It refers to explanatory understanding. Here, the sociologist attempts to understand the meaning of the act in terms of the motives of the actor. For this, efforts are made to put oneself in the shoes of the actor. For example, direct observational understanding would say that a theft has been committed through visible evidence like lost items, camera recording, etc., but explanatory understanding would dive deeper to understand why theft was committed, what is the social position of the accused thieves, were their motives of self-enrichment or vendetta, etc.

- **Misconception about Verstehen and Weber's Response:** Some thinkers critiqued Verstehen for implying the use of 'intuition', as a soft, subjective, irrational criteria replaceable with empathy, sympathetic participation or a feeling. Weber categorically rejected this idea and promoted Verstehen as a systematic and rigorous research method—a rational procedure of study.

Causality

For a complete understanding of social action, Weber argued that one must also study the cause and origin of an actor's motives. Here, he advocated the use of methods closer to the positivist approach. He aimed to discover connections between events and to establish resultant causal relationships. By causality, he implied the probability that an event will be followed by another event. For example, in his study of Protestant Ethic and the Spirit of Capitalism, Weber made the following observations:

(i) He suggested that ascetic protestantism preceded capitalism (an event followed by another event).

(ii) He went further to assess the motives of individual protestants and concluded that when individuals indulge in similar actions, large scale changes occur.

Weber also followed a multi-causal approach and admitted that Protestantism is one of the causal factors for the rise of capitalism. Causality can only reflect probability, the 'degree' to which a likely outcome can occur, not certain concrete relationships. For example, if x occurs, it is probable that y will occur. This middle approach between nomothetic and idiographic approaches came to be known as Weber's adequate causality.

Types of Social Action

Weber identified four types of social action based on his ideal-type methodology. This typology provides a framework for understanding the different motivations and reasons behind human behaviour in social contexts.

(i) **Zweckrational (Rational-Purposeful Action):** This type of social action is characterized by individuals acting in a rational, goal-oriented, and calculated manner. They weigh the costs and benefits of different actions and choose the one that best serves their interests or objectives. Zweckrational action is driven by a clear purpose or goal and is often associated with economic and bureaucratic activities. For example, decisions to invest in stock market, real estate, etc., are based on careful assessment of profit and loss, etc.

(ii) **Wertrational (Value-Rational Action):** In this type of social action, individuals act based on deeply held values, beliefs, or ethical principles. Their actions are guided by a commitment to certain values and principles, and they are willing to pursue these values even if it doesn't result in the most efficient or pragmatic outcomes. Value-rational action is often seen in religious or moral contexts. For example, actions of holding protests, conducting campaigns, etc., as part of India's freedom struggle were driven by values related to liberty, equality and fraternity.

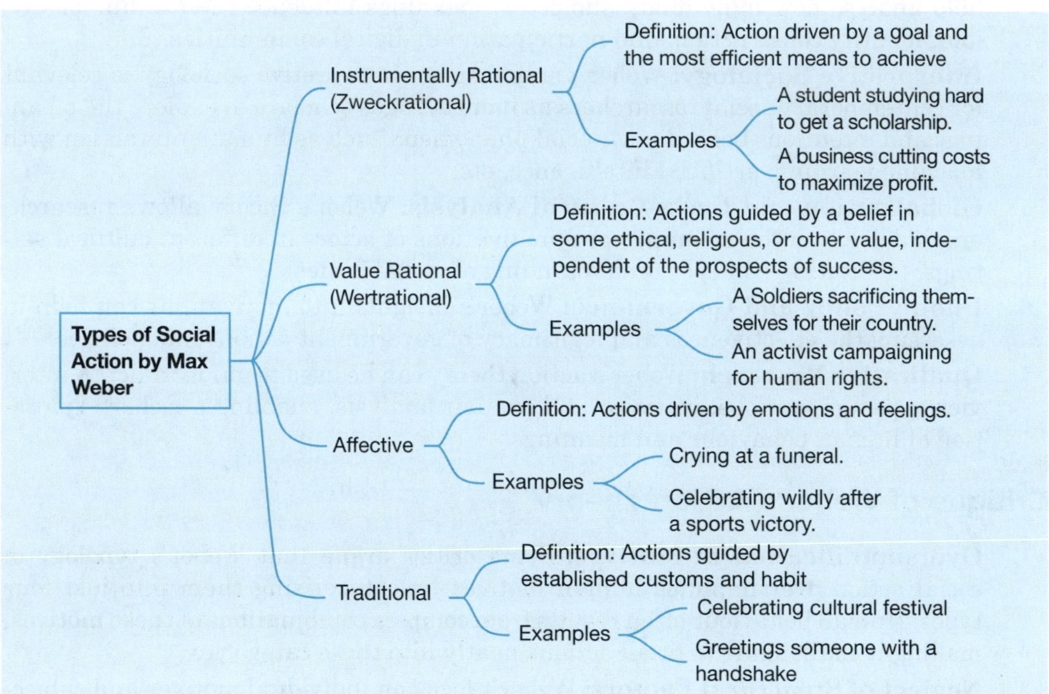

(iii) **Affective (Emotional) Action:** Affective action is driven by an individual's emotional state, such as love, anger, passion, or fear. In this type of action, emotions play a significant role in motivating behaviour. Affective actions may not always be rational or value-based but are instead influenced by the individual's emotional state at a given moment. For example, expression of grief on someone' s death, making a grand gesture to make someone happy – these all are driven by one's underlying emotions of empathy, love, etc.,

(iv) **Traditional Action:** Traditional action refers to behaviour that is based on long-established customs, rituals, or traditions. People engage in traditional action because it is consistent with the practices and norms of their society or culture. Tradition often guides these actions, even if they no longer serve a clear rational or value-based purpose. For example, actions such as performing traditional rituals in wedding ceremonies, fasting during specific days, making specific meals during festivals, etc., all fall in this category.

Relevance of Weber's Action Theory in Present Times

1. **Understanding Complex Motivations:** Weber's theory provides valuable insights into the multifaceted nature of human behaviour, particularly in an increasingly diverse and interconnected world.
2. **Organizational Analysis:** Weber's concepts, such as different types of action help in classifying human behaviour in terms of patterns and therefore at a larger, organizational level.
3. **Social Media and Digital Culture:** In the digital age, Weber's approach can help analyse how individuals' subjective meanings influence their online behaviour, identity construction, and participation in digital communities.
4. **Interpretive Sociology:** Weber's emphasis on interpretive sociology is relevant for contemporary social researchers as it encourages scholars to explore the meanings and intentions behind new social phenomena such as human interaction with machine learning, artificial intelligence, etc.
5. **Globalization and Cross-Cultural Analysis:** Weber's theory allows researchers to delve into the meanings and motivations of actors in different cultural settings, facilitating a deeper understanding of global issues.
6. **Public Policy and Governance:** Weber's insights into motivations can help in assessing the effectiveness and legitimacy of government actions and policies.
7. **Qualitative Research:** Weber's action theory can be used to guide in-depth interviews, participant observations, and content analysis, enabling a richer exploration of human behaviour and meanings.

Critique of Weber's Action Theory

1. **Oversimplification of Motives:** Some critics argue that Weber's typology of social action oversimplifies human motives by categorising them into just four types. Human behaviour often results from complex combinations of these motives, making it challenging to fit all actions neatly into these categories.
2. **Neglect of Structural Factors:** Weber's focus on individual motives and subjective meanings is criticized for downplaying the role of structural factors, such as societal norms, institutions, and power relations.
3. **Limited Predictive Power:** Weber's emphasis on understanding individual meanings and motives may provide valuable insights into historical and cultural contexts but doesn't offer strong predictive capabilities for future social behaviour.

4. **Eurocentric Bias:** Some critics claim that Weber's work is Eurocentric, primarily focused on Western societies, which might not be applicable to non-Western or diverse cultural contexts. This bias limits the theory's universality and applicability.
5 **Incomplete Macro-level Analysis:** Weber's theory is criticized for its predominant focus on micro-level social actions and meanings.
6. **Difficulty in Empirical Application:** Critics suggest that Weber's typology can be challenging to apply empirically, as it relies heavily on understanding subjective meanings. This subjectivity makes it difficult to quantify and measure in a precise and replicable manner.

Ideal Types

Point to Note

'An ideal type is formed by the one-sided accentuation of one or more points of view and by the synthesis of a great many diffuse, discrete, more or less present and occasionally absent concrete individual phenomena, which are arranged according to those one-sidedly emphasized viewpoints into a unified analytical construct. In its conceptual purity, this mental construct... cannot be found empirically anywhere in reality.'

Max Weber

In simple words, an ideal type is a concept constructed by a social scientist according to his/her interests and theoretical orientation to capture the essential features of some social phenomenon.

Features

(i) It is a heuristic device, a 'measuring rod', a 'yardstick' that can be used to empirically study some specific aspect of the social world.

(ii) It can be used for comparison of the concerned social phenomenon with the empirical reality to bring out divergences and similarities. For example, an ideal type of bureaucracy can be compared with the observations of real-world bureaucracy.

(iii) The ideal type is exaggerated and so the reality diverges from it. The social scientist can then study 'causes' for such divergences, for example, why is the bureaucracy in a certain society not as efficient as the ideal type bureaucracy. The reasons could include logical fallacies, strategic errors, misinformation, emotions, etc.

(iv) The term 'ideal' does not refer to a utopian version of reality, rather to the fact that the form described in the concept is rarely to be ever found in the real world.

(v) It need not be positive or correct, it can just as well be negative or morally repugnant.

(vi) They should make sense in themselves, their components should be compatible with each other and they should aid us in making sense of the real world.

(vii) They can be used to describe both static and dynamic entities – example, both bureaucracy and bureaucratization.

(viii) It cannot be a timeless concept and needs to evolve as the society too is constantly changing.

How is an Ideal Type to be Constructed?

An ideal type can be constructed in the following two ways:

(i) They are to be derived inductively from the real world of 'social history', not deductively from abstract theory.

(ii) They should neither be too general nor too specific, for example, in case of religion, the ideal type should not be of an individual's religious experience but of intermediate phenomena such as Calvinism, Methodism, baptism, etc.

Max Weber's concept of 'Ideal Types' is a pivotal methodological tool in sociology. It represents a mental construct that delineates the essential features of social phenomena, aiding in the analysis and understanding of complex social realities. While it is true that ideal types do not correspond directly to reality, their value lies in their heuristic function.

An ideal type is a hypothetical construct that encapsulates the purest forms of social phenomena. It serves as a benchmark against which actual social realities can be compared and analysed.

Ideal types are abstractions and simplifications, deliberately accentuating certain elements while omitting others. They are not empirical descriptions but conceptual tools designed to provide clarity and facilitate comparative analysis. For instance, Weber's famous ideal types of bureaucracy, capitalism, and authority (traditional, charismatic, and rational-legal) are not found in their pure form in reality but represent a synthesis of their most salient characteristics.

Utility of Ideal Types and its Criticism and Limitations

Heuristic Value: Ideal types enable sociologists to dissect and understand social phenomena by providing a clear framework. For example, Weber's ideal type of bureaucracy highlights characteristics such as hierarchical structure, rule-bound administration, and merit-based advancement. While no real-world organization perfectly fits this model, it helps in evaluating and understanding deviations and similarities in actual bureaucratic structures.

Analytical Utility: By using ideal types, researchers can isolate the core components of complex social phenomena, facilitating the study of cause and effect relationships. For instance, Weber's analysis of the Protestant Ethic and the Spirit of Capitalism used ideal types to demonstrate how religious values could influence economic behaviour.

Criticisms and Limitations: Critics argue that ideal types, being abstract, may oversimplify the complexities of social life. They may also introduce biases by emphasizing certain features over others, potentially distorting reality. However, Weber acknowledged these limitations, asserting that ideal types are not final truths but provisional tools subject to refinement.

Max Weber's ideal types, though mental constructs that do not correspond directly to reality, are invaluable in the field of sociology. They provide a structured means to analyse and understand the intricate and multifaceted nature of social phenomena. Despite their abstract nature, ideal types facilitate comparative analysis, offering insights into the underlying structures and dynamics of social life. Their heuristic and analytical utility outweighs the criticisms, affirming their continued relevance in sociological research.

According to Hekman, Weber offered a variety of ideal types, some of which included:

1. **Historical Ideal Types:** Phenomenon found in a particular historical epoch (for example, a slave market, the estate system, sati tradition, etc.).
2. **General Sociological Ideal Type:** They cut across historical periods and societies, for example, bureaucracy.
3. **Action Ideal Type:** Pure ideal types of action based on certain motivations, for example – affectual action guided by emotions (as discussed above).
4. **Structural Ideal Type:** Forms acquired by causes and consequences of social action, for example – traditional domination, charismatic authority, patriarchy, etc.

Contemporary Relevance of Weber's Ideal Type Theory

Ideal types can be constructed and used to analyse contemporary phenomena in different ways:

1. **Analysing Political Leadership:** For instance, political scientists use the 'charismatic leader' ideal type to evaluate leaders like Nelson Mandela or Mahatma Gandhi who were able to influence numerous followers.
2. **Understanding Market Structures:** The 'perfect competition' ideal type helps economists assess real-world markets, such as e-commerce platforms, to identify how closely they align with this competitive model.
3. **Evaluating Bureaucratic Organizations:** Researchers and management consultants use the 'iron cage of bureaucracy' ideal type to evaluate how closely modern institutions, like government agencies or multinational corporations, resemble Weber's conceptualization of bureaucracy.
4. **Analysing Social Media Behaviour:** The 'digital influencer' ideal type is used to understand individuals who gain popularity and influence on platforms like Instagram or YouTube, shedding light on their typical characteristics and actions.

Contemporary Examples

1. **Bureaucracy:** In India, the Indian Administrative Service (IAS) represents a bureaucratic system, though it deviates from Weber's ideal type due to issues like political interference and corruption.
2. **Charismatic Authority:** The leadership of Mahatma Gandhi during India's independence movement serves as an example of charismatic authority, where his personal qualities and vision inspired a mass movement.
3. **Traditional Authority:** The British monarchy exemplifies traditional authority, where legitimacy is derived from historical customs and hereditary succession.

4. **Rational-legal Authority:** The functioning of the United Nations is an example of rational-legal authority, where procedures and rules guide operations and decision-making processes.
5. **The Protestant Ethic:** The work culture in Silicon Valley, emphasizing innovation, hard work, and economic success, reflects the ideals of the Protestant ethic.
6. **Capitalism:** The economic systems of the United States and Germany are illustrative of capitalism, although with variations in regulatory and welfare policies.
7. **Feudalism:** Medieval Europe's social structure during the Middle Ages is a classic example of feudalism, characterized by the relationship between lords and vassals.
8. **Patriarchy:** In many traditional societies, including some rural areas in India, patriarchal structures remain prominent, influencing social norms and family dynamics.
9. **Democracy:** Modern democracies such as those in Scandinavian countries, which emphasise equality, social welfare, and civic participation, approximate the ideal type of democracy.
10. **Caste System:** Though officially abolished, remnants of the caste system in India still influence social interactions and opportunities, albeit with significant deviations from the historical ideal type.

Critique

Being a conceptual tool, Weber's ideal type is subject to criticism for its inability to be used as an effective tool in all situations

1. **Lack of Precision:** Critics argue that Weber's ideal types can lack precision and operational clarity. For example, when applying the ideal type of 'charismatic authority' to contemporary leaders, it may be challenging to objectively determine and compare the presence and extent of charisma in real-world figures.
2. **Limited Generalisability:** Weber's ideal types are often criticized for their limited generalisability. For instance, the 'rational-legal authority' ideal type, while suitable for analysing bureaucratic systems, may not fully capture the complexities of governance in non-Western contexts.
3. **Subjectivity:** Critics contend that the creation of ideal types relies heavily on the sociologist's subjectivity. The development of an 'entrepreneurial personality' ideal type may vary among researchers, potentially leading to biased or inconsistent analyses.
4. **Historical and Cultural Bias:** Weber's ideal types may carry historical and cultural biases, as they were developed in a specific time and context. For example, applying the 'Protestant work ethic' ideal type to non-Western societies may not account for alternative cultural influences on economic behaviour.
5. **Limited Prescriptive Value:** Some critics argue that Weber's ideal types lack prescriptive value. While they offer valuable tools for analysis, they do not inherently provide solutions or policy recommendations. For example, the 'iron cage of bureaucracy' ideal type highlights issues but does not offer guidance on improving bureaucratic systems.

Weber's Ideas on Social Stratification, Authority, Bureaucracy

Stratification, in sociology, refers to the hierarchical arrangement of individuals or groups within a society based on various factors like wealth, power, social status, or access to resources. Weber saw stratification as multidimensional. The possibility of people ranking high on one or two of the social stratification indicators and low on the other provided a more sophisticated analysis.

As opposed to Marx who identified only class-based division, Weber identified three factors of class, status and power.

Class

- Weber saw class as a group of people whose shared situation is a possible basis for action by the group.
- Class situation occurs in the presence of the following three conditions:
  (i) A number of people have in common a causal component of their life chances.
  (ii) This component is represented exclusively by economic interests in the possession of goods and opportunities for income.
  (iii) This component is represented under conditions of commodity or labour markets.
- Thus, a class is not a community but a group of people in the same economic situation.

Status

- Status groups are amorphous communities.
- Status situation is defined by every component, which is determined by a specific, positive or negative, social estimation of honour. Status relates to a style of life. It refers to consumption of goods while class refers to economic production.
- Class and status are not necessarily linked to one another.

Party

- It is related to the political dimension.
- To Weber, 'parties are structures struggling for domination.'
- They may exist both in the state and outside in social clubs.
- They may or may not represent class and status but they are always oriented towards the attainment of power.

Point to Note

Max Weber used the term 'life chances' to refer to the opportunities and possibilities that individuals or groups have in life, particularly in the context of social stratification and inequality. Life chances are influenced by various factors, including social class, economic resources, education, social status, and access to opportunities.

Aspect	Class	Status	Power
Definition	Economic position based on ownership, control of resources, and market position.	Social prestige, honour, or respect within a society or social group.	Ability to influence or control others, make decisions, and impose one's will.
Primary Concern	Distribution of wealth, income, and economic opportunities.	Social hierarchy, cultural capital, and social recognition.	Exercising authority and control over others or social institutions.
Basis of Formation	Economic factors such as income, wealth, occupation, and socioeconomic class.	Social factors like reputation, family background, education, and occupation.	Can be political, economic, or social, depending on the context.
Mobility	Possible through changes in economic circumstances, education, and career opportunities.	Difficult to change without radical shifts in social status.	Subject to fluctuations based on political developments and alliances.

Weber has been contrasted with Marx on ideas related to social stratification. A brief comparison between the two is represented below:

Aspect	Weber's Theory of Social Stratification	Marx's Theory of Social Stratification
Key Theorist	Max Weber	Karl Marx
Basic Unit of Analysis	Multiple factors, including class, status, and power.	Primarily economic class (relations to means of production).
Central Focus	Interplay of multiple factors such as economic class, social status, and power in shaping social hierarchy.	Economic class and its relation to the means of production; conflict between capitalists and workers.
Class Structure	More complex and nuanced, encompassing multiple classes and strata based on economic, social, and political power.	Simpler, primarily divided into bourgeoisie (capitalists) and proletariat (working class).
Causes of Inequality	Multiple factors, including economic, social, and political forces.	Primarily rooted in economic exploitation by capitalists.
Class Mobility	Possible through changes in economic circumstances, education, and career opportunities.	Struggles and revolution were seen as essential for proletariat to achieve a classless society.
View on Capitalism	Acknowledges the role of capitalism and its economic aspects but considers non-economic factors as well.	Sees capitalism as the root of class-based exploitation and inequality.

Aspect	Weber's Theory of Social Stratification	Marx's Theory of Social Stratification
Role of Conflict	Recognizes that conflicts can arise from various sources including class, status, and power.	Central focus on class struggle between the bourgeoisie and proletariat.
Concept of Exploitation	Acknowledges economic exploitation but also highlights non-economic aspects, such as social privilege.	Primarily concerned with economic exploitation of workers by capitalists.

Authority and Its Types

Weber defined domination as the probability that certain commands will be obeyed by a group of people. He defined authority as a legitimate form of domination. His study of authority is linked to his concern for a solution to the social problems as a result of capitalism.

Although he was critical of modern capitalism, he did not advocate revolution. He had faith in political leaders, not masses or bureaucrats. He placed the nation above all else, even above democracy and parliamentarism. He preferred democracy not because he believed in the masses but because it offered maximum dynamism and the best milieu to generate political leaders. He developed a comprehensive framework to analyse legitimate forms of domination, which he termed 'Herrschaft.' Weber's analysis revolves around three distinct types of legitimate domination, each grounded in different sources of legitimacy.

As a result, he identified different types of authority that existed to manage large social structures and take care of the masses. According to him, the three legitimate bases of authority included: rational, traditional and charismatic.

Rational-legal Authority

This is the type of authority which achieves rational coordination of the work of numerous individuals in the pursuit of large-scale goals and tasks. It is formed through legal mechanisms, either by law or official decree, and hence enjoys legitimacy irrespective of the personal identity of its occupants.

Traditional Authority

It is based on the claim by the leaders and a belief on part of the followers. There is virtue in the sanctity of age-old powers and rules. The leader is a personal master and the administrative staff consists of personal retainers driven by a sense of loyalty.

Weber used ideal-types to differentiate between two early forms of traditional authority:

1. Gerontocracy – Rule by elders
2. Primary patriarchalism – Leaders who inherit their positions
3. A more modern type has been identified as the third type – Patrimonialism (traditional domination with an administration and military force. For example, in countries like North Korea)

4. A more modern form is feudalism

Weber argued that structures of traditional authority constituted an impediment to the rise of rational economic structures in particular, capitalism.

Charismatic Authority

Weber's sense of charisma was not dependent on the qualities of the leader but on the group of disciples and the way they define the charismatic leader. The process through which the concerned person is set apart and seen as someone possessing supernatural or superhuman powers is what distinguishes the person.

Weber saw charisma as a revolutionary force which brought about changes in the minds of the actors, causing a subjective or internal reorientation.

Another revolutionary force that Weber was much more concerned with was formal rationality. While charisma was seen as bringing about an internal change, formal rationality was seen as bringing about an external change – first changing the structures of society then changing the thoughts and actions of individual actors.

Charismatic Organizations and Routinization of Charisma

Weber saw staff of a charismatic leader to be inferior to the staff in a bureaucratic organization. With the death of the charismatic leader, Weber argues, though the staff tries hard to retain the old charisma but it is difficult to routinize it and still keep it as charisma. Routinization involves transformation of some kind. Either the authority transforms into traditional authority or into a rational-legal authority or in some form of institutionalized charism, such as the Catholic church.

Weber went so far as to predict the death of charisma in the modern world and called for rationality as the most irresistible and important revolutionary force in the modern world.

Authority in the Real World

Weber recognized that in the real world, any specific authority involved a combination of all three forms of authority.

FYI

Weber's Rationalization Theory

It has been difficult to extract a clear definition of rationalization from Weber's work. He defined rationality with regard to types of action—means-ends and value rationality. In essence, it denotes the application of rational, rule-based, and calculable methods to various aspects of human life. According to Donald Levine, Weber was interested in 'objectified rationality', which refers to the organization of society, particularly in cases of bureaucratic institutions, in accordance with a rational and efficient system of rules, procedures, and structures.

Stephen Kalberg identified four basic types of objectified rationality in Weber's work:

(a) **Practical Rationality:** This kind of rationality exists when people accept the given realities and according to their own pragmatic and egoistic interests, calculate the most expedient ways of dealing with the difficulties that life presents. It restricts itself to the everyday routine and opposes anything that transcends it. It is trans-civilizational and trans-historical.

(b) **Theoretical Rationality:** It involves cognitive efforts to master reality through abstract concepts rather than through action. It involves processes such as logical deduction, induction, attribution of causality and the like. This type of rationality is related to sorcerers, priests, philosophers, judges and scientists. It requires the actor to transcend daily reality to understand the world as a meaningful cosmos.

(c) **Substantive Rationality:** It involves direct action through a choice of means to ends within the context of a system of values. One value system is no more substantively rational than another. It is also trans-civilizational and transhistorical. For example, actions dictated by religious values of Hinduism, Islam, Christianity, etc., terrorists guide their actions by certain values and so do the soldiers protecting a country.

(d) **Formal Rationality:** Kalberg considers this the most important. It involves means-ends calculation and occurs with reference to 'universally applied rules, laws and regulations'. It reflects the rationality of industrial capitalism and bureaucratic administration. According to Weber, bureaucratic rationalization first changes the material and social orders and through them the people, by changing the conditions of adaptation and the opportunities of adaptation, through a rational determination of means and ends. As opposed to other forms of rationality, formal rationality only arose in the West with the coming of industrialization.

(e) **Calculability:** Emphasis on quantification, measurement, and numeric assessment.

(f) **Efficiency:** Focus on the most effective means to achieve predetermined ends.

(g) **Predictability:** Processes and outcomes become uniform, standardized, and consistent across contexts.

(h) **Control through Non-human Technologies:** Bureaucracies and capitalist enterprises increasingly replace or regulate human labour with technical systems and procedures.

(i) **Reduction of Uncertainty:** Organizational rules and technologies minimise unpredictability, especially by constraining human behaviour.

(j) **Irrationality of Rationality:** A paradox: rational systems can generate alienation, disenchantment, and a loss of meaning (e.g., the 'iron cage' of rationality).

According to Weber, substantive rationality is the only type of rationality with an emphasis on a methodical way of life. It can further give rise to formal rationality with its emphasis on rules, efficiency and calculability. For example, Calvinism.

Rationalization

Weber's concept of rationalization describes the process by which traditional methods and values are replaced by those based on efficiency, calculability, and predictability.

Contemporary Examples

In India

- **Education System:** The Indian education sector is increasingly adopting standardized testing and performance metrics, reflecting rationalization.
- **Healthcare:** Technological advancements and data-driven decision-making are transforming healthcare delivery, making it more efficient and standardized.

In the World

- **Business Practices:** Global companies employ data analytics and AI to optimize operations, exemplifying rationalization.
- **Public Services:** E-governance initiatives in countries like Estonia streamline administrative processes, enhancing efficiency and accessibility.

Bureaucracy

As the purest example of rational-legal authority and of zweckrational action, Weber described bureaucracy as an ideal-type. According to Weber, a bureaucracy is capable of achieving the highest degree of efficiency and is the most rational known means of exercising authority. It is superior to any other form in terms of precision, stability and stringency of discipline. It is applicable to all kinds of administrative tasks and makes possible a high degree of calculability of results. As per him, bureaucracies will be the dominant institutions of capitalist industrial society due to their 'technical superiority' in comparison to other forms of authority.

Point to Note

Features of Weber's Ideal-typical Bureaucracy

1. It consists of a continuous organization of functions/offices bound by rules.
2. Each office has its own sphere of competence, obligations, authority and means/resources to do the job.
3. The offices are arranged in a hierarchy.
4. Each office has technical qualifications which job holders must be trained in.
5. The available means of production are not owned by the position-holders but are there simply so that they can do the job properly.
6. The position is not appropriated by the holder, but belongs to the organization.
7. Administrative acts, decisions and rules are recorded in writing.

Though Weber saw bureaucratization as an inevitable and a necessary phenomenon, he also expressed concerns regarding bureaucracy, such as:

(i) Red tapism can make dealing with bureaucracy trying and difficult.
(ii) The rationalization (process of seeking definite goals through carefully calculated means and removal of all obstacles) that dominates all aspects of bureaucracy can threaten individual liberty.
(iii) Rational calculation reduces every worker to a cog in the bureaucratic machine.
(iv) Bureaucracies are escape-proof and hardest to destroy.
(v) Individual bureaucrats cannot simply leave the bureaucracy.
(vi) In times of crisis, bureaucratic leaders may prove to be ineffective as they are trained to follow orders rather than to take initiatives.
(vii) In capitalist society, top bureaucrats may be influenced by the interests of the capitalists.

FYI

Iron Cage of Bureaucracy

Max Weber's concept of the 'iron cage of bureaucracy' reflects the paradoxical consequences of rationalization and bureaucracy in modern society. According to Weber, the process of rationalization, which includes the implementation of bureaucratic systems for efficiency and control, can lead to unintended and often undesirable outcomes. The 'iron cage' metaphor describes a situation in which individuals and organizations become trapped by the very systems they create. Bureaucracies, while designed to increase predictability and efficiency, can become so rule-bound and rigid that they stifle creativity, individuality, and meaningful human interactions. As a result, people may find themselves constrained by the bureaucratic structures they intended to serve them

Critique: According to Ray and Reed, while iron cage could be one possibility, another possibility is that of people becoming increasingly concerned with the end goals of the organizations. If people emphasise democratic control and engage in deeper discussions, the legitimacy of ends will depend on wider consensus. Thus, the iron cage model is not inevitable and it can definitely be challenged.

The Iron Cage

Weber warned about the potential negative consequences of rationalization, referring to the 'iron cage' of bureaucracy, where individuals become trapped in systems of efficiency and control.

Contemporary Examples

In India

- **Bureaucratic Red Tape:** The complexity and rigidity of bureaucratic procedures often hinder innovation and responsiveness in government institutions.
- **Corporate Work Culture:** The increasing pressure on employees in large corporations to meet targets and adhere to strict protocols reflects Weber's iron cage.

In the World

- **Surveillance Society:** The widespread use of surveillance technology and data monitoring in countries like China exemplifies the iron cage, where individual freedoms are curtailed for the sake of control.
- **Work-life Balance:** In highly industrialized nations, the emphasis on productivity and efficiency often leads to burnout and a compromised work-life balance.

FYI

Weber's Solution to Bureaucratic Problem and how Bureaucracy is Better in Capitalism than in Socialism

According to Weber, in capitalism because the owners are not bureaucrats, they will be able to control the latter. In socialism, on the other hand, even the top level leaders will be bureaucrats. Thus, individual freedom and creative liberty will still be better preserved under capitalism where bureaucratization can be reasonably controlled. His solution to excessive bureaucratic control lay in regulation by professional and publicly-elected politicians who held the top posts. Besides them, those standing outside the bureaucratic system such as the scientists, intellectuals and even capitalists can control the stifling rationalization of bureaucracy to some degree.

However, Weber admitted that even politicians could ultimately come to depend on the bureaucrats due to the latter's expertise and knowledge control. Hence, he suggested that bureaucrats should be made accountable to a strong parliamentary government through parliamentary committees who could regularly cross-examine the top civil servants.

Ethic of Responsibility vs Ethic of Conviction: Ethic of responsibility involves a commitment to values while rationally making choices to meet certain ends whereas ethic of conviction involves a commitment to an unconditional demand or higher value without any rationality.

Comparison of Weber's Iron Cage and Marx's Alienation

Aspect	Weber's Iron Cage	Marx's Alienation
Core Concept	Rationalization and bureaucratization	Exploitation under capitalist production
Focus of Analysis	Society's emphasis on efficiency and control	Economic and social conditions of labour
Nature of Confinement	Bureaucratic structures and formal rules	Alienation from the product, process, self, and others
Scope of Impact	Affects individuals across various societal institutions	Primarily concerns the working class and labour relations
Key Characteristics	Rationalization Bureaucracy Loss of freedom and individuality	Alienation from the product Alienation from the process Alienation from self Alienation from others
Examples	Corporate environment with rigid protocols Standardized testing in education	Factory work with repetitive tasks Gig economy with lack of job security
Dehumanization	Yes, through impersonal efficiency and control	Yes, through detachment from labour and exploitation
Loss of Autonomy	Yes, due to bureaucratic constraints	Yes, due to exploitative labour practices
Systemic Constraints	Bureaucratic and rationalized systems	Capitalist economic structures

Similarities

- **Dehumanization:** Both concepts describe processes that dehumanize individuals, reducing them to mere components within larger systems.
- **Loss of Autonomy:** Individuals in both scenarios experience a loss of control over their work and lives.
- **Systemic Constraints:** Both theories highlight the constraints imposed by broader economic and social structures, limiting personal freedom and creativity.

Differences

- **Focus of Analysis:** Weber's iron cage centers on the rationalization and bureaucratization of society, while Marx's alienation focuses on the capitalist mode of production and its impact on labour.

- **Nature of Confinement:** The iron cage is characterized by bureaucratic efficiency and rationalization, whereas alienation stems from exploitation and economic disenfranchisement.
- **Scope of Impact:** The iron cage affects individuals across various societal institutions (e.g., government, education, corporations), while alienation primarily concerns the working class and their relation to production.

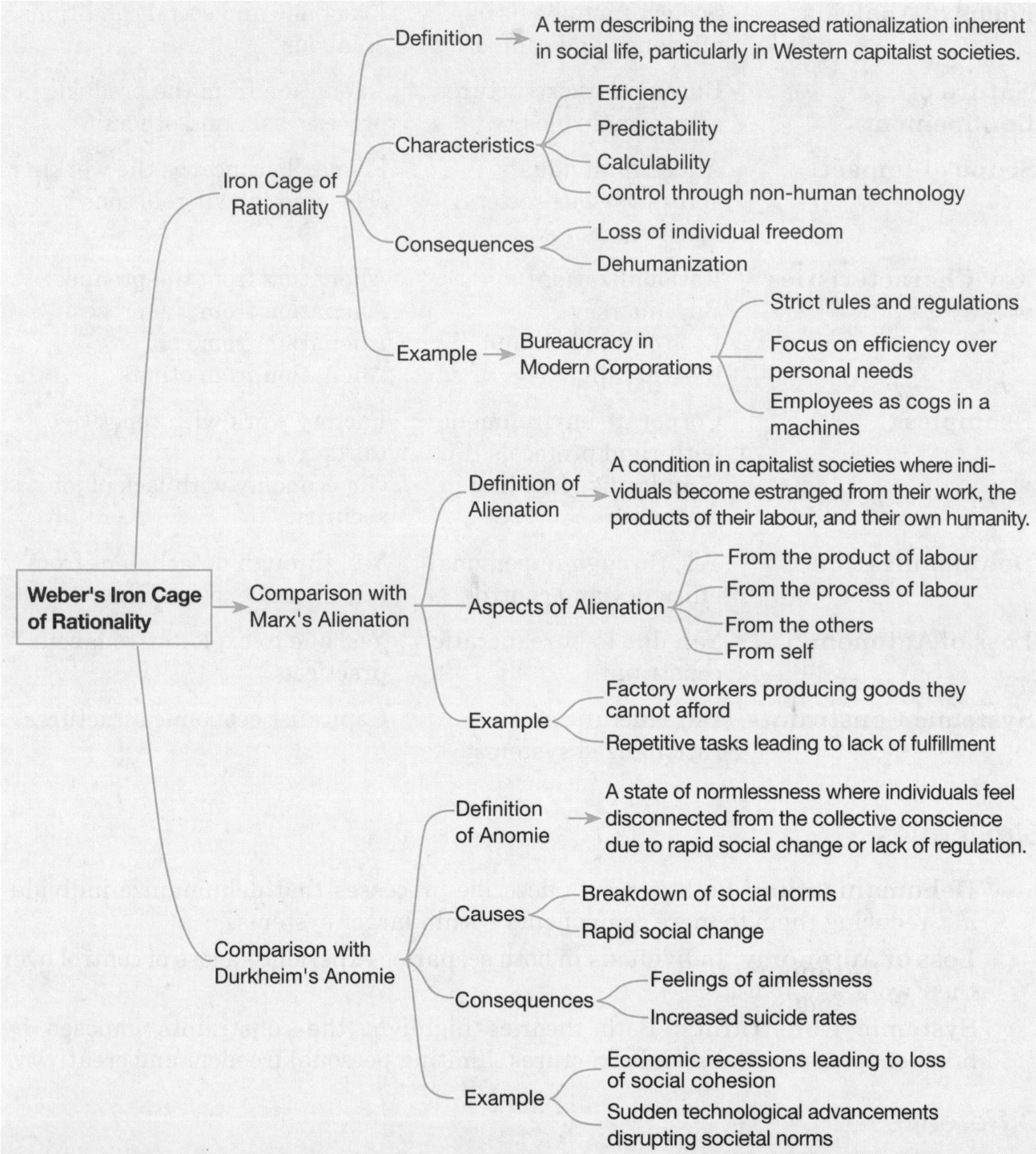

Weber's ideas on bureaucracy continue to hold relevance in the present times. However, they have also been subject to critique with the changing needs and functional diversions.

S. No.	Contemporary relevance	Critique
1.	Bureaucratic structures are still prevalent in government agencies and large private corporations.	Weber's one-size-fits-all approach fails to achieve the objectives in different settings. Many global businesses now emphasise flat organizational structures and agile approaches, deviating from the traditional bureaucratic hierarchy. Post modernists like Stewart Clegg argue that post-Fordist firms are quite flexible and that bureaucracy is not a dominant form of organization.
2.	Weber's idea of hiring based on merit and qualifications is critical in contemporary civil services and private sector organizations which continue to hold assessments and interviews for the same.	Despite merit-based recruitment, bureaucracies are accused of being highly inefficient, slow and corrupt.The rational pursuit of goals does not take into account the values necessary for better functioning, like honesty, punctuality, etc.
3.	Bureaucratic principles like impartiality and standardized procedures continue to stay relevant in legal systems.	Bureaucracies are accused of exploiting the common masses and giving preferential treatment to those in power.

Protestant Ethic and the Spirit of Capitalism

Weber traced the impact of ascetic Protestantism, particularly Calvinism (a major branch of Protestantism), on the rise of the spirit of capitalism. He sought to understand how this religious ethic influenced the development of capitalism in the Western context.

Weber linked the Protestant ethic to a system of ideas known as the 'spirit of capitalism.' This is different from being linked to 'structures' of capitalism. According to Weber, religious philosophy of Protestantism provided an ideological basis to its practitioners to adopt certain beliefs and behaviours which proved conducive to the development of capitalism in the West. It is to be noted that Weber gave importance to both cultural and material realms in his historical analysis as opposed to Marx who held materialism responsible for both social and ideological changes. As per Weber, ideas like those in the realm of religion can develop independently of material changes and then go on to influence the latter in different ways. Marx, however, saw economic production as the basis of origin for everything else.

What is the Spirit of Capitalism?

The spirit of capitalism refers to a moral and ethical system that emphasises economic success. It transformed the pursuit of profit from an individual act motivated by greed into a moral crusade, which was critical for the expansion of profit-seeking and the emergence of capitalism. It involves various interrelated ideas, including the rational pursuit of profit, avoidance of life's pleasures, diligence in business, frugality, punctuality, fairness, and the duty to increase wealth ceaselessly. It is more than individual ambition; it becomes an ethical imperative.

How did Protestantism Lead to the Development of such a Spirit?

How did Protestantism Lead to the Development of the Capitalist Spirit?

- **Doctrine of Predestination (Calvinism):** Calvinism, a branch of Protestantism, taught that individuals were predestined either for salvation or damnation. Since this destiny was unknowable, it created deep anxiety and uncertainty among believers.
- **Economic Success as a Sign of Salvation:** To manage this uncertainty, Calvinists came to interpret material success and diligence in worldly callings as possible signs of being among the elect. Prosperity and disciplined labour thus became moralized as evidence of divine favour.
- **Ethics to Attain Economic Success:** Calvinism required self-control, systematic life, and an integrated round of activities, especially in business. This contrasted with the mediaeval Christian ideal, where isolated acts of atonement were practised to secure salvation. Calvinism emphasized a life of good works integrated into a unified system.
- **High Value for the Ethical Middle-Class Person:** Calvinism highly valued the sober, middle-class, self-made individual. It instilled a strong work ethic and appreciation for systematic, continuous work in a worldly calling.
- **Moral Economic Pursuit Led to Large Scale Profit-driven Capitalist Structures:** Calvinism's religious valuation of systematic work and its emphasis on asceticism played a significant role in the expansion of the spirit of capitalism. It transformed economic pursuit into a moral duty. Capitalists felt that their pursuit of economic interests was not solely driven by self-interest but was an ethical obligation. This allowed ruthless economic pursuits and silenced critics who couldn't reduce these actions to self-interest.
- **Exploitation of Workforce:** Calvinism provided capitalists with a workforce that was diligent and industrious, dedicated to their work as a divine purpose willed by God. This allowed capitalists to raise the level of exploitation.
- **Legitimation of Inequality:** Calvinism legitimized social stratification, reassuring capitalists that the unequal distribution of wealth was a divine dispensation.

Capitalism Beyond Religion: Weber's Reflections

Weber did not view capitalism without reservations. He criticized it for producing specialists without spirit and sensualists without heart, leading to a shallow civilization. He also saw capitalism in modern society as no longer dependent on, although certainly influenced by, religion.

While he was primarily focused on the impact of Calvinism on capitalism, he acknowledged that religion and economic conditions have a reciprocal influence on each other. However, he chose not to address this aspect in 'The Protestant Ethic.'

Why Capitalism didn't Arise Elsewhere?

Weber claimed that capitalism in its pure form only emerged in the West. He found similar favourable material conditions in other societies but found other structural barriers to the rise of capitalism in different contexts, such as China and India.

The Case of China

According to Weber, although China possessed many of the material prerequisites for capitalism, including acquisitiveness, industry, capacity for work, powerful guilds, and a growing population, capitalism did not develop in China due to the following reasons:

Structural Barriers

(i) **Community Structure:** Chinese communities were structured around rigid kinship bonds called sibs. These sibs were conservative and self-contained, promoting small landholdings and a household-based economy, inhibiting market development.

(ii) **State Structure:** The Chinese state was patrimonial, governed by tradition, and lacked a rational and calculable system of administration. It had few formal laws for commerce, and officials often bought offices for profit, affecting efficiency.

(iii) **Language:** The Chinese language, according to Weber, was not conducive to systematic thought or logical thinking, which impeded the development of a rational capitalist system.

Religious Barriers

(i) **Confucianism:** Confucianism emphasized literary education and the importance of literary knowledge for social status and office. It created a class of literati who valued cultural and literary pursuits over practical economic activities. The literati cared little for the economy and saw actual administration as beneath them.

(ii) **Confucian Worldview:** The Confucian worldview was centred around acceptance of the existing social order and conventions. Material success and wealth were not considered signs of salvation, leading to the acceptance of the status quo.

(iii) **Attitude Towards Work:** Confucians were discouraged from thrift and viewed active engagement in profitable enterprises as morally dubious. Wealth was prized, but the appropriate goal was a good position rather than high profits.

(iv) **Taoism:** Taoism was a mystical Chinese religion where the supreme good was seen as a state of mind, not a result of real-world conduct. Taoists did not engage in rational action to change the external world, and Taoism's 'Do not introduce innovations' principle discouraged major changes.

(v) **Lack of Tension and Conflict:** Both Confucianism and Taoism lacked the tension and conflict that would motivate individuals to engage in innovative actions to change the world or develop capitalism.

The Case of India

With regard to India, Weber identified the following as hindrance to the development of capitalism:

(i) **Caste System:** Weber identified structural barriers in India, with a particular focus on the caste system which posed overwhelming barriers to social mobility and limited opportunities for individuals to engage in activities conducive to capitalism.

(ii) **The Upper-caste Ethos:** The Brahmins, the highest caste, adhered to an ethos that encouraged them to avoid vulgar occupations and emphasized elegance in manners and conduct. Their religious worldview promoted indifference to worldly affairs. The highly literary education of the Brahmins was different from practical, technical knowledge needed for capitalism.

(iii) **Hindu Religion:** Hinduism, the dominant religion in India, featured the central idea of reincarnation. Hindus believed that one's caste in the current life was determined by their past life's behaviour. Strict adherence to caste rituals earned merit for the next life. Hinduism did not emphasise innovation in this world, as the focus was on spiritual pursuits and attaining a higher caste in the next life. Activity in the economic sphere was not seen as a means of achieving salvation.

In India

- **Entrepreneurial Spirit:** The rise of start-ups in cities like Bengaluru can be partially attributed to a work ethic similar to Weber's Protestant Ethic, driven by innovation and a desire for economic success.
- **Cultural Shifts:** Economic liberalization in the 1990s led to a shift in values towards individual success and entrepreneurship, aligning with Weberian ideals.

In the World

- **Asian Economies:** Countries like South Korea and Japan exhibit work ethics that resonate with Weber's thesis, contributing to rapid industrialization and economic success.
- **Western Capitalism:** The United States continues to embody the Protestant Ethic, with a cultural emphasis on hard work, individualism, and economic success.

Critique

Weber's theory of religion has been critiqued in relation to the following points:

1. **Overemphasis on Protestant Ethics:** Critics argue that while religious values may have played a role, other factors such as economic, political, and cultural developments were also significant contributors to capitalism.
2. **Misinterpretation of Non-western Religions:** Weber's theory has been criticized for neglecting the influence of non-Western religions in shaping economic and social behaviours. For instance, caste system, some argue, was originally meant to stabilise social order through functional division of labour. The system was originally meant to be open and traditions like the *Jajmani* system ensured rural communities meet their needs through cooperation and interdependence.
3. **Simplification:** Critics argue that the impact of religious beliefs on economic actions is complex and varies across different historical and cultural contexts, making it difficult to generalise Weber's findings.

4. **Causality versus Correlation:** Weber's theory highlights the correlation between Protestant values and capitalist development but does not establish a clear causal link. Critics argue that correlation does not necessarily imply causation, and other factors may have contributed to the observed economic changes.
5. **Historical Accuracy:** Some historians have questioned the historical accuracy of Weber's claims about the Protestant Reformation's direct influence on capitalism. They point out that his evidence is often anecdotal and not based on comprehensive historical data.
6. **Ethnocentrism:** Weber's Eurocentric perspective has been criticized for assuming that the Western experience is the standard by which all societies should be measured. This ethnocentrism can limit the applicability of his theory to non-Western contexts.
7. **Ignoring the Role of Structural Factors:** Some critics argue that Weber's theory places too much emphasis on individual beliefs and values while neglecting the influence of structural factors, such as economic policies, institutions, and class dynamics, in shaping capitalist systems.

Comparison of Durkheim, Marx and Weber with Regard to their views on Religion

Aspect	Emile Durkheim	Karl Marx	Max Weber
Perspective on religion	**Functionalism:** Religion serves a fundamental role in creating and maintaining social order and cohesion. It provides moral values and reinforces collective conscience. Religion is a sacred version of society itself.	**Conflict Theory:** Religion is considered an 'opiate of the masses' that reinforces class-based inequalities. Religion diverts attention away from economic injustices and legitimises the power of the ruling class.	**Interpretive Sociology:** Examined religion as a social system of ethical ideas and explored its impact on emergence and sustenance of modern capitalist society in different countries.
Forms that religion takes	Durkheim distinguishes between the sacred (associated with the divine, religious rituals) and the profane (everyday, non-religious).	Marx sees religion as part of the superstructure of society, reflecting economic and class relations. Religion is part of the ideological apparatus that supports the economic base. It is a reflection of economic realities.	Weber explored the concept of the 'disenchantment' of the world, where traditional religious beliefs are replaced by rationality and secularization.

Aspect	Emile Durkheim	Karl Marx	Max Weber
Role in society	Durkheim views religion as a central institution that integrates and regulates society, providing a moral framework and shared values. It has a community of believers with shared rituals and an institution, such as the Church.	Marx sees religion as a tool used by the ruling class to maintain social order and control the working class. He refers to it as the 'opium of the masses' that helps the proletariat cope with their suffering.	Weber views religion as an integral part of social life that provides meaning, values, and norms. It also influences economic and political aspects of society and can in turn be influenced by them.
Relationship to capitalism	Durkheim's work on religion is not explicitly tied to capitalism.	Marx is critical of religion in the context of capitalism, arguing it can serve as a form of false consciousness.	Weber explored the protestant ethic and its influence on the development of capitalism. He highlighted ideas which either favoured or hindered the emergence of capitalism in different societies, like that of the West, China, India, etc.

Religion and Social Change

Weber's studies on the interplay between religion and social change, particularly in his work 'The Sociology of Religion,' provide insights into how religious beliefs can influence economic behaviour and societal transformation.

In India

- **Hindu Reform Movements:** Organizations like the *Arya Samaj* and the *Brahmo Samaj* have historically sought to reform Hindu practices, promoting social change.
- **Religious Pluralism:** The coexistence and interaction of diverse religions in India influence social policies and communal harmony, driving social change.

In the World

- **Islamic Banking:** In many Muslim-majority countries, Islamic banking principles align with Weber's ideas, showing how religious beliefs shape economic practices.
- **Liberation Theology:** In Latin America, liberation theology merges Christian teachings with social activism, advocating for the poor and driving political change.

Conclusion

Max Weber made significant contributions to sociology by introducing the concept of social action, the ideal type method, and his influential work on bureaucracy and the Protestant Ethic. His emphasis on understanding the subjective meaning behind human behaviour has shaped modern sociological inquiry. However, his theories have faced criticism, including his Eurocentric perspective, overemphasis on individual values, and historical accuracy. Despite critiques, Weber's work continues to inform sociological thought, offering valuable insights into the complexities of social phenomena, capitalism, and the rationalization of modern societies.

TALCOTT PARSONS (1902–1979)

A Brief Biographical Sketch

Talcott Parsons, born in 1902 into a religious and intellectual family, became one of the most influential figures in twentieth-century sociology. In 1927 he joined Harvard University as an instructor, where he remained until his death in 1979. Parsons played a central role in introducing European thinkers such as Max Weber to American audiences and achieved early prominence with the publication of *The Structure of Social Action* in 1937. By 1951, with the release of *The Social System*, he had established himself as the leading voice of American sociology. However, during the late 1960s his work came under sustained criticism from emerging radical and conflict theorists who saw him as politically conservative and overly committed to the status quo. Yet the 1980s witnessed a resurgence of interest in his writings, which went on to influence not only mainstream sociologists but also critical theorists such as Jürgen Habermas. Parsons is most closely associated with functionalism, and like Durkheim, he sought to answer the enduring question of how social order is possible. He argued that social life is fundamentally characterized by mutual advantage and peaceful cooperation rather than mutual hostility and destruction.

Parsons' Theory of Social Action

Talcott Parsons, a key figure in functionalist sociology, developed a comprehensive theory of social action that Emphasises the structured and purposeful behaviour of individuals within a social system. His theory of social action is framed within the context of the larger social system, emphasizing the interconnectedness of various elements of society.

Key Components

1. **Actor:** The individual who performs the action.
2. **Means:** The resources or methods used to achieve the ends.

3. **Ends:** The goals or objectives of the action.
4. **Norms and Values:** The cultural standards and expectations that guide actions.
5. **Situational Conditions:** The external environment that influences the action.

Parsons argues that social action is always goal-oriented and occurs within a normative framework. Actions are guided by norms and values that are internalized by individuals through the process of socialization.

Examples from India

- **Reservation Policies:** The implementation of reservation policies in educational institutions and government jobs is a significant example of social action aimed at achieving social equality. These policies are based on the normative values of social justice and aim to uplift marginalized communities.
- **Marriage Practices:** Traditional norms still influence marriage practices, where caste considerations play a crucial role in the selection of spouses. Despite modern legal frameworks, these actions reflect deep-seated cultural norms and values.
- **Campaign for Sanitation:** Swachh Bharat Abhiyan, launched by the Indian government, this campaign aims to improve sanitation across the country. It reflects a goal-oriented social action aimed at public health and hygiene, guided by the normative value of cleanliness. Citizens' participation in building toilets and cleaning public spaces exemplifies collective action influenced by both governmental norms and public awareness campaigns.

Examples from the World

- **Fight for Equality:** The Civil Rights Movement of the 1960s, led by figures like Martin Luther King Jr., is a prime example of social action aimed at achieving racial equality. The movement was guided by the normative values of justice and equality and employed means such as non-violent protests and legal challenges to dismantle segregation.
- **Global Climate Strikes:** The global climate strikes, inspired by activists like Greta Thunberg, represent a contemporary example of social action. These strikes aim to address climate change and are driven by the normative value of environmental sustainability. The means include public demonstrations and advocacy for policy changes to mitigate environmental degradation.

Contemporary Examples

- **Against Sexual Harassment:** The #MeToo movement, which gained global momentum in the late 2010s, is a powerful example of social action against sexual harassment and assault. The movement is guided by the normative values of gender equality and justice. Through social media campaigns and public testimonies, it aims to change societal attitudes and policies regarding sexual misconduct.

- **Promoting Digital Literacy:** In India, the Digital India initiative aims to transform the country into a digitally empowered society. This initiative reflects social action geared towards technological advancement and digital inclusion, with the normative value of progress and modernization. Activities under this initiative include promoting digital literacy, improving internet connectivity, and providing e-governance services.

Parsons' theory of social action provides a framework for understanding how individual actions are shaped by broader social structures and cultural norms. By examining examples from India and around the world, we can see how goal-oriented actions are influenced by situational conditions and guided by normative values. These actions, in turn, contribute to the maintenance and transformation of social systems.

Aspect	Max Weber	Talcott Parsons	Contemporary Examples
Basic Definition	Weber defines social action as an action that takes into account the actions and reactions of other individuals and is thereby oriented in its course.	Parsons views social action as a process in the actor-situation system, which includes the actor's motivational orientation, the actor's goal, and the situational conditions.	When a person uses social media to promote a cause, considering how their actions will influence others and be influenced by them.
Types of Action	1. Instrumentally rational (goal-oriented) 2. Value-rational (determined by a belief in the inherent value of an action) 3. Affectual (guided by emotions) 4. Traditional (habitual)	1. Instrumental (goal-oriented) 2. Expressive (emotional expression) 3. Moral (value orientation) 4. Cognitive (belief orientation)	1. Campaigning for environmental protection (Instrumental) 2. Participating in a public vigil for a tragedy (Expressive) 3. Protesting for civil rights (Moral) 4. Attending a religious service (Cognitive)
Motivation	Focusses on subjective meaning that the individual attaches to their actions.	Emphasises the role of norms and values in guiding action, assuming a system of normative regulation that shapes the 'ends' and 'means' of action.	Using hashtags on social media for awareness campaigns like #MeToo where the subjective experience (Weber) and the societal norms (Parsons) both play crucial roles.

Aspect	Max Weber	Talcott Parsons	Contemporary Examples
Social System	Less emphasis on systemic structures in his concept of social action, which is more focused on individual behaviour.	Strong focus on the system of social actions where the actions are seen as part of a broader societal system, heavily influenced by social norms and institutional roles.	Corporate Social Responsibility (CSR) initiatives where businesses engage in social good driven by both individual leadership decisions and broader societal expectations (Parsons).
Influence on Theory	Weber's theory has greatly influenced the development of symbolic interactionism and ethnomethodology.	Parsons' work laid the groundwork for structural functionalism, influencing subsequent theories about the system's needs and functional prerequisites.	Modern movements like Black Lives Matter can be analysed through Weber's lens of individual actions creating social change, or Parsons' perspective of systemic function and dysfunction.

Value Consensus

Values provide a general conception of what is desirable and worthwhile. If members share common values, they will likely share a common identity, which will further provide a basis for unity and cooperation. Shared values also lead to common goals, which provide guidance in specific situations. For instance, values of nationalism and patriotism lead citizens to defend their country in times of crisis. Thus, value consensus forms the fundamental integrating principle in society. It refers to the phenomenon of members sharing similar values leading to a shared sense of identity and movement towards collective goals.

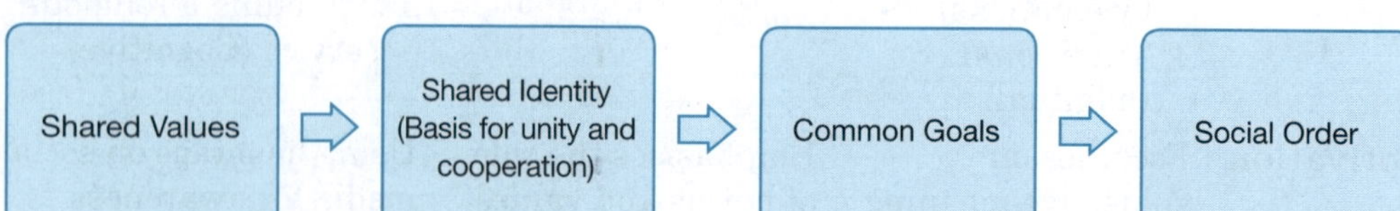

Parsons's Conception of Value Consensus

Society as a Social System

Parsons sought to answer the problem of establishing social order through structural functionalism. He only worked on the issue of 'social change' towards the later part of his career. Parsons gave the theory of action systems to explain social order. His action systems are not found in the real world, rather act as analytical tools to describe the real world.

According to Parsons, a social system has the following features:

1. A plurality of individual actors interacting with each other.
2. The interaction occurs in a situation which has at least a physical or environmental aspect.
3. Actors interact with other individuals, their environment and their circumstances. Actions are influenced by social context.
4. Actions are driven by the actors' desire to maximise their happiness or satisfaction (optimization of gratification) through the most rewarding outcomes.
5. Such interactions occur through commonly shared cultural symbols, meanings, norms and beliefs.

Social System

Parsons defined a social system as a complex of interacting components that form a unitary whole, where the actions of individuals are coordinated through a set of structured relationships involving norms and values. In simpler terms, a social system is like a big machine where each part (or person) plays a role that keeps the machine running smoothly. These roles are guided by rules and shared values that everyone generally agrees on.

Think about a university. It is a social system composed of various actors (students, faculty, administration) who interact within a framework of rules (academic regulations, codes of conduct) and shared goals (education, research). Each person's actions—attending classes, grading papers, administering programs—are coordinated to help the university function as a whole.

Status-Role Complex

Parsons used the 'status-role' complex as the basic unit of the social system. It is a structural component as opposed to interaction which is a micro-level process. Status-role indicates the status or the structural position of the actor and the accompanying role or set of functions that the actor performs in that position.

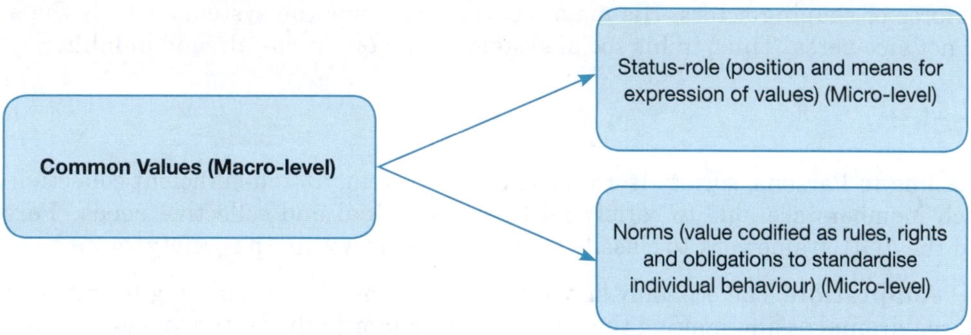

Even though Parsons talked about actors, his main concern was large-scale systems and their relationship to one another (societal functionalism).

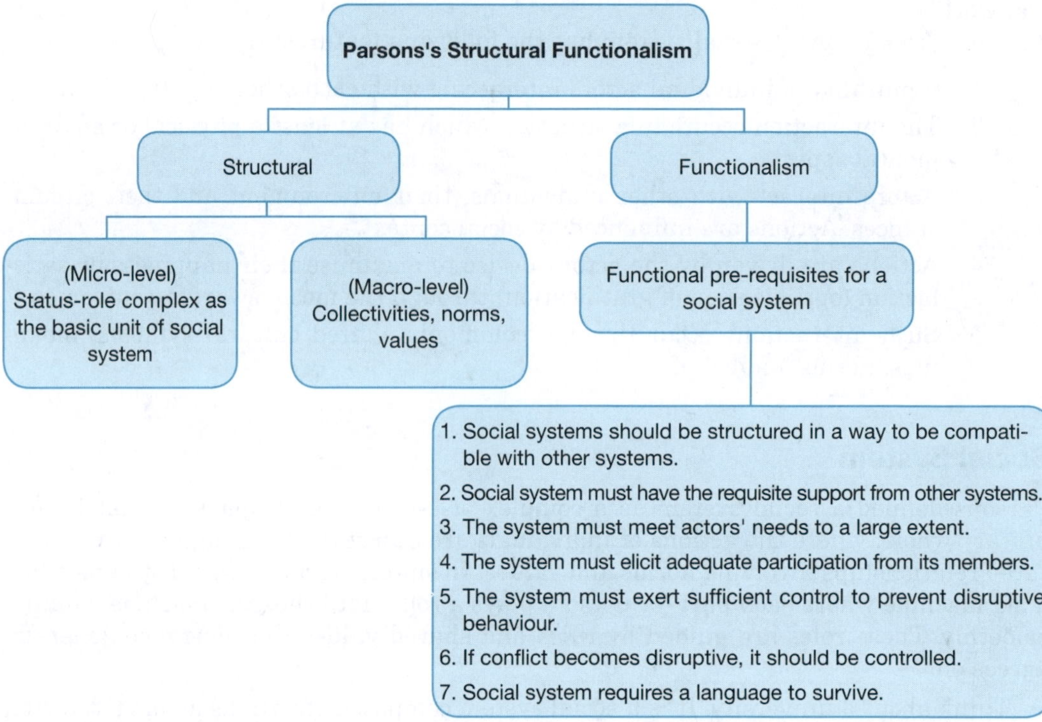

Actors and Social Systems

Parsons was concerned with the transfer of societal norms and values to actors through socialization and internalization. As per him, when collective value orientations become integrated with individual need-dispositions, pursuit of individual goals too will serve the societal interests. Parsons did take note of individual variation and deviance but did not deem them strong enough to threaten the integrity of the system. He advocated social control to induce conformity and a range of role opportunities to allow expression of different personalities. He pushed for a flexible social system rather than a rigid one. Parsons was criticized for seeing actors as passive recipients and socialization as the sole force of shaping actors. His major concern was how the system controls the actor and not vice-versa. Thus, in his social system, social order was already in-built.

Society

According to Parsons, society is a type of social system, a ' self-sufficient collectivity in which members are able to satisfy all their individual and collective needs.' Parsons used the AGIL framework to classify four subsystems within the society.

1. **Adaptation:** The economy subsystem is responsible for adapting to the external environment and making the environment adapt to the system needs.

2. **Goal Attainment:** The polity subsystem identifies primary goals for the society and allocates power and resources to achieve them.

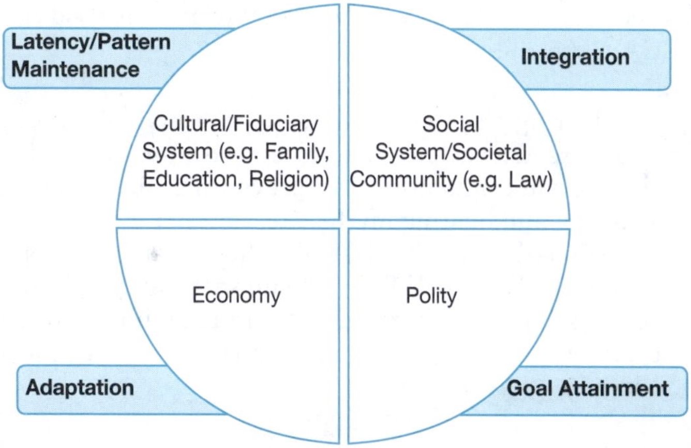

3. **Integration:** The social subsystem/societal community fosters coordination between actors, actors and subsystems and between subsystems through application of institutionalized norms, rules, law, etc.
4. **Latency/Pattern Maintenance:** The cultural/fiduciary subsystem transmits commonly shared values, norms, symbols, beliefs, etc., from the system to the individual actors and also into other subsystems to maintain and foster consensus.

Parsons also spoke of symbolic media of interchange which circulated in all systems as a common link. For instance, he identified money not just as a material commodity but as a media of interchange symbolising interdependence, a resource to control the environment, achieve goals and determine power.

Relevance

Parsons's theory of social system is relevant in explaining how society maintains its stability and order. The AGIL scheme can be used to analyse several problems in the present times and give direction to how different subsystems should function to restore equilibrium.

1. **Adaptation:**
   - **Example 1:** Climate change poses a significant risk today. Applying the AGIL framework, adaptation would involve societal efforts to develop sustainable practices, implement environmental policies, and invest in green technologies to cope with changing climate conditions.
   - **Example 2:** The COVID-19 pandemic led nations to quickly adapt to the new situation by implementing various measures such as lockdowns, mask mandates, etc. New global arrangements and platforms like the UN, WHO, etc., with speedier research, vaccine production and distribution strategies led to creation of a stronger health landscape.
2. **Goal Attainment:**
   - **Example:** Every nation sets the goal of eliminating poverty and enabling every citizen to meet their basic needs. Consequently, the governments formulate

policies that aim to increase access to education, food security, job opportunities, and social services. In India's case, this has been attempted through legislations like Right to Education Act, 2009; National Food Security Act, 2013, MGNREGA, 2005, etc.

3. **Integration:**
   - **Example 1:** During the Covid pandemic, the mainstream media subsystem functioned to spread awareness and integrate efforts of the State and the public in achieving the common goal of preventing virus transmission, availing help to the needy and busting myths, etc.
   - **Example 2:** Globally, during crises like the Ukraine-Russia war, Israel-Gaza war, etc., platforms like the UN coordinate with various agencies and States to integrate efforts to provide humanitarian relief, build pressure for ceasefire on warring countries, etc. Organizations like UNSC, etc., are also equipped with powers to impose legal sanctions.
4. **Latency:**
   - **Example:** Social issues like racial or gender inequality demand latency mechanisms. For instance, movements like #MeToo or Black Lives Matter aim to shift societal attitudes and norms regarding gender equality and racial justice, contributing to long-term cultural changes.

More Examples

Adaptation (A)

- **Tech Startups:** In the fast-paced tech industry, startups continuously adapt by innovating new products or services to meet changing consumer demands and technological advancements. For example, a tech startup might pivot from developing desktop applications to mobile apps as smartphone usage increases.
- **Public Health Systems:** During the COVID-19 pandemic, public health systems had to adapt quickly by scaling up testing facilities, modifying hospital capacities, and rolling out vaccination programs to manage resources effectively and respond to the health crisis.

Goal Attainment (G)

- **Non-Governmental Organizations (NGOs):** NGOs like Greenpeace set clear environmental goals, such as reducing plastic waste or combating deforestation, and mobilise resources and campaigns to achieve these objectives.
- **Government Policies on Education:** Many governments aim to increase educational attainment by implementing policies that provide free or subsidized education, scholarships, and digital learning platforms to reach wider populations.

Integration (I)

- **Corporate Social Responsibility (CSR):** Companies integrate their business operations with social welfare activities, such as Google's environmental sustainability practices, which not only aim to reduce carbon footprints but also enhance their corporate image and stakeholder relations.

- **Urban Planning:** Modern urban planning integrates residential, commercial, and recreational areas to enhance the quality of life. Well-designed cities ensure that different community needs—such as transportation, housing, and leisure—are harmoniously integrated.

Latent Pattern Maintenance (L)

- **Cultural Festivals:** Events like the Diwali in India or Thanksgiving in the USA play a crucial role in reinforcing cultural norms and values, strengthening community ties, and ensuring the continuity of these traditions.
- **Educational Institutions:** Schools and universities not only impart knowledge but also play a critical role in socialising young people into societal norms and values through curricula that include civic education, ethical conduct, and community service.

Parsons also classified social systems into different types based on their value orientations:

1. **Particularistic Ascriptive:** Roles are assigned based on attributes like gender and age. Traditional societies often exhibit this pattern.
2. **Particularistic Achievement:** Roles are assigned based on individual achievement but within the context of group values. Parsons saw this in Chinese culture.
3. **Universalistic Achievement:** Roles are assigned based on individual merit in a democratic framework. Modern industrial societies exemplify this type.
4. **Universalistic Ascriptive:** Roles are assigned based on ideological conformity rather than individual merit. Totalitarian societies reflect this pattern.

Critique

Talcott Parsons's theory of social system has faced critique, and some argue that it may fall short in analysing certain real-world events. Here are specific critiques with examples.

1. **Overemphasis on Stability:** Parsons tends to emphasise social stability, which may not fully capture the dynamics of rapid social change.
   Example: The Arab Spring (2010–2012) saw widespread protests and political upheaval in the Middle East, leading to multiple large-scale conflicts like the Syrian civil war; the rise of Islamic State - Iraq and Lebanon, insurgency in Iraq and the following civil war; the Egyptian Crisis, coup, and subsequent unrest and insurgency; the Libyan Crisis; and the Yemeni Crisis and subsequent civil war. Parsons' theory might struggle to explain the sudden and disruptive nature of these events.
2. **Oversimplification of Functional Equivalence:** Parsons uses one theory to explain every society. The assumption of functional equivalence of the four subsystems across different societies oversimplifies the complexities and unique characteristics of diverse cultures.
   Example: The challenges faced by Western democracies may differ significantly from those in non-Western societies. Applying a uniform framework might overlook culturally specific factors influencing social systems. For example, secularism is interpreted differently in the USA and in India, which reflects in how religion functions in the two countries.

3. **Status Quo and Limited Attention to Conflict:** Parsons' focus on consensus and equilibrium may downplay the role of conflict in shaping social systems. His bias towards social equilibrium could be seen as promoting status quo, resisting the necessary change.
   Example: The theory might struggle to explain social movements like anti-government protests in Hong Kong, where conflict is central to social dynamics. Similarly, countries like North Korea maintain social order through repression of human rights. Pressure from other countries and international organizations has failed in changing the state of affairs there.
4. **Gender Bias and Family Role Assumptions:** Parsons' model assumes traditional gender roles and may not adequately address evolving family structures and gender dynamics.
   Example: The rise of single-parent households, LGBTQ+ families, and changing gender roles challenges the traditional nuclear family model in ways that Parsons' theory may not account for.
5. **Neglect of Power Dynamics:** The theory's treatment of power dynamics is limited, and it might not fully address how power structures shape social systems.
   Example: Instances of political corruption or authoritarian rule, such as in cases like the rise of populist leaders, reveal the significance of power dynamics that may not be fully captured by Parsons' framework.
6. **Lack of Empirical Studies:** Parsons' sociology was based on a general theoretical system rather than on real-life, smaller, empirical studies. Some critics have argued that this approach restricts the practical application of his theories in understanding real-world social phenomena.

Social Change

- **Paradigm of Evolutionary Change:** Parsons gave a positive model of social change through his evolutionary theory. It assumes that as society evolves from simple to complex, it grows to be better able to cope with its problems. Though he did not characterise his theory as unilinear, he did identify three broad evolutionary stages—primitive, intermediate and modern; on the basis of cultural dimensions. The transition to every successive stage is marked by a cultural development.

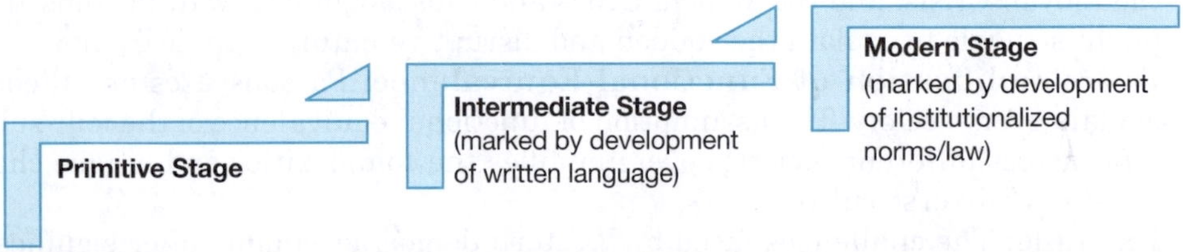

According to Parsons, social change occurs, but within a framework that tends to preserve the system's stability and order. Here's a breakdown of how he conceptualized social change.

1. **Evolutionary Change**: Parsons believed that social change often occurs through an evolutionary process. This is not in the biological sense but rather in terms of social structures adapting over time. He suggested that societies develop through certain evolutionary stages, each representing an advancement in that society's ability to deal with its environment and internal complexities. For instance, moving from traditional to modern societies involves changes in the legal system, market economy, educational systems, and democratization.
2. **System Needs:** Social change, according to Parsons, must address the needs of the system, which are adaptation, goal attainment, integration, and latent pattern maintenance (the AGIL scheme). Changes in one aspect of society are often related to adjustments in other aspects to maintain the system's stability. For example, as technological innovations (Adaptation) increase, educational systems might need to evolve to prepare individuals for new types of jobs (Goal Attainment), which may require reforms in policy and curriculum (Integration) that align with societal values and future visions (Latent Pattern Maintenance).
3. **Change through Differentiation and Integration:** Parsons argued that change typically occurs through a process of differentiation and integration. Differentiation refers to the development of increasingly specialized structures within a society. As societies grow more complex, these specialized structures must then be integrated into a cohesive whole. For example, as a healthcare system becomes more complex, integrating various specialties, it necessitates more sophisticated administrative and regulatory mechanisms to coordinate these services effectively.
4. **Adaptation to External and Internal Pressures:** Change can also be a response to external pressures (such as economic crises, wars, or global pandemics) and internal pressures (like social movements, demographic shifts, or cultural innovations). While Parsons emphasises stability, he acknowledges that these pressures can necessitate significant adjustments in a society's structure to maintain systemic balance.
5. **Role of Values and Norms:** For Parsons, values and norms are central to understanding social change. Changes in societal norms and values can lead to changes in social structures. For instance, shifts in attitudes towards gender equality have led to changes in the legal and organizational frameworks that promote gender equality in education and the workplace.

Contemporary Examples

1. **Digital Transformation:**

   In the contemporary context, consider the digital transformation as an example of social change. This transformation involves adaptation (development and integration of new technologies), goal attainment (enhancing connectivity and efficiency), and integration (creating policies and regulations for digital operations). Meanwhile, latent pattern maintenance is observed as societies renegotiate norms and values around privacy, work, and communication in the digital age.

2. **Legal System Adjustments:**
   - **Change:** The legalization of same-sex marriage in many countries.
   - **Parsons' Perspective:** This legal change reflects a shift in societal values and norms, representing latent pattern maintenance as it aligns legal frameworks with evolving societal beliefs. Integration is also critical here as the new legal status must be harmonized with existing laws regarding marriage, inheritance, and family rights.
3. **Economic Policies:**
   - **Change:** Implementation of green economy strategies, such as subsidies for renewable energy and penalties for high carbon emissions.
   - **Parsons' Perspective:** These policies are examples of adaptation to environmental challenges and goal attainment in pursuing sustainability goals. They require integration into the broader economic system and entail latent pattern maintenance by embedding new environmental values into economic practices.
4. **Urban Development:**
   - **Change:** The development of smart cities, integrating IoT technologies to enhance efficiency in transportation, energy use, and municipal services.
   - **Parsons' Perspective:** This represents adaptation to new technological capabilities and goal attainment in making cities more livable and sustainable. The integration of these technologies into everyday urban life is crucial, as is maintaining the latent pattern of innovation and progress in urban planning.
5. **Cultural Shifts**
   - **Change:** Increasing acceptance and visibility of diverse cultural identities and lifestyles, such as multiculturalism and LGBTQ+ rights.
   - **Parsons' Perspective:** This cultural shift shows latent pattern maintenance as societal values evolve towards inclusivity and diversity. The integration of these values into formal structures like anti-discrimination laws and educational policies reflects societal adaptation and goal attainment in fostering an inclusive environment.

The Cybernetic Hierarchy of Control

The cybernetic hierarchy of control is based on the idea that certain subsystems in a society have more control over maintaining order and directing change than others. According to Parsons, these subsystems are arranged in a hierarchy from the highest (most control over information) to the lowest (most control over energy). Here's how these levels are typically organized.

1. **The Cultural System:** At the top of the hierarchy, the cultural system is concerned with the maintenance of societal values and the transmission of knowledge. It provides patterns for behaviour and establishes norms, which guide the other subsystems. This system is crucial for controlling the goals and directional movements of society.

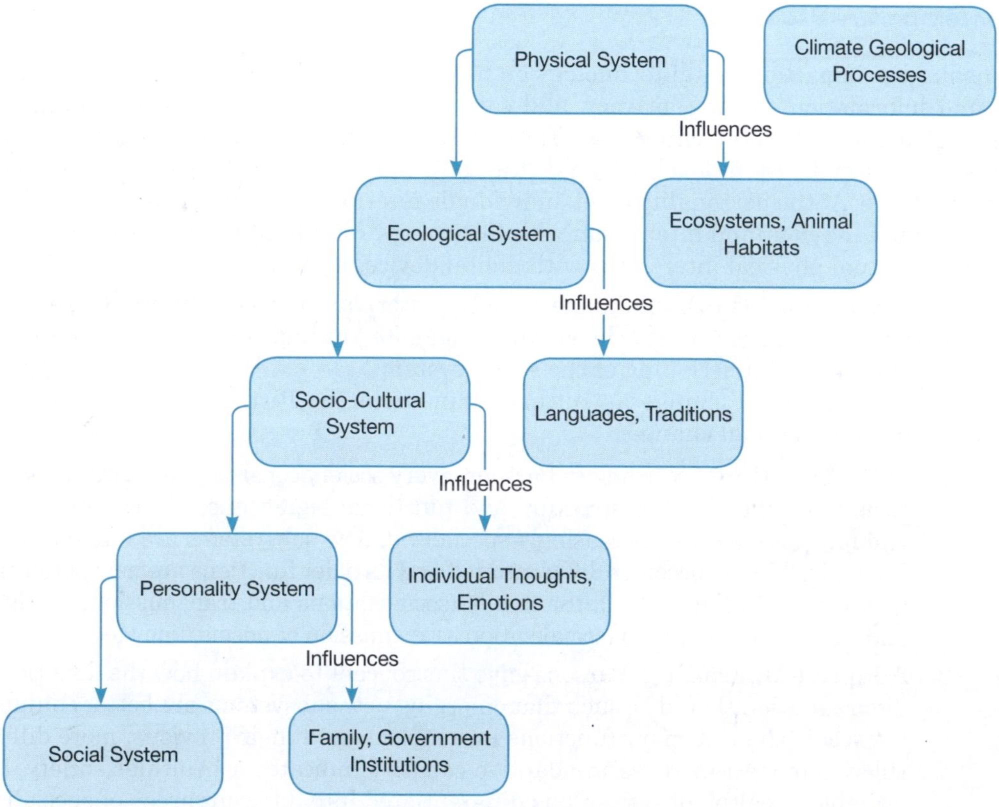

2. **The Social System:** Below the cultural system, the social system organises interactions between actors (individuals or organizations). It translates the values and norms of the cultural system into social roles and institutions, facilitating coordination and adaptation within the society.
3. **The Personality System:** This system deals with individual personalities and behavioural processes. It involves the internalization of societal norms and values by individuals, ensuring that their motivations and actions are aligned with societal expectations.
4. **The Behavioural Organism:** At the bottom of the hierarchy, the behavioural organism refers to the physical and biological aspects of human actions. This includes the capacities and limitations imposed by the human body, which influence how individuals can physically interact with their environment.

Application and Contemporary Example

Application

In Parsons' view, each level in the hierarchy controls the flow of information and energy downward, while feedback from the lower levels can affect adjustments at the higher levels. For instance, cultural values (top) shape social norms and roles (next level), which in turn influence individual behaviours and actions (further down), and are ultimately manifested in physical actions and interactions (bottom).

Contemporary Example

Consider the impact of digital technology on modern society. At the cultural level, values around information sharing, privacy, and connectivity influence how societies regulate and interact with digital technologies. These values are translated into laws and regulations at the social system level, which dictate how individuals and organizations should behave online. At the personality level, individuals internalise these norms, which shapes their online behaviour and interaction with technology. Finally, at the behavioural organism level, actual physical interaction with digital devices occurs.

This hierarchy helps to explain the complex interplay between different aspects of society and how changes at one level can propagate through others, influencing the overall structure and functioning of the social system.

Besides studying social change as cultural transitions, he further gave the following concepts to explain social change:

1. **Differentiation:** According to Parsons, every society consists of a series of subsystems that differ in both structure and functional significance. As society evolves and functions become increasingly specialized, new subsystems are differentiated. Example, religion becomes differentiated and its older functions are now performed by the state (social control), the family (socializations and transmission of values) and the education system (socialization, transmission of norms, knowledge, etc.).
2. **Adaptive Upgrading:** Parsons gave this concept to explain how the direction of differentiation should be such that emerging new subsystems are better equipped to execute their primary functions in comparison to their previous, more diffuse subsystems. An increase in adaptive capacity indicates a healthier society. For example, health subsystem has differentiated into different areas of specialization–insurance, primary healthcare, secondary healthcare, homeopathy, allopathy, etc., and each of these subsystems is equipped to solve specific problems.
3. **Moving Equilibrium:** Parsons admits that in practical life, no social system is perfect. In his AGIL scheme, any disturbance in any one of the sub-systems creates a reaction from the other interrelated subsystems too. This reaction is directed towards restoring the social equilibrium and the disturbance-reaction equation creates a change, however small, in the entire system. Thus, social change is the process of moving equilibrium. For example, the 9/11 terrorist attack, though happened in one country, it created disturbance all over the world impacting the political system, economy and cultures. Every step in its aftermath was taken to restore the USA's position as a superpower and prevent any similar future events.
4. **Pattern Variables:** According to Parsons, cultural changes like changes in values lead to the broadest patterns of change in a society. For example, he argued that the structure of modern societies owes much to values inherited from ancient Israel and classical Greece. To further explain this effect, he identified two sets of cultural values which he called pattern variables A and B. These pattern variables answer the most basic questions, like, how should people be selected for different roles? What rules should govern different forms of relationships? Whose interests should take a priority—the group or the individual's? etc.

Pattern Variables A	Pattern Variables B
Ascription–Status is determined by one's birth in a particular family, caste, tribe, etc.	**Achievement**–Status is earned through one's efforts in education, workplace, etc.
Diffuseness–Relationships between people satisfy a large range of needs. For example, a relationship between mother and child, husband and wife, etc.	**Specificity**–Relationships between people satisfy particular needs. For example, doctor-patient, teacher-student, etc.
Particularism–Individuals act differently towards particular people. For example, loyalty towards family not towards strangers, cooperation within the community while suspicion towards the outsiders, etc.	**Universalism**–Individuals act according to universal principles. For example, a cop arresting their family members if necessary, following equality before law; a child going through a meritorious selection process to attain the same or even better job than the father's.
Affectivity–Immediate gratification. People act to satisfy their desires as soon as possible. For example, indulging in merriment today, not worrying too much about tomorrow.	**Effective neutrality**–Dayed gratification. People postpone acting on desires to get better rewards in the future. For example, saving money to buy car, property, etc.
Collective orientation–Group's interests are placed above individual self-interests. For example, an individual who has broken community rules is ostracized.	**Self-orientation**–People pursue their own interests first, rather than of their social groups. For example, in love marriages, individuals give priority to their own preferences rather than their community's.

- According to Parsons, barring family life, pattern variables A are characteristic of simple societies while those in set B are characteristic of modern societies. Thus, social change is movement from variables A to variables B. Any disturbance in this movement could lead the society to stagnate. For example, the persistence of the caste system in India prevents the actualization of true merit.

Problem with Social Change

According to Parsons, the differentiation occurring as part of social change could lessen social integration. However, this problem can be overcome through 'generalization of values'. Thus, even though new subsystems emerge, efforts should be made to generalise values that govern all other subsystems. For example, value of universalism can guarantee upholding of fundamental rights everywhere, value of individualism can lead to a more competitive and efficient market economy, value of effective neutrality can better prepare both the actors and the system for future economic emergencies, etc., like it happened during financial crisis of 2008 and COVID crisis of 2020. Cultures where people had sturdy saving habits were able to weather the crisis with better resilience.

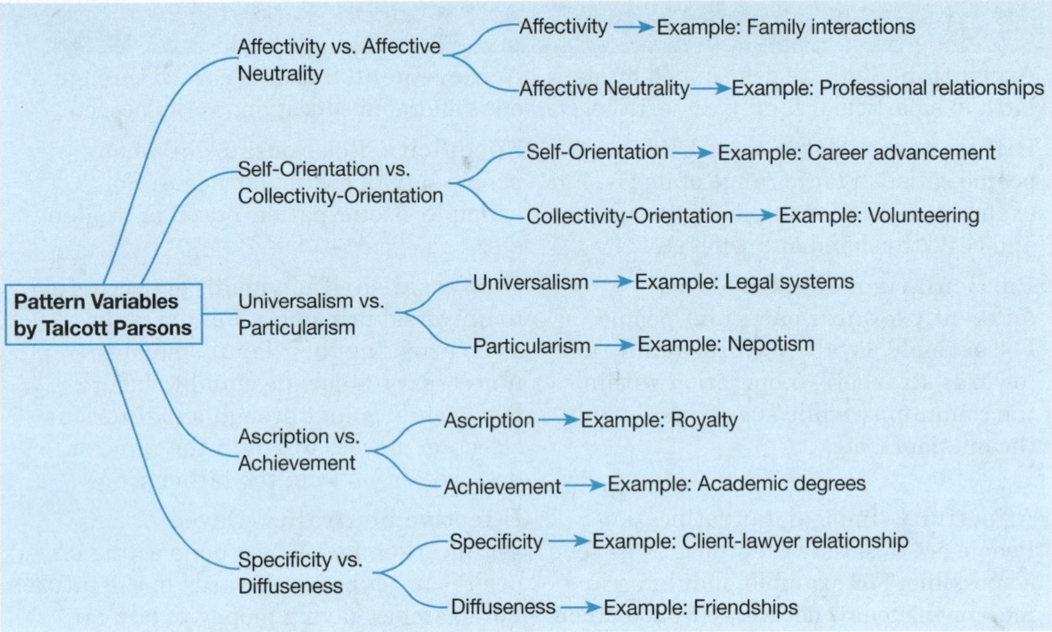

Relevance

1. **Specialization:** The modern society lays emphasis on expertise to solve emerging problems. Parsons's concepts of differentiation and adaptive upgrading are useful in this regard. For example United Nations has several specialized agencies like Food and Agriculture Organization, International Labour Organization, International Monetary Fund, etc., to cater to demands of different sectors.
2. **Moving Equilibrium in an Ever-changing World:** Though the world saw a devastating pandemic in 2020-2021, the social equilibrium was soon restored in many of the previous ways. For instance, people returned to their old ways of functioning and very few retained the habit of wearing masks. The changes that have occurred in all subsystems include: health and environment becoming priorities in budget allocation, environment becoming a key politically rallying point in both domestic (for example, pollution, free water, waste management, etc.) and in international arenas, stronger implementation of legal instruments like phyto-sanitary measures in cross-country trade, conservation measures in species' trade, etc., and culturally, sanitation and cleanliness have become important values which are tied up with societal goals.
3. **Pattern Variables to Explain Modern Changes**
   (a) Understanding Social Roles through Diffusion and Specificity
      (i) **Example:** In professional settings, the pattern variable of specificity versus diffuseness helps understand specific roles like of a Data Analyst or more flexible and broad responsibilities such as those involved in Human Resources.

(b) Balancing Affectivity and Effective Neutrality
  (i) **Example:** Advertising industry encashes on people's tendencies to immediately gratify their desires related to fashion, food, etc., while banking sector encourages people to invest in saving instruments such as Fixed Deposits.

(c) Particularism vs. Universalism in Moral Judgements
  (i) **Example:** Legal systems often navigate the tension between instances of upholding universal values such as right to life (example - of a mother by permitting abortion) and considering particular situations such as giving death sentence to a terrorist to send out a social message against violence.

(d) Collectivity vs. Self-Orientation in Group Dynamics
  (i) **Example:** Teamwork in organizations involves finding a balance between prioritizing the collective goals (meeting company's targets) and recognizing individual contributions and needs (promotion, appraisal, etc.).

Critique

Parsons's theory of social change has been subject to critique on several fronts as listed below:

1. **Debate on Upgrading vs Downgrading:** Society's evolution from simple to modern has not necessarily led to better conditions. Economic changes have increased production but they have also led to environmental degradation. The technological changes, for instance, have brought in more comforts and convenience, compressing both space and time, but they also pose threats in the form of disintegration, cybercrimes and the apocalyptic prophecies of humans becoming secondary beings to artificial intelligence.
2. **Specialization and Fragmentation of Knowledge:** As more specialized subsystems have emerged, knowledge has become increasingly fragmented. Thus, specialized systems to generate more with less labour and time do not take into account the negative effects on working conditions, unemployment, waste generation, etc. Similarly, in education, the division between natural and social sciences prevents students from developing a well-rounded perspective on various types of issues.
3. **Oversimplification:** Complex changes cannot be captured in two sets of cultural values. Parsons claims that the transition from Pattern Variables A to B is applicable in all areas of modern society except family life. However, in reality, traditional values are predominant in several areas in all known societies, even the most modern ones.

   - Ascription, for instance, plays an influential role through the monarchy in the UK, majority students who complete higher education in the US come from racially and economically privileged backgrounds.
   - Similarly, specificity and particularism do not necessarily represent efficiency and progress as is visible in societies like that of Japan where hectic work culture has increased isolation and alienation among people.

- Collective-orientation has taken different forms like increasing jingoism, waging of wars, refugee exodus, etc., and self-orientation has mistakenly led people to revel in self-promotion through social media, impacting attention spans, self-esteem levels and quality of interactions.

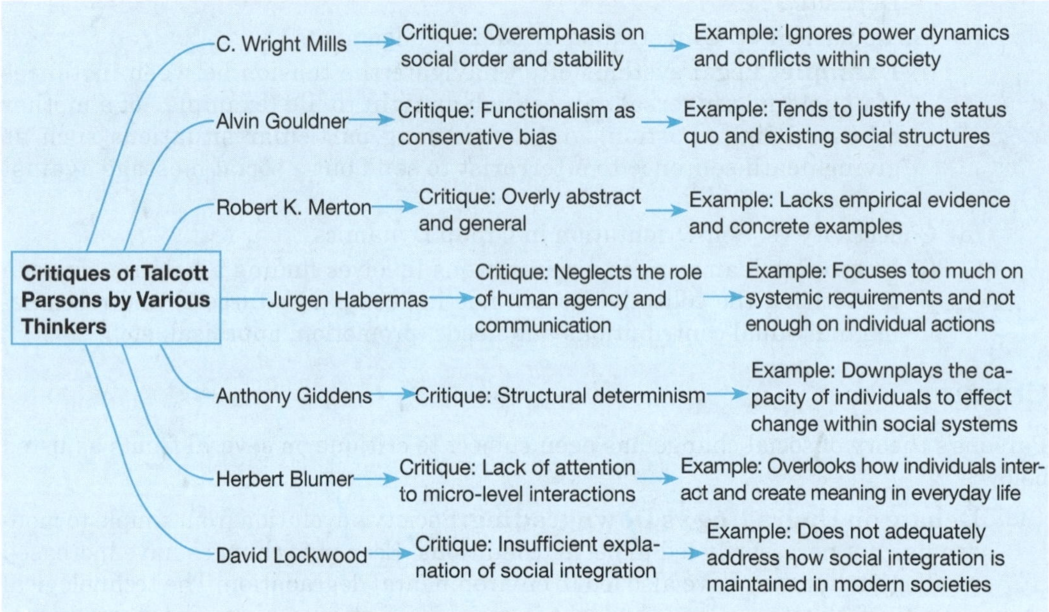

Conclusion

Talcott Parsons, a prominent figure in sociology, made significant contributions to the field through his structural-functional perspective. His theory emphasized the importance of social systems, pattern variables, and the AGIL paradigm in understanding the functioning and stability of societies. While influential, Parsons' work has faced criticism for its perceived limitations in addressing issues of power, cultural diversity, and social change.

GEORGE HERBERT MEAD (1863-1931)

A Brief Biographical Sketch

George Herbert Mead was born in Massachusetts, USA, in 1863 into an academically inclined family. His father served as a professor at Oberlin College, where Mead himself completed his Bachelor's degree in 1883. Trained primarily in philosophy and its application to social psychology, Mead pursued graduate studies at Harvard in 1887 and later studied at the universities of Leipzig and Berlin. In 1894, at the invitation of John Dewey, he joined the University of Chicago, where he remained for the rest of his career. By 1900 he began teaching a course in social psychology, which eventually evolved into an advanced course during 1916–17; student notes from these lectures later formed the basis of his posthumously published classic *Mind, Self and Society*. Mead continued to teach until 1930, but in 1931 he passed away from heart failure. His work has had a profound influence on the development of contemporary sociology, particularly in shaping the tradition of symbolic interactionism.

Micro-approach

- Mead is indeed a micro-sociologist. His work on symbolic interactionism focuses on everyday interactions, symbols, and the social genesis of the self.

Act (Four Stages)

- Mead outlined four stages of an act: **Impulse → Perception → Manipulation → Consummation**. This is accurately reflected in the diagram.
- Source: Mead, *Mind, Self, and Society* (1934).

Social Processes → Self and Mind

- Mead emphasizes that **mind and self emerge from social processes**, not pre-exist them. The diagram shows this relationship correctly.

Mind as Conversation of Gestures

- Mead described 'mind' as arising from the **conversation of significant gestures**, i.e., symbols used in communication with others and internally. The diagram's split ('Outside with others / Within-to oneself') matches this idea.

Self as Subject and Object

- Mead defines the self as the ability to see oneself both as subject and object — accurately shown in the diagram.

Stages of Development of Self

- Mead distinguished between:
  - **Play Stage** (child takes role of specific others, e.g., pretending to be mother, teacher)
  - **Game Stage** (child learns rules and perspectives of many others, leading to the idea of the **Generalized Other**)
- These stages are correctly represented in the diagram.

'I' and 'Me'

- Mead divided the self into two aspects:
  - **'Me'**: the socialized, habitual, conformist side — linked with conformity and coordination.
  - **'I'**: the spontaneous, creative, unpredictable side — linked with innovation and social change.

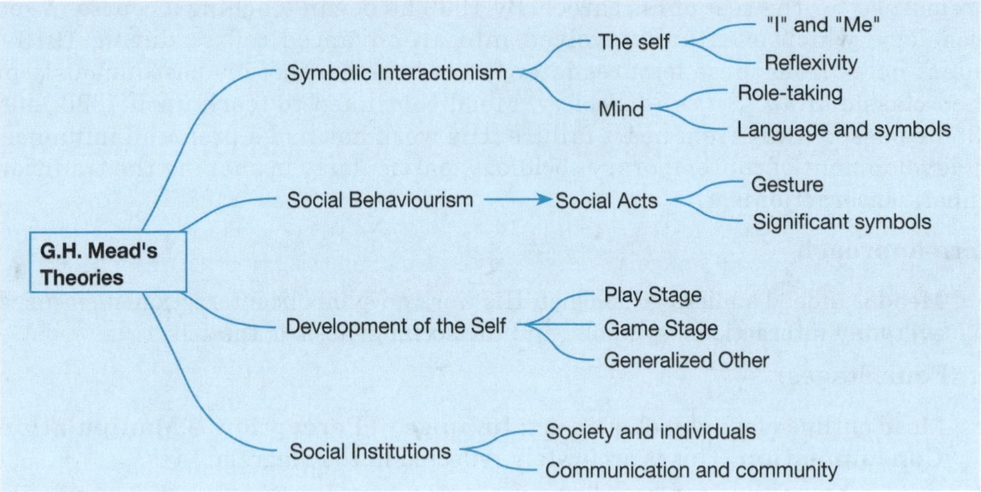

Symbolic Interactionism

Symbolic interactionism as a theoretical paradigm consists of a set of related ideas and principles that govern human relations at a micro or individual level. It aims to combine the social aspects with the psychological aspects of individual members and studies majorly two things–a) how large scale and collective social processes impact individual identities and b) how individuals, as independent and free-thinking agents, create and alter social reality in a simultaneous manner. The interaction between society and individual, therefore, is complex and involves dialectically interrelated components.

The basic postulates of symbolic interactionism include:

(i) Humans have capacity for thought.

(ii) The capacity for thinking allows humans to do two things- i) interact with others and ii) interact with themselves.

(iii) The interaction occurs through meanings and symbols, which are themselves learned and shaped through social interactions.

(iv) The shared meanings in social interactions constitute the framework for social groups and societies.

(v) Humans retain the ability to modify the meanings and symbols according to their interpretation of the situation.

(vi) This interpretation is possible due to human ability to interact with others and with oneself.

(vii) Interaction, in turn, continues to shape capacity for thought.

Thus, these postulates are all dialectically interrelated, one impacting the other across time, space and cultures.

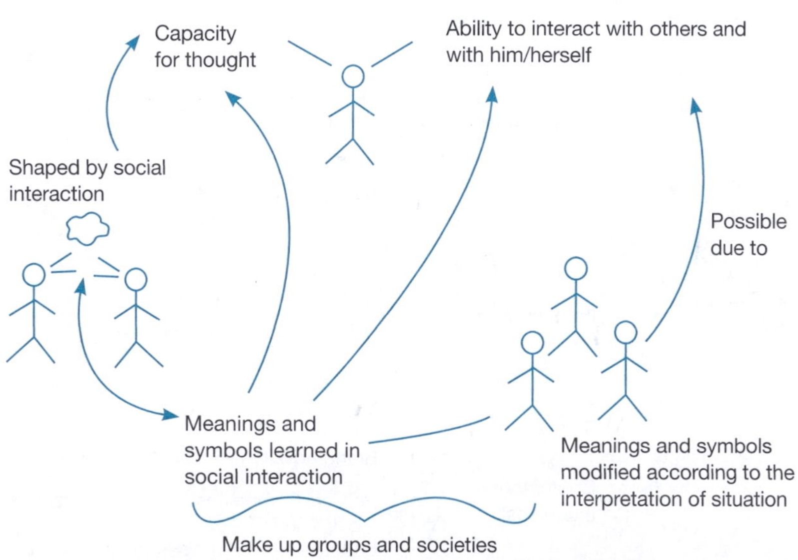

Basic Principles of Symbolic Interactionist Theory

Mead and Symbolic Interactionism

George H. Mead was one of the early prominent thinkers associated with the development of the symbolic interactionism approach. His ideas have been said to derive from the following two key strands of thought:

(i) **Philosophical Realism:** It emphasises on the impact of society and social processes on mental capacity of human beings.

(ii) **Social Behaviourism:** It emphasises study of unobservable aspects of human behaviour - what happens in the mind of the actor between the stimulus and the response. Mead saw a clear difference between animals and humans; in that the latter had the capacity to self-reflect through the use of language before deciding on any action.

Mead's book–*Mind, Self and Society* contains some groundbreaking insights which form the foundation of his theory of self and identity. The related ideas are shared below.

1. **The 'Social' as the Cause of 'Emergence':** Mead gave priority to the society. He defined society as the social processes that represent an organized set of responses. According to him, humans do not have minds or selves in the beginning and these only 'emerge' from society. The whole (society) is prior to the part (individual). Coming first, the social group leads to the development of self-conscious mental states.

2. **Humans as Actors:** Mead argued that humans have distinct capacities that distinguish them from animals. He gave the concept of 'act' as the most primitive unit of his theory. Although both humans and animals act, Mead was interested in how the two differed in this regard. His conceived of act as comprising of the following four stages:

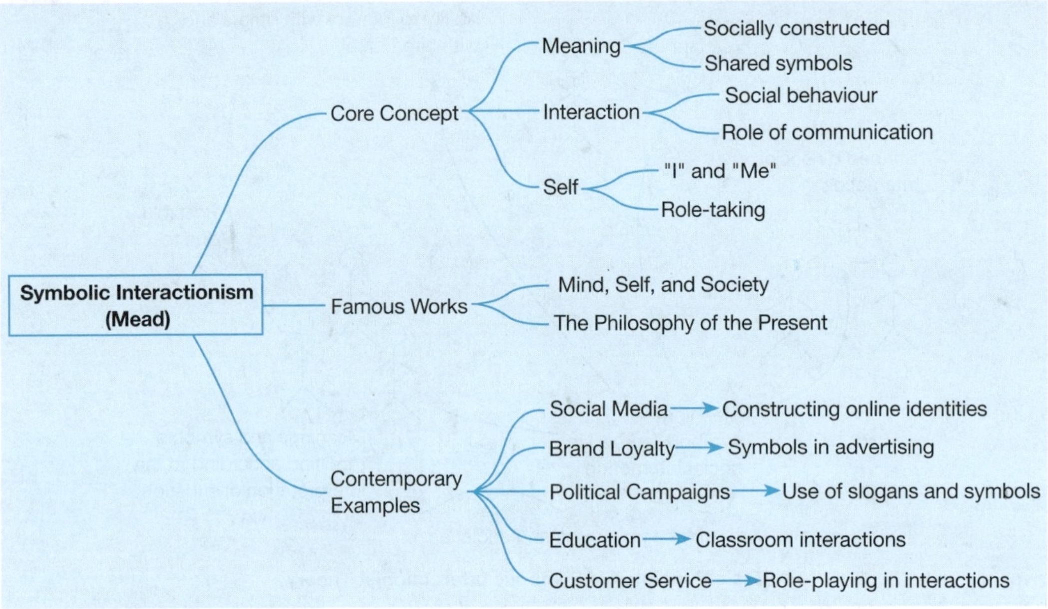

(i) **Impulse:** This involves both actors and the environment. An impulse represents an immediate sensuous stimulation and actor's reaction in acknowledging the stimulus. For example, the feeling of hunger is an impulse.

(ii) **Perception:** This involves incoming stimuli as well as mental images. For example, the impulse of hunger may have developed after the actor saw food in his environment, or it may have developed internally and now the actor is visualising food in his mind to satisfy his impulse.

(iii) **Manipulation:** This includes taking action with regard to the perceived object. So, the actor may come across a range of food options in his environment. As he perceives them, he is also thinking in his mind over what he would like to have, what choices to make. This stage is influenced by the actor's past experiences, present situation and a concern over future outcomes. For example, the actor may let go of something delicious because he wants to make a healthier choice.

(iv) **Consummation:** This refers to the final stage of taking action that will ultimately satisfy the original impulse. In this instance, it will include the action of eating.

In theorising his concept of 'act', Mead portrays humans as 'thinking beings' and puts his focus on the processes occurring between stimulus and response.

Social Acts and Interaction

Mead defines social act as one that involves a) two or more persons, and b) significant gestures and symbols.

As per Mead, gesture is the most basic mechanism of any social action. He classifies gestures into physical and vocal. Additionally, they can be either unconscious (made without any conscious thought) or conscious (made with prior thought). Physical gestures are common to both humans and animals. In case of physical gestures, the actor is not able to view themselves as they are performing the gesture. But in case of vocal gestures, the actor is able to listen to themselves as they speak. Thus, vocal gestures allow actors to be subjects (as speakers) and also objects (listeners to their own speech as well as to others' gestures). This simultaneous activity allows human actors to do multiple things at once–interact with others, interact with themselves, interpret the situation and also modify their gestures as per their own interpretation. For Mead, these became the focus of study. He further studied gestures through the concept of 'Significant symbols'.

Significant Symbols

Mead was majorly focused on gestures with meanings, which led him to devise the concept of significant symbols. He defined significant symbols as gestures which:

(i) only humans can make

(ii) arouse in the individual who is making them the same kind of response that they are supposed to elicit from those to whom the gestures are addressed

Fulfilling these two conditions, Mead argues Language. Language is a system of significant symbols which is used only by humans and has shared meanings among its users. So for example, when one says a chair or table, humans will create the same, not necessarily identical, mental image. Language performs another function of stimulating both the speaker as well as the people that the speaker is talking to. It makes human thinking possible. Mead defines thinking as 'an internalized or implicit conversation of the individual with himself.' Thus, conversation takes place both outside and inside. The concept of significant symbols becomes the basis for the theory of 'symbolic interaction'. Mead has talked about meaningful vocal gestures such as symbols, which make interaction–both within and outside–possible.

Mind and Self

Mind

As per Mead, mind is not a structure or a thing that is intrinsic to every being. Rather, it emerges from society and has the capacity to constantly evolve. He gives the following characteristics of mind:

(i) Mind is a process; an inner conversation with one's self.

(ii) It is a social phenomenon and is not found within from the beginning.

(iii) The social process precedes the mind. Therefore, as per Mead, it is not possible to have a mind without getting exposed to some form of social process.

(iv) Mind gives the individual the ability to call out in himself not simply a single response of the other but the response of the community as a whole.

(v) Similarly, the mind gives the ability to give an organized response to the overall community. Thus, the mind can function to give response from the community to self and from self to the community. It acts as a dynamic duo existing as a continuous conversation.

(vi) The mind is pragmatic and is always oriented towards problem-solving.

Self

As per Mead, lower animals and human infants do not have selves. So, just like the mind, the self too originates from the social. Mead refers to self as the peculiar 'ability' to be both subject and the object. This ability develops from the process of communication among and within humans. It arises through social activity and social relationships. It cannot emerge without social experiences, but once developed, can continue to exist without social contact.

FYI

Reflexivity

It refers to the ability to put ourselves unconsciously into others' places and to act as they act. Through reflexivity, people are able to examine themselves as others would examine them. People do not experience themselves directly but take on the role of others. Such reflexivity constitutes the mechanism for the development of the self.

Relationship between the Mind and the Self

The mind and the self are dialectically related. The mind is a process involving conversation within and outside and the self is the ability to be both the subject and the object (as perceived by others) simultaneously. Thus, the mind becomes the constitutive element for the self. When we converse with ourselves, we take on different roles. When we converse with others, we are constantly interpreting the situation to alter our responses. The mind and the self therefore are enmeshed with each other.

Origin of Self

Mead traces the genesis of the self through two stages in childhood development:

1. **Play Stage:** In this phase, children learn to take the attitude of particular others, like parents, to themselves. In this stage, a limited self develops as the child can take only the roles of distinct others, children are still in the process and hence, lack definite personalities.
2. **Game Stage:** In this phase, the child learns to take the role of everyone else involved in the game. For example, in cricket, a player can take into account the roles of multiple other players. In this stage, a definite personality starts to emerge. The limited self transforms into a coherent self. The game stage leads to the development of 'generalized other'.

Generalized Other

It refers to the attitude of the entire community. So while in play stage, the child learns the attitude of only select individuals like his parents, in the game stage, the child grows to think like the entire community. This allows for the possibility of abstract thinking and objectivity. In one's actions, one is able to think of the response that would come collectively from the society. So, for instance, a person who wishes to marry would know that while his parents would be okay if he chose his life partner, his community might have a different response. According to Mead, the process of education aids in internalization of the common habits of the community. So, for instance, young cadets in the Army are trained to follow its rules and regulations. A soldier is guided more by army as an institution than by his/her own personal values and experiences.

Thus, according to Mead, to have a self, one must be a member of the community and be directed by the attitudes 'common' to the community. It is important to note here that Mead conceptualises self in relation to generalisable responses of the community. So, while all members may not think alike, most members will be able to give a shared response. It is this majority response which gets internalized during the game stage and completes the formation of self.

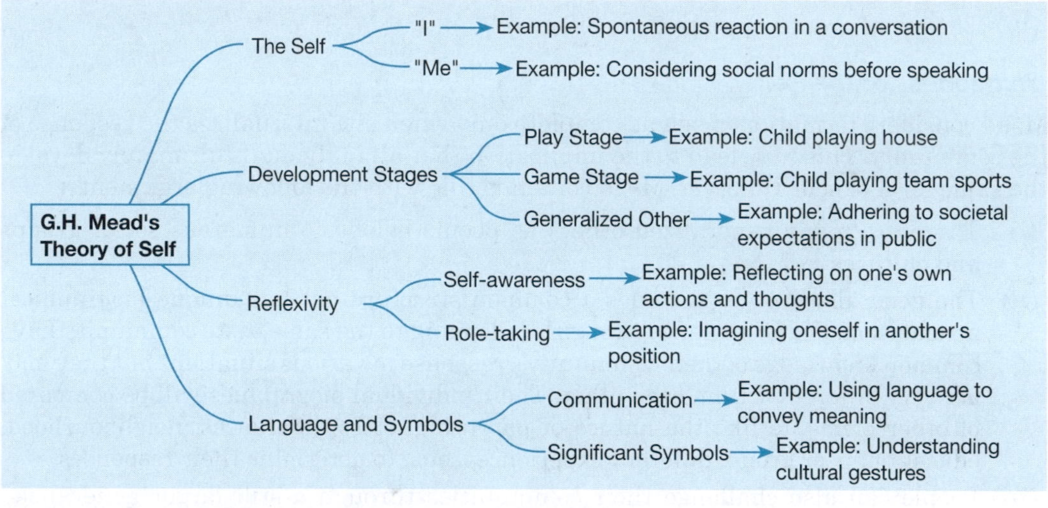

Society's Dependence on the Self

1. **Collective Behaviour and Social Norms:** While the self is shaped by society, societal norms and structures are concurrently shaped by the actions and interactions of individuals. Collective behaviours and shared meanings emerge from individual actions and interactions. Through this dynamic process, society evolves and adapts, reflecting the continuous interplay between individual and collective identities.
2. **Social Institutions and the Self:** Social institutions, such as family, education, and religion, play a crucial role in shaping individuals' self-concepts. These institutions provide the frameworks within which social interactions occur, guiding the development of the self. Conversely, individuals contribute to the perpetuation and transformation of these institutions through their actions and interactions.

3. **Social Media and Identity:** In contemporary society, social media platforms exemplify the twin-born nature of self and society. Individuals curate their online identities through interactions on these platforms, while societal norms and trends are influenced by the collective behaviours exhibited online. The feedback loop between individual self-presentation and societal trends on social media illustrates Mead's theory vividly.
4. **Cultural Evolution:** Cultural practices and norms evolve as individuals negotiate their identities within a society. For example, shifts in gender roles and expectations are both a result of individual actions challenging traditional norms and the collective redefinition of these norms through societal discourse. This evolution demonstrates the mutual shaping of self and society.

Functions of the Self

(i) It allows people to meet other people's expectations.

(ii) It makes people avoid inefficiencies as they view themselves from the perspective of others.

(iii) It generates greater coordination in society as a whole.

(iv) The social groups operate more effectively.

Uniqueness of the Self

Mead considers formation of self as complete only when one internalises the response of the community. This may lead to the implication that all individuals ultimately develop the same form of self. However, Mead contends this with the following arguments:

(i) There are many generalized others as people belong to numerous social groups and cultures.

(ii) The generalized other provides a common structure but has unique biographical articulation. So, for instance, two girls belonging to the same caste community have common knowledge of their community's response in various situations but they may act very differently from each other. Their individual biographies will be composed of other elements like the nature of parenting, class differences, neighbourhood, education, peer group, different experiences, etc., to determine their responses.

(iii) People can also challenge their communities through a still larger generalized other. Learning to take on the role of the community might not always translate into conformity and compliance. For instance, Raja Ram Mohan Roy challenged the culture of idol worship through a larger generalized other of worshipping a single, formless God.

Aspects of the Self

Mead proposes that there are two aspects to the Self : 'I' and 'Me'

1. **I:** The 'I' constitutes the immediate response of an individual to others. It is the incalculable, unpredictables and the creative aspect of the self. Because it is not pre-planned, it is only known in one's memories, once it has been performed. According to Mead, its features include:
   - It is a key source of novelty in the social process.

- It is the storehouse of a person's most important values.
- It helps in the realization of the self.
- It helps us to develop a 'definite personality'.

2. **Me:** The 'Me' refers to the organized set of attitudes of others which one himself assumes. It is the 'generalized other' which one adopts as a result of one's social experiences. Its features include:
   - It makes conventional, habitual and conformist individuals.
   - It involves conscious responsibility.
   - Through 'me', the society exercises social control to dominate the individual's 'I' aspect.

S. No.	I	Me
1.	Characteristic of modern societies	Was predominant in primitive societies
2.	Incalculable, unpredictable and innovative	Conventional and habitual
3.	Innovator – Formation of definite personality and realization of self	Conformist – Yearns to meet other people's expectations
4.	It reflects the individual's most important values.	It reflects social control.
5.	It makes social change possible.	It allows the individual to live comfortably within social groups through greater coordination.

Society and Institutions

Through Mead's conception of mind and self, it becomes easier to understand his usage of the term 'society'. So, in Mead's theory, society is what comprises the a) organized response of the community b) the 'me' aspect of the self and c) the processes which precede mind and self. This idea is connected to Mead's definition of social institutions. As per him, when the whole community acts towards individuals under certain circumstances in an identical way, it is called 'formation of the institution'. For example, Khap Panchayats are not recognized legal institutions but they act as bona fide institutions for the relevant caste members. Similarly, when a 15-year old Greta Thunberg sat in front of the Swedish Parliament every school day for three weeks in August, 2018, as a mark of protest against inaction on the climate change, it led to formation of a global institution with many coming in support and starting a full-fledged Fridays for Future movement.

Critique

Mead's work has been criticized on the following counts:

1. **Lack of Empirical Evidence:** Some critics have questioned the validity of his ideas and their real world application as his work has rested heavily on theoretical arguments rather than empirical evidence.

2 **Confusing and Vague Terminology:** The overlapping traits of mind and self, confusing terminology like emergence, etc., have made it difficult to understand his ideas in a clear manner. For example, it is not clear how his concept of generalized other is different from the concept of socialization as given by structural functionalists. His writing has been criticized for lacking coherence.

3. **Overemphasis on Social Process and Neglect of Individual Agency:** Mead has been criticized for over-emphasizing the role of social processes in the formation of mind and self. His own student Herbert Blumer chose to present individuals with more agency and freedom in their development. Besides, human development is a complex phenomenon and cannot be solely attributed to social experiences.

4. **Neglect of Other Factors:** Marxist thinkers, such as Louis Althusser, have criticized Mead for neglecting the economic base and focusing excessively on ideological superstructures.

5. **Neglect of Processes Shaping Social Reality:** While Mead's main argument centres on how interactions constitute social groups and impact individuals, mentally and socially, he fails to acknowledge the numerous other forces that shape social processes. Michel Foucault and other post-structuralist thinkers have criticized Mead for not adequately addressing power relations and the role of discourse in shaping social reality.

6. **Gender Bias:** Mead's ideas on I and Me do not take into account the intersectional nature of identity. Feminist scholars like Dorothy Smith and Harriet Martineau have pointed out how Mead's theories may not adequately account for the experiences of women and the gendered nature of social interactions. His theory talks of organized response but fails to look at the unequal power relations and historical injustices that determine such responses.

7. **Cultural relativism and downplay of historical context**: By acknowledging that there could be many generalized others, Mead safely treats all cultures equally and avoids the role of forces like colonialism and imperialism in shaping distinct societies and individual behaviour.

Conclusion

George H. Mead's contributions include the development of symbolic interactionism, emphasizing symbols and language in shaping human behaviour. His theory of the self-explores how individuals form identity through social interaction and the internalisation of societal expectations. Despite incoherence in conveying some of his ideas and excessive focus on impact of social processes and interactions, Mead's work provides a foundational understanding of how individual identity is formed in various stages and contributes to the dynamics of society.

ROBERT K. MERTON (1910-2003)

A Brief Biographical Sketch

Robert King Merton (1910–2003) is widely regarded as one of the most influential figures in functionalism and structural functionalism. Born on 4 July 1910 in Philadelphia, Pennsylvania, he completed his undergraduate studies at Temple University in 1931, earning a degree in both sociology and engineering. He then pursued graduate studies at Harvard University, where he was shaped by the intellectual influence of Talcott Parsons and Pitirim Sorokin, and received his Ph.D. in sociology in 1936. Merton's early essay '*Social Structure and Anomie*' (1938) introduced the foundations of his **Strain Theory**, which explained deviance in relation to the disjunction between cultural goals and institutional means. His seminal book *Social Theory and Social Structure* (1949) further advanced sociology by introducing the concepts of **manifest and latent functions**, providing a framework for analyzing the intended and unintended consequences of social practices. In the late 1950s and 1960s, Merton made pioneering contributions to the sociology of science, exploring the processes of innovation, priority disputes, and the diffusion of scientific ideas. Over his long career, he received numerous accolades, and his theories continue to shape contemporary sociological thought. Merton passed away on 23 February 2003 in New York City, leaving behind a lasting intellectual legacy that bridged classical theory and modern sociological research.

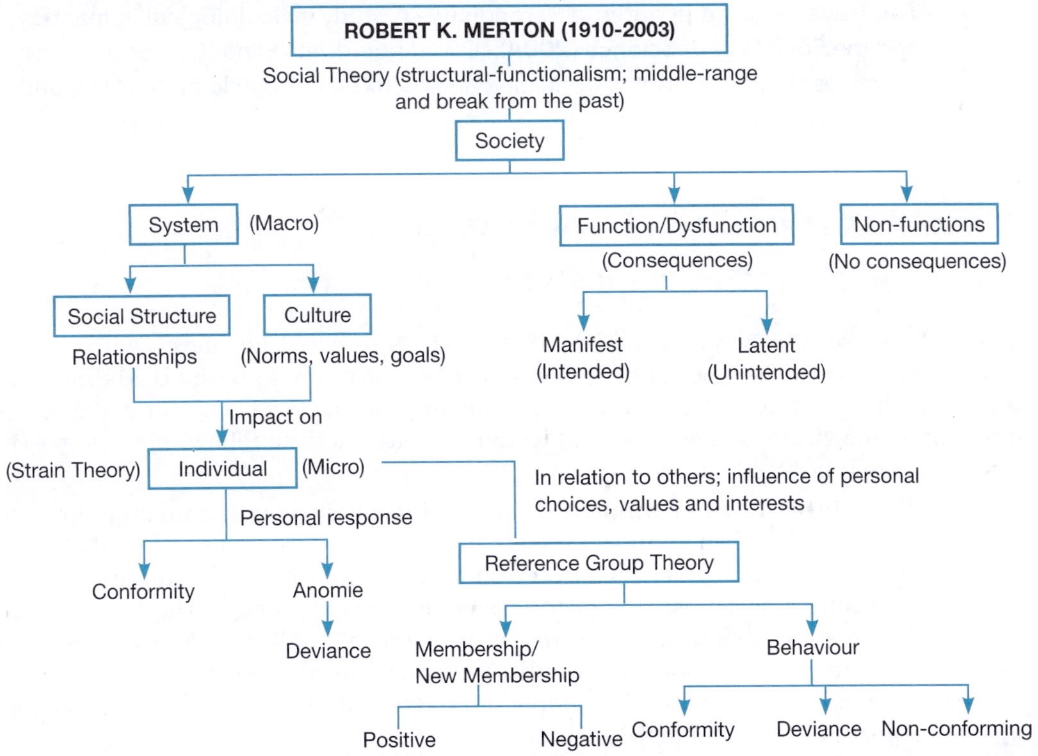

FYI

Major Books by Robert K. Merton

1. **Social Theory and Social Structure (1949)** - This is perhaps Merton's most influential work, where he introduced many of his key concepts such as 'manifest and latent functions,' 'reference groups,' and 'middle-range theory.'
2. **On The Shoulders of Giants: A Shandean Postscript (1965)** - In this book, Merton explores the concept of intellectual and scientific progress, tracing the famous phrase 'standing on the shoulders of giants' through history.
3. **The Sociology of Science: Theoretical and Empirical Investigations (1973)** - This collection of essays delves into the sociology of science, examining how social factors influence scientific research and knowledge production.
4. **Sociological Ambivalence' (1976)** - Here, Merton explores the inherent contradictions and conflicts within social roles and institutions, emphasizing the concept of ambivalence in social behaviour.
5. **On Social Structure and Science (1996)** - This book is a compilation of Merton's writings, covering a wide range of topics including social structure, the sociology of science, and theoretical sociology.
6. **The Travels and Adventures of Serendipity - A Study in Sociological Semantics and the Sociology of Science (2004)** - Co-authored with Elinor Barber, this work examines the concept of 'serendipity' and its role in scientific discoveries and sociological theory.

Merton's Criticism of Functionalism of Early Social Anthropologists

Though a structural-functionalist himself, Robert Merton did not agree with all the assertions made by earlier social anthropologists like Talcott Parsons and B. Malinowski. He argued that such assertions were based majorly on abstract, theoretical systems rather than empirical testing. This led Merton to contradict the following three postulates related to functionalism:

1. **The Postulate of Functional Unity of Society:** It argued that all standardized social and cultural beliefs in the society are functional to society as a whole and also to the individuals. However, Merton stated that while this may be true for small, primitive societies; this postulate cannot be extended to the larger, more complex modern societies. For example, religion in smaller societies acted as a force of unity and cohesion but in multi-religious, pluralistic societies of the modern age, it can be detrimental to individual freedom and safety as has been visible in instances of riots and mob lynching.

2. **The Postulate of Universal Functionalism:** It states that 'all' standardized social and cultural forms have a 'positive' function. Merton argued that in the real world, not every custom, belief, practice, structure, etc., has a positive function. For example, patriarchy is a dominant cultural form across most known societies and has been a contributing factor to the continuing gender-based inequality and discrimination.
3. **The Postulate of Indispensability:** It argued that all standardized forms were not only positive in function but also indispensable to the whole, implying that they were necessary. Merton argued that there are alternatives available and we should be able to consider that. For example, the traditional family model has been heteronormative in nature but societies today are looking at the possibility of normalising families with same-sex couples, single parents, etc. Similarly, from the earlier binary division of male and female, India also recognizes transgenders as the third gender today.

Merton's Contributions to Sociology

Merton's sociological work can be categorized into several key areas:

1. **Theory of Deviance: (Strain Theory):** Merton proposed that societal structures can pressure individuals to commit deviant acts. This theory is encapsulated in his typology of modes of individual adaptation: conformity, innovation, ritualism, retreatism, and rebellion. These modes describe different responses to the disjunction between culturally prescribed goals and the socially structured means of achieving them.
2. **Reference Group Theory:** Merton introduced the concept of reference groups, groups to which individuals compare themselves and against which they evaluate their own behaviour and status.
3. **Manifest and Latent Functions:** Merton distinguished between the intended (manifest) and unintended (latent) functions of social actions. This analytical distinction allows sociologists to uncover the broader and often hidden implications of social behaviours and institutions.

Middle-Range Theories

Merton is particularly renowned for advocating the development of middle-range theories. These are theories that lie between minor but necessary working hypotheses and all-encompassing systematic efforts to develop a unified theory that will explain all the observed uniformities of social behaviour, social organization, and social change. Middle-range theories are more modest, focusing on specific aspects of social life.

Why Merton Chose Middle-Range Theories?

1. **Practicality and Empirical Orientation:** Merton believed that grand theories, such as those proposed by Talcott Parsons, were too abstract and removed from empirical observation. Middle-range theories, in contrast, are more closely connected to observable phenomena and are thus more testable through empirical research.

2. **Flexibility and Relevance:** Middle-range theories can be adapted and refined in the light of new data. This adaptability makes them particularly useful for studying complex and dynamic social phenomena.
3. **Bridge Between Micro and Macro:** These theories provide a crucial link between macro-level structures (like institutions) and micro-level interactions (like individual behaviours), offering a more comprehensive understanding of social dynamics.
4. **Cumulative Knowledge:** By focussing on specific issues, middle-range theories contribute incrementally to the body of sociological knowledge. This cumulative approach allows for the gradual construction of more comprehensive theories.

Examples of Middle-Range Theories

1. **Strain Theory:** Merton's own strain theory is a prime example of a middle-range theory. It specifically addresses the social conditions that contribute to deviant behaviour without attempting to explain all aspects of deviance.
2. **Social Mobility:** Theories explaining patterns and determinants of social mobility within specific societies or historical periods are middle-range theories. These theories do not seek to explain all aspects of social stratification but focus on specific pathways and mechanisms of mobility.
3. **Role Theory:** The study of how individuals fulfill societal roles, and the conflicts and tensions that arise from these roles, is another middle-range theory. This approach provides insights into the dynamics of role-taking and role conflict without claiming to explain the entirety of social structure.
4. **Reference Group Theory:** Merton's reference group theory examines how individuals' attitudes and behaviours are influenced by the groups they compare themselves to. This theory addresses a specific aspect of social psychology and social behaviour.

Function and Its Types

According to Merton, the earlier structural functionalists confused subjective motives of individuals with functions of social structures. For example, the function of marriage from the perspective of the participant could be fulfillment of the need for companionship, but as an objective consequence, marriage serves the function of socialization of children for the maintenance of society. Merton defined functions as 'those observed consequences which make for the adaptation or adjustment of a given system.' This definition implied positive contribution in the maintenance of the system. However, structures and practices could contribute in other ways too. To highlight those, Merton, in addition, developed the following concepts:

1. **Dysfunction:** When structures and institutions have negative consequences for other parts of the system. For example, caste system in India once was the basis of division of labour to ensure smooth occupational interdependence. However, the structure has had more dysfunctions with regard to creating inequality in terms of access to opportunities and resources, discrimination like untouchability related practices, honour killing in instances of inter-caste marriages, etc.

2. **Non-functions:** These refer to consequences that are no more relevant to the system and may simply exist as 'survivals' from historical times. For example, under the Indian Aircraft Act, 1934, kites were also aircraft and you needed to obtain a permit as required for an airplane. Under the Indian Treasure Trove Act, 1878 you could have been jailed if you were found with anything worth more than ₹10 and did not report it to a revenue officer. While many archaic laws have been repealed in recent years, some irrelevant ones still remain.
3. **Net Balance:** It reflects whether positive functions outweigh the negative ones or vice versa. However, such assessment is difficult to calculate and is highly subjective. Its usefulness lies in showcasing relative significance. For instance, in asking questions like, on balance, will legalization of same-sex marriage be more functional or dysfunctional for the society?
4. **Levels of Functional Analysis:** Recognizing that assessing functionality or dysfunctionality at a societal level is too complex and difficult, Merton proposed having levels of functional analysis such as organization, institution or group. For example, legalising same-sex marriage may be deemed inappropriate by the traditional, heteronormative groups, it will be functional for the LGBTQ+ community in terms of gaining basic civic rights and safe expression of identity.
5. **Manifest and Latent Functions**: Merton analysed functions in terms of consequences (positive, negative, irrelevant) and in terms of intentions. When intended, they are called manifest functions and when not intended, they are called latent functions. The concept of latent functions is related to another idea of unintended consequences. Peter Berger has called this 'debunking'–to look beyond the stated intentions and see the real effects.

   For example, while the manifest function of Hopi ceremonials was to cause abundant rainfall, the latent function was to bring together scattered members and create more unity and solidarity through collective participation.

   Similarly, in the modern times, while the manifest function of environmental regulations is to protect the environment and keep it clean, the latent function results in spurring innovation in the market economy with the development of sustainable fashion, clean technologies, increased expenditure in Corporate Social Responsibility, etc. It should be noted that latent functions constitute just one type of unanticipated consequences and are not synonymous with them.

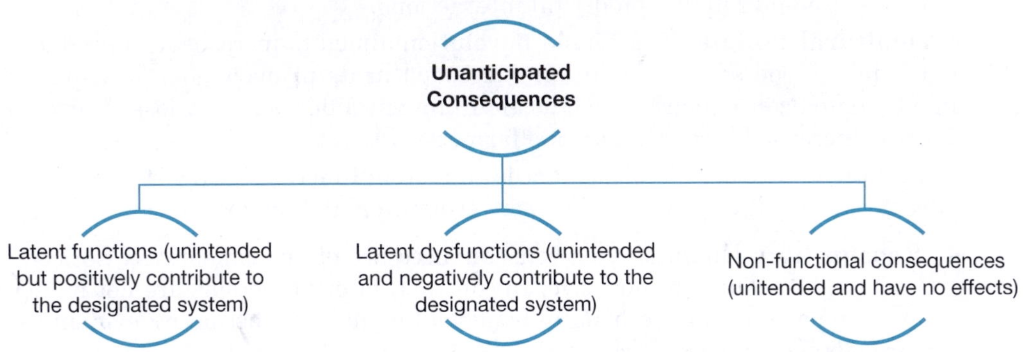

Aspect	Manifest Function (Intended/ Recognized)	Latent Function (Unintended/ Unrecognized)	Dysfunction (Negative Consequence)
Education System	Educate the populace and prepare for employment.	Networking opportunities among students.	Stress and anxiety among students due to pressure.
Healthcare System	Improve health and treat diseases.	Employment opportunities in healthcare sectors.	High costs can lead to financial strain for patients.
Social Media	Facilitate communication and information sharing.	Creation of influential social movements.	Spread of misinformation and privacy issues.
Urban Development	Provide organized living spaces and infrastructure.	Increased property values due to improved amenities.	Gentrification and displacement of lower-income residents.
Public Transportation	Provide affordable travel within and between cities.	Reduction in individual carbon footprints.	Overcrowding and underfunding leading to poor service quality.

Unanticipated Consequences

This refer to outcomes that are not foreseen or intended by the actors involved in a social action. These consequences can be either positive or negative and arise because the complexities of social systems make it difficult to predict all possible outcomes.

Examples

1. **Technological Advancements:** The introduction of smartphones intended to facilitate communication and access to information. However, an unanticipated consequence has been the rise in social isolation and mental health issues due to excessive use and reliance on digital interactions.
2. **Agricultural Policies:** The Green Revolution aimed to increase food production and improve food security. While it succeeded in its primary goal, it also led to unanticipated consequences such as environmental degradation, loss of biodiversity, and increased inequality among farmers.

   While both unanticipated consequences and latent functions deal with unintended outcomes, they differ primarily in their recognition and impact:

   - **Recognition:** Unanticipated consequences are often immediately noticeable and can be positive or negative. In contrast, latent functions are not immediately apparent and are usually beneficial or neutral, becoming evident only through deeper sociological analysis.

- **Impact:** Unanticipated consequences can disrupt or reinforce social systems, sometimes requiring new strategies to mitigate negative effects. Latent functions, however, typically sustain the existing social structure by fulfilling unacknowledged roles that contribute to social stability.

Critique

1. **Overemphasis on consensus and functional approach:** Critics argue that Merton's framework assumes a high degree of functional integration in society, emphasizing how various structures contribute to the maintenance of the entire system. This perspective neglects the existence of conflicting interests and power dynamics.

   Example: In education, the manifest function may be knowledge transmission, but latent functions can include social stratification and reproduction of inequalities to ensure those in the upper class retain their power. Conflict theorists like Pierre Bourdieu critique this functionalist perspective, highlighting how education can reinforce social hierarchies.
2. **Neglect of intersectionality:** Feminist theorists argue that Merton's framework does not adequately address gender power dynamics in various institutions.
3. **Static view of functions:** Merton's framework assumes a static view of functions, not accounting for changes over time or the dynamic nature of social institutions. What may be functional today may become dysfunctional after some time.

   Example: In the evolution of technology, the manifest function of a new invention may be apparent, but its latent functions, such as unintended social consequences or ethical dilemmas, may become evident only over time. Social thinkers like Albert Borgmann critique functionalism for its limited temporal perspective.

Merton's Strain Theory (Social Structure, Anomie, Conformity and Deviance)

Merton analysed the relationship between culture, structure, anomie and resultant deviance in his 1938 work, *Social Structure and Anomie*. Merton defined culture as 'that organized set of normative values governing behaviour which is common to members of a designated society or group' and social structure as 'that organized set of social relationships in which members of the society or group are variously implicated.' According to Merton, anomie occurs 'when there is an acute disjunction between the cultural norms and goals and the socially structured capacities of members of the group to act in accord with them.'

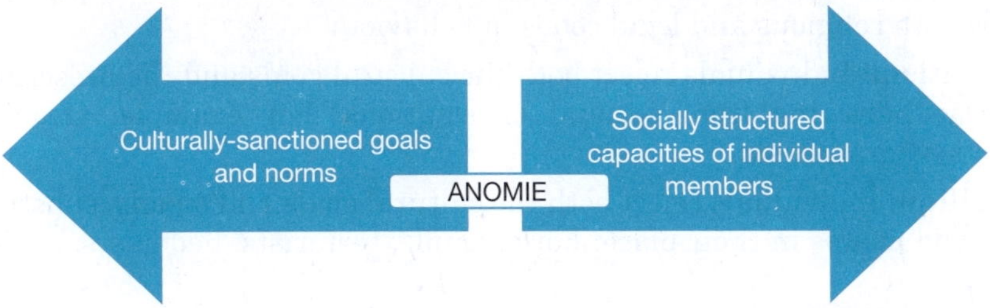

Merton gave the example of the American dream which values materialistic achievements as a cultural goal. However, the available structural means are variably spread across different segments. The social position of many, for example Blacks, Hispanics, etc., restricts their chances to achieve the culturally desired goal. The absence of legitimate means and the persistent desire to reach the top creates a sense of deprivation and frustration–a strain. This strain is representative of the anomie (disjunction between cultural goals and institutionalized means), which leads to deviant behaviour in the form of crime and other illegal activities such as robbery, Ponzi schemes to defraud people, using corrupt ways to make money, etc. The relation between unemployment and increased crime can thus be explained.

In Indian society, high value is placed on working in the government sector. However, strict competition for limited seats implies that majorly those who have the resources to avail good education and guidance can make themselves eligible for these jobs. This disjunction leads people to deviate and indulge in illegal activities such as bribery, leaking of examination papers, generating fake educational degrees, etc.

In another example, the cultural system of urban India requires workers to be punctual and more efficient in their daily schedules. This can only be achieved if the connecting paths between homes and offices are easy to access and allow for smooth travel. Structurally, due to growing congestion and haphazard planning, the traffic system is still overwhelmed. Moreover, due to lack of adequate education and lax attitude, different people regard the traffic rules differently. As a result, people often breach traffic lights and violate these rules. In more recent times, it was highlighted how delivery executives of platforms like Zomato, Swiggy, etc., met with accidents as they were often in a hurry to meet the 30-minute delivery timeline.

Thus, when there is disjunction between culture (norms and goals) and structure (available means), the resulting anomie creates the negative consequence of deviance.

According to the Strain Theory, a person can resort to five types of adaptive responses with regard to the relation between cultural goals and available structural means. These are explained below:

1. **Conformity:** Individuals accept both the cultural goals and the prescribed means. For example, a student studies hard and secures a respectable job.
2. **Innovation:** Individuals accept the cultural goals but reject or modify the means, often resorting to unconventional or criminal methods. For example, a hacker who opts to earn more money by hacking into others' accounts.
3. **Ritualism:** Individuals abandon the cultural goals but continue to adhere strictly to the legitimate means. For example, a sage may give up worldly pursuits and yet follow both religious and legal codes in behaviour.
4. **Retreatism:** Individuals reject both the cultural goals and the prescribed means, often withdrawing from societal expectations. For example, alcoholics, drug addicts, vagrants, etc.
5. **Rebellion:** Individuals reject both the cultural goals and means, substituting new goals and means in their place. For example, terrorists, hedonists, anti-work proponents, etc.

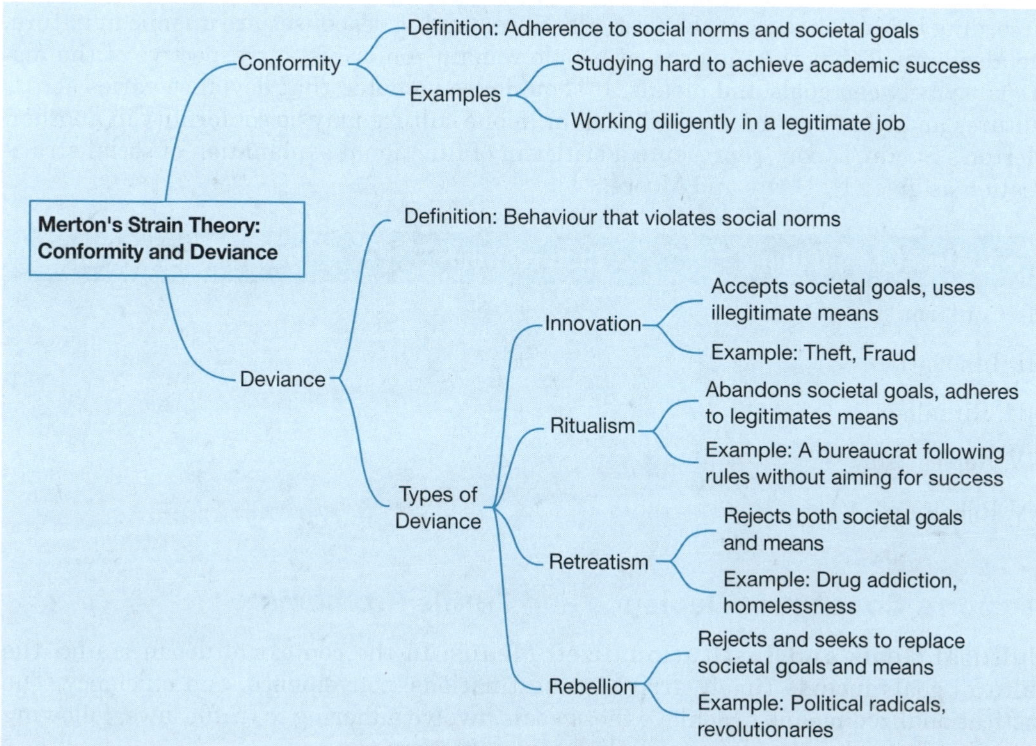
Merton's Strain Theory: Conformity and Deviance
Conformity
Definition: Adherence to social norms and societal goals
Examples
Studying hard to achieve academic success
Working diligently in a legitimate job
Deviance
Definition: Behaviour that violates social norms
Types of Deviance
Innovation
Accepts societal goals, uses illegitimate means
Example: Theft, Fraud
Ritualism
Abandons societal goals, adheres to legitimates means
Example: A bureaucrat following rules without aiming for success
Retreatism
Rejects both societal goals and means
Example: Drug addiction, homelessness
Rebellion
Rejects and seeks to replace societal goals and means
Example: Political radicals, revolutionaries

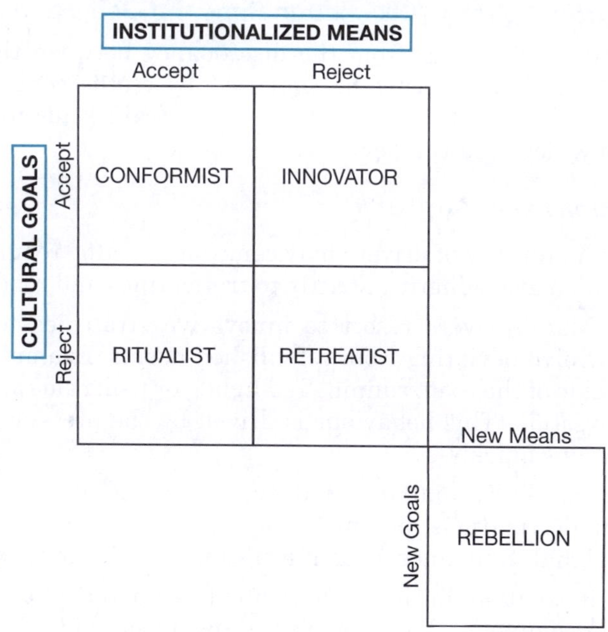
INSTITUTIONALIZED MEANS
Accept
Reject
CULTURAL GOALS
Accept
Reject
CONFORMIST
INNOVATOR
RITUALIST
RETREATIST
New Means
New Goals
REBELLION

According to Merton, except the first, all the remaining responses are anomic in nature. He also argued that the majority of people remain conformists irrespective of the discrepancy between goals and means. It should also be noted that deviance varies across cultures and what may be deemed deviant in one culture may be conformity in another. Merton's Strain Theory represents a criticism of functional explanation of social stratification as given by Davis and Moore.

Modes of Adaptation	Cultural Goals	Institutionalized Means
I. Conformity	+	+
II. Innovation	+	–
III. Ritualism	–	+
IV. Retreatism	–	–
V. Rebellion	±	±

Merton's Concept of Deviance and Traffic Problems

Cultural Goals and Institutionalized Means: In the context of urban traffic, the cultural goals include timely arrival at destinations, convenience, and efficiency. The institutionalized means to achieve these goals involve adhering to traffic laws, following road signals, and maintaining orderly driving practices.

Strain in Urban Traffic Context (Disjunction Between Goals and Means)

The strain in urban traffic arises from the discrepancy between the desire to reach destinations quickly and the constraints imposed by traffic congestion, inadequate infrastructure, and enforcement of traffic laws. This strain leads to various modes of adaptation, some of which result in deviant behaviours.

Modes of Adaptation in Urban Traffic

1. **Conformity:** A minority of drivers may conform to traffic regulations despite the congestion and delays, adhering strictly to traffic rules and road safety norms.
2. **Innovation:** Many drivers resort to innovative strategies to navigate traffic, which often involve deviating from established norms. Examples include driving on the wrong side of the road, running red lights, or using sidewalks and shoulders to bypass congestion. This behaviour is driven by the pressure to save time and reach destinations quickly.
3. **Ritualism:** Some individuals may adhere to traffic rules without any hope of reaching their destinations on time. This might be seen in drivers who rigidly follow traffic signals and lanes, even if it means significant delays.
4. **Retreatism:** Retreatism in the traffic context can manifest as avoidance of peak traffic hours or complete reliance on alternative modes of transport, such as bicycles or walking, to escape the pressures of urban traffic.

5. **Rebellion:** In some cases, groups or individuals may engage in acts of protest against the existing traffic system, advocating for changes in traffic management, better infrastructure, or improved public transport options. These actions represent a rejection of current goals and means, proposing new solutions to the traffic problem

Examples Illustrating Merton's Concept

1. **Innovative Driving Behaviours:** Urban India often witnesses drivers using unconventional methods to beat traffic, such as jumping lanes, overtaking from the left, or using unauthorized shortcuts. These behaviours reflect an innovative adaptation to the strain caused by traffic congestion and inadequate enforcement.
2. **Non-compliance with Traffic Laws:** Due to inconsistent enforcement of traffic regulations, many drivers choose to ignore traffic signals, speed limits, and lane discipline. This non-compliance is an innovative response to the pressure of reaching destinations on time in a congested environment.
3. **Alternative Transport and Retreatism:** Faced with the frustration of navigating congested roads, some individuals may retreat by avoiding peak traffic hours or relying entirely on alternative modes of transport such as bicycles, walking, or even ride-sharing services to escape the pressures of urban traffic.

Addressing Traffic Problems Through Merton's Lens

Applying Merton's concept of deviance to urban traffic problems helps identify the root causes of deviant driving behaviours. The primary cause is the strain between the cultural goal of efficient and timely travel and the inadequate means provided by the urban infrastructure and enforcement mechanisms.

Policy Implications

1. **Improving Infrastructure:** Addressing the infrastructure deficit by expanding and maintaining roads, improving public transportation, and developing efficient traffic management systems can help alleviate the strain on drivers and reduce the need for deviant behaviours.
2. **Enhancing Enforcement:** Strengthening the enforcement of traffic laws through the use of technology (e.g., traffic cameras, automated fines) and increasing the presence of traffic police can deter drivers from engaging in innovative, non-compliant behaviours.
3. **Public Awareness Campaigns:** Educating the public about the importance of traffic rules and the dangers of deviant driving behaviours can foster a culture of conformity and compliance with traffic laws.
4. **Encouraging Alternative Modes of Transport:** Promoting the use of public transportation, cycling, and walking by making these options more attractive and accessible can reduce the strain on road infrastructure and decrease the prevalence of deviant driving behaviours.

Difference Between Durkheim and Merton's Views on Anomie

Aspect	Durkheim's Anomie	Merton's Strain Theory
Theorist	Émile Durkheim	Robert K. Merton
Definition of Anomie	Anomie is a breakdown of social norms, a state of normlessness or confusion, leading to a lack of regulation in society.	Anomie is a condition resulting from a disjunction between societal goals and the legitimate means available to achieve them. Merton focusses on the strain individuals experience in pursuing cultural goals.
Causes of Anomie	Rapid social change and disruption in societal norms, especially during periods of industrialization. Changes to social structures through large scale events are responsible.	Merton's focus is on the strain, deprivation and frustration that individuals experience. The unequal social structures and their discrepancy with goals are responsible.
Functions of Anomie	Durkheim sees anomie as a social pathology that can lead to increased rates of suicide and deviance.	Merton suggests that anomie can lead to various adaptations, such as conformity, innovation, ritualism, retreatism, or rebellion, depending on how individuals respond to the strain.
Social Integration	Durkheim emphasises the importance of social integration and collective conscience in preventing anomie.	Merton acknowledges the role of social structure but places greater emphasis on the strain-inducing aspects of the societal structure that limit the capacities of individuals.
Emphasis on Goals	Durkheim's focus is on the collective conscience and shared values, with less emphasis on specific societal goals.	Merton's theory centres on the pursuit of culturally approved goals.
Application	Durkheim's theory is more macro-level, examining societal conditions and their impact on individuals in large numbers.	Merton's theory operates at both macro and micro levels, emphasizing the interplay between societal structures and individual responses.
Examples	Durkheim's classic study on suicide rates in different social contexts illustrates the impact of anomie.	Merton's Strain Theory can be applied to various contexts, such as understanding crime rates, educational attainment, and the consequences of societal expectations on individuals.

Critique

1. Critics argue that Merton's theory is culturally biased, rooted in the American Dream, and may not be universally applicable.

   Example: In non-Western societies, the goals of success and the means to achieve them may be perceived differently. Subaltern studies scholars, like Ranajit Guha, critique universalizing theories that do not consider diverse cultural contexts.
2. Critics challenge the assumption that deviance is solely a response to strain, overlooking instances of deviance without apparent strain.

   Example: White-collar crime, committed by those in high socio-economic positions, may not be easily explained by Merton's strain theory. Conflict theorists like Edwin Sutherland argue that power differentials and opportunity structures play a more significant role in such deviance.
3. Interactionists like Howard Becker have argued how deviance is not simply a behavioural response. One could be labelled deviant even when one is not. Also, one could be deviant in one culture and not in others.
4. Scholars like Lemert and Laurie Taylor have argued that deviance is a weapon used by the powerful to suppress resistance and does not reflect the consensus of society on what is considered wrong or illegal.
5. Merton fails to consider other causes for anomie apart from disjunction between goals and means. For example, crisis situations like a war or environmental emergencies can cause strain.
6. Albert Cohen in Deviance and Control, 1966 has argued that deviance is specific to sub-cultures rather than individual level phenomenon. He also stated that Merton failed to explain non-utilitarian crimes like vandalism which are symbolic in nature and do not intend to achieve any personal goal.
7. According to the ecological approach of the Chicago school, deviance varies area wise within a city, region, nation, etc., depending upon a combination of factors - economic, social, cultural, etc.
8. Deviance as a behavioural response has psychological roots as well. The same individual could respond differently at different times to the same social stimulus. Thus, it is not solely determined by cultural and social factors.

Generation of Deviant Subcultures

Deviant subcultures emerge predominantly through the innovative mode of adaptation, where individuals accept societal goals but resort to illegitimate or non-normative means due to perceived barriers to legitimate opportunities. This process is typically influenced by various socio-economic factors:

1. **Blocked Opportunities**
   - Individuals from disadvantaged socio-economic backgrounds often face significant obstacles in accessing education, employment, and other legitimate avenues for success. This blockage can lead to frustration and the adoption of alternative, often deviant, strategies to achieve societal goals.

- For instance, the emergence of gangs and criminal organizations in economically deprived urban areas can be seen as a response to blocked opportunities, where members seek financial success and social status through illicit means.

2. **Socialization and Peer Influence**
   - Within certain communities, deviant behaviour can become normalized and reinforced through social interactions and peer influence. When individuals associate predominantly with others who engage in or endorse deviant activities, these behaviours become an accepted part of their subculture.
   - An example is the development of drug subcultures, where individuals learn and adopt behaviours related to drug use, distribution, and associated criminal activities through their social networks.
3. **Reaction to Societal Norms**
   - Deviant subcultures can also form as a reaction against societal norms and values perceived as oppressive or irrelevant. Members of these subcultures may reject mainstream societal expectations and create their own sets of norms and values.
   - The punk subculture of the 1970s, with its emphasis on anti-establishment sentiments and distinct styles of dress and music, exemplifies a cultural rebellion against prevailing social norms.

Merton's analysis provides a nuanced understanding of how societal structures and cultural dynamics contribute to the formation of deviant subcultures. By identifying the strain between cultural goals and institutionalized means, Merton highlights the socio-economic and psychological pressures that drive individuals towards deviant adaptations. This framework underscores the importance of addressing systemic inequalities and providing equitable opportunities to mitigate the emergence of deviant subcultures.

Theory of Reference Group

In his book, *Social Theory and Social Structure* (1949), Robert Merton gave the theory of reference group behaviour. We all are a part of different groups. A group is a network of relationships, such as a family, a group of friends, a practice group, etc. Merton gave three defining characteristics of a group - a) it consists of a number of people who frequently interact with one another, b) there is a pattern of expectations that all members of the group feel obligated to fulfil and c) the members are identified as belonging to the group by their fellow members and other non-members.

A reference group is one to which a person refers to in order to evaluate their achievements, their role performances, their aspirations and ambitions. It can be both–a membership group as well as a non-membership group. For a person, a reference membership group such as the family tells them whether what they do is right or wrong, and reference non-membership groups such as celebrities, cricketers, politicians, etc., create a sense of deprivation through comparison in privileges, standards of living, etc. Positive reference group is one whose lifestyle, values and norms one attempts to emulate, to which one wishes to belong while negative reference group like criminal gangs, drug addicts, alcoholics., etc is one which one resists, one which involves motivated rejection.

Merton identified several types of reference groups, each serving different purposes:

1. **Primary Reference Groups:** These are close-knit groups such as family and close friends that have a profound impact on an individual's values and self-identity.
2. **Secondary Reference Groups:** These include larger, more impersonal groups like colleagues or classmates, which influence behaviour but to a lesser extent than primary groups.
3. **Membership Reference Groups:** Groups to which an individual currently belongs, such as a university community or a professional organization.
4. **Aspirational Reference Groups:** Groups to which an individual aspires to belong but is not currently a member, such as a prestigious club or a high-status profession.
5. **Avoidant (or Dissociative) Reference Groups:** Groups that an individual does not want to belong to and uses as a standard to avoid certain behaviours or attitudes.

To explain deprivation further, Merton gave the following concepts:

1. **Relative Deprivation:** Merton in his work, *The American Soldier* (1949) explained how a soldier looks at himself through comparison with his peers. He argues that happiness and deprivation are not absolutes rather they depend on the scale of measure and frame of reference. For example, married soldiers think they are deprived of the freedom that their unmarried counterparts enjoy, unmarried soldiers think they are deprived of the emotional support that their married counterparts have. Thus, deprivation becomes relative in a sense that it depends on the group one is using for comparison purposes.
2. **Anticipatory Socialization:** It refers to adoption of lifestyle and values of non-membership positive reference groups to one day be able to officially become their member. Merton introduced the concept of anticipatory socialization, where individuals adopt the values and behaviours of a group they aspire to join. This process helps in easing their transition into the new group but can also lead to role conflict and marginalization if the individual fails to gain entry into the aspirational group.
3. **Reference Individuals and Role Models:** People aspire to be like certain individuals when the entire group does not hold much appeal. For example- actors as a group may not be desirable, but stars like Amitabh Bacchan or Rajnikant enjoy a massive following. A reference individual is different from a role-model. The latter, according to Merton, is more restricted in scope and offers identification in selected areas. For instance, an aspiring actor could treat Amitabh Bacchan as their role-model. But in case of a reference individual, their values and behaviours are approximated in several areas of one's life, even to the point of identifying with the individual's smile, mannerisms, etc.

Factors governing selection of non-membership reference groups

- The group's capacity to confer prestige in the larger society
  Example- IAS officers as a reference group for their power and influence
- The 'isolates' of membership groups choose to emulate values and norms of individuals of other groups
  Example- a person whose father wants him to join family business chooses to become an actor instead
- The 'openness and mobility' of social systems
  Example - in an open society where merit and hard work are recognized, choosing other reference groups becomes easier
- Norms and values that one is interested in
  Example- one may aspire to live like a celebrity and yet say no to leather-made products because they care for animals.

4. **Functionally Optimum Degree of Visibility:** Merton admits that it is impossible to have complete knowledge of the norms, values and actual role-performance of members of the reference group. This introduces an element of uncertainty and scepticism. Thus, it is common for many parents to discourage their children to choose to become actors as they are uncertain of all that lies beneath the glamour. Hence, Merton calls for a functionally optimum degree of visibility which could provide, if not full, but still an accurate picture of the reference group.
5. **Non-conformity as a Type of Reference Group Behaviour**: According to Merton, conformity is adhering to the in-group's ideals and norms while non-conformity is either rejection of the in-group's norms or adherence to the out-group's norms. Non-conformity is not deviant behaviour though.

Non-conformity	Deviance
1. The non-conformist announces his dissent.	1. The deviant is the criminal who does not declare his dissent.
2. The non-conformist challenges the legitimacy of norms and expectations and rejects them. He is not an opportunist.	2. The criminal does not have the courage to challenge the legitimacy of norms. For example - he does not agree that theft or murder is right but merely finds it more convenient to violate the rules to benefit himself.
3. The non-conformists believe that they are gifted with a 'higher morality' and that they should change the norms of the group.	3. The criminal does not have any such vision of morality.

Contemporary Examples

1. **Social Media Influencers:** In today's digital age, social media influencers serve as powerful aspirational reference groups. Many individuals, especially younger generations, compare themselves to influencers and adopt their lifestyles, fashion choices, and behaviours in hopes of achieving similar social status and recognition.
2. **Professional Organizations:** For professionals, membership in prestigious organizations such as the American Medical Association or the Bar Association serves as a reference group. These organizations set standards for professional behaviour and achievement, influencing members' career aspirations and ethical standards.
3. **Fitness Communities:** Fitness communities, both online and offline, act as reference groups for individuals aiming to improve their health and fitness. Members often compare their progress to others in the group, adopt workout routines, and follow dietary guidelines promoted by the community.
4. **Educational Institutions:** Students often use their educational institutions as reference groups. For instance, attending an Ivy League university can serve as a reference point for academic and career aspirations, influencing students' study habits, extracurricular activities, and career choices.
5. **Corporate Culture:** In the corporate world, companies with strong cultures, such as Google or Apple, serve as reference groups for other businesses and employees. These companies set benchmarks for innovation, work environment, and employee benefits, influencing practices and aspirations in the broader industry.

Critique

1. **Simplistic view of influence:** Critics argue that Merton's theory oversimplifies the influence of reference groups on individual behaviour.

   Example: In consumer behaviour, reference groups may influence choices, but social psychologists like Herbert Kelman argue that different processes, such as identification or internalization, play distinct roles in determining the impact of reference groups.
2. **Limited exploration of diversity within reference groups:** Merton's theory tends to treat reference groups as homogeneous entities, neglecting the diversity within groups.

   Example: Feminist critics argue that Merton's theory does not adequately consider the diversity of women's experiences within reference groups. Kimberlé Crenshaw's intersectionality framework highlights the importance of considering multiple social identities in understanding influence.
3. **Neglect of agency:** Critics argue that Merton's theory may downplay individual agency in the face of reference group influence.

   Example: Social psychologists like Albert Bandura emphasize the role of self-efficacy and personal agency in resisting or accepting reference group norms. The social cognitive theory provides a more nuanced perspective on individual decision-making.

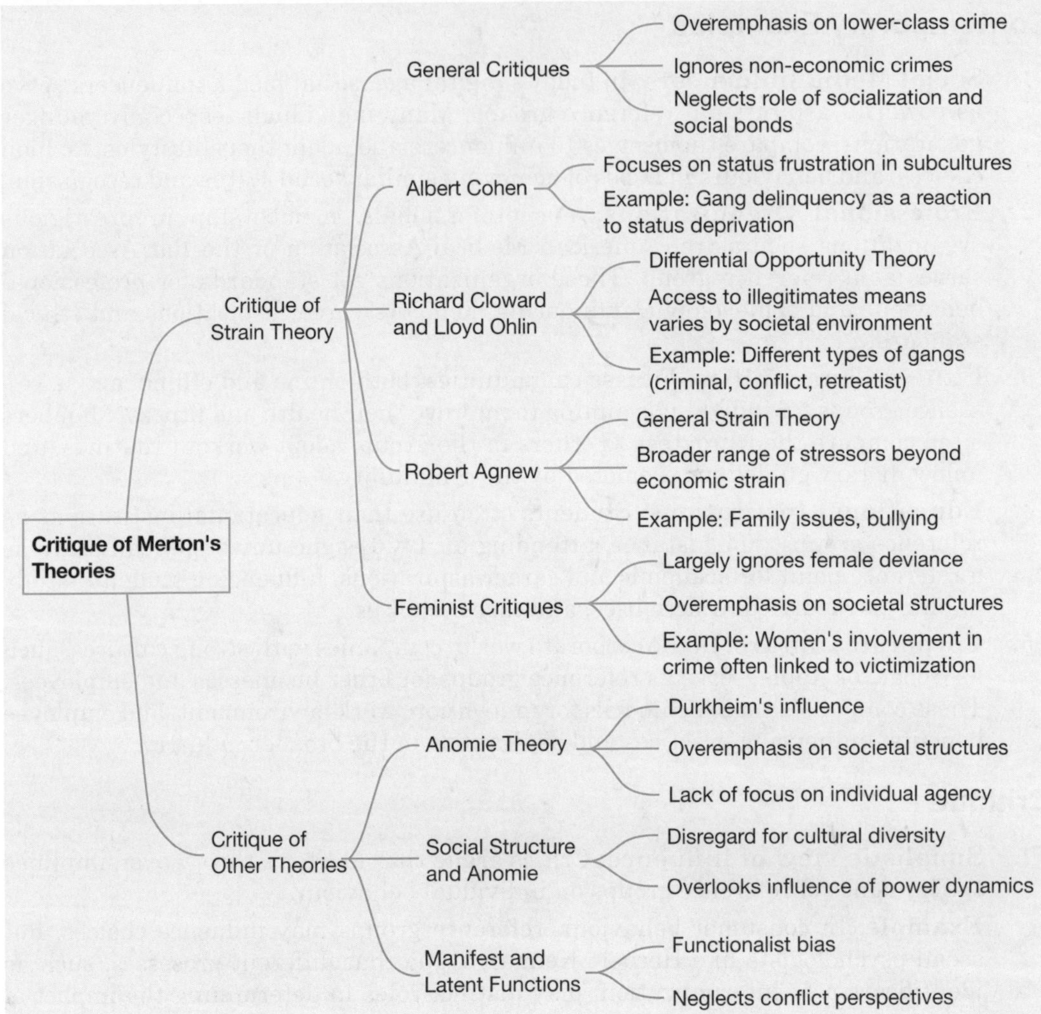

Conclusion

Despite criticisms, Merton's legacy lies in his efforts to bridge micro and macro perspectives, exploring the interplay between societal structures and individual responses. His work has inspired further research and debate within sociology, enriching our understanding of how social structures influence behaviour and how individuals navigate societal expectations.

Previous Years' Questions

2024

1. What are the 'basic and irreducible' functions of the family as proposed by Talcott Parsons? Explain. (10 Marks)
2. Describe the main idea of Max Weber's book, '*The Protestant Ethic and the Spirit of Capitalism*' as a critique of Marxism. (20 Marks)
3. Critically explain the salient features of 'alienation' as propounded by Karl Marx. (10 Marks)
4. Describe various characteristics of a 'social fact'. How is rate of suicide a social fact according to Durkheim? (10 Marks)
5. Explain G.H. Mead's idea of development of 'self' through the 'generalized other'. (10 Marks)
6. How is 'power' different from 'authority'? Discuss various types of authorities as theorized by Max Weber. (10 Marks)

2023

1. What is historical materialism? Examine its relevance in understanding contemporary societies. (20 marks)
2. Is Weber's idea of bureaucracy a product of the historical experiences of Europe? Comment. (10 marks)
3. Explain Max Weber's theory of social stratification. How does Weber's idea of class differ from that of Marx? (20 marks)
4. Is Weber's idea of bureaucracy a product of the historical experiences of Europe? Comment. (10 marks)
5. Explain Max Weber's theory of social stratification. How does Weber's idea of class differ from that of Marx? (20 marks)
6. Is reference group theory a universally applicable model? Elucidate. (10 marks)

2022

1. Durkheim argued that society is more than the sum of individual acts. Discuss. (10 marks)
2. Critically examine how Durkheim and Merton explicate Anomie. (20 marks)
3. Critically examine the relevance of Durkheim's views on religion in contemporary society. (10 marks)

4. Durkheim argued that society is more than the sum of individual acts. Discuss. (10 marks)
5. Critically examine how Durkheim and Merton explicate Anomie. (20 marks)
6. Critically examine the relevance of Durkheim's view on religion in contemporary society. (20 marks)
7. Critically analyse Parsons's views on society as a social system. (20 marks)
8. According to Mead, the idea of self develops when the individual becomes self-conscious. Explain. (20 marks)
9. Critically examine how Durkheim and Merton explicate anomie. (20 marks)

2021

1. Explain whether Durkheim's theory of Division of Labour is relevant in the present day context. (10 marks)
2. Critically examine the dialectics involved in each mode of production as propounded by Karl Marx. (20 marks)
3. Explain whether Durkheim's Theory of Division of labour is relevant of the present day context. (10 marks)
4. Critically examine the dialetics involved in each mode of production as propounded by Karl Marx. (20 marks)
5. Critically examine Max Weber's theory of social stratification. (10 marks)
6. Do you agree with Max Weber's idea that bureaucracy has the potential to become an iron cage? Justify your answer. (20 marks)
7. Do you think Talcott Parsons gave an adequate theory of social change? Justify your answer. (10 marks)
8. Critically examine Max Weber's theory of social stratification. (10 marks)
9. Do you agree with Max Weber's idea that bureaucracy has the potential to become an iron cage? Justify your answer. (20 marks)
10. Do you think Talcott Parsons gave an adequate theory of social change? Justify your answer. (10 marks)
11. With suitable examples, explain how conformity and deviance coexist in a society as propounded by R.K. Merton. (10 marks)

2020

1. Critically analyse Durkheim's views on elementary forms of religious life and role of religion. Also discuss the consequences of religious revivalism in contemporary society. (20 marks)

2. According to Durkheim, 'The major function of education is the transmission of society's norms and values.' Discuss. (20 marks)
3. What are the problems in observing social facts in Durkheim's views? (10 marks)
4. How does Marx view social conflict as an essential element of social change? (20 marks)
5. Critically analyse Durkheim's views on elementary forms of religious life and role of religion. Also, discuss the consequences of religious revivalism in contemporary society. (20 marks)
6. According to Durkheim, 'The major function of education is the transmission of society's norms and values.' Discuss. (20 marks)
7. What are the problems in observing social facts in Durkheim's views? (10 marks)
8. How does Marx view social conflict as an essential element of social change? (20 marks)
9. 'Ideal types' of Max Weber are mental constructs, they do not correspond to reality. Give your views. (10 marks)
10. Analyse the relevance of pattern variables in the study of social change. (10 marks)
11. 'Ideal types' of Max Weber are mental constructs, they do not correspond to reality. Give your views. (10 marks)
12. Analyse the relevance of Pattern Variables in the study of social change. (10 marks)
13. What are the reactions of R.K. Merton to the functionalism of social anthropologists? Bring out the limitations of latent functions. (20 marks)

2019

1. What is the Marxist concept of 'fetishism of commodities'? (10 marks)
2. What is 'reserve army of labour'? Present the position of feminist scholars on this. (20 marks)
3. Compare and contrast the contributions of Marx and Weber on social stratification in capitalist society. (20 marks)
4. How well do you think Tonnies, Weber, Durkheim and Marx predicted the character of modern society? (10 marks)
5. What is the Marxist concept of 'fetishism of commodities'? (10 marks)
6. What is 'reserve army of labour'? Present the position of feminist scholars on this. (20 marks)
7. Compare and contrast the contributions of Marx and Weber on social stratificaiton in capitalist society. (20 marks)
8. How well do you think Tonnies, Weber, Durkheim and Marx predicted the character of modern society? (10 marks)

9. Compare and contrast the contributions of Marx and Weber on social stratification in capitalist society. (20 marks)

10. How well do you think Tonnies, Durkheim, Marx and Weber predicted the character of modern society? Critique. (10 marks)

11. Differentiate between life chances and lifestyle with suitable examples. (10 marks)

12. Compare and contrast the contributions of Marx and Weber on social stratification in capitalist society. (20 marks)

13. How well do you think Tonnies, Durkheim, Marx and Weber predicted the character of modern society? Critique. (10 marks)

14. Differentiate between life chances and lifestyle with suitable examples. (10 marks)

15. According to Mead, 'We play a key role in our own socialization.' Explain. (20 marks)

16. What, according to Merton, is the difference between 'unanticipated consequences' and 'latent functions'? Give examples to elaborate. (10 marks)

17. How, according to Merton, are deviant subcultures generated? (20 marks)

2018

1. Explain Durkheim's basic arguments on suicide. Can you analyse high suicide rates of contemporary Indian society with Durkheim's theory? (20 marks)

2. Does collapse of functionalism and bankruptcy of Marxism coincide with the rupture of modernity? Discuss. (20 marks)

3. What is the difference between anomie in Merton and Durkheim? Explain. (10 marks)

4. According to Marx, how are human beings alienated from their human potential and what does he suggest to change this? (20 marks)

5. In what way did Durkheim perceive religion as functional to society? (10 marks)

6. Explain Durkheim's basic arguments on suicide. Can you analyse high suicide rates of contemporary Indian society with Durkheim's theory? (20 marks)

7. Does collapse of functionalism and bankruptcy of Marxism coincide with the rupture of modernity? Discuss. (20 marks)

8. What is the difference between anomie in Merton and Durkheim? Explain. (10 marks)

9. According to Marx, how are human beings alienated from their human potential and what does he suggest to change this? (20 marks)

10. In what way did Durkheim perceive religion as functional to society? (10 marks)

11. Distinguish between fact and value in Weber's Protestant Ethic and the Spirit of Capitalism. (10 marks)

12. How can Parsons's AGIL framework be used to analyse key problems in a society? Discuss. (20 marks)
13. Distinguish between fact and value in Weber's Protestant Ethic and the Spirit of Capitalism. (10 marks)
14. How can Parsons's AGIL framework be used to analyse key problems in a society? Discuss. (20 marks)
15. Do you think 'I' and 'Me' are central terms in Mead's work? (10 marks)
16. What is the difference between anomie in Merton and Durkheim? Explain. (10 marks)

2017

1. Discuss distinct sociological method as adopted by Durkheim in his study of suicide. (20 marks)
2. Analyse Marxian concept of historical materialism as a critique of Hegelian dialectics. (20 marks)
3. Give an assessment of the Durkheimian notion of sacred and profane in sociology of religion. (10 marks)
4. Discuss distinct sociological method as adopted by Durkheim in his study of suicide. (20 marks)
5. Analyse Marxian concept of historical materialism as a critique of Hegelian dialectics. (20 marks)
6. Give an assessment of the Durkheimian notion of sacred and profane in sociology of religion. (10 marks)
7. What is Weberian critique of Marxian notion of social stratification? (20 marks)
8. Critically analyse Talcott Parsons' conception of 'pattern variables'. (10 marks)
9. What is Weberian critique of Marxian notion of social stratification? (20 marks)
10. Critically analyse Talcott Parsons' conception of 'pattern variables'. (10 marks)
11. What is the difference between anomie in Merton and Durkheim? Explain. (10 marks)

2016

1. Evaluate Marx's ideas on mode of production. (10 marks)
2. 'Social conflict is both a cause and consequence of social change.' Explain. (10 marks)
3. How is Durkheim's theory of religion different from Weber's theory of religion? (20 marks)
4. Evaluate Marx's ideas on mode of production. (10 marks)
5. 'Social conflict is both a cause and consequence of social change.' Explain. (10 marks)

6. How is Durkheim's theory of religion different from Weber's theory of religion? (20 marks)

7. Examine Max Weber's method of maintaining objectivity in social research. (20 marks)

8. How is Durkheim's theory of religion different from Weber's theory of religion? (20 marks)

9. Describe the functional prerequisites of a social system as given by Talcott Parsons. Examine in the context of university as a social system. (20 marks)

10. Examine Max Weber's method of maintaining objectivity in social research. (20 marks)

11. How is Durkheim's theory of religion different from Weber's theory of religion? (20 marks)

12. Describe the functional prerequisites of a social system as given by Talcott Parsons. Examine in the context of university as a social system. (20 marks)

13. Analyse the manifest and latent functions of 'the security of tenure of bureaucrats' in the light of Merton's theory. (20 marks)

2015

1. Differentiate between Marxian and Weberian theories of social stratification. (20 marks)

2. Elabourate the views of Durkheim on 'The Elementary Forms of Religious Life.' (10 marks)

3. Differentiate between Marxian and Weberian theories of social stratification. (20 marks)

4. Elabourate the views of Durkheim on 'The Elementary Forms of Religious Life.' (10 marks)

5. What concepts did Weber use to analyse legitimate forms of domination? (10 marks)

6. Discuss the role of Calvinist ethic in the development of Capitalism. (20 marks)

7. Differentiate between Marxian and Weberian theories of social stratification. (20 marks)

8. How is social equilibrium maintained in Parsonian framework? (20 marks)

9. What concepts did Weber use to analyse legitimate forms of domination? (10 marks)

10. Discuss the role of Calvinist ethic in the development of Capitalism. (20 marks)

11. Differentiate between Marxian and Weberian theories of social stratification. (20 marks)

12. How is social equilibrium maintained in Parsonian framework? (20 marks)

13. 'Self and society are twin born.' Examine the statement of Mead. (10 marks)

14. Anomie is rooted in social structure. Explain with reference to R.K. Merton's contribution. (10 marks)

2014

1. Identify the similarities and differences between Marx's theory of alienation and Durkheim's theory of anomie. (20 marks)
2. For Marx, class divisions are outcomes of 'exploitation'. Discuss. (10 marks)
3. What are the distinctive features of social organization of work in slave society? How is it different from feudal society? (10 marks)
4. 'According to Durkheim, the essence of religion in modern society is the same as the essence of religion in primitive society.' Comment. (10 marks)
5. According to Marx, capitalism transforms even the personal relationships between men and women. Critically examine with illustrations from the contemporary Indian context. (10 marks)
6. Identify the similarities and differences between Marx's theory of alienation and Durkheim's theory of anomie. (20 marks)
7. For Marx, class divisions are outcomes of 'exploitation'. Discuss. (10 marks)
8. What are the distinctive features of social organization of work in slave society? How is it different from feudal society? (10 marks)
9. 'According to Durkheim, the essence of religion in modern society is the same as the essence of religion in primitive society.' Comment. (10 marks)
10. According to Marx, capitalism transforms even the personal relationships between men and women. Critically examine with illustrations from the contemporary Indian context. (10 marks)
11. How is objectivity different from value neutrality? Discuss with reference to Weber's views on methodology. (10 marks)
12. 'According to Max Weber, 'class' and 'status' are two different dimensions of power'. Discuss. (20 marks)
13. How does Weber use the notion of 'ideal types' in his theory of bureaucracy? (20 marks)
14. 'Power is not a zero-sum game.' Discuss with reference to Weber's and Parsons' views. (20 marks)
15. How is objectivity different from value neutrality? Discuss with reference to Weber's views on methodology. (10 marks)
16. 'According to Max Weber, 'class' and 'status' are two different dimensions of power'. Discuss. (20 marks)

17. How does Weber use the notion of 'ideal types' in his theory of bureaucracy? (20 marks)

18. 'Power is not a zero-sum game.' Discuss with reference to Weber's and Parsons' views. (20 marks)

19. Using Mead's theory of symbolic interactionism, discuss the stages in formation of gender identity. (10 marks)

20. How could one use Merton's concept of deviance to understand the traffic problem in urban India? (10 marks)

21. Using Merton's concepts of manifest and latent functions, explain the persistence of corruption in Indian society. (10 marks)

2013

1. Critically examine the functionalist tradition in Sociology. (20 marks)
2. Analyse the salient features of historical materialism. (10 marks)
3. Compare Karl Marx with Emile Durkheim with reference to the framework of 'division of labour'. (20 marks)
4. How do Karl Marx and Max Weber differ in terms of their analysis of social stratification? (20 marks)
5. Critically examine the functionalist tradition in Sociology. (20 marks)
6. Analyse the salient features of historical materialism. (10 marks)
7. Compare Karl Marx with Emile Durkheim with reference to the framework of 'division of labour'. (20 marks)
8. How do Karl Marx and Max Weber differ in terms of their analysis of social stratification? (20 marks)
9. Examine the salient features of Weberian bureaucracy. (10 marks)
10. How do Karl Marx and Max Weber differ in terms of their analysis of social stratification? (20 marks)
11. Examine the relevance of Parsonian social system in the present society. (10 marks)
12. Examine the salient features of Weberian bureaucracy. (10 marks)
13. How do Karl Marx and Max Weber differ in terms of their analysis of social stratification? (20 marks)
14. Examine the relevance of Parsonian social system in the present society. (10 marks)
15. Critically analyse the contributions of G.H. Mead to symbolic interactionism. (20 marks)

CHAPTER

5

Stratification and Mobility

In this Chapter

- Equality, Inequality, Hierarchy, Exclusion, Poverty and Deprivation
- Theories of Social Stratification
- Dimensions of Social Stratification-Class
- Social Mobility
- Types of Mobility
- Sources and Causes of Mobility
- Previous Years' Questions

Social Stratification and Mobility

What is Social Stratification?

According to Anthony Giddens (2009), social stratification is a concept which is used to describe inequalities that exist between individuals and groups in a society. It refers to both a system and a process. It is a system of evaluative ranking of social units in terms of relations of superiority and inferiority. It is a process of placing units in a hierarchy which is governed by certain norms and principles with the aim objective to distribute social advantages among the units. Giddens summarises stratification as 'structured inequalities between different groupings of people.'(2009)

The most common way to imagine stratification is via class, that is through distribution of material resources. However, society is also stratified according to age, gender, race, caste, ethnicity, religion and other such factors. In sociology, we study stratification of 'groups' and how they have access to unequal rewards based on their position in the system. So, for example, a Scheduled Caste woman might have access to less opportunities than an upper caste man. Even as individuals, they belong to certain social categories such as gender, caste, etc., which determine their chances to better their lives.

What are the Major Types of Social Stratification?

Historically, the following types of systems of social stratification have been known to exist:

1. **Age-set System:** This type of stratification was common in stateless societies such as those of Masai and Nandis of East Africa. People who belonged to a certain range of years were put into one age-set. The age-set determined their role and authority. When one grows in age, one also transitions to a different age-set, like from junior to senior warriorhood, and from junior to senior elderhood. This transition occurs in a collective group and hence, everyone is able to occupy positions of authority at one point. It provides an open system of mobility where one's movement up the social ladder happens in accordance with one's age.
2. **Slave System:** Though this system of stratification does not legally exist anymore, it illustrates how societies have been divided since ancient times through the concept of human ownership based on artificial notions of superiority and discriminatory rules by those in power. Ancient slavery existed in ancient Rome and Greece where slaves were usually the foreign prisoners of war. In New World Slavery, colonial expansion and racist exploitation led to human ownership through denial of economic, political and social rights. Slavery was abolished in the 19th century in the UK and the USA but continues to exist in more varied forms in different parts of the world. Examples include - forced labour, child labour, human trafficking, domestic servitude, etc.
3. **Estate System:** This type of system was characteristic of feudal societies in Medieval Europe. The defining features included: a) each estate had its own set of rights defined by law, b) the difference between estates was marked by punishment given for identical offences, c) a hierarchy existed within each estate in which at the top, was a royal family and military aristocracy. At par with them,

was the clergy or the priesthood, who were allied with the nobility. Below them, ranked the merchants and the craftsmen who later became the middle-class and at the bottom, were the landless serfs and the peasants d) each estate was managed through the control of property/land and hereditary transmission of property rights among the aristocracy and the nobility e) the estate system was marked by division of labour (the nobility was to protect all, the priesthood was to pray for all and the serfs were to produce food for all) f) this system reinforced political and economic inequalities as the burden of taxes fell on those at the bottom – the serfs and the merchants, while the upper strata enjoyed domination. The estate system came to an end with the transition to capitalism.

4. **Caste System:** This system of stratification is unique to India, although some of its features are found in other forms of stratification. Its main characteristics include: a) First one is religious basis based on which the caste system is traced to certain Hindu religious texts dictating how society should be organized, b) membership is fixed and hereditary, the ascriptive identity cannot be changed, c) promotes endogamy in terms of marriage, commensality, contracts, etc., d) originally was based on occupational specialization, e) fixed hierarchy dictating the superiority of some castes over others. In terms of abstract classification, caste system refers to the fourfold *varnas – Brahmins, Kshatriya, Vaishyas and Shudras*. A fifth category which lies outside the system include the *Avarnas* or the Untouchables. At the operational level, caste system exists in terms of local communities called *jatis* which are more in number and have their own specific rules.

5. **Class System:** It refers to a social hierarchy based primarily on the differences in wealth, income and consumption patterns. As opposed to other types of stratification which are closed and rigid, this system is open and allows for vertical mobility. It has been of most significance in the capitalist society as a result of processes of industrialization and urbanization. According to Max Weber, classes are distinguished from each other on the basis of wealth, power and lifestyle. All industrial societies have been known to have three distinct classes – upper class, middle class and lower class. As for the rural society, Daniel Thorner identified three classes namely *maalik* (proprietors who own the land), *kisaan* (working peasants who own small parcels of land) and *mazdur* (labourers who do not own any land).

6. **Race System:** Race is a biological concept used to refer to a large category of people who share certain inherited physical characteristics such as colour of skin, type of hair, facial features, etc. In sociology, race is studied as a system of classification wherein a group of people are endowed with certain social attributes on the basis of their appearance. For instance, during the apartheid regime of South Africa, physical characteristics were believed to be linked to moral, intellectual and other non-physical attributes. In countries like the USA too, slavery system was built on the basis of racist discrimination in which the blacks were treated as inferior. The colonization process led by European countries like the UK was also driven by notions of racial superiority and 'White man's burden' to civilise other inferior and backward races in their colonies. The Aryan theory too remains controversial in its beliefs about racial purity. One of the theories on genesis of caste system in India relates to division between the immigrating Aryans and the native dasyas.

7. **Ethnic System:** Ethnicity refers to common cultural heritage which is learned, not inherited. The ethnic group may share a common language, history, national origin or lifestyle. So while race is based on common physical traits, ethnicity is based on common cultural traits. Ethnicity is wider and may most likely include a homogenous racial group.

Ace Your Answers!

1. *What is the difference between race and ethnicity? Illustrate through relevant examples.*
2. *Discuss the nature of ethnic conflicts in contemporary India. (Manipur, Nagaland)*
3. *Has class-based stratification eclipsed caste discrimination in India?*
4. *What are the modern forms of slavery? Mention the steps that have been taken to address them.*
5. *The situation of domestic workers in India is representative of multiple forms of stratification. Elaborate.*

What is the Source of Social Stratification?

The early primitive societies have been considered the most egalitarian in nature as the focus in them was on 'subsistence'. According to conflict theorists, with the generation of 'surplus', social stratification came into the picture as people now started figuring out more ways of investing and making money. The resultant differences in lifestyle and wealth accumulation led to increased competition. According to functional theorists, on the other hand, social stratification emerged from the need to better organize society and ensure its proper functioning through a) specialized division of labour and, b) role allocation.

Key Concepts Associated with Social Stratification

Equality

According to the Collins dictionary, equality refers to the state or situation wherein all members of a society, group or family have the same status, rights and responsibilities. For sociological understanding, the Cambridge Dictionary of Sociology talks about four types of equality:

(a) **Ontological Equality:** This type of equality is supported by Natural Law philosophers and human rights advocates who believe that 'all human beings are born free and equal in dignity and rights' (UN Universal Declaration of Human Rights)

(b) **Equality of Opportunity:** This type of equality emphasises talent over inheritance. It calls for provision of access to important social institutions such as higher education to all, regardless of what one's family possesses. The argument is that social roles should be open to achievement and competition.

(c) **Equality of Condition:** This refers to adoption of certain strategies which will reduce the limitations on equality of opportunity. For instance, state measures such as taxation for wealth distribution, market regulation, affirmative action, etc.

(d) **Equality of Outcome:** This type of equality focuses on giving the same reward regardless of the individual need or performance. For example, the idea of Universal Basic Income, employment guarantee for every person, etc. Generally, societies are unable to achieve equality of outcome as some form of inequality is considered functionally necessary for filling up important roles and positions.

Ace Your Answers!

The Preamble of the Constitution of India talks about securing to all citizens - equality of status and opportunity (among other things). Reflect on the following: a) Is it possible and desirable to achieve equality of status in India? b) What steps has the Indian government taken to promote equality of opportunity?

Inequality

Inequality refers to the state or situation wherein members of a group, family or society have different rights, responsibilities and advantages, and also differential access to material resources. Inequality includes a certain degree of discrimination which puts certain segments at a relatively disadvantageous position. Such discrimination not only contributes to oppression of some but also reinforces unfair structures of power, maintaining the stronghold of few.

Ralf Dahrendorf in a famous essay – 'On the Origins of Social Inequality' distinguished four types of inequality (Cambridge Dictionary of Sociology).

(a) Natural differences of kind such as colour of the skin, eyes, one's height, etc.

(b) Natural differences of rank-based on talent or intelligence. For instance, theories of biological determinism and racial superiority argue that some groups are born with a superior intelligence and ability. The principle of hereditary nature of intelligence thus reinforces hierarchies. This was most evident in mid-20th century Britain wherein intelligence testing was used as a tool to justify not increasing investments on expanding secondary education. Intelligence Quotient IQ has been criticized for its inherent biases and failure to take into account social obstacles. In 1952, Brian Simon had shown how intelligence testing via IQ (Intelligence Quotient) upheld a form of school organization and teaching that prevented secondary education for all.

(c) Social differentiation based on division of labour which is a system of occupational segregation on the nature of one's work. For example, the Jajmani system in traditional India.

(d) Social stratification which includes rank ordering of individuals based on prestige and wealth Though Dahrendorf distinguished these types, stratification has come to include various dimensions which go beyond wealth and prestige, such as gender, race, ethnicity, etc. Thus, including other forms of inequality as well.

Ace Your Answers!

1. What is the difference between natural inequality and social inequality? Is IQ an objective tool for testing intelligence?
2. Critically examine the *Jajmani* system as a form of division of labour.

Hierarchy

It denotes the ranking of multiple strata in a society placed one above the other on the basis of certain factors like wealth (class hierarchy), power (political hierarchy), purity and pollution (caste hierarchy), tradition (religious hierarchy), biological traits (gender-based hierarchy), etc. Hierarchy forms the basis of social stratification as it is representative of inequality and power imbalance. It results into unequal opportunities and unequal rewards, further reinforcing hierarchies. While hierarchies represent domination and subordination, difference represents mere existence of diversity. So, while two groups may be different from each other, they may not necessarily be placed in terms of ranking in relation to each other.

Exclusion

It refers to practices that deny the targeted people involvement in general social, economic, cultural and political activities of the society and exercise of certain rights. It is systematic and prevents actualization of equality of opportunity for all as a result of structural constraints. The social exclusion is involuntary, i.e., exclusion is practised regardless of the wishes of those who are excluded. For example, even though public restaurants are supposedly accessible to all members of the public, the restaurants still reserve the right to restrict the entry of any individual, who are most likely from the underprivileged sections. Similarly, in institutions like Army, factors like gender and sex can be used to regulate entry of women into different posts. In earlier times and in certain rural areas still, the so-called upper castes control entry of other caste members in terms of access to public places like temples, ponds, rivers, etc. It is often argued that the excluded sections themselves do not wish to participate but in actuality, the prolonged discrimination discourages the members to an extent that they then stop trying to be included. Social exclusion is exercised by those in power to keep the weaker sections out and is often institutionalized through laws, customs, rules and regulations, etc.

Ace Your Answers!

1. What are the modern forms of 'Untouchability' that promote social exclusion?
2. Can you think of some important judgments in the past decade that have sought to curb social exclusion?
(Eg. Sabarimala verdict, Judgment on permanent commission to women, etc.)

Poverty

It refers to the condition of 'not having access to those things which are considered 'normal' or 'basic' within a given society.' (Giddens & Sutton) As a concept, it emerged in the early 20th century with Seebohm Rowntree's work on poverty in York. Poverty can be understood in two ways - absolute and relative. Absolute poverty deals with material subsistence- the basic conditions, such as food, shelter and clothing that must be met to sustain a reasonably healthy existence. Sociologists are more interested, however, in relative poverty which deals with the overall standards of living in a society. Poverty in this case is culturally defined and recognizes that what may be considered essential in one society may not be so in others. Social groups that are more likely to be found living in poverty include children, older people, women and some ethnic minorities. The prevalence of poverty is explained via two approaches:

(a) **Blame the Victim Theory:** Wherein individual lifestyle and attitude is blamed for their poor living conditions. In the 1980s, American sociologist Charles Murray coined the term 'underclass' to refer to sections of people with a dependency culture on welfare benefits and a tendency to avoid entering work

(b) **Blame the System Theory:** This looks at social processes which create conditions of poverty. In the 1930s, R.H. Tawney theorized that poverty is an aspect of social inequality (see Giddens & Sutton) and hence, instead of changing individual attitudes, focus should be on structural changes such as policy interventions to reduce income inequality, better access to quality education for all, national minimum wage, child care income, etc. Economic restructuring such as excessive privatization, increase in indirect taxes, decline in manufacturing or unforeseen events like famine, droughts, etc., can also lead to poverty.

Dimensions of Poverty and Social Exclusion

1. **Economic Exclusion**
   - **Income Poverty:** Low income restricts access to essential goods and services, such as housing, healthcare, and education.
   - **Employment Exclusion:** Unemployment or underemployment limits individuals' financial stability and career progression.

2. **Social Exclusion**
   - **Social Networks:** Poor individuals often lack access to social networks that can provide support and opportunities.
   - **Stigmatization:** Stereotypes and negative perceptions can lead to discrimination, further isolating the poor.
3. **Cultural Exclusion**
   - **Cultural Capital:** Limited access to cultural resources, such as education and cultural activities, prevents full societal participation.
   - **Identity and Belonging:** Marginalized groups may struggle with identity and societal acceptance.
4. **Political Exclusion**
   - **Lack of Representation:** Poor individuals often have limited political influence and representation.
   - **Policy Impact:** Policies may not address the needs of the poor, perpetuating exclusion and inequality.

Deprivation

Deprivation refers to a state of deficiency that impedes social progress. The concept of cultural deprivation, for instance, posits that certain cultures possess inherent deficiencies that hinder economic and social advancement. Some scholars argue that values such as fatalism and antipathy toward individual wealth accumulation contribute to a "culture of poverty," which is ostensibly deprived of the necessary traits to promote progress among marginalized sections of society.

Basil Bernstein contended that the language of the poor or working-class is "restrictive," lacking elaborative codes of communication, thereby reducing their chances of advancement. Similarly, Pierre Bourdieu emphasized that the dominated class, due to its inability to appropriate "legitimate" forms of culture, is deprived of opportunities for advancement. Bourdieu posited that the dominant class defines what constitutes "legitimate" or high-status culture. This includes specific tastes, knowledge, behaviours, and cultural practices. According to Bourdieu, the dominated or lower classes are often unable to access or fully appreciate this "legitimate" culture due to their different socialization and limited resources.

It is crucial to note that deprivation functions as both a cause and a consequence of social inequality. As certain sections of society wield more power than others, their cultures and ideas become dominant and more pervasive. The imposition of these dominant ideas on others, coupled with the unequal distribution of benefits, deprives marginalized sections of the necessary resources to ascend the ladder of social mobility.

Here are the primary dimensions of deprivation within social stratification:

1. **Economic Deprivation**
   - **Income Inequality:** Unequal distribution of income results in varying standards of living. Lower-income groups face difficulties in affording basic needs such as food, clothing, and shelter.
   - **Wealth Disparity:** Wealth accumulation varies significantly among social classes, impacting individuals' ability to invest in education, health, and property.

2. **Educational Deprivation**
   - **Access to Education:** Lower socio-economic groups often have limited access to quality education, perpetuating cycles of poverty and hindering upward mobility.
   - **Educational Attainment:** Disparities in educational attainment lead to unequal job opportunities and income levels.
3. **Health Deprivation**
   - **Healthcare Access:** Socio-economic status affects access to healthcare services. The poor often face barriers to quality healthcare, leading to higher morbidity and mortality rates.
   - **Nutritional Deficits:** Lower-income groups may lack access to nutritious food, resulting in malnutrition and related health issues.
4. **Social Deprivation**
   - **Social Networks:** Poor individuals often lack robust social networks that can provide support, opportunities, and information.
   - **Social Capital:** The ability to leverage social connections for personal or professional gain is often limited among the lower classes.
5. **Cultural Deprivation**
   - **Cultural Capital:** Access to cultural knowledge, skills, and education is often stratified, with higher classes having greater cultural capital.
   - **Cultural Participation:** Opportunities to participate in cultural activities, such as art, music, and literature, are often limited for the economically disadvantaged.
6. **Political Deprivation**
   - **Political Representation:** Marginalized groups often have less political representation and influence, leading to policies that may not address their needs.
   - **Civic Participation:** Lower classes may have fewer opportunities or resources to engage in political and civic activities.
7. **Spatial Deprivation**
   - **Housing Quality:** Lower socio-economic groups often live in substandard housing with poor infrastructure and limited amenities.
   - **Neighbourhood Effects:** Living in impoverished neighbourhoods can limit access to quality schools, jobs, and healthcare facilities, reinforcing social stratification.
8. **Gender Deprivation:**
   - **Gender Pay Gap:** Women, particularly in lower socio-economic classes, often earn less than men, exacerbating economic deprivation.
   - **Gender Roles:** Traditional gender roles can limit opportunities for education and employment for women, contributing to broader social and economic inequalities.

Illustrative Examples

1. **India's Rural-Urban Divide:** Rural populations often face economic, educational, and healthcare deprivation due to limited access to resources and opportunities compared to urban areas.

2. **Racial and Ethnic Minorities in the US:** African Americans and Hispanic communities experience significant disparities in income, education, healthcare, and political representation, leading to systemic deprivation.
3. **Caste System in India:** Lower castes, particularly Dalits, face historical and systemic deprivation across economic, educational, health, and social dimensions, often resulting in severe marginalization and exclusion.

Four Social Processes Associated with Social Stratification

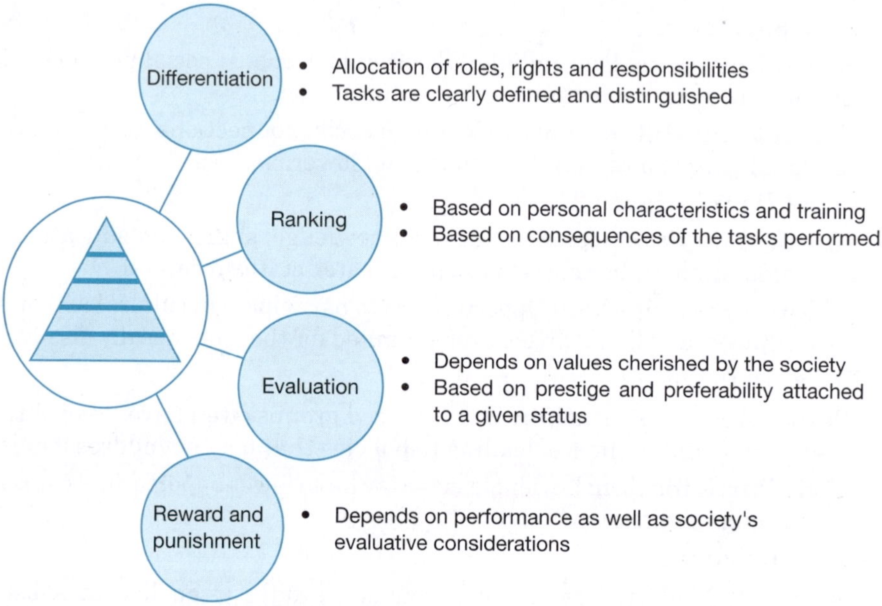

Theoretical Approaches to Social Stratification

Theory	Key Proponents	Basic Premise	Mechanism of Stratification	Examples
Functionalism	Kingsley Davis, Wilbert Moore	Social stratification is necessary for the proper functioning of society. It ensures that the most qualified individuals fill the roles that are most important for the society's survival.	Roles are allocated based on the skills and abilities of individuals, leading to unequal rewards.	In many professions like medicine or law, individuals undergo extensive education and training, which society rewards with high status and income.

Theory	Key Proponents	Basic Premise	Mechanism of Stratification	Examples
Conflict Theory	Karl Marx	Stratification arises from the conflicts between different social classes, primarily the bourgeoisie (capitalists) and the proletariat (workers). It benefits those at the top and oppresses those at the bottom.	Ownership and control of resources lead to power differentials and exploitation.	In industrial societies, factory owners (bourgeoisie) exploit workers (proletariat) to maximise profits, maintaining power through control of resources.
Weberian Theory	Max Weber	Stratification is multidimensional and includes class (economic), status (social), and party (political power). These dimensions interact to influence one's overall social position.	Class is determined by one's market situation; status by social honour and lifestyle; party by power within an organization.	A high-ranking military officer may have significant political power (party) and social prestige (status) but may not be wealthy (class).
Cultural Capital Theory	Pierre Bourdieu	Stratification is maintained through cultural capital, which includes non-economic resources such as education, intellect, style of speech, and appearance.	Cultural capital is transmitted across generations, reinforcing social positions.	Elite schools often produce students who possess the cultural capital valued by elite universities and prestigious employers.
Feminist Theory	Ann Oakley, Sylvia Walby	Stratification is rooted in patriarchy, with gender being a primary organizing principle of social inequality.	Gender roles and norms perpetuate inequalities in various social institutions.	The gender pay gap in many societies where women are systematically paid less than men for similar work.
Intersectionality Theory	Kimberlé Crenshaw, Patricia Hill Collins	Social stratification is a complex interplay of multiple social identities such as race, gender, class, sexuality, etc.	Intersecting identities create unique experiences of advantage and disadvantage.	African American women in the US may face compounded disadvantages due to both racism and sexism.

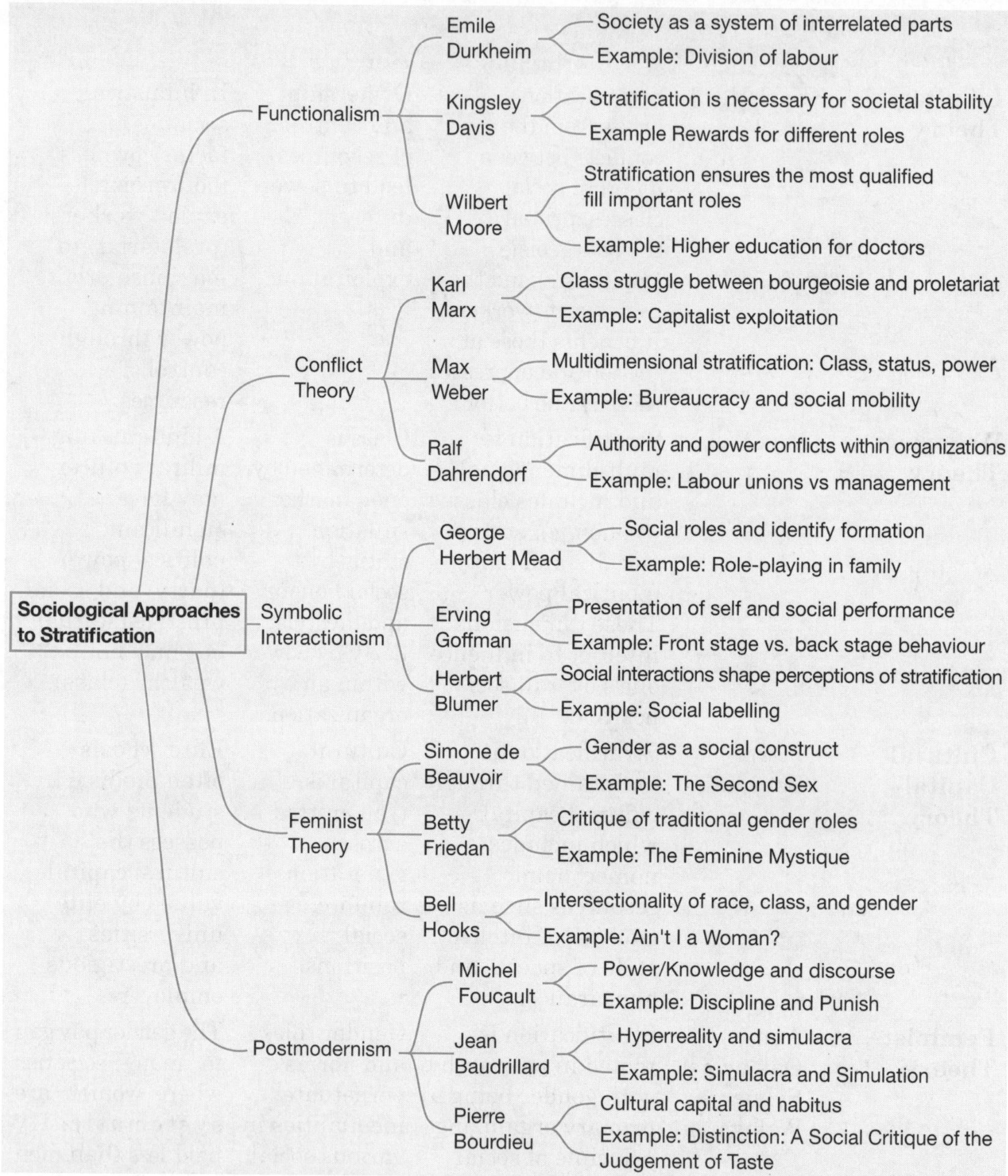

Structural-Functionalist Theory

Functional theorists of stratification, Kingsley Davis and Wilbert Moore stress the necessity of stratification. Basic premise of functional approach is that, one person cannot do everything. People depend on each other for fulfillment of different tasks. Different people perform different tasks according to their respective intent and ability. Different tasks are valued differently in the society. As such, people performing such tasks are valued and rewarded differently so that the most capable ones are correctly allocated the tasks. The differential reward pattern automatically gives rise to stratification and hierarchy.

What Do They Propose?

Davis and Moore proposed the following points:

- Stratification is a universal phenomenon.
- It serves a positive function and is necessary for societal survival.
- All societies need fulfillment of certain functional pre-requisites to survive, one of which is 'role- allocation and performance. Stratification fulfills this objective.
- Some positions are functionally more important than others. People differ in terms of their talent and ability while positions differ in terms of their importance for survival and maintenance of the society.
- More important positions require certain specialized skills and people possessing such skills are limited.
- Social stratification serves as the mechanism through which the society ensures that the most important positions are carefully filled by the most able and qualified persons.
- Since these top positions require extensive training and deferral of gratification, they also receive the highest rewards in terms of prestige and money.
- The differential rewards act as motivation to draw in the most talented and also for those who fill these positions to do their job efficiently and conscientiously.
- Thus, stratification helps in proper functioning of the society.

How Does One Decide Whether a Position is Functionally Important?

According to Davis and Moore, the importance of a position can be measured in two ways:

1. It can be measured by 'the degree to which a position is functionally unique' such that there are no other positions which can perform the same function satisfactorily. For example, a judge is functionally more important than a stenographer who records the judgments
2. The second measure of importance is 'degree to which other positions are dependent on the position I question'. For example, both faculty and administrative staff are dependent on the principal for directions

Thus, according to Davis and Moore, social inequality is an inevitable feature of human society and differential reward system is key to its maintenance and proper functioning.

What are the Criticisms?

Melvin M. Tumin has given the most comprehensive criticism of Davis and Moore's ideas on stratification:

1. **Functional Importance:** Tumin dismissed the idea that the most rewarded positions are also the most important. He argued that 'some labour force of unskilled

workmen are as indispensable in a factory as some labour force of engineers'. There is no objective way of measuring functional importance, rather it is more a matter of opinion.

2. **Power and Rewards:** Tumin argued that differences in pay and prestige between different occupational groups may be due to differences in power rather than their functional importance. For example, corporate workers get handsomely paid because of the power of capitalist enterprises in a consumerist society. On the contrary, a farmer struggles to generate enough income due to lack of bargaining power despite the functional importance.
3. **The Pool of Talent:** Tumin criticized the assumption that only a limited number of people possessed the required talents and abilities for the most important positions on three grounds: a) there is still no effective way of measuring talent b) there is no proof that exceptional talent is required for these positions and c) the talent pool may be larger than assumed and thus may not require a system of unequal rewards
4. **Training:** Tumin argued that the period of training should not be seen as a sacrifice compensation for which is provided for the rest of one's life. Even a student gets time for leisure and self-development and can make up for the lost earnings in ten years of work.
5. **Motivation:** Tumin criticized the idea that unequal rewards motivate individuals. Rather, the social stratification system acts as a barrier, especially in the closed systems. The caste system, for instance, prevents those in the hierarchically lower categories from accessing opportunities due to their ascribed status. An untouchable has no chance of becoming a priest despite having a similar potential. Similarly, Blacks have been historically discriminated against, depriving them of the chance to prove their mettle. Even in the open class system, those belonging to the lower classes may not be exposed to the same opportunities as their counterparts of upper class.
6. **Misuse of Power:** Tumin also argues that those in power erect barriers to prevent certain sections from accessing their positions, thereby creating high demands for their services and thus increasing the associated rewards. For example, even though there is a need for greater number of doctors in India, in proportion, the available number of seats for medical courses is still quite less. Similarly, the All India Judicial Service has failed to become a reality despite the abysmal state of recruitment in subordinate judiciary in the country. Attempts at conducting a centralized exam have failed to fructify due to lack of consensus among the stakeholders.
7. **Inequality of Opportunity:** Tumin argued that by its very nature, social stratification maintains social inequality by limited the access of those born in the lower strata to the opportunities that are readily available to those born in the higher strata.
8. **Social Division:** Tumin argued that far from aiding in proper functioning of society, social stratification actually is a divisive force. It excludes a large section from equal participation in social activities and increases hostility and suspicion between groups. The disintegrating effect is visible in instances of crime, riots, corruption, suicides, etc.

Are their theory relevant in contemporary times?

Ace Your Answers!

1. What changes can a caste census bring into the existing system of social stratification in India?
2. Do you think Davis and Moore's theory on differential reward system and effective role allocation applies to politics? Does politics attract the most talented and the most able to occupy political positions?
3. Is the reward system in entertainment industry in proportion to its functional importance?

Weberian Theory

Max Weber is popular for giving a more nuanced theory of social stratification. He recognized three bases of group formation in modern societies as opposed to Marx's one. They are explained below:

1. **Class:** According to Weber, people who belong to the same class share the same 'market situation'. They share the same position in the market economy and as such share similar economic rewards and similar 'life chances' (chances of obtaining those things which are deemed desirable by the society). Like Marx, Weber saw the division of classes between those who owned the means of production and those who did not. However, Weber also recognized the market situation of propertyless groups who offer different skills and services with differing market values. Overall, Weber distinguished the following four types of classes:
   (i) The propertied upper class
   (ii) The property-less white collar workers
   (iii) The petty bourgeoisie
   (iv) The manual working class
2. **Status:** It refers to the unequal distribution of 'social honour' between different groups. Those who are accorded similar levels of social prestige by society's members and also share similar lifestyles belong to the same status group. Members are aware of their common status situation and place restrictions on how the outsiders can interact with them. The exclusion of some people from membership of a status group is known as social closure. For example, in the caste system in India, people's identity of belonging to a specific caste remains the same throughout their life. Castes are closed groups disallowing entry of outsiders through various ways, for example marriage, eating and socializing restrictions, etc. Another example of social closure is South Africa's Apartheid system which promoted racial

segregation in public places, marriages, etc. Even in certain occupations, status groups can erect barriers to entry for others. For example, nepotism in Bollywood creates a more challenging and an uneven playing field for new actors who do not belong to traditional film families.

- How are class and status groups linked?
  - (i) Class influences one's status but it is not necessary that those who share the same class situation will also belong to same status group. For example, a famer and a businessman owning same levels of property may have very different lifestyles and hence, different status situation. Similarly, a Government official may earn less than a corporate employee and yet earn more prestige in the society.
  - (ii) Status groups may create divisions between classes. In a study conducted in Banbury, Oxfordshire in the 1950s, Margaret Stacy found that members of the working class distinguished three status groups within that class: a) the 'respectable working class', 'the ordinary working class' and the 'rough working class'
  - (iii) Status groups can cut across class divisions. For example, homosexuals belonging to different class divisions come together to unite and fight for their rights; very often, large, small and mid-sized farmers come together to fight against any unwanted policy intervention; netizens come together to voice collective opinion on controversial issues such as war, human rights issues, etc.

3. **Party:** According to Weber, parties are groups which are specifically concerned with making policies and with making decisions in the interest of the group's membership. They are concerned with the acquisition of social power. They could range from political parties to pressure groups, professional associations to trade unions. They could or could not be influenced by class and status. For example, Bharatiya Samajwadi Party emerged as a patron of the Dalit and underprivileged castes members of which have historically occupied a lower class and status situation in the social hierarchy. On the other hand, pressure groups like Association for Democratic Reforms (ADR) do not represent interests of one particular class or are representative of one singular status but believe in challenging power to prevent arbitrary governance. Organizations such as Rashtriya Swayamsevak Sangh might not represent one class but do represent members who share similar status situation in terms of religion, lifestyle, etc.

As per Weber, the interplay between class, status and party remains complex and varies according to social context and time period.

Marxist Theory

For Marx, social stratification is associated with the formation of classes. Classes, as per Marx, refer to strata or groups of people with shared interests and same relationship to means of production. In all stratified societies, there are two types of classes namely ruling class and subject class. The ruling class owns and controls the means of production (land, capital, labour power, machinery) while the subject class sells its labour to survive. Other institutions such as the legal and political systems are instruments of ruling-class domination.

1. **Classes Across Historical Epochs**

- **Primitive Communism:** There were no classes during this stage as it was based on 'subistence economy'. Production took place for the purpose of fulfillment of basic needs. Everyone was a producer as well as consumer and there was widespread egalitarianism.

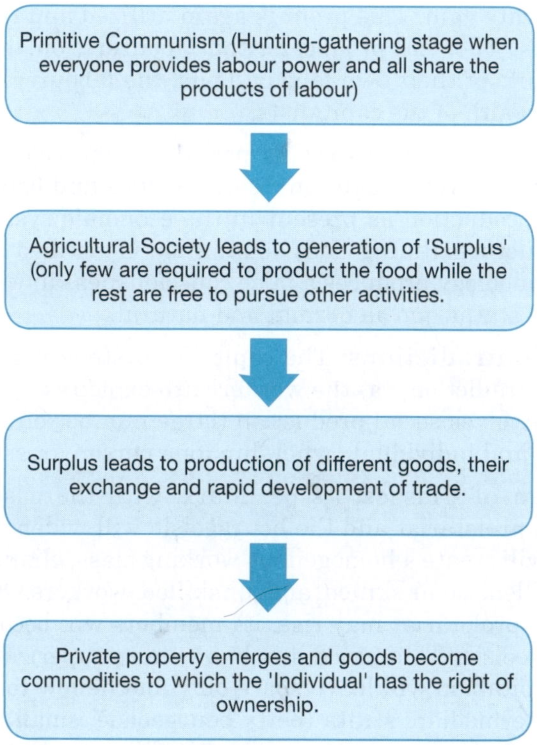

- **Ancient Society:** During this stage, the society was divided between the classes of masters and slaves. The source of power was control over knowledge which dictated division of society between the superior, more civilized ones and the inferior, so-called savage ones.
- **Medieval Society:** During this stage, the society was divided between the classes of landlords and serfs. The source of power was control over 'land'.
- **Capitalist Society:** During this stage, the society is divided between the classes of bourgeoisie and the proletariat. The source of power is control over 'capital' in the form of finance, technology, buildings, etc.

  Stratification in modern capitalist society is characterized by the following features:

- **Minority vs Majority:** According to Marx, a small minority of people owns the means of production and controls the majority of the masses. Thus, there is a small, powerful class dominating a numerically large, weaker class.
- **Dependency and Conflict:** Both classes are dependent on each other while being at conflict with each other. Without the ownership of means of

production, the wage labourers depend on the capitalists for wages to survive. Without being producers themselves, the capitalists depend on the labourers for labour power to fuel production. However, capitalists gain at the labourers' expense. The non-producer capitalists exploit the labourers. The former sell the commodities at high prices but pay the labourers low wages. The difference between the two—the excessive profit/surplus value—is amassed by the capitalist for private gain. This profit is again utilized and re-invested to generate more surplus. The real producers, the labourers, on the other hand, do not enjoy the fruits of their own labour. Thus, the labourers' exploitation contributes to the wealth of the capitalists.

- **Power and Superstructure:** As per Marx, the economic base determines the superstructure of institutions, social values and belief systems. Thus, the relations of production as present in the economic system get reproduced in the superstructure. Ruling class domination is justified by these systems. The ruling class ideology produces a false consciousness in which both classes tend to accept the status quo as normal and natural.
- **Inherent Contradictions:** The capitalist system of stratification is riddled with two contradictions: a) the workers are exploited by the capitalists and b) capitalism involves social production (large number of workers work together in a factory) and individual ownership (one person amassing all profits)
- **Polarization of Classes:** As per Marx, with the passage of time the gap between the proletariat and the bourgeoisie will widen. The increasing use of machinery will create a homogenous working class, eliminating the differences between skilled, semi-skilled and unskilled workers. Even though the real wages of the proletariat may rise, its members will become poorer in relation to the bourgeoisie. This process is known as pauperization. The competitive nature of capitalism will leave space only for the few to survive and will suppress the intermediate strata (petty bourgeoisie, small business owners) into the proletariat. The surviving companies will grow larger and capital will be concentrated into few hands.

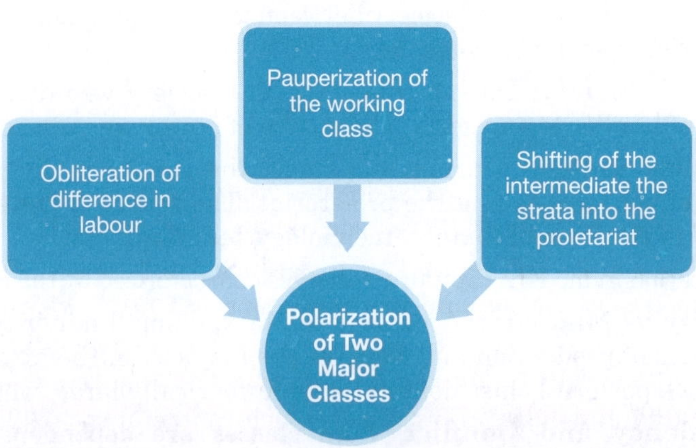

2. **Stratification and Social Change:** According to Marx, social change in societies occurs in two ways.
   - **Minority vs Minority:** In the first case, a new social group develops superior forces of production. For instance, capitalism emerged from the struggle between feudal aristocracy and the emerging capitalist class (merchants, industrialists, etc.). Both groups are minorities.
   - **Minority vs Majority:** This case is particularly relevant for capitalism. Due to its inherent contradictions and conflict of interests, the oppressed class-in-itself (class whose members share the same relationship to means of production and live in false consciousness) transform into class-for-itself through class consciousness, class solidarity and class struggle (the members fully realise the true nature of situation and exploitation, develop a common identity, recognizes their shared interests and unite to take collective action to overthrow the ruling class)
3. **Classless Society and Stage of Communism:** Marx envisioned a classless communist society as the last and final stage following capitalism. In this stage, means of production and all property will be communally owned. So Marx did see an end to social stratification, when all members will share the same relationship to means of production.

Critique

Even though Marx's theory has proved immensely useful in explanation of classes, his theory has been subjected to the following criticism:

- The sole consideration of economic factors as the basis of stratification ignores other relevant factors such as culture, power, religion, gender, ethnicity, race, etc.
- Marx fails to account for the situations when legal and political systems act independently of the economic system.
- The division between ruling and subject class over-simplifies stratification which is more nuanced and depends on the characteristics of each society
- His argument that the inherent contradictions within capitalism will eventually lead to its collapse did not prove true. Capitalism continues to thrive though occasionally, as on events like the Asian crisis of the 1990s, the Global Financial Crisis of 2008, his theory has proven correct.
- The polarization of classes does not account for a sizable expansion in 'middle class' which actually prevents occurrence of any class struggle.
- Concepts like pauperization and obliteration of differences do not account for reduction in poverty levels and increasing specialization with the emergence of different kinds of jobs.
- His theory fails to take into account phenomena like environmental emergencies, political apathy and cultural processes which contribute to exploitation of different sections of people.

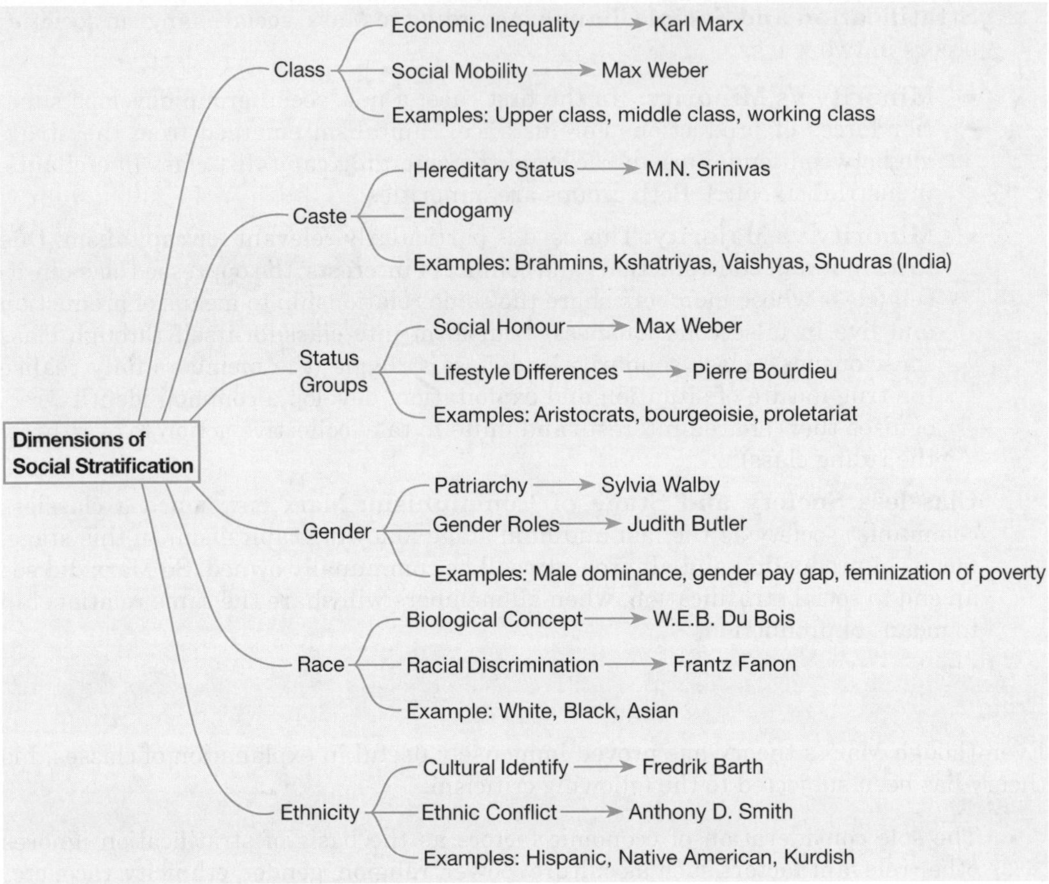

Dimensions of Social Stratification

Social Stratification of Class

Class as a dimension of social stratification is primarily concerned with the economic differences among groups based on their relationship to the means of production. Karl Marx, a central figure in defining this concept, argued that class is determined by one's role in the production process (i.e., whether one owns production or works for owners). Marx's dichotomy between the bourgeoisie (capitalists who own the means of production) and the proletariat (workers who sell their labour) underscores the inherent conflict and inequality in capitalist societies.

In contemporary society, class distinctions can be seen in differing access to resources like education, healthcare, and housing. For instance, the higher socioeconomic classes often have better access to quality education, leading to higher-paying job opportunities. This perpetuates a cycle of wealth and advantage, exemplified by the Ivy League schools in the United States, where a significant percentage of students come from affluent families.

Sociological Approaches

Max Weber expanded on Marx's ideas by introducing the concept of class status and party, emphasizing that property (class), prestige (status), and power (party) are separate but related sources of power and social stratification. Pierre Bourdieu further developed this understanding through concepts of cultural capital (e.g., tastes, skills, manners), social capital (networks, connections), and economic capital, which influence one's class position.

Critical Perspectives

Contemporary sociologists like Erik Olin Wright have evolved the concept of class through the theory of contradictory class locations, which recognizes the diverse and overlapping identities individuals may hold within the class structure (e.g., managers who both wield power and sell their labour).

Social Stratification of Status Groups

Status groups, a term popularized by Weber, refer to groups formed around the prestige and honour accorded to their lifestyle, which can be distinguished by education, ethnicity, or religion. Unlike class, which is economically grounded, status groups are more about social esteem and the monopolization of ideal or material resources (e.g., prestigious education).

An example of a status group in modern society could be the 'old money' families, whose social position is maintained through legacy and lifestyle rather than just economic power alone. Clubs and societies exclusive to Ivy League alumni also exemplify how status groups operate, maintaining social exclusivity beyond economic capabilities alone.

Sociological Approaches

Weber's analysis of status groups emphasises the role of symbolic elements and lifestyle in their formation. Contemporary sociologists have studied how cultural consumption (like art, music, and literature) serves as markers of status group membership, aligning with Bourdieu's theory of distinction, where tastes become a means of social and class differentiation.

Critical Perspectives

The intersection of status with race, ethnicity, and gender has been explored by sociologists like Patricia Hill Collins and Kimberlé Crenshaw, who discuss how status is not merely about honour but also about intersectional identities influencing one's access to social privileges.

Gender and Social Stratification

- For a long period of time, research on social stratification was gender-blind. However, it has also been acknowledged that there is no known society where men, at least in some social aspects, do not possess more wealth, influence and social status than women. Men had a superior standing to women even in hunter-gatherer societies where there were no classes. Gender-based inequality has been more historically deep-rooted than class-based divisions.

- This form of stratification is rooted in theories of biological determinism and natural functionalism which support the role of men as the bread-winners and of women as home-makers. According to feminist scholar, Ann Oakley the concept of 'sex' indicates natural biological differences but 'gender' is a social construct. It refers to a set of role expectations which have historically and almost universally benefitted men and allowed them to dominate over women. Although post modernists like Jacques Derrida and Lacan have dismissed the idea of having a grand theoretical framework for analysing gender-based stratification, following perspectives can shed a light on the subject.
- **Gender and Class:** Gender and class-based divisions have continued to overlap with each other. Even in modern societies, the material condition of most women, it is argued, is determined by the position of their fathers or husbands. Goldthorpe (1983) in his class-scheme upheld the conventional position which suggested that because paid work by women is relatively insignificant in comparison to men, they remain in a subordinate position in the labour force and their class position is primarily determined by the economic position of the men that they depend on. This argument, however, has been criticized on the following grounds:
  - In many households, women's income is instrumental in maintaining the economic position of the household and determines its class position.
  - Even in situations where the woman is earning less than her husband, her occupation could influence the class position of her husband as well as of the household. For example, in India, the wife is a Government teacher and husband a self-employed shopkeeper, even though the wife may be earning less, her occupation will have more influence in the overall position of the family
  - The proportion of households in which women are the sole breadwinners are increasing.
  - Marxists have suggested that under capitalism, more women are entering the labour force and gender-based stratification will end in communism wherein even women will communally owned the means of production.
  - Some like Frank Parkin and Helen Meyer have dismissed the idea of women as a class. Parkin has argued for family to be the basis of stratification and see women as an integral part of it. Meyer has called for terming women as a minority.
- As a result of the above arguments, Goldthorpe's scheme has been modified to reflect the preponderance of women in certain situations.
- Intersectionality, a concept introduced by Kimberlé Crenshaw, is crucial in understanding how gender intersects with other identities like race, class, and sexuality, to create unique experiences of disadvantage and discrimination. This perspective helps in understanding the multi-layered experiences of people who are often marginalized in society.
  - **Simone de Beauvoir:** In her seminal work, *The Second Sex* (1949), de Beauvoir argued that women have historically been treated as the "Other" and

subjected to a socially constructed inferiority. She highlighted how cultural norms and societal expectations perpetuate gender inequality.

- **Betty Friedan:** In *The Feminine Mystique* (1963), Friedan explored the dissatisfaction of many housewives in the United States, calling attention to the limitations imposed on women by traditional gender roles. Her work sparked the second wave of feminism, emphasizing women's rights and opportunities.
- **Judith Butler:** Butler's book, *Gender Trouble* (1990), introduced the concept of gender performativity. She argued that gender is not a fixed attribute but rather an ongoing performance shaped by societal norms and expectations. Butler's work challenged the binary view of gender.
- **Raewyn Connell:** Known for her theory of hegemonic masculinity, Connell, in works like *Masculinities* (1995), examined how certain forms of masculinity dominate over others, contributing to the persistence of gender inequality. Her work has been influential in understanding the dynamics of gender power relations.
- **Sharmila Rege:** Rege's contributions to feminist sociology in India include her focus on Dalit feminism. In *Writing Caste/Writing Gender* (2006), she highlighted the intersectionality of caste and gender, emphasizing that Dalit women face unique forms of oppression not experienced by upper-caste women.
- **Leela Dube:** An anthropologist, Dube's work has been pivotal in understanding the intersections of kinship, caste, and gender. Her studies, such as *Anthropological Explorations in Gender: Intersecting Fields* (2001), provided insights into how these factors shape women's lives in Indian society.
- **Nancy Fraser:** Fraser's concept of "participatory parity" argues for a comprehensive approach to justice that includes redistribution, recognition, and representation. Her work, such as *Justice Interruptus* (1997), addresses the need for structural changes to achieve gender equality.
- **Patricia Hill Collins:** In her work *Black Feminist Thought* (1990), Collins introduced the concept of intersectionality, emphasizing that experiences of oppression are interconnected and cannot be understood in isolation. She focussed on the experiences of African American women, linking race, gender, and class.

- **Two-fold Stratification:** Women are attached to a two-fold stratification in relation to men and in relation to other women. It operates within the family and outside it. In relation to men, this stratification manifests as patriarchy which legitimises subordination of women at different levels. This is visible in economic division of labour and also in social institutions such as marriage, property inheritance, etc.

- **Relation between Wages and Empowerment:** Blood and Hamblin in their 'Effect of the Wife's Employment on the Family Power Structure, 1968', argued that gender stratification is not necessarily altered by women's participation in economic roles. Their decision-making power within the family determines their level of empowerment. Unfortunately, their roles as mother-wife remain the predominant one while the main decisions are still taken by men.

- **Gender and Occupation:** Scholars like Blackburn and Stewart in their 'Women, Work and Class Structure, 1977' have shown how women are restricted to certain select occupations which are often low-paid and part-time. This is true for even communist countries like Russia. In their 1970s study of the socialistic communal unit - Kibbutz of Israel, Lionel Tiger and Joseph Shepher discovered that even there the work was divided in a way that men tended to outdoor activities like agriculture, construction, etc., while women were restricted to nursing, teaching and kindergarten.
- **Beyond male-female debate:** In the past few decades, gender-based stratification has come to include LGBTQ+ community as well. Same-sex marriages are being accorded legal recognition in many countries and there are more debates on having more inclusive social initiatives.

Point to Note

Gender stratification in India includes:

1. Women in economic sector
2. Women and safety
3. Women and politics
4. Women and legal rights

Ethnicity and Social Stratification

- The term ethnicity is used to refer to non-biological traits such as shared culture, history, language, patterns of behaviour and beliefs that provide members of a group a sense of common identity. Ethnicity refers to shared cultural practices, perspectives, and distinctions that set apart one group of people from another. The essential components of ethnicity include common ancestry, language, history, society, culture, or nation. Unlike race, which is often perceived as rooted in physical characteristics, ethnicity is tied to cultural expression and identification.
- In sociology, ethnicity can be explored through the lenses of symbolic interactionism, which examines the daily interactions through which ethnic boundaries are maintained, and conflict theory, which looks at how societal power dynamics enforce ethnic hierarchies and inequalities.
- Ethnic stratification depends on the processes that the society has undergone. These processes could include assimilation, melting pot, pluralistic coexistence or antagonistic coexistence.
  - In assimilation, the minority group gets absorbed in the ways of the majority group leading to blending of identities. For example, in the late 19th and early 20th centuries, large numbers of immigrants arrived in the United States from various countries, including Italy, Ireland, Germany, and Eastern Europe. Over time, these immigrant groups went through a process of assimilation into American society. They adopted English as their primary language, embraced American cultural practices. Similarly, the rapid urbanization and

migration of rural populations to urban centres in China have led to a form of assimilation. Migrants from rural areas may adopt urban lifestyles, language, and cultural practices as they integrate into the urban environment.

- The melting pot simply refers to a metaphorical idea that in a culturally diverse society, different ethnic, cultural, and national groups come together, blend, and contribute to the formation of a new, homogeneous culture. For example - Singapore is often referred to as a melting pot due to its multicultural population consisting of ethnic Chinese, Malays, Indians, and various other communities. The government promotes a policy of multiculturalism and social integration. While individuals may retain their cultural practices, there is an emphasis on a shared national identity and a common understanding of citizenship.
- The pluralistic coexistence refers to the simultaneous existence of diverse groups such as in India, while antagonistic coexistence refers to the atmosphere of hostility, conflict and mutual suspicion within which ethnically diverse groups exist such as those of Tamils and Sinhalese in Sri Lanka.
- Glazner argued that ethnicity will not fade away but will resurge as a reaction to the forces of modernization.

Critical Perspectives

Transnational perspectives on ethnicity, such as those by Arjun Appadurai and Benedict Anderson, discuss how ethnic identities can transcend geographical boundaries, forming imagined communities that maintain distinctive cultural identities in a globalized world.

FYI

Ethnicity in India

India is an incredibly diverse country with a multitude of ethnic groups, linguistic communities, and cultural traditions. While the Constitution of India enshrines principles of equality and prohibits discrimination on the basis of religion, race, caste, sex, or place of birth, the complex interplay of historical, social, and political factors still influences ethnic dynamics.

1. **Regional and Linguistic Identity:**
   - The demand for the creation of separate states or autonomous regions based on linguistic identity is a recurring theme. For instance, the movement for a separate state of Telangana in 2014, carved out of Andhra Pradesh, was driven by linguistic and regional identity considerations.
   - The Gorkhaland movement is a political movement in the Darjeeling hills of West Bengal, India, where the demand for the creation of a separate state named "Gorkhaland" has been a long- standing issue. The movement is primarily associated with the ethnic Gorkha community, who are of Nepali origin and have a significant presence in the region.

- The demand of the Meitei community to be included in the Scheduled Tribe category led to large-scale violence in the state of Manipur in 2023. The ethnic clashes broke out between the members of the Meitei community and of other tribes, prominent among which were the Kukis. The conflict of interest was the concern on part of the Kukis that grant of ST status to the Meities will further harm other tribal groups. The status will allow the Meitie members to purchase land in the hill-side ultimately pushing the other tribes out.

2. **Identity Politics:** For example, political parties sometimes use ethnicity and identity as tools for mobilization. This can involve the representation of specific ethnic or regional groups in politics, with parties aligning themselves with particular communities to garner support. This is evident in various states where identity-based politics plays a crucial role in elections. Some of the political parties include: Dravida Munnetra Kazhigham (DMK) of Tamil Nadu, Asom Gana Parishad of Assam, Shiv Sena of Maharashtra, Sikkim Krantikari Morcha of Sikkim, etc.
3. **Naxalism:** Consolidation of ethnic interests have led to internal civil strife in the form of naxalism in states of Chhattisgarh, Telangana, Andhra Pradesh, etc.
4. **Language and Cultural Assertion:** Ethnic identities are fiercely protected while conserving one's identity, language usage, etc. For example - the three-language formula attracted protests from the Southern states when it was initially suggested to make Hindi a compulsory language in all schools. This was seen as an imposition of North Indian culture on Southern states where Dravidan languages have primarily been used.
5. **Migration:** Ethnic clashes occur when influx of migrants threatens the interest of native inhabitants. For example, The "Assam Accord of 1985," was signed between the Government of India and leaders of the Assam Movement, after a mass agitation that took place in the state of Assam during the early 1980s. The movement was primarily focused on the issues of illegal immigration from Bangladesh and its impact on the demographic and socio-political landscape of Assam.

Race and Social Stratification

- In common parlance, race is used to refer to a category of individuals labelled and treated as similar because of common physical traits, such as skin colour, skeletal structure, colour and texture of hair, and shape of eyes, nose, or head. It is commonly portrayed as an inherited and permanent biological characteristic that can be used to divide people into mutually exclusive groups.
- But the concept of race isn't nearly so straightforward. For instance, Australian Aborigines have black skin and 'Negroid' facial features but also have blond, wavy hair. (Newman, 2018) There are no universal racial categories. South Africa has

four legally defined races—black, white, coloured, and Indian—but in England and Ireland the term black is used to refer to all people who are not white.

- Therefore, for most sociologists, race is more meaningful as a symbolic category than as a biological or genetic one. It is indicative of the characteristics that a society selects to distinguish one ethnoracial group from another to shape social rankings and determine access to important resources. For instance, Jews, the Irish, Italians, and even some Germans were once defined as members of inferior races. They came to be seen as 'white' only when they entered the mainstream culture and gained economic and political power. (Newman, 2018)
- Theories on racial stratification:
  (i) One theory suggests that physical differences acquired a racist shape with the arrival of racial nomenclature and technologies.
  (ii) Ethnocentrism (the phenomenon of considering one's own culture as superior to others) creates in-group and out-group. This has resulted in relegating certain racial groups to subordinate positions through misuse of power and force. For example, the policy of White Man's Burden led to oppression of non-Whites during the colonization.
  (iii) According to O.C. Cox in his *Class, Caste and Race*, 1959, racial stratification is a product of capitalist system. Racism has been used as a tool to exploit people for cheap labour and for generating massive profits. For example, indigenous people from India, Africa, etc., were made to work on large plantations under the slavery system, to fulfil trade related objectives of the colonising countries.
- Racism is the worst form of racial stratification. Apartheid in South Africa was a practice which segregated Whites and non-Whites in all aspects of public activity. The segregation was worsened by restrictions which were exclusively placed on the non-Whites. Similarly, in colonial India, the Criminal Tribes Act served to stigmatise certain tribes and indigenous peoples with distinct cultures and practices that were not clearly understood by the Britishers.
- Racism continues to manifest as discriminatory beliefs, attitudes, practices, and policies based on perceived racial or ethnic differences.
  - The killing of George Floyd in 2020, sparked widespread protests and renewed discussions about the persistent and systemic racism in the USA.
  - In various countries, including some in Europe, there have been instances of xenophobia and discrimination against immigrants.
  - Islamophobia is a form of racism that targets individuals of Muslim faith. Incidents such as the Christchurch mosque shootings in New Zealand in 2019 and other attacks on mosques reflect the rise of Islamophobic sentiments.
  - Racial profiling by law enforcement is a global issue. In countries like the U.S., individuals from minority communities, particularly Black and Hispanic populations, often face higher rates of stops, searches, and use of force by the police compared to their white counterparts.
  - People from the northeastern states of India and tribal communities often face discrimination and racial profiling in other parts of the country. Stereotyping, harassment, and cultural insensitivity contribute to their marginalization.

- Colorism, where individuals are discriminated against based on the color of their skin, is prevalent in India. Fairness creams and advertisements that promote lighter skin as desirable contribute to reinforcing these biases.

- Critical race theory, developed by scholars like Derrick Bell and Kimberlé Crenshaw, emphasises that racism is embedded within the fabric of society and existing legal frameworks, which perpetuate racial inequality. This approach advocates for recognizing historical and systemic injustices to address contemporary racial disparities.

Critical Perspectives

Postcolonial theory, as discussed by Frantz Fanon and Homi Bhabha, explores how colonial legacies have perpetuated racial hierarchies and stereotypes, influencing how race is perceived and enacted globally, underscoring the global dimension of racial stratification.

The unequal distribution of resources is often motivated by racism, the belief that humans are subdivided into distinct groups so different in their social behaviour and mental and physical capacities that they can be ranked as superior or inferior.

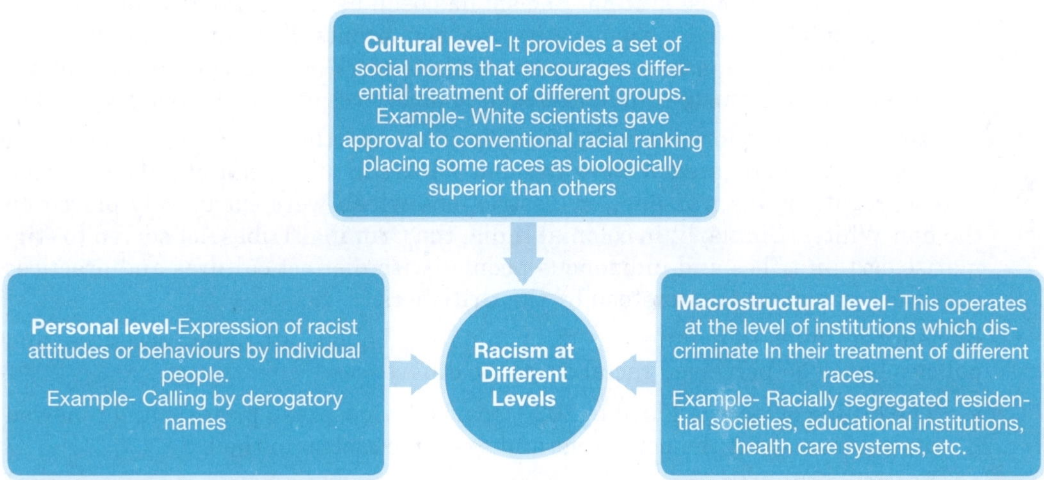

Social Mobility

Social mobility refers to the movement of individuals and groups within a stratification order between different socio-economic positions. It was first examined systematically by Pitrim Sorokin in his book, *Social Mobility* (1927). His fundamental concern was with 'social structure' within which movement takes place and he conceived of social structure to consist of classes.

Before Sorokin, Max Weber defined social class as the 'totality of all class situations in which individual and generational mobility is easy and typical.'

Sources and Causes of Mobility

The causes of social mobility are complex and can be categorized into structural and individual factors.

Structural Causes

1. **Educational Opportunities**
   - **Access to Quality Education:** A well-functioning education system that provides equal opportunities for all, regardless of socio-economic background, can be a significant driver of social mobility.
   - **Affirmative Action Policies:** Policies that promote equal access to education and provide affirmative action for underrepresented groups can contribute to increased social mobility.
2. **Economic Factors**
   - **Economic Growth:** A growing economy often creates more job opportunities, leading to upward mobility for individuals who can access those opportunities.
   - **Labour Market Policies:** Policies that support fair labour practices, workers' rights, and job training programs can enhance economic opportunities and contribute to social mobility.
3. **Social Policies**
   - **Welfare Programs:** Well-designed social welfare programs can act as a safety net, reducing the impact of economic hardships on individuals and families.
   - **Healthcare Access:** Access to healthcare can influence an individual's ability to maintain good health, work, and pursue opportunities.
4. **Legal and Political Environment**
   - **Equal Rights and Opportunities:** Legal frameworks that ensure equal rights and opportunities for all citizens contribute to social mobility.
   - **Anti-discrimination Laws:** Legislation against discrimination based on race, gender, or other factors helps create a level playing field.
5. **Technological Advancements**
   - **Technological Innovation:** Advancements in technology can create new industries and jobs, providing opportunities for individuals to acquire new skills and move up the social ladder.
   - **Digital Inclusion:** Ensuring access to and proficiency in digital technologies can enhance economic opportunities in a technologically driven society.

Individual Causes

1. **Education and Skills**
   - **Educational Attainment:** Higher levels of education and skill acquisition can increase an individual's competitiveness in the job market and contribute to upward mobility. In their study on social mobility, Blau and Duncan (*The American Occupational Structure,* 1967) showed how parents transmit their social standing to their children mainly by influencing their children's education. (Turner, 2006)

- **Lifelong Learning:** A commitment to continuous learning and skill development can enhance an individual's adaptability to changing job requirements.

2. **Work Ethic and Ambition**
    - **Hard Work and Initiative:** Individuals who demonstrate a strong work ethic, ambition, and initiative often have better prospects for career advancement. Peter M. Blau and Otis Dudley Duncan's research (*The American Occupational Structure,* 1967) had apparently demonstrated that educational background and early work experiences were more important than social origin (class) in determining mobility chances. (Turner, 2006)
    - **Entrepreneurship:** Starting one's business or pursuing entrepreneurial ventures can create opportunities for upward mobility.
3. **Networking and Social Capital**
    - **Social Connections:** Building and leveraging social networks can provide access to valuable opportunities, mentorship, and information.
    - **Professional Associations:** Active involvement in professional associations and communities can expand one's network and open doors to new opportunities.
4. **Personal Choices and Decision-Making**
    - **Life Choices:** Responsible life choices, such as delaying parenthood until after education and establishing a career, can positively impact social mobility.
    - **Financial Management:** Sound financial decisions, such as saving and investing wisely, can contribute to long-term economic mobility.
5. **Geographic Mobility**
    - **Willingness to Relocate:** Being open to relocating for job opportunities can enhance an individual's chances of finding better employment.
    - **Globalization:** In a globalized world, individuals with skills that are in demand internationally may have increased mobility.

Types of Mobility

1. **Vertical and Downward Mobility:** Vertical mobility refers to the movement up or down the socio-economic scale. Someone who gains property, income or status is upwardly mobile while someone who loses the same and moves in the opposite direction is downwardly mobile. Downward mobility is less common than vertical mobility and is often associated with psychological problems, anxieties and redundancy. Downwardly mobile people find themselves unable to sustain the lifestyle that they have become accustomed to or are unable to cope with incoming changes, for example, technological advancements making it tough for mid-career professionals to transition to better career opportunities. For example, in 1967, a large-scale social mobility study was conducted in America by Peter Blau and Otis Dudley Duncan. They concluded that there was very much vertical mobility in the United States but it was majorly in occupations quite close to each other. 'Long range mobility' was found to be rare. The reason was that there was much more rapid growth in white-collar and professional jobs. Blau and Duncan found that education and training played a significant role in an individual's success.

In their view, upward social mobility is characteristic of industrial societies and contributes to overall social stability and integrity. However, since the study was conducted on 20,000 males, it lacked gender balance – a major criticism of most social mobility studies.

2. **Lateral Mobility:** It refers to geographical movement between neighbourhoods, towns and regions. For example, migrants moving to other regions and states for better job opportunities. Lateral mobility and vertical mobility are often combined.

3. **Intergenerational Mobility:** Intergenerational mobility compares children's occupational achievements with those of their parents. For example, a rickshaw puller's son becoming an IAS officer is an example of intergenerational mobility. Similarly, research in America showed that Baby Boomers (the generation of children born immediately after World War II), for the most part, achieved upward intergenerational mobility: On the whole, they amassed more wealth during the course of their lives and consequently moved up the social class ladder. (Norton, 2022) Studies have also shown how mobility depended on various factors such as policy changes, geographical areas, time period, the larger socio-economic environment, etc. A study identified five characteristics of high mobility areas: less residential segregation, less income inequality, better schools, greater social capital, and greater family stability. (Norton, 2022)

4. **Intragenerational Mobility:** Intragenerational mobility is concerned with an individual's movement within their own lifetime. It can be measured in two directions: a) horizontal mobility: It refers to changing of jobs within a social class. For example – a person working as a teacher shifts to different schools or starts their own coaching institution is an example of horizontal mobility. b) vertical mobility : It refers to the upward or downward movement along a social ladder leading to a change in class status. For example, if a teacher marries the CEO of a large company, they may experience upward vertical mobility or a shopkeeper accumulates and invests more capital to open new branches and create a larger nation-wide brand also experiences vertical mobility. The greater the mobility between generations or over the life-course, the more open the society is regarded to be.

5. **Structural Mobility:** It occurs when large numbers of people move up or down the social ladder because of structural changes in the society as a whole, particularly when the economy is affected by large-scale events. For example, during the Great Depression of the early 1930s, huge numbers of upper- and middle-class people suddenly found themselves among the poor. Conversely, the LPG (Liberalization, Privatization and Globalization) reforms of the early 1990s led to creation of a new and expanded middle class in India.

   In industrial societies, the study of social mobility is typically concerned with the structure of occupations. According to Robert Erikson and John Goldthorpe in The Constant Flux (1992), when compared with pre- industrial societies, the industrial societies are characterized by high rates of social mobility, upward mobility predominates over downward mobility, mobility opportunities are more equal across groups and rates of mobility and the degree of equality of opportunity increase over time.

Ace Your Answers!

1. IMF's Gita Gopinath has said that Generative Artificial Intelligence (AI) may lead to flattening of the pay structure in the future. What repercussions, do you think, will AI have on occupational structure and social mobility?
2. Have initiatives like Digital India impacted social mobility in India?
3. During COVID-19, the social stratification system, both at the domestic and global level, became starker than ever. Elaborate.

Open and Closed System

1. **Open system:** It refers to a social system with ample opportunities for people to move from one social strata to another. For example, the class system in capitalistic industrial societies is considered an open system wherein meritocratic selection and one's hard work result in one's movement up the ladder of social classes. It is based on efforts and achievement.
2. **Closed system:** It refers to a social system with very little opportunity to move from one strata to another. For example, India's caste system is based on ascription wherein one's identity is determined by one's birth in a particular community. In olden times, one's caste also influenced one's occupation and thus made movement up the socio-economic ladder difficult. One's caste identity still remains fixed although legal and policy changes have allowed for economic changes in one's status. America's slavery system is another example of a closed system. It prevented Blacks from gaining socio-economic privileges through discriminatory policies of residential and occupational segregation.

Aspect	Open Systems	Closed Systems	Mixed Systems
Examples	Scandinavia (e.g., Sweden, Norway)	Saudi Arabia (historically)	United States
	Canada	North Korea	United Kingdom
	Nordic Model countries (e.g., Iceland)	India (Caste system)	

Aspect	Open Systems	Closed Systems	Mixed Systems
Characteristics	Social mobility, meritocracy, equal opportunities	Limited mobility, ascribed status, hereditary factors	Mixed elements of social mobility and barriers
	Equal emphasis on education and welfare	Restricted opportunities based on social background	
	Emphasis on diversity and inclusivity	Government control, limited freedoms	
Challenges	Despite openness, challenges in income inequality	Perpetuation of social inequality and discrimination	Income inequality, systemic issues
		Limited opportunities for certain groups	Class distinctions, challenges in social mobility

Constraints to Social Mobility

1. **Role of historical experiences:** Nathan Glazer, Professor Emeritus at Harvard University, has argued that, because black Americans had suffered so profoundly in the past from slavery, they have not experienced the upward social mobility enjoyed by other ethnic communities who have prospered in the American Dream. (Turner, 2006)
2. **Social mobility is a result of a combination of several favourable factors:** In the classical 'status- attainment' model of social mobility, associated with the work of Peter Blau and Otis Dudley Duncan (The American Occupational Structure, 1967), individual inequalities in opportunity and reward reflect family background, individual attainment (such as education), and sociodemographic attributes (such as race / ethnic group memberships), or even such idiosyncratic factors as physical attractiveness. (Turner, 2006)
3. **Social closure:** It refers to the means by which groups protect access to certain scarce resources. For example, in 2019 news broke of a college admissions scandal in which a number of already privileged families bribed college admissions officials and consultants in order to get their kids into selective schools like Yale, Stanford, and Georgetown. (Norton, 2022)
4. **Class structure of industrialized societies still not open:** Goldthorpe and his colleagues (R. Erikson and J. Goldthorpe, *The Constant Flux*, 1992) demonstrated that, although rates of absolute social mobility had increased, this was largely due to changes in the occupational structure, as the expansion of professional and managerial occupations (together with the decline in working-class occupations)

meant that an increasing proportion of higher-level jobs will have to be filled from below. However, relative rates of social mobility, that is, the relative chances of achieving a service-class occupation depending on class of origin, had remained remarkably stable.

Impact of Artificial Intelligence on Social Stratification

The advent of Artificial Intelligence (AI) and related technologies is heralding significant changes across various domains, particularly in the economic sphere. These technological advancements have the potential to reshape social stratification profoundly. This essay examines how AI might alter social stratification by affecting employment, income distribution, and social mobility.

Employment and the Labour Market

AI's integration into the economy is transforming the labour market. Automation and AI are replacing routine and repetitive tasks, leading to job displacement in certain sectors. For instance, manufacturing and administrative roles are increasingly automated, resulting in job losses for workers in these fields. This phenomenon disproportionately affects low-skilled workers who may lack the qualifications to transition into new roles created by AI.

However, AI also creates new job opportunities in fields such as data analysis, AI programming, and robotics. These positions typically require advanced technical skills and higher education levels. Consequently, individuals with access to quality education and training are more likely to benefit from the AI-driven job market, while those without such access may find themselves marginalized. This dichotomy can exacerbate existing social inequalities, reinforcing class stratification.

Income Distribution

The impact of AI on income distribution is multifaceted. On one hand, AI can enhance productivity and economic growth, potentially increasing overall wealth. On the other hand, the benefits of AI-driven growth are often unevenly distributed. High-skilled workers and those who own or invest in AI technologies are likely to see significant income gains. In contrast, low-skilled workers may experience wage stagnation or decline due to job displacement and increased competition for the remaining low-skilled jobs.

This divergence can lead to a widening income gap between different social strata. The economic elite, who control AI technologies and possess the skills to thrive in an AI-driven economy, may accumulate greater wealth. Meanwhile, the working class and economically disadvantaged groups may face heightened economic insecurity, further entrenching social stratification.

Social Mobility

AI's impact on social mobility is closely linked to education and skill acquisition. Access to education and training in AI and related technologies is crucial for upward mobility in an AI-driven economy. However, disparities in educational resources and opportunities can hinder social mobility for disadvantaged groups. For instance, urban areas with better-funded schools and more access to technological resources are better positioned to equip students with the skills needed for future job markets compared to rural or underfunded areas.

Moreover, the high cost of education and training programs in AI-related fields can be a barrier for individuals from lower socio-economic backgrounds. Without targeted interventions and policies to promote inclusive education and skills development, AI may reinforce existing social hierarchies, making it more difficult for individuals from disadvantaged backgrounds to ascend the social ladder.

In conclusion, the integration of AI and related technologies into the economy has the potential to significantly alter social stratification. By transforming the labour market, influencing income distribution, and affecting social mobility, AI can both create opportunities and exacerbate existing inequalities. Policymakers must address these challenges by promoting inclusive education, equitable access to technological resources, and policies that support workers transitioning to new roles. Such measures are essential to ensure that the benefits of AI-driven growth are broadly shared and do not reinforce social stratification.

Previous Years' Question

2024

1. Analyse the changing nature of caste as a status group. (10 Marks)
2. What is social mobility? Critically examine the classification of 'closed' and 'open' models of social stratification. (10 Marks)
3. How does a multicultural society accommodate diversities of all kinds- ethnic, linguistic and religious? Discuss its major challenges. (10 Marks)

2023

1. Do you think that the boundary line between ethnicity and race is blurred? Justify your answer. (10 marks)
2. How is poverty a form of social exclusion? Illustrate in this connection the different dimensions of poverty and social exclusion. (20 marks)
3. Explain Max Weber's theory of social stratification. How does Weber's idea of class differ from that of Marx? (20 marks)
4. Does women's education help to eradicate patriarchal discriminations? Reflect with illustrations. (10 marks)

2022

1. How do sociologists construct gender in their analysis on social inequality? (10 marks)
2. Discuss social mobility in open and closed systems. (10 marks)
3. Social stratification is claimed to contribute to the maintenance of social order and stability in society. Critically assess. (20 marks)

2021

1. Critically examine Max Weber's theory of social stratification. (10 marks)
2. Explain the concept of social mobility. Describe with suitable illustrations how education and social mobility are related to each other. (20 marks)

2020

1. How are hierarchy and exclusion the major impediments in the transformation of societies? Discuss. (20 marks)
2. Critically assess social mobility in closed and open systems. (10 marks)

2019

1. Davis and Moore made it clear that social stratification is a functional necessity and also an unconscious device. Discuss. (10 marks)
2. Modernization presupposes class society; however, caste, race and ethnicity are still predominant. Explain. (20 marks)
3. Compare and contrast the contributions of Marx and Weber on social stratification in capitalist society. (20 marks)
4. Why is gender a dimension of social stratification? How does gender intersect other dimensions of social inequality based on caste, class, race and ethnicity? (20 marks)

2018

1. What is the difference between natural and social inequality? Give examples from caste and class dimensions. (10 marks)
2. Evaluate if social stratification is functional for society. (10 marks)
3. Is social mobility possible in closed systems of stratification? Illustrate from research work. (10 marks)

2017

1. Examine gender, ethnicity and race as major dimensions of social stratification. (20 marks)

2016

1. 'Vertical mobility brings structural change even in a closed system.' Comment. (10 marks)
2. Elucidate the basic premises of Davis's structural-functional theory of social stratification. How far is it relevant in understanding contemporary Indian society? (20 marks)
3. Discuss the relationship between poverty and social exclusion. (10 marks)

Right Approach

2024 - Q 2

How does a multicultural society accommodate diversities of all kinds—ethnic, linguistic and religious? Discuss its major challenges. (10 Marks)

Introduction: A multicultural society embraces and accommodates diversity in ethnicity, language, and religion by promoting inclusivity, tolerance, and respect for differences. In such societies, policies and social structures are designed to support pluralism and protect minority rights, fostering social harmony.

Body:

Accommodating Diversity in Multicultural Societies

1. **Policies of Inclusivity and Tolerance:** Governments often adopt multicultural policies to ensure equal representation and rights for diverse groups. For instance, Canada and Australia emphasize multicultural policies, ensuring minority groups have equal opportunities.
2. **Legal Protections and Language Rights:** Laws are enacted to protect linguistic diversity and religious freedom. In India, the Constitution grants linguistic minorities the right to preserve their language and culture, and allows religious minorities to manage their institutions. This aligns with the views of sociologist Will Kymlicka, who argues for 'group-differentiated rights' to safeguard cultural diversity.
3. **Promotion of Intercultural Dialogue:** Events, educational programs, and public campaigns promote understanding among diverse groups. This approach is inspired by Amartya Sen's concept of 'plural monoculturalism,' where different cultures co-exist while interacting positively with each other.

Challenges of Multicultural Societies

1. **Social Integration:** Integrating diverse groups while preserving cultural identities is challenging, often leading to identity conflicts.
2. **Rising Ethnic Tensions:** Differences can lead to ethnic or religious tensions, as seen in European societies with immigrant populations facing social and economic marginalization.
3. **Balancing Universalism and Particularism:** Accommodating group-specific rights without compromising national identity remains a critical issue.

Conclusion: While multicultural societies promote inclusivity and diversity, balancing distinct identities with social cohesion remains challenging. Effective policies, intercultural dialogue, and legal protections are essential to fostering unity in diversity.

2022 - Q 1

How do sociologists construct gender in their analysis on social inequality? (10 Marks)

Introduction: Sociologists view gender not merely as a biological category but as a social construct that shapes and reinforces social inequality. Gender, as a social institution, organizes society by assigning different roles, expectations, and resources to men and women, often resulting in unequal power dynamics.

Body:

Gender as a Social Construct

1. **Symbolic Interactionism:** Sociologists like Erving Goffman argue that gender is performed through daily interactions, where individuals 'do' gender according to societal norms. These performances reinforce traditional roles, often placing men in dominant positions and women in subordinate roles.
2. **Feminist Theory:** Feminist sociologists such as Ann Oakley and Judith Butler emphasize that gender is constructed through socialization, education, media, and other institutions. Butler's concept of 'gender performativity' highlights how repeated acts create and sustain gender identities, which are often hierarchical.
3. **Gender and Structural Inequality:** Functionalists like Talcott Parsons viewed gender roles as complementary, but conflict theorists like Sylvia Walby critique this perspective, arguing that gender roles perpetuate inequality. Walby's concept of 'patriarchy' suggests that social structures, from the family to the workplace, systematically advantage men.

Impact on Social Inequality By constructing gendered roles and norms, society limits opportunities for women and gender minorities, affecting education, employment, and political representation. This construction of gender reinforces social stratification, making it a central focus in analyzing social inequality.

Conclusion: Through the lens of symbolic interactionism, feminist theory, and structural analysis, sociologists reveal how gender is socially constructed and linked to broader patterns of inequality, highlighting the need for transformative social change.

CHAPTER
6

Work and Economic Life

In this Chapter

- Works and Economic Life
- Social Organization of Work in Different Types of Society
  - Slave Society
  - Feudal Society
  - Industrial Capitalist Society
- Formal and Informal Organization of Work
- Labour and Society
- Previous Years' Questions

Introduction

According to Anthony Giddens, work can be defined as 'carrying out of tasks, requiring the expenditure of mental and physical effort, which has as its objective the production of goods and services that cater to human needs'. It can be either paid or unpaid. An occupation or job is work done in exchange of regular salary or wages. Work forms the basis of the economic system in all societies. Work is not synonymous with a paid job. Non-paid labour such as household work, caring for the elderly and children in one's own home, etc., also economically contribute to the continuation of societies. Voluntary work is another kind of non-paid work, intended to do social good. Both the experience of work and what work actually means for people varies across regions in different societies.

An economic system consists of institutions that provide for production of goods and services. As societies have evolved, so have the economic systems. As we have learned in the previous units, Marx has in fact traced the evolution of society to developments in the field of economic production. Here are the various definitions of work:

1. **Economic Activity:** Work is primarily seen as economic activity that generates income and sustains livelihoods.
2. **Social Activity:** It is a social process that structures daily life, creates social relationships, and builds community bonds.
3. **Identity and Status:** Work contributes to one's identity, social status, and sense of purpose.
4. **Power and Control:** It reflects power dynamics and control within the workplace and broader society.
5. **Cultural and Symbolic Meaning:** Work has cultural significance and symbolic meanings that vary across societies.

Aspects of Work

1. **Division of Labour**
   - **Emile Durkheim:** Differentiates between mechanical solidarity (simple societies with similar work roles) and organic solidarity (complex societies with specialized work roles).
   - **Karl Marx:** Focuses on the division of labour in capitalist societies, leading to alienation.
2. **Alienation**
   - **Karl Marx:** Describes how workers are alienated from their labour, the products they create, and their own potential due to capitalist exploitation.
3. **Rationalization**
   - **Max Weber:** Highlights the role of rationalization and the Protestant work ethic in the development of capitalism and its impact on work ethics.
4. **Social Integration and Solidarity**
   - **Emile Durkheim:** Views work as essential for social cohesion and integration, particularly in modern, industrial societies.

5. **Adaptation and Evolution**
   - **Herbert Spencer:** Sees work as an adaptive process that evolves with societal changes and contributes to social progress.
6. **Gender and Work**
   - **Feminist Sociologists:** Analyse how gender roles and inequalities shape the experiences and valuation of work, both paid and unpaid.
7. **Cultural Context**
   - **Indian Sociologists (e.g., M. N. Srinivas, A.R. Desai):** Examines how work is influenced by caste, community, and agrarian structures in the Indian society.

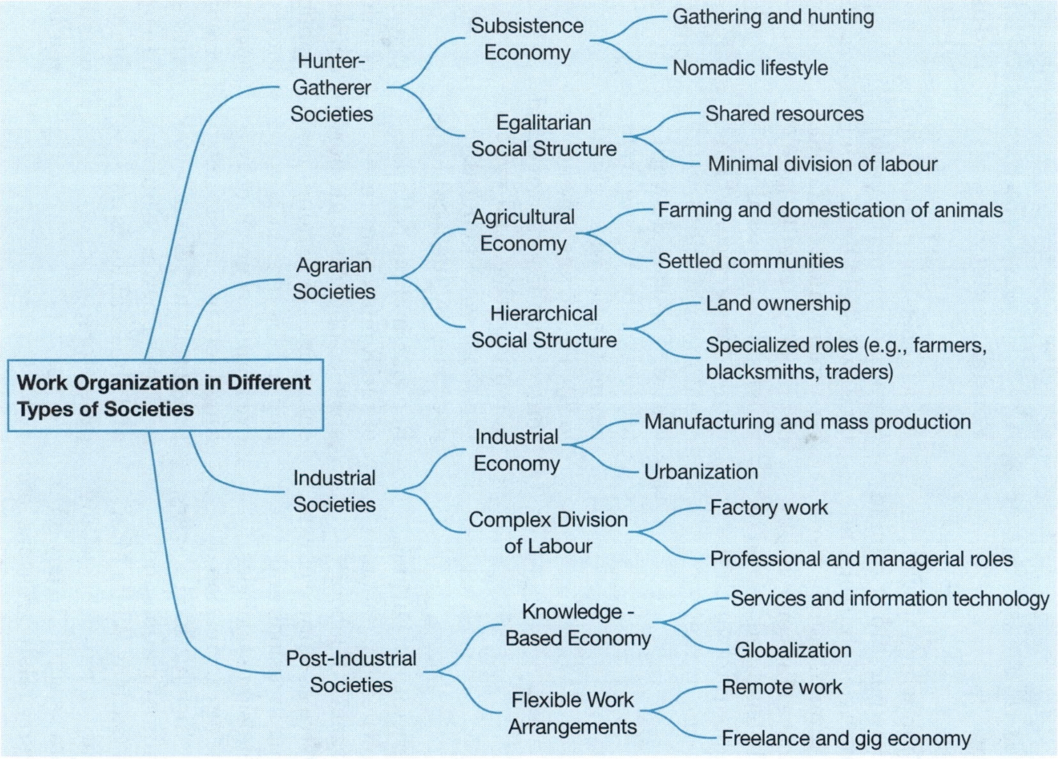

Social Organization of Work in Different Types of Society

Work in any society is not just governed by economic needs and systems but also social rules, obligations and hierarchies. In a way, how people are placed in different occupations, how classes are generated and institutionalized and how overall economic systems develop have both sociologically macro and micro aspects. Thus, social organization of work refers to patterning of activities which people indulge in to ensure their survival. Such organization is dictated by a host of factors.

Let us understand and simultaneously compare how work was socially organized in three different types of society—slave, feudal and industrial-capitalist. Some of the following ideas have been discussed in the previous units through the classic sociological thinkers (Marx, Weber, Durkheim, Parsons, etc.).

Aspect	Traditional		Modern
	Slave Society	**Feudal Society**	**Industrial-capitalist Society**
Definition	A social set-up in which it was the law permitted ownership of human beings as property or chattel, and wherein such human beings were deprived of most rights enjoyed by free persons. It legalized 'forced or involuntary labour' in which the slave is tied to the owner	A social set-up in which fief (a piece of property, usually land) was held by A social set-up in which fief (a piece of property, usually land) was held by a vassal in return for service, which could include military duties. The vassal swore fidelity to the person from whom the fief was held (the lord). There was absence of central public authority and administrative, and judicial functions were generally exercised by the local lords.	
Cause of emergence	Factors like agricultural surplus, unequal land ownership, labour shortage, emergence of labour intensive industries, capture of war prisoners during invasions and conquests, expansionist policies, population pressures, creation of legal systems which justified slavery, ideology of dehumanization and discrimination (such as White Man's burden), inability to pay debt, selling family members as slaves to pay off debt or for poverty related reasons, etc.	Reasons include collapse of the Roman empire, absence of central authority, emergence of regional lords and nobles to gain power over lands, concept of two kingdoms in Christianity promoted the idea of two centres of power: Church and the local lords as protectors.	Reasons include decline of feudalism, emergence of merchants and traders as budding capitalists, internationalization of trade, opening up of global markets, invention of new technologies with scientific revolution (steam engine, spinning jenny, etc.), beginning of mass manufacturing with industrial revolution in 18th century, etc.

Aspect	Traditional		Modern
Time period	Has existed in various forms throughout history, starting from 18th century BCE in China to as late as 19th century CE.	Characteristic of the Middle Ages with peak activity between 5th to 12th century CE.	Mid 18th century to present.
General features of society	• The economic system relied on slaves for production in dominant areas such as agriculture and mining. • Slaves were also employed in domestic service. • The legal system defined the status of slaves, their limited rights and powers of the slaveholders. • Slaves were treated as property, movable or immovable.	• An overwhelmingly agrarian economy, with limited money exchange. • The Church exercised enormous power. • The society was divided on the basis of services a section could provide to the other in return for protection or revenues.	• The largest shares of the economy are occupied by manufacturing and service-based industries, although some societies continue to rely heavily on agriculture • Two class system - The class system majorly consists of the capital-owning bourgeoisie and the labour-owning proletariat. • The capitalists employ labourers for wages. Labourers work to generate profits that are amassed and re-invested by the capitalists to generate more profits. • Private ownership - The law allows capitalists to own and invest capital as they deem fit. • Competition - The capitalists compete with each other to maximise profits. • Market mechanism and minimal government intervention

Aspect	Traditional		Modern
Social hierarchy	• The hierarchy consisted of slaves at the bottom, followed by free labourers and a minority elite or aristocracy at the top.	• Largely, the social order was dominated by the "three estates" or the "three orders" of feudal society—"those who make war" (miles, knights), "those who pray" (priests, monks) and "those who labour" (peasants, serfs). At the top was the king	• While the capitalist society has been seen by Marxists to consist of two main classes –bourgeoisie and proletariat, thinkers like Weber have also spoken of a sizeable middle class.
Means of production	• Slavery provided 'dependent labour' to work on the 'estates' owned by the masters. The property was both land and human beings. • While slaves were integral for generating incomes, they were also 'consumption goods' who had to be maintained to keep the system running. • The international slave trade treated slaves as 'commodities', who were needed not just for economic purpose but also as status symbols.	• The fief or property was the source of all power. • The king was at the top but relied on aristocrats for management of fiefs. • The aristocrats further loaned the fiefs to knights in return for military duties. • The knights managed the fiefs through the help of peasants who did the actual labour on the land to produce food for the remaining groups.	• Capital in the form of finance, property, technology, buildings, machinery, infrastructure, etc.

Aspect	Traditional		Modern
Relations of production	• The master-slave relationship was legalized and was characterized with domination and power. • The slave often lacked ownership of even the clothes that he/she was wearing. • In some societies, the master had control over the slave's reproductive choices too. • There is no evidence to show if slavery contributed to economic upliftment of society. • Since slaves had no rights or means to survive on their own, they were dependent on their masters for survival, while masters depended on the slaves to maintain the status quo. In a way, the oppression of slaves was ensured through their participation. • A slave was usually an outsider, someone from another race or nationality. The inferior treatment towards the slave was also directed towards the slave's cultural origins.	• It was a system of inter-dependence with peasants bearing the heaviest burden. • The kings, lords, knights and priests enjoyed their privileges at the expense of the peasants/serfs.	• Marxists see the relationship between bourgeoisie and proletariat as of domination and exploitation. • However, unlike the traditional societies, labourers are neither tied to a person or to land. • They are tied to wages and contracts through voluntary consent. • The economy is divided between formal and informal sectors, so in some sectors the relations are regulated by State sanctioned rules, in others they are not.

Aspect	Traditional		Modern
Wealth distribution	Highly unequal, law treated the slave as an 'object' and allowed masters to own both physical and human property.	Highly unequal, while the position of serf was relatively better than the slave, they were still exploited. Although in terms of classes, the priests also enjoyed enormous power and wealth without actually owning the land.	• Unequal but less in comparison to earlier societies. • The expansion of the middle class has allowed people to earn for themselves and become economically prosperous. • Right to property is a legal right. • Intergenerational mobility is possible.
Stratification (Ideas by Parsons)	• Based on ascription, heredity • State is complicit in creating artificial divisions		• Based on achievement, talent and meritocracy • State endeavours to establish a rights-based system through democracy, welfare measures, etc.
Alienation, solidarity and division of labour (ideas by Marx, Durkheim	• Alienation is less as integration within the class is high and workers had some control on the product as they built it from start to finish • Mechanical solidarity • Simple division of labour –people specialise in limited occupations		• Alienation is high with increase in individualism and workers only work on part of the product. • Organic solidarity • Complex division of labour – people specialise in numerous activities
Place of work	• Either home or land-related occupation sites such as mines, farms, plantations, estates, etc.		• Clear separation of home and workplace • Factories, industries, offices, etc.

Transforming the Social Organization of Work

The industrial capitalist society continues to undergo rapid changes. It has transformed the organization of work in several ways. In this regard, an understanding of the following concepts can prove useful:

Feminisation of Agrarian Workforce

- Economically, the trend towards the feminisation of work continues to be marked by women's increasing participation in the informal and low-wage sectors. According to the International Labour Organization (ILO), women's global labour force participation rate was 47.4% in 2023, compared to 72.3% for men. This shows a slight decrease from previous years, potentially influenced by the global pandemic. However, in many developing countries, women are still disproportionately represented in informal employment.
- In India, for example, the Periodic Labour Force Survey (PLFS) for 2021-2022 reported that about 75.2% of women in the workforce are engaged in the informal sector. While this shows some improvement from the 90% figure reported in 2019, it still indicates a significant overrepresentation. These jobs often lack security, benefits, and fair wages. For instance, in the garment industry, which remains heavily feminized, workers in countries like Bangladesh and India often earn well below living wage standards, though exact figures would need to be updated to reflect current economic conditions.
- From a social and cultural perspective, the shift in women's roles due to their increased workforce participation remains significant but complex. Despite their economic contributions, women continue to bear the primary responsibility for unpaid domestic labour. The United Nations' latest available data suggests that women globally spend about 2.5 times more hours on unpaid domestic and care work than men, a slight improvement from the previous 'three times' figure, but still a significant disparity.
- In India, this disparity remains pronounced. The most recent Time Use Survey in India (2021) revealed that women spend on average 5 hours and 29 minutes per day on unpaid domestic services for household members, compared to 1 hour and 37 minutes by men. While this shows a slight reduction in women's unpaid work and a small increase in men's contribution compared to the 2020 data, the 'double burden' of work continues to significantly impact women's ability to participate fully in the formal workforce and achieve career advancement.

1. **Taylorism (Scientific Management)**
   - **Developed by:** Frederick Winslow Taylor in the early 20th century.
   - **Key Concepts:** Taylorism, also known as scientific management, emphasizes efficiency and productivity through standardized work processes and division of labour. Taylor's approach involved breaking down tasks into smaller, repetitive units and timing workers to identify the 'one best way' to complete each task. Workers' roles were simplified to increase speed, with little room for individual initiative.

- **Sociological Perspective:** Taylorism views the worker as a cog in a machine, reducing the human element to mere physical labour. The approach is criticized for alienating workers (as described by Karl Marx), stripping away autonomy and creativity, and treating labour as a purely mechanistic component. This leads to what Marx called 'alienation,' where workers become disconnected from their labour, the products they create, and their own potential.

2. **Fordism**
   - **Developed by:** Henry Ford in the 1910s and 1920s.
   - **Key Concepts:** Fordism builds on Taylorism but emphasizes mass production and standardization, with assembly line production being its hallmark. Ford introduced moving assembly lines to produce standardized products, such as the Model T car, efficiently and at lower costs. To ensure stability, Ford paid his workers relatively high wages, creating a consumer base for the products they manufactured—a model often described as 'paying workers enough so they can afford to buy what they make.'
   - **Sociological Perspective:** Fordism expanded beyond factory organization to influence broader economic structures, leading to the development of the welfare state and mass consumer society. It created a stable working class with higher wages, which led to a consumer-oriented economy. However, Fordism faced criticism for reinforcing a rigid class structure, as workers had minimal control over their work processes. The repetitive, highly regimented nature of assembly-line work also contributed to worker dissatisfaction and dehumanization in the workplace.

3. **Toyotism (Lean Production)**
   - **Developed by:** Toyota in Japan in the 1950s and 1960s, particularly under Taiichi Ohno.
   - **Key Concepts:** Toyotism, also known as lean production, contrasts with both Taylorism and Fordism by emphasizing flexibility, continuous improvement (Kaizen), and just-in-time production. Toyotism empowers workers to stop the production line to address issues and encourages teamwork and problem-solving. Production is adjusted to demand, minimizing waste and focusing on quality over quantity.
   - **Sociological Perspective:** Toyotism promotes a more human-centred approach, valuing workers as active participants rather than passive labour. Unlike the repetitive and isolated tasks in Taylorism and Fordism, Toyotism advocates for skill development and involvement, allowing workers to contribute to problem-solving and process improvement. Sociologically, Toyotism aligns with post-Fordist theories of flexible specialization and networked production, reflecting a shift from rigid, standardized production to adaptable and skilled labour.

Approach	Key Feature	Worker Role	Economic Impact	Sociological View
Taylorism	Efficiency through standardized tasks	Passive, mechanistic, limited autonomy	High productivity, low wages	Worker alienation, dehumanization

Approach	Key Feature	Worker Role	Economic Impact	Sociological View
Fordism	Mass production and higher wages	Semi-passive, limited skill use	Growth of consumer society, stable economy	Stable working class, welfare economy, worker dissatisfaction
Toyotism	Flexibility, quality control, continuous improvement	Active participant, skilled problem-solver	Efficient, waste-reducing production	Worker empowerment, post-Fordist flexibility

Hawthorne Studies and Human Relations

- The Hawthorne studies conducted by Elton Mayo and his colleagues in the 1920s and 1930s shed light on the importance of human relations and social factors in the formal organization of work. The studies revealed that factors such as employee satisfaction, group dynamics, and communication patterns significantly impact worker productivity and morale.
- These findings highlighted the significance of considering social and psychological factors in the design and management of work. They led to the emergence of the human relations approach, which emphasizes the importance of employee motivation, job satisfaction, and participatory decision-making in enhancing organizational effectiveness.

Contemporary Perspectives and Flexible Work Arrangements

- In recent years, the formal organization of work has witnessed transformations due to changing economic, technological, and social contexts. Scholars such as Richard Sennett and Zygmunt Bauman have examined the impact of flexible work arrangements, such as remote work, freelancing, and temporary contracts, on the organization of work.
- Flexible work arrangements challenge traditional bureaucratic structures and provide individuals with greater autonomy and control over their work. However, they also raise concerns about job insecurity, the erosion of worker rights, and the blurring of boundaries between work and personal life.

Wright Mills' Concept of White-Collar Alienation: A Sociological Perspective

- C. Wright Mills, an influential sociologist, examined various aspects of modern society, including the experiences and challenges faced by white-collar workers.
- Mills argued that white-collar workers, unlike their blue-collar counterparts, experience a distinct form of alienation in the workplace. He suggested that white-collar alienation arises from the bureaucratic nature of office work, the hierarchical structure of organizations, and the alienating effects of mass society. While alienation is often associated with factory labour and the assembly line, Mills posited

that alienation is not exclusive to manual labour but extends to intellectual and administrative work as well.

- One key element of white-collar alienation highlighted by Mills is the separation of intellectual labour from decision-making and autonomy. White-collar workers, such as clerical staff or administrative personnel, often find themselves performing routine and monotonous tasks, with little control over the content and direction of their work. They are subject to strict rules, procedures, and hierarchical authority, which can limit their ability to exercise their creativity and problem-solving skills. This lack of meaningful participation in decision-making processes can lead to a sense of powerlessness and disconnection from the outcomes of their work.
- Moreover, Mills emphasized that white-collar alienation is exacerbated by the social isolation and impersonal relationships prevalent in bureaucratic organizations. Unlike traditional craft occupations that fostered a sense of community and shared purpose, office environments often promote individualism, competition, and impersonal interactions. White-collar workers may experience a sense of loneliness and detachment from their colleagues, leading to feelings of isolation and a diminished sense of belonging. Mills' analysis of white-collar alienation also highlighted the impact of mass society and the erosion of personal autonomy. In his book *'White Collar: The American Middle Classes,'* he argued that white-collar workers are subject to the influence of mass media, consumer culture, and societal expectations. They may feel constrained by societal norms and pressures to conform, which can further contribute to a sense of alienation and a loss of individuality.
- From a sociological perspective, Mills' concept of white-collar alienation highlights the social and structural factors that contribute to the alienating experiences of office workers. It underscores the role of bureaucracy, hierarchical structures, and the broader dynamics of modern society in shaping individuals' relationships with their work and their sense of self.
- Understanding white-collar alienation has implications for addressing issues related to job satisfaction, mental health, and overall well-being in the workplace. It calls for the recognition of the unique challenges faced by white-collar workers and the need for organizational reforms that promote meaningful engagement, autonomy, and supportive social environments. By critically examining white-collar alienation, sociologists can contribute to a deeper understanding of the complexities of work in modern society and advocate for more fulfilling and human-centred work environments.

Robert Blauner: Alienation and Technology

- Robert Blauner, an American sociologist, made significant contributions to the understanding of alienation from a sociological perspective. Blauner expanded upon Marx's concept of alienation by examining its manifestations in modern industrial societies and how it is influenced by social structures and power relations. His work offers valuable insights into the sociological aspects of alienation in contemporary society.

- In his book *'Alienation and Freedom: The Factory Worker and His Industry'* (1964), Blauner conducted a study on factory workers in the United States to explore the experience of alienation in industrial settings. He argued that alienation is not solely a result of the capitalist mode of production, but it also arises from the broader social structures and dynamics within which work is organized.
- Blauner identified two main types of alienation: 'objective alienation' and 'subjective alienation.' Objective alienation refers to the structural conditions of work that result in the separation of workers from the products of their labour and the loss of control over the production process. This includes factors such as the division of labour, mechanization, and the hierarchical organization of work.
- **Subjective alienation**, on the other hand, focuses on the psychological and emotional consequences of alienated labour. It encompasses feelings of powerlessness, meaninglessness, and a sense of being disconnected from one's work and the social world. Blauner argued that subjective alienation is influenced not only by the objective conditions of work but also by workers' perceptions, values, and expectations.
- Blauner's research revealed that the experience of alienation varied across different industries and occupations. He found that workers in highly routinized and deskilled jobs, such as assembly line workers, tended to experience higher levels of alienation. These workers faced repetitive tasks, limited autonomy, and little opportunity for creativity or personal fulfilment.
- In contrast, workers in more skilled and autonomous occupations, such as professionals or craftsmen, experienced lower levels of alienation. These individuals had more control over their work processes, greater opportunities for self-expression, and a sense of ownership over their tasks.
- Blauner's work highlighted the role of social factors in shaping the experience of alienation. He argued that factors such as technology, work organization, management practices, and power relations within the workplace influenced the degree and type of alienation experienced by workers. For example, oppressive and exploitative management practices, such as strict control and surveillance, could exacerbate feelings of alienation among workers.

Goldthorpe and Lockwood: The Affluent Worker

Key Theories: Goldthorpe and Lockwood conducted seminal research on the impact of industrialization and economic affluence on workers' attitudes and behaviours. Their study, known as the 'Affluent Worker' study, focused on workers in Luton, UK, during the 1960s.

Main Findings

1. **Embourgeoisement Thesis:** They explored whether increased wages and improved living standards led manual workers to adopt middle-class values and lifestyles.

2. **Instrumental Attitude to Work:** They found that workers viewed work primarily as a means to an end (i.e., to earn money) rather than an intrinsic source of satisfaction.
3. **Social Integration:** Despite higher wages, workers remained socially distinct from the middle class, maintaining strong ties with their working-class peers and neighbourhoods.

Implications

- The study challenged the assumption that economic affluence would lead to the dissolution of traditional class identities.
- It highlighted the persistence of class distinctions and the limited impact of economic improvements on social integration.

Serge Mallet: New Working Class

Key Theories: Serge Mallet introduced the concept of the 'new working class' in the context of advanced industrial societies. He focused on the changes in the nature of work due to technological advancements and the rise of white-collar and technical occupations.

Main Findings

1. **Technological Change:** Mallet argued that the rise of automated and technologically sophisticated industries created a new segment of workers with specialized skills and higher education.
2. **New Class Consciousness:** This new working class, consisting of technicians, engineers, and scientists, developed a distinct consciousness influenced by their role in production and their relative autonomy.

Implications

- Mallet's work emphasized the transformation within the working class itself, noting the emergence of new forms of social stratification and consciousness.
- It suggested that traditional Marxist views on the working class needed revision to account for these new occupational categories and their unique experiences.

Duncan Gallie: Occupational Change and Social Mobility

Key Theories: Duncan Gallie focused on occupational change and its impact on social mobility and job satisfaction. He examined how changes in the labour market and employment conditions affected workers' attitudes and life chances.

Main Findings

1. **Job Satisfaction:** Gallie found that job satisfaction was influenced by factors such as job security, opportunities for skill use, and autonomy at work.
2. **Social Mobility:** He examined the patterns of social mobility, emphasizing the role of education and occupational changes in facilitating upward mobility.

Implications

- Gallie's work underscored the importance of non-economic factors in shaping workers' experiences and job satisfaction.
- It highlighted the complex relationship between occupational change, social mobility, and individual well-being.

Stanley Parker: Work and Leisure

Key Theories: Stanley Parker studied the relationship between work and leisure, exploring how changes in work patterns influenced leisure activities and vice versa.

Main Findings

1. **Spillover and Compensation:** Parker identified two primary patterns: spillover, where work experiences influence leisure activities, and compensation, where leisure is used to compensate for unsatisfactory work experiences.
2. **Leisure Patterns:** He found that workers' leisure activities were often shaped by their work schedules, income levels, and job satisfaction.

Implications

- Parker's research highlighted the interconnectedness of work and leisure, suggesting that to understand one, we must consider the other.
- It provided insights into how workers balance their work and non-work lives and the role of leisure in enhancing quality of life.

FYI

Harry Braverman on the Degradation of Work in Capitalist Societies

Braverman's analysis came in opposition to Robert Blauner's work. Blauner conducted a study on the impact of automation on workers and concluded that increasing automation can help reduce the feelings of alienation among workers.

- Braverman argued that automation further estranged the workers from the production process and led to deskilling of industrial labour force.
- In both industrial settings and offices, technology led to degradation of work by limiting human creative input and turned workers into unthinking, unreflective beings.
- Braverman dismissed the idea that technologies are 'neutral' but agreed that it is the capitalists that determine how machinery is used and hence, social class division is responsible for exploitative use of technology.

- Braverman argued that since the 19th century, an era of 'monopoly capitalism' has begun in which large businesses eat up small businesses.
- Braverman argued that 'average skill levels' may have increased in comparison to previous decades, but workers had actually become largely deskilled.

Ace Your Answers!

1. Do you think Braverman's arguments can explain capitalism in the present times? Can you think of any examples of 'monopoly capitalism' in India?

Types of Organizations of Work

Formal Organization of Work

Formal organization of work refers to a structured system of rules, procedures, and practices that govern the activities of an organization or of an economy. The rules are usually set out in writing in clear and unambiguous terms. Sociologist Max Weber theorized on one of the most popular models of formal organization, the bureaucratic model, that remains one of the most applied formal organization models today. The processes of industrialization and democracy led to the establishment of formal organizations.

Features of Formal Organizations

- They are systems of coordinated and controlled activities.
- The work is governed by fixed contracts between the employee and the employer or by rules and legal statutes as determined by the Government.
- In modern societies, formal organizational structures also arise in highly institutional contexts. For instance, the entire State machinery right from the decision-making at the top to the last worker in the hierarchy is governed by fixed rules and procedures that have the backing of laws.
- The formal organizations have explicit goals and objectives, and to achieve them, there are explicit means and processes in place.
- The workers are trained in their roles and are promoted at regular intervals to take on bigger roles in accordance with their accumulated expertise and experience.
- The main advantages of formal organization of work include—balance of interests of both workers and employers, better accountability as employers are

liable for their activities and by signing of contracts workers also agree to deliver through adequate performance, protection of rights of workers through fixed wages, security of tenure, benefits such as insurance, allowances, paid leaves, etc.

Point to Note

India has several employment-related laws and legislations that companies have to follow to protect the interests of both employers and employees. The Indian Constitution grants the Central and state governments the powers to enact laws to protect the employees and foster a professional work environment. Based on the industry, nature of the work, number of employees in the company, location, and more, there are various legislations like the Industrial Disputes Act 1947 (ID Act), Factories Act 1948 (Factories Act), and Shops and Establishment Acts in relevant states (S&E Act). These laws mandate all aspects of employer-employee interaction, such as companies must keep attendance logs, different accounts for overtime wages, and file types of annual returns.

Informal Organization of Work

The informal organization of work refers to a system where workers are not governed by fixed rules but by the directions and control of the employer. It is based on social contracts in which rules are implied rather than clearly stated, and it often includes casual labour, contract labour, and domestic labour.

Features of Informal Organization of Work

- It is largely found in societies whose economies are yet to reach their full potential and where there is a huge presence of unskilled labour. The mismatch between less demand and more supply leads people to work in occupations which are unregulated.
- It is characterized by personal linkages and rapport, and it operates outside the legislations and rules of the land.
- Informal organizations are created by the will and shared identity of their members and run parallel to formal organizations.
- They consist of interpersonal relationships without any conscious structure, legal existence, or official leadership.
- The informal organization is an aggregate of norms, personal and professional connections through which work gets done and relationships are built among employees.
- Being outside the formal rules and laws of the land, the informal organizations do not guarantee protection of rights of the workers.

- Disadvantages include:
    (a) absence of security of tenure
    (b) wage disparity
    (c) increased chances of exploitation of workers especially those of the marginalized sections like women, children, scheduled castes, tribes, etc.
    (d) unethical practices and ill-governance
    (e) absence of social mobility
    (f) corruption

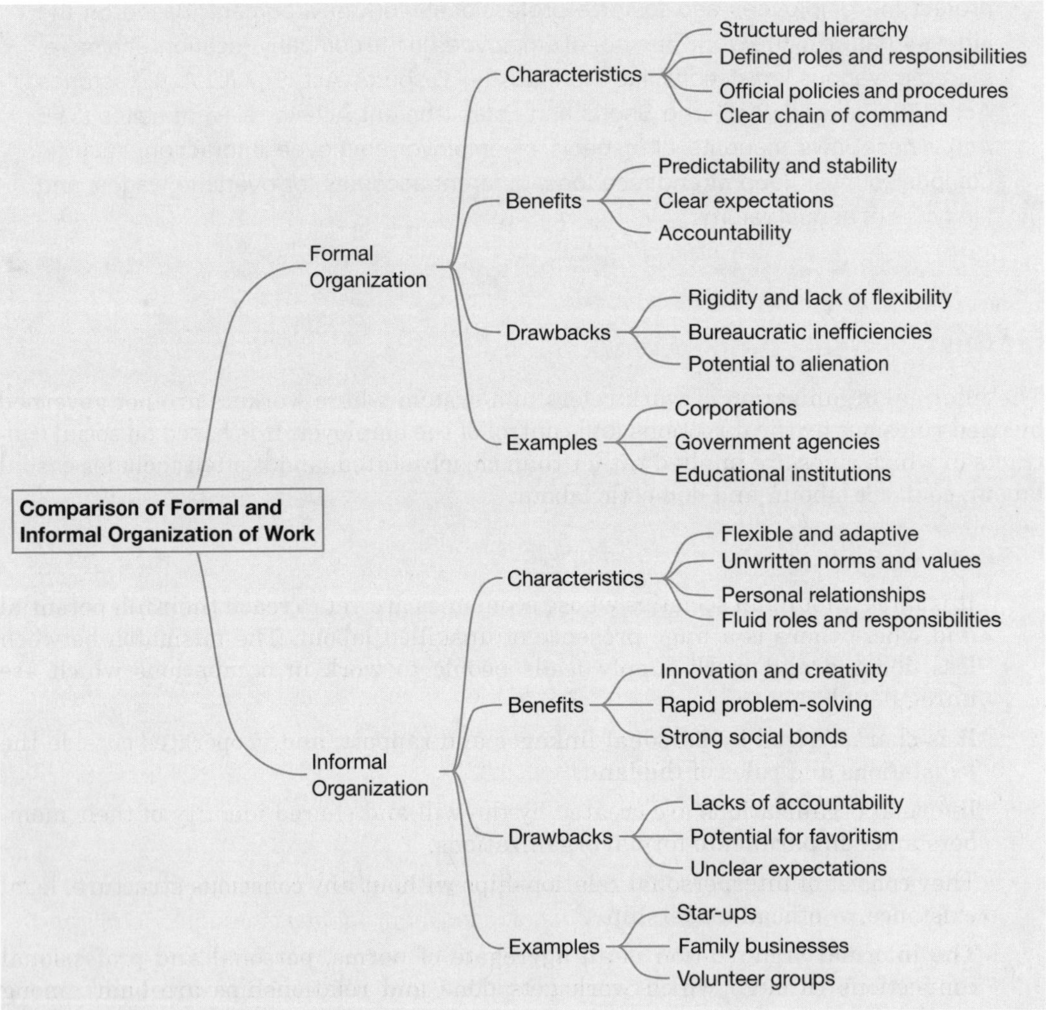

Point to Note

Formal, Informal, Organized, Unorganized

In Indian official statistical documentation, there is no mention of the term 'informal sector'. It is also not being used by the National Accounts Statistics (NAS). In fact, NAS uses the terms—organized and unorganized sector.

The organized sector is used to refer to the formal aspects of the economy, that is to companies which are registered with the government, where the employment terms are fixed and regular, and to employees who work under fixed terms and conditions. The unorganized sector refers to the informal aspects of the economy referring to those enterprises whose activities or collection of data are not regulated by any legal provision or who do not maintain any regular accounts.

FYI

Relationship between Formal and Informal Organization of Work

The relationship between formal and informal organization of work is complex and interrelated. The two can coexist within an organization, and the informal organization often complements the formal structure by facilitating communication, fostering a positive work environment, and addressing social needs of employees. Peter Blau in his work, *The Dynamics of Bureaucracy* (1963), has noted that 'Informal structures exist even in formal organizations.' In fact, many organizations begin as informal organizations and then grow up to become formal organizations.

While the formal organization provides stability and coordination, the informal organization can enhance motivation and teamwork. It is important to note that both formal and informal structures are present in most organizations, and their dynamics depend on the needs, goals, and size of the organization. This kind of relationship is visible in practical forms such as informal weekend dinners of employees, employee support groups, activity clubs in companies, etc.

Additionally, despite the existence of formal procedures and rules, most decisions at the top are taken in an informal way. A lot of recruitment happens through referrals and networking. According to Meyer and Rowan in their work Institutional Organizations: Formal Structures as Myths and Ceremony in 1977, 'formal rules and practices are often quite distant from the practices actually adopted by the members of the organization.'

FYI

The Hawthorne Studies – Importance of Informal Structures in Formal Settings

The Hawthorne Studies were a series of experiments conducted in the 1920s at the Hawthorne plant of the Western Electric Company in Illinois. These studies shifted the focus on the socio-psychological needs of the workers and the influence of work surroundings and coworkers on employees' performance. The main findings of the Hawthorne Studies included:

1. **Informal Organization:** The Hawthorne Studies revealed the importance of informal social processes within the organization. Informal groups based on occupations, friendships, and shared interests had a significant impact on employees' performance and satisfaction.
2. **Social Needs:** The studies showed that employees had social needs such as support, camaraderie, and a sense of belonging beyond material gains of money, work hours, and work conditions. These social needs were met through the formation of informal groups.
3. **Worker-Manager Relationships:** The studies highlighted the importance of worker-manager relationships. Effective management was found to be more related to understanding and addressing employees' social needs than simply focusing on improving individual output.
4. **Influence of Work Surroundings:** Although the studies initially aimed to investigate the effects of physical conditions on productivity, the researchers found that workers were more influenced by their work surroundings and coworkers.
5. **Hawthorne Effect:** The researchers found that the act of being observed modified the workers' behaviour. This came to be known as the Hawthorne effect.

These findings have influenced management strategies and overall understanding of organizational behaviour. The focus shifted from a 'man as machine' perspective to a more holistic approach.

Impacting Lives - Economy

Informal Sector in Global and India's Economy

The 2021 book, *The Long Shadow of Informality – Challenges and Policies*, supported by the World Bank Group, provides the following insights on the informal sector:

- The informal economy accounts for one-fifth of GDP and 16 percent of employment in advanced economies like the USA, UK, Japan, etc.
- In EMDEs (Emerging Markets and Developing Economies) like India, Brazil, South Africa, China, Malaysia, etc., the informal sector accounts for about a third of gross domestic product (GDP) and more than 70 percent of employment (of which self-employment is more than a half). Informality is majorly associated with under-development.
- Regardless of the nature and causes of informality, countries with larger informal sectors tend to have less access to finance for the private sector, lower labour productivity, slower physical and human capital accumulation, and smaller fiscal resources.
- Informality is also associated with higher income inequality and poverty and less progress toward the Sustainable Development Goals.
- The informal sector is, on average, less productive than the formal sector because it tends to employ more low-skilled workers; have more restricted access to funding, services, and markets; and lack economies of scale.
- Workers in the informal sector often live and work in crowded conditions and conduct most transactions in cash. They are also more vulnerable and can be driven into extreme poverty in emergency situations.
- A larger informal economy is associated with weaker economic, fiscal, institutional, and development outcomes. In countries with widespread informality, governments have limited resources and few administrative structures in place to effectively deliver well-targeted relief measures.
- People living in EMDEs with more widespread informality suffer from greater prevalence of hunger, poorer health and education, and greater gender inequality.
- There has been a decline in informality over the past three decades and has been accompanied by improvements in policy climates in EMDEs. Most EMDEs have reduced tax burdens; enhanced access to finance, education, and public services; and improved governance and regulatory quality

India's Informal Economy

- Approximately 81% of India's workforce is employed in the informal sector accounting for 52 per cent of the country's GDP. Both the traditional informal economy and the growing informality within the formal sector exemplify this phenomenon.
- The employment structure reveals a decline in the proportion of informal sector workers over time, accompanied by notable expansion in formal sector employment. This shift was primarily attributed to a decrease in agricultural employment, while all industry categories, except mining, witnessed robust growth in formal sector employment.
- The share of informal employment has increased significantly in the formal sectors of education, health, and community services. The overall rate of informal employment in the (formal) service sector has increased quickly. Within the economy, a

staggering 91.3 per cent of workers lack written contracts, paid time off, and other benefits. The proportion of informal employment within the formal sector escalated from 6.64 per cent in 2004-05 to 11.71 per cent in 2019 – 20.

- The high persistence of informality in the economy is caused by the low levels of formal education and training among informal sector workers and low wages as well as low productivity prevailing in this sector.
- **Informality as a key factor in high inequality in the country**
  - Data from the World Inequality Lab shows that the richest 70 lakh people in India earn as much as the poorest 80 crore. Not just that, but the richest 0.5% of Indians are as rich as the top 10% of people in the US, the biggest economy in the world.
  - As per different reports issued by the government, construction employs 20% SC and 24% ST, a much higher share than their proportion in the population. Among brick kiln workers, 49% of all migrant workers are Dalits, and 16% are Adivasis. Even of the remaining 35%, an overwhelming 30% are OBCs.
- **Women in informal economy**
  - Informal employment is a greater source of employment for all women workers than men in India. Within the informal economy, there are certain categories of work that are more vulnerable than others, but essential for the effective functioning of society. These are home-based workers, domestic workers, street vendors, waste pickers and construction labourers.
  - As per the PFLS Survey, among the domestic workers, which are estimated at 50 million, 75% are women who perform 'a distress-livelihood option that does not guarantee a basic minimum sustenance'. The domestic workers do not have any income security and in many situations suffer from inhumane treatment.
- Formalization as a development strategy requires stepping up investment in physical and human capital to boost productivity and the extension of social security benefits for all workers.

Ace Your Answers!

1. Give a sociological analysis of the impact of Covid pandemic on the informal sector of India's economy.

Impacting Lives - Economy

Changing Nature of Work in 21st Century

- Globally, the shift has occurred from the earlier predominant blue-collar workers in manufacturing industries to now white-collar workers in service based industries especially in advanced economies.
- The share of agriculture in a country's GDP and towards employment has gone down for most societies, with a few exceptions where despite a lower share in GDP, the sector still accounts for high employment.
- Events like the COVID pandemic have increased trends of nationalism and self-sufficiency within national economies.
- The supply chains are getting diversified beyond the traditional destinations like China known for their cheap labour, to countries like India, with its large young and semi-skilled workforce.
- Technological developments like automation, robotics, Artificial Intelligence, Machine-based learning, etc., are changing the nature of jobs that will be in-demand in the future.

Ace Your Answers!

1. It is being argued that Artificial Intelligence will take over most existing jobs in the future. According to the World Economic Forum, the skills of the future include creativity and problem-solving. Do you think the new technologies will enable humans to reach their highest potential and give them more time for leisure?
2. Contrast this with the earlier times wherein Fordism divided complex tasks and indirectly also deskilled the workers.

Important Theories on Organization of Work

Formal Organization of Work

1. **Bureaucratic Theory (Max Weber)**
   - **Key Concepts:** Bureaucracy, rational-legal authority, hierarchical structure, formal rules, and impersonal relationships

- **Explanation:** Weber's theory of bureaucracy explains the existence of formal organizations as a rational and efficient way to manage large-scale operations. Bureaucracy, with its hierarchical structure and formal rules, ensures order, predictability, and efficiency in complex societies.

2. **Scientific Management (Frederick Taylor)**
   - **Key Concepts:** Scientific analysis of work, efficiency, standardization, time and motion studies.
   - **Explanation:** Taylor's scientific management theory justifies formal work organizations by emphasizing the optimization of work processes through scientific methods. This approach leads to increased productivity, standardization, and economic efficiency, supporting the existence of structured, formal workplaces.
3. **Human Relations Theory (Elton Mayo)**
   - **Key Concepts:** Social needs, employee motivation, group dynamics, workplace relationships.
   - **Explanation:** Mayo's theory highlights the social aspects of work within formal organizations. It explains that formal structures need to consider human relations to enhance productivity and worker satisfaction, emphasizing the importance of social interactions and employee well-being in formal work settings.
4. **Structural Functionalism (Talcott Parsons)**
   - **Key Concepts:** Social systems, functions, roles, equilibrium
   - **Explanation:** Parsons' structural functionalism views formal organizations as essential components of social systems that contribute to societal stability and equilibrium. Each part of the organization has specific functions that work together to maintain order and achieve collective goals, justifying the structured nature of formal work.

Informal Organization of Work

1. **Social Network Theory**
   - **Key Concepts:** Social ties, networks, social capital, informal relationships
   - **Explanation:** Social network theory explains the existence of informal work organizations by highlighting the importance of social ties and networks. Informal relationships provide support, facilitate communication, and enhance cooperation, making informal work environments viable and resilient.
2. **Symbolic Interactionism (Erving Goffman)**
   - **Key Concepts:** Social interactions, meanings, roles, impression management
   - **Explanation:** Goffman's symbolic interactionism focuses on the everyday interactions and meanings individuals attach to their work roles. In informal settings, workers negotiate their identities and roles through interactions, making informal work organization's dynamic and adaptive.

3. **Dual Labour Market Theory**
   - **Key Concepts:** Primary and secondary labour markets, segmentation, job stability
   - **Explanation:** Dual labour market theory explains the coexistence of formal and informal work by dividing the labour market into primary (formal, stable jobs) and secondary (informal, unstable jobs) sectors. This segmentation arises from economic and social inequalities, sustaining the presence of informal work alongside formal employment.
4. **Embeddedness Theory (Mark Granovetter)**
   - **Key Concepts:** Economic actions, social context, embeddedness
   - **Explanation:** Granovetter's embeddedness theory highlights how economic actions are deeply embedded in social relationships. Informal work is explained by the trust, reciprocity, and social ties that shape economic activities outside formal structures, emphasizing the role of social context in sustaining informal work.
5. **Informal Economy Theory**
   - **Key Concepts:** Informal economy, subsistence, flexibility, survival strategies
   - **Explanation:** Informal economy theory explains the existence of informal work as a response to economic needs and survival strategies. Informal work provides flexibility and adaptability in the absence of formal employment opportunities, especially in developing economies where formal job creation may be limited.

Organized Work

1. **Labour Process Theory (Harry Braverman)**:
   - **Key Concepts:** Labour process, deskilling, control
   - **Explanation:** Braverman's labour process theory explains organized work by focusing on how work is structured and controlled within capitalist economies. Organized work is characterized by systematic control over the labour process, often leading to deskilling and increased managerial control.
2. **Neo-Marxist Theory**
   - **Key Concepts:** Class struggle, exploitation, capital accumulation
   - **Explanation:** Neo-Marxist theory explains organized work as a site of class struggle and exploitation within capitalist systems. Organized work environments are structured to maximize capital accumulation and maintain the power dynamics between capitalists and workers.

Unorganized Work

1. **Survivalist Theory**
   - **Key Concepts:** Survival strategies, economic necessity, marginalization.

- **Explanation:** Survivalist theory explains unorganized work as a response to economic necessity and marginalization. Individuals engage in unorganized work as a means of survival in the absence of formal employment opportunities and social safety nets.

2. **Dependency Theory**
   - **Key Concepts:** Economic dependency, underdevelopment, peripheral economies
   - **Explanation:** Dependency theory explains unorganized work in the context of global economic inequalities. Peripheral economies rely on unorganized work due to their dependency on developed nations, resulting in a lack of formal job creation and economic development.

Contemporary Examples

Formal Work

- **Tech Industry:** Software developers at Google or Microsoft benefit from structured job roles, regulatory compliance, and extensive employee benefits, aligning with Weber's bureaucratic theory and Taylor's scientific management principles.

Informal Work

- **Gig Economy:** Drivers for Uber or delivery personnel for DoorDash operate in flexible, network-based work environments with minimal regulation, fitting within social network theory and informal economy theory.

Ace Your Answers!

1. How is the emerging gig economy changing the formal and informal aspects of the economy?

Organized Work

- **Automobile Industry:** Workers in automobile manufacturing plants like Toyota or Ford experience structured, unionized work environments that reflect labour process theory and structural functionalism.

Unorganized Work

- **Agriculture:** Small-scale farmers in rural India work in unregulated, subsistence-based environments, exemplifying survivalist theory and dependency theory.

Labour and Society

Concept of Labour

Initially, the concept of labour emerged in the context of industrial capitalism to refer to paid employment, relationship with the capital and to collectives of workers (labour movements). Gradually though, the labour paradigm has extended beyond the core debates of industrial capitalism in the following three ways:

- First, there is a distinction between 'free' wage labour and 'unfree' forms of labour like modern slavery, bonded labour, etc.
- Second, labour has extended beyond the sphere of paid formal work to include informal forms such as domestic labour.
- Third, labour has been used to analyse the different forms of paid work in post-industrial society which include knowledge work, insecure employment and emotional labour. For example, Arlie Hoschchild in her study, The Managed Heart (1983), which was based on Delta Airlines showed how the service industry required manipulation of emotions as part of their daily work.

In another sense, the term labour has been seen in contrast to a worker on the basis of choice. It was believed that a labourer has no or less choice in comparison to an industrial worker. However, as noted above, the word 'labour' now encapsulates different types of work and workers.

Characteristics of Labour in Modern Societies

1. Human labour is only one dimension of work in modern industrial societies as the remaining is fulfilled by machines and technologies.
2. Existence of labour markets in which workers become available for hire to work for specified periods for a wage.
3. High division of labour with increasing expertise and specificity. This division is also based on social identities of caste, class, sex, etc. For example, women being a majority in domestic labour, men being a majority in construction work, marginalized members of the transgender community often have to resort to prostitution because of absence of opportunities for them in the formal labour markets, etc.
4. Rise of service sector has come with a decline in the older factory production. One of its consequences has been a decline in the trade-union movements and erosion of bargaining power of labour in the modern world.
5. Flexible production, liberal labour laws and intense global competition have also affected labour power.
6. Labour in modern times is required to be skilled in multiple areas which has resulted in labour being 'flexible'. They lack expertize in any one area, rather build up a portfolio of numerous skills. This has given choice to the workers to become eligible for work in multiple places but also makes them dispensable at will for the capitalists. Such workers are called portfolio workers.

7. The Information Technology revolution has transformed workers into machines and restricted them to cubicles, facing the screen, limiting face-to-face interaction and putting them under constant surveillance.
8. Globalization has led to high mobility of labour, transboundary movement and also shifting of workplaces to sites of cheaper production. This has led to rise of sweatshops in countries like China, Bangladesh, Vietnam, etc., where working conditions are often bad and workers mainly work at low wages in an informal capacity.

Theories

1. **Classical Sociology**
   - **Karl Marx:** Focused on the concept of labour as central to his critique of capitalism. He introduced the idea of alienation, where workers are estranged from the products of their labour, the labour process, their fellow workers, and their own potential.
   - **Émile Durkheim:** Examined the division of labour in society, proposing that it was essential for social cohesion. He distinguished between mechanical and organic solidarity in traditional and modern societies, respectively.
   - **Max Weber:** Studied the rationalization of labour in modern society, particularly through bureaucracy and the Protestant work ethic, linking it to the rise of capitalism.
2. **Conflict Theory**
   - **Ralf Dahrendorf:** Extended Marx's ideas, emphasizing the role of authority and conflict within labour relations. He argued that industrial societies are characterized by conflicts between those with and without authority.
   - **Harry Braverman:** Critiqued the degradation of work under capitalism in his seminal work 'Labour and Monopoly Capital,' highlighting the deskilling of labour through technological advancements.
3. **Functionalism**
   - **Talcott Parsons:** Viewed labour as a key component of the social system, essential for maintaining social order and stability. He focused on how different institutions contribute to the functioning of society.
   - **Robert K. Merton:** Built on Parsons' ideas, emphasizing the functions and dysfunctions of different aspects of labour in society.
4. **Symbolic Interactionism**
   - **Herbert Blumer:** Emphasized the meanings and interpretations individuals attach to their labour and work experiences. He studied how these meanings are constructed through social interactions.
   - **Erving Goffman:** Analysed the performative aspects of work, focusing on how individuals present themselves in different work roles.
5. **Feminist Sociology**
   - **Dorothy Smith:** Critiqued traditional sociology for ignoring women's experiences, focussing on the everyday lives and labour of women.

- **Heidi Hartmann:** Explored the intersection of patriarchy and capitalism, highlighting how both systems oppress women in the workforce.
- **Arlie Hochschild:** Investigated emotional labour, particularly in service industries, and how it is often undervalued and gendered.

6. **Postmodernism**
   - **Michel Foucault:** Analysed the relationship between power, knowledge, and labour, focusing on how labour practices are influenced by discourses and power structures.
   - **Jean Baudrillard:** Explored how labour and production are replaced by consumption and signs in a postmodern society.
7. **Neo-Marxism**
   - **Antonio Gramsci:** Introduced the concept of cultural hegemony, examining how dominant groups maintain control through ideology, including labour relations.
   - **Louis Althusser:** Emphasized the role of ideological state apparatuses in reproducing labour power and maintaining capitalist relations of production.
8. **Critical Theory**
   - **Jürgen Habermas:** Examined the colonization of the lifeworld by systems of money and power, affecting labour relations and communication.
   - **Herbert Marcuse:** Critiqued the one-dimensional nature of work in advanced industrial societies, arguing that it suppresses critical thinking and creativity.

FYI

Marxist Conception of Labour

While Hegel viewed labour only in terms of ideas, Marx saw labour in the material domain. According to Marx, labour is a process in which both man and nature participate and in which man of his own accord starts, regulates and controls the material reactions between himself and nature.

- Labour deals with material things but is not restricted solely to economic activities. It is intrinsic to all productive activities in which human beings are engaged to produce something which previously existed only in their imagination (objectification of purpose).
- Marx considered labour as peculiar only to humans, not animals.
- Labour is a social activity and transforms both the individual and the society.
- In capitalism, labour is not owned by workers.
- As part of his labour theory of value, Marx argued that the value of a commodity is determined by the amount of socially necessary labour time required for its production.

Criticism: Michael Burawoy rejected Marxist argument of labour being coerced to work under capitalism and argues that workers' consent is involved. Durkheim saw division of labour and labour relations in modern society as creating interdependency and new forms of integration.

Limits of the Working Day

The concept of the 'limits of the working day' is central to Marx's critique of capitalism. He argues that capitalists seek to extend the working day as much as possible to extract more surplus value from workers.

1. **Historical Struggle:** The length of the working day has been a major site of struggle between capital and labour. Workers have historically fought for shorter working hours to improve their quality of life and reduce exploitation.
2. **Legal and Regulatory Limits:** Various laws and regulations have been enacted to limit the working day. For instance, the Factory Acts in 19th century Britain were some of the first legislative attempts to regulate working hours.
3. **Capitalist Resistance:** Capitalists resist limits on the working day because longer hours mean more surplus value. They argue that such limits reduce profitability and economic growth.
4. **Impact on Workers:** Overwork can lead to physical and mental exhaustion, reducing productivity in the long run. Shorter working days are associated with better health outcomes and higher overall productivity.

Labour Commitment

Labour commitment refers to the degree of dedication, attachment, and responsibility that workers feel towards their work, their employer, and their role within the organization. It encompasses various dimensions including affective commitment (emotional attachment), continuance commitment (cost-based attachment), and normative commitment (obligation-based attachment).

Labour Commitment in the Manufacturing Industry

1. **Classical Studies:** Studies like those by Frederick Taylor on scientific management and Elton Mayo's Hawthorne experiments have highlighted how organizational practices influence labour commitment. Taylor emphasized efficiency and incentives, while Mayo focused on social factors and worker satisfaction.
2. **Human Relations Movement:** This movement stressed the importance of social factors in the workplace. It suggested that workers' commitment is enhanced by good interpersonal relations, a supportive management style, and opportunities for participation in decision-making.
3. **Job Satisfaction and Commitment:** Research in the manufacturing sector shows that job satisfaction is a significant predictor of labour commitment. Factors contributing to job satisfaction include fair wages, job security, opportunities for advancement, and a safe working environment.

4. **Impact of Technology:** The introduction of advanced technologies and automation in manufacturing has complex effects on labour commitment. While technology can lead to job enrichment and higher satisfaction for some, it can also result in job displacement and alienation for others.
5. **Case Studies:** Studies of Japanese manufacturing firms, for instance, highlight high levels of labour commitment attributed to practices such as lifetime employment, seniority-based pay, and a strong emphasis on teamwork and collective responsibility.
6. **Contemporary Challenges:** In the context of globalization and precarious employment, maintaining labour commitment has become challenging. Outsourcing, contract work, and the gig economy contribute to a decline in job security and, consequently, in labour commitment.

FYI

Ann Oakley on Gendered Domestic Division of Labour, Housework and Role of Housewife

The second wave of feminism in the West questioned the previous assumptions of housework being the exclusive preserve of women. In 1974, Ann Oakley published two related books – *The Sociology of Housework* and *Housewife*. She argued that due to industrialization, the workplace separated from the home. When work started to occur outside, home became primarily a site for consumption rather than for production of goods or services as was the case earlier. The work outside came to be perceived as 'real work' as the worker earned 'wages' for it. The work at home became largely invisible. In the conventional model then, the men assumed the responsibility to go outside and earn the wages for the upkeep of the family. The women, on the other hand, were expected to stay at home, their 'natural domain', and do all domestic tasks. The separation of workplace from home led to a gender based division of labour, creating categories for what counted as 'real work' and 'invisible work'.

Oakley also argued that because housework brings no monetary reward, women gain satisfaction and psychological rewards from meeting standards of cleanliness and order, which feel like externally imposed rules. Women also cannot leave their workplace, like men can and do not enjoy a separate leisure time. The income brought by men through their paid work creates an unequal power relationship making the women of the house dependent on men for their own and family's economic survival.

Ace Your Answers!

1. Times have changed and today, women too, whether married or unmarried, are engaged in the market economy. In comparison to previous generations, have the attitudes of the present generation changed? Is there more equalization in the realm of household work?
2. In some quarters, it is also argued that men too suffer from the pressure to provide. The term 'househusband' is now familiar to many. Yet, the role of man as a homemaker still suffers from some sort of stigma. In terms of labour, is patriarchy harmful to both men and women?
3. In the metropolitan cities of India, a significant share of housework is now being done by domestic workers, majority of which are still women. These are migrants, very often not even adults. While women are seen to work inside the house, chores outside the house such as gardening, car cleaning, driving, etc., are done by male workers. In this context, is gender the only determinant in domestic division of labour?
4. During the COVID pandemic, the concept of 'work from home' blurred the physical boundaries between home and workplace. Did it also alter the domestic division of labour?

Impacting Lives - Globalization

Impact of Globalization on Labour and Society

Positive Impacts

1. **Increased Economic Opportunities:** The outsourcing of customer service jobs to countries like India has created employment opportunities in sectors such as IT, BPO, etc. Even locally indigenous products have gained customers across countries, thereby boosting international trade while strengthening home-grown businesses.
2. **Technological Advancements:** The global sharing of technological innovations, such as advancements in information technology, has led to increased connectivity and improved efficiency.
3. **Cultural Exchange:** The popularity of films, music, and cuisine has given the opportunity to local artistes to showcase their talents beyond their local regions.

4. **Poverty Reduction:** Microfinance initiatives, supported by global networks, have empowered budding entrepreneurs in developing countries, contributing to poverty reduction.

Negative Impacts

1. **Labour Market Inequality:** The rise of gig economy platforms has led to job insecurity and the lack of workers' rights, contributing to inequality.

   In 2002, Nobel laureate Joseph Stiglitz claimed that 'globalization has become a race to the bottom, where corporations are the only winners and the rest of society, in both the developed and developing worlds, is the loser.'
2. **Exploitation of Labour:** For example, sweetshops in developing countries, producing goods for global markets, often involve exploitative labour practices.
3. **Job Insecurity:** Automation in manufacturing industries has led to job displacement and increased uncertainty for workers.
4. **Cultural Homogenization:** The dominance of Western films and fashion in global markets can contribute to the erosion of local cultural identities.
5. **Environmental Degradation:** The global demand for cheap goods has led to environmentally damaging production practices in some countries.
6. **Social Dislocation:** Rapid urbanization and industrialization in some developing countries have led to social dislocation and challenges in adapting to new economic realities.

Mitigation Strategies

1. **Labour Standards and Regulation:** The implementation of fair labour standards by international organizations can help protect workers from exploitation.
2. **Investment in Education and Training:** Countries investing in education and vocational training programs are better positioned to adapt to the changing demands of the global economy.
3. **Environmental Sustainability:** Companies adopting environmentally sustainable practices in response to consumer demands contribute to global efforts in addressing climate change.
4. **Social Safety Nets:** Countries with robust social safety nets, including unemployment benefits and healthcare support, can better cushion the impact of economic changes on vulnerable populations.
5. **Promoting Inclusive Growth:** Policies that prioritise inclusive economic growth, such as progressive taxation and social welfare programs, can contribute to a more equitable distribution of benefits.

Recent Topics of Interest in the Context of Work and Economic Life

The Debate on 70-hour Work Week

- **Capitalist Work Ethic:** Reflects the capitalist ideology promoting productivity and profitability over workers' well-being.
- **Social Stratification:** May increase inequality as only certain socio-economic groups can afford to work such long hours.
- **Health and Well-being:** Potentially detrimental effects on physical and mental health, raising concerns about work-life balance.
- **Work-life Balance:** Challenges traditional family roles and domestic responsibilities, leading to social strain.
- **Labour Rights:** Raises questions about labour rights and protections, as well as the role of unions and collective bargaining.

Trends such as Moonlighting, Quiet Quitting, and Job Hopping

- **Economic Insecurity:** These trends reflect the precarious nature of modern employment and economic insecurity.
- **Work Identity:** Challenges traditional notions of loyalty and identity tied to a single employer.
- **Work-life Integration:** Indicates a shift towards seeking better work-life balance and personal fulfillment.
- **Labour Market Dynamics:** Reflects the fluidity and flexibility of the gig economy and freelance work culture.
- **Employer-employee Relations:** Highlights changing power dynamics and the need for employers to adapt to retain talent.

Attitudes towards Work among Gen-Z Youngsters

- **Value Shift:** Gen-Z prioritises meaningful work, flexibility, and personal growth over job security and high salaries.
- **Technology Integration:** High reliance on technology and digital platforms for work and communication.
- **Workplace Diversity:** Strong emphasis on inclusivity, diversity, and social justice in the workplace.
- **Mental Health Awareness:** Greater awareness and prioritization of mental health and well-being.
- **Collaborative Work Culture:** Preference for collaboratiove and innovative work environments over hierarchical structures.

Impact of New Labour Codes in India

- **Regulation and Protection:** Aim to streamline labour regulations and enhance protections for workers, especially in informal sectors.

- **Formalization of Workforce:** Encourages the formalization of employment, offering better benefits and job security.
- **Flexibility vs. Security:** Balances flexibility for employers with security for employees, though criticisms exist regarding potential erosion of worker rights.
- **Social Security:** Expansion of social security benefits to a larger section of the workforce.
- **Industrial Relations:** Modernizes industrial relations, aiming to reduce conflicts and improve employer-employee relations.

Feminisation of Agrarian Workforce in India

- **Gender Roles:** Traditional male migration for urban employment leads to increased female participation in agriculture.
- **Economic Contribution:** Women's labour becomes crucial to rural economies, though often undervalued and underpaid.
- **Social Status:** Alters the social status and empowerment of rural women, offering both opportunities and challenges.
- **Access to Resources:** Women face barriers to accessing resources, training, and technology in agriculture.
- **Policy Implications:** Necessitates gender-sensitive policies and interventions to support female agrarian workers.
- Economically, the trend towards the feminisation of work is marked by women's increasing participation in the informal and low-wage sectors. According to the International Labour Organization (ILO), women's global labour force participation rate was 48.5% in 2018, compared to 75% for men. However, in many developing countries, women are disproportionately represented in informal employment. In India, for example, the National Sample Survey Office (NSSO) reported in 2019 that over 90% of women in the workforce are engaged in the informal sector. These jobs often lack security, benefits, and fair wages. For instance, in the garment industry, which is heavily feminised, workers in countries like Bangladesh and India often earn less than $100 per month, far below a living wage.
- From a social and cultural perspective, the shift in women's roles due to their increased workforce participation is significant but complex. Despite their economic contributions, women often continue to bear the primary responsibility for unpaid domestic labour. The United Nations reports that women globally spend roughly three times more hours on unpaid domestic and care work than men. In India, this disparity is even more pronounced. The Time Use Survey in India (2020) revealed that women spend nearly six hours a day on unpaid domestic services for household members, compared to less than one hour by men. This 'double burden' of work significantly impacts women's ability to participate fully in the formal workforce and achieve career advancement.
- Furthermore, the intersection of feminisation of work with education, urbanization, and globalization presents both opportunities and challenges. The World Bank data indicates that with better education, women are more likely to participate in the formal labour market. However, in many developing countries, there's a significant

gender gap in education, which limits these opportunities. Urbanization has led to increased female labour force participation in urban areas compared to rural settings.

- According to the PLFS, we have approximately 166 million women either working, seeking work, or available for work. Out of the population of working women, more than 90 percent work in the informal sector. They are either self-employed or casual workers, predominantly in agricultural and construction sectors. This means that they face increased exploitation, poor working conditions, lack of mobility, and higher risk of violence. This discourages women from entering the workforce.
- A recent NITI Aayog report states that women in India spend 9.8 times more time than men on unpaid domestic chores (against a global average of 2.6 as reported by UN Women). Globally, unpaid care work is the key reason that women are outside the labour force whereas for men it is 'being in education, sick, or disabled'. Additionally, deep-rooted social norms and lack of agency leave women with little choice in their employment decisions.
- A 2023 report by State Bank of India suggests that unpaid women's total contribution to the economy is around INR 22.7 lakh crore—approximately 7.5 percent of India's GDP. A working paper by the Economic Advisory Council highlights that the PLFS (Periodic Labour Force Survey) does not capture 'economically productive work done by women like poultry farming, milking of cows, etc., as part of their domestic duties'. Upon correcting for this omission, the Economic Survey 2022 – 2023 estimated an FLFPR (Female Labour Force Participation Rate) of 46.2 percent for 2020 – 21.
- The United Nations highlights that urbanization can offer more diverse employment opportunities for women, but it also exacerbates the urban-rural divide in gender-specific employment patterns. Globally, the demand for cheap labour has seen a surge in women's employment in export-oriented industries. While this has provided job opportunities, it often comes with poor working conditions and low wages, reflecting the broader dynamics of global inequality and exploitation.
- It is multifaceted, while it indicates progress in terms of women's participation in the workforce, it also highlights ongoing challenges related to economic inequality, gender norms, and the intersection of various sociological factors. Addressing these challenges requires comprehensive policies that focus not only on increasing women's employment but also on improving the quality of employment and addressing the broader socio-economic factors that influence women's work.
- Recent PLFS data shows a possible Feminisation U Hypothesis in female participation rates in India. The feminization hypothesis, also known as the feminization of poverty thesis, posits that women are disproportionately represented among the poor and that this trend is increasing over time. This concept emerged in the 1970s and has since been a significant area of study in sociology, gender studies, and economics. This hypothesis was created on the basis of a cross section of 169 countries from 1990 to 2013. It shows that the early stages of economic growth are accompanied by a decline in female labour force participation. This is because women who were previously working to make ends meet can now opt out of the workforce due to rising household incomes. However, as incomes rise further, women tend to become economically active again. And this increase in economic activity tends to be accompanied by a drop in both fertility rates and the gender education gap.

- Periodic Labour Force Survey Report 2022 – 23 released by the Ministry of Statistics and Programme Implementation on 9th October 2023 shows that the Female Labour Force Participation Rate in the country has improved significantly by 4.2% to 37.0% in 2023, as per 'usual status' concept of measuring labour force participation.

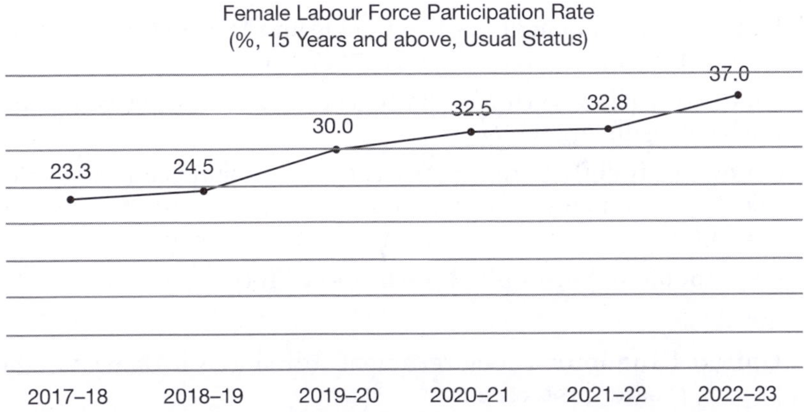

- Unlocking the full potential of women in our workforce would provide multiple times the return on initial investments made by the government and businesses. As per McKinsey Global Institute's report, India could achieve an 18 percent increase over business-as-usual GDP (USD 770 billion) by 2025.

Recent Trends Related to Women and Labour

Global Trends

1. **Gender Pay Gap and Equality Initiatives**
   - **Examples:**

     (i) **Iceland**: Iceland has implemented a law that requires companies to prove they are paying men and women equally.

     (ii) **Germany:** The Transparency in Wage Structures Act encourages employees to discuss their wages to reduce the gender pay gap.
   - **Sociological Insight:** According to feminist theory, the gender pay gap reflects systemic patriarchy and gender discrimination. Efforts to close this gap align with the feminist pursuit of gender equality, challenging traditional gender roles and advocating for equal opportunities.
2. **Rise of Women in Leadership**
   - **Examples:**

     (i) **New Zealand:** Prime Minister Jacinda Ardern's leadership has been widely recognized and praised.

     (ii) **Finland:** Sanna Marin, one of the world's youngest prime ministers, leads a coalition government dominated by women.

- **Sociological Insight:** This trend signifies a shift in societal norms and values towards gender inclusivity and the breaking down of glass ceilings. It also highlights the role of social movements and advocacy groups in promoting gender parity.

3. **Flexible Work and Remote Opportunities**
   - **Examples:**

     (i) **United States:** Companies like Google and Microsoft have adopted flexible work policies.

     (ii) **Australia:** The government has encouraged remote work to support work-life balance during the pandemic.
   - **Sociological Insight:** From a structural-functional perspective, flexible work arrangements can be seen as adaptive mechanisms that help balance societal roles and family dynamics, reducing role conflict for women.

4. **Increased Focus on Women's Health and Safety**
   - **Examples:**

     (i) **United Kingdom:** The government introduced a Domestic Abuse Bill to provide greater protection.

     (ii) **Sweden:** Known for its robust policies on gender equality and workplace safety.
   - **Sociological Insight:** The heightened focus on women's health and safety at work reflects the impact of social movements like #MeToo, which utilise collective action to challenge and change institutional practices and cultural norms regarding gender and power dynamics.

5. **Representation in STEM Fields**
   - **Examples:**

     (i) **Canada:** Programs like the Canada 150 Research Chairs are designed to attract top international talent, including women in STEM.

     (ii) **India:** Initiatives like 'Women Scientists Scheme' (WOS) encourage women to pursue careers in science.
   - **Sociological Insight:** Addressing gender disparities in STEM aligns with the conflict theory perspective, which seeks to address inequalities perpetuated by dominant groups. Encouraging women in STEM challenges the traditional gender stratification and promotes equity.

Trends in India

1. **Women in the Workforce**
   - **Examples:**

     (i) Initiatives like the 'Skill India Mission' aim to empower women through skill development.

     (ii) Organizations like SEWA (Self-Employed Women's Association) support female workers in the informal sector.
   - **Sociological Insight:** From a developmental perspective, enhancing women's participation in the workforce is critical for economic growth and social

progress. This aligns with modernization theories that link gender equality to overall societal advancement.

2. **Legislative Reforms**
   - **Examples:**

     (i) The Maternity Benefit (Amendment) Act, 2017, which extends maternity leave from 12 to 26 weeks.

     (ii) The Sexual Harassment of Women at Workplace (Prevention, Prohibition and Redressal) Act, 2013, ensuring safer workplaces.
   - **Sociological Insight:** Legislative reforms are steps toward achieving gender equality as per liberal feminist theory, which advocates for equal legal rights and protections to ensure women's full participation in public life.
3. **Education and Skill Development**
   - **Examples:**

     (i) The *Beti Bachao, Beti Padhao* initiative focuses on increasing awareness and improving the efficiency of welfare services for girls.

     (ii) The 'National Skill Development Mission' aims to create a skilled workforce, with a focus on women.
   - **Sociological Insight:** Education is a key factor in social mobility and empowerment, as posited by human capital theory. Increasing educational opportunities for women is essential for reducing gender disparities in the labour market.
4. **Microfinance and Women Entrepreneurs**
   - **Examples:**

     (i) Microfinance institutions like Grameen Bank and initiatives by NABARD provide financial services to women entrepreneurs.

     (ii) The 'Mahila E-Haat' platform facilitates direct online marketing by women.
   - **Sociological Insight:** Microfinance aligns with the empowerment theory, which emphasises enabling individuals to gain control over their lives and resources. It fosters economic independence and challenges traditional gender roles in rural communities.

Point to Note

Challenges of Informal Sector Employment

- A significant number of women in India work in sectors like agriculture, domestic work, and construction, often without formal contracts or benefits.
- Organizations like SEWA advocate for better conditions and rights for women in the informal sector.

Sociological Insight: Informal sector employment highlights the structural inequalities and the dual labour market theory, where the informal sector is characterized by low wages and poor working conditions, disproportionately affecting women.

Impact of Economic Globalization on Employment Patterns in the 21st Century

Economic globalization refers to the increasing interdependence of world economies resulting from the growing scale of cross-border trade of commodities and services, the flow of international capital, and the wide and rapid spread of technologies. This phenomenon has profoundly influenced employment patterns globally. Here are some key changes:

1. **Shift from Manufacturing to Service-Oriented Economies**
   - **Example:** In the United States, there has been a significant decline in manufacturing jobs while service sector jobs have surged. Cities like Detroit, once known for automobile manufacturing, have seen a decrease in factory jobs, whereas cities like San Francisco have experienced a boom in tech and service-related employment.
   - **Sociological Insight:** This shift aligns with Daniel Bell's post-industrial society theory, which emphasises the transition from goods-producing to service-oriented economies. It reflects a change in the labour market where knowledge and services become more critical than physical labour.
2. **Rise of the Gig Economy**
   - **Example:** Platforms like Uber, Airbnb, and Upwork have created opportunities for freelance work and short-term contracts. In India, the gig economy has provided employment opportunities for many, especially in urban areas, with companies like Swiggy and Zomato.
   - **Sociological Insight:** The gig economy exemplifies the transformation of labour relations and the rise of flexible employment. This trend can be analyzed through the lens of Karl Marx's alienation theory, where workers may feel disconnected from their work due to the lack of stable, long-term employment relationships.
3. **Outsourcing and Offshoring**
   - **Example:** Many Western companies outsource IT services, customer support, and manufacturing to countries like India, China, and the Philippines. For instance, India has become a hub for IT and back-office services, employing millions in the Business Process Outsourcing (BPO) sector.
   - **Sociological Insight:** Outsourcing and offshoring highlight the global division of labour, where countries specialise in specific sectors. This can be examined through the world-systems theory by Immanuel Wallerstein, which discusses the hierarchical structure of the global economy and the exploitation of peripheral countries by core countries.
4. **Increase in Female Labour Force Participation**
   - **Example:** Economic globalization has led to more women entering the labour force, particularly in developing countries. In Bangladesh, the garment industry employs a large number of women, providing them with financial independence.

- **Sociological Insight:** This trend can be explored through feminist theories that emphasize the economic empowerment of women as a critical step towards gender equality. It also raises issues regarding labour rights and working conditions in industries predominantly employing women.

5. **Technological Advancements and Remote Work**
   - **Example:** The COVID-19 pandemic accelerated the adoption of remote work worldwide. Companies like Google and Microsoft have implemented permanent remote work policies for many employees.
   - **Sociological Insight:** Technological advancements and the shift to remote work can be analysed using Manuel Castells' theory of the network society, where information technology facilitates new forms of social organization and work patterns.
6. **Migration and Labour Mobility**
   - **Example:** Economic globalization has facilitated the movement of labour across borders. The Gulf Cooperation Council (GCC) countries host millions of migrant workers from South Asia and Africa, working in construction, domestic work, and service sectors.
   - **Sociological Insight:** Migration and labour mobility can be examined through migration theories, such as the push-pull model, which considers economic opportunities as a major factor driving migration. It also raises issues of labour rights, exploitation, and the social integration of migrants.
7. **Changes in Labour Regulations and Standards**
   - **Example:** The European Union has implemented various directives to standardize labour regulations across member states, ensuring better working conditions and protections for workers.
   - **Sociological Insight:** Standardizing labour regulations aligns with theories of global governance and the role of international organizations in shaping domestic labour policies. It reflects a trend towards improving labour standards globally in response to the pressures of economic globalization.

Changing Nature of Work in Contemporary Societies

Redefining Formal Organization of Work

1. **Decentralization of Workspaces**
   - **Previous Norm:** Formal organizations typically operated from centralized office spaces.
   - **New Norm:** Employees work from various locations, decentralizing the physical workspace.
   - **Implication:** This change necessitates the development of robust remote work infrastructure, including communication tools, data security measures, and virtual collaboration platforms.

2. **Flexible Work Schedules**
   - **Previous Norm:** Fixed working hours and strict schedules.
   - **New Norm:** Flexibility in work hours to accommodate different time zones, personal commitments, and productivity peaks.
   - **Implication:** Organizations must adapt their management practices to monitor productivity and performance without micromanaging, focusing more on results than hours worked.
3. **Performance Measurement and Accountability**
   - **Previous Norm:** Performance was often measured by visible presence and immediate output.
   - **New Norm:** Emphasis on outcomes, deliverables, and virtual performance tracking.
   - **Implication:** New metrics and tools are required to assess productivity, manage remote teams, and ensure accountability.
4. **Human Resource Practices**
   - **Previous Norm:** Traditional HR practices focused on in-office activities, onboarding, training, and team-building exercises.
   - **New Norm:** Virtual onboarding, remote training programs, and online team-building activities.
   - **Implication:** HR departments must innovate to maintain employee engagement, culture, and morale in a virtual environment.

Redefining Informal Organization of Work

1. **Informal Communication Channels**
   - **Previous Norm:** Informal interactions occurred naturally in office settings through casual conversations, coffee breaks, and social gatherings.
   - **New Norm:** Virtual communication channels like instant messaging, video calls, and social media platforms facilitate informal interactions.
   - **Implication:** Organizations need to create virtual spaces and opportunities for informal interactions to foster camaraderie and a sense of belonging.
2. **Work-life Balance and Boundaries**
   - **Previous Norm:** Clear separation between work and personal life with distinct physical spaces.
   - **New Norm:** Blurred boundaries as home becomes the workspace.
   - **Implication:** Employees need to establish boundaries and routines to prevent burnout, and organizations must respect personal time and promote a healthy work-life balance.
3. **Employee Autonomy and Empowerment**
   - **Previous Norm:** Direct supervision and management control were prevalent.
   - **New Norm:** Increased autonomy and self-management as employees work independently from home.

- **Implication:** Trust becomes crucial, and employees need to be empowered with the necessary tools and support to manage their work effectively.

4. **Team Dynamics and Collaboration**
    - **Previous Norm:** Collaboration occurred in-person, often spontaneously.
    - **New Norm:** Planned virtual meetings and structured communication for collaboration.
    - **Implication:** Teams must adapt to new ways of working together, leveraging technology for effective communication and collaboration.

New Labour Codes

The Indian government has consolidated 29 labour laws into four broad labour codes to simplify and modernize the existing labour regulations. These are:

1. Code on Wages, 2019
2. Industrial Relations Code, 2020
3. Code on Social Security, 2020
4. Occupational Safety, Health and Working Conditions Code, 2020

Key Features

1. **Code on Wages, 2019**
    - **Key Provisions**
        - Universal minimum wage.
        - Timely payment of wages.
        - Equal remuneration for men and women.
    - **Impact**
        - **Formal Sector:** Ensures better wage compliance and equity.
        - **Informal Sector:** Aims to extend minimum wage protections to more workers, but enforcement remains a challenge.
2. **Industrial Relations Code, 2020**
    - **Key Provisions**
        - Simplified procedures for hiring and firing.
        - Provisions for strikes and lockouts.
        - Formation of unions and dispute resolution mechanisms.
    - **Impact:**
        - **Formal Sector:** Eases business operations by simplifying dispute resolution and hiring/firing processes.
        - **Informal Sector:** Minimal direct impact as informal workers are often not covered by formal industrial relations frameworks.
3. **Code on Social Security, 2020**
    - **Key Provisions**
        - Universal social security coverage including gig and platform workers.

- Maternity benefits, gratuity, and employee insurance.
- Creation of social security funds for unorganized workers.

- **Impact**
  - **Formal Sector:** Enhances existing social security benefits and compliance requirements.
  - **Informal Sector:** Potentially transformative if effectively implemented, as it seeks to extend social security benefits to unorganized workers, including gig workers.

4. **Occupational Safety, Health and Working Conditions Code, 2020**
   - **Key Provisions**
     - Health, safety, and working conditions standards across industries.
     - Provision for annual health checks and working hour regulations.
     - Welfare provisions like crèches, canteens, and first aid.
   - **Impact**
     - **Formal Sector:** Ensures improved safety and health standards, impacting worker well-being positively.
     - **Informal Sector:** Limited impact due to challenges in enforcement and the fragmented nature of informal work.

Impact on Formal Labour

1. **Simplified Compliance and Operational Flexibility**
   - The new codes streamline compliance requirements, reducing the regulatory burden on companies.
   - This can lead to increased formal employment as businesses find it easier to navigate labour laws.
2. **Enhanced Worker Benefits and Protections**
   - Improved social security provisions, better wage regulations, and occupational health standards can enhance job satisfaction and worker retention.
   - It encourages fair treatment and improved working conditions in the formal sector.
3. **Industrial Relations**
   - Simplified dispute resolution mechanisms and clearer guidelines for strikes and lockouts can lead to a more stable industrial environment.
   - However, there are concerns about the ease of firing, which could lead to job insecurity.

Impact on Informal Labour

1. **Extension of Benefits and Protections**
   - The inclusion of gig and platform workers under social security and the extension of minimum wage laws are significant steps.

- If effectively implemented, these measures can provide much-needed financial security and improve living standards for informal workers.

2. **Challenges in Implementation**
   - The fragmented nature of the informal sector and lack of formal employment contracts make enforcement difficult.
   - Informal workers often lack awareness and access to legal recourse, limiting the practical benefits of these codes.
3. **Transition to Formal Sector**
   - The new codes might encourage businesses to formalize their workforce to avail the simplified compliance processes.
   - This can potentially reduce the size of the informal sector over time, bringing more workers under the ambit of formal labour laws and benefits.

Sociological Insights

1. **Social Inequality**
   - While the codes aim to provide a safety net for informal workers, the implementation gap could widen inequalities if the benefits fail to reach the intended beneficiaries.
   - Informal workers, often belonging to marginalized communities, might continue to face socio-economic disadvantages.
2. **Gender Dynamics**
   - Improved maternity benefits and health provisions can positively impact female labour force participation.
   - However, informal women workers, especially in sectors like domestic work, may still remain outside the purview of these protections.
3. **Labour Rights and Movements**
   - The new labour codes have generated mixed reactions from trade unions and labour rights organizations, with some welcoming the reforms and others criticizing the potential for increased labour exploitation.
   - The sociological lens emphasizes the need for collective action and advocacy to ensure that the rights of both formal and informal workers are upheld.

Changing Nature of Work Due To AI and Automation

The integration of AI and automation is profoundly transforming the pattern and nature of work, affecting employment structures, worker identities, and economic life. From a sociological perspective, these changes represent a shift in how work is organized, valued, and experienced, with implications for social stratification, power dynamics, and human interactions.

1. **Job Displacement and Creation of New Roles**
   - **Impact on Traditional Jobs:** AI and automation are replacing repetitive and manual tasks, leading to job displacement, particularly in manufacturing,

retail, and administrative sectors. Routine tasks, traditionally performed by low- and medium-skilled workers, are increasingly automated, causing job losses and shifting demand toward new skill sets.

- **New Employment Opportunities:** While some jobs are disappearing, AI and automation are creating new roles in data analysis, machine learning, and technology management. Sociologically, this shift leads to occupational polarization: high-skilled, well-paid tech jobs on one end and low-paid, insecure service jobs on the other, widening social inequality.
- **Example:** The rise of e-commerce has led to a decline in retail jobs but an increase in warehouse automation jobs, reshaping the labour market and impacting social class structures as traditional jobs vanish.

2. **Redefining Skills and Worker Identity**
   - **Shift Toward Digital Skills:** With AI adoption, there's a growing demand for digital skills, analytical abilities, and technical expertise. Sociologically, this change emphasizes credentialism (value placed on formal qualifications) and creates knowledge-based hierarchies where tech-savvy workers are valued over manual labourers.
   - **Evolving Worker Identity:** As workers adapt to new technologies, their sense of identity is reshaped. Those who successfully transition to tech-driven roles may see enhanced self-worth, while those left behind experience alienation and marginalization, echoing Karl Marx's theories of alienation in industrial settings.
   - **Example:** Factory workers transitioning to automated environments may need to learn robotics programming, transforming their work identity from manual labourers to machine supervisors, altering their self-perception and place within the workforce.

3. **Flexible Work Patterns and the Gig Economy**
   - **Rise of Platform-Based Work:** AI-driven platforms (like Uber, TaskRabbit) have expanded the gig economy, where work is often short-term and task-based. This structure emphasizes flexibility but also results in job insecurity, lack of benefits, and reduced worker protections.
   - **Impact on Social Structures:** From a sociological standpoint, the gig economy shifts the traditional employer-employee relationship, promoting individualism and weakening collective labour rights. Workers become independent contractors, often without benefits, leading to precarity and insecurity, especially among lower-income groups.
   - **Example:** Food delivery platforms use algorithms to assign tasks, which limits workers' control over their schedules and wages, creating a new class of workers who are bound by digital systems rather than traditional employer-employee contracts.

4. **Surveillance and Control in the Workplace**
   - **Increased Workplace Monitoring:** AI enables constant surveillance and data collection on employee productivity, from tracking keystrokes to analyzing customer service calls. This leads to what sociologists call the panopticon

effect (drawing from Michel Foucault), where workers self-discipline under the pressure of being constantly monitored.

- **Loss of Autonomy and Privacy:** With automated monitoring, employees lose control over their work pace and privacy, creating stress and reducing job satisfaction. This shift reflects Max Weber's bureaucratization and rationalization, where human workers become components of a controlled, machine-like system.
- **Example:** Amazon's warehouse employees are monitored in real time, with algorithms setting strict performance quotas. This hyper-monitoring shapes worker behaviour, making the work environment more impersonal and increasing stress and burnout.

5. **Transformation of Work-Life Boundaries**
   - **Blurring Boundaries:** Remote work enabled by AI and digital tools has blurred the line between personal and professional lives, creating what sociologists call the **always-on culture**. This change can lead to burnout, as workers struggle to disconnect from work-related tasks and notifications.
   - **Shifting Family Dynamics:** The blurring boundaries impact family life and social interactions, as work encroaches on time traditionally reserved for personal life. This creates new forms of social stress and reshapes traditional family roles, affecting how people balance their identities as workers and family members.
   - **Example:** During the COVID-19 pandemic, remote workers found themselves working longer hours as the home became the office. This blending of roles led to increased stress and altered family interactions, highlighting the sociological impact of technology on social life.
6. **Changing Social Stratification and Inequality**
   - **Digital Divide and Inequality:** AI-driven economies favour individuals with digital skills and tech access, increasing inequality between high-skilled and low-skilled workers, and between tech-enabled economies and marginalized groups.
   - **New Class Divides:** Sociologists are observing a new 'digital elite' emerging, where those with advanced tech skills and digital capital enjoy social mobility, while those lacking such skills experience downward mobility and precarious job prospects. This creates what Pierre Bourdieu might call a new form of social capital – digital literacy and access as valuable resources.
   - **Example:** In urban areas, workers with tech skills enjoy higher-paying roles in tech industries, while in rural or low-income communities, workers without tech skills face limited job opportunities, exacerbating social inequality.

Previous Years' Question

2024

1. Define the concept of 'gig' economy and discuss its impact on the labour market and workers' social security net. (20 Marks)
2. Critically assess the impact of technological advancement and automation on the nature of work and employment. (10 Marks)
3. Describe the differing principles of work organization in feudal and capitalist societies. (10 Marks)

2023

1. Explain how economic globalization has brought changes in patterns of employment in the 21st century. (20 marks)
2. What is taylorism? Analyze its merits and demerits. (20 marks)

2022

1. Explain the implications of feminisation of work in developing societies. (10 marks)

2021

1. How has the idea of 'work from home' forced us to redefine the formal and informal organization of work? (20 marks)
2. Explain the emerging challenges in establishing gender inequality in the informal sector. (10 marks)
3. Elucidate the main problems and challenges faced by migrant labourers in the recent 'Lockdown period'. (20 marks)

2020

1. Capitalism has brought increasing informalization of work in society. Substantiate your answer. (20 marks)
2. Discuss the new labour codes and their impact on formal and informal labour in India. (20 marks)
3. What is the impact of gender division of labour on the development of society? (20 marks)

2019

1. What is informal labour? Discuss the need for and challenges in regulating informal labour in post-industrial societies. (20 marks)

2018

1. Discuss the nature of social organization of work in a capitalist society with reference to the 'Limits of the working day'. (20 marks)
2. What is labour commitment? Discuss it with reference to studies of the manufacturing industry. (20 marks)

2017

1. What do you understand by informalization of labour? Write your answer with special reference to India. (10 marks)
2. Trace the changing nature of organization of work in capitalist society over the years. (20 marks)

2016

1. Describe the nature of social organization of work in industrial society. (10 marks)
2. Globalization has pushed labour into informal organization of work. Substantiate your answer with suitable examples. (20 marks)

2015

1. Distinguish between social organization of work in feudal society and in capitalist society. (10 marks)
2. The increasing importance of the tertiary sector has weakened the importance of formal organization of work in the present times. Examine the statement. (20 marks)

2014

1. What are the distinctive features of social organization of work in slave society? How is it different from feudal society? (10 marks)

2013

1. Examine the social impact of globalization on labour and society. (20 marks)

Right Approach

2023

Q. 1 Explain how economic globalization has brought changes in patterns of employment in the 21st century. (300 words)

Approach

1. **Introduction:** Define economic globalization and briefly introduce how it has impacted employment patterns.
2. **Body:**
   - Explain key trends like the gig economy, outsourcing, and offshoring.
   - Discuss the shift from manufacturing to service sectors, particularly in India.
   - Highlight the rise of precarious work and informal employment due to globalization.
3. **Conclusion:**
   Summarize the benefits and challenges of globalization on employment and discuss the need for policies to mitigate adverse effects.

Answer:

Introduction: Economic globalization refers to the increasing integration of economies through the flow of goods, services, capital, and technology across borders. In the 21st century, globalization has significantly transformed employment patterns globally by creating new opportunities while also posing challenges for traditional labour markets.

Body:

1. **Rise of the Gig Economy:** One of the most significant changes in employment patterns is the emergence of the gig economy. Jobs in this sector are typically short-term, flexible, and often mediated through digital platforms. Companies like **Uber**, **Airbnb**, and **Swiggy** exemplify this trend, where individuals work as freelancers or independent contractors. Although it offers flexibility, the gig economy also reduces job security, health benefits, and long-term stability for workers.
2. **Outsourcing and Offshoring:** Globalization has encouraged businesses in developed countries to outsource services to nations where labour is cheaper. **India's IT and BPO (Business Process Outsourcing)** sectors have greatly benefited from this trend, creating millions of jobs. However, this has led to

job displacement in developed economies and heightened competition for lower wages in developing nations.

3. **Shift from Manufacturing to Service Sector:** With the decline of traditional manufacturing in global markets, there has been a marked shift towards service-oriented employment. In countries like India, the **services sector** now contributes more to GDP than agriculture or manufacturing. Employment in sectors such as IT, banking, tourism, and healthcare has expanded, reflecting the changing global economic landscape.
4. **Precarious Work and Informalization:** Economic globalization has also contributed to the informalization of labour, especially in developing countries. The **International Labour Organization (ILO)** reports that informal employment—where workers lack security and legal protections—has grown in response to the competitive pressures of globalization. This is particularly evident in the construction and retail sectors in India, where informal work dominates.

Conclusion: Economic globalization has fundamentally altered employment patterns in the 21st century, offering new opportunities through the gig economy and service sectors but also creating challenges such as job insecurity and informalization. While globalization drives economic growth, there is an urgent need for policies that protect workers' rights and ensure inclusive labour market growth to mitigate its adverse effects.

2015

Q 1 Distinguish between the social organization of work in feudal society and in capitalist society. (200 words)

Approach

1. **Introduction:**
   Briefly define the social organization of work in feudal and capitalist societies.
2. **Body:**
   - Highlight key features of the feudal work structure (land-based economy, serfdom).
   - Explain the capitalist work structure (wage labour, industrial production).
3. **Conclusion:**
   Summarize the primary differences between these two economic systems and their implications on work relations.

Answer:

Introduction:

The social organization of work in feudal and capitalist societies differs fundamentally in terms of production, labour relations, and social hierarchy. **Feudal society** was primarily agrarian, where landownership determined power, and the labour force consisted of serfs. In contrast, **capitalist society** is based on wage labour, industrial production, and market-driven economies.

Body:

1. **Feudal Society:** In feudal societies, the economy was **land-based**, and the system was organized around the **manor**. The feudal lord owned the land, while **serfs** (peasants) worked on the land in exchange for protection. Work was tied to the land, and social mobility was limited, with a rigid hierarchy between lords and serfs. There was no concept of wages, and the economy was largely self-sufficient.
2. **Capitalist Society**: In capitalist societies, the economy is driven by **industrial production** and market forces. Labour is **commodified**, with workers selling their labour power in exchange for wages. The relationship between the capitalist (owner) and the worker is impersonal, driven by profit maximization. Social mobility is theoretically more fluid, and the economy is integrated globally, fostering competition and innovation.

Conclusion: The feudal system was characterized by hierarchical, land-based labour tied to obligations, while capitalism is based on free wage labour, industrial production, and market exchanges. The transition to capitalism brought fundamental changes in work organization, economic relations, and class dynamics.

CHAPTER

7

Politics and Society

In this Chapter

Introduction

In sociology, power is studied from different perspectives, not just in relation to the state like in Political Science. However, major theoretical approaches have studied it in relation to institutions like the state, political parties, pressure groups, bureaucracy, etc. According to T.B. Bottomore, 'Political institutions are primarily concerned with division of power in the society.' Dowes and Hughes argue that, 'politics occurs when there are differentials in power.' Tawney (1931: 229), "Power may be defined as the capacity of an individual, or group of individuals, to modify the conduct of other individuals or groups in a manner in which he desires, and to prevent his conduct being modified in the manner in which he does not". The differentials in power refer to the ways in which power is distributed between different groups in the society. Michels believed that the craving for power is inherent in the nature of human beings. Those who acquire power, seek to perpetuate it. Against this backdrop, he propounds that democracy calls for organization, which leads to oligarchy. The trend towards oligarchic rule in party organizations is better known as the Iron Law of Oligarchy.

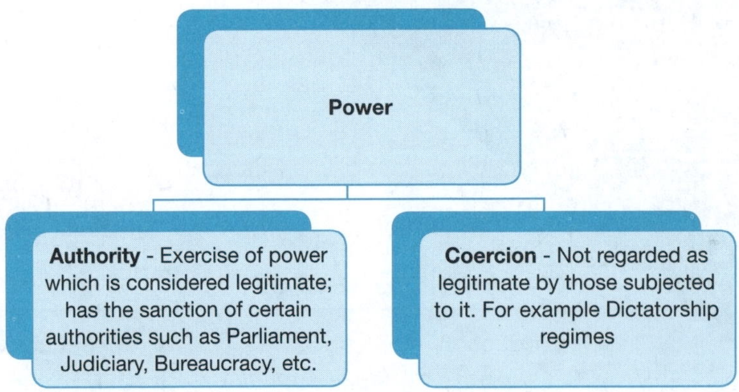

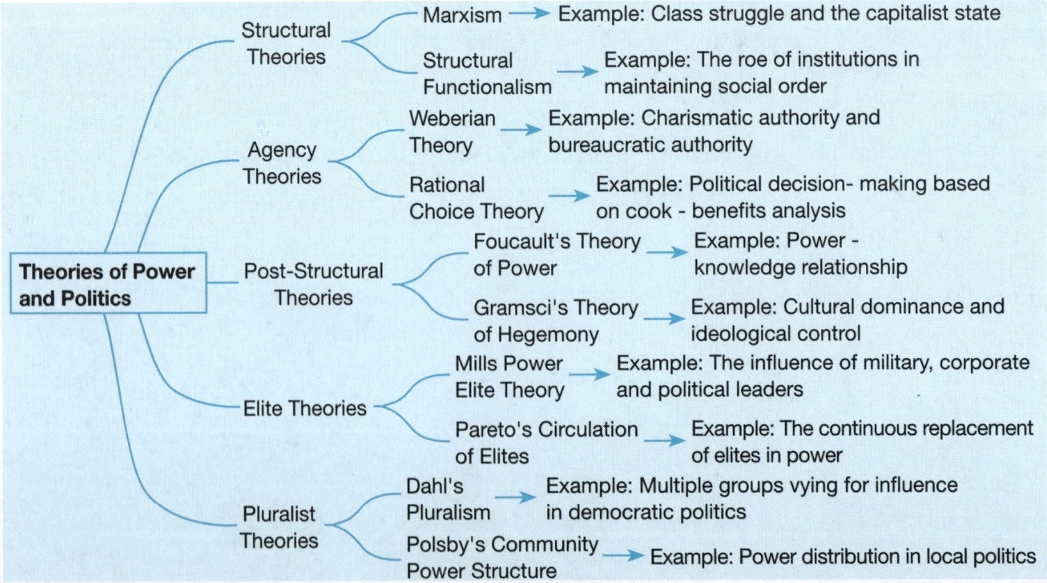

Sociological Theories of Power

Max Weber – Power and Types of Authority

- **Definition:** Weber defined power as the chance of a man or number of men to realise their own will in a communal action even against the resistance of others who are participating in that action. According to Weber (1914, 1920) 'power' (macht) as a general concept, is distinct from 'domination' (herrschaft) and a specific phenomenon. Power is defined as an actor's chance to impose his/her will on another (even against the resistance of the latter) in social relationship.
- **Implications of Weber's Definition of Power:**
  (i) **Constant-sum Concept of Power:** Weber's definition implies that those who hold power do so at the expense of others. The amount of power is fixed; therefore if some hold power, others do not.
  (ii) **Variable-sum Concept of Power:** Weber's definition also suggests that those who hold power use it to further their own sectional interests. Power is variable in the sense that it can increase or decrease.
- **Weber Distinguished Between Three Types of Authority:**
  (i) **Charismatic Authority:** Derived from the devotion felt by subordinates for a leader who is believed to have exceptional qualities. These qualities are seen as supernatural or superhuman or exceptional in comparison to other humans. For example, Alexander the Great, Napoleon, and Fidel Castro, etc.
  (ii) **Traditional Authority:** Derived from the established customs and beliefs which are considered to be right. The status is inherited and followers have feelings of loyalty and obligation to long-established positions of power. For example, nobles and monarchs in feudal system of Europe.
  (iii) **Rational-legal Authority:** Based on the acceptance of a set of impersonal rules. A legal framework supports the authority. For example, judge, tax inspector, etc.

Karl Marx—Conflict View of Power

Marx saw exercise of power in terms of coercion. According to him, the society is divided between the haves and the have nots, in which the former exercise power over the latter. The main source of power is the economic base—ownership of means of production and control of relations of production. Power is used to further the interests of the bourgeoisie at the expense of the proletariat. The ruled class accepts the power of the ruling class due to false consciousness. The only way to return the power to the people involves communal ownership of forces of production and it is possible only through revolution.

Steven Lukes—A Radical View of Power

- According to Lukes, '*A* exercises power over *B* when *A* affects *B* in a manner contrary to *B*'s interests.'
- In his radical view of power, Steven Lukes states that power has three dimensions:
  (i) **Decision-making:** Different groups exercise their influence in terms of decision-making.

(ii) **Non-decision Making:** Power may prevent discussion of certain issues or from decisions being taken about them.

(iii) **Shaping Desires:** Power can be exercised by shaping desires, manipulating the desires and wishes of social groups.

Power—A Functionalist Perspective

- Talcott Parsons views Power is a variable-sum concept or as a non-zero sum. He translated a few works of Max Weber from German into English and made important contribution to the study of power and its functions for society. The basis for functional analysis was laid by Spencer, Durkheim, Malinowski and Radcliffe–Brown.
- Parsons stated that in order for social systems to survive, value consensus is essential. From shared values, derive collective goals. The more a society is able to realize these goals, the greater the power that resides in the social system. Since goals are shared by all members of the society, power will generally be used in furtherance of the collective goals. As a result, both sides of the power relationship will benefit and everybody will gain by this arrangement. This forms the basis of cooperation and reciprocity that Parsons considered essential for the well-being and maintenance of society.
- Cooperation on a large scale requires organization and direction, which necessitate positions of command. Some are therefore granted the power to direct others. This power takes the form of authority. Those in positions of authority work for the benefit of all.
- Thus, according to Parsons, power differential is necessary to benefit all sections of the society. This has also become the basis for major criticism directed against Parsons.

Elite Theory

- Elite theories fall under two traditions—the classical (dominated by Mosca, Pareto and CW Mills) and the pluralist (dominated by Karl Mannheim, Schumpster, Anthony Downs, Robert Dahl)
- Elite theory sees power in society as being monopolized by a small minority. It sees society as divided between two groups: a small ruling minority who exercise power through the state, and the ruled majority

Classical Elite Theory—Pareto and Mosca

Elite theory was first developed by two Italian sociologists: Vilfredo Pareto (1848–1923) and Gaetano Mosca (1858–1911). Both saw elite rule as inevitable and dismissed the possibility of a proletarian revolution as proposed by Marx.

Pareto and Mosca agreed that the basis of elite rule was:

- The superior personal qualities of those who made up the elites. For Pareto, elites were more cunning and for Mosca, elites had better organizational ability. Pareto (1935) explained the concept of elite, the terms of a class of people with highest indices (referring to sign of capacity, for example, a successful lawyer has highest index, one who does not get a client has the lowest index in their branch of activity).

FYI

Vilfredo Pareto's Theory of Circulation of Elites—Lions and Foxes

Placed particular emphasis on the psychological characteristics as the basis of elite rule. Argued that there are two main types of governing elite: lions and foxes.

- Lions rule by force and possess the ability to take direct and incisive decisions. Example, Military dictatorships.
- Foxes rule by cunning and guile using diplomatic manipulation. Pareto considered European democracies representative of this type.
- Circulation of elites—Pareto believed that all elites decay in quality and rigour, become soft gradually or inflexible in decision-making. This leads to replacement of one type of elite by another, known as the circulation of elites.
- To Pareto, history is and always will be a 'graveyard of aristocracies'

Critique

- Pareto's view of history is criticized for being too simplistic. He dismisses the differences between different types of government (Western democracies, single-party communist government, fascist dictatorships, etc.) as mere variations of the elite rule while in reality this is not so.
- Pareto fails to provide an objective criterion for measuring superior qualities. Much of it depends on his subjective interpretation.
- Pareto's explanation of elite decadence fails to explain why the closed elite group of Brahmins in the Indian caste system have continued to maintain their power for hundreds of years.

Point to Note

Differences Between Pareto's and Mosca's Approach

Pareto considered the qualities required for elite rule to be the same at all times in all societies. Mosca believed that the qualities of the elites varied from society to society. For example, in one society, courage and bravery in battles could grant access to power, in another it could be the skill to acquire wealth.

While Pareto saw democracy as merely another form of elite rule, for Mosca, democracies represented an open arrangement allowing for elites to be drawn from diverse backgrounds. The interests of different sections could find voice among the elite and their decisions.

Despite these differences however, both agreed that the masses lacked capacity for self-government and required the leadership and guidance of an elite.

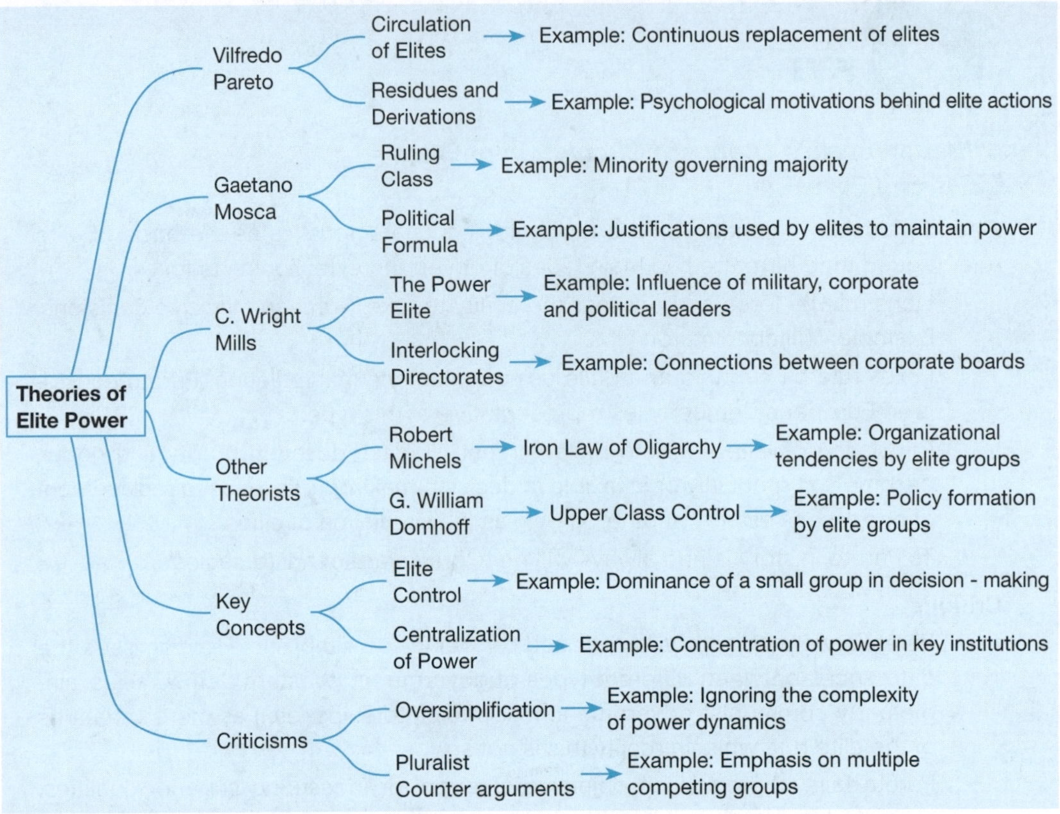

- The Elites have a better internal organization and forms a united and cohesive minority in the face of an unorganized and fragmented mass. Major decisions, even in the democratic society, are taken by the elite. Elite theorists picture the majority as apathetic and unconcerned with the major issues of the day.

Elite Theory and USA

C. Wright Mills

Mills limited his analysis to American society in the 1950s. Unlike the early theorists, Mills did not believe that elite rule was inevitable and in fact saw it as a recent development. Mills adopted a conflict version of the elite theory and saw elite rule as based on exploitation of the masses. He condemned it.

Mills' Theory—The Power Elite

Mills explained elite rule in institutional rather than psychological terms. He rejected the argument of superior psychological qualities and instead said, that the structure of the institutions was such that those at the top of the institutional hierarchy largely monopolized power. Certain institutions occupied key pivotal positions in society and the elite comprised those who held 'command posts' in those institutions.

Mills identified three key institutions:

1. The major corporations
2. The military
3. The federal government

Elite Unity

Those who occupied the command positions in these institutions formed the three elites. In practice though the interests and activities of the elites were sufficiently similar, had common social backgrounds and were inter-connected to form a single-ruling majority, which Mills termed the 'power-elite'. The power-elite involved the co-incidence of political, economic and military power.

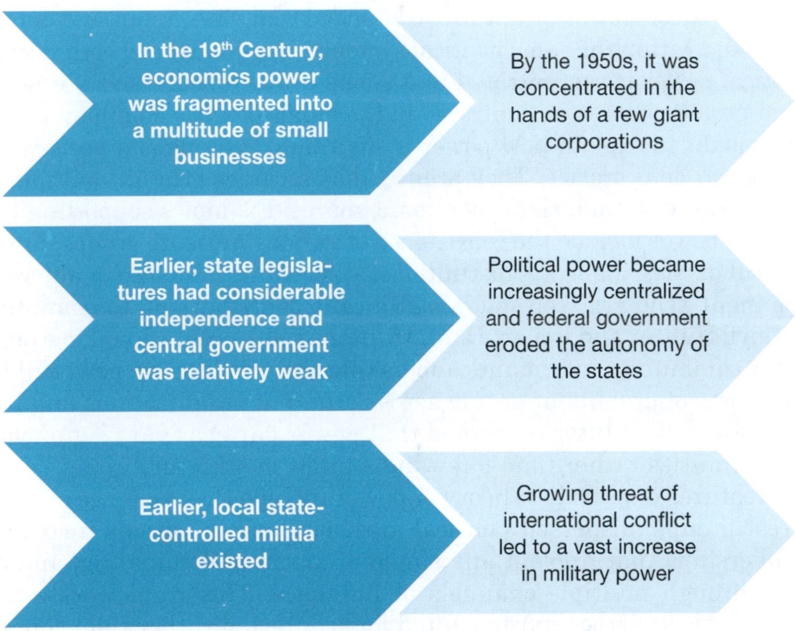

Figure Change in 'institutional landscape' leading to emergence of elites, in the context of America of 1950s

Characteristics of Power Elite

1. Similar social background of members
2. Interchange and overlapping of personnel between the three elites. For example, a politician could also be the director of a company; a military official could be a member a political committee, etc.
3. Similar education backgrounds and mixed socially in the same high-prestige clubs
4. Share similar values and sympathies which provided for mutual trust and cooperation

Elite Dominance—According to Mills, American society was dominated by a power elite that possessed 'unprecedented power and unaccountability'. Major decisions like America's entry into the Second World War, dropping of bomb on Hiroshima, etc., were taken by the power elite without referring with the masses. Even the mass media was controlled by the elite and was directed towards the passive and quiescent masses who remained unconcerned with the major issues of the day. Absence of accountability and free from popular control, the power elite pursued its own agenda of power and self-aggrandisement. David Riesman (1953) proposed the concept of veto groups (explained in terms of a diversified and balanced plurality of interest groups, each of which is primarily concerned with protecting its jurisdiction by blocking actions of other groups which seem to threaten that jurisdiction).

Pluralist Thesis of Power or Community Thesis of Power

This theory emerged as a response to elite theorists who argued that elitism and democracy are fundamentally incompatible. Pluralists contended that elite groups and democratic governance can coexist within the same political system. They challenged both the elitist assertion that political power is concentrated in a single center within society and the Marxist argument that power remains concentrated in the hands of a few dominant classes.

Pluralists sought to explain how power is distributed throughout society, particularly in modern Western democracies. They argued that societies contain multiple, competing centers of power rather than a single dominant source. Examples supporting the pluralist understanding of power include the coexistence of various pressure groups, interest organizations, political parties, and state institutions, all wielding influence in different spheres.

Two prominent scholars who made significant contributions to community power studies are Floyd Hunter and Robert Dahl. Hunter used a reputational method, selecting knowledgeable community informants and asking them to identify powerful individuals from prepared lists of prominent people across different organizations and institutions. Through this research, Hunter concluded that power patterns vary significantly across American communities rather than following a uniform structure.

The main features of pluralist theory of power include the existence of multiple competing interest groups, dispersed political authority across various institutions, overlapping memberships that prevent any single group from dominating, and democratic participation through multiple channels of influence. This framework suggests that power in democratic societies is fragmented and contested rather than concentrated in the hands of a single elite.

- The industrial society is increasingly differentiated into various social groups and sectional interests. There are diversified occupations and power held by each group.
- There are multiple groups like trade unions, professional associations and pressure groups who hold different degrees of power. Absence of a single dominating group leads to bargaining and compromising.
- Since different groups cannot compete for power directly, they field their representatives who act as elites. This situation leads to elite pluralism. Government acts like a broker to mediate between different elite groups.
- In his study 'Who Governs?' (1961), Robert Dahl found that local politics is a business of bargaining and compromise, with no single group dominating the decision-making. He showed that economic factors are not the sole factors in decision making, like Marxists argued.

- Arnold M Rose in 'The Power Structure' (1967) gave a multiple influence hypothesis. He argued that economic and political elite do not work hand in glove, as proposed by Mills.
- Karl Mannheim argued that though a policy may be seemingly formed by the purported elite, but in a democracy, there are various pulls and pressures that actually shape a policy. People do make their voices count, like during elections, which keep the elites in check.
- In 'An Economic Theory of Democracy' (1957), Anthony Downs argues that just like producers and consumers defend their interests in the market, trade unions and associations play similar roles in politics to defend the interests of their members and workers.

Critique

The pluralists have been criticized for ignoring non-decision or safe decision making. Elites take decisions in general interest keeping their own interests at a priority. According to Westergaard and Resler, power is manifested in its consequences and pluralists tend to ignore the consequences. Roberto Michels also contends that representatives of people may ultimately usurp power and act in their own vested interests, ignoring the interests of public at large.

Social Movements

Definition

Collective attempts to further a common interest or secure a common goal through action outside the sphere of established institutions. (Giddens) They are among the most powerful forms of collective action; well organized persistent campaigns.

Features

- Sustained collective action
- Organization which may include some degree of leadership and structure
- Shared objectives and ideologies
- Aim of bringing about changes on a public issue
- Can lead to counter movements in defence of the status quo. For example, campaigns of women's right to abortion have been vociferously challenged by anti-abortion activists. Similarly, Raja Ram Mohan Roy's Brahmo Samaj was countered by the conservative Dharma Sabha

Types

1. **Redemptive or Transformatory:** Aims to bring about change in the personal consciousness and actions of its individual members. For example, people in Ezhava community if Kerala were led by Narayan Guru to change their social practices
2. **Reformist:** Strive to change the existing political and social arrangements through gradual incremental steps. For example, the 1960s movement for reorganization of states and the Right to Information campaign

3. **Revolutionary:** Revolutionary attempt to radically transform social relations, often by capturing state power. For example, the Bolshevik revolution in Russia, the Naxalite movement in India, etc.

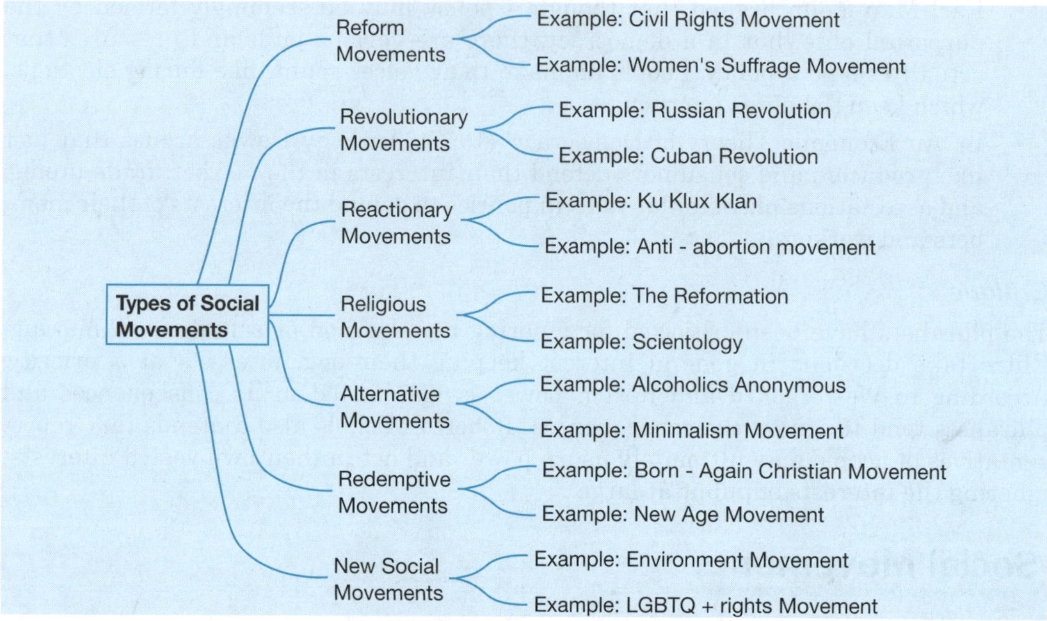

Old and New Social Movements

1. **Old Social Movements:** These majorly include the class-based movements such as the working class movements, peasant movements and the anti-colonial movements. Examples include communist movement, socialist movement, and movements that led to the creation of rights-based welfare states.
2. **New Social Movements:** These include the movements that emerged in the decades after the Second World War, in the 1960s and 1970s. These included the anti-war movement such as the one in US, joined by thousands of students, against the war in Vietnam, the women's movements and the environmental movements, etc. More on these is discussed in given sections.

Theories of Social Movements

The Chicago School—Hebert Blumer's Theory of Social Unrest

- Bumer saw all social movements as motivated by dissatisfaction with some aspects of current society; which they sought to rectify. In doing so, they were trying to build a 'new order of life'. In the beginning, social movements were amorphous and poorly organized. As a social movement develops, it acquires culture, social organization and new scheme of life. He classified two types of social movements:
  (i) **Active or Outwardly Directed:** Aiming to transform society. For example, labour movements

(ii) **Expressive or Inwardly Directed:** Trying to change the people who become involved. Examples include New Age movements. In practice however, most social movements have elements of both.

- According to Blumer, a social movement has a life cycle which has four consecutive stages:
  (i) **Stage of Social Ferment:** When people are dissatisfied or agitated about something but this is relatively unfocussed and disorganized.
  (ii) **Stage of Popular Excitement:** In this stage, sources of people's dissatisfaction are more clearly defined and understood.
  (iii) **Formalization:** In the third stage, formal organizations are created to bring about a higher level of coordination to the emerging movement and a more effective campaigning structure is put in place.
  (iv) **Institutionalization:** The movement which was originally outside mainstream politics comes to be accepted as part of the wider political and social life.

Criticism

Blumer's interactionist approach to social movements has been criticized on two counts: a) it does not explore the rational decisions and strategies of movement activists and b) the study of social movements was mainly descriptive and did not really pay enough attention to explanations connecting social movement activity to changes in the social structure.

FYI

Neil Smelser on Understanding Social Movements

- Smelser devised a theory of 'structural strain' to account for the emergence of social movements. It is a 'value-added model' of movement emergence. It suggests that social movement emerges and develops through a process of identifiable stages, with each stage adding value to the next one.
- Smelser emphasises on there being multiple causes for the emergence of social movements.
- According to Smelser, six value-added elements are necessary for the development of social movements:
  (i) **Structural Conduciveness:** All social movements occur within a wider social context and the structural context has to be conducive to movement formation. For example, it is relatively easier for social movements to develop in democratic societies than it is in authoritarian states.
  (ii) **Structural Strain:** If the social structure is conducive collective behaviour, then there needs to be a strain between people's expectations and social reality. For example, Robert Merton explained high levels of working class crime as emerging from a strain between cultural goal of material success and the available structural means.

(iii) **Generalized Beliefs:** When the first two conditions are met, it is necessary for generalized beliefs about the strain to spread among people and to convince them of the need to join and form a social movement.

(iv) **Precipitating Factors:** These are the events that act as igniting factors for protest action. For example, removal of Rosa Parks from a bus in 1955 on grounds of racial segregation became a key event in the black civil rights movement; the Nirbhaya rape incident of 2012 became a key event in women's movement on safety in India.

(v) **Mobilization of Social Action:** This happens through effective communication via the formation of an active social network.

(vi) **Failure of Social Control:** The response of authorities is a final determining factor. If the response is one of excessive suppression, the social networking can come to a halt. Sometimes, however, an overreaction by the authorities can encourage others to support the movement.

Though criticized for its structural-functionalist approach, Smelser's theory has proved useful in explaining many social movements.

Resource Mobilization Theory (RMT)

This perspective emerged in the late 1960s and 1970s America as a reaction to the social unrest theory which portrayed social movements as irrational phenomena. According to RMT, social movement participants behaved in rational ways and movements themselves were purposeful, not chaotic. RMT theorists argued that social unrest is always present in capitalist societies but this discontent transforms into effective mobilizations only when there are necessary resources available to mount effective campaigns that challenge the established order. In essence, they argue that social unrest is not enough but it is the availability of social resources that determines formation and success of a social movement.

RMT fails to explain the success of those movements which did not have sufficient amount of resources like the workers' movement of the 1930s, civil rights movement of the 1950-60 s and welfare movements of the late 1950s and early 1960s. It also fails to explain the movements who found success in the early, formative stages before being properly organized.

Relative Deprivation Theory

- **Key Thinkers:** James C. Davies, Ted Gurr
- **Associated School:** Structural-Functionalism
- **Description:** This theory posits that social movements arise when individuals or groups perceive a gap between their expected and actual conditions, leading to feelings of deprivation and discontent. James C. Davies' J-Curve hypothesis suggests that revolutions are likely to occur when a period of economic or social improvement is followed by a sharp reversal.

Resource Mobilization Theory

- **Key Thinkers:** John D. McCarthy, Mayer N. Zald

- **Associated School:** Organizational Sociology
- **Description:** This theory focuses on the resources necessary for social movements, such as money, labour, and media. It emphasises the importance of organized structures, leadership, and strategic planning in mobilizing these resources effectively. The success of social movements is seen as contingent on their ability to acquire and utilize these resources.

Political Process Theory

- **Key Thinkers:** Charles Tilly, Doug McAdam.
- **Associated School:** Political Sociology.
- **Description:** This theory argues that social movements are more likely to arise and succeed when political opportunities are favourable, such as when there is political instability, elite divisions, or reduced repression. It highlights the importance of the political environment in shaping the possibilities for social movements.

New Social Movement Theory

- **Key Thinkers:** Alain Touraine, Jürgen Habermas, Manuel Castells
- **Associated School:** Post-Structuralism
- **Description:** This theory focuses on the post-industrial, post-materialist values of newer social movements, such as those related to identity, cultural change, and environmentalism. Unlike traditional movements centred on economic issues, new social movements emphasise social and cultural concerns and often utilize decentralized, networked forms of organization.

Framing Theory

- **Key Thinkers:** Erving Goffman, David Snow, Robert Benford
- **Associated School:** Symbolic Interactionism
- **Description:** Framing theory explores how social movements construct and communicate their messages to garner support and mobilise participants. It focuses on the importance of framing issues, grievances, and solutions in a way that resonates with potential supporters. Successful framing can align a movement's goals with the values and beliefs of a broader audience.

Structural Strain Theory

- **Key Thinkers:** Neil Smelser
- **Associated School:** Structural-functionalism.
- **Description:** Based on the idea that social movements develop in response to social strain or stressors, this theory posits that movements emerge when there is significant societal strain, leading to collective action to address the issue. Strain could be economic, social, or political, and social movements are seen as a response to these stressors to restore equilibrium.

New Social Movements (NSM)

Late 1960s has been seen as a time period that ushered in a new 'type' of social movements all across the globe – student movements of the 1960s, civil rights and feminist movements of the 1960s and 70s, anti-nuclear and ecological movements of the 1980s, gay rights campaigns of the 1990s. There are four main ways in which new social movements have been seen as differing from the old:

(i) **New Issues:** For NSM theorists, these movements reflect a broad transformation from an industrial to a post-industrial society where the issues go beyond the material realm. The new issues were concerned with the 'quality of life' including the state of the global environment, animal welfare and animal rights, peaceful energy production and identity politics associated with gay rights and disabled people's movements.

(ii) **New Organizational Forms:** NSMs looked like loose networks of people with a 'many-headed' structure. This meant that even if one local group broke the law and faced prosecution, the rest of the network could carry on. NSMs lacked a formal organization as they did not seek to take over the state but looked to appeal directly to the public by working at the cultural level.

(iii) **New Action Repertoires:** A repertoire refers to all the things that a person is able to do. The main trait of NSMs in this regard is non-violent, symbolic direct actions. By adopting non-violent form of protest, NSMs take a high moral stance in relation to the forces of the state. NSM actions aim to present aspects of the society to the public that were previously unknown or unseen. For example, campaigns against nuclear and toxic waste dumping, displacement of tribals due to building of dams, etc. NSMs also make extensive use of the media and act like forms of communication.

(iv) **New Social Constituencies:** NSM activists have primarily constituted the 'new' middle class that works in the post-1945 welfare state bureaucracies, creative and artistic fields and in education (majorly students). Theorists have called it a 'rainbow coalition' – consisting of retired people, students, first time protesters, feminists, anarchists, socialists, traditional conservatives and more. The change from earlier times was that the working class was not significantly involved in NSM politics.

Point to Note

Prominent Social Movements of India

1. The National Freedom Struggle for Independence—Swadeshi Movement, Non-Cooperation Movement, Civil Disobedience Movement (satyagraha as a strategy, *Dandi* March as a precipitating event, etc.
2. Telangana struggle
3. Tebhaga movement
4. Movement to allow Dalits to enter temples
5. Movements for separate statehood—Gorkhaland, Uttarakhand, etc.
6. Anna Hazare Movement
7. Ecological movements such as the *Chipko* movement

FYI

Chipko Movement

The *Chipko* movement is an example of the ecological movement that took place in the Himalayan foothills. According to Ramachandra Guha in his book *Unquiet Woods*, villagers rallied together to save the oak and rhododendron forests near their villages. When government forest contractors came to cut down the trees, villagers, including large numbers of women, stepped forward to hug the trees to prevent their being felled. At stake was the question of villagers' subsistence. All of them relied on the forest to get firewood, fodder and other daily necessities. This conflict placed the livelihood needs of poor villagers against the government's desire to generate revenues from selling timber. The economy of subsistence was pitted against the economy of profit. Along with this issue of social inequality (villagers versus a government that represented commercial, capitalist interests), the *Chipko* movement also raised the issue of ecological sustainability. Cutting down natural forests was a form of environmental destruction that had resulted in devastating floods and landslides in the region. For the villagers, these 'red' and 'green' issues were inter-linked. While their survival depended on the survival of the forest, they also valued the forest for its own sake as a form of ecological wealth that benefits all. In addition, the *Chipko* movement also expressed the resentment of hill villagers against a distant government headquartered in the plains that seemed indifferent and hostile to their concerns. So concerns about economy, ecology and political representation underlay the *Chipko* movement.

Globalization and the Social Movement Society

- Processes have globalization have meant that systematic and much more immediate connections across national boundaries have become possible and with this, the possibility of genuinely global social movements.
- The current information age has allowed social movements around the globe to join together in huge regional and international networks comprising non-governmental organizations, religious and humanitarian groups, human rights associations, consumer protection advocates, environmental activists and others who campaign in the public interest. Internet is extensively used for this purpose, allowing for people to respond to challenges immediately, connect with a simple click, share resources and information.
- The emergence of 'world social forums' – organizations dedicated to the global operation of such activities is another aspect of globalization.
- Another dimension is the emergence of violent global social movement such as terrorist networks of Al-Qaeda, ISIS, etc.

- International social movements have emerged with the ability to coordinate international campaigns—one that is most worrying for governments and most inspiring for participants in social movements. Some observers have argued that the information age is witnessing a migration of 'power' away from nation-states into new non- governmental alliances and coalitions.

Point to Note

Netwars

International conflicts in which information and public opinion are the stakes rather than resources or territory. Participants in netwars use the Internet to spread information about corporations, government policies, etc., to international audiences who may be unaware about them. According to Manuel Castells, these movements rely on information technologies as their organizational infrastructure.

The philosophy of 'political pluralism' states that there are multiple political structures within a society to facilitate distribution of power. The political system of today's modern society is characterized by a high degree of differentiation, explicitness and functional specificity of governmental and non-governmental structures. Each of these sub-systems plays its assigned role and acts as a mutually regulative mechanism. These sub-systems—both existing within the realm of the State and outside it—are discussed below.

State

Since the time humans have lived in groups, they have devised a way to govern themselves. Even in the absence of a formal mechanism, such as stateless societies, other arrangements such as hierarchies within kinship networks have performed this function. State, in essence, refers to a political system with structures, functions and transactions, which are directed towards the control of individuals and groups in a larger social system.

Different Perspectives

Greek philosophers used to view the state 'as a natural and necessary institution coming out of the needs of human beings as a political animal.' According to Marxists, the state is an instrument of exploitation in the hands of the ruling class. Sociologists have defined the state as an association which legally maintains social order within a community. The state has also been viewed as society, divided into government and subjects, claiming, within the allotted physical area, a supremacy over all other institutions.

According to Max Weber, 'a state is a human community which successfully claims, within a given territory, the monopoly of the legitimate use of physical force.'

Essential properties of a state include:

1. **Population:** This represents a viable number of people in a state. For example, India and China with over 140 crores of people and Maldives with a little over five lakh of people are both states. States with large populations have certain

political advantage over states with very small populations as a larger population enhances a state's bargaining power in world affairs.

2. **Territory:** States need to demarcate its subjects and also needs resources to govern, and a primary source for revenue in this regard is the land (including water). It is possible to establish authority over subjects only if they live in a territory. Territory is also important because it identifies a certain population within it. As such, it provides physical limits.
3. **Government:** It is the agency of the state, and exists for carrying out the will of the state. Without a government, a state cannot function. While a government can exist without a state, a state cannot exist without a government. Government can take different forms such as democratic, totalitarian, etc., and can have different goals such as communism, socialism, capitalism, welfare ideology, etc.
4. **Sovereignty:** The word sovereignty means ultimate power. A state has the monopoly of coercive power over all individuals and institutions within its territory. No one can question this power of the state. Sovereignty also extends to the relationship with other sovereign states. No state has power to impose restriction on another state or intervene in a state's internal affairs.

State	Government
1. Abstract	Concrete
2. Supreme body	Element of the state
3. More or less permanent	Derived and limited by the terms of the Constitution
4. Sovereignty is a trait of the State	Not an attribute of the Government

Critique

- With the emergence of international bodies such as the United Nations, International Monetary Fund, World Bank, etc., the sovereignty of states has been called into question.
- Arbitrary actions such as invasions, waging of war, attacks by third parties like terrorist groups, etc., have also challenged the existence and territories of states.
- Many states have challenges of internal conflicts wherein the governed population refuses to acknowledge the supremacy of the state.
- Territorial disputes between states also continually challenge the authority of the state. For example, Palestine was not recognized as a state for a long time by the UN and other countries. China does not recognize Taiwan as a separate state.

Meaning of Nation, Nationality and Nationalism, Nation-state

Nation

The word nation is derived from the Latin word 'natio' which means 'born'. This implies that a nation is a people descended from a common stock. Mostly, a nation has been defined as a population of an ethnic unity, inhabiting a territory of a geographic unity. By ethnic unity, it is meant that a population has a common custom and a common consciousness of rights and wrongs. But in reality, the ties that bind people together into a nation are more psychological and spiritual than ethnic, linguistic or religious. A nation is the 'people's consciousness of unity.' Once this consciousness is achieved, ethnic differences do not matter. For example, Switzerland is a nation of three different ethnic groups.

State	Nation
1. People are organized for law within a definite territory	People are psychologically bound together
2. Statehood is objective; conferred through legal processes like citizenship	Nationhood is subjective, dependent on the sentiments of the people
3. Statehood is enforceable by law	Nationhood is a condition of the mind, a spiritual possession
4. A state may consist of one nation (Rumania, Albania, France) or different nations, (India, Canada).	For the same reason, a nation may be split into two or more states (North and South Korea, People's Republic of China and Republic of China)

Benedict Anderson has argued that nations are 'imagined communities' rather than concrete 'things', with diverse groups bound together by a perception or imagination of what constitutes the cultural entity to which they feel they belong. When many people act on the basis of a perceived national community, they bring about a shared national identity that binds them together

Nationality and Nationalism

- Nationality is a spiritual or psychological identification among people having common affinities like common origin, race, language, tradition or history and common political aspirations. It is a way of feeling, thinking and living together.
- Nationalism is the growth of a feeling of oneness among people based on the same attributes that contribute to nationhood and nationality. Nationalism brings together people into a nation by creating in them a sense of identity (nationality).
- Nationalism (process) leads to nationality (phenomenon).

Nation State

- It is, as the term suggests, a combination of a large community (nation) and a territorial, political form (state), creating a cultural-political entity. It is now the most widespread 'survival unit' across the world.
- Nation states have originated relatively recently with the demands of *industrialization* requiring more effective means of government and administration. This led to education in an 'official language' and development of systems of taxation and use of legitimate violence to keep the large society in order.
- While a nation is a large community, a state is the political form which guarantees that community its security. However, nations are not communities defined by

homogeneous cultures with a shared language, history and traditions. The United Kingdom, for example, is a nation state consisting of England, Scotland, Wales and Northern Ireland and has several languages and different historical traditions.

- In modern times, therefore, we have nation-states rather than just nations or just states. Within nation-states, there could be different arrangements for different communities. For instance, in Quebec (the French-speaking province of Canada) and Flanders (the Dutch-speaking area in the north of Belgium), regional political bodies have the power to take major decisions without actually being fully independent.

On the other hand, there are also nations which remain unrecognized by the states as is the case with the Tibetans in China and the Kurds, whose homeland overlaps parts of Turkey, Syria, Iran and Iraq.

Bureaucracy

Though this topic has been dealt with in detail in the previous units, we will once again summarise the most essential points here.

- It is a type of organization based on written rules, contracts and a hierarchy of positions that is very widely adopted in modern industrial societies.
- The word 'bureaucracy' was coined in 1745 as a combination of the French 'bureau' (office or writing table) and the Greek 'kratos' ('to rule') and thus means 'the rule of officials'.
- Sociological studies of bureaucracy have been dominated by the ideas of Max Weber, who created a classic 'ideal type' bureaucracy in his works.
- According to Weber, bureaucracy is the most efficient form of organization. However, he also *recognized* that it tended to stifle creativity and nullify enterprise. For Weber, the extension and expansion of bureaucracy across all formal forms of organization was inevitable and the only way of coping with the demands of modernity.

Critique

- Critics of Weber's arguments claim that he ignored the informal relationships and small-group dynamics that help make organizational life 'work'.
- Peter Blau's 1963 study of an American government tax agency found that procedural bureaucratic rules were routinely broken in the interests of 'getting the work done'. Also, group loyalties developed at lower levels of the hierarchy as an informal system of mutual help and advice.
- Zygmunt Bauman argued that Weber's concerns for bureaucracy being an 'iron cage' of rationality did not capture the full picture. He cited the German National Socialists' mass murder of Jewish populations during the Second World War. According to Bauman, it was only made possible by using the bureaucratic machinery of the modern state. It was precisely the impersonality of bureaucracies that enabled officials to avoid personal, moral responsibility.
- On the other hand, some scholars have favoured bureaucracy for its neutral and essentially neutral nature. Paul du Gay argued that many of the problems

commonly attributed to 'bureaucracy' are really caused by attempts to bypass the rules and guidelines of procedure. As per him, the bureaucratic ethos is one of equal treatment for all, and bureaucracies contain some important safeguards which prevent abuses of power by political leaders.

Contemporary Relevance of Bureaucracy

- With the global spread of capitalism, Weber's theory of bureaucracy remains relevant. However, bureaucracy in its organizational form may be undergoing change. For instance, bureaucracies have begun to allow some novel activities into the workplace. Catherine Casey has highlighted the trend for bureaucratic organizations to allow and enable the expression of spirituality at work. Some large corporations—Ford, IBM and Apple among others—support and even encourage 'spirituality at work' programmes, thereby transforming the rigid hierarchy associated with bureaucracy.
- Leisha DeHart-Davis has shown how bureaucratic procedures may actually prove beneficial for women within organizations, as they ensure that career promotions are based on capabilities and qualifications rather than on the personal ties and social networking which favour men more. In her research, women were more likely to emphasise the efficiency, legitimacy and equity of bureaucracy, while men were focused on what they saw as the excessive controls and rules.

Citizenship

It refers to a status accorded by the State to individuals within a specific nation or political community. It represents possession of certain rights and responsibilities. The concept of citizenship originated in the city states of ancient Greece, where the status of 'citizen' was limited to only select people living within the city boundary. In that sense, citizenship was a symbol of social status. In most traditional states ruled by monarchs and emperors, subject populations had no formal political rights or influence on decision-making. Today, however, most people living within the borders of a political system are citizens who have some common rights and duties. Today, citizenship is a social status granted to members of nation states on the basis of residence.

Marshall's Theory of Citizenship

T.H. Marshall saw citizenship as emerging alongside industrialization. He traced the evolution of modern notion of citizenship alongside the emergence of civil rights, political rights and social rights in successive stages as mentioned below:

- First, civil citizenship emerged with modern property ownership. It imposed certain mutual obligations on people to respect one another's right to property, leading to a mutual responsibility for the maintenance of social order.
- In the second stage, political citizenship involved the gradual extension of voting rights to working-class groups and women. Certain rights of free association were introduced, such as those allowing the formation of trade unions and ideas of free speech also emerged.

- The third stage, social citizenship, saw citizenship rights extended to social welfare. It involved a shared responsibility for collective provision of welfare and other benefits, which was earlier exclusively in the domain of the state. People were expected to contribute to the social fund used for supporting the vulnerable and, as a result, enjoyed the right to a share of the welfare safety net when they needed it.
- In recent years, some have argued that we are moving into a fourth stage, described as environmental or ecological citizenship. In this stage, citizens have new rights to a clean and safe environment but also possess a new duty not to pollute the human or natural environment.

Critique

- Marshall's conception of citizenship has been criticized for being based on the experience of one nation state, Britain. In France, Germany and other countries, citizenship did not 'evolve' in the way he describes.
- Governments in the 1980s made efforts to 'roll back the state' by cutting welfare spending. It showed that citizenship can be reversed and that there are no guaranteed rights.
- Globalization theories have challenged the nation-state-based model of citizenship. For instance, the European Union offers a regional form of citizenship which grants some rights to people panning across countries in its region, such as the right to travel and to work. The nation-states have to respect these rights. European citizens also possess the right to challenge legal decisions made at nation-state level at the regional European level.

Contemporary Relevance

- More recent political debates have focused on how to enable citizens to become more active as a means of reinvigorating politics. There is also continual pressure for the expansion of rights and responsibilities continues to all sections of the society who may be deemed as citizens but may not enjoy the benefits that come with it.
- Citizenship is also experienced differently by different generations. For instance, in Hussain and Bagguley's (2005) qualitative research in the aftermath of the 2001 'riots' in some northern English towns and cities, the authors found that the identity of being a citizen is not necessarily shared by all. Despite living in Britain, first-generation migrants from Pakistan did not generally consider themselves to be British citizens. However, second-generation British Pakistanis strongly considered themselves as British- born citizens.

Ideology

- Ideology may be defined as an integrated system of beliefs and symbols which have an appeal to the followers. It has the power to sway the sentiments of the followers. It is accepted as an article of faith by the followers. It refers to 'commonsense' ideas and widespread beliefs in asociety that serve, often indirectly, the interests of dominant groups and legitimize their position.

- A political system in general and political parties within that system, in particular may have their own ideologies. The ideologies convey to the members the nation's or parties' goals and means. The followers accept the goals without question and also become committed to the means. The degree of internalization of an ideology and of its goals and means, are influenced by political socialization of individual and the party's capacity for disciplining its members.
- Ideology may be based on political, economic or religious elements. Sometimes, ethnic and cultural elements also may provide the necessary basis for ideology.
- A political ideology can have economic and religious overtones. For example, democracy is a political ideology, communism is an economic ideology and theocracy is a religious ideology. Communism as an ideology extends to political and other fields. It is against religion and, at least in the early stages, calls for a totalitarian social structure.
- Political ideology can also have violent undertones. The rise of fundamentalism as a political ideology and terrorism as a means to achieve goals is the potential for destruction of the socio-political basis of the state and of order in society.
- In India, a combination of religious fundamentalism, ethnic and linguistic factors can be seen as a threat to democratic structure in Punjab, Kashmir, Nagaland, Manipur, North Bengal, Karnataka etc.
- Similarly, political elites belonging to dominant ethnic groups in ethnically pluralistic societies use ethnicism as a convenient ideology for achieving their political ambitions

Democracy

It refers to a political system providing for the participation of citizens in political decision-making, either directly or through the election of political representatives. It is generally seen as the political system most able to ensure political equality, protect liberty and freedom, defend the common interest and meet citizens' needs.

The word democracy has its roots in the Greek term *demokratia:* demos (people) and *kratos* (rule). Democracy is therefore a political system in which rule is by the people. Democratic rule has taken differing forms at varying times and in different societies. For example, 'the people' has been understood to mean all men, just owners of property, or adult men and women.

According to the level of participation, it has been classified into: direct and indirect democracy.

(i) In participatory or direct democracy, decisions are made by all of those affected by them. This was the original type of democracy practised in ancient Greece. A small minority of the society known as citizens regularly assembled to consider policies and make major decisions.

(ii) Representative or indirect democracy, in which decisions are taken by representatives elected by the people, has become the normal method of achieving 'rule by the people'. In national governments, representative democracy takes the form of elections to congresses, parliaments or similar national bodies.

According to the distribution of power, democracies can be classified as tutelary and political democracies.

(i) In tutelary democracy, it has all the formal norms of democracy, which includes universal suffrage, freedom of association and speech and the structural forms of democracy. But there is a concentration of power in the executive and the bureaucracy. The legislature tends to be relatively powerless and there is a lot of interference in the functioning of the judiciary. The executive wants to establish democracy only in a superficial way. The assumption is that people are not ready for the democratic process. Until the end of 1988, Pakistan was the best example of this system.

(ii) In political democracies, there are autonomous executives, legislatures and judiciary. Political parties and the media are free and competitive. There are autonomous interest groups and pressure groups. Examples are USA, UK and some of the developing countries such as India, are examples of political systems which are moving in that direction.

Countries in which voters can choose between two or more parties and in which the mass of the adult population has the right to vote are usually called 'liberal' democracies and include Britain, the USA, India, Japan and Australia.

Spread of Democracy

- Globalising processes have played an important role in spreading democracy around the world. Increasing cross-national contacts, presence of a global media and advances in information and communications technology have made people in non-democratic states aware of democratic ideals leading to more internal pressure on political elites.
- For example, in 1989, the news of the revolution in Poland travelled rapidly to Hungary, providing pro-democracy activists there with a useful model for their own protests. In 2011, the so-called Arab Spring saw a series of demonstrations and protests that forced out leaders in Tunisia, Egypt, Libya and Yemen, as well as causing a destructive civil war in Syria.
- International organizations such as the United Nations and the European Union have also played an important role and have come to put external pressure on non-democratic states to change.

Critique

- Scholars have argued that though democracy has become a preferred form of government, in many countries, it is characterized with dictator-style leadership and single-party domination. The growing majoritarianism and fundamentalism are other challenges in this regard.
- Representative democracy does not truly represent the interests of the people. For a democracy to function properly, other measures such as local-level participation, increase in literacy, strong opposition, economic well-being, etc., are also needed.
- Even in countries that have transitioned to democracy, some continue to struggle with challenges of military coup, external interference, internal conflicts and unstable governments.

Non-Government Associations—Political Parties, Interest Groups, Pressure Groups, Civil Society

Political Parties

- These are organized groups of citizens who hold common views on public issues. They act as political units, seeking to obtain control of the government with a view to further their own programme and policies. More precisely, a political party has been defined as 'an association organized in support of some principle or policy which, by constitutional means, it endeavours to make the determinant of government.'
- Political parties are essential for the working of a democratic government. They socialise the people into political behaviour, sort out the needs and aspirations of the people and place them before the people in the form of a party programme (manifesto), present the people's needs and demands before the government and provide a link between people and their elected representatives
- Political parties may differ on ideologies, and consequently, on their goals and means. The modern trend is to divide them broadly into two categories—right and left. The rightist parties are conservative and status.

  quo oriented whereas the leftist parties are revolutionary and change-oriented. In many European countries there are centrist parties which do not belong either to the right or to the left.
- Of late, religious fundamentalism has also entered the arena of political parties. Several states in the world today are under the grip of religious fundamentalism (e.g., Iran, Israel, India).
- The number of political parties functioning within a state is also an important aspect of a political system. There are states with only one political party (For example, China). There are also states with a number of parties. A few states have only two parties (e.g., UK and USA). In states with multiple parties, political coalition have emerged. In India, we have a multiparty system. In some states there are coalition cabinets.
- Communist countries and non-communist totalitarian states do not tolerate any opposition and hence, have only one political party.
- The presence of several parties competing for the loyalty of the citizens and acting as a control on one another is the strongest safeguard for democracy. If there is only one party, it can become indifferent to the needs of the people and can use its power arbitrarily, there is no check on the ruling party as it does not have to face any opposition either from the legislature or from the people.

Interest Groups and Pressure Groups

- These are associations or groups which have objectives different from those of political parties. Members of these groups may join political parties but the reason to do so is also to further their own interests than out of conviction in the party's ideology or action programme.

- Interest groups may be based on economic, ethnic, linguistic, religious, regional or other considerations.
- When an interest group converts itself into a political party or win over some members of the government (ruling party) and pressure the government to concede their demands, in such cases, the group could be considered as a pressure group.
- Interest groups and pressure groups use a number of strategies to influence the government and to get their demands accepted. These strategies include threats of direct action like boycott, threat of holding back essential services, protest closure of shops and agitation's such as street demonstrations and strikes. However, the strategy is decided by the probability of success. Interest groups play an important part in government decision-making.

Civil Society

It refers to the sphere of society made up of all those networks, voluntary associations, businesses, clubs, organizations and families formed by citizens independently of the government. In its original form, the concept of civil society can be traced right back to ancient times, when it was tied to notions of 'civility' and people treating one another with respect. However, modern conceptions of civil society originate from Alexis de Tocqueville's nineteenth-century idea of 'civic associations'. These included lodges, charities and religious groups. According to him, these associations not only performed useful functions but were also fundamental in sustaining the country's democratic culture.

- While there are disagreements about what a civil society entails, some scholars have analysed it in opposition to the other two realms of the state and the market.
- There are also disagreements about the nature of civil society. For some, it represents a space for the expression of active citizenship and a democratic bulwark against authoritarianism. In the Marxist view however, civil society is, along with remaining cultural superstructure, responsible for transmitting the ideological and cultural dominance of capitalism and its values. Though the later neo-Marxists, especially Gramsci, did acknowledge that civil society offered opportunities to build a counter-cultural challenge to capitalism and that ideological domination was never absolute.

Emergence of Global Civil Society

It is argued that with global communications and interactions becoming more common, a global civil society may be evolving. For example, campaigners against landmines, tax avoidance by multinational companies, and fundamentalist terrorists are able to link up with sympathizers around the world in global networks, especially through the Internet, and help build a global civil society.

Critique

- Civil society does not always strengthen democracy or challenge capitalism. Some voluntary groups in fact enjoy high levels of social capital – such as the National Rifle Association in the USA and have significant access to government. It gives them much more power than other groups to influence policy without having to run for election.

- The spread of the Internet is a key factor in the constitution of an emerging global civil society. However, scholar J. Naughton has shown how the huge digital divide between the information-rich and information- poor countries is a barrier to global communications. He has also claimed that though cyberspace has been seen as very different from the 'real world', in reality, the two are converging.

Ace Your Answers!

1. Reflect on the changes in the nature of democracy in the following cases:
   (a) India – Inauguration of new Parliament, rising majoritarianism, threat of fundamentalism, weak opposition, 2024 elections, dispute over 'one nation-one language', security breach in the parliament
   (b) Pakistan – Example of hybrid democracy – Intervention of judiciary and military in executive matters
2. Reflect on how global media functions as a pressure group. Do the Indian media enjoy absolute autonomy and freedom in this regard?
   [*Hint:* Recent US elections vs Twitter(X)]
3. Reflect on the changing nature of nation-state in the context of:
   (a) Russia-Ukraine war
   (b) Israel-Gaza conflict
4. What are the critical issues related to citizenship in India from a sociological point of view?
   (a) Do marginalized castes and Dalits enjoy citizenship benefits equally?
   (b) How do women perform when it comes to political participation both at the level of running elections and as a voter base?
   (c) Does the new Citizenship Amendment Act create more faultlines in Indian society on the basis of religion or is it a necessary way to delimit the citizenry for the Indian state?
5. Reforms are difficult in India as it is too much of a democracy. Do you agree with this statement? Reflect and justify your stance.

Collective Action

Collective action refers to the organized and coordinated behaviour of individuals or groups working together to achieve common goals or address shared concerns. It involves people coming together, in a structured or unstructured manner, to pursue objectives that transcend individual interests. Sociologists study collective action to understand how individuals mobilise, cooperate, and enact change within the broader social context.

Key aspects of collective action include:

1. **Shared Goals:** The shared objectives serve as a unifying force, bringing people together to work towards a common cause.
2. **Social Structure:** This includes existing institutions, power dynamics, cultural norms, and patterns of social interaction providing the context within which the collective action occurs.
3. **Organization:** This can range from informal networks and spontaneous gatherings to more formal structures such as social movements, interest groups, or advocacy organizations.
4. **Mobilisation:** It involves strategies through which individuals are recruited, activated, and brought together for collective action.
5. **Communication:** It includes the exchange of information, the creation of shared narratives, and the use of symbols and rhetoric to articulate the goals and values of the collective.
6. **Conflict and Cooperation:** Collective action often occurs in response to perceived conflicts or inequalities. Additionally, cooperation among participants is crucial for the success of the collective effort.
7. **Resource Mobilization:** Resources, both material and symbolic, play a significant role. These resources can include financial support, expertise, media attention, and public opinion.
8. **Political and Social Change:** Collective action can lead to various forms of political or social change. It may influence policies, challenge cultural norms, or contribute to the reshaping of social institutions.

Types of Collective Action

Herbert Blumer, a symbolic interactionist sociologist, introduced the concept of 'collective behaviour' and identified various types of collective action in his work, 'Critique of the Research in Social Sciences (1939)'. The four main types of collective action according to Herbert Blumer are:

1. **Crowds**
   - (a) **Casual Crowds:** These are gatherings of people who happen to be in the same place at the same time without any significant interaction. Examples include individuals waiting at a bus stop or shopping in a mall.
   - (b) **Conventional Crowds:** In these crowds, individuals come together for a specific, planned purpose, such as attending a concert, a religious ceremony, or a sports event. While there is a shared focus, interactions may be limited.
   - (c) **Expressive Crowds:** Characterized by emotional and expressive behaviour, these crowds form around occasions that evoke strong feelings, such as funerals, celebrations, or protests. Emotions play a central role in shaping collective behaviour.
2. **Publics**
   - (a) **Conventional Publics:** These are gatherings of individuals who come together to discuss a specific issue or topic. Public meetings, forums, or town hall gatherings are examples.

(b) **Action Publics:** In these situations, individuals come together to take action in response to a shared issue or concern. Activism, advocacy, and movements for social change often involve action publics that mobilise around specific causes.

3. **Masses**
   (a) **Casual Mass:** This refers to a large number of people who are exposed to the same stimulus, such as through media or a widespread event. While they share exposure, there is limited interaction among individuals.
   (b) **Public Mass:** In this context, individuals are exposed to a common stimulus, and their attention is directed toward a specific issue or event. Public opinion and sentiments are shaped by shared exposure, creating a sense of a public mass.
4. **Social Movements**
   (a) **General Social Movements:** These movements are general in nature aimed towards spreading awareness and raising mass consciousness. For example, many movements in India's freedom struggle, besides challenging British authority, also had elements of social service, abolishing caste discrimination, eliminating orthodox practices, etc.
   (b) **Specific Social Movements:** These movements are aimed towards specific goals. For examples, women's suffragette movement was aimed at securing voting rights for women.
   (c) **Expressive Social Movements:** These movements are aimed at changing the members of the movement itself. For example, Transcendental movement of Mahesh Yogi.

Protest

Protest is a form of action, either at the individual or collective level that involves public expression of dissent, dissatisfaction, or disagreement with existing social, political, or economic conditions.

Main features of protest include:

1. Opposition is the central element.
2. It can occur at individual (example, fast until death by Mahatma Gandhi against the British, by Potti Sreeramulu for Andhra state formation) or collective level (example - wrestlers' protest at Jantar Mantar, Delhi against improper functioning within Wrestling Federation of India), manifest or latent level and many involve action or inaction as a tool of protest.
3. It generally occurs in response to a prior event.
4. Modes of protest could vary from marches, vigils, torch light processions to street theatre, songs, poetry, violence and vandalism.

Here are several key sociological perspectives on protest:

1. **Symbolic Interactionism:** In the context of protest, symbolic interactionism explores the symbolic significance of protest signs, slogans, gestures, and other communicative acts.
2. **Structural-functionalism:** From a structural-functional perspective, protest can be seen as a mechanism for addressing social dysfunctions or imbalances.

3. **Conflict Theory:** Influenced by Karl Marx, this theory views protest as a response to perceived injustice and as a manifestation of class struggle or other forms of social conflict.
4. **Resource Mobilization Theory:** Resource mobilization theory focuses on the practical aspects of protest, emphasising the mobilization of resources such as money, manpower, and media attention.
5. **Political Process Theory:** It considers the role of the political environment, state responses, and the availability of channels for expressing dissent.
6. **Frame Analysis:** Frame analysis, developed by Erving Goffman, focuses on how individuals interpret and frame their experiences. Protest involves the framing of issues, grievances, and goals in a way that resonates with potential participants and the broader public.

Agitation

It is a type of action that involves intense activity undertaken by an individual or group, in order to fulfill a purpose. It can be seen as a way of creating a sense of urgency around an issue and mobilising public opinion in support of a particular cause. Agitation can also be used to challenge dominant narratives and promote alternative perspectives on social and political issues.

Main features of agitation include:

1. It can occur at individual or collective level.
2. Purpose and a sense of urgency are the central elements here.
3. Dissatisfaction is the igniting factor.
4. Generally spontaneous and ephemeral.

Feature	Protest	Agitation	Social Movement
Type	Can be at individual or collective level	Can be at individual or collective level	Institutionalized form of protest occurring at a collective level
Nature of Expression	Public demonstrations, marches, rallies, symbolic acts	Emotional, intense, disruptive actions	Diverse actions, including protests, advocacy, and more for a sustained period of time
Communication Emphasis	Explicit communication, raising awareness, garnering support	Emphasis on stirring emotions, creating a sense of urgency	Broad communication strategies, framing issues, mobilization
Level of Organization	Can vary from spontaneous to highly organized	Tends to be more spontaneous, less structured	May range from loosely organized (like on social media without any leadership) to highly structured movements (with specific leadership and planned activities)

Feature	Protest	Agitation	Social Movement
Nature of Action	Diverse, may include peaceful marches, sit-ins, petitions, boycott	More disruptive, may involve provocative or attention-grabbing tactics	Inclusive of various actions, advocacy, lobbying, marches, public processions, debates and more
Goals and Intent	Specific goals or demands, addressing particular issues	Less focused on specific policy changes, more about creating a sense of discontent or urgency	Articulates broader goals and may encompass long-term societal transformation like eradication of *sati pratha*, dowry practice
Similarities	In essence, it can be gauged that agitations are a type of protest and protests, when occurring for a sustained period of time in a more structured and institutionalized manner, take the form of a social movement.		

Revolution

Revolution refers to a sudden and transformative change in the structure and nature of society. It often involves significant changes in the social, economic, cultural, political, and technological systems. It is typically associated with fundamental changes in social structures leading to the emergence of new social orders. The term revolution first came into socio-political vocabulary in 1688 when James II was replaced with William III and the event was called—The Glorious Revolution.

According to Theda Skocpol, a prominent sociologist, social revolution is a 'combination of thoroughgoing structural transformation and massive class upheaval.' Chalmers Johnson, in his book 'Revolutionary Change,' discusses a value-based model, arguing that revolution occurs when the values realized through socialization, norms, and rules become misaligned. According to Charles Tilly, in his work European Revolutions (1993), 'A revolution is also different from similar sounding terms like revolt, uprising, rebellion or mutiny in the sense that the latter may not have a lasting impact on the society.' He further states that 'a revolution is actually an outcome of a power struggle between competing interest groups.'

Sociological theories of revolution have mainly focused on two main strands of thought: functionalism and conflict-coercion theory. Functionalism focuses on the role of social institutions and social stratification in causing revolutions, while conflict-coercion theory emphasises the role of social conflict and inequality in driving revolutionary change.

Some key aspects of revolution from a sociological perspective include:

1. **Social Institutions and Social Stratification:** These theories propose that the causes of revolutions can be found in the dynamics of social relations, including social institutions and social stratification.
2. **Value-based Models:** Some theories suggest that revolution occurs when the values that society is built on become misaligned.

3. **Comparative Historical Approach:** A comparative historical approach allows for a more nuanced understanding of the factors that contribute to revolutionary change through comparison of different historical events.
4. **Systems View:** Neil Smelser, as per his systems view of revolutions, says that 'when equilibrium in society is disturbed, revolutions take place.'

Revolutionary change is multi-faceted in nature. From a sociological point of view, revolutions can be categorized into various types based on their nature and impact on society. Some of the types of revolution include:

1. **Political Revolution:** This type of revolution involves a significant and rapid change in the political structure and governance, often leading to the overthrow of the existing government and the establishment of a new political system. Examples: French Revolution, Russian Revolution, the Iranian Revolution, etc.
2. **Social Revolution:** Social revolutions are sudden and extensive changes in the structure and nature of society, encompassing not only political systems but also society, economy, culture, philosophy, and technology. Examples include feminist movement, the Civil Rights Movement in the United States, or the Cuban Revolution (which had both political and social dimensions), etc.
3. **Cultural Revolution:** This type of revolution involves a fundamental change in the cultural values, beliefs, and norms of a society and often seeks to create a new cultural identity. Example – Renaissance (14th–17th centuries), Mao Zedong's Cultural Revolution in China (1966-76), Digital Revolution (Late 20th century – Global), etc.
4. **Economic Revolution:** An economic revolution can involve the transition from one economic system to another, such as from agrarian to industrial, or from a centrally planned economy to a market economy. Example - Industrial Revolution (18th–19th centuries – Europe and North America), Green Revolution, Post-1991 Economic reforms in India

Besides these, Jeff Goodwin, a sociologist, distinguishes between two types of revolutionary movements: conservative (reformist) and radical. Conservative or reformist revolutionary movements aim to change fewer elements of the socio-political system (examples – environmental movement, women's rights movement), while radical revolutionary movements (like French revolution, Russian revolution, etc.) want to take exclusive control of the state and fundamentally transform one or more elements of society, economy, or culture. His definition emphasises the extent of change that revolutionary movements seek to introduce.

Conditions for the rise of revolutions:

1. **Socioeconomic Inequality:** Widening gaps between social classes and economic disparities can fuel discontent and provide a foundation for collective mobilzation. Example- include the French Revolution (1789 – 1799) was fueled by economic disparities.
2. **Political Oppression:** Authoritarian rule, lack of political representation, and the suppression of civil liberties can create grievances that motivate people to seek political change. The Iranian Revolution (1979) was a response to the authoritarian rule of Mohammad Reza Shah Pahlavi.

3. **Failed Reforms:** Unsuccessful attempts at addressing social, economic, or political issues through reforms may lead to frustration and a desire for more radical solutions. The Russian Revolution (1917) was triggered by dissatisfaction with the failed reforms of the Provisional Government and the continuation of World War I.
4. **Crisis Situations:** Economic crises, food shortages, or other severe challenges can create a sense of urgency and a fertile ground for revolutionary sentiments. The Arab Spring (2010-2012) was sparked by economic challenges, high unemployment, and food shortages in several Arab countries. The economic crises in India led to the IMF-mandated LPG reforms in early 1990s.
5. **Intellectual and Cultural Shifts:** The spread of new ideas, ideologies, or cultural movements challenging the existing order can foster a climate conducive to revolutionary thinking. The Enlightenment era in Europe laid the intellectual groundwork for political and cultural transformations, contributing to the American and French Revolutions.
6. **Technology and Communication:** Advances in communication technologies, such as printing presses, social media, or mass media, can facilitate the rapid dissemination of ideas and coordination of movements. The role of social media in the Arab Spring, facilitating rapid communication and coordination among protesters.
7. **Youth Unrest:** Youth populations often play a central role in revolutionary movements, driven by aspirations for change and dissatisfaction with the status quo. The Tiananmen Square protests (1989) in China were largely driven by students advocating for political reform and democratic principles.
8. **Failure of Security Forces:** A breakdown in the loyalty and effectiveness of security forces can weaken the government's ability to suppress dissent, making it more vulnerable to revolutionary forces. : The collapse of loyalty within the Soviet military played a role in the success of the Bolsheviks during the Russian Revolution.
9. **External Influences:** Support or interference from external actors, such as foreign governments or international organizations, can influence the dynamics of a revolution. The support of the American colonies by external powers, such as France, contributed to the success of the American Revolution (1775 – 1783).
10. **Crisis of Legitimacy:** When a government loses legitimacy in the eyes of the population due to corruption, incompetence, or perceived illegitimacy, it becomes more susceptible to revolutionary challenges. The fall of the apartheid regime in South Africa (1994) was preceded by international condemnation and a loss of legitimacy for the discriminatory system.
11. **Symbolic Triggers:** Events or incidents that serve as symbolic triggers, such as a specific act of injustice or a symbolic event, can galvanize public sentiment and catalyse revolutionary movements. The self- immolation of Mohamed Bouazizi in Tunisia in 2010 served as a symbolic trigger for the broader protests of the Arab Spring.
12. **Organized Opposition:** The presence of organized opposition groups, political parties, or social movements provides a structure for coordinating and sustaining revolutionary efforts. : The role of the African National Congress (ANC) as an organized opposition was crucial in the anti-apartheid movement in South Africa.
13. **Social Movements:** Pre-existing social movements advocating for change in areas such as labour rights, civil rights, or environmental issues can converge

into broader revolutionary movements. The Civil Rights Movement in the United States (1950s-1960s) involved various social movements advocating for racial equality and justice. Similarly, the Non-cooperation movement, Civil Disobedience movement in India led to the final independence.

14. **Mass Mobilization:** The ability to mobilise a critical mass of people, often through effective leadership and communication, is crucial for the success of revolutionary movements. The People Power Revolution in the Philippines (1986) saw mass mobilization, including peaceful protests, against the authoritarian regime of Ferdinand Marcos.
15. **Historical Precedents:** Awareness of or inspiration from past successful revolutions can serve as a catalyst for present-day movements, providing a blueprint and a sense of possibility. The American Revolution itself served as a historical precedent and inspiration for later independence movements in Latin America. Similarly, revolution for freedom movement in India was inspired by similar revolutions around the world.

These conditions are interconnected and can interact in complex ways. The emergence of revolutions is often the result of a combination of these factors coming together in a particular historical context.

Relationship Between Different Types of Collective Actions

Agitation, protests, movements and revolutions are all different types of collective actions varying in purpose, organization, aims and impact. However, all of them are related to each other and often integrate with each other when it comes to actual operation. So agitation is one type of protest while protests are a regular feature of social movements. A revolution may be of a short duration but it culminates as a result of long social movements and protests.

Key Relationships

1. **Escalation Pattern:**
   - Protests → Agitation → Social Movements → Revolution
   - Not all forms necessarily progress to the next level
   - Can occur simultaneously or independently
2. **Interconnections:**
   - Protests often emerge from social movements
   - Agitation can spark both protests and movements
   - Revolutions typically incorporate all other forms
3. **Feedback Loops:**
   - Movement success can inspire new protests
   - Failed protests can lead to sustained agitation
   - Revolutionary situations can generate new movements

Previous Years' Question

2024

1. Democracy needs a vibrant culture of civil society in order to strengthen its foundation of citizenship. Comment. (10 Marks)
2. How is 'power' different from 'authority'? Discuss various types of authorities as theorized by Max Weber. (10 Marks)
3. Underline the role of social media in contemporary social movements and describe its challenges. (10 Marks)
4. How does a multicultural society accommodate diversities of all kinds—ethnic, linguistic and religious? Discuss its major challenges. (10 Marks)
5. Discuss the dimensions of power the construction and maintenance of social hierarchies in a society. (10 Marks)

2023

1. Is Weber's idea of bureaucracy a product of the historical experiences of Europe? Comment. (10 Marks)
2. What, according to Robert Michels, is the iron law of oligarchy? Do lions and foxes in Vilfredo Pareto's theory, essentially differ from each other? Substantiate. (10 Marks)
3. How is civil society used in deepening the roots of democracy? (10 Marks)
4. Do you think that the social media has brought significant changes in the forms of protest? Argue your case. (10 Marks)

2022

1. Analyse the nature of transition from ideology to identity politics in India. (10 Marks)
2. Discuss how 'environmentalism' can be explained with new social movements approach. (10 Marks)
3. Illustrate with examples the role of pressure groups in the formulation of social policies. (10 Marks)

2021

1. Critically examine the relevance of Vilfredo Pareto's theory of Circulation of Elites in the present scenario. (10 Marks)
2. Highlight the roles and function of civil society in a democratic system. (10 Marks)

2020

1. What are the theoretical models of societal power? Which one of them is most applicable in advanced industrial societies? (20 Marks)
2. 'Power is not a zero-sum game'. Discuss with reference to Weber's and Parsons's views. (20 Marks)
3. According to Mills, 'Elite's rule in institutional terms rather than psychological terms.' Comment. (10 Marks)
4. Explain democracy as an order of society. What are the factors preventing people's participation in politics? (10 Marks)
5. Examine how social movements come to an end. Illustrate with examples. (10 Marks)

2019

1. Discuss the concept of circulation of elite. (10 Marks)
2. What is civil society? Present a note on civil society engagement with science and technology policy in India. (10 Marks)
3. How is terrorism a new form of asymmetrical warfare? What are some of the challenges in trying to win the war on terrorism? (10 Marks)

2018

1. What, according to Pareto, are the basic characteristics of elites? Discuss. (10 Marks)
2. Are social movements primordial in means and progressive in agenda? Explain. (10 Marks)

2017

1. Examine the dynamics of pressure groups in multi-party political system. (10 Marks)
2. Discuss the changing interface between state and civil society in post-independent India. (10 Marks)
3. What is new in 'new social movements'? Elaborate your answer with special reference to India. (10 Marks)

2016

1. Discuss the importance of 'power elite' in democracy. (10 Marks)
2. Examine the role of protest movements in changing the status of Dalits in India. (10 Marks)
3. To what success revolution replaces the existing order of society? Discuss. (10 Marks)

2015

1. 'Globalization involves deterritorialization.' Examine with reference to the nation state. (10 Marks)
2. 'Ideology is crucial for social transformation in a democracy.' Discuss. (10 Marks)
3. Caste ideology appears to have strengthened democracy. Comment. (10 Marks)
4. Explain the conditions under which a collective action transforms into a social movement. (10 Marks)

2014

1. Distinguish between Political Parties and Pressure Groups. (10 Marks)
2. Discuss T. H. Marshall's views on citizenship. (10 Marks)
3. What do you understand by social movement? How has the mobilization by Scheduled Castes helped them in constructing a new identity? (10 Marks)

2013

1. Evaluate how do civil society and democracy mutually reinforce each other. (10 Marks)
2. Critically examine the role of civil society in democracy. (10 Marks)
3. Defines social movement. Elucidate the role of reformist movements in social change. (10 Marks)

Right Approach

2024

Q3. Underline the role of social media in contemporary social movements and describe its challenges. (10 Marks)

Introduction: Social media has become a powerful tool in contemporary social movements, enabling activists to mobilize support, raise awareness, and challenge dominant narratives. Platforms like Twitter, Facebook, and Instagram have transformed how movements operate by providing a space for collective action, rapid information dissemination, and global reach.

Body:

Role of Social Media in Social Movements

1. **Mobilization and Awareness:** Social media allows movements to mobilize large numbers of people quickly and effectively. The Arab Spring and #BlackLivesMatter movements illustrate how online platforms can amplify marginalized voices and rally supporters worldwide.
2. **Decentralized Leadership:** Unlike traditional movements with hierarchical structures, social media enables decentralized, leaderless movements. This was evident in the #MeToo movement, where individual stories collectively challenged systemic gender-based violence.
3. **Countering Censorship:** Social media provides an alternative space for dissent, especially in authoritarian societies. Activists use it to bypass state-controlled media and share unfiltered information with the world.

Challenges of Social Media in Social Movements

1. **Misinformation and Polarization:** Social media can spread misinformation and divisive content, undermining the credibility of movements and leading to polarization. False information often spreads faster than verified news, complicating fact-checking efforts.
2. **Surveillance and Censorship:** Governments and corporations monitor online activities, potentially curtailing activism. For instance, authorities may use surveillance to track activists, posing risks to privacy and freedom.
3. **Ephemeral Engagement:** The fast-paced nature of social media can lead to superficial engagement, with people participating in 'hashtag activism' without deeper commitment.

Conclusion: Social media plays a crucial role in contemporary social movements, empowering activists and challenging traditional power structures. However, the challenges of misinformation, surveillance, and transient engagement highlight the need for responsible digital activism to ensure social media remains a constructive tool for change.

2024

Q 4 How does a multicultural society accommodate diversities of all kinds-ethnic, linguistic and religious? Discuss its major challenges. (10 Marks)

Introduction: A multicultural society accommodates diversity by promoting inclusivity and tolerance across ethnic, linguistic, and religious groups. This framework aims to create harmony by respecting differences, allowing individuals to preserve their cultural identities within a shared national identity.

Body:

Accommodating Diversity in Multicultural Societies

1. **Legal Protections and Rights:** Multicultural societies like India and Canada implement legal protections to ensure the rights of minorities. In India, the Constitution protects linguistic and religious minorities, allowing them to establish and manage their educational institutions. Canada's Multiculturalism Act promotes cultural diversity and minority rights, fostering social cohesion.
2. **Policies of Inclusivity:** Countries adopt policies encouraging equal representation and participation. For example, South Africa's post-apartheid policies promote racial and ethnic inclusivity, while Singapore's housing policies ensure ethnic mixing to reduce segregation.
3. **Promotion of Intercultural Dialogue:** Events, education, and media in multicultural societies encourage understanding among diverse groups. This reflects Amartya Sen's idea of 'plural monoculturalism,' where communities coexist while fostering positive intercultural interactions.

Challenges of Multicultural Societies

1. **Social Integration:** Balancing cultural preservation with integration remains challenging. In France, debates over religious symbols in public spaces illustrate tensions between universalist and particularist values.
2. **Ethnic and Religious Tensions:** Multicultural societies can face ethnic or religious conflicts. In India, communal tensions occasionally arise, highlighting the delicate balance required in such societies.
3. **Political Exploitation of Identities:** Identity politics can lead to divisions, as seen in the United States, where ethnic and racial identities are sometimes politicized, risking social cohesion.

Conclusion: Multicultural societies accommodate diversity by providing legal protections, inclusive policies, and promoting intercultural dialogue. However, challenges like social integration, ethnic tensions, and political exploitation of identities underscore the need for balanced approaches to sustain unity in diversity.

2024

Q 5. Discuss the dimensions of power in the construction and maintenance of social hierarchies in a society.

Introduction: Power, a central concept in sociology, influences the construction and maintenance of social hierarchies in society. Sociologists view power as the ability to influence others' actions, and it operates through various dimensions—coercive, economic, cultural, and ideological—contributing to social stratification.

Body:

Dimensions of Power in Constructing Social Hierarchies

1. **Coercive Power:** Max Weber highlights the role of coercive power, where authority and control are maintained through force or threats. This is visible in authoritarian regimes that maintain hierarchy through repression and military dominance.
2. **Economic Power:** Karl Marx emphasized economic power as a fundamental dimension in maintaining class hierarchies. The capitalist class controls resources and means of production, creating a system where wealth and privileges are concentrated among the elite.
3. **Cultural Power:** Pierre Bourdieu's concept of 'cultural capital' shows how education, language, and lifestyle can maintain social hierarchies. The elite reinforce their status by monopolizing cultural assets, creating symbolic boundaries that differentiate social classes.
4. **Ideological Power:** Antonio Gramsci's theory of 'hegemony' explains how the ruling class maintains dominance by controlling cultural narratives and values. Through institutions like media and education, they shape societal beliefs, making social hierarchies appear natural and legitimate.

Conclusion: The dimensions of power—coercive, economic, cultural, and ideological—interact to construct and sustain social hierarchies. By examining these dimensions, sociologists reveal how power operates subtly and overtly to reinforce inequality, shaping the structure of society and influencing social mobility.

CHAPTER

8

Religion and Society

In this Chapter

- Sociological Theories of Religion
- Types of Religious Practices: Animism, Monism, Pluralism, Sects, Cults
- Religion in Modern Society: Religion and Science, Secularization, Religious Revivalism, Fundamentalism
- Previous Years' Questions

Introduction

Historical Accuracy of Sociology's Emergence

The claim that sociology emerged in the first half of the 19th century is well-documented in academic histories. The discipline arose as a response to massive social transformations brought by the industrial revolution, urbanization, and political upheavals in Europe. Auguste Comte coined the term 'sociology' in 1839, establishing it as a distinct field of scientific inquiry.

Archaeological Evidence for Religious Antiquity

The assertion that religion is 'as old as human societies' is supported by extensive archaeological and anthropological evidence. Prehistoric burial practices, cave art, and ritual sites indicate spiritual practices dating back tens of thousands of years, with evidence of animistic beliefs among early hunter-gatherer societies.

Institutionalization of World Religions

The description of major world religions becoming institutionalized through texts, rituals, and organizational structures is factually accurate. Historical scholarship extensively documents how religions like Christianity, Islam, Hinduism, Buddhism, Judaism, Sikhism, and Jainism developed formal institutions, sacred texts, and complex relationships with political power over centuries.

Ethnographic Accuracy of Teton Sioux Example

The example of the Teton Sioux (Lakota) and their beliefs about Wakan powers is ethnographically sound. The concept of *waka* as a mysterious, animating force permeating the universe is central to Lakota spirituality. Anthropological research confirms the distinction between worship and invocation in their religious practices.

Durkheim's Theoretical Framework

The description of Durkheim's work in *The Elementary Forms of Religious Life* (1912) accurately represents his theoretical approach. Durkheim studied Australian Aboriginal totemism, particularly the Arunta (now Arrernte) people, arguing that religion's essence lies not in belief in gods but in its social function of creating solidarity through the sacred/profane distinction.

Merton's Functionalist Analysis

The reference to Robert Merton's concept of latent functions is correctly presented. Merton distinguished between manifest functions (intended consequences) and latent functions (unintended consequences), noting that religion promotes social cohesion beyond its stated purposes, with potential functional alternatives like political ideologies.

Critical Assessment

The passage demonstrates several characteristics of academic writing:

- Uses established theoretical frameworks without personal interpretation
- Draws from recognized ethnographic sources

- Presents factual claims supported by scholarly consensus
- Maintains objective tone throughout
- References specific studies and researchers

The only potentially subjective elements are word choices and the selection of examples, which is typical of introductory textbook writing rather than personal opinion.

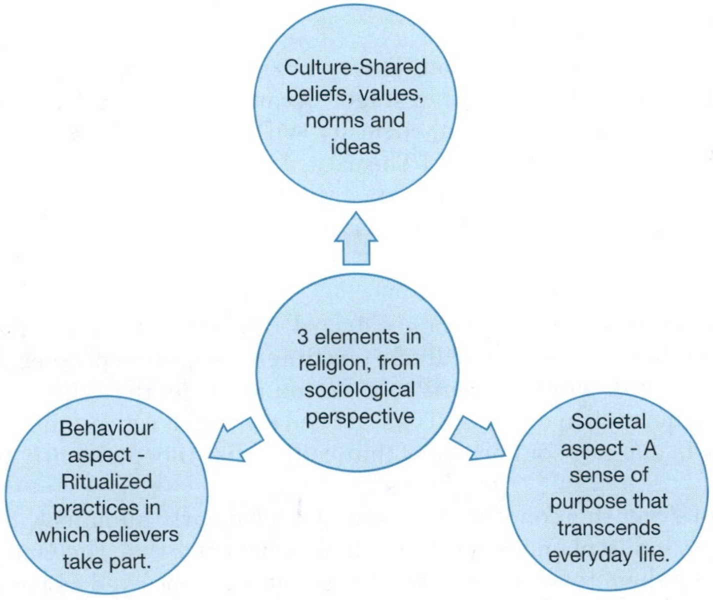

Parsons saw religion as a repository of societal values. In his famous AGIL scheme, religion contributes to latency or pattern maintenance by becoming the basis for value consensus.

Definitions

In sociology, there have been two main approaches for defining religion:

1. **Functional Terms:** For instance, Yinger defined religion as a 'system of beliefs and practices by means of which a group of people struggles with the ultimate problems of human life.'
2. **Substantive Terms:** (This is more concerned with content rather than function) For instance, Durkheim defined religion in terms of distinction between sacred and profane. Rolan Robertson defined religion in terms of 'existence of supernatural beings that have a governing effect on life.' Melford Spiro included the institutional aspect in this to say that 'religion is an institution consisting of culturally patterned interactions with culturally postulated superhuman beings.'

Sociological Theories of Religion

Sociologists have studied religion as a social construct. They are not concerned with whether God exists or whether the held religious beliefs are right or wrong, but rather with the social organization of religion, how the beliefs originated and changed over a period of time and what role religion plays in the society.

Theories of Origin

Initial theories on religion were evolutionary in character centered on understanding forms of religion during the primitive stage. Because they were based on speculation and served to satisfy the intellectual curiosity, without any substantial evidence, they are also referred to as the Intellectual Theories. Among social anthropologists, scholars like Edward B. Tylor, Herbert Spencer, Max Mueller, etc., have made important contributions in this regard.

Tylor's Theory of Animism

In his study of early human societies, Edward Burnett Tylor identified phenomena such as death and dreams as particularly puzzling to primitive peoples. Early humans would have wondered: what happens to a person after death? What accounts for the experiences people have in dreams? Tylor argued that such reflections led to the development of beliefs about a soul or spirit that could exist independently of the physical body.

According to Tylor, this concept of the soul provided early humans with explanations for various mysterious phenomena. Since it was believed that the soul animated the person—enabling them to walk, talk, and think—it was conceived as possessing special powers beyond the material world. This spiritual dimension was understood as distinct from, though connected to, the natural physical realm.

Based on these observations, Tylor defined religion as 'belief in spiritual beings.' He argued that all other dimensions of religion emerged from this fundamental belief in souls or spirits. Tylor identified animism—the belief that all things, including animals, plants, and inanimate objects, possess souls or spirits—as the earliest and most elementary form of religion. From this basic animistic foundation, he theorized, more complex religious systems gradually evolved over time.

Tylor viewed practices such as ritual sacrifice as attempts to communicate with or appease these spiritual beings, reflecting humanity's ongoing relationship with what they perceived as the spirit world. He saw animism as representing a rational attempt by early peoples to explain natural phenomena and human experiences that would otherwise remain mysterious.

Source: Tylor, Edward Burnett. *Primitive Culture: Researches into the Development of Mythology, Philosophy, Religion, Language, Art, and Custom.* London: John Murray, 1871, particularly Volume 1, Chapters 11-19.

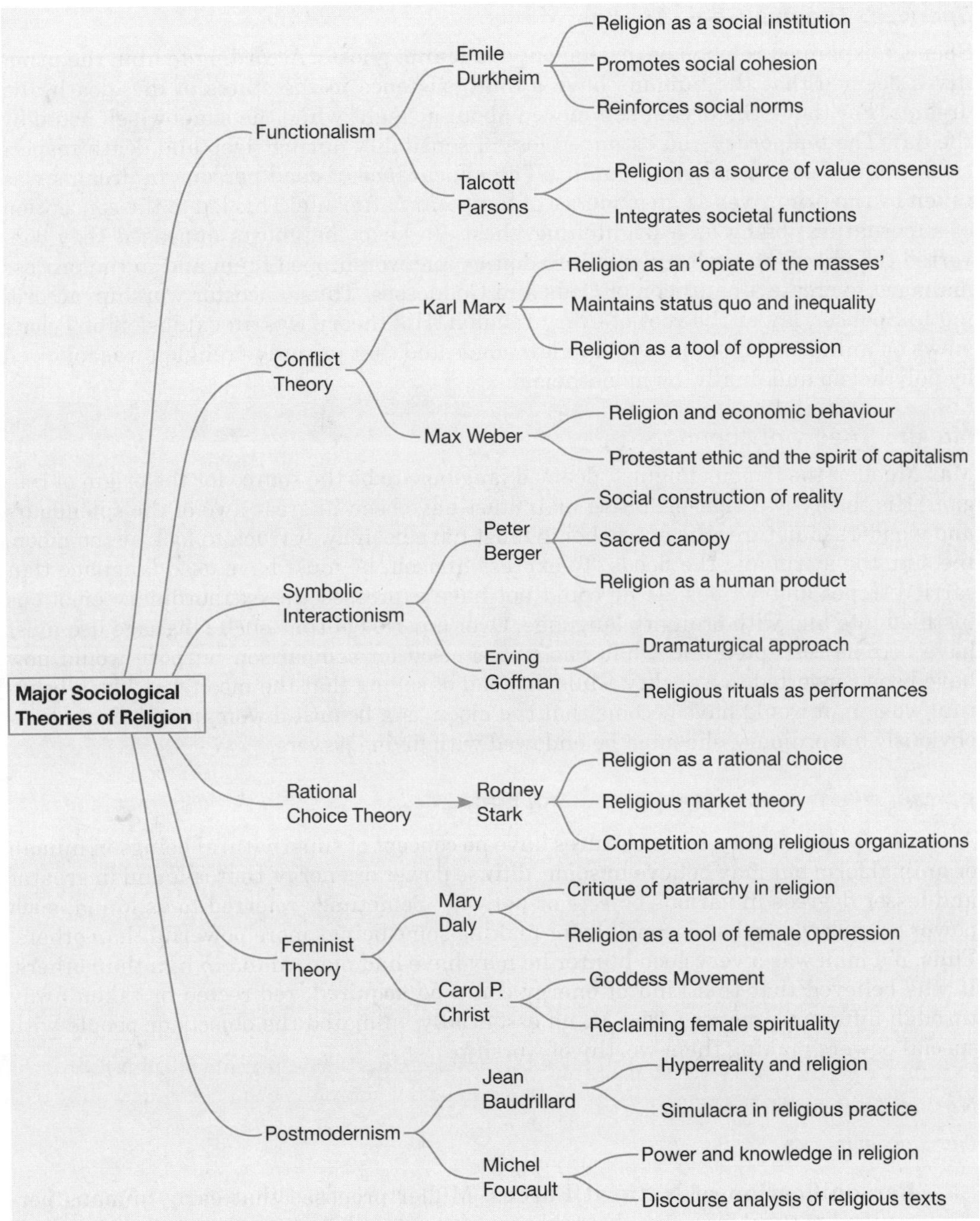
Major Sociological Theories of Religion
Functionalism
Emile Durkheim
Religion as a social institution
Promotes social cohesion
Reinforces social norms
Talcott Parsons
Religion as a source of value consensus
Integrates societal functions
Conflict Theory
Karl Marx
Religion as an 'opiate of the masses'
Maintains status quo and inequality
Religion as a tool of oppression
Max Weber
Religion and economic behaviour
Protestant ethic and the spirit of capitalism
Symbolic Interactionism
Peter Berger
Social construction of reality
Sacred canopy
Religion as a human product
Erving Goffman
Dramaturgical approach
Religious rituals as performances
Rational Choice Theory
Rodney Stark
Religion as a rational choice
Religious market theory
Competition among religious organizations
Feminist Theory
Mary Daly
Critique of patriarchy in religion
Religion as a tool of female oppression
Carol P. Christ
Goddess Movement
Reclaiming female spirituality
Postmodernism
Jean Baudrillard
Hyperreality and religion
Simulacra in religious practice
Michel Foucault
Power and knowledge in religion
Discourse analysis of religious texts

Spencer's Dreams/Ghost Theory

Spencer explained religion as arising out of a fear of ghosts. According to him, the primitives deemed that the humans have a dual existence in the states of life, death and dreams. For them, the dream-self moved about at night while the shadow-self acted by the day. The temporary and extended loss of sensibility during sleep and death respectively reinforced the notion of duality. The appearance of dead persons in dreams was taken by the primitives as an evidence of temporary after-life. This led to the conception of supernatural being as a frightening ghost. To keep the ghosts appeased they converted the ghosts of powerful men into deities and worshipped them and in the process managed to create a pantheon of Gods and Goddesses. Thus, ancestor worship, according to Spencer, lay at the root of every religion. His theory was an extension of Tylor's views on animism. His evolutionary view suggested that primitive religion was followed by polytheism and finally, by monotheism.

Muller's Theory of Language

Max Mueller, the famous linguist, deemed language to be the source for the origin of religion. His theory was that primitive man must have been in great awe of the splendours and wonders of nature. His entire being must have been awe struck to look at the moon, the sun, the storm and the floods. To express himself, he must have used language that carried tropes and similes, as he could not have expressed the extraordinary emotions instilled into him with ordinary language. Over a period of time such language use must have become corrupted and what was earlier used for comparison purpose would now have been converted to a reality. Thus, instead of saying that the moon was like a beautiful woman, it would have become that the moon 'is' a beautiful woman and since she is obviously not ordinary, she must be endowed with divine powers.

RR Marett's Theory of Animatism and Mana

According to this theory, some cultures have no concept of supernatural beings in human or animal form but may believe in some 'diffuse power or energy' that is found in greater and lesser degrees in various objects or persons. Sometimes referred to as Mana, such power or energy may be responsible for making some beings more powerful than others. Thus, if a man was a very good hunter he may have had more Mana in him than others. It was believed that this kind of energy could be acquired, redirected or taken away through different practices. The Mana essentially animated the objects or people with special powers making them worthy of worship.

Nature Theory: Max Müller

Core Concepts

1. **Personification of Natural Forces:** Müller proposed that early humans personified natural forces, such as the sun, moon, wind, and storms, attributing them with human-like qualities and supernatural powers. This personification led to the development of deities representing these natural phenomena.
2. **Mythology:** According to Müller, myths and stories about these personified natural forces formed the basis of early religious beliefs and practices. These myths

explained the origins and behaviour of natural phenomena in a way that was comprehensible to early humans.

3. **Language and Religion:** Müller emphasized the role of language in shaping religious beliefs. He argued that the way early humans described natural phenomena in poetic and metaphorical language contributed to the development of religious concepts.

Critique of Nature Theory

1. **Anthropological Critique:** Some anthropologists argue that Müller's theory overemphasizes the role of language and mythology and does not adequately account for the social and cultural functions of religion.
2. **Evolutionary Critique:** Critics suggest that Müller's focus on nature and language overlooks the evolutionary and psychological aspects of religious belief formation.

Frazer's Theory of Magic, Religion and Science

In his magnum opus, The Golden Bough, anthropologist James Frazer traced the evolution of religion in a series of stages. As opposed to earlier thinkers, Frazer believed that the earliest stage of human existence is marked by magic, then comes religion and then comes science. As per him, magic is not about prayers but about action that is directed towards controlling nature. The earliest man was aware of his needs and requirements and thus, sought to control nature, not appease her. Religion, on the other hand, contains some superior mental values that one does not expect to find among the primitives. At the last stage of human social evolution, Frazer advocated for the emergence of science as the dominant mode of thinking. In this stage, humans will be able to perceive the right causal relationships rather than the false ones as in magic.

The above theories have also been labelled as psycho-cultural theories as they traced the origin of religion to human psychological responses. These theories also suffered from Eurocentric bias as the final stage in the development of religion was equated with the state of societies as found in the Western countries and as most of the theorists belonged to the European culture.

Dominant Sociological Perspectives on Religion

Functionalist Perspective

The functionalist perspective examines religion in terms of society's needs and what role religion plays in its maintenance. Main thinkers and their contributions in this regard are mentioned below:

Emile Durkheim

In his work, The Elementary Forms of Religious Life (1912), Durkheim defined religion as 'a unified system of beliefs and practices related to sacred things, that is to say things set apart and forbidden.' He argued that the division between sacred and profane in all societies formed the basis of religion. The sacred could be anything, ranging from a tree to pebble, but it is what the object 'symbolises' is what matters.

Totemism

- Durkheim saw totemism, a form of religion present in the Arunta tribe of the aboriginals of Australia, as the simplest and purest type of religion.
    - **Totems:** Each clan had a totem, an emblem (often an animal or plant) that held religious significance.
    - **Rituals and Ceremonies:** Totemic rituals and ceremonies were central to the social life of the clan, reinforcing group solidarity and collective identity.
    - **Collective Effervescence:** During these rituals, individuals experienced a sense of collective effervescence, a heightened emotional state of collective unity and shared purpose.
- The tribe consisted of different clans. Each clan was like an extended family with certain rules (e.g., exogamy) and obligations. Each clan had a totem, which could be either a plant or animal. The drawings of the totems were called *churingas* and were considered as sacred as the totemic plants and animals themselves. The totem was symbolic of the clan and was the most scared object in aborigine rituals. Durkheim argued that since the totem symbolized the society, in worshipping the totem, people actually worshipped the society. The relationship between the sacred totem and the profane individuals is replicated when society is considered more important than the individual. The individual is dependent on the society and therefore worships it.
- **Religion and the 'Collective Conscience':** According to Durkheim, social life is impossible without shared values and beliefs which form the collective conscience. Religion reinforces the collective conscience through activities such as collective worship, religious rituals and practices in highly charged atmosphere wherein the social integration is strengthened. Durkheim also states that the practice of worshipping gods and deities emerged from the ancient practice of worshipping the ancestors' spirits. These spirits or souls represent common social values. It is an interrelated process by which individual souls are used to strengthen collective conscience, which in turn gets reinforced in individual belief systems.
- **Kumbh Mela in India:** This large-scale Hindu pilgrimage brings millions together, fostering a sense of community and shared identity among participants.
- **Criticism:** Durkheim's theory of religion has been criticized mainly on the following grounds:
    (a) the sample of aboriginal tribes was too small to be generalized.
    (b) his theory could be relevant for small, non-literate societies but not so for modern societies where there are many institutions and religion pluralism.
    (c) Malcolm Hamilton argues that religion and society could be at odds with each other as many times, religious morality and societal majoritarianism are not compatible with each other. For example, society may value consumerism and material achievements, while religion calls for contentment and austerity.

Bronislaw Malinowski

- Malinowski, through his fieldwork in the Trobriand Islands, emphasized the functional aspects of animism. He argued that animistic beliefs serve to address psychological needs and help individuals cope with the uncertainties of life, providing explanations for natural phenomena and social events.

- **Life Crises:** Malinowski notes that situations like birth, puberty, marriage and death include crises of life and produce emotions of anxiety and tension. Religious rituals are conducted around such situations to release the emotions and stress which could be destructive to the society. For example, in the case of death, a member of the society has been lost, so organization of a funeral brings together a social group to comfort the close ones of the bereaved and to reinforce social integration.
- **Prediction and Control:** Malinowski highlights a second category of events which bring uncertainty and are hard to predict. For example, in case of Trobriand Islanders, because the waters in the lagood were calm, fishing there was an easy task but in the open sea where there was uncertainty about storms, loss of life, availability of a good catch, etc., religious rituals were conducted in hopes of good fortune. Thus, religious rituals, which Malinowski referred to as magic, reduce anxiety by providing a feeling of assurance and control and because they are conducted in social groups, they also promote social solidarity.
- **Criticism:** Malinowski has been criticized for exaggerating the importance of religion. Scholars have argued that the rituals had other purposes like maintenance of prestige rather than promotion of solidarity.

Talcott Parsons

- According to Parsons, religion is a part of the cultural system (part of his Action System Theory) and provides the guidelines to direct and evaluate human behaviour in the society. The guidelines are visible in the form of norms for proper conduct. For example, Buddhism advocates the Noble Eightfold Path, which includes right view, right speech, right conduct, right effort, etc. These directions are visible in legal directions which criminalise acts such as robbery, murder, defamation, etc.
- **Social Order Through Adjustment and Boost in Self-confidence:** Like Malinowski, Parsons states that religion is useful in addressing particular areas of social life. First of these is the situation when unforeseen events, like death occur. Religion helps in adjusting to such situations. Second of these areas is where uncertainty dominates, like one does not know the resulting outcome. Religious rituals help in making one confident.
- **Meaning to Life's Events:** Parsons sees religion as providing meaning to the contradictory and frustrating events of life, such as premature death, heinous crimes, rise of the corrupt, etc. This promotes stability in the society and prevents development of pessimism.

The functionalist perspective on religion has been criticized for ignoring the dysfunctional aspects of religion—cause of conflict, divisions, oppressions, etc. The conflict between religious groups and use of violence have also not been talked about in their analysis.

Marxist Perspective

Karl Marx

- **Religion as 'the Opium of the People':** To Marx, religion was like an opiate which served to dull the pain of exploitation and alienation under capitalism in an artificial way. It does so by a) promising bliss and salvation in the afterlife if one bears the oppression in one's current life, and b) by making a virtue of the suffering. Religion justifies status quo and members make peace with the existing system of stratification as divinely ordained. This discourages the members from seeking change.

- **Religion and Social Control:** Religion acts as a mechanism of social control and reinforces class inequalities, thus is an instrument of oppression. It produces false consciousness blinding people from their true situation and seeking their real interests. It is used by the ruling class to further their own interests.
- **Criticism:**
  (i) Malcolm Hamilton has criticized limiting religion as an instrument of oppression. Religion in fact leads to more resilience.
  (ii) As opposed to Marx's vision of a socialist society in which religion will have no place, in cases of socialist Israeli kibbutzim and post-revolution communist Russia, religion continued to maintain a stronghold. Though it was discouraged in Russia, the level of faith in people's private capacity stayed intact.
  (iii) Roger O'Toole analysed Engels' work to suggest that Christianity was once a radical force for social change.
  (iv) Neo-Marxist Otto Maduro has claimed that religion has some degree of 'relative autonomy' away from the economic powers of the bourgeoisie and that it can be a revolutionary force.

Bryan S. Turner – A Materialist Theory of Religion

- Turner agreed with Marx that religion emerged from the economic base but also proposed a series of things in disagreement with him.
- Turner argued that during feudal times the peasants were indifferent to religion and were solely focused on survival. Religion was important to the rich, estate-owning feudal landlords as it legitimized loyalty in marriage so that the principle of primogeniture (transmission of property to the eldest son) could be carried out without any hindrance. Promiscuity and adultery would have threatened this system and by implication, transmission of property which was the source of all power.
- Turner sees religion as just an option for the ruling class in modern capitalistic societies. In these societies, wealth is not concentrated in the hands of a few individuals, rather with organizations.

Besides Durkheim and Marx, Weber was also a classical sociologist who contributed immensely to the study of religion. His views have been discussed in detail in the previous unit on thinkers.

Feminist Perspective

Feminist theory of religion is aligned with Marxists in seeing religion as an instrument of oppression but unlike the latter who see religion as a product of capitalism, feminists see religion as a product of patriarchy.

Religion was not always opposed to the interests of women. Karen Armstrong has argued that in early history 'women were considered central to the spiritual quest' and there were numerous female priests. In the Middle East, Asia and Europe, numerous symbols representing the Great Mother Goddess have been recovered. As per Armstrong, the position of women in religion began to decline as a result of invasions. The final death knell of goddesses came with the acceptance of monotheism—belief in a single god.

Perspective of Different Scholars

- **Jean Holm** has highlighted how women's roles in religion are mostly subordinate to men. In Japanese folk religions, women are responsible for organising public rituals but only men can take part in the public performances. In Buddhism, all monks are seen as senior to the nuns. Orthodox Judaism only allows males to take a full part in the ceremonies. In Islam, in some regions, women are not allowed to enter mosques for worship and men have made all the legal rulings. In Hinduism, only men can become Brahmanic priests. Holm recognises Sikhism as the most egalitarian religion with all positions equally open for men and women, but even there only a small minority of women occupies important positions. Holm further attributes the subordination of women in religious settings to the cultural perception of women's sexuality and their biological functions, such as menstruation and childbirth. Across religions, menstruation is often stigmatized and considered polluting, leading to the exclusion of women from sacred spaces and ceremonies during specific periods. These perceptions reinforce patriarchal control over women's bodies and limit their participation in religious life.
- **Simone de Beauvoir** in her book, *The Second Sex* (1953) notes how men have generally exercised control over religious beliefs. She also says that religion is used to deceive women. They are conditioned to be relatively passive and are portrayed by religion as closer to God even though they do not hold actual positions of power within the religion. Their role as mothers is considered a key religious duty. Their subjugation on earth, it is stated, will be compensated with equality in heaven. As a result, religion reinforces the unequal status quo.
- **Nawal El Saadawi,** an Egyptian feminist writer, in her work, *The Hidden Face of Eve* (1980), discusses female oppression in the Arab world. She argues that Arab girls are often victims of sexual aggression by men. Practices like female circumcision have been attributed to the influence of Islam. However, she also states that authentic religion discourages any such oppressive activities and it is men who distort religion to serve their own interests. Men have reinterpreted religious beliefs and with monotheism, the patriarchal structure has become stronger. According to Sadawi, women can improve their position through struggle for liberation, abandoning of patriarchal misinterpretations and emphasis on more positive aspects of Quran.

Impacting Lives - Religion

Gender Equality in Religion

Many scholars have opposed the idea that women are passive victims in the realm of religion. Religions have transformed over a period of time to give women more space for expression of power and voice.

- Alexandra Wright notes that Reform Judaism has allowed women to become rabbis since 1972.
- Some Christian religions, like Quakerism have never been oppressive to women.
- Even practices often viewed as oppressive have been interpreted differently by some scholars. Research on hijab (a form of veil) has highlighted how it can provide advantages for some Muslim women. Studies have shown it can serve as a response to Western cultural pressures, enabling the wearer to assert their religious identity, maintain cultural authenticity, and exercise personal agency. Some women report feeling protected from unwanted male attention while wearing hijab. However, this research has been criticized for often studying small samples of women who choose to veil and not adequately representing those who feel coerced into wearing it.

Recent examples:

Progressive

1. In a groundbreaking development, Tamil Nadu made history by appointing women as temple priests for the first time. Three women—Krishnaveni, S. Ramya, and N. Ranjitha—who completed their priestly training were designated as assistant priests at government-administered temples, challenging centuries-old gender restrictions in Hindu temple practices. These appointments were made at temples under the jurisdiction of the Tamil Nadu Hindu Religious and Charitable Endowments Department.
2. The Supreme Court of India declared the Islamic practice of instant triple talaq (talaq-e-biddat) unconstitutional and void on August 22, 2017, ruling it violated the fundamental rights of Muslim women under Articles 14, 15, and 21 of the Indian Constitution.

   Shayara Bano v. Union of India, Supreme Court of India, Writ Petition (Civil) No. 118 of 2016, decided August 22, 2017. Also reported in: 'Supreme Court strikes down triple talaq.' *The Times of India*, August 23, 2017.

Oppressive

1. Mahsa Amini, a 22-year-old Iranian woman, was arrested on September 13, 2022, by Iran's *Guidance Patrol*, also referred to as the morality police, for allegedly

wearing her hijab improperly --referred to as a 'bad hijab.' Subsequently, she sustained severe injuries due to alleged harassment while in custody, leading to her admission to the ICU and eventual death.

Her tragic demise sparked widespread protests across Iran and beyond, with demonstrators decrying systemic oppression and advocating for gender equality and freedom. These protests, widely recognized as the '*Woman, Life, Freedom*' movement, resonated as a symbolic fight against restrictive policies and the curtailment of women's rights. The incident remains a poignant example of resistance against oppressive cultural norms and state enforcement.

2. Female genital cutting (also known as female genital mutilation) continues to be practiced within certain Bohra communities in India, including among the Dawoodi Bohras, Alavi Bohras, and Suleimani Bohras. This practice, locally referred to as 'khatna,' typically involves the ritual cutting of a portion of the clitoris and is performed on young girls, usually between the ages of 6 and 10.

Reference:

Anantnarayan, Lakshmi, et al. 'The Clitoral Hood a Contested Site: Experiences of Women from the Dawoodi Bohra Community in India.' *Reproductive Health* 15, no. 1 (2018): 1–10.

Ace Your Answers!

While many dubbed the Supreme Court judgement on permitting women of all ages to enter the Sabarimala Temple in Kerala, there was a sizeable section of women who were against the ruling. Reflect and state the possible reasons for it.

FYI

Religion serves universal human needs by offering 'compensators' and is here to stay—Stark and Bainbridge

Rodney Stark and William Sims Bainbridge have rejected the functionalist, Marxist and feminist ideas to suggest that religion serves the needs of individuals and its importance has not diminished in industrial capitalist society.

- According to them, at the root of religion lay the human desires for scarce resources like wealth and status, and the desire for life after death.

- They argue that religion offers a 'compensator', a belief that a reward will be obtained in the distant future or in some other context. For example, the belief that there will be a Judgement day, that there will be a political revolution in the future, the belief that working hard now will lead to fame and riches, etc.
- These compensators are based on assumptions about a supernatural entity that has endowed life with meaning, and universe with a design.
- So long as religious organizations store their beliefs in the supernatural, religion will stay relevant.
- Stark and Bainbridge also refused the idea that secularization has taken place or will take place in the future.

Criticism

- Roy Wallis and Steve Bruce have argued that new religious movements have not attracted sufficient number of recruits as the older religions, showing a decline in popularity of religion in the younger generations.
- Wallis and Bruce also argue that rather than human desires, it is the society and its culture that cultivate the need for religion.
- They also criticise Stark and Bainbridge for ignoring the role of religion in maintaining status quo and unequal structures of power

Types of Religious Practices – Monism and Pluralism

Feature	Monism	Pluralism
Nature of Reality	Belief in a single ultimate reality or truth underlying all religious expressions. In Western culture, the term was coined by Christian Wolff.	Recognition of multiple and diverse realities or truths coexisting. It is opposed to exclusivism and is different from syncretism – which calls for mixing of different beliefs into one single output.
Common Essence	Assumes a shared essence or source among different religious traditions.	It acknowledges diversity and can exist in an atmosphere of freedom of religion, expression and mutual tolerance.
Interconnectedness	Emphasises the interconnectedness of various religious paths leading to the same reality.	Recognises and respects the distinctiveness of different religious paths.

Feature	Monism	Pluralism
Thinkers	Preached by philosophers like Thales, Plotinus, Adi Shankara, etc. Various sufi saints also stress upon the concept of a single all-powerful entity. E.B. Tylor contended that monotheistic religions are hallmark of a modern society. Baruch Spinoza, a 17th century philosopher, was a key influence in spreading the idea of pantheism.	Steve Bruce has said that religious pluralism undermines the basis of communal orthodoxy and is a sign of growing secularization Peter Berger has linked pluralization with modernization. Bryan Wilson has stated that with pluralization, religious values become personal values.
Examples	Islam is the most popular and widespread monotheistic religion. In pantheism, there is no strict separation between the divine and the material or natural world. Instead, the entire cosmos is considered divine or a manifestation of a single, ultimate reality. This idea is found in religions like Hinduism, Buddhism, etc. This ideology has had noted followers like William Wordsworth, Ralph Waldo Emerson, Henry David Thoreau and Einstein.	Hinduism as a religion contains various traditions like Vaishnav, Shaiv, Dwait, etc. Christianity has Calvinists, Methodists, Protestants, Catholics.
	Theological states like Iran, Afghanistan, Somalia, Israel, etc., have one specific religion endorsed by the state. Countries like Laos do not have an official religion but have a preferred religion, which in this case is Buddhism.	Multicultural societies like India, USA, Russia, etc., where diverse religious practices coexist without necessarily merging into a common essence.

Religions in the World

Totemism and Animism

These two are associated with the smaller pre-literate cultures. Totemism has been discussed above in relation to Durkheim (Refer Pg 8.6). Its modern representations are visible in the form of mascots, flags, emblems containing plants or animals as symbols, etc.

Animism, also discussed above in relation to E.B. Tylor, refers to a belief in spirits and ghosts, thought to co-exist in and populate the same world as human beings. The spirits could be perceived to be either benign or malevolent, influencing human behaviour in different aspects. According to Tylor, the primitive man saw soul to separate from the body during sleep for brief period and after death, permanently. Thus, to the primitive man, everything that underwent growth and decay, like elements in nature—trees, animals, etc., came to be associated with spirits.

Teton Sioux of America practised animistic religion in which spirits played negative role in their lives and they performed a Ghost Dance ceremony to appease them. Evans Pritchard in his study of Nuer of South Sudan found that the tribal people worshipped a Sky Spirit or High God. In India, among Hindus, ancestor worship is prevalent through notions of *pitra* and *shraadh*. According to Tylor, the 'most ancient form of animistic practice is manifested in terms of ancestor worship'. The theory of animism as given by Tylor has been criticized by the post-modernists who suggest that all societies animate their social world, not just the primitives. It is not confined to smaller cultures. For instance, in Medieval Europe, those believed to be possessed by evil spirits were persecuted as sorcerers or witches. In modern society, people develop personal relationships with elements of the objective world such as toys, pets, etc. This reflects a form of 'new animism'.

Judaism, Christianity and Islam

These three are the most influential monotheistic religions of the world and originated in the Middle East.

(a) **Judaism:** It is one of the oldest monotheistic religions, with its origins tracing back to approximately 2000 BCE with Abraham, though the unified kingdom of Israel was established around 1000 BCE. The early Hebrews were a nomadic people who migrated through the ancient Near East, including periods in Egypt, and their religious traditions developed through encounters with various regional cultures and beliefs. Jewish theology emphasizes ethical monotheism, with adherence to divine commandments and moral codes as central tenets. Throughout history, Jewish communities established themselves across Europe, North Africa, and Asia, often facing periods of persecution and displacement. When the modern state of Israel was established in 1948, it became the first nation-state to recognize Judaism as having a special status, though it does not have an official state religion in the formal sense.

References:

- Sarna, Nahum M. *Understanding Genesis: The Heritage of Biblical Israel*. New York: Schocken Books, 1966.
- Neusner, Jacob. *The Way of Torah: An Introduction to Judaism*. 7th edition. Belmont, CA: Wadsworth Publishing, 2003.

(b) **Christianity:** It originated in the 1st century CE as a sect of Judaism, with Jesus of Nazareth, an Orthodox Jew, being its central figure. Early Christians, primarily Jewish followers of Jesus, faced persecution both within the Jewish community and from Roman authorities for refusing to worship Roman gods and the emperor, which was seen as an act of defiance. Under emperors like Nero (64 CE) and Diocletian (303–311 CE), Christians were subjected to severe punishments, including executions and destruction of their places of worship. The turning point came with Emperor Constantine's conversion and the Edict of Milan in 313 CE, which granted Christians the freedom to worship. By 380 CE, Christianity became the official religion of the Roman Empire under Theodosius I, leading to its growth as a dominant cultural and religious force in Western civilization.

(c) **Islam:** Islam derives from the teachings of Prophet Muhammad dating back to 7th century CE. The pillars of Islam refer to the five essential duties of Muslims: The first is the recitation of Muslim creed on recognising no other god than Allah and Muhammad as his apostle; the second is on recitation of prayers five times a day; the third is of giving alms to the poor; the fourth is the observance of Ramadan and finally, the fifth, is the effort on part of each follower to attempt a pilgrimage to Mecca.

The Religions of the Far East

(a) **Hinduism:** The oldest of all the great religions in the world today is Hinduism, dating back to 6000 years ago. It is a polytheistic religion and is extremely internally diverse. Some of the key features of Hinduism include: the doctrine of reincarnation (samsara) and karma, a complex social stratification system traditionally known as varna and jati (often referred to as the caste system), and a remarkable diversity of beliefs, practices, and philosophical schools. Unlike some organized religions, Hinduism has historically emphasized orthopraxy (correct practice) over orthodoxy (correct belief) and generally does not engage in systematic missionary activities or proselytization.

References:

- Flood, Gavin D. *An Introduction to Hinduism*. Cambridge: Cambridge University Press, 1996.
- Klostermaier, Klaus K. *A Survey of Hinduism*. 3rd edition. Albany: SUNY Press, 2007.
- Lipner, Julius J. *Hindus: Their Religious Beliefs and Practices*. 2nd edition. London: Routledge, 2010.

(b) **Buddhism, Confucianism, Taoism:** These religions have no gods. They espouse ethical ideals to relate the believer to the natural cohesion and unity of the universe. Buddhism advocated achieving salvation through the renunciation of desire and by leading a life of self-discipline and meditation. Confucius, a 6th century teacher, taught how to adjust human life to the inner harmony of nature and focused on the veneration of ancestors. Taoism shares similar principles, stressing meditation and non-violence as means to the higher life.

Religious Organizations

Early theorists such as Max Weber, Ernst Troeltsch and Richard Niebuhr described religious organizations as falling along a continuum, based on the degree to which they are well-established and conventional: churches lie at one end (conventional and well-established), cults on the other and sects fall somewhere in the middle.

Churches and Sects

Weber and Troeltsch distinguished between church and the sect in the following manner:

Church	Sect
1. A church is a large, well-established religious body.	1. A sect is a smaller, less highly organized grouping of committed believers, usually formed in protest against what a church has become.
2. Churches have a formal, bureaucratic structure, with a hierarchy of religious officials.	2. Sects are comparatively smaller, do not always have a formal organization and lack officials. However, they often form around an inspirational leader.
3. They tend to represent the conservative face of religion.	3. Sects aim at discovering and following 'the true way', and tend to withdraw from the surrounding society into communities of their own.
4. Most adherents follow the footsteps of their parents in being the church members.	4. Members of sect regard established churches as corrupt and all members are regarded as equal participants.
5. Members are born into the tradition of the church.	5. A small proportion of people are born into sects, but most actively join them to further their beliefs.
6. For example, the Catholic Church	6. For example, Calvinists, Methodists

Denominations and Cults

To the church/sect typology, Howard Becker added further two: the denomination and the cult.

Denominations

- A denomination is a sect which has cooled down and has become an institutionalized body rather than an active protest group. Sects which survive any period of time inevitably become denominations. For example, Calvinism and Methodism were sects in their initial years of formation and over a period of time became more respectable.
- Denominations are recognized by churches as more or less legitimate and exist alongside them often cooperating harmoniously with them.

Cults

- Cults resemble sects but have different emphasis. They are the most loosely knit and transient of all religious organizations. They are composed of individuals who reject the values of the outside society. Their focus is on individual experience, bringing together like-minded individuals.

- People do not formally join a cult and are allowed to maintain other religious connections. They follow particular theories or particular ways of behaviour. Like sects, cults also form around an inspirational leader. For example, believers in astrology, transcendental meditation, believers of leaders like Osho, etc.
- What is a cult in one country may well be an established religious practice in another. For example, Christianity began as an indigenous cult in ancient Jerusalem.

Sects and Cults

Sects and cults emerge in contemporary society as responses to sociocultural and existential crises. Sects typically arise from established religious traditions, representing a protest against perceived corruption or dogmatism within the parent organization. They appeal to individuals seeking spiritual purity, moral guidance, or alternative interpretations of faith. Cults, however, are often characterized by their novel, unorthodox beliefs and charismatic leadership, forming around the quest for individual meaning, identity, or empowerment in a rapidly changing world.

Emergence of Sects and Cults in Contemporary Society

1. **Response to Sociocultural Crises:**
   - **Sects:** Often emerge as reform movements within established religions, protesting against perceived corruption or rigidity.
     Example: The Protestant Reformation led by Martin Luther was a response to the perceived excesses of the Catholic Church.
   - **Cults:** Form around new, unorthodox beliefs or practices, offering alternative spiritual or ideological frameworks.
     Example: Scientology, which promotes unique ideas about spirituality and personal growth.
2. **Factors Contributing to Their Rise:**
   - **Social Alienation:** Individuals experiencing isolation may seek belonging in these groups.
     Example: Urbanization and migration often lead to a breakdown of traditional communities, driving people toward sects or cults for support.
   - **Economic Instability:** Economic hardship prompts individuals to turn to groups promising hope and material improvement.
     Example: Cults offering prosperity theology or financial success attract economically vulnerable populations.
   - **Fragmentation of Traditional Institutions:** The weakening of family structures and religious institutions creates a vacuum for alternative affiliations.
   - *Example:* New Age movements gaining popularity as alternatives to traditional religions.
3. **Role of Charismatic Leadership:** Charismatic leaders often inspire devotion and obedience, forming the nucleus of cults.
   Example: Jim Jones and the Peoples Temple, which led to the tragic Jonestown incident.

4. **Digital Communication and Recruitment:** Social media and online platforms facilitate global reach and recruitment.
   Example: QAnon, a contemporary cult-like conspiracy group, uses digital media for propagation and membership growth.
5. **Psychological Needs:** These groups fulfill deep needs for meaning, identity, and belonging in a complex world.
   Example: The Hare Krishna movement appeals to those seeking spiritual solace and community.

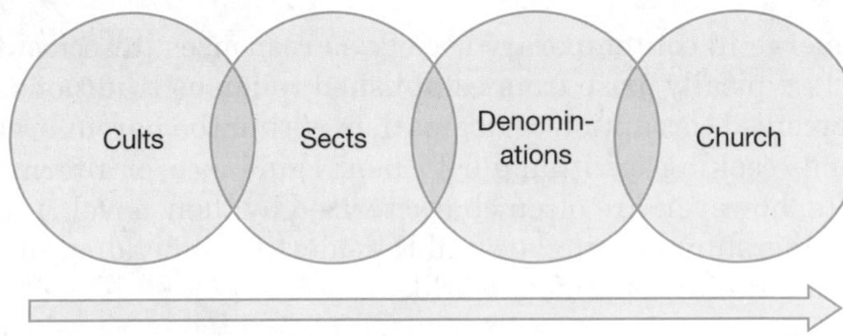

Jeffrey K. Hadden, a leading sociologist of religion, explains that nearly all of the approximately 100,000 religions that exist today started as new and often despised cults, eventually evolving into sects, denominations, and established churches as they gained acceptance and legitimacy over time.

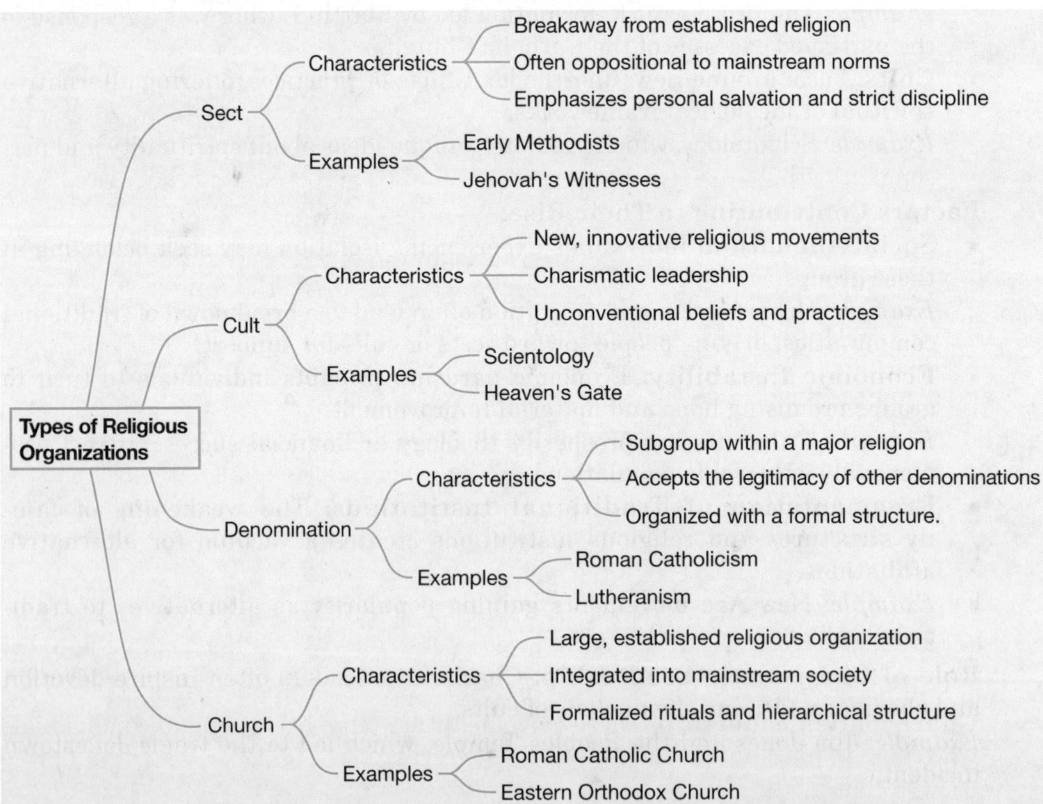

Religious Movements

A religious movement is an association of people who join together to spread a new religion or to promote a new interpretation of an existing religion. They are larger than sects and less exclusivist in membership but are not clearly distinct from them. To a degree, all sects and cults can be classified as religious movements.

Phases of Development

- **First Phase:** The movement derives its life and cohesion from a powerful leader. Max Weber classified such leaders as charismatic. Example – Jesus, Muhammad. The leaders of religious movements are usually critical of the existing religious establishment and seek to proclaim a new message. In the early years, the movement is usually fluid and lacks any established authority system. The members are normally in direct contact with the leader and together they spread the new teachings.
- **Second Phase:** This phase starts with the death of the leader.The movement now faces what Weber terms 'routinization of charisma'. To survive, it creates certain formalized rules and procedures. Many movements fade during this phase. A movement that survives and takes on a permanent character becomes a formal religious organization such as the church. The church itself at a later point might become a source of origin of other movements.

New Religious Movements

- This term is used to refer to a range of religious and spiritual activities, groups, cults and sects that have emerged alongside the established larger mainstream religions. Many new religious movements are derived from the major religious traditions. Membership in new religious movements mostly consists of converts. Members are well-educated and mostly belong to middle-class backgrounds. People who find traditional religions as ritualistic and devoid of spiritual meaning may find comfort and a greater sense of community in smaller, less impersonal new religious movements.
- The popularity of new religious movements has been explained on several accounts such as:
  (a) Some see them as a response to the processes of secularization and liberalization.
  (b) Some see them as an outcome of rapid social change.
  (c) These movements hold an appeal for the people who feel alienated from mainstream society.

Characteristics of New Religious Movements

Innovative Beliefs and Practices

New Religious Movements (NRMs) bring in new ideas and rituals that make them distinct from mainstream religions.

1. **Charismatic Leadership**: These movements are often led by dynamic individuals who claim to have unique insights or divine revelations.

2. **Personal Transformation Focus**: They emphasise personal spiritual growth and transformation.
3. **Inclusive or Exclusive Membership**: Some NRMs welcome anyone interested, while others require a high level of commitment and separation from mainstream society.
4. **Adaptability**: They tend to be flexible and can easily adapt their practices and structures.

Roy Wallis's Categorization of New Religious Movements

Sociologist Roy Wallis created a way to classify NRMs based on how they relate to society and their truth claims. His framework includes three main types:

1. **World-rejecting NRMs**
   - **Characteristics:** These groups are often critical of the current social order and advocate for drastic changes or complete withdrawal from mainstream society. They stress the need for spiritual purity and a break from worldly life.
   - **Examples:** The Unification Church (Moonies), the Children of God, and the Branch Davidians.
   - **Explanation:** World-rejecting NRMs demand a lot from their members, such as communal living and strict adherence to the group's beliefs. They view the outside world as corrupt and believe salvation lies in total commitment to the movement.
2. **World-affirming NRMs**
   - **Characteristics:** These groups accept the world as it is but offer ways for individuals to achieve personal success, enlightenment, or self-improvement. They often provide practical techniques and focus on personal development.
   - **Examples:** Scientology, Transcendental Meditation, and the Human Potential Movement.
   - **Explanation:** World-affirming NRMs give their followers tools to improve their lives within the current social structure. They are generally less demanding about lifestyle changes and more focused on helping individuals achieve personal goals.
3. **World-accommodating NRMs**
   - **Characteristics:** These movements don't fully reject or embrace the world. Instead, they aim to revive the spiritual aspects of existing religious traditions, emphasising inner spiritual life over societal transformation.
   - **Examples:** Neo-Pentecostalism and certain forms of charismatic Christianity.
   - **Explanation:** World-accommodating NRMs encourage their members to stay engaged with society while deepening their spiritual lives. They often emerge as reform movements within established religions, aiming to restore lost elements of spirituality.

Application and Relevance

Understanding NRMs helps us grasp the changing landscape of spirituality today. These movements often reflect broader social and cultural trends, showing how people seek meaning and community in modern times. Sociologists study NRMs to explore issues like authority, identity, and the impact of globalization on religious practices.

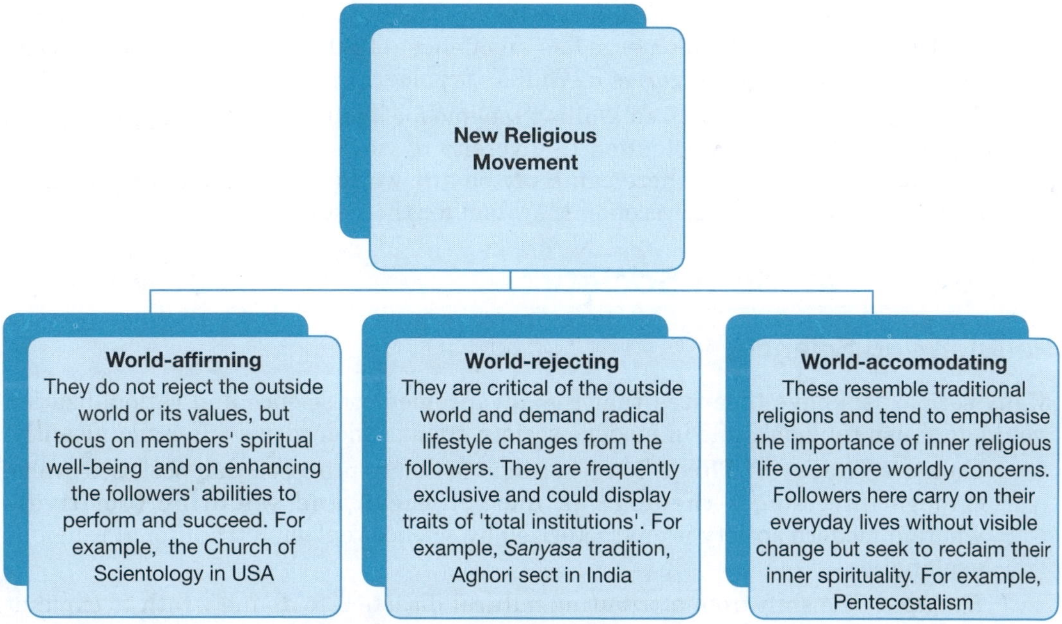

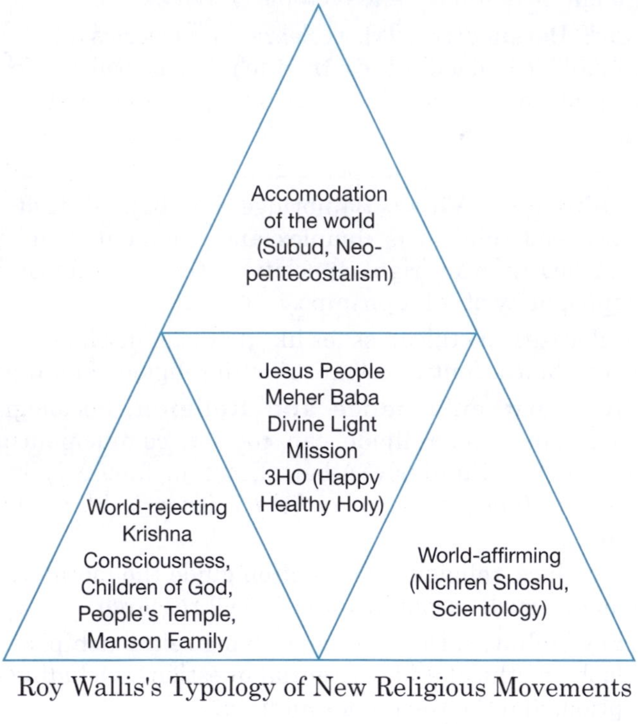

Roy Wallis's Typology of New Religious Movements

- Wallis acknowledged the limitations of rigid categorization, recognizing that religious organizations often exhibit characteristics that span multiple categories rather than fitting neatly into a single classification. He observed that many movements display hybrid features that challenge clear-cut boundaries between his three types. A notable example is the Happy Healthy Holy (3HO) organization in the United States, which emerged as an offshoot of Sikhism but incorporates elements from all three categories in Wallis's typology.
- James Beckford has criticized Wallis's scheme for its difficulty to be applied in the real world, insufficient attention to diversity of views within the movement and has questioned whether there can truly be any world-rejecting movements since all interact with the wider economic system for their survival.

Religion in Modern Society

Religion and Science

Many sociologists have theorized that the advancement of science and rationalization would diminish religion's role in modern society, though their views differ significantly:

- **Comte's Theory of Three Stages:** Auguste Comte proposed that societies evolve through three stages–**theological, metaphysical, and scientific (positive)**–wherein modern society is characterized by science replacing traditional religious explanations.

  Example: The shift from attributing natural disasters to divine wrath to explaining them through meteorology and tectonic activity.
- **Edward Tylor's Perspective:** Tylor celebrated science as a hallmark of modernity, viewing it as infallible and a direct contrast to religious beliefs. He argued that scientific reasoning promotes progress by replacing superstition with empirical evidence.
- **Herbert Spencer's Opposition:** Spencer viewed science and religion as fundamentally opposing forces --science being grounded in reason and religion in faith.
- **William Bainbridge's View:** Bainbridge highlighted that the relationship between science and religion is complex and fragmented in modern times. He argued that rather than outright opposition, the two coexist in diverse forms, reflecting a multiplicity of relationships.

  Example: The debates on ethical issues like artificial intelligence and genetic engineering often combine scientific advances with religious moral perspectives.
- **Compatibility Between Science and Religion:** Sociologist **Steve Bruce** asserted that science and religion can coexist, complementing each other in different areas of life. Similarly, Albert Einstein famously remarked, '*Science without religion is lame, religion without science is blind,*' emphasizing their interdependence.

  Example: In bioethics, religious values often guide the moral application of scientific advancements, such as cloning or stem cell research.
- **Contemporary Debates:** Despite the evolving relationship, science and religion continue to clash on ethical and existential questions, including euthanasia, cloning, contraception, and the theory of evolution.

Aspect	Role of Religion	Role of Science
Source of Authority	Sacred texts, religious leaders, divine guidance	Empirical evidence, scientific community, peer-reviewed research
Worldview and Meaning	Provides moral and ethical frameworks, existential purpose. It can be imaginative and speculative.	Describes the natural world, offers technological solutions. It is generally investigative and deliberative. Darwin's theory of evolution is in contrast to theological thinking that God is the source of all creation.
Social Cohesion	Unites communities through shared beliefs and rituals	Promotes a shared understanding of natural phenomena
Social Control	Establishes moral codes, prescribes behavioural norms	Develops laws based on empirical evidence, encourages ethical conduct
Education and Knowledge Transmission	Teaches religious doctrines, moral values. It shares knowledge on what cannot be perceived through the senses, and thus is immeasurable. Lacks universal validity.	Advances knowledge through formal education, research, and innovation. Lays emphasis on measurement and precision. Through correct methodology, can gain universal validity and reliability.
Response to Uncertainty and Anxiety	Offers spiritual comfort, explanations for the unknown	Investigates the unknown, seeks evidence-based explanations
Attitude Towards Change	May resist change to preserve traditions and doctrines. It could encourage fatalism and discourage questioning.	Embraces change, adapts based on new evidence and understanding. It is liberating and promotes the questioning of everything.
Conflict and Cooperation	Can be a source of conflict between different religious groups	Encourages collaboration in the pursuit of shared knowledge
Role in Governance	May influence political structures and laws based on religious principles	Contributes to evidence-based policy-making, technological advancements
Cultural Identity	Shapes cultural identity through religious practices and beliefs	Shapes cultural identity through scientific achievements and progress

Secularization

- The word secular is derived from the Latin word 'secular', which means the 'present age or generation'. Secularization came into use in Europe, to describe the transfer of territories previously under the control of the church to the dominion of secular authority or the state. Social thinkers have used the word secularization to indicate a process whereby the religious institutions and religious conceptions and understanding have lost control in wordly matters—economy, polity, justice, health, family, and so on.
- According to Bryan Wilson, secularization refers to the 'process of structure differentiation in which social institutions (the economy,the polity, morality, justice, education, health, and family) become recognized as distinctive concerns operating with considerable autonomy. It is a process in which conceptions of the supernatural lose their sovereignty over human affairs.'

Evolution of Secularization

- Secularization occurred in Europe in times when society was undergoing through different types of changes.
  1. **Renaissance (14th–16th Centuries):** Rational enquiry was the essence of this movement and the increasing number of people who could read and write began to work out new ideas for themselves.
  2. **Growth of Science:** The renaissance also was the period which saw the Copernican Revolution which demonstrated that the earth moved around a fixed sun. This period also saw the growth of various disciplines of science. William Harvey discovered the circulation of blood. This led to the rethinking about the human body. In Physics, Galileo Galilei, Johannes Kepler, and subsequently Issac Newton shattered the earlier metaphysical thoughts of the universe. In short, the growth of science and the application of science reduced man's dependence on religion and the divine interpretation of the universe.
  3. **Expansion of Trade and Commerce:** The 15th century AD also signaled a shift from the subsistent and stagnant economy to a dynamic and worldwide system. One of the most important results of this expansion of trade and commerce was the growth of middle class. This class, which included merchants, bankers, shipowners, became an influential and politically powerful group.
  4. **Reformation:** In the 16th century, there was a movement within Christianity to purge the medieval abuses and to restore the doctrine and the practices that the reformers believed confirmed with the Bible. This led to a breach between the Roman Catholic Church, and the reformers whose belief and practices came to be called as Protestantism. The Protestant conception of the divine made God personal. God thus receded to the personal realm.

Various Aspects of Secularization

Some scholars have argued that secularization is not strictly a modern phenomenon. It has occurred throughout history. Even in early primitive societies, supernaturalist apprehensions and explanations were mixed with empirical knowledge and rational techniques. Slowly, the process which Max Weber phrased as the 'disenchantment of the world' removed the natural phenomena of their magico-religious meaning. The modern society however has seen increasing degree of secularization, which is evident in the following aspects:

1. **Modification of Religious Practices:** Religions modify their doctrines and practices in response to the changing needs of members and other changes in the society. For example, in 1976, the Episcopal Church in the United States of America officially allowed women to become priests.
2. **Change in Religious Content:** Secularization also influences the content of religious beliefs and in doing so can lead to the development of a sect. Example Protestantism grew against the orthodoxy of Roman Catholicism and brought down religion to 'this world'
3. **Increasing Attention to Public Issues:** Secularization in religion is usually accompanied by increase in attention to public issues. For example, religious institutions get involved with running of modern hospitals and secular educational institutions or engaging in philanthropic activities.
4. **Development of Monotheistic Religions:** Monotheistic religions like Judaism and Christianity introduced a more universalistic conception of an increasingly transcendental and universal deity. In this process, the monotheistic religions heralded a process of systematization or rationalization.
5. **Decline in Participation in Institutionalized Religion:** In 'Religion in a Secular Society' (1966), Bryan Wilson argued, 'The decline in organized religion participation indicates a way in which the churches are losing the direct influence over ideas and activities of man.'
6. **Structural Differentiation:** Today, education, politics and social welfare are no longer functions of religion. Bryan Wilson has highlighted how secularization has led to the process of various social institutions becoming increasingly distinct from each other and thus increasingly free from the matrix of religious assumptions.
7. **Societalization:** In 'Secularization', Steve Bruce has compared the earlier close-knitted integrated societies with the modern, complex ones wherein large bureaucratic organizations have taken over and resultant societalization has rendered even religion subject to inquiry.
8. **Increasing Religious Pluralism:** As opposed to monotheism as a sign of rationality, the fact that multiple religions co-exist has led scholars to believe that religious loyalties are now becoming more of a matter of convenience. In such a situation, Bryan Wilson argues, religious values are no longer the values of the whole community.
9. **Growing Individualism:** Individuals today prefer to work out their own path of salvation.
10. **Desacralization:** The sacred is losing its relevance as more and more people are accessing the world in empirical and rational terms. Bryan Wilson states that men act less and less in response to religious motivation.

Point to Note

Secularization vs Secularism

Secularization refers to the process by which religious institutions, practices, and beliefs lose social and cultural significance over time, particularly in modern societies. It is a sociological phenomenon where religion's influence diminishes in public life and is often replaced by rationality and science. For example, in many Western countries, church attendance has declined, and policies are increasingly shaped by scientific evidence rather than religious doctrine.

Secularism, on the other hand, is a principle or ideology advocating the separation of religion from the state, ensuring that government functions remain neutral in religious matters and that no religion is favored over another. For instance, the Indian Constitution upholds secularism by treating all religions equally while maintaining the state's non-interference in religious affairs. In contrast, France practices *laïcité*, a stricter form of secularism that limits the public expression of religion in state institutions.

While secularization is an observable process of declining religious influence, secularism is a deliberate political and legal framework promoting religious neutrality.

Continued Relevance of Religion

- In 'The Invisible Religion' (1967), Thomas Luckmann has argued that though religion has receded from the public sphere, it is still alive. Along with Luckmann, Peter Burger also argued that conventional theories on religion narrowly focused on Christian institutions, measuring religious importance in terms of attendance at Church. They observed that religion is practiced more in a personal capacity as a means to self-realization. The belief in the 'sacred' still underlies the prevailing individualism in modern society. This phenomenon came to be known as the 'invisible religion'.
- A study by Kaufmann indicates that while church attendance has decreased, number of believers has not. Davie, 'Religion in Modern Europe' (2000) has called this 'belief without belonging'.
- Rise of new religious movements also shows that religion continues to exist in a renewed form.
- In a globalized world, religion continues to provide a central source of identity.
- Civic or civil religion continues has characterized all forms of society and continues to hold sway.
- Samuel Huntington has argued that as the world is shrinking, various civilizations are coming in increasingly close contact with each other in the process intensifying 'civilizational consciousness'. This situation is leading to the growth of 'unsecularisation'.

FYI

Peter Beyer – Globalization and Religion

Peter Beyer has defined globalization as a situation in which previously isolated civilizations and cultures are now close together, in almost unavoidable contact. This, he says, can cause two types of effects:

1. Increased danger of clashes between different cultures
2. Increased contact might reduce the differences and therefore the likelihood of conflicts

Beyer suggests that since global society involves a conflict between particularism (emphasis on distinctive characteristics of particular groups) and universalism (emphasis on similarities between people), going forward, religion may take one of the three ways:

1. It might retreat into a limited, privatized role as other sub-systems like economy and polity will have a more prominent role to play.
2. Religion can act as a central source of identity and be used for mobilization of masses to seek power and influence in alignment with nationalistic goals.
3. Religion could bring together different beliefs and faiths for common issues such as poverty, religious environmentalism, etc.

Beyer has concluded that religion will not lead to demise of religion but will limit its influence.

Case of India

- Weber had argued that as rationality and scientific thoughts increase, secularism will increase and space of religion will decrease. While it is true that religion has ceased to have a kind of hold that it had in the medieval society, secularization has not occurred uniformly all over the world.
- In India, secularization and secularism have been used in the context of nature of the state. In India, the term secularism implies that the state will not identify with any one religion but is tolerant of all religious practices. At the same time, the citizens enjoy the right to freedom of religion and worship as a fundamental right.
- T N Madan has noted that 'religion and secular cannot be separated, in other words, religion cannot be in any meaningful sense privatized.' During the national struggle for freedom, Mahatma Gandhi openly declared the necessity of religion in politics. Although deeply rooted in Hindu popular ethos, Gandhi believed in pluralism and equal respect for all religions. However, the growing extremist tendencies led to nationalism that came to defined by religion. India's partition in 1947 and Gandhi's assassination in 1948 led the Indian leaders to develop a secular ideology in order to keep politics and religion separate.

FYI

Civil Religion

- The term was first used by J.J. Rousseau in his work 'The Social Contract' (1762) and later developed by Emile Durkheim in 'The Elementary Forms of Religious Life' (1912). According to Rousseau, civic religion is the religion of the citizen – a public matter of the individual's relationship with the society and state or government. Religion of the 'man' on the other hand is a private matter between individual and God.
- Robert Nisbet has defined civil religion as 'the religious or quasi-religious regard for certain civic values and traditions found recurrently in the history of the political states.' This regard for the civic values and traditions of the political state is expressed through special festivals, rituals, creeds and dogmas which honour great personages and events of the past. For example - the celebrations of Independence Day on 15th August and Republic Day on 26th January.
- These celebrations are marked by a semi-religious fervour. They serve to heighten the sense of national and political identify of the Indian citizens and remind them of the sacrifices made by our leaders like Mahatma Gandhi, Jawaharlal Nehru, Bal Gangadhar Tilak, Bhagat Singh, Chandra Shekhar Azad and several others who fought for Independence.
- Carlton J.H. Hayes' in his Book Essays on Nationalism (1926) writes that if we examine human history, we will find that the mainspring of frequency and the force of human movements have been of 'religious emotion'. It is in this context of the sense of religion, the feeling of patriotism or nationalism, of belonging to a distinct socio-political group that we have to understand the concept of civil religion. Civil religion is the religion of an advanced modern society with higher technology. As Nisbet mentions, civil religion has been a highly visible aspect of the modern national state in the West.

- The term 'secular' does not mean separation of state from religion, but implies neutrality of state to all religions. Secularism, in India means religious equidistance, but not non-involvement. Here religion is not the determinant of Indians citizenship, it is their birthright.

Though secularism came to be an important ideal in governance, the masses in India are still steeped in religion with its myths, legends and folklore. Mobilising one's own community on religious and ethnic lines is very often the practice. The State political parties on the other hand address communities to gain support. This only reinforces the primordial identities of community and religion.

Religious Revivalism and Fundamentalism

Religious revivalism is a broader term to refer to revival of religion in a variety of ways – such as increase in religious participation, growth of organizations such as sects, cults, denominations, increased inclination to spiritual pursuit or even to radical resurgence such as in the case of fundamentalism. So, fundamentalism is a type of religious revivalism even though the two terms could be used interchangeably.

Fundamentalism refers to a belief in and strict adherence to a core set of principles, often religious, which may arise as a reaction to perceived compromises with modern social and political values. Karen Armstrong notes that 'all fundamentalisms follow a certain form: they are embattled forms of spirituality that emerge in response to a perceived crisis.' In such responses, the approach is neither democratic nor tolerant. Instead of engaging in dialogue, fundamentalism often manifests through denial, rejection, and withdrawal into a rigid belief that the 'old' ways represent the ultimate truth and goodness, while anything opposing them is viewed as evil. This worldview frames a cosmic struggle between good and evil, where 'good' is defined absolutely by the group's perspective, leaving no room for compromise. Such ideological rigidity has historically turned violent, contributing to significant conflicts, including the root causes of the World Wars.

- Fundamentalism emerged when there are drastic changes in society and change of pace which disturbs community life. This could lead to a loss of identity and rootlessness among people. In such situations, people search for hope and stability. Fundamentalism promises certitude and restitution of an earlier better age. The psychological appeal of this is too strong to be resisted.
- To achieve this earlier, better age the fundamentalist evolves a comprehensive and absolutist, rigid belief system and practice. This belief and practice promises to bring happiness. It is capable of motivating intense commitment among its followers and could be punitive to the non-believers. That is why fundamentalism very often takes on a rather aggressive, militant form where killing and terrorism are justified. Terrorism has been practiced throughout history and throughout the world. 5th century B.C. Greece recommended psychological terror against enemy populations. The Roman emperor Caligula (1st Century A.D.) used banishment, confiscation of property and execution to discourage opposition to his rule. The Spanish Inquisition (16th century) used arbitrary arrest, torture and execution to punish what was perceived as religious heresy. Robespierre openly advocated the use of torture during the French Revolution 1793-94 during the period known as the reign of terror. After the American Civil War (1861-65) the Southerners who wanted to retain slavery, set up a terrorist organization the Ku Klux Klan to intimidate supporters of freedom and Reconstruction. Terrorism was adopted by the Anarchists in the later 19th century in Europe, Russia and the United States.
- George Marsden in a comprehensive study entitled 'Fundamentalism and American Culture: The Shaping of Twentieth Century Evangelicalism' (1870–1925), explored the earliest use of the term fundamentalism. He found that the

terms fundamentalist and fundamentalism came from the name for a series of books published in 1912 which sought to bring out the fundamentals of Christian faith. These works constituted an attack upon science, especially evolutionism, liberal philosophy and liberal theology even. They were edited by popular evangelists and teachers whose intentions were to mark down those basic 'truth' which constituted the foundations of faith.

Example – Islamic resurgence in Iran – Bernard Lewis has pointed out that unlike Judiasm and Christianity which eventually became separate from the state, Islam, from the lifetime of Prophet Muhammad, was synonymous with the state. In the Iranian revolution of 1979, the then ruler Muhammad Reza Shah was overthrown because he had sided with the Western powers and had alienated the masses by separating religion from the State. It was at this juncture that leadership was provided by Ayatollah Ruhollah Khomeini. Khomeini had over the years spoken out against the policies and activities of the Shah.

- According to Steve Bruce, the following factors have contributed to the growth of fundamentalism:

  (i) Fundamentalist emerged as a reaction to the changes in traditions brought about by forces of modernization and secularization.

  (ii) Religions with single authoritative text have higher potential for fundamentalist tendencies as they offer greater scope for ideological cohesion and mobilization of people along specific beliefs.

  (iii) Threat perception or 'othering' of a common enemy can further solidify fundamentalist tendencies into concrete action.

  (iv) Presence of charismatic leaders and recruiters aids in growth of fundamentalism. Example- Abu Bakr-al-Baghdadi of the Islamic State.

  (v) Backing by the State or political parties helps fundamentalism to thrive. For example, the extremist Buddhist parties in Myanmar had a backing of the totalitarian state

- Gabriel Almond has given more factors such as unemployment, persecuted ethnic groups, radical social changes and specific historical circumstances such as colonial exploitation and nationalist fervor. For example, Iranian revolution was in reaction to colonial exploitation by the US led Western powers.

Features of Fundamentalism in the Contemporary Times

(a) Emphasis on infallibility of scriptures and doctrines

(b) God's words and the Divine law are proposed to be the basis of all aspects of society—polity, economic, social, culture, law, education apart from the domestic or personal lives of individuals.

(c) Fundamentalism does not believe in religious pluralism or in the equality of all religions.

(d) It is opposed to rationalism, humanism and secularism. It stresses on the superiority of and compliance to its own tenets.

(e) Fundamentalism equate traditional with not just right, but also 'pure'. Modern interpretations of religious beliefs are deemed to be polluted. For instance, Bhindranwala talked of the 'fallen Sikhs' due to their different lifestyles which involved haircuts and shaved faces.

(f) T.N. Madan has explained fundamentalist movements of possessing a collective character and of being led by charismatic leaders who are usually men.

(g) According to Peter Beyer, religious fundamentalism has close connections with expressions of nationalism.

(h) Fundamentalism also involves divergence of values with other religions, which may sometimes escalate into violence.

Point to Note

Fundamentalism, Traditionalism and Communalism

Traditionalism as compared to fundamentalism is quietest and it is content with pursuing religion in the sacred sphere without it spilling over into other domains particularly, the political. The element of activism is common to communalism and fundamentalism, whereas the communalists have a particular 'other', for the fundamentalists it is rather a case of 'us' versus 'the rest,' because the 'rest' is a 'general other.' Moreover, fundamentalism reaches deep into its philosophical and religious roots to define its community of believers. It looks inwards and is self-producing.

Aspect	Secularism	Seculariza-tion	Commu-nalism	Fundame-ntalism	Traditionalism
Definition	The principle of separating religion from government and public affairs.	The process by which religious institutions, practices, and beliefs lose their social significance.	A belief system that emphasises religious or ethnic community identity over national unity, often leading to conflict.	A strict adherence to specific theological doctrines typically in reaction against modernist theories.	Adherence to traditional beliefs, practices, and customs, often in opposition to change or innovation.

Aspect	Secularism	Secularization	Communalism	Fundamentalism	Traditionalism
Key Features	Equal treatment of all religions by the state. No official state religion.	Decline in religious influence on various aspects of society. Increase in rational and scientific thinking.	Prioritiz-ation of religious/ ethnic identity. Can lead to inter-group conflict and polarization.	Literal interpretation of sacred texts. Resistance to modern ideas and practices.	Preservation of cultural heritage and historical continuity. Resistance to modern influences and changes.
Examples	India: Constitutionally secular with no state religion. France: Laïcité ensuring separation of church and state.	Europe: Declining church attendance and influence in public life. Western Countries: Shift towards secular values in public policies.	India: Hindu-Muslim riots due to religious tensions. Pakistan: Sunni-Shia conflicts based on religious differences.	USA: Christian fundamentalism advocating for creationism in schools. Middle East: Islamic fundamentalism emphasizing Sharia law over secular law.	Amish communities in the USA maintaining traditional lifestyles. Japan: Shinto practices maintaining traditional rituals.
Impact	Promotes equality and non-discrimination.	Greater focus on individual rights and secular governance.	Can undermine national unity and social cohesion.	Often leads to resistance against progressive social changes.	Maintains cultural identity and social stability.
Challenges	Balancing freedom of religion with maintaining secular governance.	Potential loss of cultural heritage and community identity.	Escalation into violence and extremism.	Intolerance towards differing beliefs and cultural practices.	Conflict with modernization and progressive social policies.

Aspect	Secularism	Secularization	Communalism	Fundamentalism	Traditionalism
Relevance Today	Ensures diverse societies can coexist peacefully.	Reflects ongoing changes in belief systems and societal values.	Rising ethnic and religious tensions in multicultural societies.	Influence on political movements and policies in various regions.	Influence on conservative political and social movements.

Contemporary Trends

- In the study titled 'Strong Religion' (2003), Gabriel Almond and others had argued that different religious groups in different countries are moving towards fundamentalist ideology for different reasons.
- Victory of right-wing parties in different countries.
- In 2023, Asbury University of Kentucky, USA made news for a 24 hour prayer service that went on to last full 16 days. As days progressed, the clamour spread to other college campuses. More than 200,000 people converged on the small town of Willmore, Kentucky—a town of just 6,000 residents. In May 2023, at Pirate Coves, California, more than 4000 people were baptized at one time. This was the largest baptism in California history. These instances led many to proclaim that religious revival was growing in the United States.
- Growth of organizations like ISIS.
- The Israel-Gaza conflict has its roots in religious differences.
- Resurgence of fundamentalist organizations like Taliban in Afghanistan.
- Demands for Khalistan and agitations abroad reflect the simmering nature of militancy amongst some specific communities.
- In India, instances of religious revivalism should be analysed through instances such as (a) building of the much awaited Lord Rama Temple in Ayodhya, Uttar Pradesh; (b) multi-faith prayer ceremony at the inauguration of the new Parliament building; (c) handling of Hadia's conversion case; (d) ban on Tabacos in Karnataka; and; (e) cultural revival of religious places as part of Government planning in states such as Madhya Pradesh, etc.

Previous Year Question

2024

1. How does a multicultural society accommodate diversities of all kinds—ethnic, linguistic and religious? Discuss its major challenges. (10 Marks)
2. Discuss the concept of animism and differentiate it from naturism. (10 Marks)
3. Do modernization and secularization necessarily go together? Give your views. (20 Marks)
4. How do you understand the phenomena of the mushrooming of sects and cults in contemporary society? Discuss the factors responsible for the trend. (10 Marks)

2023

1. Highlight the differences and similarities between totemism and animism. (10 marks)
2. What functions does religion perform in a pluralistic society? (10 marks)
3. What are the new religious movements? Elaborate emphasizing their forms and orientations. (20 marks)

2022

1. Critically examine the relevance of Durkheim's views on religion in contemporary society. (10 marks)
2. Write a note on global trends of secularization. (10 marks)
3. How do little tradition and great tradition coexist in contemporary Indian society? (20 marks)

2021

1. Critically compare the views of E.B. Tylor and Max Muller on religion. (10 marks)
2. What is cult? Explain the growth of cults in the contemporary world. (10 marks)
3. Give your comments on the growth of religious revivalism in the present day context. (10 marks)

2020

1. Critically analyse Durkheim's views on elementary forms of religious life and role of religion. Also discuss the consequences of religious revivalism in contemporary society. (20 marks)

2. State the reasons for the various religious beliefs and practices in pre-modern societies. (10 marks)

2019

1. Are all world religions patriarchal? Substantiate your answer with examples. (20 marks)

Right Approach

2024

Q4. How do you understand the phenomena of the mushrooming of sects and cults in contemporary society? Discuss the factors responsible for the trend. (10 Marks)

Introduction: The mushrooming of sects and cults in contemporary society reflects a dynamic response to social, cultural, and spiritual needs in an era of rapid globalization and individualism. These groups often promise a sense of belonging, spiritual fulfillment, or solutions to existential crises, drawing followers from diverse demographics.

Body:

Factors Responsible for the Trend

1. **Alienation and Individualism:** Modern lifestyles often lead to isolation, with people turning to sects and cults for community and emotional support. Durkheim's concept of *anomie* explains this disconnect from societal norms.
2. **Spiritual Vacuum and Quest for Meaning:** Declining influence of traditional religions in urbanized societies has created a spiritual vacuum. Sects like ISKCON and cult-like organizations fill this gap by offering alternative paths.
3. **Globalization and Media Influence:** The internet and social media amplify the visibility of sects and cults, making their messages accessible globally. Groups like QAnon gained traction through digital platforms.
4. **Economic and Psychological Factors:** Economic uncertainties post-pandemic have driven people to seek stability and hope in charismatic leaders. Cults exploit these vulnerabilities.
5. **Charismatic Leadership:** Leaders like Gurmeet Ram Rahim Singh in India or NXIVM's Keith Raniere attract followers through promises of self-improvement or salvation.

Conclusion: The rise of sects and cults in contemporary society stems from alienation, spiritual quests, and the influence of media. Addressing these factors through community building and mental health awareness is essential to counter their exploitative potential.

2022

Q2. Write a note on global trends of secularization. (10 marks)

Introduction: Secularization refers to the diminishing influence of religion in public and personal spheres, often linked to modernization, urbanization, and rationalization. Globally, secularization trends vary across societies, with some regions experiencing a decline in religious influence while others witness its resurgence.

Body:

Global Trends of Secularization

1. **Western Societies:** In Europe and North America, the decline of religious adherence is evident. According to the Pew Research Center (2023), nearly 30% of adults in the U.S. identify as religiously unaffiliated, highlighting the growth of atheism, agnosticism, and humanism.
2. **Rising Secularism in Asia:** Urbanization in countries like Japan and South Korea has led to growing secular attitudes, with youth prioritizing material well-being over traditional religious practices.
3. **Resistance to Secularization in the Global South:** In Africa and parts of Asia, religion remains central to identity and community. Pentecostal movements in Africa and Islamic revivalism in the Middle East challenge secular ideologies.
4. **Globalization and Hybridization:** The interconnectedness of cultures has led to syncretism, where secular and spiritual elements coexist. For instance, spirituality-driven wellness movements in the West incorporate Eastern philosophies without formal religious affiliations.

Conclusion: Global secularization is uneven, influenced by socio-economic factors and regional histories. While the West experiences religious decline, parts of the Global South emphasize faith's role, showcasing the complexity of secularization as a global phenomenon.

CHAPTER 9

Systems of Kinship

In this Chapter

- Family, Household, Marriage
- Types and Forms of Family
- Lineage and Descent
- Patriarchy and Sexual Division of Labour
- Contemporary Trends
- Previous Years' Questions

Kinship

The kinship system refers to a set of persons recognized as relatives, either, by virtue of a blood relationship called consanguinity, or by virtue of a marriage relationship, that is called affinity. Kinship practices contribute to the maintenance of the society as a whole, aiding in its continuity over time and containing the conflicts that might potentially disrupt it. However, some customs like *sati*, female infanticide, child marriage, amniocentesis or killing of the female foetus, etc., have been dysfunctional and accordingly have been made illegal.

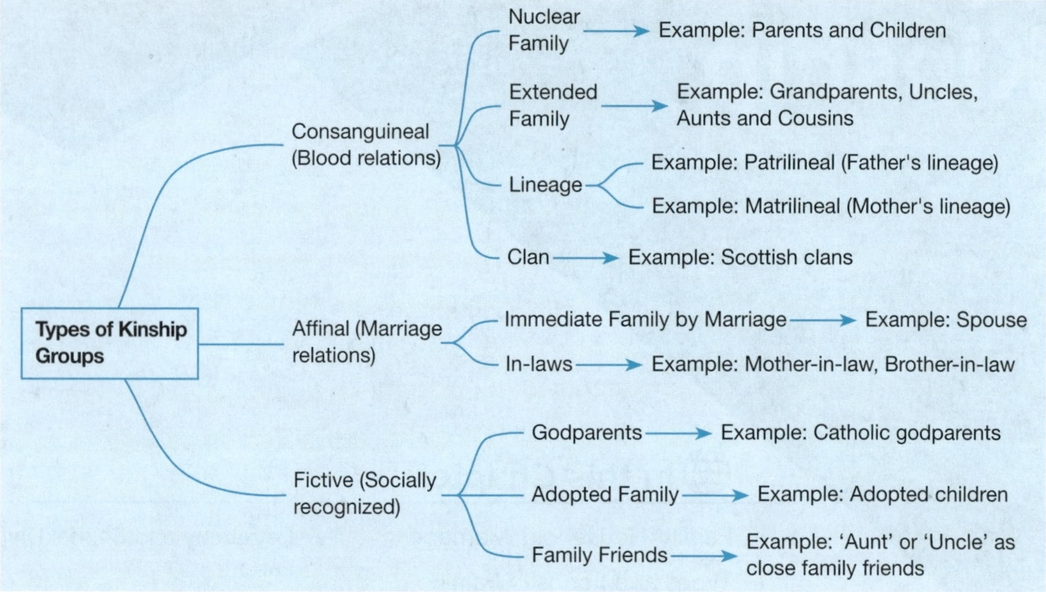

Lineage, Descent and its Principles

Lineage

Lineage can be understood in two ways:

(i) As a principle, it refers to how alignment and inheritance is chosen in a linear fashion. This arrangement is called line/lineage or *vanshavali* in Indian traditional system. For example, patrilineage (from male ancestors) or matrilineage (from female ancestors) which further create descent groups. Lineage groups are often exclusive in their membership and have common ritual observances, sometimes of a totemic nature.

(ii) Lineage also refers to a kingroup or *kula* (as is known in the traditional system) members of which can be traced back to a common ancestor whose identity is known and who is generally regarded as the founder of the group. The founder is an actual remembered person, unlike the clan where the ancestor is a mythical figure. Among the North Indian Hindus, there is an old practice of maintaining genealogical records in places like Hardiwar by Brahmin *pandits*, more commonly known as *pandas*.

Descent

Descent is the system of deriving relationships from a common ancestor. It is the rule whereby a child is socially affiliated with the group of his or her parents.

(i) **Bilateral or Cognatic Descent:** In this, the child is regarded as a descendant equally of both the father and the mother, although the titles and surnames continue to be passed down along the male line. This type of system is termed bilateral or cognatic. In this, the individual belongs simultaneously to several descent groups—those of the two parents, the four grandparents, the eight great-grandparents, and so on.

(ii) **Unilineal Descent:** In certain societies, descent is determined unilineally, meaning through a single line. This can either be patrilineal, where the child is affiliated with the father's group; or matrilineal, where the child is associated with the mother's group. In patrilineal descent, the father is often seen as the primary procreator, with the mother merely carrying the child. Conversely, in matrilineal descent, the father's role may not be recognized at all. The principle of unilineal descent provides individuals with a clear identification within a distinct social group that exists before their birth and continues after their death.

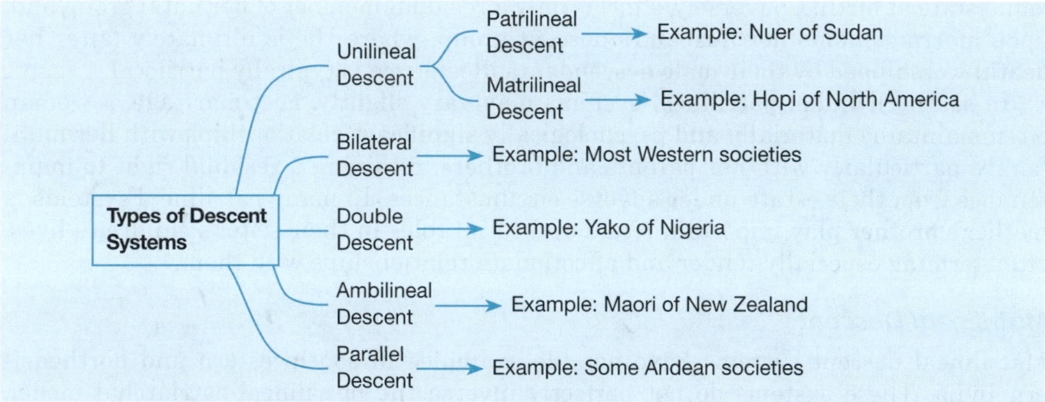

(iii) **Double Unilineal Descent:** In certain societies, children may be associated with either their mother's or father's group, depending on choice or specific aspects they inherit from each parent. For instance, they might receive property from one parent and ceremonial responsibilities from the other. This arrangement is known as Double Unilineal Descent. Members of such descent groups share a strong sense of identity, frequently addressing each other as 'brother' and 'sister.' These groups are often, though not always, marked by exogamy, meaning individuals are required to marry outside their descent group.

(iv) **Ambilineal or Cognatic Descent:** In this system, individuals decide how they want to trace back their lineage. They can do so via their father or mother or both. Parallel Descent: A rather rare rule of descent, it is sex-specific in which a boy follows patrilineal descent, and a girl follows matrilineal descent.

Functions of Descent Groups

- Unilineal descent groups tend to be 'corporate'. Their members often come together for ritual and ceremonial functions, for instance, for collective worship of lineage gods, totems or ancestors.
- The descent group has an existing built-in authority structure, with power normally exercised by senior males, and it may well own corporate property.
- An individual's economic rights and responsibilities is defined by his or her position in the descent group.
- In many societies, unilineal descent groups are also jural units, internally deciding their own disputes, and externally acting as a unified group in the conduct of feud, etc. Thus, it was common to see in societies lacking a centralized state structure that the lineage structure was often coterminous with the political structure.

Descent Systems

Patrilineal Descent

Patrilineal descent systems in India share many characteristics with similar groups globally. A boy becomes a member of his descent group and a coparcener (partner) in a joint estate at birth. Conversely, a girl is only a residual member of her natal group and, upon marriage, joins her husband's descent group, where she is ultimately (after her death) worshipped by their male descendants. Residence is typically patrilocal.

In southern India, patrilineal systems may vary slightly. Post-marriage, a woman often maintains materially and psychologically significant relationships with her natal family, particularly with her parents and brothers, retaining a residual right to maintenance from their estate under adverse circumstances. In many patrilineal systems, a mother's brother play important ritual and social roles in their sister's children's lives, often forming especially tender and affectionate relationships with them.

Matrilineal Descent

Matrilineal descent systems have notable examples in southwestern and northeastern India. These systems do not perfectly inverse the patrilineal-patriarchal model. Inheritance, while following matrilineal principles (such as passing from mother to daughter or from mother's brother to sister's son), often sees major property controlled, if not owned, by males.

Matrilineal kinship systems also present contradictions, particularly regarding residence. A man's dual role as both a father and a mother's brother can create a conflict between his affection for his own children and his jural responsibilities towards his sister's children.

Inheritance Rules

Inheritance rules generally align with the reckoning of descent in most societies, though not always directly. Often, immovable properties such as land and housing are passed from father to son, while movable properties like cash and jewellery are transferred from mother to daughter upon marriage.

Besides property, other assets like rights, obligations, esoteric knowledge, crafts, and skills may be passed down according to kinship roles. Succession to positions of authority, such as kingship, and other social roles and statuses, is frequently determined by kinship criteria. In these instances, the individual's status is considered 'ascribed' rather than 'achieved.'

Point to Note

Rules of Residence

- If husband and wife set up their own independent home after marriage, residence is said to be neolocal.
- When a wife moves into her husband's parents' home, the residence is referred to as virilocal, patrilocal, or patrivirilocal. Conversely, when a husband moves to live with his wife, it is known as matrilocal.
- Residence rules may align with or diverge from descent rules. Generally, patrilineal descent systems are associated with neolocal or patrivirilocal residence patterns.
- In contrast, matrilineal descent systems can be combined with any of the three residence types. Additionally, matrilineal systems may include avunculocal residence, where the couple resides with the mother's brother.

Patriarchy and Matriarchy

A society is considered patriarchal when certain conditions align: descent is patrilineal, major property inheritance is from father to son, residence is patrilocal, and authority is concentrated in the hands of senior males. Even in the rare matrilineal and matrilocal systems, major property is usually controlled by males, and authority is typically exercised by them, though women may enjoy higher status within the family and more decision-making power than in patriarchal systems. An exact reversal of patriarchy, termed matriarchy, has not been found anywhere in the world.

FYI

The Matrilineal Nayars of Kerala, Khasis and Garos of Assam

Among the Nayars of Kerala, men traditionally lived in large, matrilineally recruited joint families known as taravads, alongside their sisters, their sisters' children, and their sisters' daughters' children. They would visit their wives, who lived in other taravads, during the night—a practice commonly referred to as the 'visiting husband' system. The children stayed with their mother in her taravad. This system placed strong emphasis on the bond between brother and sister while de-emphasizing the husband-wife relationship. Nayar women could have multiple visiting husbands (polyandry), provided they were of the correct status, such as higher status Nayars or Namboodiri Brahmans. Similarly, Nayar men could have multiple wives (polygyny). Anthropologists have noted that the Nayar system challenges the notion that the nuclear family is a universal human institution.

There are numerous other matrilineal communities in India. For example, the Khasis of Assam practice matrilocal residence. The youngest daughter inherits the family home and resides there with her husband and their children, while the older daughter may leave upon marriage to establish new nuclear families. The husbands of these older daughters have more independent authority compared to the husband of the youngest daughter who remains in the matrilineal household.

The Garo people of Assam follow a different arrangement. In their community, marriage is matrilocal for the husband of the daughter who becomes the head of the household and its manager. There is a rule favouring cross-cousin marriage, ensuring that a man is succeeded by his sister's son, maintaining an ongoing alliance between the two linked lineages.

Distinctive features of kinship system in North India and South India, according to Iravati Karwe

Northern Zone	Southern Zone
1. In the Northern Zone, marriages are never between persons who are already closely related.	1. In the Southern Zone, there is a preference for marriage with certain categories of close kin, in particular with one or the other or both of the cross-cousins (but never parallel cousins), or even with the elder sister's daughter.
2. A rule of village exogamy (besides *gotra* and *sapinda* exogamy) exists to ensure that brides are given to and taken from other villages or towns, often at a considerable distance. The bride therefore arrives at her husband's family as a 'stranger'.	2. The marriage usually involves groups which are geographically quite proximate even from the same village (village endogamy).
3. The distinction between 'daughters' and 'brides' is very sharply emphasized in this system (as is evident in the practice of veiling), and the new bride's position is relatively vulnerable, unless she becomes the mother of a son.	3. The close relations ensure fair treatment of the bride as she is 'familiar' and like a daughter.

Distinctive features of kinship system in North India and South India, according to Iravati Karwe	
Northern Zone	**Southern Zone**
4. In this region, it is also often the case that marriages unite groups whose social status is already unequal, the wife-givers being of inferior status to the wife-takers (hypergamy), while the marriage transaction commonly (though again not always) takes the form of a 'dowry' payment.	4. The intermarrying groups are of comparable status.
5. Northern part is universally patrilineal, though patrilineal systems are also found among different communities in the southern or Dravidian zone and matrilineal systems can be found in the north-eastern areas.	5. Matrilineal system is found in communities like the Nayars of Kerala.

Though lineage and descent are often used interchangeably, there are some subtle differences between the two.

Comparison between Lineage and Descent		
Aspect	**Lineage**	**Descent**
Definition	A social group or kinship system based on tracing ancestry through a common ancestor. One can trace one's ancestor.	It is the principle by which a person is socially affiliated with a group, such as their grandparents and other ancestors. One often fails to trace one's ancestor who could be substituted with a mythical one.
Focus	Primarily focusses on the social organization of individuals who share a common genealogical ancestor	Encompasses a broader concept, including the passing down of traits, property, and social status from one generation to the next.
Nature of Connection	Emphasises the social and cultural ties among individuals who can trace their lineage to a common forebear.	Involves the biological or genealogical connection between generations, including both consanguineal (blood) and affinal (marriage) relationships.
Social Structure	Forms the basis for kinship groups and social organization within a community.	Encompasses a broader range of relationships beyond lineage, such as extended family, and other descent-based structures.
Cultural Significance	Often associated with shared rituals, ceremonies, and a sense of identity among members of the lineage.	Extends beyond social and cultural aspects, encompassing legal and economic implications related to inheritance and succession.

Aspect	Lineage	Descent
Examples	Caste-based lineages in India.	Inheritance of property or titles from parent to child. Example, the transmission of family name through generations.

The Family and the Household

Family

- Family as a concept broadly refers to the primary group comprising husband-wife (parents) and their children. This definition includes the ties of marriage between the spouses, (i.e., the parents) and of siblingship between children. Though this definition is accepted, many thinkers dispute the notion of a standard form of family.
- The two kinship links between i) parent-child and ii) siblings are found to exist in reality in various permutations and combinations, leading to the separation between nuclear/ elementary and joint/extended families.
  (i) A nuclear family is defined as a group consisting of a man, his wife and their unmarried children. Research has shown nuclear family to be of predominant type in history of Western Europe in comparison to the extended type.
  (ii) When there are additional relatives to any of the relations in the nuclear family it turns into a joint one. Thus, a joint family is a nuclear family plus all kin belonging to the side of husband and /or wife living in one homestead. The term joint and extended are used interchangeably in Sociology/Social Anthropology.
- When descent is traced through the male line, the extended/joint family is based on the extension between father-son relationship. On the other hand, an extension based on mother-daughter relationship forms a matrilineal extended/joint family. A horizontally extended family between brothers, their wives and children is called fraternal or collateral family.
- The ideal Hindu joint family consists of a man, his wife and their adult sons, their wives and children, and the younger unmarried children of the parental couple. This is called a patrilineal, patrivirilocal (the newly married couple taking residence in the husband's father's home) family. The oldest male heads the family and authority is hierarchically ordered along the lines of age and sex. In such a family, conjugal ties are considered subordinate to filial (father-son) and fraternal (relationship between brothers) ties. Members of the family are related by kinship bonds lineally or collaterally or both.
- The joint family holds property in common. However, not all members have the same right over the family property.

Common Features of a Family

- **Public as well as Private Institution:** Families function both as intimate private units and as social institutions subject to legal regulation, public policy, and societal expectations.

- **Near Universal Institution:** Found across virtually all human societies throughout history, though with significant cultural variations in structure and function.
- **Primary Agent of Socialization:** The first and most influential social group that teaches children cultural norms, values, language, and social roles.
- **Kinship-based Relationships:** Typically organized around blood relations, marriage, adoption, or other legally/socially recognized bonds.
- **Economic Cooperation Unit:** Members share resources, engage in division of labour, and provide economic support and security.
- **Reproductive and Sexual Regulation:** Provides socially sanctioned framework for procreation and sexual relationships.
- **Emotional Support System:** Offers intimacy, companionship, care during illness, and psychological security across the lifespan.
- **Status Ascription:** Determines initial social class, ethnicity, religion, and other social positions that influence life opportunities.
- **Multigenerational Continuity:** Transmits family heritage, property, traditions, and cultural practices across generations.
- **Social Control Mechanism:** Enforces behavioural norms and moral standards through informal sanctions and expectations.
- **Geographic and Residential Patterns:** Establishes household arrangements and community ties that vary by culture and economic conditions.
- According to Erving Goffman's dramaturgical notion, family is both the backstage and the front stage of a very substantial part of people's behaviour throughout their lives.
- A family may be large or small depending on the prevailing principles of organization of descent relations between the dependents of married persons.
- It is based on the principles of kinship whose members usually share a common residence. They reside in a house/homestead. This residential unit is called the household.
- Pauline Kolenda has proposed the 12 type classificatory scheme for family as follows:
  - (i) Nuclear Family, a couple with or without unmarried children
  - (ii) Supplemented nuclear family
  - (iii) Subnuclear family
  - (iv) Single person household
  - (v) Supplemented subnuclear family
  - (vi) Collateral joint family
  - (vii) Supplemented collateral joint family
  - (viii) Lineal joint family
  - (ix) Supplemented lineal joint family
  - (x) Lineal collateral joint family
  - (xi) Supplemented lineal collateral joint family
  - (xii) Other, a residual class.

Point to Note

According to Goran Therborn, the institution of family is structured by three elements:

1. Patriarchy or male dominance
2. Marriage and non-marriage in the regulation of sexual behaviour
3. Fertility and birth control measures in the production of demographic trends

Morgan's Views on Family Practices

David Morgan is a significant sociologist whose work on family practices has contributed to the understanding of family dynamics and relationships. His approach emphasises the active and routine aspects of family life rather than static structures or roles. Here's a critical analysis of his views:

1. **Family Practices:** Morgan focusses on what families do rather than what they are. This means analysing the everyday activities, routines, and interactions that constitute family life. He argues that these practices are central to understanding how families function and are maintained over time.
2. **Fluid and Dynamic Nature:** Unlike traditional views that see family as a fixed institution, Morgan views family practices as fluid and dynamic. This perspective allows for the recognition of changes and variations in family life, including different family forms and the impact of broader social changes.
3. **Relational Approach:** Morgan's work emphasises relationships and the interactions between family members. He suggests that family practices are about negotiating and managing relationships, which involves emotional work and the distribution of power within the family.
4. **Contexts of Family Practices:** He highlights the importance of context, recognising that family practices are influenced by external factors such as economic conditions, cultural norms, and social policies. This means that understanding family practices requires considering the broader societal context.
5. **Everyday Life:** Morgan places significant importance on the mundane and routine aspects of family life. By focussing on everyday activities, he argues that sociologists can gain a deeper understanding of the lived experiences of family members.

Critical Analysis

1. **Strengths**
   - **Inclusivity:** Morgan's approach is inclusive, acknowledging diverse family forms and practices. This is particularly relevant in contemporary society where traditional nuclear families are no longer the sole family model.
   - **Dynamic Perspective:** By viewing family practices as fluid, Morgan's framework is adaptable and can account for the changes and transitions that families undergo over time.
   - **Relational Focus:** Emphasizing relationships allows for a more nuanced understanding of family dynamics, considering power, emotional labour, and interpersonal negotiations.

2. **Criticisms**
   - **Ambiguity:** Some critics argue that Morgan's concept of family practices is too broad and vague, making it difficult to define and measure empirically. The emphasis on everyday activities can sometimes obscure the structural factors that shape family life.
   - **Neglect of Structure:** While focussing on practices, Morgan's approach may underplay the importance of structural aspects such as legal frameworks, economic conditions, and institutional supports that significantly impact families.
   - **Overemphasis on Routine:** Critics might say that by concentrating on the mundane and routine, Morgan's analysis risks overlooking the significant and extraordinary events that also shape family life, such as crises or major life transitions.
3. **Relevance and Application**
   - **Contemporary Relevance:** Morgan's views are highly relevant in contemporary sociology, particularly in understanding non-traditional family forms such as single-parent families, cohabiting couples, and LGBTQ+ families.
   - **Policy Implications:** His approach can inform social policies by highlighting the need to support diverse family practices rather than assuming a one-size-fits-all model.
   - **Research Implications:** For researchers, Morgan's framework encourages qualitative methodologies that capture the complexities of everyday family life, such as ethnographies and in-depth interviews.

Different Perspectives on Family

Functionalist Perspective

- **Key Proponents:** Talcott Parsons, George Murdock
- **Core Ideas**:
  - **Definition:** The family is a key institution that performs essential functions for the stability and smooth functioning of society.
  - **Functions of the Family:**
    - (i) **Socialization:** The family is the primary unit for the socialization of children.
    - (ii) **Economic Support:** Families provide financial support and economic stability.
    - (iii) **Emotional Support:** Families offer emotional care and nurturing.
    - (iv) **Reproduction:** Families ensure the continuation of society by reproducing and raising children.
    - (v) **Regulation of Sexual Activity:** Families help regulate sexual behaviour and maintain social norms regarding sexuality.
- According to Murdock, the nuclear family is a universal institution and it is a functional group indispensable to society.
- Talcott Parsons's structural, functional and comparative theory predicted an isolation, differentiation and specialization of the nuclear family as a bounded

sub-system of the American society. As per him, the family performs two basic and irreducible functions: the primary socialization of children and stabilization of adult personalities of the population. The functions performed by the wider kin group, Parsons' said would be taken over by formal institutions in the industrial society.

- Talcott Parsons identified two 'basic and irreducible' functions of the family in modern society: socialization of children and the stabilization of adult personalities. The socialization of children involves teaching cultural norms, values, and skills necessary for integration into society. This process ensures the transmission of societal values across generations, preparing children to become functional members of society. The stabilization of adult personalities refers to the emotional support provided by the family, particularly through the marital relationship, which Parsons viewed as a mechanism to reduce stress and maintain mental well-being in adults. These functions contribute to the stability and continuity of society, emphasizing the nuclear family as an ideal structure for performing these roles.
- **Criticism**
  - Parsons was criticized for assuming the white middle class American families as the ideal nuclear families. Morgan found no class, regional or religious variation in Parsons' family. Like Murdock, Parsons assumed the family to be universal. Besides, there was no exploration of alternatives to the family.
  - The harmony in family relations was also partially true. Vogel and Bell found that family tensions and conflicts, and exploitative relations do exist in families. Edmund Leach had found that members of nuclear families take immense emotional toll on each other.
  - Functionalist views have been criticized for being overly idealistic, ignoring family diversity, and underplaying conflict and power dynamics within families.

Conflict Perspective

- **Key Proponents:** Friedrich Engels, Ralf Dahrendorf
- **Core Ideas:**
  - **Definition:** The family is a site of power struggles and inequalities.
  - **Economic Power:** Engels argued that the family, especially the monogamous nuclear family, emerged to protect private property and perpetuate class inequalities.
  - **Gender Inequality:** The family reinforces patriarchal structures, where men typically hold more power and control over resources.
  - **Social Reproduction of Inequality:** Families play a role in reproducing social inequalities across generations.
- Engels' famous *The Origin of the Family, Private Property and the State* (first published in 1884) was the first Marxian attempt to analyse the family. As per him, emergence of the state and the private property led to restrictions on sexuality and sexual relations and control over women's reproduction. The monogamous family ensured the supremacy of man for undisputed paternity to enable certainty of a natural heir to the family inheritance.

- During the second feminist wave in the 1960s and 1970s, Marxian concepts were used to critique the role of women in families as producers of labour force (the basic requirement of capitalism) tied down to the domestic space without any payment for their contribution. Rowbothom elaborated how reproduction functions as a hidden subsidy to the capitalist and hidden tax on the proletariat.
- David Copper in 'The death of the family' states that reproduction and parental authority work as means for ideological conditioning for an obedient and submissive labour force. The family works as the facilitating institution for capitalism
- **Criticism:** Conflict theory can sometimes overemphasise the negative aspects of family life and may not fully account for the positive, supportive functions families often provide.

Symbolic Interactionism

- **Key Proponents:** Erving Goffman, Charles Cooley, George Herbert Mead
- **Core Ideas:**
  - **Definition:** Focusses on the day-to-day interactions and meanings that family members assign to their relationships and roles.
  - **Role of Communication:** Family life is constructed through communication and interaction, with family members constantly negotiating and redefining their roles and relationships.
  - **Identity Formation:** Families are key sites for the development of self-identity through processes like role-taking and the looking-glass self.
  - **Micro-level Analysis:** Emphasises the importance of understanding family dynamics from the perspectives of individual family members.
- **Criticism:** Symbolic interactionism may overlook broader structural factors that influence family life, focussing too narrowly on micro-level interactions.

Feminist Perspective

- **Key Proponents:** Betty Friedan, Ann Oakley, Jessie Bernard
- **Core Ideas:**
  - Advocates for gender equality through legal reforms and equal opportunities.
  - Focuses on removing barriers to women's participation in all areas of public life, including family life.
  - Critiques traditional family structures for perpetuating gender inequalities.
  - **Patriarchy and Power:** Feminist theorists argue that families are often patriarchal, with power and authority typically vested in male members.
  - **Division of Labour:** Examines how domestic labour is divided along gender lines, often leading to women's disproportionate burden of housework and childcare.
  - **Agency and Resistance:** Highlights how women resist and negotiate power dynamics within families.
  - **Diverse Family Forms:** Advocates for recognising and valuing diverse family forms, including single-parent families, LGBTQ+ families, and non-traditional households.

- **Criticism:** Some critics argue that feminist perspectives can sometimes overemphasise conflict and may not fully acknowledge the complexity of family relationships and the potential for cooperation and mutual support.

Feminist Perspective

Liberal Feminism

Key Ideas:

- Advocates for gender equality through legal reforms and equal opportunities.
- Focuses on removing barriers to women's participation in all areas of public life, including family life.

Key Thinkers:

- **Betty Friedan:** Her book '*The Feminine Mystique*' (1963) critiqued the traditional roles assigned to women and argued for greater opportunities for women outside the home.
- **Ann Oakley:** Her research on housework highlighted the unequal distribution of domestic labour between men and women.

View on Family:

- Liberal feminists argue that traditional family roles (e.g., men as breadwinners, women as homemakers) limit women's opportunities.
- They advocate for policies that support working women, such as maternity leave, affordable childcare, and anti-discrimination laws.

Example: Campaigns for parental leave policies that allow both parents to share childcare responsibilities, promoting equality in domestic labour.

Marxist Feminism

Key Ideas:

- Links the oppression of women to the capitalist system.
- Argues that women's unpaid domestic labour supports capitalism by reproducing labour power at no cost to capitalists.

Key Thinkers:

- **Friedrich Engels:** In '*The Origin of the Family, Private Property and the State*' (1884), Engels argued that the family as an economic unit supports capitalism.
- **Margaret Benston:** Highlighted the economic importance of women's unpaid labour in maintaining the capitalist system.

View on Family:

- Marxist feminists see the family as a site where women's labour is exploited.
- They emphasize how the capitalist system benefits from women's unpaid work at home, which sustains the workforce.

Example: Analysis of how women's domestic work is undervalued and unrecognized, contributing to their economic dependence on men and the perpetuation of class inequalities.

Radical Feminism

Key Ideas:

- Focuses on patriarchy as the root cause of women's oppression.
- Advocates for radical changes to eliminate male dominance in all areas of life, including family.

Key Thinkers:

- **Shulamith Firestone:** In '*The Dialectic of Sex*' (1970), Firestone argued for the abolition of the traditional family structure to liberate women.
- **Kate Millett:** In 'Sexual Politics' (1970), Millett analyzed how patriarchy is perpetuated through cultural and social institutions, including the family.

View on Family:

- Radical feminists argue that traditional family structures perpetuate patriarchy by reinforcing male dominance and control over women.
- They call for the abolition or transformation of the nuclear family to dismantle patriarchal power relations.

Example: Critique of marital rape laws that historically ignored the possibility of rape within marriage, highlighting the control men have over women's bodies in patriarchal family structures.

Socialist Feminism

Key Ideas:

- Combines insights from Marxist and radical feminism.
- Emphasizes the intersection of capitalism and patriarchy in the oppression of women.

Key Thinkers:

- **Heidi Hartmann:** Argued that capitalism and patriarchy are intertwined systems of oppression.
- **Alison Jaggar:** In '*Feminist Politics and Human Nature*' (1983), Jaggar explored the connections between economic and gender inequalities.

View on Family:

- Socialist feminists view the family as both an economic unit and a site of patriarchal power.
- They advocate for changes in both economic and social structures to achieve gender equality.

Example: Support for comprehensive social policies, such as public childcare and healthcare, that reduce women's dependence on men and the family as the primary site of care.

Black Feminism

Key Ideas:

- Emphasizes the intersectionality of race, class, and gender in understanding women's experiences.
- Critiques mainstream feminist perspectives for ignoring the unique experiences of women of color.

Key Thinkers:

- **bell hooks:** In '*Ain't I a Woman?*' (1981), hooks examined the impact of racism and sexism on Black women.
- **Patricia Hill Collins:** In '*Black Feminist Thought*' (1990), Collins introduced the concept of the 'matrix of domination' to explain intersecting oppressions.

View on Family:

- Black feminists highlight the diverse family forms and roles within Black communities.
- They stress the importance of considering the impact of racism and economic inequality on family life.

Example: Examination of how Black women often take on both breadwinning and caregiving roles, challenging the traditional gendered division of labour.

Postmodern Feminism

Key Ideas:

- Rejects universal or fixed definitions of gender and family.
- Emphasizes diversity, fluidity, and the deconstruction of traditional categories.

Key Thinkers:

- **Judith Butler:** In '*Gender Trouble*' (1990), Butler argued that gender is performative and not tied to biological sex, challenging traditional notions of family.
- **Donna Haraway:** In 'A Cyborg Manifesto' (1985), Haraway critiqued the boundaries between human and machine, nature and culture, including in family structures.

View on Family:

- Postmodern feminists argue that there is no single 'correct' family form.
- They explore how family meanings and structures vary across different cultural and historical contexts.

Example: Analysis of non-traditional families, such as LGBTQ+ families, and how they challenge conventional notions of family and gender roles.

Ecofeminism

Key Ideas:

- Links the domination of women to the exploitation of the environment.
- Advocates for a holistic approach to social and environmental justice.

Key Thinkers:

- **Vandana Shiva:** In '*Staying Alive*' (1988), Shiva connected the exploitation of women and nature to patriarchal and capitalist practices.
- **Carolyn Merchant:** In '*The Death of Nature*' (1980), Merchant explored the historical connections between environmental degradation and the subjugation of women.

View on Family:

- Ecofeminists see the family as a microcosm of broader ecological and social systems.
- They promote sustainable living practices and egalitarian family structures.

Example: Encouraging families to adopt environmentally sustainable practices and egalitarian decision-making processes to reflect ecofeminist principles.

Postmodern Perspective

- **Key Proponents:** Judith Stacey, Anthony Giddens
- **Core Ideas:**
    - **Definition:** Emphasises the diversity and fluidity of family forms in contemporary society.
    - **Individualization:** Giddens argues that contemporary relationships are characterized by greater individual choice and reflexivity.
    - **Changing Norms:** Traditional norms and roles within families are less fixed, leading to more diverse and negotiated family arrangements.
    - **Intimacy and Love:** Focuses on the transformation of intimacy, with relationships increasingly based on personal satisfaction and emotional fulfillment rather than social obligation.
- **Criticism:** Postmodern perspectives can sometimes be criticized for lacking clear theoretical coherence and for focusing too heavily on individual experiences at the expense of broader social structures.

Structural Functionalism

- **Key Proponents:** Talcott Parsons, Robert K. Merton
- **Core Ideas:**
    - **Definition:** Views the family as an institution that contributes to the stability and functioning of society.
    - **Primary Socialization:** Families are responsible for the primary socialization of children, teaching them societal norms and values.
    - **Stabilization of Adult Personalities:** Families provide emotional support to adults, helping to stabilize their personalities and maintain social order.
- **Criticism:** Structural functionalism is often criticized for being too conservative, failing to account for family diversity, and underestimating the prevalence of family conflict.

Cultural Perspective

- This perspective includes theorization on emotions, norms, values and facets such as procreation, ideology, power dynamics between family members, etc., and emphasises on household rather than family enabling a cross-cultural comparative research.
- There are attempts at understanding the ideology. For instance, the ubiquitous procreation metaphor of seed and earth, assumes the male as the active principle, while the female as the passive one. Hypergamy and hypogamy practices are

linked to this conception about parental contribution as are rules of *sapinda* exogamy. Similalrly, the level of significance attributed to different sexes is different in patrilineal and matrilineal societies.

Cooperative-Conflict Perspective

In 1960s studies showed how love, conjugality and oppression co-exist in the family alongside unequal gender relations. Feminist economists opposed the either-or approach of viewing family only as a safe haven or on the verge of complete breakdown, and instead advocated a shift to analysing dialectical relations of cooperation and conflict.

Household

According to AM Shah, the household (*ghar*) is a residential and domestic unit composed of one or more persons living under the same roof and eating food cooked in the same kitchen (hearth/*chullah*). It may so happen that not all the members of a family live in the same household all the time. Geographically distanced homes may be occupied by a few of the members of a given family. These members then reside in two or more households but they consider themselves as belonging to the same family. The household is a commensal and coresident group/ unit (with provision for the phenomenon of single person households). Thus, kin and residence rules distinguish between family and household.

Family	Household
1. It refers to a group of individuals related to each other either by consanguinity or affinity.	1. It refers to the dwelling or place of residence for one or more persons who eat food cooked from the same kitchen. It is a characteristic of the institution of family.
2. Though the concept has evolved over time, it still requires two or more people to be identified as a family. However, for residence purpose, a single member of a family could live by themselves.	2. Single person households can exist. Different members of a family can live in different households.
3. Family could be joint, nuclear or of any other type.	3. A household in itself is neither joint nor nuclear, but becomes either of these by virtue of it being under progression and regression in a developmental process. For example, a married son's moving out of his father's house in patrilineal society makes the son's house a nuclear one, or rather a separate one. A.M. Shah has used the terms 'simple and complex' for the household rather than joint or nuclear.
4. The term family is used for the group related through kinship, emotional, ritual and legal dimensions.	4. The term household is used for the residential grouping.

Views on the Family in India

Family in India has been studied through the Indological and the empirical approaches.

1. **The Textual/Indological View:** Kinship and marriage as reflected through the Hindu sacred texts, the '*Dharmshastra*' led scholars like Maine to project the Indian joint family as a surviving example of the ancient form of human family. To Maine, this patriarchal family worked as a corporation, with its members as its trustees. It is through the Indological approach that the Hindu joint family came to be considered as the ideal and often the real family in India. The Indological approach had posited the patrilineal joint family prevalent among the higher castes as the ideal Indian family.

   However, empirical evidence has revealed that the large joint family is not the universal form of family in India and as an institution is much more varied. The joint and the nuclear types of the family have been found to be Indological constructs.
2. **The Field View:** With India's political independence and following the formation of the Indian Sociological Society, the sociological study of the family experienced a transition from the book view to the field view. The field/empirical view basically highlighted how family existed in varied forms in reality, and not just in the binary of joint or nuclear.
3. **Process View (Phases of Household Development):** It proposes that family is not a static institution and goes through a development cycle which connects the phases of nuclear and joint family types. Similarly, not all nuclear families are identical nor are all joint families so. This process of the developmental cycle has been improvised by A.M. Shah's (1973) study of the household and its developmental phases. A household may experience progression and/or regression or both on the basis of birth, adoption and in- and out-marriage, and death, divorce and separation of members over a period of time. Thus, at any given time the family forms in a society are likely to vary from a single member to a large group residing together.

Point to Note

The Developmental Process of Making a Simple Household into a Complex One

According to AM Shah, the pattern of the developmental process in each society is influenced by three major factors. The first is the demographic factor, which includes the phenomena of birth, adulthood and death, the sex and number of members. The second factor is the series of explicitly-stated norms regarding the residence of various relatives in a household. The third is the pattern of interpersonal relations in a household, largely dependent on the norms or codes of proper conduct attached to kinship relationships in the household.

When a simple household becomes a complex one through addition of other family members (by birth or marriage) the process is called fusion. Similarly, when members are lost (by birth, out-marriage, migration) the household is said to undergo fission. A household goes through the process of fusion and fission, accretion and attrition; and in its wake turning itself into simple and complex one.

FYI

The Myth of Disintegration of Joint Family

Early thinkers like Engels, Morgan and Maine agreed on the evolutionary perspective which proposed that the traditional joint family in India will eventually convert into a nuclear one, and the filial ties will be superseded in importance by conjugal ties. This view was strengthened by field studies and censuses that were conducted in early 20th century. They showed that size of the Indian household was decreasing (in comparison to the textual Indological image of a large, joint Hindu family) thereby implying that the jointness was also reducing. Parsons' thesis on how industrialization had led to a small nuclear family becoming a necessity in America, was further used to substantiate these findings.

However, these arguments were devoid of serious historical data and insightful analysis. The reality was quite different.

In his work on families in South India, Milton Singer showed that the Indian industrial family was capable of adapting to Western ways and yet supporting joint family and caste values.

On the other hand, the issue of jointness was delinked from the sole criterion of joint residence. Thus, retaining the jointness of the family is possible without living jointly.

A distinction between the kinship oriented family and the residence oriented household was drawn to get more conceptual clarity.

In 1998, AM Shah showed that the proportion of joint families had remained the same, if not increased over the past several decades. Similarly, Kolenda too reiterated the popularity of the prevalence of the joint family.

Changing Nature of Family in Contemporary Times

The structure of the family has undergone significant changes in contemporary society, shaped by diverse socio-economic, cultural, and demographic factors. Traditional family structures, which were primarily joint and extended, are increasingly being replaced by nuclear, neo-local, and even child-centered (filiocentric) arrangements. This transformation reflects the impact of modernization, globalization, urbanization, and shifts in cultural norms.

Key Changes in Family Structures

1. **Decline of Joint Families:** Joint families, once the cornerstone of traditional societies, are diminishing, particularly in urban areas. Factors such as industrialization, increased mobility, and individual aspirations have made joint living arrangements less practical.

   Example: In India, the traditional joint family model has been replaced by nuclear families in urban centers like Bengaluru and Mumbai due to economic pressures and job opportunities.

2. **Rise of Nuclear Families:** Nuclear families, comprising parents and their dependent children, have become the dominant structure in many parts of the world. This change aligns with a growing emphasis on personal autonomy, privacy, and economic independence.
   Example: In the United States, nearly 70% of households are nuclear families, while in India, nuclear families constitute around 52% of all households (Census 2011).
3. **Neo-Local Residence Patterns:** Neo-locality, where couples establish a separate household after marriage, is a growing trend. It reflects shifts in marital norms and the desire for independent living arrangements.
   Example: Young couples in urban India, China, and Europe increasingly prefer living separately from their parents after marriage, valuing autonomy and reduced familial interference.
4. **Filiocentric Families:** Modern families have become more filiocentric, placing children at the center of familial decision-making and resource allocation. This trend reflects changing social priorities, including heightened focus on child welfare, education, and emotional bonding.
   Example: Middle-class families in India, China, and the U.S. prioritize investments in their children's education, extracurricular activities, and psychological well-being.

FYI

Factors Responsible for the Changes

1. **Economic Modernization:** Industrialization and urbanization have shifted economic activity away from agrarian and family-based production systems, leading to greater economic independence and the erosion of traditional family structures.
2. **Urbanization:** Migration to urban centers for employment has made nuclear and neo-local living arrangements more feasible and desirable.
3. **Educational Attainment:** Increased education, especially among women, has fostered egalitarian family structures, reduced dependence on extended kin, and promoted smaller, nuclear families.
4. **Globalization and Cultural Exchange:** Exposure to Western values of individualism and privacy through media and migration has influenced family norms, particularly in developing societies.
5. **Legal and Policy Shifts:** Changes in laws related to marriage, inheritance, and property rights, as well as welfare policies for single parents and working mothers, have influenced family structures.
   Example: India's Hindu Succession Act amendments (2005) have empowered daughters with equal inheritance rights, altering traditional family dynamics.
6. **Technological Advancements:** Technology, such as mobile communication and remote working, has enabled families to maintain connections without co-residence, facilitating neo-local and nuclear trends.
7. **Demographic Changes:** Lower fertility rates, higher life expectancy, and delayed marriages have contributed to smaller families and child-centric practices.

There has been a rise of filiocentric families also which can be explained through the following sociological frameworks and observations:

1. **Parsonian Theory of Functionality:** In modern societies, the family has evolved to focus primarily on the socialization of children and the stabilization of adult personalities. The growing emphasis on child-rearing reflects this shift.
2. **Consumerist Influence:** Global consumer culture promotes child-centered consumption, where parents invest heavily in products and services designed for children's development and comfort.
3. **Declining Fertility Rates:** As families have fewer children, parents are able to devote more attention and resources to each child, thereby amplifying filiocentric tendencies.
4. **Changing Parental Roles:** Egalitarian values have redefined parenthood as a collaborative effort between partners, with greater emphasis on nurturing and emotional bonding with children.

Marriage and its Changing Patterns

According to John Boswell, a historian of medieval Europe, ideas of romantic love, as the basis of marriage only emerged in the 18th century and have gained popularity in the post-industrial era. Before that, marriage was decided by factors of pragmatism, status enhancement, securitization of property through reproduction of heirs and political alliances. In fact, love was not the basis of marriage and only came to be connected with sexuality in modern times. Thus, even notions of romantic love are shaped by social and historical factors and are not a 'natural' part of human life.

Marriage: Definitions

1. Marriage can be defined as a socially acknowledged and approved sexual union between two adult individuals.
2. Edmund Leach considered marriage to be 'bundles of rights'. The rights included:
   (i) Legitimating offspring
   (ii) Socially approved access to the spouse's sexuality, labour and property
   (iii) Establishment of affinal relationships between persons and between groups

   However, because of lack of uniformity and countless variations, Leach has also said that 'all universal definitions of marriage are vain'.
3. Marriage has also been defined as a union between a man and a woman such that children born to the woman are the recognized legitimate offspring of both partners.
4. In the context of the Nayar community, Kathleen Gough however preferred to modify the definition of 'marriage' in the following words – 'Marriage is a relationship established between a woman and one or more other persons, which provides that a child born to the woman under circumstances not prohibited by the rules of the relationship is accorded full birth-status rights common to normal members of the society or social stratum.'

This definition enlarges the scope of viewing marriage in a broader context. It would include the case of Nuer woman-woman marriage, mentioned by Evans-Pritchard, the case of levirate unions, which consider the child as the legitimate offspring of a man other than its genitor. Levirate refers to a marriage in which a man has the obligation to marry the widow of his brother. Gazetteer of India (1965) has mentioned the prevalence of levirate alliances among the Ahir of Haryana, some Jat communities and Girijan and several castes in Uttar Pradesh and among the Kodagu of Mysore.

Ace Your Answers!

Is legitimating of children an essential condition of marriage?

5. Bohanan (1949), has discussed Dahomean marriage and distinguished the rights of a woman as a wife (rights in uxorem) from rights over the children she may bear (rights in genetricem).
6. Marriage is not only a means of sexual gratification but also a set of cultural mechanisms to ensure the continuation of the family, establishment of relationships, of alliance between persons and between groups.
   - Among the Hindus, for instance, marriage is regarded as a socio-religious duty. Ancient Hindu texts, such as the '*Dharmashastra*', point out three main aims of marriage which are: *dharma* (duty), *praja* (progeny) and *rati* (sensual pleasure).
   - Islam views marriage as '*sunnah*' (an obligation), which every Muslim must fulfill.
   - Christianity too, like other religions, holds marriage as critical to life and emphasises the establishment of a mutual relationship between husband and wife, and adhering to their duties towards each other.

FYI

In a famous comparison of several hundred societies of mid-20th century, George Peter Murdock found that polygamy was permitted in more than 80 percent of them. Majority of these societies were found in Africa and South Asia.

Change in Goals of Marriage

Goals of marriage are changing in general and for the urban and educated sections of the population in particular.

1. A clear preference for small-size family has replaced the older notions of family with a large number of children especially sons being the source of status for parents.
2. On the individual level, younger couples view marriage as a relationship for self-fulfillment rather than primarily for procreation.
3. There is also a strong protest movement among the dalit women against caste and gender violence, and against the legal recognition of only *anuloma* marriages where upper caste men marry or live with lower caste women and not *pratiloma* ones where women of higher castes marry or live with lower caste men.

Rules Regulating Marriage

1. **Incest Taboo/Rules:** Incest refers to sexual relations or marriage between closely related individuals. These rules define who is prohibited from marrying (typically immediate family members and close relatives), establishing the boundaries of permissible marriage partners. The specific degree of kinship that constitutes incest varies across cultures.
2. **Endogamy and Exogamy Rules:**
   - **Endogamy (Positive Rules):** Requirements to marry within specific social groups (caste, class, religion, ethnicity, tribe)
   - **Exogamy (Negative Rules):** Prohibitions against marrying within certain groups (clan, lineage, village, or specific kinship categories)
3. **Cross-cultural Marriage Restrictions:**
   - **Inter-caste Marriages:** Rules governing marriage across caste boundaries.
   - **Inter-religious Marriages:** Regulations concerning marriage between different faith communities.
   - **Same-sex Marriages:** Cultural and legal rules regarding marriage between individuals of the same gender.
   - **Inter-racial/ethnic Marriages:** Rules about marriage across racial or ethnic lines.
4. **Rules Applicable to Married Persons:** The negative rules are those of adultery that restrict sexual access to those already married. You may observe the positive side of rules in polygamous and the levirate or sororate or Islamic short-term marriage (*mut'a*), whereby already married persons have sexual access to specified married persons.

Patterns of Spouse Selection

Majority of the marriages in present times are either classified as arranged (which are decided by the elders and family members of prospective bride and groom) or love/self-choice (decided by the concerned prospective bride and groom themselves).

Blumberg and Dwarki identified the following patterns of spouse selection in India:

- Marriage arranged by parents or elders without consulting the boy or girl.
- Marriage chosen by the individuals themselves without consulting parents or elders.
- Marriage chosen by the individuals with parental consent.
- Marriage arranged by parents with the consent of both the boy and girl.
- Marriage arranged by parents with the consent of only one partner.

Marriage Rituals and Status

- In India, certain communities do not follow religious rites in marriage, resulting in what are known as customary marriages. These involve simple practices; for instance, in some Himalayan groups, marriage is signified by placing a ring in the bride's nose. Customary marriages are typically found in groups that allow and practice divorce and remarriage.
- The Special Marriage Act of 1954 provides for secular and civil marriages before a registrar. This act is available to all Indian citizens regardless of their religious background.

Status

Besides the transfer of the wife, two major types of material wealth transfers occur during marriage. In one type, wealth moves in the opposite direction of the bride, known as the bride price. In the other, wealth moves with the bride, known as a dowry. The demand for dowry is present in various communities, including Muslim and Christian groups.

1. **Bride Price (Bride Wealth):** Wealth flows from the groom's family to the bride's family, compensating them for the loss of their daughter's labour and reproductive capacity. This practice is common in many African, Asian, and Pacific societies (Goody & Tambiah, 1973; Schlegel & Eloul, 1988).
2. **Dowry:** Wealth accompanies the bride to her new household, typically provided by her natal family. This serves as her economic security and establishes her status in the marital home. Dowry systems are prevalent in South Asia, parts of Europe, and the Middle East (Goody, 1973; Miller, 1981).
3. **Brideservice:** The groom provides labour or services to the bride's family for a specified period, common among foraging societies (Schlegel & Eloul, 1988).
4. **Gift Exchange:** Reciprocal exchanges between families that create ongoing social bonds and obligations (Lévi-Strauss, 1949).

The demand for dowry persists across religious boundaries in South Asia, affecting Hindu, Muslim, Christian, and Sikh communities alike, often leading to dowry inflation and related social problems (Srinivas, 1984; Oldenburg, 2002).

Patriarchy and Sexual Division of Labour

Patriarchy

- The term patriarchy is 'about the power of men, a power which extends to the individual jurisdiction of men (or a man) over a family and its members, as well as the more general power of 'the male' over the organization of a social group or a society.' (Cambridge Dictionary of Sociology)
- In sociology, the first theoretical account of patriarchy is found in Engels's discussion of women's subservience to men under capitalism. Engels argued that capitalism concentrated power in the hands of a small number of men and, because the system produced more wealth than ever before, intensified gender as well as class inequality, as men passed on their wealth to their male heirs.

FYI

Theorising Patriarchy by Sylvia Walby

Walby identifies six structures through which patriarchy operates:

1. **Production Relations in the Household:** Women's unpaid domestic labour is appropriated by their husbands.
2. **Paid Work:** Women in the labour market face exclusion from certain types of work, receive lower pay, and are segregated into less skilled jobs.
3. **Patriarchal State:** The state exhibits a patriarchal bias in its policies and interests.
4. **Male Violence:** This violence is systematic and patterned rather than individualistic, with the state often complicit by failing to intervene appropriately.
5. **Patriarchal Relations in Sexuality:** Concepts like 'compulsory heterosexuality,' sexual double standards, and different rules of sexual behaviour for men and women perpetuate patriarchal control.
6. **Patriarchal Cultural Institutions:** Media, religion, and education produce representations of women through a patriarchal lens.

- In Theorising Patriarchy, 1990, Sylvia Walby has defined patriarchy as ' a system of social structures and practices in which men dominate and oppress women.' According to her, patriarchy operates at multiple levels – in discriminatory domestic relations at home, in terms of wage disparity and job allocation in the labour market, capture of political power, patterned and systematic male violence, sexual double standards, patriarchal cultural institutions like education, media, etc. Walby's analysis is the distinction between private and public forms of patriarchy. Private forms include domestic relations and intimate relations, while public forms involve paid employment, the state and politics.

- According to Ann Oakley, industrialization marked the real beginning of the modern patriarchal system when women were branded as 'housewives'.
- By the second half of the 20th century, anthropologists had generally concluded that the majority of human societies were explicitly patriarchal, in that authority, lineage, and descent were situated in men, the social function of women being as objects of the exchange process which cemented and continued social relations and structures of power.
- In the second half of the 20th century, the authority of patriarchy, and the patriarchal, has come to be contested in a number of ways. Patriarchy was identified by second-wave feminism as the conceptual apparatus, both symbolic and material, through which the social inferiority of women was maintained.
- Radical feminists frequently focus on the family as a fundamental source of women's oppression. They contend that men exploit women by depending on the unpaid domestic labour women perform in the home. Additionally, men collectively obstruct women's access to positions of power and influence in society.
- Firestone argued that men control women's roles in reproduction and child-rearing. Because women are biologically able to give birth, they become dependent on men for protection and livelihood. This 'biological inequality' is socially organized within the nuclear family.
- Other radical feminists say that male violence against women is central to male supremacy, as domestic violence, rape and sexual harassment are all part of the systematic oppression of women. Their 'objectification' through the media, fashion and advertising turns women into sexual objects whose main role is to please and entertain men. Because patriarchy is a systemic phenomenon, gender equality can only be attained by overthrowing the patriarchal order.
- According to Goran Therborn, patriarchal power within the family has declined over the 20th century:
    (a) The first time period was after the First World War when women were needed to work for the war effort and during the Russian revolution which worked in favour of egalitarian ideals.
    (b) The second was between the sexual revolution of the 1960s and the 1975 when second-wave feminism occurred.
- In Working Women Don't Have Wives (1994), Terri Apter argues that women find themselves struggling with two contradictory forces. They want and need economic independence, but at the same time they want to be mothers to their children.
- With relation to housework, the division between men and women is still highly unequal. For women who are already working, the extra work at home amounts to a 'second shift'. This state of relations wherein women have entered the workforce yet men have not agreed to doing their share of domestic tasks led Arlie Hochschild to call it 'stalled revolution'. Hochschild has suggested that women are doubly suppressed by men.
- In Feeding the Family (1991), Marjorie Devault showed how the caring activities within a household are socially constructed as women's work.

Sexual Division of Labour

Sexual division of labour refers to the process of dividing work between different people on the basis of sex and gender. Sociologists use the term 'sex' to refer to the anatomical and physiological differences that define male and female bodies. Gender, on the other hand, concerns the psychological, social and cultural differences between males and females.

R.W. Connell has given three aspects which interact to form a society's gender order namely, labour, power and cathexis (personal/sexual relationships). Just like gender and sex are socially constructed, Connell argues that gender relations are also part of an ongoing process and therefore, subject to challenge.

Women and the Workplace—A Historical View of the West

- In pre-industrial societies, productive activities and activities of the household were not separate. All members of the family participated in work and women had considerable influence in decision-making as a result of their importance in economic processes, even though they were excluded from politics and warfare.
- The movement of work to factory and its mechanization under industrialization led to the separation of home from workplace as private and public sphere respectively. As a result, women were relegated to domestic private space. This had differential effects for women of different classes and races. For example, women who belonged to the upper, privileged class enjoyed their stay at home while enjoying the services of maids and domestic servants.
- Until the 20th century, women's share in formal employment was quite low and even then only young, single women were allowed to work. Upon marriage, they were made to withdraw from the labour force.
- Women's participation in labour force increased significantly in 20th century especially during the war years when there was labour shortage.
- With a range of changes in the ensuing years—introduction of new economic policies, institutionalization of equal rights, right to vote for women, globalization, increased privatization and shift to service-based economy—the share of women in overall employment has increased in an unprecedented manner.

Three Main Inequalities for Women at Work

- **Occupational Segregation:** The overwhelming proportion of women in secretarial and caring jobs such as nursing, social work and child care. Vertical segregation occurs when women are concentrated in jobs with little authority and room for advancement. Horizontal segregation refers to the tendency of men and women to occupy different categories of job.
- **Concentration in Part-time Employment:** Part-time jobs are favoured by women due to the flexibility they offer as women also need to manage their household duties. However, part-time work carries limited opportunities such as low pay, job insecurity and limited opportunities for advancement. However, the trend has also seen a shift with more women landing lucrative professional positions and becoming equally qualified as their male counterparts.
- **Wage Gap:** The problem of wage disparity continues to persist as men are paid more than women. However, legislations in this regard have brought in changes.

Changes in the Domestic Division of Labour

- With more women entering the paid work, traditional family patterns are being renegotiated and the 'male breadwinner' model is no more the rule.
- There is a shift towards more egalitarian relationships in many households, although women continue to shoulder the main responsibility for most housework. Scholars refer to it as 'lagged adaptation' – renegotiation of domestic tasks between men and women is proceeding more slowly than women's entry into the labour market.
- Women's entry in the labour market has also enhanced their financial decision-making power.

Theories of Gender Inequality

1. **Functionalist Approach:** Its proponents include those in favour of the natural differences theory and argue that division of labour between men and women is biologically based.
   (a) George Murdock saw it both practical and convenient that women should concentrate on domestic and family responsibilities while men work outside the home.
   (b) Lionel Tiger and Robin Fox in *The Imperial Animal, 1972,* gave concept of 'Human Biogrammer'. According to them, because men have spent most of their time historically in hunting and gathering, and women in domestic and child-rearing activities, both have developed a genetic component which makes men as aggressive – therefore, suitable in the role of production outside home, and women as caring – programmed for reproduction and taking care of children.
   (c) In Talcott Parsons' view, the family operates most efficiently when females act in expressive roles, providing care, security to children and emotional support to men and when men act in instrumental roles – being the breadwinner of the family.
   (d) John Bowlby argued that if a child is separated from mother at a young age– a time known as maternal deprivation, the child runs a high risk of being inadequately socialized. Bowlby's theory has led some to argue that working mothers are neglectful ones.
   (e) **Criticism of Functionalist Approach:** Feminists have argued that there is nothing natural or inevitable about allocation of tasks. Instead, cultural socialization is responsible for conditioning men and women differently into roles. The maternal deprivation thesis has also been challenged through studies which showed that part-time employment of both parents outside home actually enhanced the educational performance and personal development of children. Parsons' theory has been criticized for condoning women's oppression at home.
2. **Feminist Approaches:** The major strands of feminism that existed in the West during the 20th century included liberalism, socialism/Marxism and radical feminism.

(a) Liberal Feminism: It looks for explanations in social and cultural attitudes. Liberal feminists do not look at subordination of women as part of a larger system, rather focus on many separate factors as contributing to inequalities between men and women. They work within the system to bring gradual reforms, such as by advocating for equal wages in the workplace, right to entry in educational institutions, etc. Their methods and goals are more moderate in comparison to the radical feminists. An early contribution in this regard was John Stuart Mill who in his essay, 'The Subjection of Women' (1869) advocated for political and legal equality between the sexes, including the right to vote.

(b) Socialist and Marxist Feminism: Socialist feminists have sought to destroy both patriarchy and capitalism. Engels argued that patriarchy has its roots in private property and that capitalism intensifies patriarchy as material wealth and power is concentrated in the hands of a small number of men. Second, capitalism thrives by turning women into mass consumers and attaching their lifestyle with increase in consumption. And lastly, capitalism relies on the free labour of women at home with caring, cleaning and raising children who will join the labour force in the future. Socialist feminists have called for restructuring of the family, end of 'domestic slavery' and introduction of some collective means of raising children.

(c) Radical Feminism : The core belief of radical feminism is that men are responsible for and benefit from the exploitation of women. Patriarchy is viewed as a universal phenomenon and family is seen as one of the primary sources of women's oppression in the society. Shulamith Firestone, an early feminist writer, argued that men control women's roles in reproduction and childrearing. Because women reproduce they become dependent on men for protection and this biological inequality is the basis of nuclear family. Firestone uses the term 'sex class' to describe women's position in society and argues that emancipation is possible only through abolition of family and associated power relations. Other radical feminists argue that male violence against women, in the form of rape, sexual harassment and domestic violence, is systemic and underlies male supremacy.

(d) Post-modern Feminism: It challenges the idea that there is unitary basis of identity and experiences shared by all women. They argue that there is no single grand theory which can explain the position of all women and even dismiss concepts like patriarchy, race or class as essentialist. According to postmodernists, all different standpoints are equally valid. The recognition of difference is central to postmodernism.

Criticism

- Liberal feminists have been criticized for their inability to deal with the root causes of gender inequality and of encouraging women to become accepting of an unequal society.

- The socialist feminists have been criticized for their impractical approach towards revolutionising the social institutions.
- Radical feminists have been criticized for assuming patriarchy as ever-present in all times and places, leaving little room for any variation. They also ignore the influence of other factors like class, race, caste, ethnicity, etc., which play a role in women's subordination.
- Postmodernists have been criticized for failing to acknowledge oppressive patterned social behaviours and processes, and for not providing any definite solutions to women oppression.

Contemporary Trends

Kinship Patterns

India

- **Urbanization and Migration:** Increasing urbanization and internal migration for education and employment have led to a decline in traditional joint family structures, with nuclear families becoming more common.
- **Transnational Families:** Due to globalization and migration, there are more transnational families where members live in different countries but maintain strong kinship ties through digital communication.

Global

- **Blended Families:** Rising divorce and remarriage rates have led to more blended families, where children may have step-siblings and step-parents.
- **Chosen Families:** Among LGBTQ+ communities and other marginalized groups, there is a trend towards forming 'chosen families' based on mutual support and care rather than biological ties.

Family Structures

India

- **Nuclear Families:** Increasingly prevalent in urban areas due to economic constraints and the need for mobility.
- **Single-parent Families:** Growing acceptance and support for single-parent families, particularly in urban centers.
- **Delayed Marriage and Childbearing:** Rising educational and career aspirations have led to delayed marriage and childbearing.

Global

- **Diverse Family Forms:** Recognition and acceptance of various family forms, including single-parent families, cohabiting couples, and same-sex families.
- **Co-residence with Elderly:** In many cultures, there is a trend of adult children living with or near elderly parents to provide care and support.

Patriarchy

India

- **Challenging Patriarchy:** Increased awareness and activism against patriarchal norms, particularly among younger generations and in urban areas.
- **Women's Movements:** Strong women's movements advocating for gender equality and challenging traditional patriarchal practices.

Global

- **Patriarchal Resistance:** While patriarchy persists globally, there is significant resistance and movements towards gender equality.
- **Legal Reforms:** Many countries have enacted legal reforms to promote gender equality and protect women's rights.

Sexual Division of Labour

India

- **Changing Gender Roles:** Urbanization and economic necessity have led to more women entering the workforce, challenging traditional gender roles.
- **Domestic Labour:** Despite changes, women continue to bear the majority of domestic labour and caregiving responsibilities.

Global

- **Work-life Balance:** Increasing emphasis on policies promoting work-life balance, including parental leave and flexible working hours, to address the sexual division of labour.
- **Shared Domestic Responsibilities:** In many societies, there is a growing trend towards shared domestic responsibilities between men and women.

Gender Inequality

India

- **Education and Employment:** Significant progress in female education and employment, yet gender disparities remain, particularly in rural areas and among disadvantaged communities.
- **Violence Against Women:** Persistent issues of gender-based violence, with ongoing efforts to address and combat these through legal and social initiatives.

Global

- **Pay Gap:** The gender pay gap remains a critical issue, with women generally earning less than men for similar work.
- **Representation:** Under-representation of women in political, corporate, and leadership roles, despite efforts to promote gender equality.
- **Sexual Harassment:** The #MeToo movement and similar initiatives worldwide have brought attention to issues of sexual harassment and assault, leading to increased advocacy and policy changes.

Impacting Lives - Marriage and Kinship

1. **Progress in Reducing Child Marriages, but Challenges Persist:** Globally, an estimated 640 million women and girls were married during childhood. South Asia accounts for 45% of all child brides, followed by sub-Saharan Africa (20%), East Asia and the Pacific (15%), and Latin America and the Caribbean (9%). India alone represents one-third of the world's child brides. Despite progress, achieving the goal of eradicating child marriage by 2030 requires a significant acceleration, with efforts needing to increase 20-fold.
2. **Emerging Trend of 'Reverse Dowry' in Andhra Pradesh:** In Andhra Pradesh, a notable shift in marriage dynamics has been observed, particularly concerning the phenomenon of 'reverse dowry.' Men engaged in traditional occupations such as farming, family-owned businesses, or other professions are increasingly being asked to provide a bride price. This reflects changing preferences in the marriage market.
3. **Live-in Relationships: Legally Valid but Socially Contentious:** The legal recognition of live-in relationships in India began in 2010 when the judiciary affirmed the protection of women in such partnerships under the Domestic Violence Act. Over the years, the legitimacy of these partnerships has been further strengthened, particularly in safeguarding the rights of children born from these unions. The Supreme Court has consistently upheld that consensual live-in relationships between two adults do not constitute any legal offense.
4. **Evolving Attitudes Toward Marriage Among Millennials and Gen-Z:**
   - **Weekend Marriages:** Weekend marriages, also known as separation marriages, are gaining popularity in Japan. In this arrangement, couples maintain separate residences and meet only on weekends, allowing them to pursue personal goals and professional responsibilities independently during weekdays. Despite sharing family duties, they do not live together for most of the week.
   - **DINKs (Dual Income, No Kids):** The trend of dual-income households without children, commonly known as DINKs, is rising globally. In the United States, approximately 43% of households followed this pattern in 2022, reflecting a 7% increase over the past decade. This shift underscores evolving priorities among couples, including financial independence and career growth.

Contemporary Issues

Judicial Interventions on Live-in Relationships

Following are the key judicial decisions on live-in relationships.

1. **S. Khushboo vs. Kanniammal & Anr (2010):**
   - The Supreme Court ruled that live-in relationships come within the right to life under Article 21 of the Constitution of India.
   - The Court stated that live-in relationships are permissible and fall within the scope of personal liberty.
2. **Indra Sarma vs. V.K.V. Sarma (2013):**
   - The Supreme Court provided guidelines for determining the legitimacy of live-in relationships.
   - It recognized that women in live-in relationships are entitled to protection under the Domestic Violence Act, 2005.
3. **D. Velusamy vs. D. Patchaiammal (2010):** The Court clarified that live-in relationships must fulfill certain conditions to be considered in the nature of marriage, such as the duration of the relationship and the intention to live as a married couple.
4. **Nandakumar vs. State of Kerala (2018):** The Supreme Court upheld the right of adults to live together, even if they are not married, emphasizing that such relationships are not illegal.

FYI

Marriage: From Tradition to Transformation

Historically, marriage was viewed as a sacramental or religious obligation. In India, Hindu marriage was defined as a *sanskar* (sacrament), signifying a sacred union. Globally, marriage often symbolized family alliances, economic security, and social status.

However, the following key transformations highlight its evolving nature:

1. **Individual Autonomy:** Marriage is no longer merely a family decision; individuals now assert greater autonomy. Love marriages and inter-caste/inter-religious unions have increased significantly, reflecting changing societal values.
2. **Legal and Structural Changes:** The recognition of same-sex marriages in several countries, the rise of cohabitation, and declining marriage rates show a shift from traditional, heteronormative frameworks to more inclusive ones.
3. **Delayed Marriages and Alternative Lifestyles:** Delayed marriages, singlehood, and live-in relationships have gained acceptance, especially in urban centres globally and in India, driven by changing priorities such as education and career.

The Shift from Ritual to Commercial Outlook

1. **The Commodification of Marriage Ceremonies:**
   - **Extravagant Weddings:** Marriage has become a status symbol, with grandiose ceremonies showcasing wealth. For instance, Indian weddings often feature destination weddings, designer attire, and luxury catering.
   - **Influence of Media:** Shows like 'Indian Matchmaking' and social media platforms promote opulence and glamor, turning weddings into spectacles.
2. **Rise of the Wedding Industry:** The global wedding industry is valued at approximately $300 billion, with India's share around $50 billion. Specialized services like wedding planners, pre-wedding photo shoots, and themed decorations emphasize consumerism over ritual significance.
3. **Digital Influence:**
   - **Marriage Apps:** Matrimonial websites and apps like Shaadi.com and Tinder reflect the digital commodification of marriage.
   - **Online Gifting and Event Streaming:** Technology facilitates commercial avenues such as virtual weddings and gifting platforms.
4. **Cultural Hybridization:** Globalization has introduced hybrid practices, such as Christian-style white weddings in India. These ceremonies often highlight a commercialized, westernized appeal over traditional rituals.

Factors Behind the Transformation

1. **Economic Factors:** Rising disposable incomes and aspirations for social mobility encourage lavish spending on weddings.
2. **Globalization and Westernization:** Exposure to global trends has influenced marriage practices, making them more about personal expression and status.
3. **Urbanization and Changing Lifestyles:** Urban living fosters individualistic attitudes, prioritizing personal preferences over family traditions.
4. **Consumer Culture:** Advertisements and social media amplify the notion of a 'dream wedding,' making consumption an integral aspect of the ceremony.
5. **Technological Advancement:** From online matchmaking to drone photography, technology plays a key role in redefining how marriages are perceived and executed.

Examples of Transformation

- **India:** The weddings of celebrities like Virat Kohli and Anushka Sharma, held in exotic foreign locales, are emblematic of the shift towards commercialized and status-oriented ceremonies.
- **Global:** The Kardashian weddings in the U.S. reflect the transformation of marriages into entertainment events, driven by media and consumerism.

Impact on Marriage and Family

Changing Perceptions

- **Acceptance of Non-traditional Relationships:** Judicial recognition of live-in relationships reflects a growing acceptance of non-traditional family forms. This shift challenges the conventional notion of marriage as the only legitimate framework for cohabitation.
- **Personal Autonomy:** Emphasizing personal autonomy and the right to choose one's partner, the judiciary promotes individual freedom over societal expectations.

Legal Protections

- **Rights and Protections:** Legal recognition of live-in relationships ensures that partners, especially women, receive protection from abuse and have rights to maintenance and inheritance, similar to those in marital relationships.
- **Domestic Violence Act:** Inclusion of live-in relationships under the Domestic Violence Act provides legal recourse for individuals facing domestic abuse.

Future of Marriage and Family in India

Diverse Family Forms

- **Plurality of Family Structures:** The future of family in India is likely to be characterized by a plurality of family structures, including nuclear families, joint families, single-parent families, live-in relationships, and same-sex partnerships.
- **Legal and Social Recognition:** Continued judicial support and evolving social norms will lead to greater legal and social recognition of diverse family forms.

Evolving Concept of Marriage

- **Marriage as a Choice:** Marriage may increasingly be seen as a choice rather than a necessity, with more individuals opting for live-in relationships due to personal preferences, economic considerations, or the desire for greater flexibility.
- **Delayed Marriages:** With more people prioritising education and careers, marriages may occur later in life, leading to an increase in live-in relationships as a precursor to or alternative to marriage.

Challenges and Adaptations

- **Cultural Resistance:** Despite legal recognition, cultural resistance to live-in relationships persists, particularly in rural and conservative areas. Overcoming deeply ingrained social norms will require continuous advocacy and education.

- **Policy Adaptations:** Policies and laws will need to adapt to address the needs and rights of individuals in diverse family structures, ensuring that protections are in place regardless of marital status.

Impact on Gender Roles and Equality

- **Redefining Gender Roles:** As live-in relationships become more accepted, traditional gender roles within households may be redefined, promoting more egalitarian relationships.
- **Empowerment of Women:** Legal protections for women in live-in relationships empower them to make choices about their personal lives without fearing social stigma or legal disadvantages.

Judicial intervention in live-in relationships marks a significant step towards modernising the concept of family and marriage in India. The future of marriage and family will likely be more inclusive and diverse, reflecting changing social values and increasing recognition of individual rights and autonomy. While challenges remain, particularly in overcoming cultural resistance, the trend towards acceptance of varied family forms is poised to continue, shaping a more progressive and flexible understanding of kinship and cohabitation in India.

Key Legal Reforms and Policies Favouring for Women Empowerment

1. **The Domestic Violence Act, 2005**
   - Provides protection to women from domestic violence by spouses or family members.
   - Offers legal recourse and support mechanisms such as protection orders and shelter homes.
2. **The Sexual Harassment of Women at Workplace (Prevention, Prohibition and Redressal) Act, 2013**
   - Aims to protect women from sexual harassment at the workplace.
   - Mandates the establishment of Internal Complaints Committees (ICCs) in workplaces.
3. **The Maternity Benefit (Amendment) Act, 2017**
   - Increases the duration of paid maternity leave from 12 weeks to 26 weeks.
   - Introduces provisions for crèche facilities and flexible working arrangements.
4. **The Prohibition of Child Marriage Act, 2006**
   - Prohibits the marriage of girls below the age of 18 and boys below the age of 21.
   - Provides for the annulment of child marriages and protection of affected girls.

5. **The Hindu Succession (Amendment) Act, 2005**
   - Grants daughters equal rights to ancestral property, similar to sons.
   - Aims to ensure gender equality in inheritance rights.
6. **The Medical Termination of Pregnancy (Amendment) Act, 2021**
   - Extends the gestation period for abortion to 24 weeks in specific cases.
   - Seeks to improve access to safe abortion services.
7. **Coparcenary Rights under Hindu Succession (Amendment) Act, 2005**
   - Ensures that daughters have the same rights as sons in ancestral property, making them coparceners by birth.
   - Provides daughters with the right to demand partition and claim their share of the property.
8. **Benefits under New Criminal Laws (Bharatiya Nyaya Sanhita) in India**
   - The BNS aims to reform and modernize the criminal justice system, with provisions that enhance the protection of women.
   - It includes stricter penalties for crimes against women, such as rape, domestic violence, and dowry-related offenses.
   - The law emphasises victim protection and speedy justice through fast-track courts.

Perspectives on Legal Reforms from Sociological Viewpoint

1. **Functionalist Perspective**
   - **Social Stability:** Legal reforms that promote gender equality are viewed as essential for the stability and functioning of society. By addressing gender disparities, these reforms contribute to social harmony and cohesion.
   - **Role of Institutions:** Institutions such as the family, workplace, and legal system play a crucial role in implementing and upholding these reforms, ensuring that women's rights are protected and promoted.
2. **Conflict Perspective**
   - **Power Dynamics:** Legal reforms are seen as a means to address the power imbalances between men and women. By challenging patriarchal structures, these policies aim to redistribute power and resources more equitably.
   - **Resistance and Backlash:** There is often resistance to these reforms from those who benefit from existing power structures. This resistance can manifest in social backlash, attempts to undermine the reforms, or non-compliance with legal provisions.
3. **Feminist Perspective**
   - **Gender Equality:** Feminist theorists emphasise that these reforms are crucial steps towards achieving gender equality. They highlight the need for continuous advocacy and activism to ensure that women's rights are recognized and enforced.

- **Intersectionality:** It is essential to consider the intersectional nature of women's experiences, recognising that factors such as caste, class, and religion also influence the impact of legal reforms on different groups of women.

4. **Symbolic Interactionism**
   - **Changing Norms and Values:** These legal reforms contribute to changing societal norms and values regarding gender roles and relations. They encourage a shift towards more egalitarian attitudes and behaviours.
   - **Everyday Interactions:** The success of these reforms depends on how they are perceived and enacted in everyday interactions. Public awareness campaigns and education play a vital role in changing attitudes and ensuring compliance.

Challenges Associated with Implementing Legal Reforms

1. **Cultural Resistance**
   - Deeply ingrained patriarchal norms and values often resist changes brought about by legal reforms.
   - Social stigma and traditional beliefs can hinder the acceptance and effectiveness of policies favouring women.
2. **Lack of Awareness**
   - Many women, especially in rural and marginalized communities, are unaware of their legal rights and the protections available to them.
   - Effective implementation requires widespread awareness and education campaigns.
3. **Enforcement Issues**
   - Inadequate enforcement mechanisms and lack of resources can limit the impact of legal reforms.
   - Corruption, bureaucratic inefficiencies, and lack of trained personnel can hinder effective enforcement.
4. **Economic Dependence**
   - Economic dependence on male family members can prevent women from seeking legal recourse or asserting their rights.
   - Empowering women economically is crucial for the success of legal reforms.
5. **Judicial Delays**
   - Delays in the judicial system can prevent timely justice for women seeking protection or redress under these laws.
   - Fast-track courts and efficient legal processes are needed to address these issues.
6. **Intersectional Disparities**
   - Women from disadvantaged groups (such as lower castes, minorities, or economically marginalized communities) may face additional barriers in accessing justice and benefiting from legal reforms.
   - Policies must be inclusive and address the specific needs of these groups.

Previous Years' Questions

2024

1. Marriage as an institution has undergone a radical transformation from 'ritual' to 'commercial' in its outlook. Explain the factors behind this change. (10 Marks)
2. What are the 'basic and irreducible' functions of the family as proposed by Talcott Parsons ? Explain. (10 Marks)
3. Modern families have not just become nuclear and neo-local, but also filiocentric. How do you explain this trend? (20 Marks)

2023

1. How do you assess the changing patterns in kinship relations in societies today? (20 marks)
2. Analyse critically David Morgan's views on family practices. (10 marks)

2022

1. Discuss various theoretical perspectives on the family. (10 marks)
2. How do you understand the relationship between patriarchy and social development? (10 marks)

2021

1. Explain how the pattern of patriarchy is being altered in a family and at the work-place in the present context. (20 marks)
2. Discuss the changing nature of kinship relations in the contemporary world. (20 marks)

2020

1. Discuss the consequences of across region marriage on kinship system in modern India. (10 marks)
2. Does the institution of marriage continue to be sacred in Indian society? (10 marks)

2019

1. What according to Irawati Karve are the major differences between North Indian and South Indian kinship systems? (10 marks)

2. In the light of judicial intervention on 'live-in relationships' , discuss the future of marriage and family in India. (20 marks)

2018

1. What are the new forms of family in developed societies? Discuss. (10 marks)
2. Define patriarchy. How does patriarchy manifest in interpersonal relations? (20 marks)
3. Distinguish between family and household with reference to the concept of development of the household. (20 marks)

Right Approach

2024

Q1. Marriage as an institution has undergone a radical transformation from 'ritual' to 'commercial' in its outlook. Explain the factors behind this change. (10 Marks)

Introduction: Marriage as a social institution has evolved significantly, transitioning from a sacred ritual emphasizing cultural and familial ties to a commercialized event driven by consumerism. This shift reflects broader socio-economic changes, globalization, and changing individual aspirations.

Body:

Factors Behind the Transformation

1. **Consumerism and Globalization:** The rise of consumer culture has turned weddings into lavish displays of wealth. India's wedding industry is estimated at $50 billion (KPMG, 2023), driven by destination weddings, designer outfits, and elaborate ceremonies inspired by global trends.
2. **Media and Celebrity Influence:** Social media platforms and celebrity weddings (e.g., Priyanka Chopra and Nick Jonas) popularize extravagant norms, creating pressure to conform. Instagram-worthy weddings prioritize visual appeal over traditional rituals.
3. **Shift in Values:** Traditional familial bonds are being replaced by individualism, leading to the personalization of weddings. Pre-wedding shoots, curated themes, and exclusive services reflect the shift from community-centric to couple-centric celebrations.
4. **Economic Drivers:** Weddings are significant economic events, employing planners, designers, and catering services. The commodification of rituals like *mehendi* and *sangeet* reflects this commercial approach.
5. **Cultural Adaptations:** Urbanization and interfaith or inter-caste marriages have redefined rituals, blending tradition with modernity. Hybrid ceremonies often focus on spectacle rather than spiritual significance.

Conclusion: The transformation of marriage from a ritual to a commercialized spectacle stems from globalization, media influence, and shifting societal values. While fostering creativity and personalization, it risks diluting cultural essence and reinforcing economic disparities.

2019

Q1. What, according to Irawati Karve, are the major differences between North Indian and South Indian Kinship systems?

Introduction: Irawati Karve, a renowned Indian sociologist and anthropologist, highlighted significant differences between the kinship systems of North and South India in her work *Kinship Organization in India*. These differences stem from variations in marriage practices, lineage structures, and cultural norms shaped by geography, history, and social organization.

Body:

Major Differences Between North and South Indian Kinship Systems

1. **Marriage Rules:**
   - **North India:** Marriage is exogamous, with strict rules against marrying within the same village or clan (*gotra*). Cross-cousin marriages are taboo.
   - **South India:** Endogamy is more common, and cross-cousin (e.g., mother's brother's daughter) and uncle-niece marriages are socially accepted.
2. **Lineage and Descent:**
   - **North India:** Follows a strict patrilineal descent system. Daughters are seen as outsiders (*paraya dhan*), with little claim to paternal property.
   - **South India:** While patrilineal, there is greater flexibility, and daughters retain closer ties to their natal family, especially in *Dravidian kinship*.
3. **Kinship Terminology:**
   - **North India:** Terminology distinguishes between paternal and maternal sides, reflecting lineage-based hierarchy.
   - **South India:** A simpler system with overlapping terms for cousins and siblings (*classificatory kinship*), emphasizing kin solidarity.

Conclusion: According to Karve, North Indian kinship is lineage-centric and rigidly exogamous, while South Indian kinship emphasizes kin solidarity, flexibility, and endogamy. These distinctions reflect deep-rooted cultural, regional, and historical differences in Indian society.

CHAPTER

10

Social Changes in Modern Society

In this Chapter

Introduction

In sociology, social change refers to the alteration of mechanisms within the social structure, characterized by changes in cultural symbols, rules of behaviour, social organizations, or value systems. This concept encompasses modifications in the social structure and social relationships, distinguishing it from physical growth or seasonal changes. Social change is a complex process influenced by various factors and perspectives.

Point to Note

Structural Changes

- **Structural Functionalism Perspective:** This view posits that society is in a natural state of equilibrium, where gradual change is necessary and desirable. It emphasises that sudden social change can disrupt this equilibrium, necessitating adjustments in different parts of society to maintain stability.
- **Weberian Theory of Social Change:** This theory highlights the unpredictable nature of social change, suggesting that there is no inherent law governing its specific forms. It emphasises the difficulty in predicting exact forms of social change.

Cultural Changes

- **Conflict Theory Perspective:** This approach views social change as essential to reduce social inequality and address existing problems within the status quo. It advocates for sudden social change through protests or revolutions to eliminate social disparities.
- **Marxist Theory:** This theory links changes in modes of production to shifts in class systems, leading to further societal transformations or class conflicts

An example of social change in the context of structural and cultural changes can be seen in the evolution of family structures. Over time, societies have transitioned from traditional joint family structures to more nuclear family setups, reflecting a shift in social organization and relationships. This change signifies both a structural adjustment in family units and a cultural transformation in the dynamics of familial interactions and functions

Societies undergoing social change often experience a range of conflicts and tensions, driven by shifts in social norms, economic structures, and political landscapes. These conflicts manifest as resistance to change from certain segments of society and adaptation or endorsement from others, creating a complex dynamic that can both challenge and progress societal development.

FYI

Approaches to Studying Social Change in India

1. **Evolutionary Approach:** This perspective views social change as gradual and continuous, with changes occurring over a long period through evolutionary processes. Examples include the shift from traditional joint family structures to nuclear families in India.
2. **Cultural Approach:** This approach focuses on changes in cultural values, norms, and institutions. It emphasises the role of cultural factors in shaping social change, such as the influence of Mahatma Gandhi's non-violent social revolution in India.
3. **Structural Approach:** This perspective examines changes in social structures, including institutions, property relations, economic pursuits, and role distribution. It highlights the impact of structural changes on social relationships and the social system

One major area of conflict arises from generational differences. Older generations may cling to traditional values and norms, while younger generations push for changes that reflect modern ideologies and technologies. This can lead to a societal split, as seen in issues like climate change, where younger populations tend to advocate more strongly for drastic environmental policies compared to older ones. The global climate strikes, led predominantly by youth, exemplify this generational divide, with young activists like Greta Thunberg becoming symbols of this movement.

Economic shifts are another source of tension, particularly evident in regions transitioning from agrarian to industrial or from industrial to post-industrial societies. Such transitions often displace large segments of the workforce, leading to unemployment and social unrest. The rise of automation and artificial intelligence has sparked debates and anxiety about job security, exemplified by the 'yellow vest' protests in France. Political changes also generate conflict, as existing power structures are challenged by new actors and ideologies. The Arab Spring is a poignant example, where demands for political reform led to widespread protests, uprisings, and, in some cases, armed conflict across several Arab countries. Cultural conflicts also emerge with social change, particularly around issues of identity and rights. The increased visibility and rights for LGBTQ+ communities have prompted significant backlash in many parts of the world. In some countries, this has led to legislative advances and greater social acceptance, while in others, it has resulted in strengthened opposition and even regressive policies, underscoring the deeply entrenched cultural norms that can resist change.

These examples highlight the multifaceted nature of societal conflicts during periods of change. Each conflict, while disruptive and challenging, also reflects the evolving values and priorities of a society, demonstrating a continuous, though often contentious, drive toward reshaping societal norms and structures.

Theories of Social Change

Social change refers to significant alterations over time in behaviour patterns, cultural values, and norms. Various theories have been developed to explain the processes and mechanisms through which social change occurs. Here are some of the major theories:

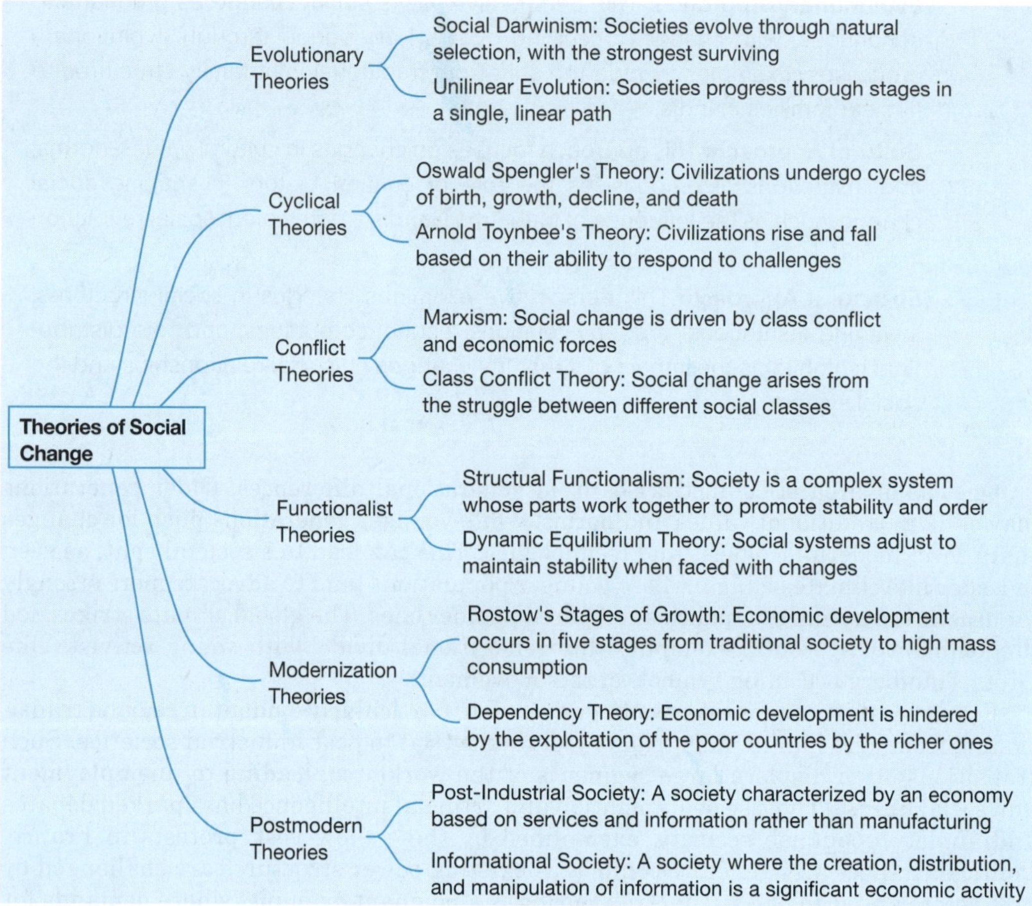

Evolutionary Theories

Evolutionary theories of social change suggest that societies progress through a series of stages in a unilinear or multilinear manner, much like biological evolution.

- **Unilinear Evolutionary Theory:** This theory posits that all societies pass through the same sequence of stages of development, typically from savagery to civilization.
  - **Example:** The classical evolutionary theory proposed by Lewis Henry Morgan, which divides human development into stages: savagery, barbarism, and civilization.

- **Multilinear Evolutionary Theory**: This theory acknowledges that different societies may take different paths to reach similar levels of complexity. It doesn't assume a single sequence of stages.
  - **Example:** Julian Steward's theory of cultural ecology, which considers how different societies adapt to their environments in unique ways.

Primitive → Traditional → Modern

August Comte's Law of Three Stages

- **Theological Stage:** Human thought is dominated by religious beliefs and superstitions. Societies are structured around divine laws and supernatural explanations.
- **Metaphysical Stage:** Abstract principles and philosophical reasoning take precedence. This stage represents a transitional phase where people begin to question religious dogma.
- **Positive Stage:** Scientific understanding and empirical evidence become the basis for knowledge. Societies prioritise rationality, logic, and observation.
- **Example:** The Enlightenment period in Europe, which emphasized reason and science over religious and superstitious explanations.

Herbert Spencer's Evolutionary Theory

- **Simple to Complex:** Societies evolve from simple, undifferentiated structures to complex, differentiated ones.
- **Homogeneity to Heterogeneity:** There is a movement from homogeneity (similarity) to heterogeneity (diversity) in social institutions and roles.
- **Integration and Differentiation:** Increased differentiation of social structures and integration of complex societal functions.
- **Example:** The transition from hunter-gatherer societies to industrialized nations.

Karl Marx's Historical Materialism

- **Stages of Economic Development:** Societies progress through a series of stages based on the mode of production and class relations.
- **Stages:**

Primitive Communism → Slave Society → Feudalism → Capitalism → Socialism → Communism

- **Class Struggle:** Each stage is characterized by class conflicts that drive social change and lead to the next stage.
- **Example:** The industrial revolution leading to the rise of capitalism and the subsequent labour movements pushing for socialism.

Modernization Theory

- **Traditional to Modern Society:** Societies develop through a process of modernization, which involves industrialization, urbanization, and rationalization.

- **Characteristics of Modern Societies:** Technological advancement, high levels of education, democratic institutions, and secular values.
- **Developmental Stages:**

Traditional society → Preconditions for take-off → Take-off → Drive to maturity → Age of high mass consumption

- **Example:** The rapid development of East Asian countries like South Korea and Taiwan in the late 20th century.

Talcott Parsons' Structural Functionalism

- **Social Evolution:** Societies evolve by increasing their capacity to adapt to the environment and maintaining stability.
- **Differentiation and Integration:** As societies develop, they create more specialized institutions that perform distinct functions, leading to increased social integration.
- **Value Generalization:** Societies progress by developing more generalized values and norms that integrate diverse social groups.
- **Example:** The evolution of educational systems to meet the needs of increasingly complex industrial societies.

Cyclical Theories

Cyclical theories propose that societies go through cycles of rise, decline, and fall, much like the natural cycles observed in seasons or life stages.

Oswald Spengler's Decline of the West

- **Cultural Life Cycle:** Societies undergo a lifecycle similar to living organisms, including birth, growth, maturity, and decline.
- **Cultural Phases:**

Cultural inception → Cultural growth → Cultural maturity → Cultural decline → Cultural death

- **Example:** Spengler viewed Western civilization as being in its decline phase, similar to the fall of the Roman Empire.

Arnold Toynbee's Study of History

- **Challenge and Response:** Civilizations rise in response to challenges and their ability to respond creatively.
- **Stages:**

Growth → Breakdown → Disintegration → Reconstitution

- **Civilizational Cycles:** Civilizations experience cycles of growth and decline based on their responses to existential challenges.
- **Example:** The fall of the Byzantine Empire and the rise of the Ottoman Empire in response to new political and military challenges.

Pitirim Sorokin's Social and Cultural Dynamics

- **Cultural Fluctuations:** Societies alternate between ideational (spiritual and religious) and sensate (materialistic and secular) cultural systems.
- **Cultural Types:**

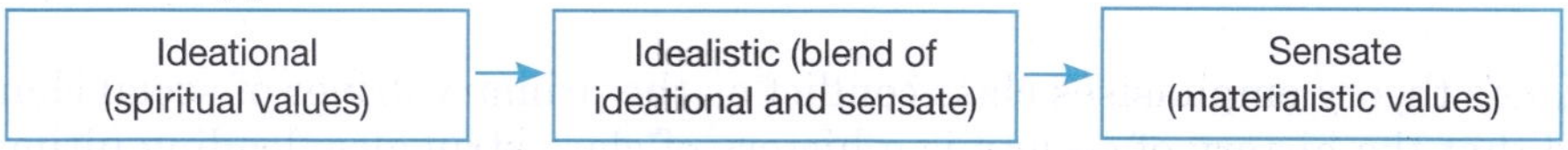

- **Example:** The Renaissance period as a transition from the ideational culture of the middle ages to the sensate culture of the modern era.

Vilfredo Pareto's Circulation of Elites

- **Elite Cycles:** Societal change is driven by the cyclical replacement of ruling elites.
- **Elite Types:** Foxes (cunning, manipulative leaders) and lions (forceful, authoritative leaders)
- **Elite Circulation:** Society oscillates between periods dominated by foxes and periods dominated by lions.
- **Example:** The periodic shifts in political power in Italy between different elite groups during the Renaissance.

Ibn Khaldun's Theory of Asabiyyah

- **Social Cohesion and Decline:** Societies rise and fall based on their level of social cohesion (asabiyyah).
- **Cycle:**

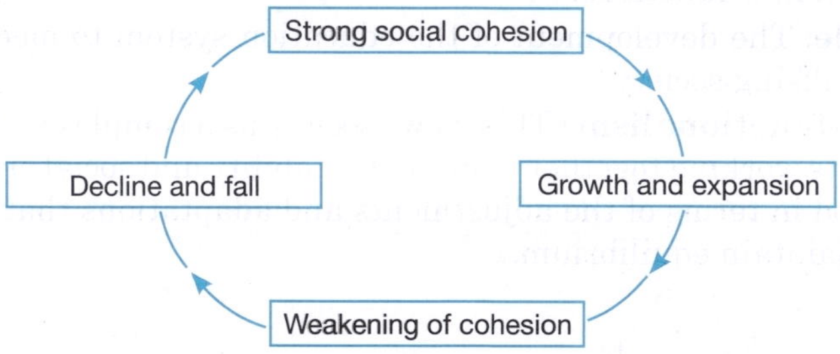

- **Example:** The rise and fall of the Arab Caliphates, where strong tribal unity initially led to expansion and eventual decline due to weakening cohesion.

Aspect	Linear Theories	Cyclical Theories
Direction	Unidirectional, progressive	Repetitive, cyclical
Nature of Change	Cumulative, irreversible	Non-linear, repetitive
Key Thinkers	August Comte, Karl Marx, Modernization theorists	Oswald Spengler, Arnold Toynbee, Pitirim Sorokin
Societal Path	From simple to complex	Rise, peak, decline, renewal
Example	Industrialization in Western Europe	Rise and fall of the Roman Empire

Conflict Theory

Conflict theories focus on the role of social conflict and power struggles as drivers of social change.

Marxist Theory

Karl Marx's theory emphasises class conflict as the primary driver of social change. He believed that the history of society is a history of class struggles, leading ultimately to the overthrow of capitalism and the establishment of socialism.

Example: The Russian Revolution of 1917, where the working class overthrew the ruling class.

Weber's Theory of Rationalization

Max Weber focussed on the process of rationalization, where traditional ways of thinking are replaced by an emphasis on efficiency and formal rules.

Example: The shift from traditional to rational-legal authority in modern societies, exemplified by bureaucratic organizations.

Functionalist Theory

Functionalist theories view social change as a gradual process of adjustment where social institutions adapt to maintain societal stability and equilibrium.

- **Parsons' Theory of Social Systems:** Talcott Parsons suggested that societies evolve through a process of differentiation and integration, where new institutions arise to fulfill new functions.
  - **Example:** The development of the education system to meet the needs of an industrialising society.
- **Structural-functionalism :** This views society as a complex system with interdependent parts working together to promote stability and social order. Social change is understood in terms of the adjustments and adaptations that occur within this system to maintain equilibrium.

Key Thinkers

- **Talcott Parsons:** One of the foremost proponents of structural-functionalism, Parsons developed a comprehensive framework to analyse the functions of social structures and their role in maintaining societal stability.
- **Emile Durkheim:** Often considered a precursor to structural-functionalism, Durkheim's work on social solidarity and the functions of social institutions laid the groundwork for later theorists.

Key Features

1. **Functional Necessity:**
   - Every social structure or institution has a function that contributes to the stability and functioning of society.
   - Functions can be manifest (intended and obvious) or latent (unintended and hidden).

2. **Equilibrium and Stability:**
    - Societies strive for a state of equilibrium where institutions and structures function harmoniously.
    - Social change occurs when there is a disturbance in this equilibrium, prompting adjustments to restore stability.
3. **Adaptation:**
    - Societies must adapt to internal and external pressures to maintain stability.
    - Adaptation involves changes in social institutions, norms, and roles to meet new needs and challenges.
4. **Integration:**
    - Effective integration of different parts of society is crucial for maintaining social order.
    - Social norms, values, and institutions play a key role in integrating diverse elements of society.

Examples

1. **Education System:**
    - **Function:** Transmits knowledge, skills, and cultural values to the next generation.
    - **Adaptation:** Changes in educational curricula and teaching methods in response to technological advancements and labour market needs.
2. **Family Institution:**
    - **Function:** Socialises children, provides emotional support, and regulates sexual behaviour.
    - **Adaptation:** Transformation of family structures (e.g., increase in single-parent households) in response to changing social norms and economic conditions.

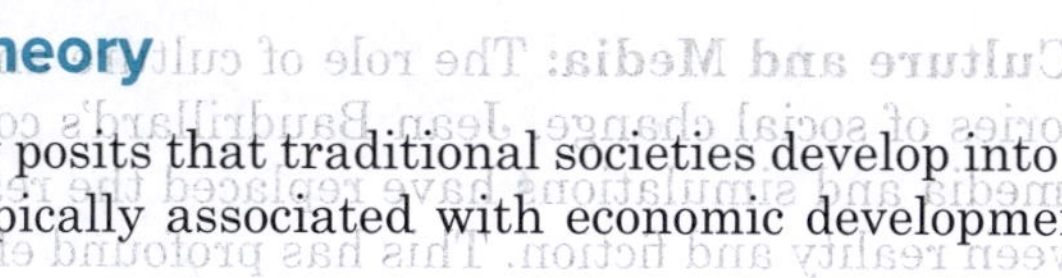

Modernization Theory

Modernization theory posits that traditional societies develop into modern ones through a series of stages, typically associated with economic development, urbanization, and cultural change.

Rostow's Stages of Economic Growth

W.W. Rostow proposed that societies move through five stages of economic growth: traditional society, preconditions for take-off, take-off, drive to maturity, and age of high mass consumption.

Example: The rapid industrialization and modernization of South Korea in the later half of the 20th century.

World-Systems Theory

World-systems theory, developed by Immanuel Wallerstein, argues that social change occurs within a global context. It divides the world into core, semi-periphery, and periphery countries, highlighting how economic and political power dynamics drive change.

Example: The exploitation of peripheral countries by core countries through colonialism and global capitalism, leading to uneven development.

Diffusion Theory

Diffusion theories focus on how cultural elements, ideas, and technologies spread from one society to another, influencing social change.

Example: The spread of democratic ideas and practices from Western societies to other parts of the world, leading to democratization movements in various countries.

Postmodernism Theories of Social Change

They emerged as a critical response to modernist theories, which emphasise progress, rationality, and the overarching narratives of history. Postmodernism, by contrast, challenges these grand narratives and focuses on the fragmented, diverse, and subjective nature of reality. This perspective has significant implications for understanding social change, emphasizing the role of culture, media, and ideology in shaping societal transformations.

Key Features

1. **Fragmentation and Plurality:** Postmodernism rejects the idea of a single, unified narrative of social progress. Instead, it highlights the plurality of experiences and identities. Social change is seen as non-linear and multi-faceted, with different groups experiencing change in varied and often contradictory ways.
2. **Deconstruction of Grand Narratives:** Postmodern theorists like Jean-François Lyotard argue that grand narratives, such as the Enlightenment or Marxism, are metanarratives that impose a false sense of coherence and order. Postmodernism deconstructs these narratives, revealing the underlying power structures and ideological biases.
3. **Emphasis on Culture and Media:** The role of culture and media is central in postmodern theories of social change. Jean Baudrillard's concept of hyperreality illustrates how media and simulations have replaced the real world, blurring the boundaries between reality and fiction. This has profound effects on social behaviour, perceptions, and identities.
4. **Decentralization and Local Narratives:** Social change is understood as a series of localized, contextual shifts rather than broad, systemic transformations. Michel Foucault's focus on the micro-politics of power and knowledge demonstrates how change occurs through localized struggles and discourses rather than through top-down processes.

Examples

1. **Digital Revolution and Social Media:** The advent of the internet and social media epitomises postmodern social change. These technologies have decentralized information dissemination, allowing diverse voices to be heard. Movements like #MeToo and Black Lives Matter gain traction through digital platforms, showcasing how fragmented yet powerful narratives can drive social change.
2. **Consumer Culture and Identity:** In a postmodern society, consumer culture plays a pivotal role in shaping identities. Individuals construct their identities through consumption patterns and lifestyle choices rather than traditional social structures. This is evident in the rise of subcultures and niche markets, where people express their identities through specific consumer preferences.
3. **Globalisation and Hybridization:** Postmodernism views globalization not just as economic integration but as a cultural hybridization process. Cultural exchange leads to the blending of traditions, creating new, hybrid cultural forms. This can be seen in the global spread of popular culture, where local and global influences merge to create unique cultural expressions.
4. **Decentralized Political Movements:** Contemporary political movements often reflect postmodern characteristics. The Occupy Wall Street movement, for instance, lacked a centralized leadership and a single ideological framework. Instead, it was a coalition of diverse groups with varied grievances and goals, united by a common opposition to economic inequality and corporate power.

Hegel's Theories of Social Change

Georg Wilhelm Friedrich Hegel's theory of social change is rooted in his dialectical method, which posits that development and progress occur through a process of thesis, antithesis, and synthesis.

Key Features

- **Dialectical Process:**
  - **Thesis:** Represents an initial idea or condition.
  - **Antithesis:** Contradicts or challenges the thesis.
  - **Synthesis:** Resolves the conflict between thesis and antithesis, resulting in a higher level of understanding or a new condition.

Historical Development

Hegel viewed history as a rational process in which the World Spirit (Geist) realises its freedom and self-consciousness through a series of dialectical stages. Each stage represents a progression towards greater freedom and rationality.

Absolute Spirit

The culmination of the dialectical process is the realization of the Absolute Spirit, where individual freedom and universal ethical life are fully actualized. This stage represents the ultimate reconciliation of individual and collective interests.

Examples

- **Master-Slave Dialectic:**
  - **Thesis:** The existence of a master who dominates the slave.
  - **Antithesis:** The slave's realization of self-consciousness and desire for freedom.
  - **Synthesis:** The development of a society where mutual recognition and freedom are achieved.
- **Development of Political Systems:**
  - **Thesis:** Absolute monarchy as an initial form of governance.
  - **Antithesis:** The emergence of democratic ideals challenging monarchical rule.
  - **Synthesis:** The establishment of constitutional democracies that balance authority and individual freedoms.

Development and Dependency in Sociology

In sociology, the concepts of development and dependency are crucial to understanding the dynamics of economic and social change within nations. Development theories focus on the processes and policies that lead to economic growth, improved living standards, and social progress. Dependency theory, on the other hand, critically examines the relationship between developed and developing countries, highlighting the systemic inequalities and historical exploitation that perpetuate underdevelopment.

Development Theories

Development theories encompass a range of approaches aimed at explaining and fostering economic and social progress. Key theories include:

1. **Modernization Theory:** This perspective suggests that development follows a linear path from traditional to modern societies. It emphasises the adoption of Western technologies, values, and institutions as prerequisites for development.
2. **Human Development Theory:** This approach, popularized by the United Nations Development Programme (UNDP), focuses on improving human well-being through education, health, and equitable access to resources, beyond mere economic growth.
3. **Sustainable Development:** Emerging in response to environmental degradation, this theory advocates for development that meets present needs without compromising future generations' ability to meet their own needs. It integrates economic, social, and environmental dimensions.

Dependency Theory

Dependency theory emerged as a critique of modernization theory, primarily advanced by Latin American scholars such as Andre Gunder Frank and Fernando Henrique Cardoso. It argues that underdevelopment in poorer nations is a result of their historical exploitation and economic dependence on developed countries. It is also known as development of underdevelopment concept. Key aspects include:

1. **Historical Context:** Colonialism and imperialism established a global economic system where resources flowed from the periphery (developing countries) to the core (developed countries), creating a cycle of dependency.
2. **Economic Relationships:** Trade patterns and international economic policies often favour developed nations, keeping developing countries in a subordinate position. This dependency is perpetuated through mechanisms like unequal exchange and debt.
3. **Structural Constraints:** Developing countries often face structural limitations such as lack of infrastructure, technological gaps, and capital shortages, hindering their ability to achieve autonomous development.

Context of India

India's development trajectory offers a complex interplay of both development and dependency dynamics.

1. **Post-Independence Development:** Following independence in 1947, India adopted a mixed economy model with significant state intervention. The focus was on self-reliance through industrialization, land reforms, and import substitution.
2. **Economic Liberalization:** The 1991 economic reforms marked a shift towards liberalization, privatization, and globalization. These reforms accelerated economic growth, but also increased India's integration into the global economy, raising concerns about new forms of dependency.
3. **Current Challenges:** Despite impressive growth rates, India faces persistent challenges such as income inequality, regional disparities, and environmental degradation. Dependency theory can be applied to understand issues like reliance on foreign technology, capital, and markets.

The interplay between development and dependency theories provides a comprehensive framework to analyse the socio-economic trajectories of nations. In the context of India, while significant strides have been made in development, the challenges of dependency persist, highlighting the need for balanced and inclusive policies that address both internal and external dynamics of growth.

Development of Underdevelopment

André Gunder Frank, a prominent dependency theorist, introduced the concept of 'development of underdevelopment' in the 1960s. His theory critiques the traditional modernization theory, which suggests that underdeveloped countries can achieve development by following the same path as developed countries. Instead, Frank argues that the current state of underdevelopment in many countries is not a natural stage, but a result of historical and ongoing economic exploitation and unequal power relations.

Core Argument

Frank's theory is rooted in the historical context of colonialism and the global capitalist system. He posits that the economic development of core (developed) countries is intrinsically linked to the underdevelopment of the periphery (underdeveloped) countries. According to Frank, the exploitation began during colonial times when European powers extracted resources and wealth from their colonies. This exploitation continued post-independence through neocolonial practices and the global capitalist system.

Mechanisms of Underdevelopment

1. **Extraction of Resources:** During colonial times, colonies were used primarily for their raw materials. The wealth generated from these resources was funnelled to the colonisers, leaving the colonies impoverished.
2. **Unequal Trade Relations:** Post-independence, the newly formed nations found themselves in a disadvantaged position within the global trading system. They exported raw materials and imported expensive finished goods, perpetuating a trade imbalance.
3. **Dependence on Foreign Investment:** Developing countries often rely on foreign investments from developed countries. These investments primarily benefit the investors and lead to the outflow of profits from the host countries, perpetuating economic dependency.
4. **Debt Dependency:** Many developing nations accumulate significant debt to fund development projects. The high-interest rates and conditionalities imposed by international financial institutions like the IMF and World Bank often lead to further economic hardship.

Criticism of Frank's Theory

1. **Overemphasis on External Factors:** Critics argue that Frank's theory places too much emphasis on external factors while neglecting internal factors such as governance, corruption, and social structures that also contribute to underdevelopment.
2. **Static Model:** Frank's model is considered static as it does not account for the dynamic nature of development. Some countries have managed to transition from underdeveloped to developed status, suggesting that the model does not fully explain the complexity of development.
3. **Neglect of Agency:** By focussing on structural constraints, the theory underestimates the agency of developing countries to effect change and development through appropriate policies and reforms.

Examples

1. **Latin America:** Frank's theory was primarily based on his observations of Latin America, where countries like Brazil and Argentina experienced significant economic exploitation by foreign corporations and unequal trade relations that stymied their development.
2. **Africa:** Many African countries continue to grapple with the legacy of colonial exploitation, resource extraction, and unfair trade practices. The debt crisis in countries like Zambia and Ghana exemplifies the ongoing cycle of dependency and underdevelopment.

3. **Asia:** Countries like India and Indonesia, despite substantial economic growth, still face significant challenges related to their colonial past and dependency on foreign technology and investment. However, the success stories of South Korea and Taiwan, which transitioned to developed status, challenge the universality of Frank's theory.

André Gunder Frank's 'development of underdevelopment' provides a critical lens to understand the persistent poverty and economic struggles in many parts of the world. While it has faced criticism for its deterministic approach and overemphasis on external factors, it remains a valuable framework for analysing the historical and structural roots of global inequality. Understanding these dynamics is crucial for formulating policies that address both external and internal factors contributing to underdevelopment.

World-Systems Theory, developed by sociologist Immanuel Wallerstein in the 1970s, expands on Dependency Theory to offer a more comprehensive analysis of global economic systems. It categorises nations into core, semi-periphery, and periphery, highlighting the complex and dynamic interactions between these regions. This theory provides a nuanced understanding of global inequality and the mechanisms that sustain it.

Core Concepts of World-Systems Theory

1. **Structure of the World Economy:** World-Systems Theory divides the global economy into three tiers:
   - **Core Countries:** These are highly industrialized, wealthy nations with advanced technological infrastructure. They dominate global trade and finance, often exploiting other regions for labour and resources.
   - **Semi-Periphery Countries:** These nations exhibit characteristics of both core and periphery countries. They are typically industrialising and may exploit peripheral regions while being exploited by core countries.
   - **Periphery Countries:** These are less-developed nations, often relying on the export of raw materials and labour-intensive goods. They are the most vulnerable to economic exploitation and external control.
2. **Historical Development:** The theory emphasises the historical evolution of the world economy, tracing back to the emergence of the capitalist world system in the 16th century. It argues that colonialism and imperialism laid the groundwork for contemporary global inequalities.
3. **Economic and Political Dynamics:** World-Systems Theory highlights how core countries maintain their dominance through economic practices, political strategies, and military power. It also shows how semi-periphery countries aspire to ascend to core status, while periphery countries struggle to overcome structural constraints.

Illustration with Examples

- **Global North and South Divide:** The global North (core) and South (periphery) divide exemplifies the unequal distribution of wealth and power. Core countries like the United States, Germany, and Japan control major financial institutions (e.g., IMF, World Bank) and dictate terms of international trade. Peripheral countries in Africa, Latin America, and parts of Asia often face terms of trade that favour core countries, perpetuating their economic dependence.

- **Brazil (A Semi-Periphery Example):** Brazil illustrates the role of a semi-periphery country. It has a diverse economy with significant industrial and agricultural sectors. While Brazil exploits resources from less-developed neighbours, it also depends on technology and capital from core countries. Its position allows it to benefit from both exploitation and cooperation but also subjects it to pressures from both core and periphery dynamics.
- **African Resource Extraction:** Many African countries, such as the Democratic Republic of Congo (DRC), are situated in the periphery. The DRC is rich in minerals like cobalt and coltan, crucial for high-tech industries. Core countries and multinational corporations often control the extraction and export processes, leading to significant economic benefits for the core, while the DRC remains underdeveloped and politically unstable.

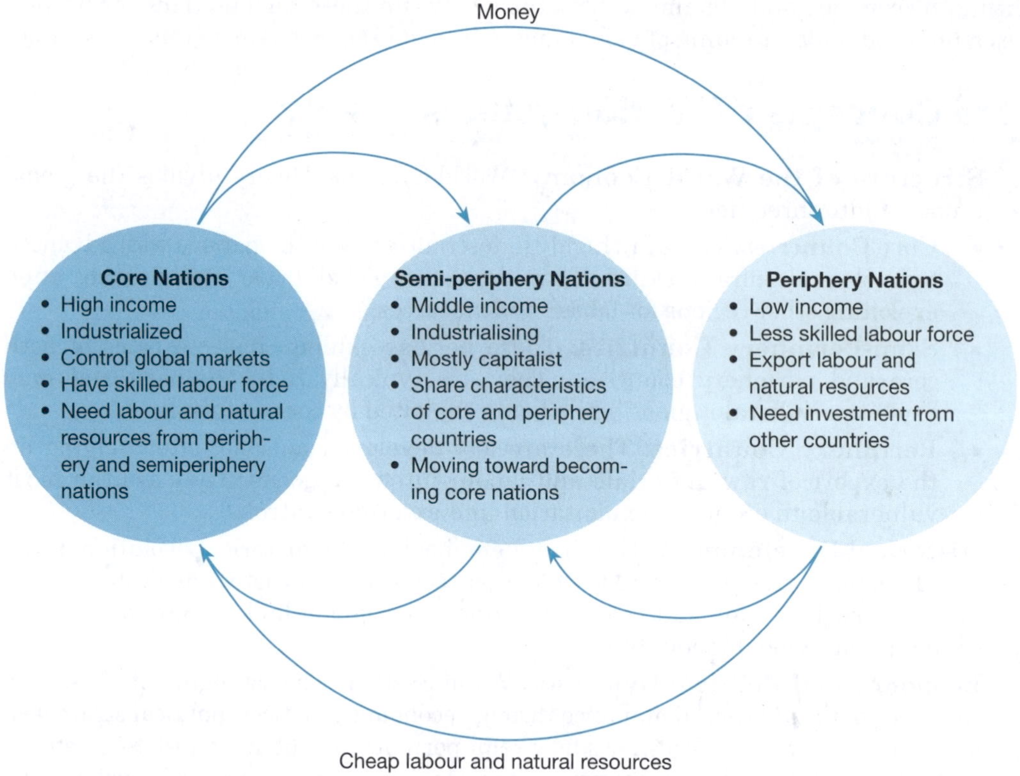

Relevance and Critique

World-Systems Theory remains relevant for understanding contemporary global inequalities. It underscores the interconnectedness of global economies and the persistent structural barriers that hinder development in peripheral regions. Critics argue that the theory can be overly deterministic and may not fully account for the agency of individual nations or local variations.

Conclusion

World-Systems Theory, within the framework of Dependency Theory, provides a robust analytical tool for examining the global economic system. By categorising nations into core, semi-periphery, and periphery, it reveals the structural inequalities and historical processes that sustain global disparities. Illustrations from Brazil and Africa highlight the practical applications and ongoing relevance of this theoretical approach.

Limitations of Theories of Social Change

1. **Unilinear Theory**
   - **Assumption of Single Path:** Suggests that all societies progress through the same stages of development, which does not account for diverse cultural, historical, or geographic factors. For instance, the belief that all societies move from primitive to advanced stages doesn't reflect the unique developmental paths of indigenous cultures.
   - **Ethnocentrism:** Often rooted in Eurocentric perspectives, assuming Western-style development is ideal. This ignores alternative paths like the unique socialist development in Cuba or mixed-economic models in Scandinavian countries.
   - **Rigid Stages of Development:** Fails to explain deviations or reversals in societal progress, such as the collapse of highly developed ancient civilizations like the Maya.
2. **Evolutionary Theory**
   - **Linear Assumptions:** Implies societies evolve in a straightforward, linear progression, ignoring regressive or multi-directional changes. For example, the rapid industrialization of Japan was followed by significant setbacks in World War II, challenging a purely linear view of progress.
   - **Ethnocentrism:** Often promotes Western progress models, overlooking the diverse paths of non-Western societies, such as Bhutan's pursuit of Gross National Happiness instead of GDP growth.
   - **Determinism:** Reduces the role of individual or collective agency in driving change. For instance, the French Revolution dramatically altered societal structures in ways unforeseen by any linear development model.
3. **Conflict Theory**
   - **Reductionism:** Simplifies social dynamics to class or power struggles, which might ignore factors like technological advancements. For example, the rapid growth of tech companies like Amazon reflects more than just class conflict—it includes innovation and globalization.
   - **Overemphasis on Conflict:** Focuses on inevitable conflicts and overlooks periods of harmony, such as the post-World War II social unity in many countries, despite structural inequalities.
   - **Ideological Bias:** Often criticized for its anti-capitalist perspective, which may limit objective analysis. For instance, the success of certain capitalist economies in improving standards of living can challenge a purely conflict-based view.

4. **Functionalist Theory**
   - **Conservatism:** Justifies existing structures by viewing them as necessary for stability, which can hinder social progress. For instance, caste-based roles in traditional Indian society were viewed as functional but led to entrenched inequalities.
   - **Neglect of Conflict:** Emphasizes social harmony, underestimating the role of conflict in driving change, such as the Civil Rights Movement, which involved substantial conflict to reform U.S. societal norms.
   - **Static View:** Struggles to explain rapid societal shifts, like the digital transformation sparked by the COVID-19 pandemic, which disrupted traditional structures.
5. **Cyclical Theory**
   - **Lack of Predictive Power:** Describes social cycles without accurately predicting future changes. The rise and fall of civilizations, such as the Roman Empire, fits this model but lacks a predictive explanation.
   - **Oversimplification:** Reduces social change to repetitive cycles, which may not apply universally. For example, Japan's post-WWII recovery and rapid economic rise are unique and don't fit a simple cyclical pattern.
   - **Deterministic Nature:** Implies inevitability in societal rise and fall, which can discourage proactive social reforms, like the economic liberalization that helped lift millions out of poverty in China.
6. **Modernization Theory**
   - **Western-Centric Bias:** Assumes that modernization must follow Western models, which may disregard unique paths taken by countries like Singapore, which blended state intervention with market practices.
   - **Dependency Issues:** Encourages reliance on Western economic models, which can perpetuate dependency in developing nations. For instance, many African economies remain heavily dependent on Western aid, limiting independent growth.
   - **Environmental Concerns:** Promotes industrialization, which often leads to unsustainable practices. The industrial rise of China, for example, brought both economic growth and significant environmental degradation.
7. **Dependency Theory**
   - **Overemphasis on External Factors:** Focuses on external exploitation, sometimes neglecting internal factors. For example, South Korea's shift from an agrarian to an industrial economy involved significant domestic policy reforms, not just external influences.
   - **Limited Agency for Developing Nations:** Implies that poor nations lack autonomy. However, countries like Rwanda have pursued independent development paths, balancing foreign investments with local priorities.
   - **Static Structure:** Does not easily account for upward mobility in the global economic hierarchy, as seen with China's transformation from a peripheral economy to a global power.

8. **World-Systems Theory**
   - **Complexity and Ambiguity:** Difficult to apply practically due to its broad global focus. For instance, categorizing China's role in the world economy is complex, as it operates both as a core and peripheral actor in different contexts.
   - **Inflexibility in Categories:** The rigid core-periphery model may not accurately capture changing dynamics, such as India's rising influence in the technology and services sectors.
   - **Overgeneralization:** Tends to overlook unique country-specific factors. For example, the economic rise of the 'Asian Tigers' does not fit neatly into the core-periphery framework due to their distinctive development strategies.
9. **Social Movement Theory**
   - **Fragmentation:** Multiple theoretical approaches can lead to fragmented understanding, making it difficult to form a unified perspective on social movements like Black Lives Matter, which combines identity, race, and class-based grievances.
   - **Reactive Focus:** Often analyzes movements in response to current issues, potentially underestimating forward-looking movements. For example, climate activism targets future sustainability more than immediate change.
   - **Challenges in Measurement:** Difficult to measure impact, as effects are long-term and dispersed. For instance, the feminist movement has influenced policies globally, but its effects vary significantly by country.

Agents of Social Change

Social change refers to significant alterations over time in behaviour patterns, cultural values, and norms. These changes can have profound impacts on society and are often driven by various agents of social change. These agents can be individuals, groups, or institutions that influence and steer social transformations. The primary agents of social change include:

1. **Individuals and Leaders:** Charismatic leaders and influential individuals can drive social change by inspiring others and leading movements. Examples include Mahatma Gandhi in India, who played a pivotal role in the Indian independence movement, and Martin Luther King Jr. in the United States, who was instrumental in the Civil Rights Movement.
2. **Social Movements and Activist Groups**: Organized groups and social movements often advocate for changes in social, political, and economic systems. The feminist movement, environmental movement, and LGBTQ+ rights movement have significantly altered societal norms and policies.
3. **Political Institutions and Government**: Governments and political institutions can enact laws and policies that facilitate social change. For instance, the Civil Rights Act of 1964 in the United States outlawed discrimination based on race, colour, religion, sex, or national origin, leading to significant social progress.

4. **Economic Forces and Market Dynamics**: Economic changes, including industrialization, globalization, and technological advancements, profoundly impact societal structures. The shift from agrarian economies to industrial and post-industrial societies has transformed social relations and living conditions.
5. **Technology and Innovation**: Technological advancements and innovations drive social change by altering how people live, work, and communicate. The advent of the internet and social media has revolutionized information dissemination and social interactions.
6. **Cultural Institutions:** Cultural institutions, including media, arts, and religion, play a crucial role in shaping societal values and norms. The portrayal of diverse cultures and perspectives in media can challenge stereotypes and promote inclusivity.
7. **New Ideas and Values:** These can emerge from various sources, including scientific discoveries, technological advancements, and cultural shifts. These new ideas can challenge existing social norms and values, leading to social movements that aim to bring about change. For example, the feminist movement in the 1960s and 1970s was driven by new ideas about gender equality and women's rights, which challenged traditional gender roles and social norms.
8. **Demographic Changes:** Demographic changes, such as changes in population size, age distribution, or geographic distribution, can also contribute to social movements. For instance, the growing youth population in the 1960s in the United States contributed to the civil rights movement, as young people were more likely to be involved in activism and social change. Similarly, the increasing number of women in the workforce in the 1970s and 1980s led to the women's liberation movement.
9. **Religious Factors:** Religious beliefs and practices can also play a significant role in social movements. For example, the Christian values of love and equality were central to the civil rights movement in the United States, as Reverend Martin Luther King Jr. and other religious leaders used these values to advocate for racial equality and social justice. Similarly, the Islamic values of social justice and equality have driven social movements in many Muslim-majority countries, such as the Arab Spring movement. Protestant ethics according to Max Weber brought about industrialization.

Education and Social Change

Education is a powerful agent of social change. It influences individuals and societies by imparting knowledge, fostering critical-thinking, and promoting values and skills necessary for societal progress. The role of education in social change can be understood through the following dimensions:

1. **Promoting Social Equity and Inclusion:** Education provides individuals with the skills and knowledge to improve their socio-economic status, thereby reducing inequality. Access to quality education can bridge the gap between different social groups and promote inclusivity.

   Example: *The Sarva Shiksha Abhiyan* (SSA) in India aims to provide universal elementary education, targeting marginalized groups, including girls, children from Scheduled Castes (SCs), Scheduled Tribes (STs), and economically- disadvantaged families. This initiative has significantly increased enrollment rates and reduced gender and socio-economic disparities in education.

2. **Fostering Critical-Thinking and Innovation:** An educated populace is better equipped to question existing norms and practices, leading to innovation and progress. Critical-thinking skills developed through education encourage individuals to seek solutions to social problems.

   Example: Finland's education system, known for its emphasis on creativity and critical-thinking, has produced highly skilled graduates who excel in various fields, driving the country's innovation and economic growth.

3. **Enhancing Civic Participation:** Education promotes civic awareness and participation by teaching individuals about their rights and responsibilities. An informed citizenry is more likely to engage in democratic processes and advocate for social justice.

   Example: Civics education programs in schools, such as those in Japan and Germany, teach students about democratic processes, human rights, and civic responsibilities. These programs have resulted in higher rates of voter participation and civic engagement among young people.

   The University of Cape Town's (UCT) social responsiveness programs encourage students to engage with local communities, fostering a sense of social responsibility and active citizenship.

4. **Shaping Cultural and Social Norms:** Educational curricula that include diverse perspectives can challenge stereotypes and promote cultural understanding. Schools and universities can serve as platforms for social integration and cultural exchange.

   Example: Educational campaigns in Sweden and Norway focus on gender equality and inclusivity from an early age. Schools teach about gender-neutral roles, challenging traditional gender norms and promoting a more equitable society.

   In Rwanda, post-genocide educational reforms have included curriculum changes that promote reconciliation and unity among ethnic groups, helping to rebuild the social fabric of the nation.

5. **Economic Development:** Education drives economic development by creating a skilled workforce capable of adapting to changing economic conditions. Economic growth, in turn, can lead to improvements in living standards and social structures.

   Example: The emphasis on STEM (Science, Technology, Engineering, and Mathematics) education in countries like South Korea and Singapore has produced a highly skilled workforce, driving technological advancements and economic growth.

   Vocational Education and Training (VET) programmes in Germany's dual education system combine classroom learning with practical work experience, ensuring a skilled labour force that meets the needs of the economy.

6. **Health and Well-being:** Education influences health outcomes by promoting healthy behaviours and increasing access to health information. Educated individuals are more likely to make informed health choices, leading to improved public health.

Example: In Kenya, the introduction of comprehensive sex education in schools has led to increased awareness about sexual health, reduced rates of teenage pregnancy, and improved overall health outcomes for young people.

Educational initiatives by organizations like Teach For America and *Pratham* in India focus on improving literacy and numeracy skills among children, leading to better health outcomes as educated individuals are more likely to adopt healthy behaviours.

7. **Environmental Awareness and Sustainable Practices:** Environment education can create an enabling environment for social change.

   Example: Environmental education programmes in schools across Costa Rica emphasise the importance of biodiversity and conservation. These programmes have instilled a culture of environmental stewardship among the younger generation, contributing to the country's successful conservation efforts.

   The 'Eco-Schools' programme, implemented in many countries, integrates sustainability into the curriculum, encouraging students to engage in projects that promote energy conservation, waste reduction, and sustainable living practices.

8. **Gender and Equality**: Education has a profound impact on gender roles and equality. By providing equal educational opportunities for all genders, education can empower women and challenge traditional gender norms. Education can promote gender equality by teaching about women's contributions to society, challenging stereotypes, and fostering an environment that encourages both boys and girls to pursue their interests and aspirations. For instance, in societies where women are under-represented in certain fields, education can help bridge the gender gap by promoting girls' education and encouraging them to pursue careers in traditionally male-dominated fields.

Different Perspectives on Education as an Agent of Social Change

Structural Functionalism views education as a vital institution that contributes to the overall functioning of society. According to this perspective, education imparts essential skills and values that help individuals integrate into society and perform their roles effectively. For instance, schools teach skills such as language, numeracy, and vocational and technical skills, which enable individuals to participate in the workforce and contribute to the economy (Durkheim, 1956).

Functionalism in schools emphasises the role of education in socialization and the inculcation of values. For example, schools teach children how to cooperate, coexist, and manage conflicts, which helps them become law-abiding citizens later in life. Additionally, schools instill values such as competition and individualism, which are characteristic of American society (Parsons, 1951).

Symbolic Interactionism Focuses on the Interactions and Meanings that individuals create within the educational setting. This perspective highlights the role of symbols, language, and social interactions in shaping educational experiences. For instance, the physical layout of a classroom can symbolise a traditional and hierarchical approach to education, while a collaborative and student-centred approach can be symbolized by a classroom with tables arranged in a circle (Lumen Learning, 2024).

Labelling theory, a part of Symbolic Interactionism, emphasises how labels can significantly impact a student's schooling. For example, a student labelled as a low achiever may struggle to overcome this label and achieve their full potential. This theory also highlights the role of power dynamics in labelling, as those in power often apply labels that can be difficult to shake off (Merton, 1968).

Critical pedagogy, rooted in Marxist perspectives, emphasises the need to challenge dominant power structures and social inequalities within education. This approach encourages students to question and critique the status quo, promoting social change and justice. For instance, critical pedagogy can help students recognise and challenge the systemic barriers that prevent certain groups from achieving their full potential (Giroux, 1983).

According to Weber, education can either reinforce or challenge existing social hierarchies. For example, education can provide opportunities for social mobility, but it can also perpetuate social inequalities by reinforcing existing power structures (Weber, 1922). **Institutional theory views education** as an institution that is shaped by its social and historical context. This perspective emphasises the role of institutions in shaping individual behaviour and outcomes. For instance, the structure and culture of a school can influence student outcomes, with institutions that promote inclusivity and support often leading to better educational outcomes (Meyer & Rowan, 1977).

Macrosocial perspectives focus on broad societal structures and trends, while microsocial perspectives examine individual interactions and behaviours. Meso-social perspectives, on the other hand, examine the interactions between individuals and larger social structures. For example, a macrosocial perspective might analyse the impact of globalization on education, while a microsocial perspective might examine how teachers interact with students in a classroom (Robson, 2024).

Science, Technology and Social Change

In modern society, the interplay between science, technology, and social change is profound and multifaceted. Advances in these fields often lead to shifts in social structures, behaviours, and norms, reflecting a dynamic process that reshapes the very fabric of communities.

Historically, technological innovations have been catalysts for economic and social transformations. The Industrial Revolution, powered by advancements in mechanical engineering and chemistry, radically altered societal structures, shifting populations from rural agrarian societies to urban industrial ones. This not only changed the economic landscape but also social dynamics, including family structures, work environments, and social mobility.

Sociologists have developed various theories to explain the relationship between science, technology and social change:

- **Evolutionary Theory:** This views technological development as the primary driver of social progress, increasing the scale and complexity of human societies over time.
- **Conflict Theory:** It suggests that technology empowers certain groups (e.g. the wealthy) while disempowering others, leading to social inequality and class conflict.

- **Functionalist Theory:** It sees technology as increasing the efficiency and specialization of social institutions, which helps maintain social stability.

The advent of information technology in the late 20th century marked a significant milestone in technological impact on society. The internet, a cornerstone of modern information technology, has democratized access to information, bridged vast geographical gaps, and facilitated new forms of human interaction. Social media platforms like Facebook, Twitter, and Instagram have redefined how people communicate and interact, influencing everything from political movements to personal relationships.

Example: A poignant example of this is the Arab Spring (2010 – 2012), where social media played a critical role in organizing protests and broadcasting local events to a global audience. This illustrates the power of technology in mobilising societal change, particularly in challenging traditional power structures and advocating for democracy.

Biotechnology and Health: Extending Life and Ethics

Biotechnology has brought about significant social change, particularly in the health sector. Innovations such as CRISPR gene editing and biopharmaceuticals have not only extended life expectancies but also presented new ethical dilemmas and social challenges. For instance, the ability to edit human embryos raises profound ethical questions about the extent of human intervention in natural processes.

Example: The rapid development and deployment of COVID-19 vaccines highlight the capability of biotechnology to respond to global health crises. This not only changed the trajectory of the pandemic but also affected international relations and global health policies, emphasizing the need for equitable access to life-saving technology.

Artificial Intelligence and Automation: Reshaping Employment

Artificial intelligence (AI) and automation represent another frontier of technology-induced social change. AI technologies are transforming job markets, with automation replacing routine jobs, creating demand for new skills, and altering workforce dynamics.

Example: In the automotive industry, AI-driven automation has shifted the skills required, moving from traditional manufacturing roles to more technology-focussed positions. This transition necessitates significant shifts in education systems and labour policies to manage the social implications of technological unemployment.

Conclusion

Science and technology continue to be powerful drivers of social change, shaping how individuals live, work, and interact. While they bring numerous benefits, such as increased efficiency and new capabilities, they also pose challenges that require careful management to ensure equitable and ethical outcomes. Moving forward, it is crucial for policymakers, business leaders, and communities to work together to harness the benefits of scientific and technological advancements while mitigating their potential downsides. This collaborative approach is essential in navigating the complex landscape of social change driven by scientific and technological progress.

Rupture of Modernity

The rupture of modernity refers to the profound changes in social, economic, and intellectual life that began in the late 19th and early 20th centuries and accelerated after World War II. This period saw the decline of traditional social structures, the rise of individualism, and the fragmentation of cultural and intellectual life. Modernity's emphasis on progress, rationality, and universal truths was increasingly questioned, leading to the rise of postmodernism, which emphasized plurality, relativism, and the deconstruction of grand narratives. The decline of functionalism and Marxism coincides with the rupture of modernity as both theories were products of the modernist project. Functionalism's focus on social order and stability and Marxism's emphasis on economic determinism and class struggle were increasingly seen as inadequate in explaining the complexities of late modern societies. The shift towards postmodern perspectives, which emphasise diversity, contingency, and the fluidity of social life, reflects the broader intellectual and cultural transformations associated with the rupture of modernity. The collapse of functionalism and the perceived bankruptcy of Marxism are intertwined with the rupture of modernity, as all three phenomena reflect the broader shift away from the grand narratives and stable structures of the modernist era towards the fragmented, fluid, and contested realities of the postmodern world.

Cultural Lag

Cultural lag is a sociological concept introduced by William F. Ogburn in his 1922 work 'Social Change with Respect to Culture and Original Nature.' It refers to the period of adjustment when non-material culture (values, beliefs, norms) struggles to catch up with rapid changes in material culture (technology, tools, infrastructure). This lag can lead to social problems and conflicts as society adapts to new technological advancements. Cultural lag occurs because material culture evolves quickly, driven by technological innovations, while non-material culture is more resistant to change. This discrepancy creates a gap or 'lag' between the two, leading to a period of maladjustment. Ogburn's theory suggests that this lag is a common societal phenomenon and can help explain and predict social problems.

Cultural lag remains highly relevant in contemporary society, as technological advancements continue to outpace changes in social norms and values. Several modern examples illustrate this phenomenon:

1. **Social Media and Privacy:** The rapid proliferation of social media platforms has outpaced the development of social norms and legal frameworks regarding privacy. While technology allows for unprecedented connectivity and information sharing, it has also led to significant privacy concerns and ethical dilemmas. Society is still grappling with issues like data breaches, cyberbullying, and the ethical use of personal information.
2. **Artificial Intelligence (AI):** AI technologies, such as facial recognition and autonomous vehicles, have advanced rapidly. However, the ethical, legal, and social implications of these technologies are still being debated. Issues such as bias in AI algorithms, job displacement, and the ethical use of AI in surveillance highlight the lag between technological capabilities and societal readiness to address their consequences.

3. **Climate Change and Environmental Policies:** Technological advancements in renewable energy and sustainable practices have progressed, but societal attitudes and policies have been slow to adapt. Despite the availability of green technologies, widespread adoption is hindered by existing economic interests, political resistance, and cultural inertia. This lag exacerbates environmental degradation and climate change impacts.
4. **Healthcare Innovations:** Advances in medical technology, such as gene editing (CRISPR) and telemedicine, have outpaced the development of ethical guidelines and regulatory frameworks. The rapid introduction of these technologies raises questions about their long-term effects, accessibility, and ethical use, leading to societal debates and policy lags.

Previous Years' Question

2024

1. Critically examine the roles of science and technology in social change. What is your opinion on their increasing trend in 'online' education and teaching? (10 Marks)
2. Discuss various theories of social change. Explain the limitations of unilinear theory of social change. (10 Marks)
3. Critically examine the World-Systems theory of Immanuel Wallerstein in terms of development and dependency of various nations. (10 Marks)

2022

1. Trace the trajectory of development perspectives on social change.

2021

1. Critically examine the contribution of dependency theories in understanding the present global scenario.

2020

1. Technology has accelerated the process of development and dependency. Discuss.

2019

1. Feminist scholars argue that 'New media' is masculine and hence reinforces structural hierarchies rather than reconfiguring them. Comment.
2. Criticise A.G. Frank's 'development of underdevelopment'.

2018

1. Does collapse of functionalism and bankruptcy of Marxism coincide with the rupture of modernity? Discuss.
2. Is the theory of cultural lag valid in present times? Discuss.

2017

1. Assess the role of mass media as an agent of social change.
2. Examine any two theories of social change in detail.

2016

1. 'Social conflict is both a cause and a consequence of social change' Explain.
2. 'Social change can be brought about through development'. Illustrate from the contemporary situation of India.

2013

1. Illustrate the conflicts and tensions experienced by societies undergoing social change.
2. Critically examine the cultural theories of social change with suitable examples.

2012

1. Write short note on the following from a sociological perspective: Theory of Cultural Lag – Ogburn and Nimkoff.
2. 'Revolutionary changes have some specific characteristics.' Discuss with examples.

2011

1. Write short note on Development and Dependency from a sociological perspective. (In about 150 words)
2. 'Social support mechanism needs to be strengthened for effective implementation of development programmes.' Comment.
3. Discuss World System Theory in the context of modern society.

2010

1. Examine the social dimensions of displacement induced by development.

Right Approach

2024

Q1. Critically examine the roles of science and technology in social change. What is your opinion on their increasing trend in 'online' education and teaching? (10 Marks)

Introduction: Science and technology play pivotal roles in driving social change by reshaping societal structures, improving living standards, and influencing behaviours. From the Industrial Revolution to the Digital Age, technological advancements have transformed communication, healthcare, and education, among other fields, facilitating social progress and altering cultural norms.

Body:

Roles of Science and Technology in Social Change

1. **Empowerment and Access:** Technology provides access to information, enabling individuals and communities to improve their knowledge and skills. The spread of mobile technology has empowered rural communities in India, enhancing access to education and healthcare.
2. **Economic Transformation:** Technological advancements lead to industrialization and economic development, creating new job opportunities and shifting labour dynamics. For instance, IT advancements in India have driven economic growth and global integration.
3. **Cultural Shift:** Technology influences social values and norms. Social media, for example, has changed how people interact and express themselves, impacting both personal relationships and activism.

Opinion on 'Online' Education and Teaching Online education, fueled by technology, provides flexible learning opportunities and democratizes access to quality education. The democratization of knowledge through MOOCs and digital platforms aligns with Bourdieu's concept of cultural capital, potentially reducing educational inequalities. However, the digital divide, as highlighted by contemporary sociologists like Jan van Dijk, creates new forms of social stratification. However, it also has challenges. In India, digital divides hinder access for marginalized communities, raising equity concerns. Additionally, online education lacks face-to-face interaction, potentially impacting social skills and learning outcomes.

Conclusion: Science and technology are powerful agents of social change, driving economic, cultural, and educational transformation. While online education offers increased accessibility and convenience, it must address challenges like digital inequality and social isolation to ensure inclusive and effective learning.

2018

Q2 Is the theory of cultural lag valid in present times? Discuss. (10 Marks)

Introduction: The theory of cultural lag, proposed by sociologist William Ogburn, argues that material culture (technological advancements) often evolves faster than non-material culture (values, norms), creating a 'lag' between the two. This theory suggests that societal adjustments to new technologies can be slow, leading to conflicts and social issues.

Body:

Validity of Cultural Lag in Present Times

1. **Technological Advancements and Social Adjustment:** With rapid advancements in areas like AI, genetic engineering, and social media, society often struggles to adapt. For instance, while genetic editing technologies like CRISPR advance quickly, ethical and regulatory frameworks lag behind, raising concerns about safety and morality.
2. **Digital Transformation and Social Norms:** The rise of social media illustrates cultural lag, as privacy concerns and mental health impacts are only now being widely discussed. Older social norms struggle to adapt to the dynamics of online interactions, leading to issues like cyberbullying and data misuse.
3. **Environmental Technology and Attitudes:** Despite advancements in green technology, widespread cultural shifts toward sustainability are gradual. Ogburn's theory is evident here, as societies struggle to align behaviours with environmental needs despite technological solutions.

Conclusion: The theory of cultural lag remains relevant as societies continuously face the challenge of adjusting values and norms to match rapid technological change. While technology progresses at a fast pace, social, ethical, and legal frameworks require time to adapt, making cultural lag a persistent reality in contemporary society.